THE AMERICAN PAST
Conflicting Interpretations of the Great Issues

VOLUME II

THE
AMERICAN PAST

CONFLICTING INTERPRETATIONS
OF THE GREAT ISSUES

SECOND
EDITION

VOLUME II

Edited by Sidney Fine & Gerald S. Brown

The Macmillan Company, New York   Collier–Macmillan Limited, London

Second Printing

Earlier edition, entitled *The American Past,* Volume II, © copyright 1961 by
The Macmillan Company.
Library of Congress catalog card number: 65-15184
THE MACMILLAN COMPANY, NEW YORK
COLLIER–MACMILLAN CANADA, LTD., TORONTO, ONTARIO
Printed in the United States of America

To Jean and Dorothy

PREFACE
TO THE SECOND EDITION

The present edition retains the basic pattern of organization of the first edition, the reception of which by teachers and students alike has been most gratifying to the editors. Approximately one third of the selections in this edition are new. Some of the new selections replace pieces of historical writing used for the same topics in the first edition; others have been paired to form entirely new topics. The new selections, in addition to sharpening the focus of conflict and enhancing the teachability of the work, help to keep *The American Past* abreast of the scholarship in American history that has become available since the appearance of the first edition.

The editors are pleased to express here their gratitude to both teachers and students for their helpful comments on the first edition.

Sidney Fine
Gerald S. Brown

PREFACE TO THE FIRST EDITION

This book has three main features: it brings into sharp focus the major issues of the American past; it presents conflicting interpretations of these issues; and it draws for its selections upon historical literature which is often relatively inaccessible to the college student. The literature presented here is taken from the professional historical journals, from periodicals of a more general nature, and from monographs and other works. Each of the items selected, in the editors' view, makes a distinct, individual contribution to our knowledge of a controversial historical problem.

For each of the great issues selected, two historians present either directly conflicting interpretations or interpretations which illuminate the whole problem from complementary, but essentially different, approaches or emphases. A glance through the table of contents will show that many of the writers represented here are among the great historians of this century. One of the purposes which the editors had in view in bringing this body of historical writing together was to introduce American college students to good historical writing upon their own past, in a sense, by their own historians, men who, in the overwhelming majority, are still living and are still active in the profession. Each historian is represented by a substantial piece of writing within the limits of which he could, so to speak, move around and develop his interpretation in some depth and with that degree of sophistication which characterizes the mature writing of history. The editors have deliberately avoided the snippets and shreds and the mélange of primary and secondary materials which so often typify volumes of this kind. It is hoped that it is history with style and meaning which is presented here.

The seventeen pairs of selections in Volume I, edited by Gerald S. Brown, pertain to the period before 1865; the seventeen pairs of selections in Volume II, edited by Sidney Fine, to the years since Appomattox. The two volumes are designed to supplement the textbook and the lectures in the survey course in American history. Each pair of selections is preceded by a brief introduction which places the two interpretations in their historical and historiographical setting and which points up the nature of the conflict between them. It is expected that the selections will serve to stimulate discussion and thought concerning the principal themes of American history, and will help to give the reader an appreciation of the nature of the historical process and of the variety and the richness of contemporary historical writing.

S. F.

G. S. B.

CONTENTS

I

Radical Reconstruction in the South: Blackout of Honest Government or Battle for Democracy?

II

The American Businessman as Robber Baron: Fact or Fiction?

xi

Contents

III

Immigration and Racism: Was Race a Valid Basis for Immigration Policy?

IV

The Turner Thesis: "Is It . . . a Valid Key to the Meaning of American History?"

V

The Populists: Provincial Nativists or Liberal Democrats?

Contents

VI

Politics in the Gilded Age: Cynicism or Modest Improvement?

VII   *Feb 2*

The Spanish-American War: Did the American Businessman Influence the Decision for War?

VIII

Theodore Roosevelt as Legislative Leader: Success or Failure?

IX   *Feb 23*

Woodrow Wilson and Progressivism: Did the South Help Make Wilson an Advanced Progressive?

Contents

X

The United States and World War I, 1914–1917:
Did the Wilson Administration
Pursue a Policy of Neutrality?

XI

The Defeat of the Versailles Treaty:
Who Was Responsible, Wilson or Lodge?

XII

The Literature of the 1920's: A Trivial Literature
or a Literature of "Useful Innocence"?

Contents

Contents

XVI

The Korean War: Who Was Right, Truman or MacArthur?

XVII

A Catholic Is Elected President: What Factors Determined the Outcome of the 1960 Election?

THE AMERICAN PAST
Conflicting Interpretations of the Great Issues

VOLUME II

I

*Radical Reconstruction
in the South:
Blackout of Honest Government
or Battle for Democracy?*

INTRODUCTION

No aspect of the history of Reconstruction has so engaged the interest of historians as the character of the governments established in the South as the result of Congressional (Radical) Reconstruction policy. The fact that Negroes, for the first time in Southern history, played a part in these governments has made still more controversial what would undoubtedly have been a controversial matter under any circumstances. To many historians of Reconstruction, the period of Radical Reconstruction in the South was a time of unmitigated horror, the blackest chapter in the history of the South. Other historians of the era, in contrast, have stressed the accomplishments of the Radical governments and have challenged at several points the contentions of those who deplore the composition and the activities of the Radical regimes.

The two selections that follow exemplify the nature of the historical controversy concerning Radical Reconstruction in the South. Professor E. Merton Coulter, born in North Carolina, finds little to praise and much to condemn in the record of the Radical governments in the South. He is particularly critical of the part the Negroes played in these governments, a development that he believes should be "shuddered at, and execrated." Coulter, basically, is in agreement with the so-called Dunning school of Reconstruction historians, who have tended to view Reconstruction in the South as a struggle between good white Democrats and a coalition of bad Republicans, carpetbaggers, scalawags, and Negroes.

Taking issue with the point of view expressed by Coulter, Northern-born Professor Carl N. Degler summarizes the findings of scholars who have challenged some of the stereotypes of Reconstruction for which Dunning and his followers were to a degree responsible. Degler stresses the democratic aspects of Radical Reconstruction and attacks what he regards as the "myths" of Reconstruction historiography.

Blackout of Honest Government

Congress had set up new state governments because, as it claimed, the Johnson states were illegal and did not protect life and property. New leaders under new constitutions now took charge; the elimination of the old Southern leaders, from top to bottom, had been the heart of the Congressional plan. Would Congressional governments succeed better than Johnson governments—or even nearly as well?

Intent upon filling the thousands of offices made vacant, the delegates of the constitutional conventions maneuvered themselves into the best ones, and set up machinery which controlled the rest. In some of the states a few Conservatives slipped into minor offices. Governors were empowered to fill most of the local offices by appointment; legislatures could declare offices vacant and provide for filling them to their liking; and returning boards, a new Radical device for counting ballots, could manipulate the votes to bring about any desired result. In addition to the state offices, there were Federal positions to be filled, both elective and appointive—Congressmen, judges, customs collectors, revenue agents, and postmasters. As noted, all elective offices the Radicals controlled and all appointive offices fell into their hands when President Johnson gave way to Grant in 1869. Now all Southern officialdom became a powerful Radical machine. Even Federal judges became miserably partisan and corrupt. John C. Underwood in Virginia thoroughly disgraced himself in the proceedings relative to the trial of Jefferson Davis and by his political manipulations; Richard Busteed in Alabama debauched his bench through a rich harvest of bribes in cases brought before him by collusion; and Edward H. Durell in Louisiana became so completely a part of the corruption in that state that he resigned to escape impeachment.[1]

From E. Merton Coulter, *The South During Reconstruction, 1865–1877* (vol. VIII of *A History of the South*, ed. by Wendell Holmes Stephenson and E. Merton Coulter; Baton Rouge: Louisiana State University Press, 1947), pp. 139–161. Reprinted by permission.

[1] These judges had been appointed before the Radicals took charge of the South. Avary, *Dixie after the War*, 237–44; Fleming, *Civil War and Reconstruction in Alabama*, 744; John W. Burgess, *Reconstruction and the Constitution, 1866–1876* (New York, 1902), 270–71. Nordhoff, *Cotton States*, 85, said the Alabama election law set up "one of the most perfect machines for political fraud that I have ever heard of." In Plaquemines

Most of the people who filled the many offices were untrained and untried —Scalawags, Carpetbaggers, and Negroes. Had the times been normal their duties would have been onerous and complicated; with the times out of joint they took the easy road and speedily buried themselves in corruption. Carpetbaggers filled a majority of the higher offices. In the first elections in the seven states admitted in 1868, four of the governors, ten of the fourteen United States Senators, and twenty of the thirty-five Representatives were Carpetbaggers. Throughout the whole period of Reconstruction nineteen Carpetbaggers went to the Senate. Some of the outstanding ones who held high offices were: in South Carolina, Daniel H. Chamberlain, native of Massachusetts and educated at Harvard and Yale colleges, mostly honest, but succumbing ultimately to party necessities, and B. Frank Wittemore, also from Massachusetts, thoroughly corrupt, and expelled from Congress; in Mississippi, Adelbert Ames, son-in-law of Benjamin F. Butler, resigning the army to enter politics, crusading and inept, fleeing the governorship to escape impeachment; in Louisiana, Henry Clay Warmoth of Illinois, entering the political scene poor and retiring rich, and William Pitt Kellogg, born in Vermont and growing up in Illinois, leading his adopted state government into a blackout of honesty; and in Arkansas, Powell Clayton, passing from a disgraced governorship to the United States Senate.[2]

Although the Carpetbaggers played an important part in every state, they were not uniformly strong. In Virginia, North Carolina, Georgia, Tennessee, and Texas, the Scalawags came to be dominant, and, therefore, all that was reprehensible in Radical rule in the South should not be placed on Northern importation. The pestilences of the times knew no limits either geographical or racial; native-born white Southerners became as corrupt as Carpetbaggers, and only in South Carolina and Louisiana did the Negroes ever have a majority in any legislature.

And yet the most spectacular and exotic development in government in the history of white civilization was to be seen in the part the Negroes played in ruling the South—longest to be remembered, shuddered at, and execrated. An English traveler could hardly believe his senses as he saw the Negroes made "King, Lords, and Commons, and something more," and in

Parish, Louisiana, one name out of every seven and one-half people in the white population was put on the registration books, but one name out of every three and one eighth of the colored people received a place on the list. Many of the names were, of course, fictitious; out of forty-eight names drawn on a jury, thirty-six were nonexistent. *Ibid.*, 66.

[2] Dunning, *Reconstruction*, 120; Reginald C. McGrane, *Foreign Bondholders and American State Debts* (New York, 1935), 313; C. Mildred Thompson, "Carpet-Baggers in the United States Senate," in *Studies in Southern History and Politics*, 161–66. Warmoth, whose salary as governor was $8,000 a year, admitted making over $100,000 his first year in office. By 1872 his wealth was estimated at $500,000 to $1,000,000. Fleming (ed.), *Documentary History of Reconstruction*, II, 39. So outraged did some communities feel that they refused to let officials take their seats. Stearns, *Black Man of the South*, 212–40.

South Carolina he observed "a proletariat Parliament . . . the like of which could not be produced under the widest suffrage in any part of the world save in some of these Southern States." As a Southerner saw the South's predicament, "What a white commune was in France we all have seen; what a negro commune is in America our eyes have also witnessed. Both made war on intelligence and social distinctions, both brought chaos in their train." [3]

Though the Northern Radicals instituted Negro suffrage and officeholding in the name of justice, they were thoroughly insincere in their protestations; for in the first place few of the Northern states allowed the Negroes to vote and none ever promoted a Negro into any office, however intelligent the Negro or however lowly the position. Furthermore, the Radical national government, unrestrained by state laws or suffrage requirements, waited long to appoint Negroes to office in the North. Seeing these inconsistencies, a delegation of Negroes, representing both North and South, begged President Grant in 1869 to select some Northern Negroes.[4] A Southerner prayed that "some Boston Sambo may be appointed postmaster in that city so that the Puritans of that place may get a dose of the physic they have prepared for the South." [5] Why had no Negro been elected to office in the North? "Why has such a negro, for example, as Frederick Douglass," asked a Southerner, "never been sent by the Radicals of New York to represent his city of Rochester in the Legislature of the State or in the Congress of the nation?" [6] Until a Negro should sit in Congress, representing a Northern state, "and a score of colored men shall sit in the Legislature of each of the New England States, then, and not till then," said a Missourian, "will the black man be as well treated in those Radical regions, as he is now treated in the rebel States of the South." [7]

Carpetbaggers were as little desirous of promoting Negroes into high office in the South as their Northern colleagues were in their states; and Scalawags, actuated by racial antipathies more than Carpetbaggers, objected to Negroes holding any offices. Both were quite desirous that Negroes vote— but not for Negroes. A Georgia Negro wrote Charles Sumner that there was no other place in the Union where there were so "many miserable hungry unscrupulous politicians . . . and if they could prevent it no colored man would ever occupy any office of profit or trust." He later wrote, "I am tired of being used as stepping-stones to elevate white men alone to office and would like to vote for some competent colored man" to go to the United States Senate.[8] A convention of Negroes in Macon re-

[3] Somers, *Southern States since the War*, 41; *Southern Magazine*, XIV (1874), 587.
[4] Montgomery *Alabama State Journal*, May 22, 1869.
[5] Dalton *North Georgia Citizen*, May 27, 1869.
[6] Augusta *Weekly Chronicle & Sentinel*, September 16, 1874.
[7] *Missouri Republican*, quoted *ibid.*, June 8, 1870.
[8] Belcher, Augusta, Ga., to Sumner, April 5, 1869, in Sumner Papers, Box 94, No. 9; Belcher to Sumner, February 3, 1870, *ibid.*, Box 96, No. 99.

solved in 1868 that they did not recommend the colored man "to be satisfied with being a mere pack horse, to ride white men into office, whether
he [sic] is the exponent of our sentiments or not; no, it would be better
that we did not have the Ballot." [9] Even so, Negroes frequently held offices
far beyond their capacity to administer them.

In South Carolina, Florida, Mississippi, and Louisiana the Negroes
reached the zenith of their power, but in no state was a Negro ever elected
to the governorship, though in South Carolina, Mississippi, and Louisiana
Negroes became lieutenant governors. In Mississippi the lieutenant governor, Alexander K. Davis, frequently acted as governor during the absence
of Ames; and in Louisiana, Lieutenant Governor Pinchback succeeded to
the governorship if it be admitted that in the jigsaw puzzle of politics in
that state Governor Warmoth was legally impeached and removed. All
other state offices in some state at one time or another were filled by Negroes
—but in only one state was a justice of the Supreme Court a Negro. South
Carolina elevated to this position Jonathan Jasper Wright, a colored Carpetbagger from Pennsylvania.[10] The great majority of Negro officeholders were
local officials—such as constables, justices of the peace, county superintendents of education, etc.—though in all the states there was a sprinkling
of Negroes in the legislatures, ranging in number from only one in Tennessee to a majority in some of the sessions of the South Carolina legislature.
It was a bitter comment among Negroes that Brownlow, the most Radical
of native Southerners, saw to it that few of their race attained office in
Tennessee.

White members of most state legislatures disliked the presence of Negroes;
in Georgia in 1868 resentment gained the ascendancy and the white members, Radicals and Conservatives, banded together and expelled them. In
later sessions when they reappeared at the behest of Congress and the army,
the editor of the legislative manual merely recorded their names without the
customary biographical sketches, explaining that there was nothing to say
about them beyond their having been waiters, bootblacks, and cotton-field
hands. He slyly admitted another motive: "though Congress could compel
him to associate with negroes in a deliberative body, sit beside them in railroad cars, etc., neither Congress, Military Government, a triple Reconstruction nor even another amendment to the national patch-work, the United
States Constitution, could compel him to publish their biographies in this
book." [11]

A considerable number of Negroes were appointed to Federal positions
in the South, such as postmasters and mail agents; but the highest Federal

---

[9] Macon *American Union*, October 9, 1868.
[10] Robert H. Woody, "Jonathan Jasper Wright, Associate Justice of the Supreme Court
of South Carolina, 1870–77," in *Journal of Negro History*, XVIII (1933), 114–31.
[11] Alexander St. Clair-Abrams, *Manual and Biographical Register of the State of Georgia
for 1871–2* (Atlanta, 1872), vi.

service performed by Negroes was in Congress. Southerners looked with some degree of complacency on Negroes going to Congress, for there Northerners would see Negro rulers in operation and would be forced to associate with them. Since Negroes would not make corn, or cotton, or sugar, it might be that they would make laws. "We want negroes to be so thick in Congress," said a Virginian, "that a man standing on the wharf at Aquia Creek, with a favorable wind, could smell them. We want their wool to be knee-deep in the halls of Congress, and we do not want any one there who is not five times blacker than the ace of spades." [12]

In the summer of 1868 a South Carolina Radical inquired of Charles Sumner whether he thought it would "injure the republican party in the North and West if [we] were to send some colored men to Congress." [13] It was apparently not considered bad politics, for during the next dozen years seven Southern states sent as Senators and Representatives twenty-eight Negroes. The greatest number at any one time was eight in 1875. The states sending Negroes were North Carolina, South Carolina, Georgia, Florida, Alabama, Mississippi, and Louisiana. Mississippi sent the first one in the person of Hiram R. Revels, as Senator, born a free Negro in North Carolina. Only two Negro Senators ever served in Congress, both from Mississippi. Pinchback, the Louisiana mulatto, succeeded in getting himself elected both to the House and Senate for overlapping terms, but he was not seated in either place. Some of these Negro Congressmen did creditable service, but others became either echoes of their Radical masters or disgusting troublemakers. Their service did not recommend their race to the South or even to the North, for not until the twentieth century did a Negro sit in Congress from any Northern state.[14]

It would have been remarkable had Negroes shown any conspicuous ability as lawmakers and rulers, though they were better than there was reason to expect; but even so, much of their performance was either grotesque or puerile. Psychologically and in every other respect the Negroes were fearfully unprepared to occupy positions of rulership. Race and color came to mean more to them than any other consideration, whether of honest government, of justice to the individual, or even of ultimate protection of their own rights. Negroes on juries let color blind them, and they rejected the wisest counsel, Northern and Southern, against banding together politically, instead of dividing on issues and policies of government. Of course, many white Conservatives made it difficult for them to do otherwise; but Negroes proscribed their own race if any voted Democratic—their preachers excom-

---

[12] Richmond *Times,* quoted in *Southern Cultivator,* XXIV (1866), 61.

[13] W. B. Nash, Columbia, S. C., to Sumner, August 22, 1868, in Sumner Papers, Box 87, No. 18.

[14] Samuel D. Smith, *The Negro in Congress, 1870–1901* (Chapel Hill, 1940), 3–9, 45, 137–44; William A. Russ, Jr., "The Negro and White Disfranchisement during Radical Reconstruction," in *Journal of Negro History,* XIX (1934), 171–92.

municating them, their womenfolk bringing all tneir feminine powers to play against them, and Loyal Leagues intimidating and doing violence to them.[15] Their idea of the new order was

> De bottom rail's on de top,
> An' we's gwine to keep it dar.[16]

Radical leaders impressed their views on the Negroes. An Alabama editor said, "The Radicals are now trying to persuade the Southern negroes that it was very cruel and inhuman to rescue them from the dinner pot—that it would have been much better for them had their forefathers been eaten in Africa. Perhaps it would. If they intend to let carpet-baggers and scallawags lead them by their noses forever we are sure it would have been. Any man had better be eaten than a 'born fool' forever or the father of a generation of fools." [17]

Most Negro officeholders were more to be pitied than blamed, but a few blatant, dishonest, insolent megalomaniacs discredited all. A Carpetbagger characterized Henry M. Turner, preacher, politician, and presider at many Negro conventions, as "a licentious robber and counterfeiter, a vulgar black-guard, a sacrilegious profaner of God's name, and a most consummate hypocrite." Yet the Negroes elected him to the Georgia legislature—"if he had received his deserts, he would have gone to the Penitentiary"; he was "a thief and a scoundrel, and yet they voted for him." "If the colored people have not the elements of morality among them sufficiently to cry down such shameless characters, they should not expect to command the respect of decent people anywhere." [18] One Southerner told Sumner that he treated Negroes kindly, "but to Sit still and allow an ignoramus to represent me in government Councils I am not going to do it & you know that no sense-ble [sic] man will." [19] Another, seeing the humorous side of a Negro candidate, said, "Ike has no 'book larnin', but he bakes an excellent wheat pone, and knows how to drive a hack." [20]

General William S. Rosecrans, amidst a Confederate atmosphere at White Sulphur Springs, asked General Lee, in writing, whether he thought the

---

[15] As an example of a sensible attitude, a Negro candidate wrote, "I am for peace and harmony, and utterly opposed to any discussions having a tendency to excite bad feeling between any classes of society; and in canvassing the District I shall so conduct myself as to merit that respect and kindness which has always been shown me." Greenville *Southern Enterprise*, April 1, 1868.

[16] King, *Great South*, 453.

[17] Montgomery *Weekly Advertiser*, August 18, 1875. This is part of a Radical handbill to impress Negroes: "Every man knows that the Republican Party, under the lead of God, President Lincoln and General Grant, freed the whole colored race from slavery; and every man who knows anything, believes that the Democratic party will, if they can, make them slaves again." Dalton *North Georgia Citizen*, September 10, 1868.

[18] Macon *American Union*, December 29, 1870; June 15, 1871.

[19] Unsigned letter, Ft. Gaines, Ga., to Sumner, October 5, 1868, in Sumner Papers, Box 87, No. 74.

[20] Tallahassee *Sentinel*, September 2, 1867.

South must in reality be ruled by "the poor, simple, uneducated, landless freedmen" under the corrupt leadership of whites still worse. Lee and thirty-one other prominent Southerners signed an answer declaring their opposition, basing it on no enmity toward freedmen, "but from a deep-seated conviction that at present the negroes have neither the intelligence nor other qualifications which are necessary to make them depositories of political power." [21] The minority report of a Congressional committee declared, "History, till now, gives no account of a conqueror so cruel as to place his vanquished foes under the domination of their former slaves. *That was reserved for the radical rulers in this great Republic.*" [22]

South Carolina and Louisiana, apart from Haiti, were the world's classic examples of Negro rule, but worse than Haiti, for the black emperors of that benighted country ruled over black people who had never known any other kind of rule but bad. The general character of Negro government in these states was dismal and devastating in the extreme. It meant that the protection which civilized communities had received from their governments was at an end. Heretofore, if conditions should become too bad there was always an irreducible minimum of intelligence to which an outraged people could turn for redress; in these states that irreducible minimum miraculously had been reduced to nothing, for no appeal could be made to ignorant Negro majorities. One of the first questions put to a stranger coming to New Orleans to see the sights was whether he had seen the Negro legislature in action; and *Appletons' Hand-Book of American Travel* advised tourists that a peep into the statehouse in Columbia would "be intensely interesting and should not be missed by those who desire to see the negro in the role of a statesman." [23]

Specifically, the South Carolina House in 1873 consisted of 124 members, of whom 23 were Conservatives. Of the remaining 101 Radicals, 94 were Negroes. The Negroes thus outnumbered the whites more than three to one, though the Negro population of South Carolina was only slightly larger than the white. The Negro legislators were of all shades, from the lightest mulattoes to the blackest negroids, fresh from the kitchen and the field, in clothing ranging from secondhand black frock coats to the "coarse and dirty garments of the field." The white members did or said little, stunned by what they saw and heard—voluble, jabbering Negroes, always raising points of order and personal privilege, speaking a half dozen times on the same question, and repeating themselves constantly without knowing it. A South Carolinian viewed the scene for a time and as he turned away ex-

---

[21] Augusta *Weekly Constitutionalist*, September 16, 1868.

[22] *Ku Klux Conspiracy*, I, 438. "Now, we have as our rulers the vilest of mankind, whom no gentleman would allow to enter his kitchen," said the *Land We Love*, VI (1868–1869), 174.

[23] Charles H. Jones (ed.), *Appletons' Hand-Book of American Travel, Southern Tour* . . . (New York, 1874), 132.

claimed, "My God, look at this! . . . Let me go." A Northern newspaper-man who came down to see this amazing spectacle declared it was "barbarism overwhelming civilization by physical force" and "a wonder and a shame to modern civilization." A black parliament representing a white constituency—the only example in all history! [24]

Saddled with an irresponsible officialdom, the South was now plunged into debauchery, corruption, and private plundering unbelievable—suggesting that government had been transformed into an engine of destruction. It was fortunate for the South that its officials were bent on private aggrandizement and personal gain, rather than on a fundamental class overturning which would have resulted in confiscations and an upset of civilization. This condition was, therefore, nothing more than the Southern side of the national picture. Corruption permeated government from the statehouse to the courthouse and city hall—though in local government there was a tendency for more honesty to assert itself under the closer scrutiny of the people. Yet it is probably true that New Orleans suffered as much from misgovernment as Chicago and Boston did from fire.

The variety of means used to debauch government and plunder the public treasury bespeaks the vivid imaginations and practical ability of the perpetrators. Every seceded state came under the withering hand of Radical rule, but it was reserved to South Carolina, Louisiana, and Arkansas to suffer most. Legislatures piled up expenses against their impoverished states to fantastic heights. In Florida the cost of printing in 1869 was more than the entire cost of the state government in 1860; and the legislature sold for five cents an acre 1,100,000 acres of public land held in trust. The Georgia legislature bought from a favored agent in Atlanta an unfinished opera house for $250,000, previously sold for much less, to convert it into a capitol building. In Arkansas a Negro was given $9,000 for repairing a bridge which had originally cost $500. Brownlow of Tennessee, too palsied to sign his name, gave wide authority to others to attach his signature to state bonds with results easily imagined. In South Carolina the legislature bought for $700,000 land worth $100,000 for resale to Negroes; it issued $1,590,000 worth of bonds with which to redeem $500,000 worth of bank notes, and paid $75,000 to take a state census in 1869, although the Federal census was due to be taken the following year, which cost only $43,000; it voted extra compensation of $1,000 to the speaker for his efficient service when he lost $1,000 on a horse race; it paid for lunches, whiskies and wines, women's apparel, and coffins charged by the legislators to legislative expenses; and Governor Scott while drunk was induced by a fancy lady in a burlesque show to sign an issue of state bonds. The Louisiana legislature was extremely ingenious in devising means of spending the state's money: Before the war its sessions had cost on an average of $100,000 but under

---

[24] Pike, *Prostrate State,* 10–16.

Radical rule they cost about $1,000,000, half of which was for the mileage expenses and salaries of the members and clerks; its printing bill under three years of Warmoth's rule was $1,500,000 although previously it had never amounted to more than $60,000 for a year; to provide a capitol building it paid $250,000 for the St. Louis Hotel, recently sold for $84,000; it chartered the Mississippi Valley Navigation Company and purchased $100,-000 worth of stock in it, though it never organized to do business; it chartered a Society to Prevent Cruelty of Animals, whose activities turned out to be rustling stray animals in New Orleans and holding them for $5.00 a day charges to the owners and arresting horses left standing in the streets while their riders were transacting business in the shops; and the chief justice was a party to the sale of a state-owned railroad for $50,000 on which had been expended more than $2,000,000, refusing to sell it at a higher price to bidders whom he did not favor. The cost of clerks and assistants amounted to as much as the total expenses of wartime sessions; legislatures created new offices and increased the salaries of the old ones and created new counties for the spoils that went with them; governors pardoned criminals for pecuniary and political reasons, and legislation was regularly bought and sold, one Louisiana legislator demanding the price of his vote though he had been absent—and so the record of corruption could be extended ad infinitum.[25]

Whether or not the purpose of Radical Reconstruction was to place "the negro and the almighty dollar in the sanctionary of the Constitution," [26] there was ample evidence in Southern state documents of the intention to do both. Yet these constitutions were considered then and since as proof of the desires of the framers to promote true democracy and economic recovery. Whatever the motives, the results were devastating to honest government, for they opened up to dishonest speculators, Northern and Southern, the exploitation of Southern credit in the name of railroad development. In these robberies stand high the names of George W. Swepson and Martin S. Littlefield in North Carolina and Florida, Hannibal I. Kimball in Georgia, and John C. and Daniel N. Stanton in Alabama. In every state there were individuals or groups that seized their opportunities.

The process was simple and appeared entirely divorced from corruption: in fact, it was nothing new, for it had been used in the South before the war and directly following, before the Radicals had secured control of the government. It consisted merely in the state lending its credit to private

---

[25] *Ibid.*, 49, 191–97, 199, 213; Nordhoff, *Cotton States*, 31, 43, 47, 56, 59, 60, 62; Ella Lonn, *Reconstruction in Louisiana After 1868* (New York, 1918), 30, 34, 50, 87; Davis, *Civil War and Reconstruction in Florida*, 648–50, 666–67, 670–71; Robert H. Woody (ed.), "Behind the Scenes in the Reconstruction Legislature of South Carolina: Diary of Josephus Woodruff," in *Journal of Southern History*, II (1936), 78–102, 233–59; Simkins and Woody, *South Carolina during Reconstruction*, 113, 134–40; Coulter, *William G. Brownlow*, 376–77.

[26] Minority report, *Ku Klux Conspiracy*, I, 525.

companies in their efforts to construct railroads, by buying their stock, by guaranteeing the payment of railroad bonds, and by giving them a fixed sum for each mile constructed, and in the last two methods taking a mortgage on the railroad. A Georgia Conservative said, "[It] is now quite apparent that the public mind has, with very considerable unanimity, accepted 'State aid' as the true policy of the State"; [27] and an Alabama Radical agreed that it was *"in no sense a party measure."* [28] It was only through the dishonesties of state officials that the great stench in railroad aid arose. In violation of law they delivered bonds before the railroads were built, and the dishonest promoters sold these bonds for what they could get and never built the roads. Sometimes legislatures also loaned more per mile than the roads were worth when finished, so that even with the roads turned over to the states, considerable losses were suffered. The amount usually allowed was from $10,000 to $15,000 a mile, to be paid as ten-mile units were completed. Counties also lent their credit. A Chicago editor declared that guarantees were claimed "and generally obtained for anything which had two parallel bars of iron, however light, upon any apology for a road-bed," and, he might have added, for nothing at all.[29] Every state suffered under these dishonesties except Mississippi, where there was a constitutional provision against state aid, but the legislature got around it by making outright gifts to certain favored companies.[30]

North Carolina authorized almost $28,000,000 of railroad bonds and actually delivered over $17,500,000; on account of ill-kept records, Alabama could never determine the amount of her issues, but it has been estimated from $17,000,000 to $30,000,000; a ring of twenty men controlled the charters of eighty-six railroads in Arkansas and got state loans to the amount of $5,350,000, to which was added $3,000,000 in levee bonds that railroads could claim by making their roadbeds serve as levees; Georgia lent to railroad companies $5,733,000; and so the story goes.[31] It should be remembered that these issues were not total losses, for where they were not delivered there could be no loss, and where the railroad had been built the state when forced to foreclose on defaulted bonds became the owner of the road. Some of the states after the raids had been made passed constitutional amendments forbidding aid to private companies.

Railroad rings used other means to reap rich harvests, such as bribing legislatures to sell their railroad holdings for practically nothing, as in

---

[27] Augusta *Weekly Chronicle & Sentinel,* July 20, 1870.

[28] Montgomery *Alabama State Journal,* December 18, 1869.

[29] *Railroad Gazette: A Journal of Transportation* (Chicago), IV (1872), 87.

[30] Garner, *Reconstruction in Mississippi,* 289.

[31] *Weekly Columbus Enquirer,* July 25, 1871; Augusta *Weekly Chronicle & Sentinel,* July 19, 1871; Somers, *Southern States since the War,* 82 ff.; Nordhoff, *Cotton States,* 30, 58; McGrane, *Foreign Bondholders and American State Debts,* 294–95; Albert B. Moore, "Railroad Building in Alabama during the Reconstruction Period," in *Journal of Southern History,* I (1935), 421–34, 437–38.

cratic governments were never able to determine exact amounts, and many later commentators have been unscientific in their appraisals. South Carolina's debt has been estimated from $15,700,000 to $29,100,000; North Carolina's and Alabama's as high as $30,000,000; and Louisiana's at $50,597,000, one fourth for the benefit of the state and the rest "squandered, or done worse with." Many bond issues were sold at a small fraction of their face value. Confusion has arisen because writers have not indicated what part of the debts was secured by railroads and other valuable property and the part that represented values evaporated and gone forever. The amount of debts piled up by local divisions, such as counties and cities, is past finding out, with many records gone and others widely scattered. Irrespective of amounts, it cannot be doubted that the South underwent fearful financial punishment under Radical rule.[39]

Another source of money, either to spend or to steal, was taxation. Since taxing is used more than bond issuing for the ordinary expenses of government, it was to be expected that taxes should be higher after the Civil War than before. This is so on account of the many additional services governments undertook to perform for the people. Education was now provided free for all people; more institutions such as insane asylums and poorhouses were set up; and the cost of administering justice was vastly increased. Formerly, if a slave committed a serious crime he received thirty-nine lashes, at no expense to the planter or the state; now, when Negroes committed crimes their arrest, trial, and punishment brought on expenses which the state must pay.

In ante-bellum times Southerners had never been subjected to burdensome taxes, and little of their revenue had been secured from land. In South Carolina in 1859 all agricultural lands were assessed for taxation at slightly more than $10,000,000, whereas lots and buildings in Charleston alone were listed at $22,000,000. With the coming of the Radicals, land was made to bear a greatly increased amount of the tax burden—and not on account of the ease in levying the tax or by simple accident. It was by special design, for those who set the taxes had little land, or, indeed, little property of any sort; but, as they wanted land, they saw that high taxes would depress its value and probably lead to its confiscation by the state for unpaid taxes. Here the Negroes and poor whites would find an easy road to landownership. Joseph H. Rainey, a South Carolina colored Congressman, said, "Land in South Carolina is cheap. We like to put on the taxes, so as to make it cheap!" [40] The amount of land advertised for taxes increased with the carry-

---

[39] Nordhoff, *Cotton States*, 29, 57, 95; Coulter, *William G. Brownlow*, 375–77; Fleming, *Civil War and Reconstruction in Alabama*, 571–86; Davis, *Civil War and Reconstruction in Florida*, 679; Simkins and Woody, *South Carolina during Reconstruction*, 45, 148–85; Beale, "On Rewriting Reconstruction History," *loc. cit.*, 816. Vicksburg's debt rose from $13,000 in 1869 to $1,400,000 in 1874. Garner, *Reconstruction in Mississippi*, 328 ff.

[40] New Orleans *Weekly Times*, June 6, 1874.

ing out of this program, until whole sections of some states were for sale. In Mississippi about a fifth of the state was advertised for taxes; in St. Landry Parish, Louisiana, there were 821 sales of land for taxes from 1871 to 1873; in Arkansas a book of 228 pages, reprinted from an advertisement taking up sixteen sheets in a large-sized newspaper and costing for one insertion $12,312, was required to list the delinquent lands there.[41]

In some places the tax rate, state, county, and city, ran as high as 50 mills, equivalent to 5 per cent of the assessed value of the property. Though property values in the eleven states which had composed the Confederacy were in 1870 less than one half what they were in 1860, the amount of taxes paid was more than four times the total in 1860. A South Carolinian who had paid a tax of fifty cents on his lands before the war, now paid $15; another complained that he was forced to sell his last cow to provide money for his taxes. And one of the most discouraging features of Radical taxes was that much of the money was stolen by the collectors. More than a half million dollars of taxes collected in 1872 in Florida were never turned into the treasury.[42] This situation led outraged landholders in many sections of the South to call taxpayers' conventions, one in Louisiana adopting the name of the Tax Resisting Association, which begged its tormentors for relief and sought more practical methods of obtaining it. When Negroes secured land they began to take the white man's point of view on high taxes. The worst tax atrocities came in the South after 1870, but even with its highest taxes it paid little higher rates than were levied in some of the Northern states. In 1870 Illinois had a rate of 45 mills, when the average for the eleven former Confederate States at that time was only 15 mills. The poverty of the South as compared with the North is strikingly shown in this fact: in 1870 the state of New York with a rate of 24.6 mills collected $48,550,000, whereas the whole former Confederate states collected only $32,227,529, state, county, and municipal.[43]

Assuredly, then, Radical government had not given the South that protection of property promised in the first Military Reconstruction Act; did it do any better in protecting life? In a war-ridden region like the South there was destined to be violence irrespective of the efforts of governing authorities to prevent it—whether they be Johnson Conservatives or Grant Radicals. After the Radicals took hold, violence instead of subsiding increased, and for reasons not foreign to provocative actions by the new rulers. Negro militia, which were organized in many of the states, incited violence as much as they promoted law and order; Loyal Leagues incited Negroes into incendiarism and racial clashes. Pistol toting became a custom, and it was

---

[41] Raymond *Hinds County Gazette,* June 7, 1867; August 17, 1870; December 27, 1871; Little Rock *Weekly Arkansas Gazette,* January 16, 1872.
[42] *Compendium of the Ninth Census, 1870* (Washington, 1872), 640; *Compendium of the Tenth Census, 1880,* II, 1509; *Ku Klux Conspiracy,* I, 439.
[43] *Ku Klux Conspiracy,* I, 228–29.

said that Colt's arms factory was kept busy supplying the Southern trade. Former Governor Perry of South Carolina wrote the Radical Governor Robert K. Scott, "Every week and every day we hear of houses, barns, gin-houses and stores being destroyed and robbed by the midnight incendiary." [44] In one issue of an Upper South Carolina newspaper appeared rewards for the burners of the stables of eight different men, and the machine shop of another. "There seems to be no limit to the insolence of the Carolina negroes," declared a Georgia editor. "They have been taught to regard the whites as their enemies and, having the power, let pass no opportunity to inflict annoyance or insult." [45]

Called into existence by violence, the Ku Klux Klan added to it; riots of serious proportions broke out widely over the South, some provoked by the Klan and others not. Rufus B. Bullock, Radical governor of Georgia, admitted that crimes against Negroes increased from an average of seventeen a month before his administration to forty-six after he took hold.[46] One issue of a state paper carried proclamations of the Governor offering rewards of $15,000 or more for lawbreakers.[47] Early in his administration, 300 armed Negroes "led on by the vermin, black and white, native and imported," incited a riot by attempting to enter Camilla. It was estimated that 150 people were killed at various times in Jackson County, Florida, alone; and Negroes started the most serious riot in Alabama's history when at Eufaula they tried to prevent a member of their race from voting the Democratic ticket. Negroes in Vicksburg provoked a race riot in which a hundred former Federal soldiers and other whites took part, and in which three dozen Negroes were killed. In Louisiana under its miserable travesty on government there was no end of riots and lesser violence—the Colfax riot in which fifty-nine Negroes and two whites were killed, the Coushatta violence in which five Radical officeholders were murdered, and the famous New Orleans uprising of 1874 which was not unlike a Parisian revolution. So bad were conditions that General Sheridan who was sent to preserve law and order, to the amazement of sane people everywhere, asked for permission to declare banditti those Louisianians whom he cared to dispose of without further ado. In North Carolina a unique band of lawbreakers known as the Lowrie Gang seem to have suffered little hindrance probably because of their Radical leanings.[48]

---

[44] Greenville *Enterprise,* April 12, 1871; April 3, 1872.

[45] Augusta *Weekly Chronicle & Sentinel,* January 7, 1874.

[46] Thompson, *Reconstruction in Georgia,* 257; W. H. McWhorter, Greensboro, Ga., to Sumner, May 14, 1869, in Sumner Papers, Box 92, No. 176; Tunis G. Campbell, Atlanta, to Sumner, April 19, 1869, *ibid.,* Box 94, No. 45.

[47] Marietta *Journal,* February 10, 1871.

[48] Rhodes, *History of the United States,* VII, 112–22; Nordhoff, *Cotton States,* 48, 54, 79; James J. Farris, "The Lowrie Gang—An Episode in the History of Robeson County, N. C., 1864–1874," in Trinity College Historical Society *Papers* (Durham, 1897–), Ser. XV (1925), 55–93.

Though it might appear that Radicals would be discredited by arguing violence in the South under their own rule, yet they did so with a great show of statistics to prove it. Their purpose was to induce the Federal government to send in troops to uphold their tottering regimes, or to "wave the bloody shirt" in the North to influence elections there. Governor Warmoth asserted that 3,000 Democrats killed 200 Radicals in the St. Landry riot of 1868; and for the Congressional elections of 1874 Representative Joseph R. Hawley of Connecticut got a list of Alabama atrocities from Charles Hays, an Alabama Radical Representative, which he used to great effect until the New York *Tribune* proved them to be myths. A meeting of Radicals from nearly all the Southern states came together this same year in Chattanooga to compile a stunning list of atrocities for the same election campaign.[49] Lucius Q. C. Lamar, Democratic Representative from Mississippi, asked these embarrassing questions: "When you point me to acts of violence, I acknowledge and deplore them; but I ask you, who has governed the States where this violence occurs, for the last ten years? Have we? Who have taxed us, controlled our legislatures, filled our courts, received the patronage of the Federal Government, ruled over us at home, and represented us here?"[50]

Radical Reconstruction had failed in every particular in which the Radical Congress had accused the Johnson governments. Radical rule in Louisiana had produced effects "which in ten years have sunk this fertile and once prosperous State into a condition of decay which it has taken Turkish misgovernment some centuries to bring about in the East."[51] And the people of New Orleans were described by a Northern traveler: "Ah! these faces, these faces;—expressing deeper pain, profounder discontent than were caused by the iron fate of the few years of the war! One sees them everywhere; on the street, at the theater, in the *salon,* in the cars; and pauses for a moment, struck with the expression of entire despair—of complete helplessness, which has possessed their features."[52] Alluding to the New Orleans uprising of 1874, the *Nation* said there was no instance in modern times "in which the insurgents had more plainly the right on their side," and when the Federal troops were sent to put it down, this journal declared that the Austrians in their seventy years of tyranny in Italy had never

---

[49] Henry C. Warmoth, *War, Politics and Reconstruction: Stormy Days in Louisiana* (New York, 1930), 67. See also, Montgomery *Weekly Advertiser,* January 20, 1875; Macon *American Union,* September 25, 1868; Columbus (Miss.) *Press,* September 26, October 13, 17, 24, 1874; Nordhoff, *Cotton States,* 18. Henry B. Denman, New Orleans, wrote Zachariah Chandler from New Orleans, March 11, 1872, that four fifths of the whites there "hate the National Government with a bitterness that can hardly be realized and not possibly expressed or described." Zachariah Chandler Papers, V, Nos. 1072–73.

[50] Edwin A. Alderman *et al.* (eds.), *Library of Southern Literature* (New Orleans, Atlanta, Dallas, 1907–1923), VII, 2973.

[51] *Southern Magazine,* XVI (1875), 430.

[52] King, *Great South,* 34.

"marched on so bad and despicable an errand." [53] An observer saw in Alabamans a despair "more dreadful and depressing than the negro ignorance." [54]

The more intelligent Negroes were beginning to see that their own fate lay buried with that of their Conservative white neighbors, and some of them began to avoid the Radicals and eschew politics entirely. Richard Harvey Cain, a Negro editor in Charleston, said, "When the smoke and fighting is over, the negroes have nothing gained and the whites have nothing left, while the jackals have all the booty." [55]

Also, it should not be assumed that there was no stern opposition and righteous indignation in the North against this Radical withering up of the South. The Democratic party platform in 1868 was strong in its denunciation, and Horatio Seymour, its candidate for President, condemned the barbarous rule of the Radicals. Frank Blair, the vice-presidential nominee, repenting that he had marched through Georgia with Sherman, threatened violence against Radical Reconstructionists. As for Federal commanders, Rosecrans, Sherman, George H. Thomas, George G. Meade, Winfield S. Hancock, George B. McClellan, Don Carlos Buell, Henry W. Slocum, John A. McClernand, William S. Franklin, and others either were silently ashamed or expressed their abhorrence of what was going on.[56] The editor of *Scribner's Monthly* saw Southerners in despair and he blamed the Federal government: "They feel that they were wronged, that they have no future, that they cannot protect themselves, and that nothing but death or voluntary exile will give them relief." [57] The editor of the *Nation* by 1870 had come to view the South with a light different from that of 1865. In the South the people had almost forgotten "that in free countries men live for more objects than the simple one of keeping robbers' hands off the earnings of the citizen." [58] There people were worse off than they were in any South American republic; for in the latter place tyrants could be turned out through the right of revolution, but the South with the army on its back could no longer resort to this ancient remedy. Southerners must continue to suffer enormities "which the Czar would not venture toward Poland, or the British Empire toward the Sautals of the Indian jungle." [59] The North

---

[53] *Nation*, XIX (1874), 199.

[54] King, *Great South*, 333.

[55] Charleston *Missionary Record*, quoted in Augusta *Weekly Chronicle & Sentinel*, November 22, 1871.

[56] Randall, *Civil War and Reconstruction*, 797–98.

[57] *Scribner's Monthly*, VIII (1874), 368.

[58] *Nation*, XIX (1874), 132. South Carolina had produced "not one, but a swarm of little Tweeds and little Butlers, some white and some black." *Ibid.*, XVIII (1874), 247.

[59] *Ibid.*, 326. "They are 'ex-rebels,' but they are not thieves. They have owned slaves, and revolted in defense of slavery; but they are influential, economical, and trustworthy in the management of State affairs, and it was of the first importance not only to the negro, but to the whole Union, that, during the transitional or reconstructive period following the war, they should neither be driven into hostility to the local government nor prevented from giving it the benefit of their experience and ability." *Ibid.*, XII (1871), 212.

with all its charities to the South had done less good than the Carpetbaggers had done harm.[60] Schurz had learned much since his first visit to the South in 1865. He saw fearful acts perpetrated against the South, all in the name of patriotism, and particularly in Louisiana, "a usurpation such as this country has never seen, and probably no citizen of the United States has ever dreamed of." [61]

---

[60] Said the *Nation*, XIV (1872), 197: "Seven years have gone over us since the close of the war, and, instead of occupying this precious season with endeavors to re-establish prosperity and to sow the seeds of peace which, in another generation, would ripen into good-will and forgetfulness, we have averted our eyes from the whole problem, refused to listen to the complaints of men whose hands we have tied, and have fallen back upon the lazy belief that in some way this great country is bound to go through."

[61] King, *Great South*, 93.

Dawn Without Noon

Carl N. Degler

In May of 1954, many Americans suddenly realized, despite the fact that almost ninety years had passed since the War for the Union, that the sounds and clashes of that struggle were still echoing. The Supreme Court's decision that Negroes are entitled to equal status with whites in the public schools of the nation was but the latest of the efforts, beginning as far back as the time of Appomattox, to find for the Negro in America a place consistent with the national heritage of freedom and equality.

For a full two hundred years the character, the status, and the future of the great majority of black men in America were defined and molded by the institution of slavery. Then abruptly, within the course of four years of war, this customary and legal guide to race relations was completely swept away; white and black men alike had to set about establishing a new relationship. The determination of what that relationship should be has been slow, unsteady, and at times agonizing. Today, almost a century after the enunciation of the Emancipation Proclamation, it has still not been

---

finally determined; it is still capable of arousing deep-seated emotions among Americans.

1. EQUALITY BY FORCE

The first attempts to carve out a place for the black man in a white-dominated America were undertaken in the dozen years after 1865, which have since come to be called the Reconstruction period. That era, despite the cataclysmic character of the War for the Union, is best understood as a continuation of the history of the previous thirty years. The conflicts of the Reconstruction period are deeply rooted in the previous generation of sectional struggle over the issue of Negro slavery. The war, it is true, removed slavery from the congressional debates as effectively as it destroyed it in the South, but it failed to reconcile the opposite moral values which lay behind the two sections' conceptions of what slavery was and what the Negro was.

Many of the northern Radical Republicans, for example—men like Ben Wade, Charles Sumner, Thaddeus Stevens, William Fessenden, and John Bingham—had been in Congress during the antislavery struggle in the 1850's. They were still there when the Reconstruction of the former Confederacy was begun. For such men, the experiences of the years of antislavery and nationalistic agitation made it unthinkable that the South should be restored to the Union untouched by the fires in which they themselves had been tempered. And what was true of the leaders was true of thousands of ordinary men of the North whose lives were permanently altered by the moral fervor of the antislavery crusade and the emotionalism of the great War for the Union.

But the South, too, had a history by which its people had been molded. The Southerner's image of the Negro was shaped by the slave past, and its contours were shaken not at all by the rhetoric of the antislavery North or by the guns which finally destroyed the "peculiar institution." When the South came to legislate a status for the freedman, it would understandably draw upon the experience under slavery.

Under such circumstances, the cessation of hostilities between the sections brought not peace, but a political cold war, one which was more full of hate, bitterness, and misunderstanding than the hot war which preceded it. Since neither section had been able to transcend its historically derived conceptions about the nature of the Union, it was hardly to be expected that either would be able to rise above its history when dealing with the emotionally charged question of the freed Negro.

As the war overturned American thinking about slavery and the nature of the Union, so the Reconstruction re-educated the American people on the place the Negro should occupy in the United States. When the war ended, the position of the newly freed black man was ambiguous throughout the

21

nation. In the North, though he was a citizen, society discriminated against him, and he was denied the ballot in all states except New York and five in New England. Moreover, as a measure of the North's attitude, within the previous five years the people of several northern states had overwhelmingly refused to extend the vote to Negroes. In the South, the Negro's ambiguous position was summed up in the fact that he was neither a slave nor a citizen.

But within half a decade, under the driving will of the Radical Republicans all this was reversed. The adoption of the Fourteenth and Fifteenth Amendments to the Constitution signified that the Negro was now to be a full citizen, equal in civil rights and voting privileges with white men. Insofar as modern Americans take pride from this inclusion of the Negro in the American dream of equality and opportunity, then it is to the Radicals that they are indebted. For it was solely because of the Radicals' control over the South that the requisite number of states were brought to ratify the two amendments. If not written into the Constitution then, when the conservative South was powerless to resist and the North was still imbued with its mission of reform, then the principle of Negro equality would probably never have been included in the national charter. This achievement of the Radicals is at least as much a part of the legacy of Reconstruction as the better-known corruption and the imposition of alien rule.

The accomplishment of the Radicals is especially noteworthy because the obstacles were so formidable—not only in the South, but in the North as well. We have already seen that few states in the North in 1865 were prepared to grant Negroes the privilege of participating in the government. The North did, however, believe that the war had put a final end to Negro slavery. It was when that decision seemed to be challenged by the vanquished South that the equalitarian Radicals were presented with an opportunity to enlarge the area of the Negro's rights and privileges. . . .

To compel the South to accept Negro suffrage was to ask of that region more than the North at that time appeared willing to give.[1] But the North's opposition to Negro voting was deceptively weak, as the rapidity with which the Fifteenth Amendment was ratified demonstrated. In February, 1869, less than two years after Negro suffrage was imposed upon the South, the Fifteenth Amendment was on its way to the states. Ratification, with the assistance of the now Radicalized southern states, was achieved within thirteen months thereafter. By a combination of persuasion and emotion in the North, and ruthless suppression in the South, the Radicals had completed their revolution. In the eyes of the national Constitution the former slave was now a full citizen, equal before the law and in possession of the ballot.

---

[1] As late as 1868, only four states outside of New England and New York granted the suffrage to Negroes: Nebraska, Iowa, Minnesota, and Wisconsin. Colorado and Connecticut had rejected Negro suffrage in 1865; Ohio and Kansas did so in 1867; Missouri and Michigan in 1868.

2. HOW BLACK WAS BLACK RECONSTRUCTION?

But, it will be said, the price the South and the nation paid for this ideal of equality was outrageously high. And because the history of Reconstruction in the South has been so overlaid with myth and emotion, it is necessary at this point to digress somewhat in an attempt to put that unhappy decade into some perspective.

There is a myth of Reconstruction history to which most Americans, Northerners and Southerners alike, give credence. In brief outline it goes something like this. In 1867, a vengeful Congress placed the southern states under a military despotism which supported by its bayonets an alien regime in each of the states, composed of white adventurers—the carpetbaggers and scalawags—and their ignorant Negro allies. For a decade thereafter, the story continues, these regimes looted the treasuries of the southern states, impoverished the region with high taxes, denied the southern white people any say in their own governance, and spread terror throughout the Southland. Not until the withdrawal of federal troops in 1877, it is said, did this nightmare end and decency in government return to the South. As in most myths, there is some truth in this one; but a balanced picture of Reconstruction is quite different.

For one thing, though it is common to think of Reconstruction as lasting the ten years from 1867 to 1877, the actual duration of the military and Radical regimes varied considerably from state to state. Democratic or conservative governments came to power in Virginia and North Carolina as early as 1870 (in fact, Virginia never experienced a true Radical civilian government at all); in Georgia in 1871; in Texas, Arkansas, and Alabama in 1874; in Mississippi in 1876. Only South Carolina, Florida, and Louisiana depended upon the withdrawal of federal troops in 1877 for the overthrow of their Radical government. In brief, Radical Reconstruction, including the military phases as well as the civilian, lasted as short as three years in two states and as long as ten years in only three.

Because it is so often assumed that Radical Reconstruction was synonymous with military rule, the role of the Army in the South during this period must be precisely understood. Under the congressional plan of Reconstruction as set forth in the acts of 1867, the South was divided into five military districts, each under a major general. It was the responsibility of these generals to oversee the establishment of registration lists for voters for the constitutional conventions and the election of new governments in the states of their districts. Once this was accomplished, civil governments based on the new constitutions would assume power. Generally, the ending of military rule roughly coincided with the date at which Congress admitted the state to the Union. Thus military rule ended in 1868 in all of the southern states except Virginia, Texas, and Mississippi, and in those states it was over in 1869 or 1870. (Only in Georgia was military rule ever imposed again.) Often, it must be admitted, the Radical civil governments required or utilized the aid of militia and sometimes the federal troops to support their regimes, but this does not mean that an extraconstitutional government was in power. For the greater part of Radical Reconstruction, then, the southern states were under civil, not military, government, and, in most cases, these were governments which conservative white Southerners could influence with their votes. Indeed, it was by losing elections that many of the Radical governments fell into conservative hands before 1877.

But even when the southern states were under the military, it should not be assumed that the government was corrupt, oppressive, or unfair toward the whites. Contrary to the usual conception of the military occupation of the South, the number of troops actually stationed in the whole region was very small. No more than 20,000 men were involved in the whole "occupation," of whom fully 7,000 were concentrated in the two states of Louisiana and Texas. No garrison, except those in Richmond and New Orleans, which contained 1,000 each, numbered more than 500 men. The relative weakness of the military force, of course, is a measure of the southern acceptance of northern control.

Though weak in man power, the military was supreme in law. In fact, the whole machinery of government and law was at the disposal of the Army; its authority was final. But the aquiescence in this on the part of the Southerners—for there was no organized opposition—is weighty testimony to the relative fairness of the administration. "It would be hard to deny that, so far as the ordinary civil administration was concerned," William A. Dunning, the authority on Reconstruction and no friend of the Radicals, has written, "the rule of the generals was as just and efficient as it was far-reaching. Criticism and denunciation of their acts were bitter and continuous; but no very profound research is necessary in order to discover that the animus of these attacks was chiefly political. . . ." There is good reason for believing, he continued, "that military government, pure and simple, unaccompanied by the measures for the institution of Negro suffrage, might have proved for a time a useful aid to social readjustment in the South, as preliminary to the final solution of political problems."

Even later, when the federal troops intervened in the South, it was with care and with a concern for fairness to the whites. President Grant in 1871, much disturbed by the attacks of the Ku Klux Klan upon Negroes, prevailed upon Congress to pass an act to aid in the suppression of the violence. Only once, however, did the President invoke the broad powers which Congress granted; this was in the famous incident of the nine counties of South Carolina in 1871. But even in this instance, Grant was careful enough to have the Attorney General investigate the situation in the area before he acted, and the President withdrew his order for one county when he found he was mistaken as to the disorders and conditions there.

In the prosecution of Southerners for infractions of the so-called enforce-

24

ment acts, passed in 1870–71 to assist in the suppression of opposition to Negro suffrage, the federal courts tried hard to be fair. Out of the hundreds of cases against whites for infringements of these laws, there were relatively few convictions. One authority, William W. Davis, a Southerner, has estimated that only about 20 per cent of the cases under the acts resulted in conviction; and about 70 per cent of them were dismissed or nolle-prossed. "The Federal courts," Davis has written, "insisted on reasonable testimony, and the judges, with some notorious exceptions, were generally fair in their rulings." Moreover, he added, "White judges were inclined toward leniency in judging the white man prosecuted under the force acts on the testimony of black men." In summary, then, it would seem that justice was obtainable for the white man even during the grimmest days of so-called Black Reconstruction.[2]

Perhaps the explanation most commonly offered for the ascendancy of the Radicals and the Negroes in southern state governments is that the conservative whites were disfranchised at the same time the Negroes were enfranchised. As a literal and nonquantitative statement, this is true, but as an explanation it will not hold water. At no time were sufficient whites deprived of the ballot to permit the Negroes and Northerners to take over the governments of the southern states by default.

Before the numbers involved can be discussed, the two different kinds or phases of disfranchisement must be understood. The first was during military rule, when Congress stipulated that those who had deserted federal office for the Confederacy or had voluntarily given aid to that cause were to be denied the suffrage and officeholding. Though it is impossible to obtain a completely accurate record of the number disfranchised under this rule (thousands of whites, for example, refused to register as a form of protest, but they are sometimes counted as disfranchised), the figure usually accepted is 150,000 for the whole South. This is to be compared with a total registration for whites in 1868 of about 630,000. Regardless of the size of the figure, under this disfranchisement only two elections were held, that for the choosing of the delegates to the state constitution conventions and that for the selection of the officers of the new governments created under the constitutions. After that, the qualifications for voting would be those decided upon in the conventions and written into the new constitutions. And that was the second phase of disfranchisement.

Again, contrary to the usual opinion, the states, on the whole, in their Radical-dominated conventions were not as ruthless in disfranchisement as

---

[2] Even a work as critical and penetrating as W. J. Cash, *The Mind of the South,* published as recently as 1941, contains exaggerated presentations of what happened during Reconstruction. "For ten years the courts of the South were in such hands that no loyal white man could hope to find justice in them as against any Negro or any white creature of the Yankee policy; for twenty years and longer they continued, in many quarters, to be in such hands that such justice was at least doubtful."

one might expect. And those which were, found that their disabling clauses were removed before ratification. In the end, only Louisiana, Alabama, and Arkansas actually enforced suffrage and officeholding restrictions against whites; the other seven states placed no legal obstacle in the way of white voting. Finally, it should be noted that the number of southern leaders upon whom the disabilities of the Fourteenth Amendment were visited was greatly reduced as early as 1872. At that date no more than 750 Southerners, those who had occupied high office under the United States in 1860–61 and had deserted to the southern cause, were still barred from officeholding. The disabilities against these men were not removed until the time of the Spanish–American War.

In view of the foregoing, it is illusory to look to white disfranchisement for an explanation of the electoral successes of the Radicals in the southern states. Rather it has to be sought in the fact that many whites did not vote, either in protest or because of indifference, while many Negroes did, either from understanding of the issues or from compulsion from their white and Negro leaders. It should not be forgotten, in this regard, that the proportion of Negroes in the southern states was uniformly greater at that time than it is now. Three states, for example—Louisiana, South Carolina, and Mississippi—contained a majority of Negroes, and one would expect, everything being equal, to encounter a Negro-Radical majority in those states. Moreover, a comparison of the number of Negroes registered in 1868 in each of the southern states with the number of Negro males over twenty-one as listed in the Census of 1870 discloses that only in Alabama was the actual number of Negro registrants out of line with the potential number as counted in the census. In all the other states the registration figures are plausible and not the result of obvious padding or fraud.

This is not to suggest that fraud did not occur in Reconstruction elections any more than it is meant to convey the impression that New York City elections at this time were innocent of fraud; undoubtedly there was much in both places and on both sides of the political fence. The purpose here, rather, is to show that there is solid justification for the strong showing which the Radicals made at the polls and that it is not to be casually attributed to the "counting out" of the whites. As a matter of fact, even under military-run registration in 1868, white voters outnumbered Negro voters in Georgia, Virginia, Texas, and North Carolina, a fact which rather effectively demolishes the argument that military reconstruction disfranchised the white majorities. Yet, of the two phases of disfranchisement, this was the stricter.

Looming over all discussions of Reconstruction, whether by Southerners or Northerners, is always the question of Negro domination. Surely, in the fear-ridden mind of the South, the unforgettable evil of Reconstruction was the participation of the Negro in government. Actually, though, aside from the exercise of the suffrage, which will be left until later, the Negro played a relatively minor political role in the Reconstruction of the southern states.

Indeed, so limited were the number of offices available to Negroes that some of the Negro leaders, one southern authority has written, complained to their white mentors that their race was getting too few plums of office. Often northern whites who came to the South did not look with favor upon Negroes in office, and Southerners who collaborated with the Radicals, retaining, at least in part, their southern-born attitudes on race, were chary of permitting too many Negroes to hold office.

Negroes, of course, did hold some offices under Reconstruction; in fact, outside of the position of Governor, which no Negro held in any state, black men filled each executive office at one time or another. In only one state, however, was a Negro a member of the Supreme Court; that was in South Carolina. The vast majority of Negro officeholders, however, were local officials like county superintendents of education and justices of the peace.

Contrary to the legend, Negroes did not dominate the legislatures of the southern states. The popularity of James S. Pike's sensational and partisan book, *The Prostrate State,* a contemporary description of the South Carolina legislature, has fostered the erroneous conclusion that such a body was typical of Radical regimes. In truth, Negroes were a majority in the legislatures of South Carolina and Louisiana only, and even there not for all the sessions of the period. Negroes were also a minority in all of the constitutional conventions called under the military, except, again, in the instance of South Carolina, and in Louisiana, where the whites and Negroes were equally divided. (South Carolina and Louisiana stand out in this regard because each contained a large and old city in which lived numbers of free Negroes who had some education and experience outside of slavery.)

Perhaps if there had been Negro domination, Reconstruction in the southern states would have been milder, for in both the conventions and the legislatures of the states the Negro members were the opposite of vindictive toward the whites. "I have no desire to take away any rights of the white man," said Tom Lee, delegate to the Alabama Constitutional Convention in 1867, "all I want is equal rights in the court house and equal rights when I go to vote." Even in the Negro-dominated legislature of South Carolina, there was no disfranchisement of whites beyond that prescribed for officeholding in the Fourteenth Amendment. Whenever the question of amnesty for Confederates came up in the United States Congress, where several Negroes sat during Reconstruction, the Negroes were usually found on the side of leniency toward the white man.

The South Carolina convention was extreme and unrepresentative of its sister conventions when it sought to ban terms of opprobrium like "Nigger" and "Yankee." South Carolina was also out of line with the other states when it provided for racially integrated schools; only two other states followed that example. For the overwhelming majority of Southerners, Reconstruction did not involve the mixing of races in the public schools. Nor did it mean the legalization of intermarriage between the races; the ante-bellum statutes prohibiting such unions were retained by the Radical regimes. The Negroes, in the main, wanted equality, not dominance.

Among the advantages which Radical Reconstruction brought to the southern states were the new constitutions which the Negroes and Radical whites wrote in each of the states. These organic laws stand up well upon comparison with earlier and subsequent ones in the South. As E. M. Coulter of the University of Georgia, and no friend of Reconstruction Radicals, has written, "The Constitutions finally turned out were much better than the Southerners had ever hoped for: in fact, some of them were kept for many years after the whites again got control of the governments." Generally they were "more democratic than the documents they supplanted, made so by increasing the electorate through Negro suffrage, requiring the total population as the basis for representation, reducing the terms of office, and by adding such principles as homestead exemptions and non-imprisonment for debt." The constitutions also provided for "free education for all and favored the economic development of the South," Coulter concludes.

Unquestionably, the evil most often charged against Reconstruction was the extension of the suffrage to a people the overwhelming majority of whom had only recently emerged from the dependent status of slavery. It is true that Negro suffrage in the South, aside from the intense fears it stirred up in the whites, was conductive to fraud, deception, and, at the very least, thoughtless voting. But viewed through the glasses of hindsight and with the recognition that universal suffrage is fundamental to a democratic society, the enfranchisement of the Negro appears considerably less "radical" today. The insouciant manner in which the suffrage was proffered to former slaves and the universality of the extension are certainly open to question, but the elementary justice of some form of Negro suffrage cannot be denied by any sincere advocate of democratic government.[3]

Unfortunately, on the matter of the suffrage, neither white Southerners nor northern Radicals were prepared to adjust their conception of the Negro to reality. Though some free Negroes were obviously capable of voting intelligently in 1865, as Lincoln, for example, recognized, and most Negroes would be after the mentally crippling effects of slavery had had a chance to be outgrown, few Southerners could shed their blanket view of the Negro

---

[3] It should not be thought that illiteracy was one of the legitimate arguments against Negro suffrage. Thousands of southern whites enjoyed the franchise even though they could neither read nor write. In 1880, for example, white illiterates averaged over a quarter of the population in Georgia, Alabama, and North Carolina. J. T. Trowbridge, the journalist, who made a tour of the South in 1865–66, concluded that the Negroes should be granted the suffrage. "They are," he wrote, "by all moral and intellectual qualifications, as well prepared for it as the mass of poor whites in the South." In a good number of states of the Union at this time, even immigrants were granted the vote prior to their acquisition of citizenship. The only valid argument against universal Negro suffrage, it would seem, was the lack of independent experience which was inherent in the Negro's former slave status.

as an incompetent. "The fact is patent to all," a South Carolina convention of whites asserted in 1867, "that the Negro is utterly unfitted to exercise the highest functions of the citizen." The South would not change. "Left to itself," southern historian Francis Simkins has concluded, "the region would not have accorded the Negro the vote or other manifestations of equality. . . ."

On the other hand, the northern radicals, fearful that the South, once back in the Union, would deny the vote to all Negroes, and especially desirous of creating a large number of new Republicans, went to the other extreme and decreed universal Negro suffrage. This solution, however, overlooked the obvious disabilities which slavery had temporarily stamped upon a majority of the Negroes and seriously underestimated the tenacity of the historically ingrained racial feeling of the whites. Today the only comfort which can be drawn from the thoughtless and opportunistic policy of the Radicals is that it did provide a means for the inclusion of the Negro in the electorate, even if the means almost smothered the ideal with disrepute.

Radical Reconstruction in the South left a more permanent monument than the Negro's transient experience in public office and a nobler one than the southern white's nightmares of racial amalgamation. This was the laying of the foundation of southern free public education. Almost all of the Reconstruction conventions and legislatures erected or revived systems of free public education—a not insignificant manifestation, it might be noted parenthetically, of the Radical propensity for making over Dixie in the image of the North. In most of the southern states, these Reconstruction efforts in behalf of public education remained after 1877 to become the bases upon which post-Radical governments built their school systems. Though the South had always had some free schools and even some local public-school systems, free education as it was known in the North by the 1850's began in the South only after the War for Southern Independence.

The other educational achievement of Radical Reconstruction in the South was the conversion of the whites to the view that Negro education was not only desirable but a necessity. This was largely the work of the Freedmen's Bureau. Prior to Radical Reconstruction in Georgia, for example, as Mildred Thompson has pointed out, the postwar government provided public education only for whites. Education for the Negroes was viewed as a waste of effort and perhaps even dangerous. All over the South in 1865–67, northern whites who attempted to instruct Negroes were subject to attack and violence. The blazing Negro schoolhouse of this period was the predecessor of the later burning cross.

Despite such opposition, the Freedmen's Bureau succeeded in establishing Negro schools before 1867. At its height, the Bureau operated over 4,000 primary schools, 74 normal schools, and 61 industrial schools for Negroes. George Bentley, a recent historian of the Bureau, concludes that by 1867 Negro and white alike in the South had come to accept the necessity for public education of the former slave. "Certainly in this respect," Bentley observes, "the Bureau had performed a commendable service for the Negroes, for the South and for the nation."

By the time the reader has gotten this far in the "other side" of Reconstruction, he is probably somewhat annoyed at the absence of references to the well-known corruption and fraud so much a part of the conventional picture of the period. He is convinced that this noisome aspect will be conveniently forgotten. There is no denying the disreputable character of all too many of the Radical state governments. Certainly the history of Louisiana, South Carolina, Florida, and Alabama during this period provide rather painful examples of what corruption can be and what government should not be.

But again it is necessary to emphasize that the total picture is not all dark. Mississippi, for example, under Radical Republican rule enjoyed a government as administratively honest as most Democratic ones, and in some ways decidedly more honest. "The only large case of embezzlement among the state officers during the post-bellum period," writes James Garner, the historian of Mississippi Reconstruction, "was that of the Democratic state Treasurer in 1866." Mildred Thompson, writing about her native state, says that in comparison with states like Alabama and South Carolina, Georgia under Radical Reconstruction "shows a marked moderation in her government, a lesser degree of reconstruction evils, less wanton corruption and extravagance in public office, less social disorder and upheaval. In Georgia," she concludes, "Negroes and carpet-baggers were not so conspicuous, and conservative white citizens were better represented."

Though Virginia escaped entirely the period of Radical Reconstruction which other southern states endured after the cessation of military rule, she did not escape extravagance. In 1869, the first and last election under military rule brought the defeat of the Radicals in a free polling. But under the conservatives who then took office, Virginia contracted as staggering a public debt as those run up in the Radical-dominated states. Even the usual stories of the high taxes imposed by the Radical governments in the various states are susceptible of a different interpretation when put into some perspective. In 1870, for instance, when the average tax rate for the southern states was 15 mills, that of Illinois was 45.

The fradulent dealings of the Radical regimes appear less exceptional and noteworthy if they are placed within the context of the times. For instance, it is instructive to realize that after the end of Reconstruction, each of the conservative Democratic governments in Georgia, Alabama, Virginia, Mississippi, Louisiana, and Tennessee had treasurers or other officials who absconded with or embezzled state funds, the individual defalcations often running to half a million dollars. Then, of course, the years of Reconstruction also included the Tweed swindles in New York City, in which perhaps over $100 million was robbed from the public treasury. And on the national level, the frauds and stealings carried out under the unseeing eye of President Grant serve to round out the picture.

Though not at all excusing the Radical frauds, the corrupt climate of the times does make it clear that the Radical pilferings were little more than particular instances of a general postwar phenomenon. And once this fact is grasped, it becomes apparent that it is not corruption which has fastened disrepute upon these short-lived regimes, but the fact that Negroes participated in them. "Corruption and extravagance increased the intolerance with which the Negro regimes were regarded," southern historian Francis Simkins has written, "yet even if these regimes had shown exemplary statesmanship they would have been unacceptable to white Southerners as long as Negroes comprising any part of them were regarded as political equals."

3. CASTE WILL OUT

The tragedy of Reconstruction is that it failed. Rather than liberating the South from its fear of the Negro, Reconstruction exacerbated it; instead of re-establishing a two-party political system, it further fastened a benumbing single party upon a region which once had led the nation in political creativity. Yet neither that section nor the North was alone responsible for the failure; both have to bear the national burden—the South for its intransigent conservatism, the North for its bungling idealism.

As is apparent today, it was imperative in those first years after Appomattox that a way be found whereby the nation and the Negro might confidently look forward to the former slave's full and equal participation in American life. But the unique opportunity of those first years was squandered. Neither Southerners nor Northerners were capable of disenthralling themselves, as Lincoln had counseled; both continued to act within their historically determined attitudinal patterns. Lincoln himself, for that matter, failed to grasp the crucial nature of the postwar era, so far as the Negro was concerned. His plan for the rapid restoration of the southern states indicated that he was quite prepared to throw away the single opportunity for realizing that equalitarian precepts of the Declaration of Independence to which he so often referred. And though the Radicals succeeded in enshrining in the Constitution their vision of equality for all, thereby illuminating the path the nation was ultimately to follow, they were woefully unequal to the complicated and delicate task of implementing their vision. Having failed to meet the problem of the Negro at its inception, Americans have been compelled to grapple with it in each succeeding generation down to our own day.

The inability of the Radicals to translate their equalitarian ideals into reality through the use of force[4] brought an end to the first phase of the

---

[4] At the risk of seeming to condone the often cynical methods employed by the Radi-

search for a place for the Negro in America. During the years which followed, the South was left free to work out for itself what it considered the
Negro's proper niche. Contrary to popular conceptions of Reconstruction
and its aftermath, the South was neither united nor decided on what that
position should be. The evolution of the region's place for the Negro would
take another generation.

---

cals in the South, the principle behind Reconstruction deserves some attempt at a
defense. It is a common argument that force cannot change ideas or dissolve prejudices,
and that, therefore, from the outset Reconstruction flew in the face of experience. It
is true that ideas are best changed by sincere, inner conversion, but this is not always
possible; and weak as enforced conversion may be as a foundation on which to build
sympathy and understanding, it is sometimes the only alternative. In both Japan and
Germany after 1945, the western powers, notably the United States, undertook to impose
certain concepts and forms of democratic life upon the defeated peoples. The only
essential difference between these efforts to change people's minds by compulsion and
that of Reconstruction was in method; the modern effort was, all things considered,
intelligently and efficiently handled. The principle, however, was precisely the same as
that which animated Radical Reconstruction in the South. It would seem that only
those who oppose the principle of forcible democratization of Germany and Japan
can consistently condemn the leaders of Radical Reconstruction for trying to solve by
force, albeit ineptly, the problem of the black man in a white America.

II

*The American Businessman
as Robber Baron:
Fact or Fiction?*

INTRODUCTION

Of the many changes in American life during the last three or four decades of the nineteenth century few were as significant as the growth and the industrialization of the American economy. As explanations of these momentous developments, historians have stressed such factors as the abundance of America's natural resources and the availability of labor, capital, and transportation facilities. They have been uncertain, however, regarding the importance to assign to the human factor, to business leadership, as a cause for the remarkable expansion of the American economy.

Influenced by the writings of such persons as Henry Demarest Lloyd, Charles A. Beard, and Vernon L. Parrington, by the Progressive movement's critique of certain aspects of "big" business, and by the collapse of the nation's economy in 1929, many historians have been highly critical of America's business leadership during the post-Civil War era and have placed particular emphasis in their accounts of the economic history of the period on the unethical practices that businessmen allegedly employed. Businessmen have been viewed, to quote Hal Bridges, as being "on the whole, a set of avaricious rascals who habitually cheated and robbed investors and consumers, corrupted government, fought ruthlessly among themselves, and in general carried on predatory activities comparable to those of the robber barons of medieval Europe." [1]

Of late, however, an increasing number of American historians have become critical of the robber baron approach to the study of the American businessman. They have tended to view this type of treatment as vastly oversimplified and as unmindful of the important contributions of American entrepreneurs to the growth of the American economy. Numerous historical studies of recent years, many of them of a biographical nature, have emphasized the creative accomplishments of American business leaders and have explained business behavior in terms that contrast markedly with the conventional robber baron approach to the American business history of the post-Civil War era.

In the first of the selections on this topic, Professor John Tipple, although making a fresh appraisal of the subject, continues to find validity in the robber baron label for the businessmen of the latter decades of the nineteenth century. He links the business leaders of the era with the emerging giant corporation, which he depicts as antithetical to traditional American values and as striving for monopoly power. His stress is clearly on the busi-

---

[1] Hal Bridges, "The Robber Baron Concept in American History," *Business History Review*, XXXII (Spring 1958), 1.

nessman's selfish pursuit of wealth rather than on his constructive accomplishments.

John Chamberlain wrote The Enterprising Americans, *from which the second selection is taken, to counterbalance the robber baron treatment of American business history and out of a conviction that business has been the "guiding thread" in the nation's development.*[2] *He concedes that the Gilded Age had its "shameful aspects," but he believes that its virtues have been insufficiently appreciated. Focusing on Cornelius Vanderbilt, John D. Rockefeller, and Andrew Carnegie, he emphasizes the services that they rendered to the American public, but he is not unmindful of the questionable tactics that they sometimes employed in seeking their goals. Unlike Professor Tipple, he is impressed with the continued operation of market forces even in fields where monopoly was alleged to have triumphed.*

[2] John Chamberlain, *The Enterprising Americans: A Business History of the United States* (Harper Colophon Books; New York: Harper & Row, 1963), pp. ix–x.

The Robber Baron in the Gilded Age:

Entrepreneur or Iconoclast?

John Tipple

It is more than coincidence that the beginning of the Robber Baron legend, the portrayal of the big businessman as a warlike brigand cheating and plundering his way to millions, was contemporaneous with the inauguration of the corporation as the major instrument of business control in the United States. After the Civil War, the large corporation had begun manifestly to dominate the American economic scene; and in those same years, Charles Francis Adams, Jr., launched his first assault against the "Erie robbers," and his brother, Henry Adams, warned of the day when great corporations, "swaying power such as has never in the world's history been trusted in the hands of mere private citizens," would be controlled by one

From "The Robber Baron in the Gilded Age," by John Tipple, in *The Gilded Age*, edited by H. Wayne Morgan, copyright 1963 by Syracuse University Press, Syracuse, New York. All rights reserved. Pp. 14–37, 246–250 man or combinations of men who would use these new leviathans to become masters of the nation.[1]

Such dangerous potentialities had not been recognizable earlier because prior to the Civil War the majority of businesses had operated as local enterprises, usually as individual proprietorships, partnerships, or as small closed corporations in which ownership and control were almost invariably synonymous.[2] Under usual circumstances, the power and influences of the businessman had been limited to the immediate environs of operation and, at the very most, seldom extended beyond state boundaries. Equally important was the fact that there existed among most businessmen of prewar days a nearly universal desire and a practical necessity for community esteem, and this governed their conduct, keeping their ventures well within the limits of individual responsibility and tending to restrain any untoward actions or irresponsible profiteering on their part. Ante-bellum criticisms of the businessman, therefore, were few and sporadic. What disapproval there was usually focused on the speculator or stock gambler, and was no doubt often inspired by an agrarian distrust of big-city ways.[3]

The bloody struggles of the Civil War, however, helped bring about revolutionary changes in economic and political life. The war needs had created almost insatiable demands for manufactured goods—arms, munitions, clothing—and had offered some manufacturers unsurpassed opportunities to make vast fortunes. More important than the immediate profits, however, was the stimulus of massive military demands, leading the entrepreneur to new concepts of the power and possibilities of large-scale enterprise: "The great operations of war, the handling of large masses of men, the influence of discipline, the lavish expenditure of unprecedented sums of money, the immense financial operations, the possibilities of effective cooperation, were lessons not likely to be lost on men quick to receive and apply all new ideas." [4] Though the war prevented general economic expansion, the new ideas were profitably applied to the peacetime economy which followed.

With the rich resources of the trans-Mississippi West lying open to private exploitation, the businessman had singular opportunities for achieving vast wealth. Before him spread an immense untapped continent whose riches were his virtually for the taking; and, most opportunely, new means to turn this stupendous wealth to profitable account were at hand. A host of new inventions and discoveries, the application of science to industry, improved methods of transportation and communication were ready to assist the

---

[1] Charles F. Adams, Jr., and Henry Adams, *Chapters of the Erie and Other Essays* (Boston, 1871), p. 134.

[2] Adolph Berle, Jr., and Gardiner Means, *The Modern Corporation and Private Property* (New York, 1932), pp. 10–17.

[3] Cf. Frederick Jackson, *A Week in Wall Street by One Who Knows* (New York, 1841); James K. Medbery, *Men and Mysteries of Wall Street* (Hartford, 1870).

[4] Adams and Adams, *Chapters of Erie*, p. 135.

businessman in his ventures, but all of these aids would have been valueless to him had he not had the effective means to put them to work. The practical agency to meet these unprecedented entrepreneurial demands on capital and management proved to be the corporation, for the stockholding system provided immense capital beyond the reach of any individual and, at the same time, the corporate hierarchy presented a feasible solution to the greatly augmented problems of management.

Certainly the corporation was no novelty in this country. It had served political as well as economic purposes in seventeenth-century America, and as an instrumentality of business its use antedated the discovery of this continent. Seldom before, however, in the history of the United States had the corporation been put to active use on such a large scale. From a relatively passive creature of legalistic capitalism, it was transformed by fusion with technics into a dynamic system spearheading American economic expansion.

The impact of the newborn corporation on American society was almost cataclysmic. Although in the first few decades of its existence the modern corporate system probably enabled this nation to develop more wealth than in any other period since the discovery of America, it also brought about a revolution of tremendous potential, menacing not only hallowed economic theories and usages but threatening to ride like a great tidal wave over the traditional social and political beliefs of American democracy. Its size alone was sufficient to change fundamental social and economic relationships; by sheer magnitude the large industrial corporation overshadowed the society around it. Of the newly formed United States Steel Corporation an awed commentator wrote at the turn of the century: "It receives and expends more money every year than any but the very greatest of the world's national governments; its debt is larger than that of many of the lesser nations of Europe; it absolutely controls the destinies of a population nearly as large as that of Maryland or Nebraska, and indirectly influences twice that number." [5] Most significantly, this enormous concentrated economic power normally gravitated into the hands of a few, raising up a corporate ruling class with almost unlimited authority.[6]

Though the meteoric rise of the so-called Robber Baron to unheralded positions of power was inseparably bound to the large corporation, there were other factors behind his sudden emergence into popular view as the outstanding phenomenon of nineteenth-century business life. One of the most important of these was a stable government dedicated to the preservation of private property and devoted to an ambiguous concept of laissez faire. Through political alliances, principally with the Republican party, the big businessman consolidated his economic triumphs. Although in the

---

[5] Ray Stannard Baker, "What the United States Steel Corporation Really is and How it Works," *McClure's*, 18 (1901), p. 6.
[6] Berle and Means, *The Modern Corporation*, pp. 2–6.

past the commercial and manufacturing interests of the North had received favors from the federal government in the form of bounties to fisheries and protective tariffs, after the defection of the South they were in the envied position of a pampered only child; and a dotingly partisan Congress bestowed upon them, among other things, new and higher tariffs and a series of favorable banking acts. The economic supremacy of the North had been guaranteed by military victory in 1865, but it was doubly insured by the actions of the radical Republicans during the process of southern reconstruction. The Fourteenth Amendment, whether intended for such purposes or not, was used by the courts to protect the corporation and to prevent attempts by the states to undermine its position of power.[7] The election of General Grant to the presidency in 1868 and 1872 backed by the leading representatives of the business community, the great financiers and speculators, politically secured the issue of northern prosperity. Despite the panic of 1873, there were obvious signs that the business of the country had, as the *Nation* put it, "adapted itself to the situation created for it by Republican legislation."[8] Within this artificial paradise, private profits were sacred. The inheritance tax had expired in 1870, the income tax was abandoned in 1872, and an attempt to revive it in 1894 was invalidated by the Supreme Court in 1895.[9] Corporate or excess profits taxes did not exist, and by 1890, the bulk of the revenue of the United States government was derived from customs duties and excises on liquor and tobacco, all taxes upon the nation's consumers.[10] Under such idyllic conditions, stock market volume attained the million share mark in December, 1886, and industrial capital almost doubled itself every ten years.[11]

In an untrammeled preserve for self-seeking such as the United States in the late nineteenth century afforded, the dedicated businessman could make money on an unprecedented scale. Though John D. Rockefeller never quite became a billionaire, his fortune in 1892 reportedly amounted to $815,647,-796.89.[12] Andrew Carnegie did nearly as well. The profits from his industrial empire in the decade 1889 to 1899 averaged about $7,500,000 a year and, in 1900 alone, they amounted to $40,000,000.[13] In the following year he sold out his interest for several hundred million dollars.[14] Such fortunes, exceptional even for those days, emphasized the prolific wealth available to

---

[7] Charles Wallace Collins, *The Fourteenth Amendment and the States* (Boston, 1912).
[8] *The Nation*, September 30, 1880, p. 232.
[9] *Pollock vs. Farmers' Loan and Trust Co.*, 157 U. S. 429, 158 U. S. 601.
[10] *Annual Report of the Secretary of the Treasury 1890* (Washington, 1890), p. xxi.
[11] *Commercial and Financial Chronicle, December 18, 1886*, 739; *U. S. Census 1910* (Washington, 1913), VIII, 32–33; Willard Long Thorp, *Business Annals* (New York, 1926), 129–30.
[12] Allan Nevins, *A Study in Power: John D. Rockefeller, Industrialist and Philanthropist*, 2 vols. New York, 1953), II, 613.
[13] James H. Bridge, *The Inside History of the Carnegie Steel Company* (New York, 1903), p. 295.
[14] *Ibid.*, p. 364.

the big businessman in the United States. In 1892, two New York news-papers engaged in a heated contest to count the number of American mil-lionaires, the *World* uncovering 3,045 and the *Tribune* raising it to 4,047.[15] Regardless of the exact total, millionaires were becoming fairly common. By 1900, for instance, the Senate alone counted twenty-five millionaires among its members, a fact which was an invitation to some suspicious folk to dub that august body the "Rich Man's Club" and the "House of Dol-lars."[16]

This sudden leap of big businessmen into new positions of wealth and power caught the public eye, and to the American mind accustomed to thinking primarily in terms of individuals, the big businessman stood out as the conspicuous symbol of corporate power, in his popular image en-compassing not only his personal attributes and failings but combining also the more amorphous and impersonal aspects of the business organization by which he had climbed to fortune. Just as Adolph Hitler and Joseph Stalin were held later to typify their respective countries, so the diminu-tive Andrew Carnegie came to represent the entire steelmaking complex of men and decisions which bore his name, the lean, ascetic John D. Rocke-feller to personify Standard Oil, the bulbous nose and rotund figure of J. P. Morgan to signify the whole of Wall Street with its thousands of operators, its ethical flaws, and its business virtues. When big businessmen came under attack as Robber Barons, they were attacked not for their per-sonal failings, though they had them as well as the lion's share of wealth, but as the recognizable heads of large corporations. It is perhaps notable that when Carnegie and Rockefeller gave up their business careers and be-came private citizens taking no active part in corporate affairs, the rancor against them almost ceased. Instead of being censured for their past actions, which had been widely and vehemently criticized, they were praised as bene-factors and good citizens. Public castigation of the steel trust was lifted from "Little Andy" to fall upon the broader shoulders of Charles Schwab, and the odium of monopoly which had surrounded his father was inherited by John D. Rockefeller, Jr. Only as the active and directive heads of great corporations, and not as subordinates or members of a business elite, were big businessmen branded "Robber Barons" and indicted for alleged crimes against society.[17]

If the big businessman was not resented as an individual but as a power symbol wielding the might of the great corporation, the provocative ques-tion arises why there was such resentment against the corporation. The

---

[15] *The Tribune Monthly*, 4 (1892), p. 92; Sidney Ratner (ed.), *New Light on the History of Great American Fortunes* (New York, 1953), pp. xviii–xxiii; Tarbell, *The Nationalizing of Business*, p. 113.

[16] David Graham Phillips, *The Shame of the Senate;* reprint from *Cosmopolitan*, 1906, pp. 2, 94.

[17] *See* John Tipple, "Who Were the Robber Barons?" which is forthcoming.

answer is that the large industrial corporation was an anomaly in nine-teenth-century America; there was no place for it among existing institutions and no sanction for it in traditional American values.

In this country all the institutions and values had been built about the social and political concept of the free individual. Born to the natural rights of life, liberty, and property, he was originally subject only to the law of nature. By being or becoming a member of society, the individual did not renounce his natural rights because this gift of God could not be alienated, but submitted to certain restraints beyond those imposed by nature for the evident good of the whole community. The basis of this ideology was of course the presumed constancy of nature in moral as well as physical opera-tions, and the universal efficacy of its laws. By asserting that these inevitable laws of nature constituted truth and by setting out from the will of God or nature, eighteenth-century Americans sought to erect an inviolable system proceeding from natural causes and therefore not subject to human error. Fanciful as they may seem, these were nonetheless the accepted premises of government and society inherited by Americans of the nineteenth century.

Obviously in such a closed system there was no ready place for the large industrial corporation which was neither an individual nor a natural mani-festation. As an artificial person created by charter and comprising many individuals and their wealth, the corporation not only was not an individual but was infinitely greater in size and power than the isolated individual about whom American society had been conceived. Unlike the individual, moreover, the corporate body was not ordinarily exposed to natural hazards of decay and death, having in effect been guaranteed immortality by the society which fathered it; hence where individual accumulation of wealth and power was limited to a lifetime, corporate possibilities were almost limitless—freed from death, and incidentally from death dues and inherit-ance taxes, the corporation was in a position to wax strong upon the accu-mulated lifetimes and earnings of many individuals. A further complication, the hazard of which increased directly in proportion to corporate size and power, was that the corporation as an unnatural creation was born without natural reason—"the common rule and measure God hath given mankind" —and was therefore not intrinsically subject to the governance of nature. In ideological terms, the corporation, since it could not be counted upon to follow the moral precepts of nature, was an outlaw to the society which spawned it.

What was to be done with such a monster? Either the corporation had to be made to conform to American institutions and principles, or those institu-tions and principles had to be changed to accommodate the corporation. This was the dilemma first seriously confronted by Americans during the Gilded Age and the issue that set off the great movement of introspection and reform which was to activate and enrapt the American people for the next fifty years.

Most flagrantly apparent to Americans of the post-Civil War era was the destructive effect of the large corporation upon free competition and equal opportunity. According to the accepted theory, which was a projection of the doctrines of liberal democracy into the economic sphere, the ideal economy—the only one, in fact, sanctioned by nature—was made up of freely competing individuals operating in a market unrestricted by man but fairly ruled by the inexorable forces of natural law. Just as the ideal polity was achieved by bargaining among free and equal individuals under the benevolent eye of nature, so it was assumed that in economic affairs impartial rivalry between individual entrepreneurs, free competition, would automatically serve the best interests of society as a whole by preventing anyone from getting more than his fair share of the wealth. And in early nineteenth-century America, this self-regulating mechanism did seem to work. Where businesses and factories were small, prices and output along with wages and profits did rise and fall according to supply and demand, and every man appeared to have equal opportunity to compete with every other man. Even after the war, the individual businessman in the interests of self-preservation was forced by and large to observe the common rules of competition. Ordinarily his share of the market was too small to permit any attempt at price control unless he joined with others in a pool, a trade association, or another rudimentary price-fixing agreement. Uusually, however, the average businessman eschewed trade agreements, not out of theoretical considerations, but for the practical reason that such coalitions did not work very well, suffering as many of them did from mutual distrust and the pursuit of centrifugal aims. But what was true in a world of individual proprietors and workers was not necessarily true for the giant corporation which possessed greater unity of control and a larger share of the market and was therefore in the powerful position either to dictate prices or to combine successfully with one or two other corporations in monopolistic schemes. Indicative of what often happened was the terse statement appearing in the *Commercial and Financial Chronicle* in 1886: "Representatives of the various coal companies met at the house of Mr. J. Pierpont Morgan this week, and informally decided to limit coal production and maintain prices." [18] Thus by bringing to bear superior economic force which to a great extent invalidated the customary tenets of the free market, the large organization put the big businessman in the favored position of operating in an economy dedicated to the idea of freely competing individuals, yet left him unhampered by the ordinary restrictions. Under such auspicious circumstances, it is not surprising that he soon outdistanced his unorganized rivals in the race for wealth.

This markedly unfair advantage did not go unchallenged. As the earliest of the large corporations in the United States, the railroads were also the

---

[18] *Commercial and Financial Chronicle*, 43 (March 27, 1886), p. 393.

first to come under concentrated attack. The immense extension of the railways after the Union victory in 1865 and the crucial nature of their operations as common carriers to the nation exposed their activities to the widest public scrutiny and subjected their mistakes or misdeeds to considerable publicity. Popular resentment against the railroads in the early 1870's grew hottest in the farming states of the Midwest, but indignant reports came from all over the country accusing the railroads of using their monopoly power to the impediment of equal opportunity. A most frequent criticism, common to both East and West, was that railway superintendents and managers showed unreasonable favoritism by discriminating between persons and places, offering rate concessions to large shippers, charging more for short than long hauls, and giving preferential treatment to large corporations in the form of secret rebates and drawbacks. That these preferential rates might sometimes have been forced upon the railroads by pressure from business made little difference. The popular consensus was not only that this elaborate system of special rates denied the little man equal opportunity with the rich and influential, breaking the connection between individual merit and success, but that the ultimate effect was to extend further monopoly by preventing free competition among businesses where railway transportation was an important factor.[19]

The Standard Oil Company was generally conceded to be the outstanding example of a monopoly propagated in this manner, the charge being that the determining factor behind Rockefeller's spectacular conquest of the oil business had been this railway practice of secrecy and favoritism which had aided his company and ruined others. By collecting rebates on their own shipments and drawbacks on those of their competitors, Standard had gained virtual control of oil transportation and was therefore in a position to regulate the prices of crude and refined oil, with the detrimental result, so Henry Demarest Lloyd charged, that by 1881, though the company produced only one-fiftieth of the nation's petroleum, Standard refined nine-tenths of the oil produced in the United States and dictated the price of all of it.[20]

As the whipping boy among trusts, Standard undoubtedly had more than its share of criticism; and yet, by contemporary standards of competition, it would seem that the corporation was fairly adjudged a monopoly. Through the testimony of H. H. Rogers, an executive of the company, the Hepburn Committee in 1879 was able to establish the fact that 90 to 95 per cent of all the refiners in the country acted in harmony with Standard Oil.[21] In

---

[19] James F. Hudson, *The Railways and the Republic* (New York, 1886), pp. 25–66; A. B. Stickney, *The Railway Problem* (St. Paul, 1891), pp. 27–35; Frank Parsons, *The Railways, the Trusts, and the People* (Philadelphia, 1906), pp. 25–56.

[20] Henry Demarest Lloyd, *Lords of Industry* (New York, 1916), p. 2; Ida M. Tarbell, *The History of the Standard Oil Company*, 2 vols. (New York, 1904), II, 111.

[21] *Report of the Special Committee on Railroads* (Albany, 1879), pp. 49–50. (*Hepburn Report*).

1886, the monopolistic proclivites of the oil trust were attested to by the Cullom Committee:

> It is well understood in commercial circles that the Standard Oil Company brooks no competition; that its settled policy and firm determination is to crush out all who may be rash enough to enter the field against it; that it hesitates at nothing in the accomplishment of this purpose, in which it has been remarkably successful, and that it fitly represents the acme and perfection of corporate greed in its fullest development.[22]

Similar convictions were expressed by a New York senate committee before which Rockefeller and other executives testified in 1888.[23] Four years later, in 1892, the Supreme Court of Ohio declared that the object of the Standard Oil Company was "to establish a virtual monopoly of the business of producing petroleum, and of manufacturing, refining and dealing in it and all its products, throughout the entire country, and by which it might not merely control the production, but the price, at its pleasure." [24]

These earlier findings were reaffirmed by new investigations undertaken at the beginning of the twentieth century. In 1902, the United States Industrial Commission reported that Standard, through its control of pipe lines, had been able practically to fix the price of crude oil; and in 1907, the commissioner of corporations supported and amplified this conclusion. While admitting that the company might fall short of an absolute monopoly, the commissioner pointed out that its intentions were nonetheless monopolistic: "There has been apparent throughout their operations a definite, persistent policy of exclusive domination of the petroleum industry." [25] In 1911, the United States Supreme Court confirmed this allegation, observing that "no disinterested mind" could survey the history of the Standard Oil combination from 1870 onward "without being irresistibly driven to the conclusion that the very genius for commercial development and organization . . . soon begot an intent and purpose . . . to drive others from the field and to exclude them from their right to trade and thus accomplish the mastery which was the end in view." [26]

Far from regarding the intricate system of business combination that he had developed as a monster to be curbed or destroyed, a big businessman such as Rockefeller looked proudly upon his creation as a marvel of beneficence, an extraordinary and distinctive expression of American genius. And Carnegie contended "not evil, but good" had come from the phe-

---

[22] Senate Reports, 49th Congress, 1st Session, no. 46, p. 199. (*Cullom Report*).

[23] *New York Senate Report,* no. 50 (1888), p. 10.

[24] *State of Ohio vs. Standard Oil Company,* 49 Ohio State 137.

[25] *Report of the Commissioner of Corporations on the Petroleum Industry* (Washington, 1907), I, xvi. (*Smith Report*).

[26] *Standard Oil Co. of New Jersey et al. vs. United States,* 221 U. S. 1.

nominal development of the corporation; he and others pointed out that the world of his day obtained goods and commodities of excellent quality at prices which earlier generations would have considered incredibly cheap. Now, maintained Carnegie, the poor enjoyed what the richest could never before have afforded. Therefore, he said, "Objections to the foundations upon which society is based are not in order because the condition of the race is better with these than with any other which has been tried." [27]

In defending himself against the charge of subverting American values and institutions, the big businessman supported his actions as being entirely in keeping with the business requisites of the day. Rather than engaging in a conscious conspiracy to undermine equal opportunity, he had sought only the immediate and practical rewards of successful enterprise, rationalizing his business conduct on the pragmatic level of profit and loss.

Instead of deliberately blocking free competition, big businessmen maintained that their actions were only natural responses to that immutable law. Charles E. Perkins, president of the Chicago, Burlington and Quincy Railroad Company, denied the deliberate misuses of power by the railroads in the matter of establishing rates. The truth was, said Perkins, that the price of railroad transportation, like all other prices, adjusted itself. Discriminatory practices were viewed as part of an inevitable conflict between buyer and seller and as a necessary result of competition.[28] Likewise, the payment of rebates and drawbacks was regarded as simply one method of meeting the market. In answer to the accusation that the railroads had made "important discriminations" in favor of Standard Oil, an executive of that company replied, "It may be frankly stated at the outset that the Standard Oil Company has at all times within the limits of fairness and with due regard for the law sought to secure the most advantageous freight rates and routes possible." [29] Rockefeller went on record as saying that although Standard had received rebates from the railroads prior to 1880, the reason was that it was simply the railroads' way of doing business. Each shipper made the best bargain he could, hoping to outdo his competitor. Furthermore, said Rockefeller, this traffic was more profitable to the railroads than to the Standard Oil Company. He claimed that whatever advantage the oil company gained in its constant efforts to reduce freight rates was passed on in lower costs to the consumer. Just as his company later justified certain alleged misdemeanors as being typical of the sharp practices prevailing in the oil fields in the early days, so Rockefeller exonerated the whole system of rebates and drawbacks on the grounds that

---

[27] Andrew Carnegie, "Wealth," *North American Review,* 168 (June 1889), pp. 657, 654; *The Gospel of Wealth* (New York, 1900), p. 5.

[28] *Cullom Report,* appendix, pp. 213–15.

[29] Ralph W. and Muriel E. Hidy, *Pioneering in Big Business 1882–1911* (New York, 1955), pp. 678–79; cf. 43.

everybody was doing it, concluding cynically that those who objected on principle did so only because they were not benefiting from it.[30]

Yet despite his public rationalizations, the big businessman's attitude toward competition was ambivalent. On the one hand he lauded it as economic theory, but on the other he sought to deny it by his practical actions. From the first viewpoint, there was no such thing as an absolute monopoly; there was always the threat of latent competition. Whenever a trust exacted too much, competitors would automatically appear, regardless of the perils that might threaten them.[31] Theoretically, competition as a natural law would survive the trusts. "It is here; we cannot evade it," declaimed Carnegie. "And while the law may be sometimes hard for the individual, it is best for the race, because it insures the survival of the fittest in every department."[32]

In practical matters, however, the big businessman conducted himself as if the law had long since become outmoded, if not extinct. Progressive opinion in the business world heralded the growing monopolistic trend as a sign of economic maturity. Increased concentration in capital and industry was defended not only as necessary but as inevitable.[33] Monopolistic practices in general were upheld in business circles on the grounds that they prevented disastrous competition and in the long run benefited, rather than plundered, the public by maintaining reasonable rates and prices.[34] "There seems to be a great readiness in the public mind to take alarm at these phenomena of growth, there might rather seem to be reason for public congratulation," announced Professor William Graham Sumner of Yale. "We want to be provided with things abundantly and cheaply; that means that we want increased economic power. All these enterprises are efforts to satisfy that want, and they promise to do it."[35] As did Sumner, so many big businessmen believed that, practically at least, the rise of the trust in industry and commerce had proved the superiority of combination over competition.

Though the claim was not always true, the business virtues of economy and efficiency were stated to be the chief advantages of the trust. Because the combination was spared the folly and wastefulness of unrestrained competition, there were alleged to be huge savings in cross freight, advertising, sales, and executive expenses. Similarly, the survival of only the most pro-

---

[30] John D. Rockefeller, *Random Reminiscences of Men and Events* (New York, 1909), p. 112.

[31] John Bates Clark, "The Society of the Future," *Independent*, 53 (July 18, 1901), pp. 1649–51.

[32] Carnegie, "Wealth," *North American Review*, 168 (June 1889), p. 655.

[33] John Moody, *The Truth About the Trusts* (New York, 1904), p. v.

[34] *See* appended testimony to *Cullom Report*.

[35] William Graham Sumner, "The Concentration of Wealth: Its Economic Justification," *Essays of William Graham Sumner* (New Haven, 1934), II, 166.

ductive forms of business resulted in greater efficiency and cheapened production which in turn meant higher wages and lower prices.[36] In this respect, Standard Oil was represented as a model trust. According to its supporters, it had been formed to curb speculation, waste, and overproduction; and, as Standard took pains to inform stockholders, the company owed its success not to illegal or reprehensible methods but to efficient organization.[37]

In his account of the birth of America's first great trust, Rockefeller advanced a generalization common to big businessmen of his day—that combination arose in response to economic necessity. Like all such generalizations, it was accurate up to a point, but was not universally applicable. Nevertheless, Rockefeller's description of the founding of Standard Oil is an interesting description of the genesis of monopoly from the big businessman's viewpoint. In the beginning, Rockefeller related, because refining crude petroleum was a simple and easy process and because at first the profits were very large, all sorts of people went into it—"the butcher, the baker, and the candlestick maker began to refine oil." And it was only a short time before the market was glutted and the price fell until the trade was threatened with ruin. At that moment, said Rockefeller, "It seemed absolutely necessary to extend the market for oil . . . and also greatly improve the processes of refining so that oil could be made and sold cheaply, yet with a profit." So, Rockefeller concluded with easy logic, "We proceeded to buy the largest and best refining concerns and centralize the administration of them with a view to securing greater economy and efficiency." [38] Though the birth pangs of Standard Oil obviously have been softened and somewhat simplified in the telling, it was on essentially this same basis that Carnegie explained the genesis of trusts in manufactured articles.[39]

Clearly the operative point of view that consolidation of capital and industry was indispensable to the successful execution of the tasks which had devolved upon modern business was the one embraced by big businessmen. In principle most of them agreed with the blunt statement of America's leading financier: "I like a little competition," J. P. Morgan was quoted as saying, "but I like combination better." [40] To the big businessman the choice was not between competition and monopoly, but between fighting to

---

[36] This view had extensive support in the business world. For a useful compendium see James H. Bridge, *The Trust: Its Book* (New York, 1902). *See also* Jonathan P. Dolliver, "Facts About Trusts: Arguments for Protection," *American Industries*, 2 (May 16, 1904); Franklin Head (ed.), *Chicago Conference on Trusts* (Chicago, 1900).

[37] J. C. Welch and J. N. Camden, "The Standard Oil Company," *North American Review*, 136 (February 1883), pp. 181–200; Hidy and Hidy, *Pioneering in Big Business*, pp. 658, 680.

[38] Rockefeller, *Reminiscences*, pp. 81–82. Copyright 1909, Doubleday & Co., Inc.; copyright renewed 1936, John D. Rockefeller. Quoted by permission.

[39] Andrew Carnegie, "The Bugaboo of Trusts," *North American Review*, 148 (February 1889), pp. 141–42.

[40] *Literary Digest*, 45 (December 28, 1912), p. 1213.

secure a monopoly by driving out competition in a bitter, destructive war and trying to obtain price control through industry-wide agreement.

Many, nevertheless, still paid lip service to the abstraction, though most had already rejected competition in practice. That this ideological discrepancy widely prevailed in the business community has been pointed out by Edward Kirkland: "Obviously there was an awkward contradiction between the belief in competition and the fact of consolidation, between natural laws which men could no more direct than 'they could make water run up hill' and the willed alterations in business organization brought about by trust and holding company, between law as immutable and law as growth and evolution." [41]

This glaring incongruity between business behavior and business theory ridiculed the notion that such economic generalizations as free competition were natural "laws," timeless and placeless, and entitled to sanctity. Rather than a competent expression of fact, the hedonistic theory of a perfect competitive system had turned out to be simply an expedient of abstract reasoning.

What in earlier and more halcyon days had been attributed to the benign operation of the law of competition had been, in most instances, an absence of competition. Before the Civil War, competition was virtually dormant in many parts of the United States largely because of intervening geographical factors, and where it did exist, it usually operated on a local rather than a national scale, cushioning a large portion of the economy from the hardships of rigorous competition. The limitation of the nation's transportation system, for example, often allowed local businessmen a certain amount of monopoly power; and, as Hans Thorelli has pointed out, backward communications, particularly a lack of reliable market information, also had a similar effect.[42] The trouble in many localities was that there was not always enough competition. These imperfections of competition in the ante-bellum period, however, tended to be eliminated by tremendous postwar advances in transportation and communication. Business rivalry also was intensified by the application of new technology to industry and nationalized by the substitution of the big interstate corporation for smaller local individual and partnership enterprises. The immediate outcome was competition with a vengeance and the inauguration of a species of commercial warfare of a magnitude and violence unheralded in economic history. In the long run, the brutal realities of this cut-throat struggle turned out to be unpalatable to the public and big businessmen alike, but while the latter sought to shield themselves by erecting monopolistic barriers, the American people continued to extol the virtues of free competition and to

---

[41] Kirkland, *Dream and Thought in the Business Community*, p. 27. (Cornell University Press.)

[42] Hans B. Thorelli, *The Federal Antitrust Policy* (Baltimore, 1955), p. 66.

look back fancifully toward an earlier, more ideal state of economic affairs which, if anything, had been distinguished by a notable lack of competition.

That faith in the mythical virtues of competition prevailed widely during most of this period there can be no doubt. The majority of the American people took it for granted that competition was the normal way of life in business.[43] Henry Demarest Lloyd, an outstanding critic of big business, found it highly paradoxical that the American people who were so inalterably opposed to anarchy in politics should have led in advocating it in business; and what was worse in his opinion was that Americans had accepted industrial anarchy as their ideal of economic conduct.[44] Free competition was the shibboleth of practically all reform movements except the Socialists. It spurred the Grange, motivated the Single-Taxers and the Populists, and dominated the economic thought of the Progressives. Most of them desired or, more importantly, thought they desired, free competition. On this matter there existed no clear partisan line. Members of Congress proclaimed "the norm of a free competition too self-evident to be debated, too obvious to be asserted." [45]

The belief in competition was essentially an assertion of economic egalitarianism which took its stand midway between the Gospel of Wealth and the Social Gospel, adopting neither the doctrine of stewardship by the chosen few nor the sweeping substitution of cooperation for competition.[46] In origin, it was a subtle interweaving of the Anglo-Saxon belief that the common law, as well as natural law, always favored competition over monopoly and native American opposition to privilege.[47] Some of the basic materials in this complex were clearly derived from classical economic theory. The economists whose works were most widely read in the United States in the nineteenth century were Adam Smith, John Stuart Mill, and David Ricardo, and their laissez faire attitude toward monopoly dominated the teaching of economics in this country. "All our education and our habit of mind make us believe in competition," said the president of Yale. "We have been taught to regard it as a natural if not a necessary condition of all healthful business life. We look with satisfaction on whatever favors it, and with distrust on whatever hinders it." [48] The Darwinian theory of biological evolution was also generally interpreted as supporting popular notions about competition and individual initiative, although the accord between classical economics and evolutionism was more apparent than real.[49] Without doubt this ingrained habit of economic reasoning retarded

[43] See Ibid., pp. 500–54.
[44] Henry Demarest Lloyd, Wealth Against Commonwealth (New York, 1899), p. 496.
[45] Walton Hamilton and Irene Till, Antitrust in Action (Washington, 1940), p. 6.
[46] Thorelli, The Federal Antitrust Policy, p. 556.
[47] Frederick Pollock, The Genius of the Common Law (New York, 1912), p. 95.
[48] Arthur T. Hadley, Railroad Transportation: Its History and Its Laws (New York, 1885), pp. 69–70.
[49] Richard Hofstadter, Social Darwinism in American Thought 1860–1915 (Philadelphia, 1945), p. 201.

public understanding of the new financial and industrial order, but, regardless, it was the belief that proved more important than its actual relevance; for it was sentiment, not fact, that prompted American action against big business.[50]

On the question whether the corporation had to be made to conform to American institutions and principles, or those institutions and principles had to be changed to accommodate the corporation, the American people almost unanimously declared for the first. If economic despotism was the outcome of unchecked corporate growth, then the corporate monster must be brought under control. For most, the way out was the way back. The American economy must be restored to a former golden time of competitive capitalism when the older individualistic values held sway, and the common man was free from the monopolistic pressures of the behemoth corporation.

The way backward, however, was not to be all the way. Completely breaking the trusts was rejected by the more realistic who urged instead that the trusts be permitted but regulated. Somewhat paradoxically, they proposed to liberate competition by imposing new restrictions in the name of freedom, suggesting thereby that they were not too sure that unrestrained competition would prove to be the economic panacea they sought. Practically, however, they justified the theoretical incongruity of their stand on the moral grounds that such restrictions were to be imposed only to prevent *unfair* competition. Apparently it never seriously occurred to them that to acknowledge the defective working of natural law against the forces of corporate immorality was, in reality, an ingenuous admission that the sacrosanct principle of competition was in the long run invalid. Wilfully blind to the logical inconsistencies of their position, the majority clamored for government regulation in the interests of equal opportunity, agreeing almost to a man with the stern dictum: "We must either regulate . . . or destroy." [51]

Responding to popular demand, Congress in 1890 passed the Sherman Act "to protect trade and commerce against unlawful restraints and monopolies," thus converting an economic myth into public policy. According to the ideology behind this law, there existed a direct cause and effect relationship between competition and monopoly. If the monopolistic obstacles in business were removed, the trend would immediately reverse itself, and full and free competition would automatically reinstate itself. Despite the stark realities of the growing trust and combination movement of the late 1880's, it was the public's overwhelming confidence in the efficacy of this self-regulating mechanism that set the tone of all subsequent federal action, whether conceived in terms of regulation or trust-busting.[52] Facts, however,

---

[50] John Lydenburg, "Pre-Mucking: A Study of Attitudes Toward Politics as Revealed in American Fiction from 1870 through 1901" (Cambridge: Harvard University, unpublished dissertation, 1946), p. 59.

[51] Lloyd, *Wealth Against Commonwealth*, p. 496.

[52] S. R. 59, January 10, 1900; B and D, 951.

proved otherwise. The Sherman Act, even when bolstered by later legislation, failed utterly to halt the combination movement or reverse its trend, making evident the ineptitude of any legislation that regards competition as a self-perpetuating and natural guarantor of economic justice rather than an intellectual hypothesis without institutional support.

Instead of arresting monopoly as intended, the principal effect of legalizing the myth of competition was to encourage the growth of large combinations by deflecting the attack upon them into purely ideological channels. Since 1890, federal antitrust laws have stood as a symbol of the American democratic belief that "the only proper type of society is composed of unorganized competitive individuals," and all attempts to curb big business by government action have represented nothing more than a ritual clash between an anachronistic ideal and a modern need. "In this atmosphere," wrote Thurman Arnold, "the antitrust laws were the answer of a society which unconsciously felt the need of great organizations, and at the same time had to deny them a place in the moral and logical ideology of the social structure." [53]

Though seemingly the corporation had been made to conform to American institutions and principles by means of antitrust laws, in actuality those institutions and principles had been changed to accommodate the giant corporation. By declaring the corporation to be an individual like any other and to have natural rights of life, liberty, and property, the Supreme Court in 1886 had seriously invalidated that basic concept of American society, the free individual.[54] Although this doctrine could be logically applied only to the individual as proprietor, partner, or even operating owner of a small company, the jurists ignored the intrinsic conflict between the individualistic myth and the corporate reality, thus evoking the strained future efforts of the Supreme Court to dress "huge corporations in the clothes of simple farmers and merchants." [55] In establishing the legal fiction that the large corporation was a person before the law and therefore entitled to the rights and privileges of a citizen, the court not only undermined the ideal of the morally responsible individual by extending the individualistic ethic to the amoral impersonality of the modern corporation, but in the long run subordinated that ideal to the right of property. For to accord a legal robot equal rights with a living person in the holding and protection of property under the Constitution was to exalt corporate property above the individual person and to pervert the traditional faith in individualism into a juridical sophism. And as the course of American legal history from 1886 to the 1930's amply discloses, such was the ultimate effect of the personification of the corporation.

---

[53] Thurman W. Arnold, *The Folklore of Capitalism* (New Haven, 1937), p. 211.
[54] *Santa Clara Co. vs. Southern Pacific Railroad Co.*, 118 U. S. 394.
[55] Arnold, *The Folklore of Capitalism*, p. 189.

Thus, in condemning the trusts as "dangerous to Republican institutions" and in branding corporate leaders as Robber Barons "opposed to free institutions and free commerce between the states as were the feudal barons of the middle ages," aroused Americans of the Gilded Age had clearly seized upon the major issue.[56] Whether they thoroughly understood or not, they had somehow recognized that American society with its individualistic traditions was engaged in a life-and-death struggle with the organized forces of dissolution. The business and industrial concentration once welcomed as implementing the promise of America had become a juggernaut threatening the very foundations of the nation. There was more individual power than ever, but those who wielded it were few and formidable. "These modern potentates" were scathingly denounced by Charles Francis Adams, Jr., great grandson of President John Adams, for the autocratic misuse of that power in complete defiance of both government and individuals. Writing in 1871, he foresaw ominous developments for the future:

> The system of corporate life and corporate power, as applied to industrial development, is yet in its infancy. . . . It is a new power, for which our language contains no name. We know what aristocracy, autocracy, democracy are; but we have no word to express government by monied corporations. . . . It remains to be seen what the next phase in this process of gradual development will be. History never quite repeats itself, and . . . the old familiar enemies may even now confront us, though arrayed in such a modern garb that no suspicion is excited. . . . As the Erie ring represents the combination of the corporation and the hired proletariat of a great city; as Vanderbilt embodies the autocratic power of Caesarism introduced into corporate life, and as neither alone can obtain complete control of the government of the State, it, perhaps, only remains for the coming man to carry the combination of elements one step in advance, and put Caesarism at once in control of the corporation and of the proletariat, to bring our vaunted institutions within the rule of all historic precedent.[57]

Yet the public already sensed that something had gone wrong with American institutions and values. Instinctively, with less understanding than Adams, they felt that somewhere, somehow, the old rules had been broken. Behind their growing animosity to the big businessman was the feeling that in some way he was cheating his countrymen, and the belief was becoming fairly common that the attainment of extreme wealth was incompatible with honesty. "The great cities," Walt Whitman wrote in 1871, "reek with respectable as much as non-respectable robbery and scoundrelism." [58] There

---

[56] See H. S. Commager (ed.), *Documents of American History*, 2 vols. in 1 (New York, 1949), II, 78.
[57] Adams and Adams, *Chapters of Erie*, pp. 96–99.
[58] Mark Van Doren (ed.), *The Portable Walt Whitman* (New York, 1945), p. 400.

were no doubt moral men of wealth, but in the Gilded Age many Americans were increasingly inclined to agree with Thomas A. Bland who in *How to Grow Rich* suggested, "In all history, ancient and modern, the examples of men of honest lives and generous hearts who have become rich . . . is so rare as to be exceedingly exceptional, and even these have invariably profited largely . . . by the labor of others." [59]

Very revealing in this regard was the portrayal of the big businessman in contemporary fiction. It was to be expected that the socialist writers would depict him as a "criminal of greed" or an "economic monster" who with other "business animals" preyed upon the life of the nation. Oddly enough, however, in an age when the corporation made unprecedented achievements in production and organization to the enrichment of countless Americans, when big business was the acknowledged power in national affairs, when monetary success was widely favored as a legitimate goal, scarcely a single major novelist of the period presented the big businessman as a hero or even in a favorable or flattering light. Except for a very few hack writers of the Horatio Alger stamp, the business or industrial leader was consistently portrayed as powerful and capable, but invariably as an enemy of American society.[60] To a limited extent this may have reflected the bias of the aesthetic or creative temperament against the pragmatic money-maker, but the big businessman was in disfavor with a much larger section of American society than a mere handful of literary cranks and social theorists. Obviously there must have been some reason for this enmity.

In the popular mind, the vices of lying and stealing were legendarily associated with Wall Street. The big businessmen who dominated "the street" were regarded by some as the ethical counterparts of the pirate and buccaneer. By the simple devices of "stock-watering" or the issuance of fictitious securities not backed by capital assets, big businessmen were generally believed to have stolen millions of dollars from the American people. In characterizing this type of fraudulent stock issue, it was alleged: "Magnificent bubbles were blown into prismatic and profitable radiance with nothing more substantial than borrowed phials of oil and deeds of property, whose only value consisted in the durable nature of the parchment and the abundant stamps wherewith they were adorned." [61] Among the more jaundiced, it became something of a habit to speak of the men of Wall Street as though they had barely skirted prison bars. "If the details of the great reorganization and trustification deals put through since 1885 could be laid bare," contended Thomas W. Lawson, a financier turned critic, "eight

---

[59] As quoted in Irvin G. Wyllie, *The Self-Made Man in America* (New Brunswick, N. J., 1954), p. 147. (By permission, Rutgers University Press.)

[60] Edward Everett Cassady, "The Business Man in the American Novel: 1856 to 1903" (Berkeley: University of California, unpublished dissertation, 1939), p. 199.

[61] Medbery, p. 282; Fowler, p. 299.

out of ten of our most successful stock-jobbing financiers would be in a fair way to get into State or federal prisons." [62]

The truth was that the iniquity of Wall Street was not merely legendary, but had firm basis in fact. Though not all speculators were swindlers nor all speculation gambling, only a small number of the stock exchange transactions during this period could be termed unquestionably of an investment character. The vast majority were virtually gambling.[63] Many corporations, although offering huge blocks of stock to the public, issued only the vaguest and most ambiguous summary of assets and liabilities. While this was not iniquitous in itself, such secrecy too often cloaked fraud. Such business conduct certainly was not calculated to give the lie to Henry Demarest Lloyd's embittered charge, "Wall Street robs us, waters and capitalizes the plunder, and sells back to us at high prices what it took from us for nothing, and then we fondle the quotations as evidence of our wonderful prosperity." [64]

The men at the top who had used the corporate device to make millions did not see it this way at all. They justified their millions on the ground that they had fairly earned it.[65] Cornelius Vanderbilt at the age of eighty-one boasted that he had made a million dollars for every year of his life, but added that it had been worth "three times that to the people of the United States." [66] Apparently some others shared his belief, for in his book *The Railroad and the Farmer,* Edward Atkinson made practically the same statement, asserting that the gigantic fortune of the older Vanderbilt was but a small fraction of what the country gained from the development of the railway system under his genius.[67] The Reverend Julian M. Sturtevant of Illinois College also envisioned the Vanderbilts and Astors of the world as "laborers of gigantic strength, and they must have their reward and compensation for the use of their capital." [68] Carnegie, a multimillionaire himself, maintained that great riches were no crime, insisting, "Under our present conditions the millionaire who toils on is the cheapest article which the community secures at the price it pays for him, namely, his shelter, clothing, and food." [69]

Most Americans, however, did not so readily accept the big businessman's

---

[62] Thomas W. Lawson, *Frenzied Finance* (New York, 1905), p. 174.

[63] See *Report of Governor Hughes' Committee on Speculation in Securities and Commodities* (Albany, 1909), pp. 4, 15; Alexander D. Noyes, "The Recent Economic History of the United States," *Quarterly Journal of Economics,* 19 (June 1905), pp. 167–209.

[64] Lloyd, *Lords,* p. 341.

[65] W. A. Croffutt, *The Vanderbilts and the Story of Their Fortune* (Chicago, 1886), p. 129.

[66] Francis A. Walker, "Democracy and Wealth," *Forum,* 10 (September 1890), p. 245.

[67] Joseph Dorfman, *The Economic Mind in American Civilization* (New York, 1949), III, 73.

[68] Andrew Carnegie, *The Empire of Business* (New York, 1902), p. 140.

[69] Henry George, *Progress and Poverty* (New York, 1880), pp. 174–75; Lyman Abbott, "Industrial Democracy," *Review of Reviews,* 4 (June 1890), p. 662.

evaluation of himself. Though some recognized that the big businessman in pursuing private ends had served national prosperity, the majority felt that he had taken extravagant profits entirely out of proportion to the economic services he had rendered. Rockefeller's millions were thought to be typical of the fortunes made by the Robber Barons, representing "the relentless, aggressive, irresistible seizure of a particular opportunity, the magnitude of which . . . was due simply to the magnitude of the country and the immensity of the stream of its prosperous industrial life." [70] The feeling was general that the great fortunes of all the railroad magnates, Vanderbilt, Gould, Harriman, Stanford, and the rest, of Carnegie, Morgan, and other big businessmen owed their vastness not so much to the remarkable personal qualities of the men involved as to special privilege which had enabled them to turn the abundant natural resources and all the multitudinous advantages offered by a growing nation into a private preserve for their own profit.

The public at large was not clearly aware of it, but the chief instrument of special privilege was the corporation. Though public franchises and political favoritism played a large part in the aggrandizement of the Robber Barons, in the money-making world of late nineteenth-century America special privilege invariably meant corporate privilege. It was the corporation that enabled Vanderbilt to unify his railroads while making large speculative profits on the side, and it was the same device which made it possible for men like Rockefeller to create and combine private enterprises embodying new technological and financial techniques while diverting enormous profits to themselves. The corporation may have been the constructive power behind the building of the cross-country railroads, but it was also the destructive instrument used by Jay Gould, Tom Scott, Collis P. Huntington and others to convert them into quick money-making machines with no regard for their obligations as public carriers.[71]

If corporate power was a dominant factor in the climb of these big businessmen to riches and notoriety, the problem remains of establishing the relationship of these individuals to the corporation. Judging by their business conduct, either they were not fully cognizant of the tremendous power placed in their hands by the corporation with single men controlling "thousands of men, tens of millions of revenue, and hundreds of millions of capital"; or they chose wilfully to exert this prodigious force for their own private benefit regardless of the consequence to the nation or its ideals. Unhappily most of those labeled Robber Baron by their contemporaries fell into the latter category.[72] Cornelius Vanderbilt, for example, held the

[70] Burton J. Hendrick, "The Vanderbilt Fortune," *McClure's Magazine,* 19 (November 1908), pp. 46–62.

[71] New York State, *Assembly Documents,* 1867, No. 19, pp. 205–10.

[72] John Tipple, "The Anatomy of Prejudice: The Critical Foundations of the Robber Baron Legend" (Stanford: Stanford University, unpublished dissertation, 1958), pp. 15–17.

law in contempt and, except where his own interests were involved, had little regard for the consequences of his actions, manipulating and remorselessly watering every corporate property he got his hands upon. One year after he took over the New York Central railroad, he increased the capitalization by $23,000,000, almost every cent of which represented inside profits for himself and friends. When admonished that some of his transactions were forbidden by law, he supposedly roared, "Law! What do I care about the law? Hain't I got the power?" [73] That this was clearly his point of view was confirmed by his testimony before the committee on railroads of the New York State Assembly in 1869.[74] But Vanderbilt's methods were in no way exceptional. Practically all of the biggest businessmen of the time made their millions in similar fashion. Of twenty-four who because of notoriety and conspicuous power might be regarded as "typical" Robber Barons, all to a greater or lesser degree combined the role of promoter with that of entrepreneur. Stock manipulation along with corporate consolidation was probably the easiest way to wealth that ever existed in the United States, and the exuberance with which the promoters of the Gilded Age threw themselves into it proved that they were well aware of its golden possibilities.

As a consequence of these reckless corporate maneuverings, however, public opinion turned against the big businessman. While from a corporate point of view the conduct of the money-makers was often legal although ethically dubious, the American public did not see it this way, and they often felt cheated. Puzzled and disenchanted by the way things had turned out, the American people not only questioned the way every millionaire got his money, but were quite ready to believe that behind every great fortune there was a crime. While the exact nature of the crime, its legality or illegality, escaped them, they knew when they had been robbed, and the classic statement of this feeling of outrage was written into the Populist platform of 1892: "The fruits of the toil of millions are boldly stolen to build up colossal fortunes for a few, unprecedented in the history of mankind; and the possessors of these, in turn, despise the Republic and endanger liberty." [75]

Inchoate as were these charges, they were nonetheless accurate. The wealth created by millions was being selfishly appropriated by a few, and the Robber Barons by their irresponsible use of the corporation, essentially a supralegal abstraction above the traditional laws of the land, were undermining American institutions and individualistic values by rendering them impotent in face of their hot pursuit of wealth. If big businessmen like

---

[73] Frederick A. Cleveland and Fred W. Powell, *Railroad Promotion and Capitalization in the United States* (New York, 1909), p. 141.

[74] New York State, *Assembly Documents, op. cit.*

[75] As quoted in Edward Stanwood, *A History of Presidential Elections* (Boston, 1892), pp. 474–78.

John D. Rockefeller were attacked as Robber Barons, it was because they were correctly identified as destroyers, the insurgent vanguard of the corporate revolution.

The Gilded Age

John Chamberlain

The panic year of 1873 marked the height—or the trough—of the Gilded Age, so-called in the satirical novel that Mark Twain and his Hartford neighbor, Charles Dudley Warner (known as Deadly Warning to some of his contemporaries), wrote in collaboration. The Twain-Warner story, which catches a period in the clear aspic of comic overstatement, is a compendium of all the more dubious business practices of its time: it tells how a hilariously fantastic booster, Colonel Beriah Sellers, puts his best brains to work luring a railroad into laying tracks from "nowhere to nowhere" in order to make a real-estate killing out of the Missouri mudhole of Stone's Landing; and the scene of its Washington chapters is scarcely changed at all from the reality of stock-distribution scandals that in the Crédit Mobilier case reached as high as the vice presidency.

True enough, *The Gilded Age* is not wholly devoted to satirizing business; it has for its hero a quite legitimate enterpriser, a sound and honorable young engineer named Philip Sterling who ensures himself a fortune by mastering the subject of geology and actually mining Pennsylvania coal without benefit of lobby or subsidy. But who is Sterling to compete for attention against the flamboyance of Colonel Sellers? What could he do to build an image of industrial probity in the "General Grant" period of scroll-saw architecture, convoluted walnut furniture, flickering gas jets, and brass spittoons? The very atmosphere of the Gilded Age—built on smoky coal and disfigured by the first fumbling attempts of architects to learn the true uses and limitations of strange new building materials (the country was departing from the age of wood)—makes us all too willing to believe the worst of the period that has been variously referred to as "the era of brass knuckles" and "the time of the great barbecue." So ingrained has the folklore become that William Allen White has suggested in all solemnity

From John Chamberlain, *The Enterprising Americans: A Business History of the United States* (Harper Colophon Books; New York: Harper & Row, 1963), pp. 140–161. Reprinted by permission.

that the men of the seventies cultivated beards for no better reason than to hide their naked shame.

And, indeed, the age had its shameful aspects. There was nothing very secret, however, about the contemptuous piracy practiced by the stock gamblers of the late sixties and seventies. Giving no quarter to each other, the rascals of the stock market conducted their raids with such brazen humor ("Nothing is lost save honor," said one of them) that the backward-looking writer in a more circumspect age is stopped in his tracks and looks for nothing else. So it is that we know far more today about the picturesque skulduggeries of Daniel Drew, Jim Fisk, Jay Gould, and other market high-binders of that type than we do about the creative accomplishments of men to whom these stock gamblers were anathema. One forgets, if one ever knew, that the vampirish Jay Gould, who made money by sucking many an enterprise dry, was too much even for the parvenu Vanderbilts, who refused to invite him to their social affairs. This despite the fact that Gould was a builder in Cornelius Vanderbilt's own image in at least a few of the enterprises he bought into, such as Western Union and the Union Pacific Railroad.

That the age had its pushing qualities was admitted by a brother novelist of Mark Twain, William Dean Howells. But Howells, as a social historian, forebore to be comic about what he glimpsed around him; he knew that "push" was an inevitable part of a life of lusty change. Speaking of the Boston business scene, which he knew at first hand, he wrote: "Before 'Appomattox' the banker and merchant appeared upon State Street, the business center, about ten in the morning, conventionally dressed, precise in movement and habituated to archaic methods. Within six months after the fall of the Confederacy the financial centers of the 'Hub,' vitalized by the inflow of new and very red blood, had taken on the aspect which is familiar to this generation. Everything that interfered with serviceable activity was set aside. Tall hats and long coats disappeared. . . . New names appeared at the head of great industrial enterprises. Boys who had gone to the War as junior officers had brought back honorable titles which vouched for responsibility, character, and daring. . . . You can't, if you will, hold down a Captain, a Colonel . . . who has earned and won the admiration of the public, and who has tested his worth." As for Howells' own fictional businessman and colonel, the self-made paint manufacturer Silas Lapham, he is, though a trifle coarse by Brahmin standards, a thoroughly likable and honest fellow. Since Howells was not an inventive novelist, somebody must have sat for the portrait.

If Howells had been writing of post-Civil War New York City, the center of the new Kingdom of Push, he might have mused upon the fading of such old families as Beekmans, Rhinelanders, and Brevoorts from the active business scene. As Burton J. Hendrick, our pioneer historian of the Age of Big Business, has pointed out, the U. S. was to hear less and less henceforward from landlord millionaires like William B. Astor (worth $6 million), or James Lenox ($3 million). The old New York merchant aristocracy—William Aspinwall ($4 million from shipping), John Haggerty ($1 million from auctioneering), Japhet Bishop ($600,000 in hardware), William L. Coggeswell ($500,000 as a wine importer)—was on its way to superannuated respectability. A. T. Stewart, who had made $2 million in dry goods, and Phineas T. Barnum ($800,000 from exhibiting Jumbo and Tom Thumb and acting as impresario for singer Jenny Lind) would still manage to stir others to emulation, but in the coming age the word "merchant prince" had an increasingly archaic ring.

In the swift change from old to new, one representative of the pre-Civil War order managed not only to survive the shift but to dominate it. Quite in line with the ethics of his age, the New York Central's Cornelius Vanderbilt did not scruple to use even the most outright trickery to get control of properties he wanted. Legislators, to him, were holdup men who had to be bribed to keep them from selling out to his opponents, who in most cases happened to be Fisk, Drew and Gould, the pirates of the Erie Railroad "ring." But the old Commodore was no vulture; and when he owned something he worked relentlessly at its physical improvement, provided, of course, that he intended to keep it.

Way back in 1833, when he was a young steamboat man, the Commodore had been injured in a railroad accident in New Jersey. He disliked railroads, and thought to have little to do with them. At the age of sixty-nine, however, sensing that his beloved river steamboats had seen their best days, the Commodore swallowed his distaste for the Iron Horse and decided to become a railroad man. Taking some of the $20 million he had made on the rivers and oceans, he quietly bought up the shares of the Harlem Railroad running out of New York City and the Hudson River Railroad leading north to East Albany. This gave him a right-of-way all along the east bank of the Hudson, with terminal facilities right in the heart of Manhattan Island. Later, using guile to depress the shares of the New York Central, which ran between Albany and Buffalo (the wily Commodore had publicly announced his discovery of an ancient law on the statute books that made it illegal to deliver his own Hudson River Railroad passengers to the Central's depot across a bridge at Albany), the old ex-ferryman from Staten Island got control of the Central at a price he could afford. Stock control of the Canada Southern, the Lake Shore, and the Michigan Central eventually followed—and the first important integration of east-west systems was thereby accomplished.

A lusty and superstitious fellow, Vanderbilt took a thirty-year-old second wife at the age of seventy-five, bickered with his children (ten out of thirteen survived both his tempers and his death), summoned up the ghost of the dead Jim Fisk to get advice on stock manipulation (it must have been good, for when Vanderbilt himself died in 1877 he was worth some $100 million), and proposed that a large monument should be reared in New York's Central Park to commemorate the two greatest Americans, George Washington and Cornelius Vanderbilt. But amid all his egotistical cavortings the Commodore relaid the Central's tracks from New York to Chicago with new steel rails, built strong steel bridges, threw away the picturesque pre-Civil War Iron Horses in favor of a drabber but more efficient type of locomotive, and cut the time of the New York–Chicago run from fifty hours to twenty-four. Whether the Commodore's son, William H. Vanderbilt, ever actually said, "The public be damned!" is a point still disputed by historians. But on one thing there can be no dispute: the public was served by the new trains on the Commodore's New York–Chicago tracks. If Cornelius was a robber baron, the country needed more like him. Old "Corneel" may have watered the Central's stock. But as fast as he watered it he solidified it —and the worst that can be said about him is that he was a shrewd capitalizer of future earnings.

Meanwhile, to the south of the territory covered by the ring-ridden Erie and the well-managed New York Central, the Pennsylvania system was built up in the sixties and the seventies under the wise and circumspect direction of J. Edgar Thomson. If Thomson was not averse to turning a quick deal to his own private advantage on occasion, he kept this aspect of his character quite apart from his rigorously ethical concern for the Pennsylvania's economic health. In 1859 the Pennsylvania consisted largely of the Main Line from Philadelphia to Pittsburgh—but within ten short years Thomson had expanded the system until it comprised nearly a thousand miles in the state of Pennsylvania itself and (by virtue of leasing the Pittsburgh, Fort Wayne & Chicago line) had reached the shores of Lake Michigan. Not satisfied with the single terminus of Chicago in the West, Thomson formed a holding company to acquire other lines, notably the Cleveland & Pittsburgh Railroad and the so-called "Pan Handle" route, which linked Pittsburgh with both Cincinnati and St. Louis. Thomson's management ended in 1874, but he passed on to his successor, Thomas A. Scott (who was, incidentally, Andrew Carnegie's friend and boss), a property quite capable of weathering the long depression that began in 1873. To quote John Moody, the Pennsylvania "was the first American railroad to lay steel rails and the first to lay Bessemer rails; it was the first to put the steel firebox under the locomotive boiler; it was the first to use the air brake and the block signal system; it was the first to use in its shops the overhead crane"— and from 1859 to the end of the nineteenth century (and after) it never skipped a dividend. Moreover, unlike its great competitor for freight originating in the new Pittsburgh area, the Baltimore & Ohio Railroad (which in times of stress paid dividends out of capital), the Pennsylvania paid all its dividends out of earnings, with the stockholders themselves keeping a tight rein on management.

The records of both the New York Central and the Pennsylvania were in marked contrast to that of the Erie, whose mulcting by Drew, Fisk, and Gould is often cited as "typical" of Gilded Age railroading. And few post-Civil War railroads were as badly served as the pre-Civil War New York and New Haven Railroad, whose president—Robert Schuyler—issued 17,752 shares of unauthorized stock and sold them to his own brokerage house before skipping the country.

For decades after the Civil War the railroads were to remain the greatest business of the nation, and even as late as 1898, as Bernard M. Baruch was to note, "something like 60 per cent of the securities listed on the Big Board were of railroads." (By 1914 they had declined to less than 40 per cent of the Stock Exchange listings, by 1925 to 17 per cent, and by 1957 to 13 per cent.) For better or worse, the railroads became implicated with the pioneer giant corporations in other fields—with Western Union (for it was along their rights-of-way that telegraph lines were strung), with Andrew Carnegie's successive steel companies (the Pennsylvania was such a good customer of Carnegie's that he named a big mill after the railroad's J. Edgar Thomson), and with Rockefeller's Standard Oil through tank car manipulation and the notorious rebate system.

The first big "trust" was the Standard Oil Co., which grew so fast and with such seeming disregard for popular criticism of its tactics that it found itself a prime political target from the 1870's until the time of its dissolution into a number of component companies by the Supreme Court in 1911. Just why the first industrial giant should have been so hated is a mystery if the question is tackled from the standpoint of the consumer. Buyers always liked the company's product—they proved it by rushing to substitute petroleum kerosene for the old coal-oil and whale-oil illuminants. And buyers did not have any particular reason to complain of Standard's pricing policy: not only did kerosene cost less than the older fluids, but it had to meet the competition of the Welsbach gas burner and Mr. Edison's carbon-filament electric-light bulb. Standard Oil could not have imposed a lighting monopoly even if it had tried.

If the consumer had no real quarrel with Standard Oil, however, other producers had. Standard offended a nation's traditional competitive ethics —and the company made itself thoroughly hated by people who never bothered to square their liking for the products of mass production with the fact of big enterprise itself. In his main objective—which was to achieve what the economists were soon to be calling "economies of scale"—the youthful John D. Rockefeller was right. But his very zealotry provoked fear: a people who were used to small regional businesses could not understand Rockefeller's passion for nipping off all the buds on the rosebush of oil so that his own American Beauty Rose, the Standard, could grow to absolute perfection. Besides the zealotry, which seemed inhuman, there was the Rockefeller secrecy. In pursuing his objective, with muffled footfalls and sudden blows in the dark, the silent little man from Cleveland seemed to have come out of the Sicily that spawned the Mafia.

Curiously, the "monster" who provoked such spasms of fear was, in actuality, a very simple person. As the son of old Bill Rockefeller, a genial cancer quack from upstate New York, John D. was bent on becoming what his father was not. He lived simply (he never owned a yacht or a race horse), he followed his mother in reading the Bible, he was generous with his money (notably to the Baptist University of Chicago) even before the pioneer public-relations counselor Ivy Lee convinced him that he should be ostentatious about his benefactions, his family life would have been worthy of emulation anywhere, and wherever he could he bought out competitors on generous terms in preference to squeezing them into the dust. As for the oil business, which was stupidly wasteful when Rockefeller first decided to make it his vocation, it was, through his orderly approach to things, eventually to learn much that was of value to itself.

In 1860, John D. Rockefeller, then a twenty-year-old junior partner in the Cleveland commission firm of Clark & Rockefeller, visited Pennsylvania's Venango County, where the first drilled oil well had yielded its black wealth the year before. He came as the agent for Cleveland businessmen who had been impressed with the young merchant's sobriety and his ability to judge a balance sheet. What the businessmen wanted was some guidance to investment possibilities in a region that had brought the bonanza feeling far closer to the East than it had ever been before.

What Rockefeller found when he got to the Oil Creek region of Venango was enough to fill his fastidious soul with acute distaste. Oil, in that last pre-Civil War year, was a raffish, up-and-down business, and had been so from the very start. It had had its origins in medical quackery as white men, posing as Indian doctors, put the skimmings from Pennsylvania creeks into eight-ounce bottles and hawked them as a sure cure for "cholera morbus, liver complaint, bronchitis, and consumption." Using by-product oil from salt wells, the greatest of the "Seneca oil" Barnums, Doc Samuel Kier, had made a big enterprise of selling the stuff as "medicine" long before anyone had thought of drilling a well directly to get at it.

The transformation of Pennsylvania "rock oil" into an illuminant dates from a day in the 1850's when George H. Bissell of New York took a specimen to Yale's professor of chemistry, the younger Benjamin Silliman, and asked him to analyze it in his laboratory. In a scientific classic, Silliman reported that "rock oil" could be refined into a better illuminant than oil squeezed from coal tar, cannel coal, asphalt, or "albertite" bituminous rock, all of which went under the generic name of coal oil. But how to get the oil out of the earth? Bissell had seen a picture of a salt-well derrick on a Kier Seneca oil advertisement but he had not acted on it. One of Bissell's associates, the New Haven banker James Townsend, was the man of action who dispatched a New Haven Railroad conductor named Colonel E. L. Drake (he had a free railroad pass) to Titusville in Venango County with instructions to dig a well directly into oil-bearing strata. Using a salt-well driller's tools, Drake made his soon-to-be-famous strike in 1859. Despite the distractions of the Civil War the Oil Creek region of Pennsylvania took off from a standing start and by 1869 was producing 4,800,000 barrels yearly. Meanwhile the price of crude oil zoomed and plummeted crazily as the race between new wells and new oil uses went first one way and then another.

Watching the boom-bust careers of well drillers as they wildcatted, the young John D. Rockefeller decided that the producing end of oil was nothing in which a sane man should invest his funds. His advice to the Cleveland businessmen was to keep out of the oil country; refining was obviously a much safer thing. He himself returned home to put a few thousand dollars into a small refinery run by a man named Samuel Andrews, who seemed to have better refining methods than others in the business. When the new firm of Rockefeller & Andrews promised to be far more profitable than the commission-merchant business, Rockefeller lost no time in transferring his eggs to a single basket. The pious, orderly young man quickly took on new partners, men who had capital and a knowledge of refining; and with every enlargement of the business the unit cost of producing and marketing a gallon of kerosene was decreased.

Under its various names (it had become Rockefeller, Andrews & Flagler by 1868), the Rockefeller company pushed its integration forward, backward, and sidewise, making its own barrels in its own cooperage plants, shipping its products in large quantities, and plowing most of the profits back into the business. By 1870 Rockefeller and his partners were doing about a fifth of all the refining in the Cleveland area. The partners celebrated their success by organizing the Standard Oil Co. of Ohio, with Rockefeller taking 2,667 shares of the new stock and Henry M. Flagler, Samuel Andrews, S. D. Harkness, and brother William Rockefeller taking 1,333 shares each.

Standard of Ohio was advantageously placed to weather the fall in prices that came with the seventies; and with the bankruptcy of many marginal concerns it would in any event have achieved a continually expanding share of the business of providing a growing country with kerosene. But this was not enough for Rockefeller, who dreamed of bringing permanent stability to his appallingly chaotic trade. He hated what he called the "idiotic, senseless destruction," "the wasteful conditions" of competition. By convincing his fellow Clevelanders of the advantages of combination, Rockefeller, in the first two years after the formation of Standard of Ohio, had managed to absorb all but five out of a total of some twenty-five local refineries. He pressed on to take in the largest refineries in Pittsburgh, Baltimore, Philadelphia, and New York, buying up distressed competitors in the depression years of 1873 and after.

It was the fact that nobody seemed able to resist Rockefeller when he really decided he wanted a company that scared the life out of refiners who wished to remain independent. In defending his methods of "persuasion," Rockefeller put it this way in later years: "Every refiner in the country was invited to become a member of the Standard Oil Company . . . The Standard . . . turned to them with confidence and said: 'We will take your burdens, we will utilize your ability, we will give you representation; we will all unite together and build a substantial structure on the basis of co-operation.'" But to the 1870's, this sort of explanation was just so much soft soap. To bring recalcitrants into line, something more than an offer to assume "burdens" was employed. For example, when Rockefeller tried to move in on the refiners of the western Pennsylvania oil region itself, where he was regarded as a usurper and an outsider, he found that deviousness was the only solution to his problem. Deaf to his pleas for "co-operation and conservation," the Titusville operators hung him in effigy and sought to band against him. By 1875, John D. Archbold, a local refiner who had opposed Standard, had succeeded in putting some twenty-five of the Titusville independents into a big combination—the Acme Oil Co.—which would presumably be able to compete with Standard on its own terms. The curses and lamentations in Titusville were loud when it was subsequently disclosed that Acme had secretly become a Standard Oil subsidiary.

Beyond such manipulations, Rockefeller invoked a still more dread device for forcing his opponents to join with him "or else." This device has gone into the history books as the South Improvement Co. To the end of his life Rockefeller insisted that he did not start the South Improvement Co. himself. Even so, Rockefeller, his brother William, Henry Flagler, and others high up in Standard of Ohio owned 900 of the South Improvement Co.'s 2,000 shares. The working control of South Improvement was theirs.

One South Improvement Co. proposition was to exact rebates running up to 50 per cent of the carrying charges on all of its oil transported by the Pennsylvania, the Erie, and the New York Central. This was quite in line with the conventional railroad practice of the day. Virtually all manufacturers of the time considered it quite legitimate to get special discounts for bulk shipments and for a guarantee of a steady flow of business. It was an "economy of scale." But the South Improvement contract contained something that went far beyond the rebate. It read: "The party of the second part [i.e., the railroad] will pay to the party of the first part [the South Improvement Co.] . . . on all oil transported for others, drawbacks." The word "drawback" signified that out of the regular freight rates paid by South Improvement's competitors a fourth to a half would be handed over by the railroad to Rockefeller and his mates. Even to the moral code of 1872 this seemed sheer industrial murder. When the Oil City *Derrick* printed a list of the South Improvement Co.'s directors under a caption, "Behold 'the Anaconda' in all his hideous deformity," righteous indignation swept the oil fields and flamed out toward the state capitals of Pennsylvania and New York. And when the newspapers ferreted out the South Improvement contract and published it, the frightened railroads quickly promised that all future oil shipments would be on a basis of equality for everybody.

In response to the angry clamor, the Pennsylvania legislature revoked the South Improvement Co.'s charter in April of 1872—and that particular adventure in exacting special tribute from a common carrier to throttle competition was at an end. But Rockefeller had already used the tacit threat of the South Improvement contract to bring the Cleveland refiners into his combination—and these eggs, once scrambled, remained an inextricable part of the dish. Moreover, Rockefeller's resolve to "stabilize" the oil market by eliminating competition remained inexorable, and the Standard empire continued to grow. It was "common knowledge" to the oilmen of the eighties that Standard had a firm grip on some 90 per cent of the refining business. It also controlled all the major pipelines, and all the oil cars on the Pennsylvania Railroad. Its tank-car control was to increase through its domination of the Union Tank Line, called Rockefeller's "secret weapon" by Albert Z. Carr.

How had all this been accomplished? The enabling trick was the "trust," an ingenious legal device that had been cooked up by a young Pennsylvania lawyer named Samuel C. T. Dodd. Dodd had first come to Rockefeller's notice as a vigorous opponent of the South Improvement Co. Asked to become the Standard Oil lawyer at a time when his voice was failing and incapacitating him for courtroom work, the young Pennsylvanian took the job with the understanding that he would keep the company within the law in all future attempts to bring stability to oil marketing. Dodd knew, of course, that property could be turned over to "trustees": it was done every day by people who wished to pass on their estates to wards and minor children with some continuing provision for wise control. Why not, so Dodd argued, why not adapt this ancient device to the peculiar circumstances of the oil business? Why not let the less able oilmen put their properties in "trust," with Standard Oil Management acting as custodian?

The first Standard Oil trust was a small committee of nine men headed by Rockefeller himself and Flagler. To this committee of nine the owners of a wide variety of oil companies had surrendered their stock certificates and voting rights, receiving in exchange "trust" certificates that entitled them to dividends pro rata on general earnings. The committee took it upon itself to settle all questions relating to price and volume over an area of several states.

The "trust" form of organization necessarily imposed a "line and staff" administration on Standard Oil, and from the line-and-staff idea there sprouted many of the modern techniques of combining "bigness" with efficiency. The management of operations under the trust agreement had necessarily to be delegated to the executives of the individual corporations. But the top committee kept control of planning and policy functions. Committees of specialists advised the executive committee. Uniform accounting and reporting were adopted, functional committees set standards of performance, and the drive to cut costs and to realize "economies of scale" was pushed by top executives who traveled throughout Standard's empire.

The Standard Oil Co. of Ohio was eventually outlawed, in 1892, by the Ohio State Supreme Court. By this time, however, the sovereign state of New Jersey had rewritten its corporation law to permit companies chartered at Trenton to own stock in other corporations. Under a holding-company dispensation, the newly incorporated Standard Oil of New Jersey simply took over where the old Dodd-devised "trust" had left off. Jersey Standard was the *de facto* boss unit in a new combination created by shuffling some ninety companies into twenty.

The story of how John D. Rockefeller brought industrial "bigness" to America has been told so often from the "monopoly" angle that two big points bearing on his success have been quite obscured. The first point is that the silent little man from Cleveland was perhaps the nineteenth century's most able competitor. The second point is that Standard, though it had 90 per cent of the refining capacity at its monopolistic peak, was unable to keep competition from returning to the field as the twentieth century approached.

As a competitor Rockefeller was positively savage, and Standard became known, whether truthfully or not, as the company that "cut to kill." But price cutting was not the whole of the story. Rockefeller was the first really to push research, hiring a German chemist named Herman Frasch, who showed him how to refine a marketable product from the sulfurous crude "skunk oil" of the new Lima-Indiana field, the first to be opened up outside the Appalachian district. And in overseas markets Standard was the leader in providing "oil for the lamps of China."

For all the fearsome Rockefeller power, however, other men fought him and remained in business. The Pews of Sun Oil, a company that got its start in Ohio in the mid-eighties, built up a compact and powerful rival organization. Lewis Emery Jr., who hated the whole Rockefeller tribe, built two pipelines (one for refined oil, one for crude) from the Pennsylvania fields to the Delaware River for his Pure Oil Co., and, unlike other pipeline builders, kept his creation out of Rockefeller hands. The emergence of these companies proved that Standard Oil could be fought right on Rockefeller's own home grounds. Then, after 1901, the year in which a Yugoslav immigrant named Anthony Luchich—or Lucas—pounded his drill deep into a salt dome at Spindletop on the Gulf Coast of Texas and opened up a geyser of oil that caught fire and burned for days, the Rockefellers could no more dominate oil than King Canute could dominate the tides. Two Pittsburghers, John H. Galey and Colonel J. M. Guffey, had backed Lucas financially, and when they in turn ran out of money, Guffey went hat in hand with the Spindletop prize to the Mellons. No strangers to oil (a Mellon had once built a pipeline and had unloaded it on Rockefeller at a profit of $2 million), the Mellons liked the prospects. The result was the Mellon-backed J. M. Guffey Petroleum Co., the forerunner of Gulf Oil. This time the Mellons, who kept 40 per cent of Guffey for themselves, had no intention of selling out to Rockefeller.

Standard tried to operate in Texas through the Waters, Pierce Oil Co., a southwestern marketing concern, but it was too late to head off the newcomers. Soon the Texas Co.—the forerunner of Texaco—was in the field. Gulf and Texas moved quickly into the new gasoline market at a time when Standard was still pretty much committed by its technological investment to kerosene. The rise of the new independents was accomplished some years before the Supreme Court invoked the Sherman Act of 1890 to force the dissolution of the Standard Oil holding company into its constituent parts. This occurred in 1911. When he heard of the Supreme Court decision, the elder J. P. Morgan growled that it would take more than a court order to force Rockefeller to compete against himself. But the Rockefeller companies were already competing against many new companies, both in Texas and in the new mid-continent, California, and Illinois fields. Moreover, Standard had already been challenged overseas by the Royal Dutch/Shell combination and by the Nobels in the Russian Caucasus. It was nature and the inexorable workings of the market, not the Supreme Court, that had brought about the end of the dominance of the first great American "trust."

A second road to bigness in the late nineteenth century was followed by the Carnegie Steel Co., which grew from a small west Pennsylvania axle forge run by two Prussian immigrants, the Kloman brothers, to become the major unit in the formation of J. P. Morgan's United States Steel Corp. in 1901. Andrew Carnegie was merely one among many steel-company men before the 1873 depression; he was not even among the first to exploit the new Bessemer-Kelly process of blowing cold air through molten iron to make a superior grade of metal. But Carnegie had a genius for riding hard times—and with every depression his organization gained in strength.

An immigrant boy from Dunfermline, Scotland, where his father, a hand weaver, had been displaced by the new machine looms, Andy Carnegie was used to adversity. Instead of crying about the sad fate of his family, the young Scot, transplanted to Pennsylvania, cheerfully set to work at the age of thirteen as a $1.20-a-week bobbin boy in a cotton mill. Given an opportunity to keep the books of the mill because he wrote a "fair hand," Andy, with three other boys of his Allegheny City neighborhood, walked into

Pittsburgh all through one winter to be tutored in the mysteries of double entry, which was his substitute for a high-school education in mathematics.

The habit of biting off more than he was immediately compelled to chew persisted. When he quit his cotton-mill job to become a telegraph messenger boy he became a kibitzer of the Morse operators, learned their code, and got away with handling an important message without authorization. Installed as a Western Union operator on his own account, he ingratiated himself with Tom Scott, the superintendent of the Pennsylvania Railroad's new Pittsburgh division, by giving special attention to his messages. Scott liked the "little white-haired Scotch devil" and put him on the railroad payroll as his private operator at $35 a month. When a railroad accident tied up traffic one day in Scott's absence, Andy broke the rules all over again and got things running by issuing "train orders" in his boss's name.

Instead of firing Andy as he should have for an incredible breach of railroad discipline, Scott was entranced by the boy's nerve. He began to throw investment opportunities Carnegie's way. Borrowing money from a bank, Carnegie took a one-eighth share in the Woodruff Sleeping Car Co.—and, fortuitously or not, Woodruff was soon building more and more sleepers for the Pennsylvania. During the Civil War the wide-awake Andy helped Scott coordinate the railroad and telegraph services of the War Department. He kept his eyes and ears open for investment opportunities so well that, in 1863, he was able to record an annual income of $47,860, with only $2,400 coming from his railroad salary. The biggest chunk of dividends—$17,868 —came from the Columbia Oil Company, into which he had bought with his sleeping-car profits.

Carnegie's memorandum of income for 1863 mentions $4,250 through "T.M.C. from Kloman," and $7,500 from J. L. Piper and Aaron Shiffler, manufacturers of iron railway bridges. "Kloman" was, of course, the maker of an excellent railroad-car axle, and the "T.M.C." who is so cryptically mentioned was Thomas M. Carnegie, Andy's brother. Andy had joined the Kloman and the Piper and Shiffler iron companies as a sleeping partner, presumably in order to keep his dual connection with the Pennsylvania and two of its suppliers from becoming the subject of gossip.

Carnegie first took an active part in the Kloman axle company by accident, when he tried to mediate a quarrel between the suspicious Andrew Kloman and a partner. This air of casual adventitiousness seemed to set the tone for Carnegie's connection with the iron-and-steel business for years to come. Yet underneath the apparent negligence there was a definite pattern to everything the young capitalist did after he finally quit the Pennsylvania Railroad in 1865. By indirection Carnegie went swiftly to his goal. He set up an office in New York, not as a steelman but as a bond broker. He spent much of his time in travel, cultivating literary men, philosophers, English royalty, and U. S. Senators who were in a position to grant him a high steel tariff. Somehow, though no one could quite fathom the process, his control of the various steel companies in which he was so distantly interested always seemed to increase.

Indignant historians, put off by Carnegie's colossal vanity in taking credit from others, have endlessly reiterated that it was Andrew Kloman who really built up the firm of Kloman & Phipps in the Civil War period; that it was William Coleman, the father-in-law of the younger brother, Thomas M. Carnegie, who first proposed that a Carnegie enterprise—the Edgar Thomson mill—be set up to make steel rails at Braddock, Pennsylvania, by the new Bessemer process; that it was Captain Bill Jones, a refugee from the Cambria Iron Works at Johnstown, who supplied the managerial ability that made the Edgar Thomson mill so profitable; that it was the relatively late newcomer Henry Clay Frick, owner of the rich Connellsville coke fields, who persuaded the Carnegie organization to become a tight vertical trust, commanding its own sources of coke and iron ore as well as its mills; that it was the hardboiled Frick, once again, who took on the unpleasant task of breaking the hold of the Amalgamated Association of Iron and Steel Workers at the Homestead mill when Carnegie was hiding in Scotland from the consequences of having written that the great law of the workingman was "Thou shalt not take thy neighbor's job."

All of the allegations that Carnegie grew rich on the labors and ingenuity of men who knew considerably more about steel than he did are perfectly true. But if it hadn't been for Andy Carnegie's peculiar character there would have been no glue to hold the whole vast enterprise together in those years when the Bessemer process was displacing the old puddling processes only to give way in turn to the great open-hearth furnaces of the modern mill. In this whole development Carnegie exhibited a unique talent for moving in and taking control when the time was ripe. In 1871 he scoffed when William Coleman and Thomas Carnegie proposed entry into the Bessemer field. Running off to Europe on a bond-selling expedition for an Iowa railroad, Carnegie left Coleman and brother Thomas to dig up capital for their new enterprise as best they could; he, Andy, would have nothing to do with it. Though the Bessemer patent situation had long since been straightened out, and though good Bessemer rails were already being made at Cambria and in Chicago, Andy thought an investment in Bessemer converters would be "pioneering." And his rule, often stated, was that "pioneering don't pay."

But while Carnegie was wandering around Europe, two things happened. First of all, he managed to dispose of $6 million of the railroad bonds, which gave him a profit of $150,000 that he had to invest somewhere. Second, he discovered that the British believed in the Bessemer rail; indeed, they delighted to point to one particular piece of Bessemer track that had been doing business on the Midland Railway at Derby for fifteen years and was still far from needing replacement. Sailing quickly for home, Carnegie offered to put all of his European commissions into Coleman's and Thomas Carnegie's venture. This sum was more than enough to give Andy belated command of the Edgar Thomson project. By 1878, when the Carnegie enterprises were recapitalized, Carnegie had 59 per cent of the stock in his own hands.

Another remote control coup of Carnegie's was responsible for bringing the greatest steel man of the age, Captain Bill Jones, into the Edgar Thomson management. Loafing in New York, Carnegie picked up some gossip about a labor dispute at Cambria which, obscurely, seemed to involve the company's operating bosses. Knowing that Cambria had had a long experience with the Bessemer process, Carnegie hastened to Pittsburgh with the suggestion that the heads of the Cambria departments be hired to run the Edgar Thomson. This is what brought Jones into the Carnegie organization. And along with Jones came a whole corps of trained Bessemer men.

By such intelligent opportunism Carnegie dominated his industry even though he knew little of the technical details of steelmaking. His chronic absence from Pittsburgh gave him all the more opportunity to sell Pittsburgh's products; he was, as Burton Hendrick has pointed out, "perhaps the greatest commercial traveler this country has ever known." When it was to his advantage to do so, the opportunistic Carnegie entered steel price and production pools. When the advantage ran out, however, he was the first to quit. He absorbed the Duquesne Steel Co. after spreading what today would be termed commercial libel against it. He forced his partners to sign an "ironclad" agreement that they would return their stock to the company at book value if, by any chance, they proposed either to retire or resign. He kept the steel tariff as high as he could for as long as he could, and if a railroad would give him a rebate he was not averse to accepting it. But none of these things really accounted for the basic profitability of the Carnegie enterprises. What counted was that Carnegie kept the organization on its toes: the cost of production was constantly lowered by men whom Carnegie often set at each other's throats to make new records. Young men like Charlie Schwab—the "young geniuses" of Carnegie's verbal adulation—were generously rewarded for enterprise, acquiring partnerships by acquiring stock they paid for on easy terms out of earnings. Whenever a depression came, Carnegie bought out his rivals, ending up in the nineties with a completely integrated company that owned or leased its Mesabi ore beds, its limestone and coke sources, its Great Lakes freighters, its docks and railroad lines, and its great mills at Braddock, Homestead, Duquesne, and Beaver Falls. Despite a fierce quarrel with Frick, and despite his inability to tolerate anybody near the throne very long, Carnegie could still truly suggest for his epitaph, "Here lies the man who knew how to get around him men who were cleverer than himself."

The proof of the Carnegie pudding was in the eating. Profits, which had been at the rate of $2 million per year in the early eighties, had jumped to

$5 million in 1890, and had risen to $40 million by 1900. This immense profitability derived from the fact that Carnegie had a grip on the bulk of crude-steel production in the U. S. Even so, his position was not entirely impregnable. For one thing, the Chicago steel area, where Captain Eber B. Ward had rolled Bessemer rails as early as 1865, was producing ingots, and in the late nineties this production increased with the organization of the Federal Steel Co. More seriously, Carnegie found himself harassed by the creation of wire, tube, tinplate, bridge-making, and other fabricating companies which threatened to build basic-ingot capacity in preference to buying from Carnegie mills. If Carnegie had been a younger man he might have met this threat head-on by building his own fabricating facilities. But he felt drained after his quarrel with Frick, and besides he had always had an ambition to retire with honor and become a great philanthropist. "The man who dies . . . rich," he had once written, "dies disgraced."

What allowed Carnegie to fulfill his philanthropic ambitions (and still die rich) was the intervention of powerful outside financial forces. The investment banker, J. P. Morgan, who had been busy consolidating the nation's railroads, began toward the turn of the century to fix his attention on the steel business, and the outlines of a new Goliath, which was to become U. S. Steel, were already taking shadowy shape in his mind. Obviously the Carnegie properties were crucial to such an enterprise. One evening late in 1900, at a famous dinner at the University Club in New York City, Carnegie's man, Charles Schwab, painted such a glowing picture to Morgan of the future of steel that Morgan asked him to name a price for the Carnegie mills. Whether Carnegie consciously set out to bait Morgan is still argued by the historians of steel. In any event, a deal quickly followed in which Carnegie received $492 million in U. S. Steel bonds and stocks in exchange for all of his properties. He himself took $225 million in 5 per cent gold bonds; the rest of the exchange went to his "young geniuses."

As had happened with the Standard Oil empire, the formation of U. S. Steel in 1901 invited the most bitter public attack against monopoly—an attack that was to continue through the beginnings of the new century and has recently been renewed by the Kennedy administration. Actually, as events turned out, this new colossus of steel was to prove as vulnerable to market forces as the Standard Oil trust. In its early years U. S. Steel had 65 per cent of the market; this was to dwindle to 45 per cent in 1914 and 30 per cent today. This would hardly have surprised Carnegie, who wrote: "Whenever consolidations . . . or syndicates, or Trusts, endeavor to circumvent . . . [competition] it always has been found that after the collision there is nothing left of the panaceas, while the great laws [of the market] continue to grind out their consequences as before. . . ." But at the time of the creation of U. S. Steel, things looked different. . . .

III

Immigration and Racism:
Was Race a Valid Basis
for Immigration Policy?

INTRODUCTION

One of the truly great epic themes of American history is the movement of peoples to the United States from all over the world. Between 1820 and 1959 more than 40 million persons migrated from other lands to take up residence in the United States. Among the great nations of the world, the United States is pre-eminently a nation of immigrants.

Until the 1880's immigrants were, in the main, welcomed in the United States, although there were occasional manifestations of nativist resentment. Beginning in the 1880's, however, opposition to immigration began to gather force and to translate itself into legislation designed to restrict the inflow of those wishing to come to the United States. Increasingly, the opposition to immigration came to be based on racial grounds. The immigrants from southern and eastern Europe, in particular, the so-called "new" immigrants, were declared to be of racial lineage inferior to that of the "old" immigrants, who had originally populated the country. The new immigrants, it was consequently argued, posed a threat to the well-being and, indeed, to the very survival of the native stock. Racist views of this sort constituted the ideological underpinning of the percentage and quota laws of the 1920's that all but closed the gates of the United States to further immigration.

The theme of immigration and the related subject of ethnic relations within the United States have attracted the attention not only of historians but also of social scientists in general. The sociologist Henry Pratt Fairchild was particularly interested in these questions and contributed importantly to the literature of the field. In 1926 Fairchild published The Melting-Pot Mistake, *a work which has been described as both an "epitaph" to, and a "qualified summation" of, the type of race thinking that influenced the immigration legislation of the 1920's.[1] In the chapter from this book that follows, Fairchild dwells on the "racial significance" of the shift from the old to the new immigration and views with alarm the racial "mongrelization" of the "typical American mixture." He lauds the determination of the American people "to keep the racial tone of the population about what it was at the time of the Declaration of Independence."*

More than any other American historian, Professor Oscar Handlin has been concerned with the problem of ethnic relations and group life within the United States. In the selection that follows, most of which was originally part of a memorandum prepared for the President's Commission on Immigration and Naturalization (1952), Handlin summarizes the contemporary scientific view of the concept of race and concludes with regard to the prob-

---

[1] John Higham, *Strangers in the Land: Patterns of American Nativism, 1860–1925* (New Brunswick: Rutgers University Press, 1955), p. 327.

lems of alcoholism, insanity, crime, and intelligence that "There is no evidence that the immigrants have been inferior to the natives, no evidence that the new immigrants have been inferior to the old, and no evidence that immigration has produced any social deterioration in the United States."

A New Menace

Henry Pratt Fairchild

Beginning about 1882 . . . a marked change in the situation began to develop. Certain new streams of immigration, which had hitherto trickled in almost unnoticed, began to swell to portentous proportions. Foremost among these were the currents from Italy, Austria-Hungary, and the Russian Empire and Finland. Streams smaller in proportion but of immense volume in the total came from various of the Balkan states, Portugal, Turkey, Greece, etc. Even after they began to increase these currents remained below the older ones for a number of years. Italy, which had never sent more than nine thousand before 1880, in that year raised its contribution to over 12,-000, and in 1882 sent 32,159, a very considerable body of people, but quite trifling compared with the delegations from the United Kingdom and Germany. The movement from Austria-Hungary, previous to 1880, had reached about the same maximum as that from Italy, but in that year it rose to over 17,000 and two years later to over 29,000. The Russian Empire still lagged behind, sending only 16,918 in 1882.

It is not necessary for present purposes to make a detailed inquiry into the causes of the sudden expansion of these streams. The development of transportation facilities by land and water, the spread of popular education and geographical knowledge, the extending reputation of the United States as the land of promise, and the gradual development of a spirit of independence and initiative among the peasants of southern and eastern Europe all played their part. The important fact is that, having once received the impetus, these streams continued to grow until, in a very short time, they dominated the situation. As the "new immigration" increased the "old immigration" diminished, not only relatively but absolutely. The records set by the United Kingdom, Germany, and the Scandinavian countries were never equaled again. The definite turn of the balance came about the year

From Henry Pratt Fairchild, *The Melting-Pot Mistake* (Boston: Little, Brown and Company, 1926), pp. 107–135.

1896. From that time on until the outbreak of the Great War a larger and larger majority of the total flow was claimed by the new immigration. In 1914 the old immigration amounted to only 13.6 per cent of the entire number. It seems evident that forces were at work which, if they had not been interrupted by the War, would in a few years have reduced the old immigration almost to zero.

The question of immediate interest is: What was the racial significance of this radical change in the sources of immigration? Were the immigrants of the past generation simply continuing to rebuild the American population along the original lines? Were they notably altering the proportions of the racial composite? Were they introducing some entirely new elements? The answer to these questions is to be found in the racial composition of the people of the countries of southern and eastern Europe, a most baffling field of investigation, to be sure.

The outstanding feature of the racial situation in these lands is the very small proportion of Nordic blood represented in their populations. This by itself means that immigration from these sources tends inevitably to reduce the Nordic proportion in the American population. In its place will be substituted primarily Mediterranean and Alpine elements. . . .

This would have been an important fact in itself. But more was involved than that. Eastern and southeastern Europe have been the scene of a long series of invasions, coming in general from the east. The best known of these, probably, because the most spectacular, is that of the Huns, but there were several others much more fateful as regards the racial makeup of the region than the Huns. Prominent among these are the Avars, the Bulgars, the Magyars, and the Turks. Without attempting to go into the complicated and somewhat obscure history of these movements, it appears that many if not most of them had their origin in that remarkable Turki or Tartar stock which has contributed out of its abundant fecundity to the population of so many remote regions. This stock appears to be essential Mongoloid in its racial affiliations, so that the lands which were the immediate sufferers from these invasions must have received important permanent additions of Mongoloid stock, however effectively the fact may be concealed by the processes of race mixture, and the modification of cultures. It follows that immigration from these regions has the effect of introducing into the American population considerable strains of Mongoloid germ plasm, just how extensive no one can tell, but certainly sufficient to be of great importance.

A further factor to be considered in connection with the new immigration is the Hebrews. To just what extent the Hebrews are to be considered a race it is impossible to say. There is a marked difference of opinion, not only on the part of non-Hebrew students, but also of many leaders of Hebrew thought. Their remarkable combination of culture and religion, or culture dominated by religion, with its restrictions and prescriptions, and their remarkable faithfulness to these restrictions have perpetuated a degree of inbreeding which has kept them related in kin to an extraordinary extent in view of all their manifold wanderings and vicissitudes. Yet it is inconceivable that in the course of all these wanderings and residence in various lands, there should have been no admixture of blood, and it seems quite certain that at times numerous outside groups have been Judaized as a whole. One thing, at least, is sure; the great bulk of Hebrew immigration in recent years has been from eastern Europe, so that if it is not actually a separate race, it is definitely affiliated with the new immigration.

The conclusion is that, beginning about 1882, the immigration problem in the United States has become increasingly a racial problem in two distinct ways, first by altering profoundly the Nordic predominance in the American population, and second by introducing various new elements which, while of uncertain volume, are so radically different from any of the old ingredients that even small quantities are deeply significant. A somewhat vague, but widespread and rapidly growing popular appreciation of this fact contributed largely to the general support of the immigration law of 1924.

A new problem of group unification, therefore, was created by the typical immigration of the last generation. Instead of facing national complications alone, the United States was confronted with the additional problem of race mixture. To get even a partial idea of all that this involved it is necessary to consider in some detail what the nature of race mixture is, and what results may be expected to follow when numbers of persons representing two or more different racial stocks are put in close territorial contact with each other.

We have observed that the qualities of race are carried in the germ plasm; that in a given stream of germ plasm they remain constant and unchanged from generation to generation; and that the only way they are modified is by putting them together in different combinations. The basic elements are never changed. It follows that, no matter how closely associated representatives of different races may be, there will be no change in the racial characteristics of any of them unless physical matings take place. Social contacts and associations alone, even though continued over many generations, will produce no alteration in racial qualities. . . .

The question then is, under what conditions do matings take place among associated racial groups, and what is the character of the products of those matings? The answer to the first part of this question is that some matings will take place under almost any conceivable conditions. Doctor Harry H. Laughlin, in a statement before the House Committee on Immigration and Naturalization, summed the matter up in the following words: "The committee of the Eugenics Research Association has had the matter in hand, and has failed to find a case in history in which two races have lived side by side for a number of generations and have maintained racial purity. Indeed, you can almost lay it down as an essential principle that race mixture takes place whenever there is racial contact." [1] The reasons for this are obvious. As has been observed, the prevailing opinion among scientists is that all races of men are descended from a single original stock, and are still to be considered as belonging to a single species. At any rate, all existing data seem to indicate that fertile unions are possible among all human races, and that the sexual impulse knows no racial boundaries. . . .

It follows that a country receiving large contingents of foreigners of different races, especially if they are not too widely separated, need have no doubt as to the processes of race mixture—they will go on spontaneously without encouragement, and in spite of impediments. To the extent to which they are retarded—which may, to be sure, be a very important extent —the causes are to be found more in national feeling than in racial feeling. This will be considered later. What such a country really needs to concern itself about is the effects of race mixture. This is a profoundly important problem concerning which, unfortunately, it is as yet impossible to state conclusions with certainty. The difficulties of carrying on experiments with human beings, and the scanty information that exists with reference to the "natural experiments" which have taken place at various times and places, leave the question as to the final effect of the mixing of human races quite unsettled. For our tentative conclusions we are forced to rely very largely upon the analogies furnished by experiments and observations upon the lower animals and plants. Fortunately, these are analogies in which we may place a high degree of confidence. For, as already repeatedly emphasized, race mixture is strictly a biological process, and in his biological processes man is closely akin to other types of living organisms. This is particularly striking in matters pertaining to reproduction, in which certain general principles run through all species, down almost to the very lowest forms. It is reasonable to assume, therefore, that facts of heredity which are universal, at least in the higher forms of animal life, will be carried over into the human field.

From the point of view of the transmission and inheritance of definite traits, the significant fact is that the germ plasm contains an enormous multitude of small particles, called "genes" or "determiners," the capacity and function of which is to cause the appearance of certain particular traits in the body of the individual. For each separate trait there is a particular determiner which may be present singly or doubly. The determiners never combine or fuse, but maintain a continuous and independent succession through unlimited generations of the species. As a result, each separate trait is inherited independently. The human body, therefore, may be thought of as a sort of mosaic, composed of a multitude of separate traits, each due to the presence of a particular type of determiner in one or the other, or both,

---

[1] Biological Aspects of Immigration, Sixty-Sixth Congress, Second Session, April 16–17, 1920, page 15.

of the two germ cells out of the union of which it has grown. Practically speaking, half of the determiners come from the mother and half from the father. Half of those which come from the mother, or one quarter of the total, are derived from the maternal grandfather, and half from the maternal grandmother; half of those from the father are derived from the paternal grandfather and half from the paternal grandmother. And so on in multiples of two back through indefinite generations of ancestry.

If we can imagine the mating of two persons of absolutely pure stock of different races, each of the offspring would receive half of its determiners from the germ plasm of one race and the other half from the germ plasm of the other race. In other words, they would all be strictly half-breeds. It does not follow that in appearance they would be an exact mean in all particulars between the two original types. Sometimes one determiner of a given type is dominant over the other determiner and so the bodily trait corresponding to that type of determiner shows a greater resemblance to one parent than to the other. But in the germ plasm which is passed on to the next generation the determiners remain evenly divided between the two racial sources. When we come to consider the mating of mixed races the outcome is by no means so simple. Various combinations are possible in the offspring. The significant fact is that out of thousands of matings between representatives of different racial stocks, whether pure or mixed, the offspring as a whole will in the long run display the characteristic features of all the different races in approximately the same proportions that they occurred in the total group of parents.

The phrase "race mixture" then, unlike so many popular phrases, accurately describes the process to which it is commonly applied. The product of the mating of different racial stocks really is a mixture. It may be compared to pouring together various chemically inert liquids—water, milk, wine, ink, etc. If the resulting mixture is thoroughly stirred, it will have the appearance of a smooth homogeneous liquid. But every separate molecule remains just what it was before the mixing took place; there is just as much water, just as much milk, just as much wine, just as much ink, as there was at the beginning. The analogy with race mixture is particularly close if some of the ingredients—like milk, for instance—are themselves mixtures, corresponding to mixed races. . . .

But two great questions remain: What kind of a substance are you going to have when the fusion is complete? And what are you going to do with it?

Taking the latter of these queries first, it has been aptly observed that a melting pot implies a mold. The object in fusing the various ingredients is to get them into a plastic state so that they may be cast into a predetermined form which they will thereafter retain permanently. In this respect the analogy of the melting pot as applied to races in America obviously breaks down completely. The assumption is that the mixture itself is the final goal;

there is nothing even remotely corresponding to a mold into which it is to be poured.

Much more important than this, however, is the question as to the character of the mixture itself. On this point, the champions of racial amalgamation for the most part beg the question. They seem to assume that if it can be proved that racial fusion will eventually be complete, that settles the matter. Nothing more need be said. They ignore the consideration as to whether the molten mass will be good for anything. True, certain sweeping statements are made to the effect that mixed races are superior to either of the originals, especially if the latter are not too far apart, and some efforts are made to bolster up this assertion by reference to various of the great civilizations of history. But these are mostly *ex cathedra* pronouncements, without a semblance of support by any factual evidence. It is, indeed, as already stated, a matter about which we know very little. The various cases of race mixture about which information is available are so complicated by social and environmental factors, often of a very unfavorable kind—as, for instance, in the case of the racial nondescripts in the seaports of the world —that it is practically impossible to isolate the results of purely racial factors. Consequently, it is easy to assert that the environmental factors are the ones responsible for the poor results, and that if these racial crosses had been given half a chance they would have been at least the equals of either of their parents.

Here, again, biology fortunately comes to our aid. The mixing of races among plants and animals has been carried on to a very vast extent, and many definite principles and rules have been worked out. Only the simplest and most fundamental need concern us here. First of all it should be recognized that many of the most beautiful, most useful, and generally finest types of plants and animals are crosses. The crossing of races is not necessarily disastrous. But these desirable crosses are either the result of long experimentation with various combinations or else of the union of carefully selected varieties chosen deliberately for certain traits which they possess and which promise to blend to advantage. No breeder would expect to improve his stock by random crossing with any variety that chanced to present itself. In other words, the desirable crosses are just as definite in their racial composition as the pure varieties.

More than this, the plant or animal breeder knows that the indiscriminate mixing of a large number of varieties can be expected to produce just one result—the mongrel. This is true even though the different varieties themselves may each be of a high type. The reason for this is clear. As remarked above, the germ plasm carried by every individual contains two classes of genes, first, those that are common to all the members of his species and give him the characteristic features of his species, and second, those that are peculiar to his own variety or race, and mark him off as a member of that particular kin-group. The varieties of the various species have been produced by specialization in the germ plasm. In wild plants and animals this specialization is produced by the general processes of natural selection; in domesticated creatures it is the result of the manipulations of the breeder, usually with a definite type or program in mind; and in man it is the outcome of the processes of race formation which have already been discussed. Accordingly, when a large number of different varieties are bred together the tendency is for the specialized genes to neutralize or cancel each other, and for the common general genes to support each other and intensify the corresponding qualities. The result to be looked for in the offspring is therefore a primitive, generalized type—often spoken of as a "reversion," "atavism," or "throwback."

There is every reason to believe that these rules hold good for man in his biological aspects. Many mixtures of human races have taken place, and some of them seem to have not only definite traits, but desirable traits according to certain widely accepted criteria. The combination of a large amount of Nordic with smaller proportions of Mediterranean and Alpine has certainly produced a type with outstanding characteristics; in the judgment of many persons (specifically those who are members of it) it is a type of peculiar excellence. This is the English type and it is the American type. It remained the prevailing type of the immigrants to America up till nearly the close of the nineteenth century. It is certainly a notable type, with a remarkable record of achievement in the past and promise of achievement for the future. Whether one likes the type or not, it is at least a known quantity. And it is a highly specialized type.

The change in the character of immigration which developed within the past generation and a half signalized the beginning of the process of mongrelization of this type. This process was not nearly so extreme in degree or rapid in rate as it would have been if we had not definitely excluded, by various means, the Chinese, Japanese, and Hindus as soon as their respective numbers begin to reach serious proportions, and if the immigration of Negroes and Malays had not been negligible in proportions for reasons which need not delay us here. Nevertheless, the new arrivals were sufficiently different, not only in their racial proportions but in their basic elements, to threaten the existing type with annihilation. What the resulting product would have been at the end of two centuries can not be definitely determined, nor can it be positively asserted that it would have been inferior to the present type. The latter is largely a matter of taste. It is almost certain that it would have been a much less specialized type, resembling much more closely a more primitive stage of human evolution. If any one, contemplating this probability, is led to deplore the check to such a development he is of course fully entitled to his own views.

It should be emphasized that this process of mongrelization takes place regardless of whether or not the component elements are of a high type. If we must have a symbol for race mixture, much more accurate than the figure of the melting pot is the figure of the village pound. If one can imagine a pound from which no dog was ever rescued, and in which all the denizens were free to interbreed at will, and into which dogs of every variety were introduced continuously for many dog generations, he will have an excellent representation of the racial situation of a country which receives all races of immigrants indiscriminately. The population of the pound, after a few generations, would be composed, aside from the newcomers, exclusively of mongrels. And this would be true even though none but thoroughbreds—Airdales, Greyhounds, Chows, Pekinese, Cockers, Doberman-Pinschers, etc.—had been placed within its confines. Mongrelization implies no inferiority on the part of the original constituents. So in a human society the prediction of a mongrel population as the almost certain product of a free-for-all immigration policy carries no more slur against the foreign elements than against the natives. It simply means a loss of specialization on all sides.

Now whether this loss of specialization, or mongrelization, among human stocks is a thing to be desired or a thing to be shunned is a matter partly of knowledge, partly of judgment, partly of taste. There is certainly a good deal to be said for the mongrel. As a canine, he is tough, resourceful, and remarkably able to take care of himself. It may be that as a human he would display corresponding features. According to the New York *Times:*

> Dr. Henry Fairfield Osborn, who presides over the American Museum of Natural History, extols the wholesome boyhood of the caveman. He figures, in effect, that old Peter Cro-Magnon's son had a better preparation for life than, say, J. Bleeker Knickerbocker's child, now at Princeton.[2]

While this, being a matter of environment, has nothing to do directly with race, there may be those who believe that by native qualities themselves the Cro-Magnon youngster, and his father as well, were better equipped to cope with difficult situations than their highly specialized descendants, and that if modern man, having achieved an extraordinarily efficient economic culture, could now reduce his own internal mechanism to a simpler and more primitive form, he would be more able to get some real comfort out of life.

But few dog lovers regard the mongrel as the most admirable product of canine evolution, and few members of any of the more highly specialized human groups are likely to look with favor upon the submergence of the distinctive traits of their stock beneath a flood of Cro-Magnon or Neanderthal humanity. At any rate there is this to be said: Whatever the qualities of the races of to-day may be, good or bad, they are at least known. The qualities of a future composite race are not known. It is conceivable that

---

[2] March 29, 1925, Section 9, page 2.

they might be good. But it is also wholly possible that they might be very bad. It is a very widespread, and probaly salutary, human trait that

> makes us rather bear those ills we have
> Than fly to others that we know not of.

Furthermore, in this respect it is never too late to mend. If the progress of future scientific research should establish the fact that indiscriminate race mixing is desirable, or that certain definite crosses can be depended upon to produce good results, it would be relatively easy by deliberate social policies to promote whatever combinations the evidence called for. But, on the other hand, if racial mixture is actually allowed to take place, and then the results are found to be undesirable, it is virtually impossible to correct the mistake. The false steps could not be retraced. It is as impossible to unmix races as to unscramble the proverbial egg. This whole matter of race mixture seems to be one where it is quite legitimate to apply the good old maxim, "In case of doubt, don't."

It is probably an evidence of the sound judgment of democracies, to which reference has already been made, that the people of the United States, by successive steps, have expressed their determination to keep the racial tone of the population about what it was at the time of the Declaration of Independence. Each time that the threat of dilution by a widely different race has appeared it has been met decisively. The first instance was furnished by the Chinese immigration, which began to assume noteworthy proportions soon after the middle of the last century. At first these quaint, exotic strangers received a hearty welcome. They filled a useful place in the woman-less organization of the mining camps. But as their numbers increased the sentiment rapidly changed, and a demand for their total debarment arose which eventually culminated in the Chinese Exclusion Acts. The next widely different race to present itself was the Japanese. Exactly the same psychological development took place. A primary attitude of welcome on the part of the American people rapidly gave place to bitter opposition as the numbers of immigrants increased, and in the end the movement was virtually stopped by means of the famous Gentlemen's Agreement. At about the same time a rising current of Hindus was checked, first by a severe interpretation of the general immigration law, by which every Hindu was assumed to be either a polygamist or likely to become a public charge, or both, and later, in 1917, by the "geographical delimitation clause," which marks out an arbitrarily bounded "barrèd zone," including large sections of Asia and most of the South Sea Islands from which no immigrants are permitted to come. Thus before the end of the Great War immigration to the United States had been definitely restricted, practically speaking, to the white and African races. This is an incongruous and anomalous combination, the *raison d'être* of which is to be found in the history of the Negroes in this country. In point of fact, there has never been more than a very

small immigration of African blacks. If this current had ever reached conspicuous proportions there is little doubt that some effective means would
have been discovered and applied to check it.

It must be confessed that the means by which the non-white races have
been excluded, and the character of much of the popular agitation in the
matter, leave much to be desired. But bad means, contrary to many pious
platitudes, not infrequently produce good results, and there can be no doubt
that the policy of keeping this as far as possible a white man's country is
fully justified in the event. At least, the native citizen of the older American stock finds it difficult to think without a shudder of what the situation
would be in this country to-day if there had been no check to Oriental immigration for the past one hundred years.

The outstanding feature of the post-War sentiment of the American people was the conviction that the mere exclusion of the non-white races did not
go far enough in racial discrimination. It was more and more strongly felt
that there must also be some definite measures to check any further dilution
of the typical American mixture, any alteration in the basic proportions of
the various sections of the white race. It was realized that while there is not
in any accurate sense an "American race," the components of the American
people are decidedly limited in variety, and combined in characteristic proportions, and that this racial composite must be held largely responsible for
the development of an American culture distinctly agreeable at least to
Americans. The destruction of this characteristic racial foundation held
potentialities of change in American institutions and cultural values which
the bulk of the citizens did not care to face. A detailed examination into
the causes of this alteration in attitude would take us too far afield. The
War itself doubtless had a great deal to do with it. The bright searchlight
which the great conflict turned upon social relations threw into bold relief
the truth of many obscure problems. Probably the continued insistence of
the special students of the question had its effect upon public opinion,
bringing, among other things, a better comprehension of the real nature of
racial factors. Whatever the causes, the fact is that racial considerations
played a wholly unprecedented part in the post-War agitation about immigration. The popular voice demanded not only a positive reduction in
the total volume of immigration, but a reapportionment of such immigration as there was so as to bring the "old immigration" once more into predominance, that is, to provide that immigration, however voluminous,
should leave the racial proportions of the American people intact.

In seeking to meet this demand, Congress, most of the influential members of which were already thoroughly persuaded, adopted a device which
had been suggested many years before, and which has now become widely
familiar as the "percentage" or "quota" plan. This idea, as embodied in
temporary legislation which ran for three years, provided that the total
immigration of persons of a given nationality in any fiscal year should be

limited to three per cent of the foreign-born persons of that nationality who were resident in the United States in 1910, as reported by the census of that year. The question will probably at once arise, why, if this legislation was a response to a demand for racial discrimination, was it expressed in terms of nationality? The answer is simple. As has already been shown, our actual knowledge of the racial composition of the American people, to say nothing of the various foreign groups, is so utterly inadequate that the attempt to use it as a basis of legislation would have led to endless confusion and intolerable litigation. So Congress substituted the term nationality, and defined nationality as country of birth. It is clear, then, that "nationality," as used in this connection, does not conform exactly to the correct definition of either nationality or race. But in effect it affords a rough approximation to the racial character of the different immigrant streams. Certainly it had the result of drawing the great bulk of our immigration once more from those countries out of which our original population had been built up.

This discriminatory effect of the quota principle was due to the fact that the old immigration, though coming in only small numbers in recent years, had been coming for so long that it had built up large reservoirs of foreign-born population by 1910, while the new immigration, though of enormous volume in the two decades just before the census of 1910, had been coming for so short a time that its base numbers were small. Thus a three per cent quota admitted considerably more immigrants from northwestern Europe than had actually been coming in recent years, but only a fraction of those from southern and eastern Europe.

By the time Congress was ready to put the principle of restriction in permanent form in 1924, advanced thought on the question had reached the point where it was recognized that quotas based on foreign-born residents exclusively were illogical and themselves discriminatory against the old stock. It was realized that the native population had at least as good a right as foreigners to be considered in determining the composition of the immigration of the future. If the goal was to preserve the racial character of the American people, why not go at it directly? The proposal was therefore made that instead of quotas based on foreign-born residents there should be a flat total of one hundred fifty thousand set for the quota countries, and that this total should be distributed among the quota countries in the same proportions as persons deriving their origin from each country respectively were found among the residents of the United States by the census of 1920. This is called the principle of "national origins," nationality once more being defined as country of birth. The task, then, is to make an estimate of the foreign sources of the total population of the country, clear back to the first white settlements, and to express this estimate in terms of the proportions of the population of 1920 attributable to each foreign country respectively. The annual total of one hundred fifty thousand is to be apportioned pro rata. In order that time might be allowed for the making of this estimate it was provided that this plan should not go into effect for three years, that is until the fiscal year beginning July 1, 1927. In the meantime, the old quota plan is continued, the percentage, however, being reduced to two, and the census of 1910 being replaced by that of 1890, which obviously has the effect of prodigiously favoring the old immigration, as it was meant that it should.

All of these provisions apply only to the Eastern Hemisphere. The countries of both of the American continents and the adjacent islands are at present left without numerical restriction at all. This plainly leaves a large loophole for racial admixture in the future. It also seems to convey a peculiar implication as to the relative desirability of the peoples of Mexico and the West Indies, for instance, and those of Italy or Roumania. Of course the fact is that something more than racial considerations led to the decision to exempt our neighbor countries from quantitative regulation. Nevertheless, the possibilities of serious race mixture involved in a heavy migration from the regions to the south of us are so great that there has already developed a vigorous sentiment in favor of bringing all countries under some form of quota regulation, and it is wholly probable that the next few years will see a definite maximum fixed to the migration of persons of every nationality.

As far as we can look into the future, then, it appears that the race problem in the United States will be confined to the unification of the various elements already established here. Further additions represented by the immigration of the future will involve few complications of a truly racial character. With reference to the sections of the white race already included in the American population, there is little doubt that the process of unification by amalgamation will go on steadily and irresistibly, until at the end of a few generations racial differentiation will have been practically wiped out, and the population of the country will once more present a racially homogeneous aspect. And we may hope that, diverse as the present varieties may be, the proportions of the definitely esoteric elements are sufficiently small so that the degree of resulting mongrelization will not be enough to reduce seriously the racial effectiveness of the American people.

What Happened to Race?

Oscar Handlin

Science, which created race as an intellectual concept, also helped destroy it. For it is the strength of science to contain within itself the means of its own redemption. The dedication to truth which animates the scholar's inquiry again and again brings him back to a reinvestigation of the evidence. Respect for the evidence raises in each man's mind questions as to the interpretations he builds upon it. The process of re-examination acquired more importance than ever before as scientists became aware of the degree to which their own preconceptions influenced their conclusions.

The result was a complete revision of the basic ideas upon which the old notion of race rested. The scholarship of the past thirty years has touched at many points upon the matters dealt with in the Dillingham and the Laughlin reports.* It has coped far more adequately with the patterns of prejudice and the problems of race, with the course of immigration through American history, with the nature of the economic and social adjustments of migrants, and with the extent to which intelligence, education, crime, insanity, and other social disorders vary among the diverse groups of the American population. Large areas, of course, still remain open for investigation; and at some place the evidence is inconclusive. But enough data is available to permit a fresh evaluation of the fundamental conceptions to which the Dillingham Commission gave expression forty-five years ago. Such a revaluation will show the distance science has traveled since.

1. GENETICS AND THE NATURE OF RACE

Intensive research into the problems of heredity has led to a much clearer understanding of how physical traits are transmitted across the generations.

From *Race and Nationality in American Life* by Oscar Handlin, by permission of Atlantic-Little, Brown and Company. Copyright, ©, 1948, 1950, 1953, 1956, 1957 by Oscar Handlin. Pp. 188–207.

* Editor's note: The Dillingham report was the report in 1911 of the United States Immigration Commission, established in 1907 under the chairmanship of Senator William P. Dillingham of Vermont. The Laughlin report was presented in 1922 by Harry H. Laughlin, a eugenicist employed by the House Committee on Immigration. Both reports were used to support the view that the new immigrants were less desirable than the old.

In so doing the theories both of Darwin and Galton have been abandoned. The new point of departure has been the observations of an Austrian abbot who patiently tended the rows of peas in his garden. Johann Mendel, called Gregor when he became an Augustinian monk, published his conclusions in 1869; but the decades that followed were not congenial to his views, which lay disregarded for more than thirty years. Then in 1900 their relevance became compellingly clear to a number of scholars; and modern genetics is the result.

Such physical traits as the color of the eyes or hair and the pigmentation of the skin do pass through the genes from parents to children. The carriers have been identified and described. We know now that a group of individuals with common characteristics will procreate offspring with the same characteristics. Mankind is composed of a variety of populations which differ among themselves in the frequency of many genes. These Mendelian populations will reproduce themselves across time.

But these Mendelian populations differ in two critical respects from what earlier geneticists called races. They are not identical with the national, linguistic, religious, economic, or other cultural groupings into which mankind is also divided. These overlap and cut across each other's boundaries. "People with blue eyes, or with round or with oblong heads, or with heads shaped like some prehistoric skull, or fat people or people convicted for crime, or sufferers from cancer or other diseases do not form Mendelian populations." The attempt to conflate the various categories can only yield meaningless confusion.

Furthermore, the Mendelian population is not fixed, but undergoes evolutionary changes. It may split into several distinct populations, or several quite separate ones may fuse into one. A variety of social and cultural factors may break down or create gene pools. Therefore, the existence of such a grouping at a given point in time is not in itself evidence of the common descent of its members, any more than it establishes the presumption that their descendants will still be part of the same population. This is certainly a far cry from the conception of race as a fixed category, united by common descent and social as well as physical characteristics.

"Race" as a term is still useful, if properly defined. A helpful statement prepared for UNESCO by a group of distinguished biologists, psychologists, and social scientists, in 1950, outlines the points upon which there was a general consensus of opinion. Its central conclusions may be stated as follows:

Mankind is essentially one, descended from the same common stock. The species is divided into a number of populations, or races, which differ from each other in the frequency of one or more genes which determine the hereditary concentration of physical traits. Those traits are not fixed, but may appear, fluctuate, and disappear in the course of time. It is presently possible to distinguish three such races—the Mongoloid, the Negroid, and the Caucasoid—but no subgroups within them can be meaningfully described in physical terms. National, religious, geographic, linguistic, and cultural groups do not coincide with race, and the cultural and social traits of such groups have no genetic connection with racial traits. There is no evidence of any inborn differences of temperament, personality, character, or intelligence among races.

Therefore, it follows that the only meaningful basis upon which one can compare social and cultural traits is in terms of the ethnic group, which preserves its continuity to the extent that its culture passes from generation to generation through a common social environment. The inheritance of an ethnic group consists not of its biological characteristics, but of its culture.

Modern anthropology has therefore devoted more attention than was usual in earlier years to the study of cultural rather than physical differences, both in preliterate and in our own societies. These differences are viewed as the product of habits, attitudes, beliefs, and institutions developed in the course of adjustments to their environment, broadly construed, by individuals and cultural groups. Differences of this sort may persist over very long periods of time, but they are not determined by the physical traits of the men marked off by them.

Since race in the old sense is no longer an important consideration, it will be enlightening to consider the effects of persisting cultural differences upon our society, primarily in terms of the place within it of the numerous ethnic groups of which it is formed. It may be, in time, that the Negroes will still constitute a distinct group, but one marked off by its own heritage rather than by the prejudice attached to its color. Regarding the problem from that perspective, we have learned much in recent years about the effect on the nation of the heterogeneity and plurality of its population.

2. MIGRATION AND THE ETHNIC GROUPS IN AMERICAN LIFE

Diverse ethnic groups played a particularly important role in American history. In the United States, the government always left large areas of social action free for the activities of voluntary organizations. Without any compulsion toward uniformity, individuals associated with one another in religious, social, philanthropic, cultural, and economic organizations through which they preserved the distinctive differences that separated them from other Americans. These differences originated in a number of factors. Religion, for instance, was the basis of identification among such groups as the Mormons or Quakers or Jews. Color set the Negroes and Japanese apart. Most important, immigration, which brought to the United States men of diverse cultural antecedents, left them in groups based upon their common heritages, interests, and ideas.

Immigration therefore always played a central role in the formation of

American culture. From the very first settlement, it helped shape the distinctive institutions of the nation. The effects of immigration, as those are now understood, may therefore offer a clue to the continuing role of the ethnic group in the United States.

The most important contributions to the understanding of this process in recent years have emphasized its continuity. Exceptional men have often enriched our culture—the East Anglian Puritans, the forty-eighters, or the refugee scientists of the 1930's. But the mass of people who arrived in the seventeenth century were not substantially different from those who came in the eighteenth or in the nineteenth or in the twentieth. Although each of the ethnic groups which reached the New World had its distinctive cultural and social life, and although they were at different stages of development at the point of departure, the process that brought them all was the same. Their social origins and their motives were always very much alike.

It is therefore no longer possible to speak of meaningful distinctions between settlers and immigrants or between old and new immigrants. Englishmen, Germans, Italians, and Poles spoke different languages, had different habits, and were accustomed to different forms of behavior. But the kinds of Englishmen who came to the United States in the seventeenth and eighteenth centuries were very much the same as the kinds of Irish, Germans, and Scandinavians who came in the middle of the nineteenth, and these in turn were very much like the Italians, Jews, and Poles who came later.

Very largely all these immigrants were people displaced by economic changes in the structure of modern agriculture and industry. With the growth of population and with the mechanization of industry and agriculture, large numbers of artisans found their handicrafts useless and even larger numbers of peasants found no place for themselves on the land. These were the people to whom opportunity beckoned in the New World. The generating economic changes began in England and spread to the east; that accounts for the difference in the era at which various peoples began to migrate. But the process was one and continuous.

In discussing adjustment to life in the United States, it is therefore necessary to take account of both similarities and differences among the groups involved. To some extent, the qualities of the cultural heritage influenced the course of that adjustment. But more important was the nature of the opportunities open to the immigrant and the length of time afforded him for adjustment. In no case does the line between old and new seem significant.

3. THE ECONOMIC ADJUSTMENT

Properly or not, discussion of the problems of immigration has often focused on the nature of the effects on the economy. The Immigration Commission devoted the bulk of its labors to this subject; and for some Americans this has been the decisive aspect of the question. Scholarly studies have thrown considerable light on the effects of immigration on depressions, on wages, on occupational stratification and mobility, and on economic innovations.

a. *Immigration and depressions.* It was once feared that immigration, which added new hands to the labor supply, contributed to the severity of depressions. The evidence of the depression that followed the panic of 1929 points in the other direction. In the early 1930's the volume of unemployment remained high and the depression intense despite the complete curtailment of immigration. These phenomena depended upon the more general fluctuations of the business cycle rather than upon a single factor, immigration.

Furthermore, studies of the period of free migration down to 1924 have indicated the likelihood that immigration may actually have eased the effects of depression. The volume of immigration seemed to rise sharply during periods of prosperity and to sink rapidly in periods of depression. Such shifts lent fluidity to the labor supply, enabling it to expand when more hands were needed and to contract when they were not.

b. *Immigration and wages.* In the years of argument over restriction some Americans feared that immigration would tend to drive wages downward. There were some grounds for that uneasiness. As a theoretical proposition it seemed convincing that the effect of adding to the supply of labor was to drive down its cost. Furthermore, through much of the period of free immigration the average *real* wages of labor, particularly of unskilled labor, fell or were stationary.

Examined more closely, however, the relationship of immigration to labor assumes another appearance. A simple comparison of the conditions of labor in 1900 with those in 1850 has little value for this purpose. To deal with the over-all average for labor, including all unskilled labor, is not very informative as to the effects of immigration on the pre-existing labor force, because the immigrants themselves come to constitute a large part of the sample. Only by eliminating from the account the unskilled labor of the immigrants can one assess the effects of the arrival upon the natives. Such a reckoning reveals that the fate of skilled native workers improved steadily in the period of immigration. Furthermore, the coming of the immigrants, by broadening the range of opportunities at the top of the occupational ladder, actually lifted the earlier labor force to higher job levels and thus increased their income. As long as the whole economy was expansive, therefore, immigration probably raised rather than lowered the wage level of existing laborers.

In the more recent past, with wages largely set by collective bargaining, the decisive element in the determination of wage rates has been the state of labor organization in any given industry. When the opportunity has been afforded them, immigrants have shown their readiness to join unions in defense of their interests as workers. Given the continued capacity of the economy to expand in the future, a moderate amount of immigration seems no threat either to wage rates or to the unions.

c. *Immigration and occupational stratification.* Although economic opportunities in American society were open to all, some groups were more likely than others to take advantage of them. The determining factors were complex, with some, although not all of them, related to immigration.

Most immigrants entered the American economy at the lowest levels, primarily as unskilled laborers. This was the logical outcome of the situation of peasants arriving in an industrial society without capital. The lack of skill and the initial role as laborers were characteristic of the old immigrants as of the new, of the Irish and Germans as of the Italians and Poles, although the proportions differed somewhat. There were occasional exceptions, of course, as among the British immigrants of the last quarter of the nineteenth century and among the Jews a little later.

It seems clear that the occupational level of all such groups rose with the passage of time, although no general study has as yet examined with sufficient care the means through which that rise occurred or the factors which affected its rate. The groups varied considerably in their experiences; and those variations no doubt reflected differences in cultural background as well as in the availability of opportunities and the length of settlement.

That the factor last named was often crucial was shown by the findings in a survey of Newburyport, Massachusetts. Using indexes of their own contriving, the authors of that study traced the occupational status of eight ethnic groups over nine decades, from 1850 to 1933. They discovered that almost all groups raised their status in time, that relative position tended to vary with duration of settlement, and that some new immigrants (Armenians and Jews, for example) did better than the old Irish. Scattered data on home ownership and savings accounts in general supported the same conclusions.

d. *Innovations and immigration.* Finally, the possibility must not be overlooked that among any group of immigrants or their children there may be an occasional individual who by his gifts as an outsider becomes one of the long list of innovators, inventors, or entrepreneurs who have helped to stimulate American industry in the past. No test will reveal which particular group will in the future bring along a Michael Pupin, a Conrad Huber, an Ottmar Mergenthaler, or a Giuseppe Bellanca. But a society will make best use of such talented individuals if it offers them the opportunity to rise to the status at which they can use their ability, whatever their origin.

To sum up, the adverse effects of immigration seem to have been slight, the gains for Americans and newcomers, considerable. All the groups which have hitherto immigrated have had some economic difficulties in the sense that they have had to begin with the poorest jobs; but all have shown the capacity to thrive from the opportunities of American life.

4. INTELLIGENCE AND ADJUSTMENT

Among the indexes that have conventionally been used to judge the capacity of various ethnic groups for Americanization were their intelligence and education. These were long the ostensible justifications for the literacy test since, it was argued, only the fittest groups ought to be permitted to·assume the responsibilities of American citizenship.

The difficulty was to find a reliable basis for comparing the intelligence of diverse groups. The Army intelligence tests of 1917 and 1918 were inconclusive since they did not eliminate from the results the effect of differences of environment. All that could reliably be deduced from these tests was that duration of residence was a significant factor. Beyond that, there was no sound basis for establishing valid differences in intelligence among various ethnic groups.

There is a good deal of evidence of difference in educational attainment. Local data indicates that some groups are more proficient in their schooling and advance to higher grades than others. Ethnic values and background may be conditioning factors here. On the other hand, there is also evidence that the social environment is critical. Negro children who migrate from the South to the North thus show a marked rise in intelligence quotient. Furthermore, a general study of American education has shown that the most significant variable in the ability of children to profit from their schooling is the character of the social environment and the class from which they come. In all this material, there is little to suggest that any group is innately incapable of being Americanized by reason of deficiencies in its intelligence.

5. CRIMINALITY AND ADJUSTMENT

Very similar conclusions emerge from the studies of criminality in the past twenty-five years. As to total inclination to crime, the (Wickersham) National Commission on Law Observance and Enforcement found that the foreign-born committed fewer crimes than the native-born in proportion to their respective numbers in the total population. This result is plausible enough, although there must always be a good deal of difficulty in compensating for differences due to the social distribution of the groups concerned.

The commission also felt that among the foreign-born there seemed to be variations, from group to group, in the proneness to commit certain types of crimes. But its evidence, it feared, was not adequate to sustain any firm generalization.

A more recent study tended to confirm the predilection of various ethnic groups to certain types of crimes. Professor E. A. Hooton (*Crime and the Man* [Cambridge, 1939]) found that crime was not due to influences generated by race or ethnic affiliations. But given a criminal individual, the type of crime committed was likely to be determined by the character of the group from which he sprang. Certainly this factor is, in general, minor in comparison with the other social, psychological, and biological elements affecting the rate of criminality in the United States.

Juvenile delinquency now also seems less a concomitant of immigration or ethnic affiliation than formerly. Intensive investigations have not found conclusive evidence that the children of immigrants are more likely to be delinquent than the children of natives; and given equality of social environment, there is even an indication they may be less so.

Furthermore, there is now a sound basis for believing that the cultural conflict deriving from ethnic affiliations is of only slight importance in determining the incidence of juvenile delinquency, and that the more critical factors spring from the social and family environment and from the personality of the individual child.

The total trend of these investigations has been to minimize the possible influence upon criminality of immigration or of ethnic background. Certainly they supply no grounds for the fear that the new immigrants were likely to be more dangerous than the old, or the Negroes more prone to lawbreaking than the whites.

6. ALCOHOLISM AND ADJUSTMENT

Statistical measurement of the incidence of alcoholism offered the same difficulties as that of other disorders. The data was at best partial and had to be adjusted against deviations with care. Thus figures for arrests for drunkenness were not very useful since these varied enormously from place to place and were likely to affect almost exclusively the lowest social groups.

A somewhat more reliable index, though hardly a thoroughly dependable one, was the rate of commitment for alcoholic psychoses in state institutions. This offered the advantage of a relatively constant criterion and one that could be fairly well standardized. A study of New York State institutions in the 1930's used this index with good results (Benjamin Malzberg, *Social and Biological Aspects of Mental Disease* [Utica, 1940], 163 ff.). That study found that the foreign-born had a rate of 7.4 per 100,000 population while the native rate was only 3.2. But standardized to remove the influence of different age distributions, the disparity disappeared almost entirely, with the foreign and native rates nearly equal.

The distribution by specific nativity groups was striking for it showed marked variations as significant as the equality of the over-all foreign with the native rate. The maximum was for the Irish with 30.5, followed by the

Scandinavians with 7.9, the English with 4.8, the Italians, 4.3, and the Germans, 3.8. Whether these differences reflected some sort of ethnic predilection or whether they reflected differences in the social environment would be difficult to judge in the absence of any convincing theory as to the causes of alcoholism. Perhaps the most that could be said is that the immigrants as a whole did not add to the burden of the problem, although specific groups among them may have. But those groups could by no means be correlated with the old and new immigrations.

7. INSANITY

On the basis of summary rates of commitment or of first admissions it was sometimes maintained that insanity was more frequent among the foreign-born than among the native-born. A careful study has shown, however, "that such comparisons are spurious, in that they fail to account for the effects of age and other disturbing conditions." The foreign-born are older than the natives and "consequently tend to have higher rates of first admissions." Furthermore, the foreign-born are more concentrated in cities, from which the rates of commitment are higher. "When age and the urban-rural ratio are both held constant," there is practically no significant difference between the foreign- and the native-born.

Dr. Malzberg's study found instead a correlation between the incidence of insanity and "general economic conditions." To the extent that that conclusion was valid, immigration has had no perceptible effect upon the general rate of insanity.

The problem was more complicated, however. For, as in the case of alcoholism, there has been a marked disparity in the incidence of the disease among various nativity groups, with the Irish far in the lead. Furthermore, if the various types of psychoses were differentiated, it appeared that the Scandinavians were ahead in admissions for general paresis, while the Germans were in the lead in admissions for dementia praecox.

A study of draft-board rejections for mental disorders confirmed these findings (Robert W. Hyde and Roderick M. Chisholm, "The Relation of Mental Disorders to Race and Nationality," *New England Journal of Medicine*, CCXXXI [1944], 612 ff.). This study had the advantage of dealing with ethnic (second generation as well as foreign-born) rather than simply with nativity groups. It showed convincingly a difference in the susceptibility of various groups to different types of mental disorder. In view of the fact that the total foreign-born rate was not larger than the total native-born, immigration seemed to offer no threat of increased incidence of insanity in the whole population. And in view of the difficulty of establishing a ranking of the various groups that would be valid for all types of insanity, it was futile to attempt to use this as one of the elements of selection of immigrants.

From what has been said above, there seems to be the following general pattern to what we know about the problems of insanity, alcoholism, crime, and intelligence:

There is no evidence that the immigrants have been inferior to the natives, no evidence that the new immigrants have been inferior to the old, and no evidence that immigration has produced any social deterioration in the United States.

None of these relationships is based on race. All may be radically altered under the impact of the changing environment of life in the United States, and all vary to some extent with the duration of residence.

For each of the disorders mentioned there was some evidence of variation among different groups of immigrants; but no immigrant group, old or new, ranked consistently high or consistently low in all the categories. These variations, therefore, were not such as to make it possible to rank the groups in order of desirability. Significantly, there was also no evidence that relative distance from American culture was a factor of any importance in determining ultimate adjustment. That is, people like the Syrians, Armenians, and Turks, relatively more alien to native American habits and ways of life, were not significantly retarded in adjustment, given the time and opportunity. The evidence suggests rather that, like the native population, each immigrant group had its own points of strength and weakness at which it yielded to, or resisted, disorganizing pressures that originated in the environment or in personal disturbances. No group was thereby prevented from playing a constructive part in American life.

8. CITIZENSHIP

There was some disposition early in the century to criticize the new immigrants for the failure to be naturalized; the Immigration Commission, for one, lent its support to such criticism. These attacks uniformly failed to consider the factor of length of residence in the United States. When account was taken of that factor, the old immigration made no better showing than the new. A study of the percentage of foreign-born naturalized as of 1940 revealed that the various nativity groups could be ranked in an order which corresponded almost exactly with the average length of residence in the United States (F. J. Brown and J. S. Roucek, *One America* [New York, 1945], 657). The only exceptions were the natives of England and British Canada, who showed unusual reluctance to become American citizens. These findings were indirectly supported by an earlier study of New Haven which showed a correlation of naturalization with education, occupational status, and income—concomitants generally of length of residence.

Nor has there been evidence that the immigrants, or any group of them, have shirked the important duties of citizenship. The two world wars in which the United States engaged in the last forty years found these men ready to serve; their part in the armed services has been fully documented and often recognized.

9. CULTURAL CONTRIBUTIONS

An evaluation of the social experience of the immigrants to the United States must also take some account of their positive contributions to American culture. It would be pointless, however, to attempt to assess the relative merits of one group as against another. The more significant conclusion that emerges from the survey of American art, music, literature, science, theater, and sports is that every group has shown the capacity to produce individuals able to play a useful role in such endeavors. The distinctions between old and new immigrants, in retrospect, seem quite pointless. There was no basis for predicting which among the millions of men and women who landed on our shores would themselves or through their children bring the gifts that contributed to American culture. It seems certain only that without these contributions life in the United States in the past would have been far poorer than it was. In a more subtle sense, the most valuable contribution of the immigrants, old and new, was always to remind Americans of the motto on the great seal, *E Pluribus Unum, From Many One.* Their adjustment involved the achievement of unity—and yet the preservation of diversities—in American society.

What has been true of the ethnic groups set off by immigration is also true of those distinguishable by their color. A point-by-point examination of the social and cultural characteristics of the American Negroes leads to the identical conclusion as with regard to the immigrants. The black man's traits are not identical with those of the whites, just as various white groups are not identical with each other. But all those differences are primarily the products of influences emanating from the social and cultural milieu. They are not related to the physical nature of the Negro; and they constitute no barrier in the way of his occupying a fully equal place in American life.

The whole scientific basis for the race fears and hatred of the past has thus disappeared. That does not mean, of course, that all the fears and hatreds themselves have vanished, any more than the terror of the nightmare, with the waking. But the light does bring reassurance, and there is room for hope that a deeper understanding of prejudice and of its psychological, social, and historical sources will help to dissipate its effects.

That would leave America free to confront the challenges of its diverse society. For the groupings within it which have so often presented problems in the past may as often create opportunities for the future. There are encouraging indications in our own experience of the means by which those opportunities may be exploited.

The Turner Thesis:
"Is It . . . a Valid Key
to the Meaning of
American History?"

INTRODUCTION

When the historian Frederick Jackson Turner first proclaimed his cele-brated frontier thesis in 1893, his views, for the moment, attracted relatively little attention. Within a generation, however, the Turner thesis was widely accepted as the most significant explanation of American development and of the character of American institutions. Criticism of the thesis began to be voiced in the 1920's and, increasingly, in the next two decades. But criticism of Turner was met by defense of Turner, as supporters of the frontier thesis rebutted the arguments of those who found fault with Turner's views.

The Turner thesis has unquestionably stimulated a considerable amount of research on the various aspects of the westward movement and the frontier, and it has also been responsible for a substantial number of publi-cations dealing directly with the merits or shortcomings of the thesis itself. Despite the abundance of the literature on the subject, however, the author of a recent historiographical account of the thesis concludes that "no one has yet completely ascertained the many-faceted effects of the frontier on American civilization." [1]

In the first of the selections dealing with the Turner thesis, Professor Robert Riegel, a student of the westward movement and the author of a textbook in the field, summarizes and accepts most of the important criti-cisms of the Turner thesis. Riegel nevertheless believes that the frontier must have had a significant effect on American development. In the second selection, Professor Ray A. Billington, who has written a textbook on the westward movement in a Turnerian framework, asks if Turner's thesis is "still a valid key to the meaning of American history?" Although he accepts some of the criticisms of the Turner thesis, Billington nevertheless finds the thesis to be correct in the main. He concludes that the frontier process was the most important of the New World conditions explaining American development and that it "remains one essential tool—albeit not the only one—for interpreting American history."

---

[1] Gene M. Gressley, "The Turner Thesis—A Problem in Historiography," *Agricultural History*, XXXII (October 1958), 249.

Current Ideas of the Significance of the United States Frontier

Robert E. Riegel

To the European a frontier means a political boundary between two potentially hostile nations. To the resident of the United States the word frontier is more likely to suggest an unsettled area in which the advancing white man is struggling to overcome natural difficulties.[1] The United States has had its share of political boundaries, but through most of its history has had the great good fortune to feel no serious threat from the people on the other side of them. Consequently the United States until late in the nineteenth century could devote almost its entire energies to the solving of internal problems, which included the occupation of a large share of the continent. Domestic concerns loomed so large that they obscured the rest of the world.[2]

The manifold difficulties of transforming a wilderness occupied by natives possessing a simple culture into a modern industrial nation led North Americans historically to give great emphasis to economic progress. While they were highly conscious of the virtues of educational, scientific, artistic and other cultural attainments, and while they boasted, possibly a trifle too loudly, of accomplishments in such fields, they reserved their greatest energies for the amassing of material wealth, believing that the mind could work better on a full than on an empty stomach. Practically every foreign visitor of the nineteenth century noted that social distinction stemmed most frequently from business success, and that the making of a fortune was the normal goal of every intelligent and ambitious young man.

The magnificent expansion and enrichment of the United States, even though greatly dependent on fabulous natural resources, reinforced the natural tendency of all peoples to have pride in their own civilizations.

From *Revista de Historia de América*, **Number 33 (June 1952), 25–43. Reprinted by permission.**

[1] Fulmer Mood, "Notes on the History of the Word *Frontier*," *Agricultural History*, XXII (April, 1948), 78–83.

[2] This point is expanded by Carleton J. H. Hayes in his presidential address to the American Historical Association, "The American Frontier—Frontier of What?", in *American Historical Review*, LI (January, 1946), 199–210.

Citizens of the United States felt that their abilities were well above average, and that their institutions, particularly Protestant Christianity and democracy, represented the ultimates in human achievement. Above all they embraced whole-heartedly the idea of the inevitability of progress—that American civilization was destined to continue to improve until something near perfection had been achieved, and until other nations followed the American example.[3]

North Americans were quite aware of the importance of a new and virgin continent in their spectacular economic advance. Dozens of thinkers, including men such as George Washington, Thomas Jefferson, Ralph Waldo Emerson, Horace Greeley and Henry George insisted on the significance of vast, unsettled tracts of excellent land.[4] They speculated that these untouched regions provided tremendous opportunities for new wealth, including potential markets which would encourage eastern industrial development. Democracy, individualism and optimism were reinforced. European migrants were attracted in large numbers, even though more to work in the industrialized regions of the East than to occupy western farms. Opportunity seemed almost endless for those sufficiently lucky to be born in America or sufficiently ambitious to migrate. Rich farms could be obtained cheaply, business opportunities seemed unlimited, and wages remained high because of the relative scarcity of labor.

The industrial growth of the United States was interrupted from time to time by periods of depression, which led to speculations even before the middle of the nineteenth century that cheap or free western land was an outlet for the industrial eastern groups affected by the ups and downs of a money civilization. The demand arose that land be given free of charge and even that prospective migrants be loaned the money to make the trip to the West and to buy necessary equipment.[5] While the free land came in time (1862) the government never went further, and whether for this or other reasons the importance of costless land was never as great as expected. Quite certainly free land did very little in a direct way to provide for sufferers from depressions.

The generation after the Civil War saw the very rapid occupation of the American West, and a growing number of people began to worry about the probable results of the end of free land. Among those who were seriously concerned were Henry George, who devised a new system of taxation to eliminate land monopoly, and Josiah Strong, who favored aggressive over-

---

[3] Arthur A. Ekirch, *The Idea of Progress in America, 1815–1860* (New York: Columbia University Press, 1944).

[4] Lee Benson, "The Historical Background of Turner's Frontier Essay," in *Agricultural History*, XXV (April, 1951), 59–82; Herman C. Nixon, "The Precursors of Turner in the Interpretation of the American Frontier," *South Atlantic Quarterly*, XXVIII (January, 1929), 83–89.

[5] Roy M. Robbins, "Horace Greeley: Land Reform and Unemployment, 1837–1862," in *Agricultural History*, VII (January, 1933), 18–41.

seas expansion to avoid the troubles coming from too great concentration of population. Others concerned with the new situation included Alfred T. Mahan, Francis A. Walker, J .W. Powell and C. Ward Davis. The speculations of Malthus, which had seemed fantastic to many earlier Americans, now began to assume ominous possibilities.[6]

Historians had been relatively slow to become interested in the effects of cheap, arable land, and the possible results of its disappearance, but the late nineteenth century saw the emergence of a man who was to dramatize the subject and to place his imprint deeply upon a generation of American historians. The man was Frederick Jackson Turner, himself a westerner. Turner had grown up in Portage, Wisconsin, where his father was a newspaper editor, had attended the University of Wisconsin and had done graduate work at Johns Hopkins, where he had been immersed in the importance of the slavery issue in United States history and in the preconception that all Anglo-Saxon institutions could be traced from their origins in the German forests.[7]

Turner's vigorous mind and western background inspired him to question certain elements of current historiography.[8] As a patriotic Mid-Westerner he could hardly agree that all virtues should be traced to the German forests, thus making his own area but the tattered fringes of the robe of civilization.[9] Undoubtedly he read and pondered current American reactions toward the importance of free land and the dangers involved in its disappearance, even though his exact reading cannot now be identified; he certainly was influenced by Richard Ely and Woodrow Wilson.[10] Also unquestionably he read various Europeans, including most importantly the Italian economist Achille Loria, whom he later gave specific credit. While

---

[6] See Benson, *op. cit.*

[7] The best general account of the life and beliefs of Turner is Merle Curti, *Frederick Jackson Turner* (Mexico: Instituto Panamericano de Geografía e Historia, 1949); Fulmer Mood has an excellent account in *The Early Writings of Frederick Jackson Turner* (Madison, Wisconsin: University of Wisconsin Press, 1938), pp. 1–39, and is now preparing a definitive life.

[8] Turner's methods and point of view are discussed in Merle Curti, "The Section and the Frontier in American History: the Methodological Concepts of Frederick Jackson Turner," in Stuart A. Rice (ed.), *Methods in Social Science* (Chicago: University of Chicago Press, 1931), 353–367; Fulmer Mood, "The Development of Frederick Jackson Turner as a Historical Thinker," in *Colonial Society of Massachusetts Transactions*, XXXIV, 238–252; Fulmer Mood, "The Historiographic Setting of Turner's Frontier Essay," in *Agricultural History*, XVII (July, 1943), 153–155; Fulmer Mood, "The Concept of the Frontier," in *Agricultural History*, XIX (January, 1945), 24–30; Rudolf Freund, "Turner's Theory of Social Evolution," in *Agricultural History*, XIX (April, 1945), 78–87; W. Stull Holt, "Hegel, The Turner Hypothesis, and the Safety-valve Theory," in *Agricultural History*, XXII (July, 1948), 175–76.

[9] Carl Becker, "Frederick Jackson Turner," in Howard W. Odum (ed.), *American Masters of Social Science* (Chicago: University of Chicago Press, 1927), 273–318.

[10] Every writer mentions the influence of Ely; see also Wendell H. Stephenson (ed.), "The Influence of Woodrow Wilson on Frederick Jackson Turner," in *Agricultural History*, XIX (October, 1945), 249–253.

his final concepts closely paralleled many of the ideas of Loria, there is question as to whether he derived his views from the Italian, or whether he attained them independently and was pleased when he found Loria taking similar points of view.[11]

The first important statement of the Turner ideas was in a short paper called "The Significance of the Frontier in American History," which he read to a gathering of his professional colleagues in 1893. Undoubtedly he weighed each word carefully because of the personal importance of the occasion. Presumably he expressed his matured judgment, for when he republished the essay twenty-seven years later he changed not a single word, even in the footnotes. The statements contained in the essay are hence the most authoritative we have; Turner's sparse later writings expanded and applied them but made no basic changes.[12]

The viewpoint of Turner was focussed strongly on the present—possibly in part because of his newspaper background. While as an historian he was passionately devoted to the search for truth, he realized that truth was frequently a relative matter, and that each generation quite properly rewrote history to make it pertinent to existing problems.[13] He contended that the most distinctive and influential factor in the North American past was the existence of cheap and easily available land. For Turner the region of sparse settlement, where white civilization encroached on the wilderness, was the area which was most important in the creation and reinforcement of traditional American ideas and ideals. Liberty-loving frontiersmen flocked to the new lands to recapitulate the development of all civilization—hunter, trader and miner, followed by pioneer farmer, specialized farmer, and finally city dweller. These men were optimistic, nationalistic and expansionist. They were individualistic and materialistic, with a sprinklng of the lawless, but withal brave, hardy and ingenious, willing to experiment until they overcame the difficulties of each new region. They were the primary source of such American traits as individualism, democracy, inventiveness and materialism. They were the main inspiration of nationalism, and it was the frontier that was the real American melting pot, where immigrants laid aside the mental and physical habiliments of their past and emerged real citizens of a new world. The whole process developed a distinctive section

---

[11] Lee Benson, "Achille Loria's Influence on American Economic Thought: Including His Contribution to the Frontier Hypothesis," in *Agricultural History*, XXIV (October, 1950), 182–199.

[12] Frederick J. Turner, *The Frontier in American History* (New York: Henry Holt and Co., 1920), *The Significance of Sections in American History* (New York: Henry Holt and Co., 1932), *The United States 1830–1850* (New York: Henry Holt and Co., 1935); a bibliography of the Turner writings by Everett E. Edwards is included in Mood, *Early Writings, op. cit.*

[13] Good brief summaries of the Turner views are contained in Robert E. Riegel, *America Moves West* (New York: Henry Holt and Co., 1949), chap. 40, and Ray A. Billington, *Westward Expansion* (New York: The Macmillan Co., 1949), chap. 1.

of the country, which took its part in the sectional struggles that were so important in much of United States history.

Now that free land was coming to an end and the frontier disappearing, Turner felt that the future of the United States rested with his beloved Middle West of the upper Mississippi Valley. Here were preserved the great national virtues, as created and reinforced by a frontier background, which would bring salvation to an industrialized and urbanized nation. The Middle West was to be the buttress of the rights of the common man— rights to be guaranteed by the government as against heartless business corporations. Furthermore, also in accord with the so-called "Progressive" ideals of the time, United States concepts and institutions were to be spread overseas in a philanthropically conceived imperialism.

The Turner views were disseminated more by students and admirers than by Turner himself, for he wrote but little.[14] Turner was an extraordinarily inspiring teacher, attracting many able students who almost always developed passionate attachments to the master and his ideas.[15] Rather rapidly the Turnerian views were adopted by other historians and then by writers in all sorts of fields, including general literature. Quite naturally they were at times misstated and at other times asserted when they contradicted the evidence. For example, one investigator of Kansas settlement asserted dogmatically the Turner doctrine that "the agricultural pioneer tries out crop after crop until he hits on some that succeed," [16] after which within half a dozen pages he stated the observable fact that "the pioneers of this earliest period relied mainly upon crops that had proved successful in the central and eastern states." [17] Turner himself

---

[14] Among the favorable comments are Avery Craven, "Frederick Jackson Turner, Historian," in *Wisconsin Magazine of History*, XXV (June, 1942), 408–424, "Frederick Jackson Turner," in William T. Hutchinson (ed.), *Marcus W. Jernegan Essays in American Historiography* (Chicago: University of Chicago Press, 1937), "Frederick Jackson Turner and the Frontier Approach," in *University of Kansas City Review*, XVIII (Autumn, 1951), 3–17, "The 'Turner Thesis' and the South," in *Journal of Southern History*, V (August, 1939); Joseph Schafer, "Turner's Frontier Philosophy," in *Wisconsin Magazine of History*, XVI (June, 1933), 451–69, "Some Facts Bearing on the Safety-Valve Theory," in *Wisconsin Magazine of History*, XX (1936), 216–32, "Was the West a Safety Valve for Labor?", in *Mississippi Valley Historical Review*, XXIV (December, 1937), 299–314; John C. Parish, "The Persistence of the Westward Movement," in *Yale Review*, XV (April, 1926), 461–477; A. L. Burt, "Our Dynamic Society," in *Minnesota History*, XIII (March, 1932), 3–23.

[15] Edward Everett Dale, "Turner—the Man and Teacher," in *University of Kansas City Review*, XVIII (Autumn, 1951), 18–28, "Memories of Frederick Jackson Turner," in *Mississippi Valley Historical Review*, XXX (December, 1943), 339–58, "Frederick Jackson Turner, a Memoir," in *Massachusetts Historical Society Proceedings*, LXV (May, 1935), 432–440; Max Farrand, "Frederick Jackson Turner at the Huntington Library," in *Huntington Library Bulletin* (February, 1933); Edward E. Robinson, "Frederick Jackson Turner," in *North Dakota Historical Quarterly*, VI (July, 1932), 259–61; Louise P. Kellogg, "The Passing of a Great Teacher," in *Historical Outlook*, XXIII (October, 1932), 270–72; other students, previously cited, include Curti, Craven, and Schafer.

[16] Carrol D. Clark and Roy L. Roberts, *People of Kansas* (Topeka, Kansas, 1936), 17.

[17] *Ibid.*, p. 23.

would certainly have been the last person to insist on this type of uncritical acceptance of dogma, for he was a modest seeker of truth.

The stimulation provided by Frederick Jackson Turner inspired much of the ever-widening investigation of the frontier experience and its results, even though at times the discussion has been muddied by the uncritical and overly-enthusiastic support of admirers and by the objections of skeptics who have been more intent upon showing their own preeminence and in buttressing the claims of their own sections of the nation to superiority than in ascertaining the truth. Careful investigation has unveiled the sources of many of the Turner ideas, for obviously Turner was a product of the age in which he lived. His assumption that human institutional development moved inevitably from simple to complex along uniform lines, and that the whole process was similar to that of physical evolution, with man reacting to environmental conditions in predeterminable ways, was in accord with the "scientific" approach of his day—an approach which expected to produce simple "laws" of human development and behavior, and which has been called Social Darwinism. Most present authorities feel that Turner's point of view led him to oversimplify the whole frontier process and to place undue emphasis on physical environment and on uniformity of result. The newer historiography has produced certain conclusions which may be stated with assurance, but retains certain problems that only the future can solve.[18]

Migrants seeking opportunity on the cheap land of the West were generally young and vigorous, even though the age differential was not as great as many people have assumed, and there was an excess of males over females. They originated above all on farms where there was a surplus of children as compared with land. Many a farmer's son was forced to leave home to earn a decent living, and he might well have found a western farm more attractive than a factory job in one of the rising industrial centers of the East. Numerous migrants described themselves as artisans, but their specialization was much less than would have been the case at a later day, and probably a considerable share of the men had farming experience. The growing towns of the West attracted skilled and unskilled labor with their

---

[18] Among the more or less critical accounts are George W. Pierson, "American Historians and the Frontier Hypothesis in 1941," in *Wisconsin Magazine of History*, XXVI (September and December, 1942), "The Frontier and American Institutions: A Criticism of the Turner Theory," in *New England Quarterly*, XV (June, 1942), 224–55, "The Frontier and Frontiersmen of Turner's Essays," in *Pennsylvania Magazine of History*, LXIV (October, 1940), 449–78; Murray Kane, "Some Considerations on the Frontier Concept of Frederick Jackson Turner," in *Mississippi Valley Historical Review*, XXVII (December, 1940), 379–400; Frederick L. Paxson, "A Generation of the Frontier Hypothesis," in *Pacific Historical Review*, II (March, 1933), 34–51; references to other critical estimates appear elsewhere in this paper as connected with specific subject material. An interesting analysis of Turner as the product of his age is Henry Nash Smith, "The West as an Image of the American Past," in *University of Kansas City Review*, XVIII (Autumn, 1951), 29–40; see also the same author's *Virgin Land* (Cambridge: Harvard University Press, 1950).

comparatively high wages, but quite obviously the greatest demand for industrial labor came long after the frontier had disappeared except in the memories of the older inhabitants.[19]

The general pattern of development as recorded by Turner existed in the majority of areas, but there were more exceptions and greater variations than Turner mentioned. The type of frontiersman most obviously under-emphasized was the land speculator, who was omnipresent on every frontier from the Appalachians to the Pacific.[20] Many a frontier was above all a frontier of prospective cities as they were envisioned by optimistic specula-tors who were not restrained by a strict regard for truth. The speculators provided real services as the advance agents of the white agricultural fron-tier, but also made desirable land more costly for the real settlers. Most westerners uttered vigorous diatribes against speculators, but they were thinking only of wealthy easterners who did not expect to live in the re-gions where they were investing. Each westerner was himself a land specu-lator, often with greater hopes of profiting from advancing land values than from farming. After all, the whole life of a frontiersman was a specu-lation, and he could hardly have been expected to forego the most obvious opportunity for profits.

The importance that Turner attributed to free land was probably ex-cessive. Certainly farmers wanted cheap land, but they took surprisingly little advantage of the free land provided under the Homestead Act of 1862. Within recent years scholars have been investigating meticulously the acquisition of new land and its transference, so that we can now speak much more accurately than formerly about what happened to the various claims. Most of the land was acquired by means other than the Homestead Act—possibly to obtain more rapid possession and possibly to acquire better land, as from railroad grants. Furthermore, a large proportion of the men who filed under the Homestead Act never completed their claims; ap-parently many of them were interested only in selling out to later arrivals or to lumber or grazing companies.[21]

The great movements of population took place in times of prosperity rather than in periods of depression. All the evidence points in this direc-

---

[19] Charles W. Thornwaite, *Internal Migration in the United States* (Philadelphia: Uni-versity of Pennsylvania Press, 1934); Dorothy S. Thomas, *Research Memorandum on Migration Differentials* (New York: Social Science Research Council, 1938); J. C. Malin, "Local Historical Studies and Population Problems," in Caroline F. Ware (ed.), *The Cultural Approach to History* (New York: Columbia University Press, 1940), 300–347; L. D. Stilwell, *Migration from Vermont, 1776–1860* (Montpelier: Vermont Historical So-ciety, 1937).

[20] Ray A. Billington, "The Origin of the Land Speculator as a Frontier Type," in *Agricultural History*, XIX (October, 1945), 204–222.

[21] Thomas Le Duc, "The Disposal of the Public Domain on the Trans-Mississippi Plains: Some Opportunities for Investigation," in *Agricultural History*, XXIV (October, 1950), 199–204; Joseph Schafer, "The Wisconsin Domesday Book," in *Agricultural His-tory*, XIV (January, 1940), 23–32.

tion, and in fact the situation is quite evident as soon as it is given consideration. Whether the migrant were a single young man or a family, capital was needed for the trip west, to acquire land, to buy equipment, and to live until the first crop was harvested; the necessary funds were easier to acquire in good than in bad times. Moreover, depression struck the West as well as the East, with the result that a farmer was reluctant to embrace a new venture at the very time that his potential market was the worst.[22]

Much misinformation has been spread about the nature and time of migration because of Turner's rather casual reference to the frontier as a "safety valve of discontent." While his exact meaning was not made clear, various later writers assumed that he meant that groups getting along badly in the East could find opportunity in the West. These interpreters then derived the corollary that much of the westward migration was composed of industrial labor escaping eastern depressions. Regardless of what Turner had in his mind, the situation has been clarified by investigations during particular periods and for specific places. The greatest movements to the West were in periods of prosperity, and relatively few of the migrants came from the more industrialized parts of the East. The concept of an unemployed and penniless mill worker moving to take up a job or a farm in the West is difficult even to imagine.[23]

Once the more immediate application of the safety-valve concept became untenable, there arose considerable argument as to the long-run effects of the frontier, and this difference of opinion still continues to exist.[24] Many historians argue that the westward movement lessened eastern population concentration and hence retarded the development of conditions which produced industrial discontent. They point particularly to the fact that eastern wages were higher than European, and that western were higher than eastern, which they contend demonstrates the relative scarcity of labor. Other equally competent historians argue against any form of the safety-valve concept. They insist that labor troubles and general social discontent in the East was roughly parallel to that of Europe, with no indication of any great lag. They agree that the West drew population from the East, but insist that the resulting vacuum attracted European immigrants in sufficiently large numbers to equal the natural increase that would have resulted without any migration. One first rate historian goes so far as to

[22] Fred A. Shannon, "The Homestead Act and the Labor Surplus," in *American Historical Review*, XLI (July, 1936), 637–51; Paul W. Gates, "The Homestead Law in an Incongruous Land System," in *American Historical Review*, XLI (July, 1936), 652–81.

[23] Murray Kane, "Some Considerations on the Safety Valve Doctrine," in *Mississippi Valley Historical Review*, XXIII (September, 1936), 169–88.

[24] Among the more critical evaluations are Carter Goodrich and Sol Davidson, "The Wage Earner in the Westward Movement," in *Political Science Quarterly*, L (1935), 161–85, LI (1936), 61–116; C. H. Danhof, "Economic Validity of the Safety-Valve Doctrine," in *Journal of Economic History Supplement* (December, 1941), 96–106.

assert that the greatest discontent of the nineteenth century was agricultural rather than urban, and that instead of the frontier being an industrial safety valve, the city was a farming safety valve.[25]

The effect of the frontier upon its inhabitants and upon the entire United States also remains a matter of differences of opinion, although there has been a definite trend toward modifying the Turner generalizations. Everyone agrees that the West was boisterous, crude, optimistic and expansion-minded, but these were general national characteristics, and the part that the West had in creating or reinforcing them is a matter of opinion. Whether or not the West was particularly ingenious and inventive has been debated warmly. Certain innovations such as the steel plow and the self-binder came from the West, but the great bulk of both material and non-material inventions were either eastern or European. Such basic mechanical improvements as the cotton gin, the reaper, the telegraph and the telephone came from the East, while many institutional innovations such as the Sunday School, the missionary movement and the abolition crusade were European in origin. Considered merely theoretically, it is hard to conceive of the hard working frontier farmer as originating many novel ideas.

Turner's insistence that the migrant to the West was motivated heavily by a desire for freedom and an overwhelming love of individual independence is being whittled away daily. More and more historians point to the obvious fact that the average westward moving farmer was concerned mainly with acquiring wealth in the most promising fashion. His basic choice was not that of individual freedom but of an occupation in which he expected to increase his personal fortune most rapidly—hence he chose a farm in Illinois rather than a mill job in Lawrence, Massachusetts. He was looking forward to silk dresses for his wife, college for his son, music lessons for his daughter, a brick house and a fast span of horses.

Individualism had emphasis in the West, but more from necessity than desire. The frontier farmer was no hermit, and desired human companionship rather than isolation. Even on the crudest frontier he wanted help to fight the Indians and to build his house. His desire was not a log cabin in the wilderness but a comfortable home in a settled community that could provide markets, stores, banks, schools, roads and theaters. The general temper of the time was somewhat more individualistic than that of a later date, but the frontiersman ordinarily wanted neighbors, and was even anxious to obtain governmental aid in such matters as banking and the building of canals and railroads.

To Turner the westerner was a radical in both thought and actions, developing new ideas to meet new conditions. The modern trend of thinking,

---

[25] Fred A. Shannon, "A Post-Mortem on the Labor-Safety-Valve Theory," in *Agricultural History*, XIX (January, 1945), 31–33.

while far from uniform, tends to move in the opposite direction, with more and more people asserting that the West was essentially conservative.[26] True enough the westerner made some unpleasant innovations such as the sod house, was forced to develop several new techniques as in the arid parts of the West, and supported certain drastic actions for his own advantage—as free land and the elimination of Indian power; and yet the great bulk of his customs, including the building of log cabins, was derivative. More basic, however, he accepted in general the virtues and ideals which he had been taught as a youth and which were common in the United States. He was a God-fearing man along traditional lines. He joined the rest of the United States in judging success as the attainment of wealth. He respected personal property and the sanctity of contracts just as did his eastern contemporary. In fact he had moved to the West not in protest at current ideals but to attain them more quickly. His objective was the same kind of life which he had envied in his eastern neighbors.

Turner also insisted strongly that the origin of United States democracy was in the western forests, and here again his assumption has been questioned gravely. The early western settlement had comparatively small differences in wealth and position, which meant a relative equality which has sometimes been identified with democracy. But differences in social status soon appeared, and the West was seldom unified politically; for example, the Southwest long approved of slavery while the Northwest tended in the other direction. The movement for universal manhood suffrage was supported widely in the West, but it also had great backing in the East. So-called Jacksonian democracy can be understood only by a study of the East as well as the West. Popular Presidents such as Jefferson, Jackson and Lincoln, noted for their love of the common man, were elected more by eastern than by western votes.[27]

Considerable interest has been given the western support in the years around 1900 of such democratic measures as the direct primary, popular election of Senators, votes for women, the initiative, referendum and recall. In every case, however, the idea came from Europe, while the support was largely eastern, with the West itself divided. Much more important, however, is the question of whether such measures represented to any degree the influence of the frontier, which in most cases had long departed. The Wisconsin of Robert La Follette and the direct primary was a far cry from the frontier of Daniel Boone.

---

[26] C. McA. Destler, *American Radicalism, 1865–1901* (New London, Connecticut: Connecticut College, 1946); J. A. Woodburn, "Western Radicalism in American Politics," *Mississippi Valley Historical Review*, XIII (September, 1926), 143–68; Benton H. Wilcox, "An Historical Definition of Northwestern Radicalism," in *Mississippi Valley Historical Review*, XXVI (December, 1939), 377–94.

[27] Jeannette P. Nichols and James G. Randall (eds.), *Democracy in the Middle West* (New York: D. Appleton-Century Co., 1941); Benjamin F. Wright, Jr., "American Democracy and the Frontier," in *Yale Review*, XX (December, 1930), 349–65.

Very possibly a more fruitful approach to the problems of radicalism and democracy than an emphasis on frontier influence is the stressing of the desires of particular economic classes.[28] Large sections of the West have been heavily agricultural, and have quite naturally possessed the viewpoints of all such farming areas. The farmer, whether in Pennsylvania or in Kansas, has an identifiable point of view. The desire for corporation control, cheap money, low tariffs on manufactured goods and similar goals is a class matter. The main difference between Pennsylvania and Kansas, from this point of view, is that there are relatively more farmers in Kansas.

Many of the reforms credited to the West have been the products of farming distress in an increasingly industrialized world, and the influence of the frontier may well have been mainly to preserve the predominance of farming' for a longer time in particular areas. One recent authority insists that for the farmer the late nineteenth century was marked by the appearance of an international agrarian market, an international agrarian depression and an international agrarian discontent.[29] From this standpoint, the appearance of a farmers' program as it reached a high point in the Populist movement, was more an indication of changing conditions of farming than a remainder of frontier influences. The only influence of the frontier may well have been the long continuance of sparsely settled sections of the country.

The effect of the West in terms of Americanizing immigrants has been rather closely circumscribed during the past few years. Relatively few immigrants went to the frontier, preferring the high wages of the eastern cities. When they settled in the raw West they tended to collect fellow-countrymen in communities which reproduced as closely as possible the customs of the homeland. Swedish or Norwegian or German or Swiss ways of life continued with remarkable persistence on the frontier. Turner's feeling that each new frontiersman shed his old customs, started anew and became a real American appears to have been more a hope than a fact. Several historians have demonstrated very clearly the extent to which national characteristics were retained in western settlement.[30] Rather curiously one of these studies was made by an ardent disciple of Turner, and was concerned with Turner's own state of Wisconsin.

The variation in frontier conditions due to differences in national back-

---

[28] This point of view is stated clearly and simply in two reviews by Louis M. Hacker, "Sections—or Classes?," in *Nation*, CXXXVII (July 26, 1933) and "Frederick Jackson Turner: Non-Economic Historian," in *New Republic*, CXXXIII (June 5, 1935), 108; see also Charles A. Beard, "Culture and Agriculture," in *Saturday Review of Literature*, V (October 20, 1928), 272–73.

[29] Lee Benson, "The Historical Background of Turner's Frontier Essay," in *Agricultural History*, XXV (April, 1951), 59–82.

[30] Richard H. Shryock, "British Versus German Traditions in Colonial Agriculture," in *Mississippi Valley Historical Review*, XXVI (June, 1938), 39–54; Joseph Schafer, "The Yankee and the Teuton in Wisconsin," in *Wisconsin Magazine of History*, VI (1932), 125–45, 261–79, 386–402, VII (1933), 3–19.

grounds suggests that Turner placed somewhat too much emphasis on geographic and climatic factors as compared with cultural backgrounds. He created the impression that particular physical features would always produce similar results, somewhat irrespective of the backgrounds of the people involved. Quite probably he would have changed or at least modified this point of view as new evidence came to light, since he always had an open mind on his generalizations. Certainly the modern point of view is to give considerable importance to cultural backgrounds as conditioning factors in any society.

Recent years have seen increasing interest in whether frontiers in other parts of the world have shown characteristics similar to those of the American frontier.[31] Turner himself pretended to no knowledge of such comparable situations and modestly limited his generalizations to the United States, but if there is validity to his assumption that physical conditions are decisive in making the man, then comparable frontiers in other parts of the world should show well marked similarities. Further studies of the remainder of the Americas, of Australia and New Zealand, and possibly even of Europe and Africa might be illuminating.

The difficulty with comparative frontier studies is partly that they fail to exist in considerable numbers but partly also that the various regions are so different that contrasts are hard to make. Recent studies of Australia and New Zealand are typical. Both areas are very different from the United States. The Australian frontier was a big man's frontier with no free land and showed no trend toward individualism and democracy and nationalization. Similarly, the New Zealand frontier emphasized collective rather than individual action, with socialism as the end product. Whether or not such experiences have any valid impact on the Turner generalizations remains open to argument.

The question of whether Turner was correct or incorrect in his analysis of the influence of the frontier is very possibly less important than the fact that he turned men's minds from traditional and increasingly sterile investigations to fields that were fresh and rewarding. His present biographer pays particular respect to Turner as an historical thinker—"the sole example of the species in the American scene at the time." [32] Another Turner admirer asserts about the Turner frontier theory that "its soundness as well as its importance must in large measure be gauged in terms of its effects on the men of its own generation." [33] Turner arranged American history in a new pattern that stimulated men to desert some of their preconceptions and see the nation's history in a completely new light.

---

[31] Among recent studies are Norman D. Harper, "Turner the Historian: 'Hypothesis' or 'Process'?," in *University of Kansas City Review*, XVIII (Autumn, 1951), 76–86; B. Fitzpatrick, "The Big Man's Frontier and Australian Farming," in *Agricultural History*, XXI (January, 1947), 8–12.

[32] Mood, "The Historiographic Setting," *op. cit.*, 155.

[33] Craven, in *Wisconsin Magazine, op. cit.*, 423.

Current Ideas of the Significance of the United States Frontier

The United States, like other nations, is unique. Its distinctive characteristics must be the product of men of particular abilities and backgrounds operating in a certain geographic setting. An important part of the picture is certainly the long-time existence of a population frontier. Certain historians have been so anxious to correct and limit the Turner generalizations that at times they seem to deny that the frontier experience had any perceptible effect. Such an implication must be wrong. No nation living on the edge of a wilderness for most of its national existence could fail to be affected by that experience.

Turner's concept of history as the handyman of current desires may itself have been a product of his own age and not necessarily true, but evidences of its validity are exceedingly numerous. Turner himself modified the historical thinking of his day by stressing such traits as individualism and democracy, but quite properly he did not eliminate the older values—he was modifying and not replacing. The present world tends to emphasize the actions of national governments, both in the domestic and international spheres. Just as Turner predicted, historians are now engaged in the task of rewriting history to make it pertinent to the new set of values.

Turner was definitely moving along with the trends of his day, for when there appeared in his mind a possible conflict between democracy and individualism he was willing to sacrifice some of the latter to obtain more of the former; like other liberals of his day he was willing to part with some of the older individualism to accomplish the improvement of the average man, which he identified with democracy. He felt that the closing of the frontier, with the disappearance of free land and increasing urbanization, meant that the average man must more and more rely upon the government to protect him from forces which he as an individual could not control.

But did the end of the frontier really mean an important limitation of the opportunities of the average man? One of our more thoughtful present United States historians is of the opinion that individualism was limited not so much by the end of free space as by the development of machine culture and science which tended to outmode the trained amateur, and insists that the retention of individualism is the pressing problem of our age—a problem that has only slight connection with the frontier.[34]

Society can progress only to the extent that the powers and the abilities of the individual are challenged. From this point of view the study of the North American frontier is not only the study of a specific situation or even of a tradition, but a study of how human energies, both male and female, have been inspired to maximum effort, together with the results, both good and bad. The analysis of situations that have produced the greatest and most intense of human activities has particular value to the modern

---

[34] J. C. Malin, "Space and History: Reflections on the Closed-Space Doctrines of Turner and Mackinder and the Challenge of these Ideas by the Air Age," in *Agricultural History*, XVIII (April, 1944), 65–74 and XVIII (July, 1944), 107–126.

world, and the historian can perform no more useful function than to make as clear as possible the ramifications of human motivation.

How the Frontier Shaped the

American Character

Ray Allen Billington

Since the dawn days of historical writing in the United States, historians have labored mightily, and usually in vain, to answer the famous question posed by Hector St. John de Crèvecœur in the eighteenth century: "What then is the American, this new man?" Was that composite figure actually a "new man" with unique traits that distinguished him from his Old World ancestors? Or was he merely a transplanted European? The most widely accepted—and bitterly disputed—answer was advanced by a young Wisconsin historian named Frederick Jackson Turner in 1893. The American was a new man, he held, who owed his distinctive characteristics and institutions to the unusual New World environment—characterized by the availability of free land and an ever-receding frontier—in which his civilization had grown to maturity. This environmental theory, accepted for a generation after its enunciation, has been vigorously attacked and vehemently defended during the past two decades. How has it fared in this battle of words? Is it still a valid key to the meaning of American history?

Turner's own background provides a clue to the answer. Born in Portage, Wisconsin, in 1861 of pioneer parents from upper New York state, he was reared in a land fringed by the interminable forest and still stamped with the mark of youth. There he mingled with pioneers who had trapped beaver or hunted Indians or cleared the virgin wilderness; from them he learned something of the free and easy democratic values prevailing among those who judged men by their own accomplishments rather than those of their ancestors. At the University of Wisconsin Turner's faith in cultural democracy was deepened, while his intellectual vistas were widened through contact with teachers who led him into that wonderland of adventure where scientific techniques were being applied to social problems, where Darwin's

From *American Heritage*, **The Magazine of History, IX (April 1958), 4, 7–9, 86–89.** Reprinted by permission.

evolutionary hypothesis was awakening scholars to the continuity of progress, and where searchers after truth were beginning to realize the multi-
plicity of forces responsible for human behavior. The young student showed
how well he had learned these lessons in his master's essay on "The Character and Influence of the Fur Trade in Wisconsin"; he emphasized the
evolution of institutions from simple to complex forms.

From Wisconsin Turner journeyed to Johns Hopkins University, as did
many eager young scholars of that day, only to meet stubborn opposition for
the historical theories already taking shape in his mind. His principal professor, Herbert Baxter Adams, viewed mankind's development in evolutionary
terms, but held that environment had no place in the equation; American
institutions could be understood only as outgrowths of European "germs"
that had originated among Teutonic tribes in the forests of medieval Germany. To Turner this explanation was unsatisfactory. The "germ theory"
explained the similarities between Europe and America, but what of the
many differences? This problem was still much in his mind when he returned to the University of Wisconsin as an instructor in 1889. In two remarkable papers prepared during the next few years he set forth his answer.
The first, "The Significance of History," reiterated his belief in what historians call "multiple causation"; to understand man's complex nature, he
insisted, one needed not only a knowledge of past politics, but a familiarity
with social, economic, and cultural forces as well. The second, "Problems in
American History," attempted to isolate those forces most influential in
explaining the unique features of American development. Among these
Turner believed that the most important was the need for institutions to
"adapt themselves to the changes of a remarkably developing, expanding
people."

This was the theory that was expanded into a full-blown historical hypothesis in the famous essay on "The Significance of the Frontier in
American History," read at a conference of historians held in connection
with the World Fair in Chicago in 1893. The differences between European
and American civilization, Turner stated in that monumental work, were
in part the product of the distinctive environment of the New World. The
most unusual features of that environment were "the existence of an area
of free land, its continuous recession, and the advance of American settlement westward." This free land served as a magnet to draw men westward,
attracted by the hope of economic gain or adventure. They came as Europeans or easterners, but they soon realized that the wilderness environment
was ill-adapted to the habits, institutions, and cultural baggage of the
stratified societies they had left behind. Complex political institutions were
unnecessary in a tiny frontier outpost; traditional economic practices were
useless in an isolated community geared to an economy of self-sufficiency;
rigid social customs were outmoded in a land where prestige depended on
skill with the axe or rifle rather than on hereditary glories; cultural pursuits

were unessential in a land where so many material tasks awaited doing. Hence in each pioneer settlement there occurred a rapid reversion to the primitive. What little government was necessary was provided by simple associations of settlers; each man looked after his family without reliance on his fellows; social hierarchies disintegrated, and cultural progress came to a halt. As the newcomers moved backward along the scale of civilization, the habits and customs of their traditional cultures were forgotten.

Gradually, however, newcomers drifted in, and as the man-land ratio increased, the community began a slow climb back toward civilization. Governmental controls were tightened and extended, economic specialization began, social stratification set in, and cultural activities quickened. But the new society that eventually emerged differed from the old from which it had sprung. The abandonment of cultural baggage during the migrations, the borrowings from the many cultures represented in each pioneer settlement, the deviations natural in separate evolutions, and the impact of the environment all played their parts in creating a unique social organism similar to but differing from those in the East. An "Americanization" of men and their institutions had taken place.

Turner believed that many of the characteristics associated with the American people were traceable to their experience, during the three centuries required to settle the continent, of constantly "beginning over again." Their mobility, their optimism, their inventiveness and willingness to accept innovation, their materialism, their exploitive wastefulness—these were frontier traits; for the pioneer, accustomed to repeated moves as he drifted westward, viewed the world through rose-colored glasses as he dreamed of a better future, experimented constantly as he adapted artifacts and customs to his peculiar environment, scorned culture as a deterrent to the practical tasks that bulked so large in his life, and squandered seemingly inexhaustible natural resources with abandon. Turner also ascribed America's distinctive brand of individualism, with its dislike of governmental interference in economic functions, to the experience of pioneers who wanted no hindrance from society as they exploited nature's riches. Similarly, he traced the exaggerated nationalism of the United States to its roots among frontiersmen who looked to the national government for land, transportation outlets, and protection against the Indians. And he believed that America's faith in democracy had stemmed from a pioneering experience in which the leveling influence of poverty and the uniqueness of local problems encouraged majority self-rule. He pointed out that these characteristics, prominent among frontiersmen, had persisted long after the frontier itself was no more.

This was Turner's famous "frontier hypothesis." For a generation after its enunciation its persuasive logic won uncritical acceptance among historians, but beginning in the late 1920's, and increasingly after Turner's death in 1932, an avalanche of criticism steadily mounted. His theories, critics said, were contradictory, his generalizations unsupported, his assumptions inadequately based: what empirical proof could he advance, they asked, to prove that the frontier experience was responsible for American individualism, mobility, or wastefulness? He was damned as a romanticist for his claim that democracy sprang from the forest environment of the United States and as an isolationist for failing to recognize the continuing impact of Europe on America. As the "bait-Turner" vogue gained popularity among younger scholars of the 1930's with their international, semi-Marxian views of history, the criticisms of the frontier theory became as irrational as the earlier support rendered it by overenthusiastic advocates.

During the past decade, however, a healthy reaction has slowly and unspectacularly gained momentum. Today's scholars, gradually realizing that Turner was advancing a hypothesis rather than proving a theory, have shown a healthy tendency to abandon fruitless haggling over the meaning of his phrases and to concentrate instead on testing his assumptions. They have directed their efforts primarily toward re-examining his hypothesis in the light of criticisms directed against it and applying it to frontier areas beyond the borders of the United States. Their findings have modified many of the views expressed by Turner but have gone far toward proving that the frontier hypothesis remains one essential tool—albeit not the only one—for interpreting American history.

That Turner was guilty of oversimplifying both the nature and the causes of the migration process was certainly true. He pictured settlers as moving westward in an orderly procession—fur trappers, cattlemen, miners, pioneer farmers, and equipped farmers—with each group playing its part in the transmutation of a wilderness into a civilization. Free land was the magnet that lured them onward, he believed, and this operated most effectively in periods of depression, when the displaced workers of the East sought a refuge from economic storms amidst nature's abundance in the West. "The wilderness ever opened the gate of escape to the poor, the discontented and oppressed," Turner wrote at one time. "If social conditions tended to crystallize in the east, beyond the Alleghenies there was freedom."

No one of these assumptions can be substantiated in the simplified form in which Turner stated it. His vision of an "orderly procession of civilization, marching single file westward" failed to account for deviations that were almost as important as the norm; as essential to the conquest of the forest as trappers or farmers were soldiers, mill-operators, distillers, artisans, storekeepers, merchants, lawyers, editors, speculators, and town dwellers. All played their role, and all contributed to a complex frontier social order that bore little resemblance to the primitive societies Turner pictured. This was especially the case with the early town builders. The hamlets that sprang up adjacent to each pioneer settlement were products of the environment as truly as were the cattlemen or Indian fighters; each evolved economic functions geared to the needs of the primitive area surrounding it, and, in the tight public controls maintained over such essential functions as grist-milling or retail selling, each mirrored the frontiersmen's community-oriented views. In these villages, too, the equalitarian influence of the West was reflected in thoroughly democratic governments, with popularly elected councils supreme and the mayor reduced to a mere figurehead.

The pioneers who marched westward in this disorganized procession were not attracted by the magnet of "free land," for Turner's assumption that before 1862 the public domain was open to all who could pay $1.25 an acre, or that acreage was free after the Homestead Act was passed in that year, has been completely disproved. Turner failed to recognize the presence in the procession to the frontier of that omnipresent profit-seeker, the speculator. Jobbers were always ahead of farmers in the advance westward, buying up likely town sites or appropriating the best farm lands, where the soil was good and transportation outlets available. When the settler arrived his choice was between paying the speculator's price or accepting an inferior site. Even the Homestead Act failed to lessen speculative activity. Capitalizing on generous government grants to railroads and state educational institutions (which did not want to be bothered with sales to individuals), or buying bonus script from soldiers, or securing Indian lands as the reservations were contracted, or seizing on faulty features of congressional acts for the disposal of swampland and timberland, jobbers managed to engross most of the Far West's arable acreage. As a result, for every newcomer who obtained a homestead from the government, six or seven purchased farms from speculators.

Those who made these purchases were not, as Turner believed, displaced eastern workers fleeing periodic industrial depressions. Few city-dwelling artisans had the skills or inclination, and almost none the capital, to escape to the frontier. Land prices of $1.25 an acre may seem low today, but they were prohibitive for laborers earning only a dollar a day. Moreover, needed farm machinery, animals, and housing added about $1,000 to the cost of starting a farm in the 1850's, while the cheapest travel rate from New York to St. Louis was about $13 a person. Because these sums were always beyond the reach of factory workers (in bad times they deterred migration even from the rural East), the frontier never served as a "safety valve" for laborers in the sense that Turner employed the term. Instead, the American frontiers were pushed westward largely by younger sons from adjacent farm areas who migrated in periods of prosperity. While these generalizations apply to the pre-Civil War era that was Turner's principal interest, they are even more applicable to the late nineteenth century. During that period the major population shifts were from country to city rather than vice versa; for every worker who left the factory to move to the farm, twenty persons moved from farm to factory. If a safety valve did exist at that time, it was a rural safety valve, drawing off surplus farm labor and thus lessening agrarian discontent during the Granger and Populist eras.

How the Frontier Shaped the American Character

Admitting that the procession to the frontier was more complex than Turner realized, that good lands were seldom free, and that a safety valve never operated to drain the dispossessed and the malcontented from industrial centers, does this mean that his conclusions concerning the migration process have been completely discredited? The opposite is emphatically true. A more divergent group than Turner realized felt the frontier's impact, but that does not minimize the extent of the impact. Too, while lands in the West were almost never free, they were relatively cheaper than those in Europe or the East, and this differential did serve as an attracting force. Nor can pages of statistics disprove the fact that, at least until the Civil War, the frontier served as an indirect safety valve by attracting displaced eastern farmers who would otherwise have moved into industrial cities; thousands who left New England or New York for the Old Northwest in the 1830's and 1840's, when the "rural decay" of the Northeast was beginning, would have sought factory jobs had no western outlet existed.

The effect of their exodus is made clear by comparing the political philosophies of the United States with those of another frontier country, Australia. There, lands lying beyond the coastal mountains were closed to pioneers by the aridity of the soil and by great sheep ranchers who were first on the scene. Australia, as a result, developed an urban civilization and an industrialized population relatively sooner than did the United States; and it had labor unions, labor-dominated governments, and political philosophies that would be viewed as radical in America. Without the safety valve of its own West, feeble though it may have been, such a course might have been followed in the United States.

Frederick Jackson Turner's conclusions concerning the influence of the frontier on Americans have also been questioned, debated, and modified since he advanced his hypothesis, but they have not been seriously altered. This is true even of one of his statements that has been more vigorously disputed than any other: "American democracy was born of no theorist's dream; it was not carried in the *Susan Constant* to Virginia, nor in the *Mayflower* to Plymouth. It came out of the American forest, and it gained a new strength each time it touched a new frontier." When he penned those oft-quoted words, Turner wrote as a propagandist against the "germ theory" school of history; in a less emotional and more thoughtful moment, he ascribed America's democratic institutions not to "imitation, or simple borrowing," but to "the evolution and adaptation of organs in response to changed environment." Even this moderate theory has aroused critical venom. Democracy, according to anti-Turnerians, was well advanced in Europe and *was* transported to America on the *Susan Constant* and the *Mayflower*; within this country democratic practices have multiplied most rapidly as a result of eastern lower-class pressures and have only been imitated in the West. If, critics ask, some mystical forest influence was responsible for such practices as manhood suffrage, increased authority for

117

legislatures at the expense of executives, equitable legislative representation, and women's political rights, why did they not evolve in frontier areas outside the United States—in Russia, Latin America, and Canada, for example —exactly as they did here?

The answer, of course, is that democratic theory and institutions were imported from England, but that the frontier environment tended to make them, in practice, even more democratic. Two conditions common in pioneer communities made this inevitable. One was the wide diffusion of land ownership; this created an independent outlook and led to a demand for political participation on the part of those who had a stake in society. The other was the common social and economic level and the absence, characteristic of all primitive communities, of any prior leadership structure. The lack of any national or external controls made self-rule a hard necessity, and the frontiersmen, with their experience in community co-operation at cabin-raisings, logrollings, corn-huskings, and road or school building, accepted simple democratic practices as natural and inevitable. These practices, originating on the grass roots level, were expanded and extended in the recurring process of government-building that marked the westward movement of civilization. Each new territory that was organized—there were 31 in all—required a frame of government; this was drafted by relatively poor recent arrivals or by a minority of upper-class leaders, all of whom were committed to democratic ideals through their frontier community experiences. The result was a constant democratization of institutions and practices as constitution-makers adopted the most liberal features of older frames of government with which they were familiar.

This was true even in frontier lands outside the United States, for wherever there were frontiers, existing practices were modified in the direction of greater equality and a wider popular participation in governmental affairs. The results were never identical, of course, for both the environment and the nature of the imported institutions varied too greatly from country to country. In Russia, for instance, even though it promised no democracy comparable to that of the United States, the eastward-moving Siberian frontier, the haven of some seven million peasants during the nineteenth and early twentieth centuries, was notable for its lack of guilds, authoritarian churches, and all-powerful nobility. An autocratic official visiting there in 1910 was alarmed by the "enormous, rudely democratic country" evolving under the influence of the small homesteads that were the normal living units; he feared that czarism and European Russia would soon be "throttled" by the egalitarian currents developing on the frontier.

That the frontier accentuated the spirit of nationalism and individualism in the United States, as Turner maintained, was also true. Every page of the country's history, from the War of 1812 through the era of Manifest Destiny to today's bitter conflicts with Russia, demonstrates that the American attitude toward the world has been far more nationalistic than that of non-frontier countries and that this attitude has been strongest in the newest regions. Similarly, the pioneering experience converted settlers into individualists, although through a somewhat different process than Turner envisaged. His emphasis on a desire for freedom as a primary force luring men westward and his belief that pioneers developed an attitude of self-sufficiency in their lone battle against nature have been questioned, and with justice. Hoped-for gain was the magnet that attracted most migrants to the cheaper lands of the West, while once there they lived in units where co-operative enterprise—for protection against the Indians, for cabin-raising, law enforcement, and the like—was more essential than in the better established towns of the East. Yet the fact remains that the abundant resources and the greater social mobility of frontier areas did instill into frontiersmen a uniquely American form of individualism. Even though they may be sheeplike in following the decrees of social arbiters or fashion dictators, Americans today, like their pioneer ancestors, dislike governmental interference in their affairs. "Rugged individualism" did not originate on the frontier any more than democracy or nationalism did, but each concept was deepened and sharpened by frontier conditions.

His opponents have also cast doubt on Turner's assertion that American inventiveness and willingness to adopt innovations are traits inherited from pioneer ancestors who constantly devised new techniques and artifacts to cope with an unfamiliar environment. The critics insist that each mechanical improvement needed for the conquest of the frontier, from plows to barbed-wire fencing, originated in the East; when frontiersmen faced such an incomprehensible task as conquering the Great Plains they proved so tradition-bound that their advance halted until eastern inventors provided them with the tools needed to subdue grasslands. Unassailable as this argument may be, it ignores the fact that the recurring demand for implements and methods needed in the frontier advance did put a premium on inventiveness by Americans, whether they lived in the East or West. That even today they are less bound by tradition than other peoples is due in part to their pioneer heritage.

The anti-intellectualism and materialism which are national traits can also be traced to the frontier experience. There was little in pioneer life to attract the timid, the cultivated, or the aesthetically sensitive. In the boisterous western borderlands, book learning and intellectual speculation were suspect among those dedicated to the material tasks necessary to subdue a continent. Americans today reflect their background in placing the "intellectual" well below the "practical businessman" in their scale of heroes. Yet the frontiersman, as Turner recognized, was an idealist as well as a materialist. He admired material objects not only as symbols of advancing civilization but as the substance of his hopes for a better future. Given economic success he would be able to afford the aesthetic and intellectual pursuits that he felt were his due, even though he was not quite able to appreciate them. This spirit inspired the cultural activities—literary societies, debating clubs, "thespian groups," libraries, schools, camp meetings—that thrived in the most primitive western communities. It also helped nurture in the pioneers an infinite faith in the future. The belief in progress, both material and intellectual, that is part of modern America's creed was strengthened by the frontier experience.

Frederick Jackson Turner, then, was not far wrong when he maintained that frontiersmen did develop unique traits and that these, perpetuated, form the principal distinguishing characteristics of the American people today. To a degree unknown among Europeans, Americans do display a restless energy, a versatility, a practical ingenuity, an earthy practicality. They do squander their natural resources with an abandon unknown elsewhere; they have developed a mobility both social and physical that marks them as a people apart. In few other lands is the democratic ideal worshiped so intensely, or nationalism carried to such extremes of isolationism or international arrogance. Rarely do other peoples display such indifference toward intellectualism or aesthetic values; seldom in comparable cultural areas do they cling so tenaciously to the shibboleth of rugged individualism. Nor do residents of non-frontier lands experience to the same degree the heady optimism, the rosy faith in the future, the belief in the inevitability of progress that form part of the American creed. These are pioneer traits, and they have become a part of the national heritage.

Yet if the frontier wrought such a tranformation within the United States, why did it not have a similar effect on other countries with frontiers? If the pioneering experience was responsible for our democracy and nationalism and individualism, why have the peoples of Africa, Latin America, Canada, and Russia failed to develop identical characteristics? The answer is obvious: in few nations of the world has the sort of frontier that Turner described existed. For he saw the frontier not as a borderland between unsettled and settled lands, but as an accessible area in which a low man-land ratio and abundant natural resources provided an unusual opportunity for the individual to better himself. Where autocratic governments controlled population movements, where resources were lacking, or where conditions prohibited ordinary individuals from exploiting nature's virgin riches, a frontier in the Turnerian sense could not be said to exist.

The areas of the world that have been occupied since the beginning of the age of discovery contain remarkably a few frontiers of the American kind. In Africa the few Europeans were so outnumbered by relatively uncivilized native inhabitants that the need for protection transcended any impulses toward democracy or individualism. In Latin America the rugged terrain and steaming jungles restricted areas exploitable by individuals to the Brazilian plains and the Argentine pampas; these did attract frontiersmen, although in Argentina the prior occupation of most good lands by government-favored cattle growers kept small farmers out until railroads penetrated the region. In Canada the path westward was blocked by the Laurentian Shield, a tangled mass of hills and sterile, brush-choked soil covering the country north and west of the St. Lawrence Valley. When railroads finally penetrated this barrier in the late nineteenth century, they carried pioneers directly from the East to the prairie provinces of the West; the newcomers, with no prior pioneering experience, simply adapted to their new situation the eastern institutions with which they were familiar. Among the frontier nations of the world only Russia provided a physical environment comparable to that of the United States, and there the pioneers were too accustomed to rigid feudal and monarchic controls to respond as Americans did.

Further proof that the westward expansion of the United States has been a powerful formative force has been provided by the problems facing the nation in the present century. During the past fifty years the American people have been adjusting their lives and institutions to existence in a frontierless land, for while the superintendent of the census was decidedly premature when he announced in 1890 that the country's "unsettled area has been so broken into by isolated bodies of settlement that there can hardly be said to be a frontier line" remaining, the era of cheap land was rapidly drawing to a close. In attempting to adjust the country to its new, expansionless future, statesmen have frequently called upon the frontier hypothesis to justify everything from rugged individualism to the welfare state, and from isolationism to world domination.

Political opinion has divided sharply on the necessity of altering the nation's governmental philosophy and techniques in response to the changed environment. Some statesmen and scholars have rebelled against what they call Turner's "Space Concept of History," with all that it implies concerning the lack of opportunity for the individual in an expansionless land. They insist that modern technology has created a whole host of new "frontiers"— of intensive farming, electronics, mechanics, manufacturing, nuclear fission, and the like—which offer such diverse outlets to individual talents that governmental interference in the nation's economic activities is unjustified. On the other hand, equally competent spokesmen argue that these newer "frontiers" offer little opportunity to the individual—as distinguished from the corporation or the capitalist—and hence cannot duplicate the function of the frontier of free land. The government, they insist, must provide the people with the security and opportunity that vanished when escape to the West became impossible. This school's most eloquent spokesman, Franklin D. Roosevelt, declared: "Our last frontier has long since been reached. . . . Equality of opportunity as we have known it no longer exists. . . . Our task now is not the discovery or exploitation of natural resources or necessarily producing more goods. It is the sober, less dramatic business of administering resources and plants already in hand, of seeking to reestablish foreign markets for our surplus production, of meeting the problem of under-consumption, of adjusting production to consumption, of distributing wealth and products more equitably, of adapting existing economic organizations to the service of the people. The day of enlightened administration has come." To Roosevelt, and to thousands like him, the passing of the frontier created a new era in history which demanded a new philosophy of government.

Diplomats have also found in the frontier hypothesis justification for many of their moves, from imperialist expansion to the restriction of immigration. Harking back to Turner's statement that the perennial rebirth of society was necessary to keep alive the democratic spirit, expansionists have argued through the twentieth century for an extension of American power and territories. During the Spanish-American War imperialists preached such a doctrine, adding the argument that Spain's lands were needed to provide a population outlet for a people who could no longer escape to their own frontier. Idealists such as Woodrow Wilson could agree with materialists like J. P. Morgan that the extension of American authority abroad, either through territorial acquisitions or economic penetration, would be good for both business and democracy. In a later generation Franklin D. Roosevelt favored a similar expansion of the American democratic ideal as a necessary prelude to the better world that he hoped would emerge from World War II. His successor, Harry Truman, envisaged his "Truman Doctrine" as a device to extend and defend the frontiers of democracy throughout the globe. While popular belief in the superiority of America's political institutions was far older than Turner, that belief rested partly on the frontier experience of the United States.

These practical applications of the frontier hypothesis, as well as its demonstrated influence on the nation's development, suggest that its critics have been unable to destroy the theory's effectiveness as a key to understanding American history. The recurring rebirth of society in the United States over a period of three hundred years did endow the people with characteristics and institutions that distinguished them from the inhabitants of other nations. It is obviously untrue that the frontier experience alone accounts for the unique features of American civilization; that civilization can be understood only as the product of the interplay of the Old World heritage and New World conditions. But among those conditions none has bulked larger than the operation of the frontier process.

V

The Populists:
Provincial Nativists
or Liberal Democrats?

INTRODUCTION

The years from 1865 to 1896 were largely years of agrarian discontent in the United States. Beset by economic difficulties and troubled over both the decline in their political power and the relatively greater social and economic advantages available to the city dweller, the farmers attempted to promote their common interests by resort to organization. The movement of agrarian protest culminated in the 1880's and 1890's in the Populist revolt, the name given to the farmers' alliances, established largely during the 1880's, and to the People's party, formed in 1892. In 1896 the Populists threw in their lot with the Democrats and supported William Jennings Bryan in his losing campaign against William McKinley.

Until relatively recent times historians have dealt rather kindly with Populism and the Populists: they have stressed the liberal aspects of the Populist cause and have tended to link Populism with the reform movements of the twentieth century, such as Progressivism. This was very much the angle of vision of John D. Hicks, The Populist Revolt *(Minneapolis: University of Minnesota Press, 1931), long regarded as the standard work on the subject. Following World War II, however, various social scientists questioned the prevailing view of the Populists and began to see in Populism, broadly conceived, the source of much that was evil and distasteful in American life. The Populists, these scholars concluded, had been "neurotic, anxious, ethnocentric, anti-Semitic, and fear-ridden and . . . their kind of democracy was noxious since it later produced McCarthy. They had not been torchbearers of democracy but incipient fascists." [1]*

Among the historians who have portrayed the dark side of Populism, the most influential has been Richard Hofstadter. Much more cautious in his approach to the subject than the social scientists referred to above, Professor Hofstadter, in the first of the selections on Populism that follow, concedes that there is "much that is good and usable in our Populist past." He contends, however, that the limitations of Populism have been overlooked, and it is upon its "unseen blemishes" that he focuses his attention. He sees Populists as backward looking, committed to a conspiracy theory of history, suspicious of the "stranger," indulging in "a kind of rhetorical anti-Semitism," and tending to be jingoist and bellicose.

In his book The Tolerant Populists, *from which the second selection on this topic is taken, Walter T. K. Nugent is particularly concerned with the relationship between Populism in Kansas and "non-American ideas, groups, and persons." As the title of the book suggests, the evidence presented by*

---

[1] Walter T. K. Nugent, *The Tolerant Populists: Kansas Populism and Nativism* (Chicago: University of Chicago Press, 1963), p. 5.

*Nugent contradicts the Hofstadter view of the Populists at every point.
Nugent cautions his readers, however, that his findings are limited to Kansas
Populism, and he makes no effort to extend his conclusions to Populists in
other parts of the country.*

The Folklore of Populism

Richard Hofstadter

I. THE TWO NATIONS

For a generation after the Civil War, a time of great economic exploitation
and waste, grave social corruption and ugliness, the dominant note in American political life was complacency. Although dissenting minorities were
always present, they were submerged by the overwhelming realities of industrial growth and continental settlement. The agitation of the Populists,
which brought back to American public life a capacity for effective political
indignation, marks the beginning of the end of this epoch. In the short
run the Populists did not get what they wanted, but they released the flow
of protest and criticism that swept through American political affairs from
the 1890's to the beginning of the first World War.

Where contemporary intellectuals gave the Populists a perfunctory and
disdainful hearing, later historians have freely recognized their achievements
and frequently overlooked their limitations. Modern liberals, finding the
Populists' grievances valid, their programs suggestive, their motives creditable, have usually spoken of the Populist episode in the spirit of Vachel
Lindsay's bombastic rhetoric:

> Prairie avenger, mountain lion,
> Bryan, Bryan, Bryan, Bryan,
> Gigantic troubadour, speaking like a siege gun,
> Smashing Plymouth Rock with his boulders from the West.

There is indeed much that is good and usable in our Populist past. While
the Populist tradition had defects that have been too much neglected, it
does not follow that the virtues claimed for it are all fictitious. Populism

was the first modern political movement of practical importance in the United States to insist that the federal government has some responsibility for the common weal; indeed, it was the first such movement to attack seriously the problems created by industrialism. The complaints and demands and prophetic denunciations of the Populists stirred the latent liberalism in many Americans and startled many conservatives into a new flexibility. Most of the "radical" reforms in the Populist program proved in later years to be either harmless or useful. In at least one important area of American life a few Populist leaders in the South attempted something profoundly radical and humane—to build a popular movement that would cut across the old barriers of race—until persistent use of the Negro bogy distracted their following. To discuss the broad ideology of the Populists does them some injustice, for it was in their concrete programs that they added most constructively to our political life, and in their more general picture of the world that they were most credulous and vulnerable. Moreover, any account of the fallibility of Populist thinking that does not acknowledge the stress and suffering out of which that thinking emerged will be seriously remiss. But anyone who enlarges our portrait of the Populist tradition is likely to bring out some unseen blemishes. In the books that have been written about the Populist movement, only passing mention has been made of its significant provincialism; little has been said of its relations with nativism and nationalism; nothing has been said of its tincture of anti-Semitism.

The Populist impulse expressed itself in a set of notions that represent what I have called the "soft" side of agrarianism. These notions, which appeared with regularity in the political literature, must be examined if we are to re-create for ourselves the Populist spirit. To extract them from the full context of the polemical writings in which they appeared is undoubtedly to oversimplify them; even to name them in any language that comes readily to the historian of ideas is perhaps to suggest that they had a formality and coherence that in reality they clearly lacked. But since it is less feasible to have no labels than to have somewhat too facile ones, we may enumerate the dominant themes in Populist ideology as these: the idea of a golden age; the concept of natural harmonies; the dualistic version of social struggles; the conspiracy theory of history; and the doctrine of the primacy of money. . . .

The utopia of the Populists was in the past, not the future. According to the agrarian myth, the health of the state was proportionate to the degree to which it was dominated by the agricultural class, and this assumption pointed to the superiority of an earlier age. The Populists looked backward with longing to the lost agrarian Eden, to the republican America of the early years of the nineteenth century in which there were few millionaires and, as they saw it, no beggars, when the laborer had excellent prospects and the farmer had abundance, when statesmen still responded to the mood of the people and there was no such thing as the money power.[1] What they meant—though they did not express themselves in such terms—was that they would like to restore the conditions prevailing before the development of industrialism and the commercialization of agriculture. It should not be surprising that they inherited the traditions of Jacksonian democracy, that they revived the old Jacksonian cry: "Equal Rights for All, Special Privileges for None," or that most of the slogans of 1896 echoed the battle cries of 1836.[2] General James B. Weaver, the Populist candidate for the presidency in 1892, was an old Democrat and Free-Soiler, born during the days of Jackson's battle with the United States Bank, who drifted into the Green-back movement after a short spell as a Republican, and from there to Populism. His book, *A Call to Action,* published in 1892, drew up an indictment of the business corporation which reads like a Jacksonian polemic. Even in those hopeful early days of the People's Party, Weaver projected no grandiose plans for the future, but lamented the course of recent history, the growth of economic oppression, and the emergence of great contrasts of wealth and poverty, and called upon his readers to do "All in [their] power to arrest the alarming tendencies of our times." [3]

Nature, as the agrarian tradition had it, was beneficent. The United States was abundantly endowed with rich land and rich resources, and the "natural" consequence of such an endowment should be the prosperity of the people. If the people failed to enjoy prosperity, it must be because of a harsh and arbitrary intrusion of human greed and error. "Hard times, then," said one popular writer, "as well as the bankruptcies, enforced idleness, starvation, and the crime, misery, and moral degradation growing out of conditions like the present, being unnatural, not in accordance with, or the result of any natural law, must be attributed to that kind of unwise and pernicious legislation which history proves to have produced similar results in all ages of the world. It is the mission of the age to correct these errors in human legislation, to adopt and establish policies and systems, in accord with, rather than in opposition to divine law." [4] In assuming a lush natural order whose workings were being deranged by human laws, Populist writers were again drawing on the Jacksonian tradition, whose spokesmen also had pleaded for a proper obedience to "natural" laws as a prerequisite of social justice.[5]

---

[1] Thomas E. Watson: *The Life and Times of Andrew Jackson* (Thomson, Ga., 1912), p. 325: "All the histories and all the statesmen agree that during the first half-century of our national existence, we had no poor. A pauper class was unthought of: a beggar, or a tramp never seen." Cf. Mrs. S. E. V. Emery: *Seven Financial Conspiracies which have Enslaved the American People* (Lansing, ed. 1896), pp. 10–11.

[2] Note for instance the affectionate treatment of Jacksonian ideas in Watson, op. cit., pp. 343–4.

[3] James B. Weaver: *A Call to Action* (Des Moines, 1892), pp. 377–8.

[4] B. S. Heath: *Labor and Finance Revolution* (Chicago, 1892), p. 5.

[5] For this strain in Jacksonian thought, see Richard Hofstadter: "William Leggett,

Somewhat akin to the notion of the beneficence of nature was the idea of a natural harmony of interests among the productive classes. To the Populist mind there was no fundamental conflict between the farmer and the worker, between the toiling people and the small businessman. While there might be corrupt individuals in any group, the underlying interests of the productive majority were the same; predatory behavior existed only because it was initiated and underwritten by a small parasitic minority in the highest places of power. As opposed to the idea that society consists of a number of different and frequently clashing interests—the social pluralism expressed, for instance, by Madison in the *Federalist*—the Populists adhered, less formally to be sure, but quite persistently, to a kind of social dualism: although they knew perfectly well that society was composed of a number of classes, for all practical purposes only one simple division need be considered. There were two nations. "It is a struggle," said Sockless Jerry Simpson, "between the robbers and the robbed." [6] "There are but two sides in the conflict that is being waged in this country today," declared a Populist manifesto. "On the one side are the allied hosts of monopolies, the money power, great trusts and railroad corporations, who seek the enactment of laws to benefit them and impoverish the people. On the other are the farmers, laborers, merchants, and all other people who produce wealth and bear the burdens of taxation. . . . Between these two there is no middle ground." [7] "On the one side," said Bryan in his famous speech against the repeal of the Sherman Silver Purchase Act, "stand the corporate interests of the United States, the moneyed interests, aggregated wealth and capital, imperious, arrogant, compassionless. . . . On the other side stand an unnumbered throng, those who gave to the Democratic party a name and for whom it has assumed to speak." [8] The people versus the interests, the public versus the plutocrats, the toiling multitude versus the money power—in various phrases this central antagonism was expressed. From this simple social classification it seemed to follow that once the techniques of misleading the people were exposed, victory over the money power ought to be easily accomplished, for in sheer numbers the people were overwhelming. "There is no power on earth that can defeat us," said General Weaver dur-

Spokesman of Jacksonian Democracy," *Political Science Quarterly,* Vol. XLVIII (December 1943), pp. 581–94, and *The American Political Tradition,* pp. 60–1.

[6] Elizabeth N. Barr: "The Populist Uprising," in William E. Connelley, ed.: *A Standard History of Kansas and Kansans,* Vol. II, p. 1170.

[7] Ray Allen Billington: *Westward Expansion* (New York, 1949), p. 741.

[8] Allan Nevins: *Grover Cleveland* (New York, 1933), p. 540; Heath, op. cit., p. 27: "The world has always contained two classes of people, one that lived by honest labor and the other that lived *off* of honest labor." Cf. Governor Lewelling of Kansas: "Two great forces are forming in battle line: the same under different form and guise that have long been in deadly antagonism, represented in master and slave, lord and vassal, king and peasant, despot and serf, landlord and tenant, lender and borrower, organized avarice and the necessities of the divided and helpless poor." James A. Barnes: *John G. Carlisle* (New York, 1931), pp. 254–5.

ing the optimistic days of the campaign of 1892. "It is a fight between labor and capital, and labor is in the vast majority." [9]

The problems that faced the Populists assumed a delusive simplicity: the victory over injustice, the solution for all social ills, was concentrated in the crusade against a single, relatively small but immensely strong interest, the money power. "With the destruction of the money power," said Senator Peffer, "the death knell of gambling in grain and other commodities will be sounded; for the business of the worst men on earth will have been broken up, and the mainstay of the gamblers removed. It will be an easy matter, after the greater spoilsmen have been shorn of their power, to clip the wings of the little ones. Once get rid of the men who hold the country by the throat, the parasites can be easily removed." [10] Since the old political parties were the primary means by which the people were kept wandering in the wilderness, the People's Party advocates insisted, only a new and independent political party could do this essential job.[11] As the silver question became more prominent and the idea of a third party faded, the need for a monolithic solution became transmuted into another form: there was only one *issue* upon which the money power could really be beaten and this was the money issue. "When we have restored the money of the Constitution," said Bryan in his Cross of Gold speech, "all other necessary reforms will be possible; but . . . until this is done there is no other reform that can be accomplished."

While the conditions of victory were thus made to appear simple, they did not always appear easy, and it would be misleading to imply that the tone of Populistic thinking was uniformly optimistic. Often, indeed, a deeply-lying vein of anxiety showed through. The very sharpness of the struggle, as the Populists experienced it, the alleged absence of compromise solutions and of intermediate groups in the body politic, the brutality and desperation that were imputed to the plutocracy—all these suggested that failure of the people to win the final contest peacefully could result only in a total victory for the plutocrats and total extinction of democratic institutions, possibly after a period of bloodshed and anarchy. "We are nearing a serious crisis," declared Weaver. "If the present strained relations between wealth owners and wealth producers continue much longer they will ripen into frightful disaster. This universal discontent must be quickly interpreted and its causes removed." [12] "We meet," said the Populist platform of 1892, "in the midst of a nation brought to the verge of moral, political, and material ruin. Corruption dominates the ballot-box, the Legislatures, the Congress, and touches even the ermine of the bench. The people are demoralized.

---

[9] George H. Knoles: *The Presidential Campaign and Election of 1892* (Stanford, 1942), p. 179.

[10] William A. Peffer: *The Farmer's Side* (New York, 1891), p. 273.

[11] Ibid., pp. 148–50.

[12] Weaver, op. cit., p. 5.

. . . The newspapers are largely subsidized or muzzled, public opinion silenced, business prostrated, homes covered with mortgages, labor impoverished, and the land concentrating in the hands of the capitalists. The urban workmen are denied the right to organize for self-protection, imported pauperized labor beats down their wages, a hireling standing army, unrecognized by our laws, is established to shoot them down, and they are rapidly degenerating into European conditions. The fruits of the toil of millions are boldly stolen to build up colossal fortunes for a few, unprecedented in the history of mankind; and the possessors of these, in turn, despise the Republic and endanger liberty." Such conditions foreboded "the destruction of civilization, or the establishment of an absolute despotism. . . ."

II. HISTORY AS CONSPIRACY

. . . There was something about the Populist imagination that loved the secret plot and the conspiratorial meeting. There was in fact a widespread Populist idea that all American history since the Civil War could be understood as a sustained conspiracy of the international money power.

The pervasiveness of this way of looking at things may be attributed to the common feeling that farmers and workers were not simply oppressed but oppressed deliberately, consciously, continuously, and with wanton malice by "the interests." It would of course be misleading to imply that the Populists stand alone in thinking of the events of their time as the results of a conspiracy. This kind of thinking frequently occurs when political and social antagonisms are sharp. Certain audiences are especially susceptible to it—particularly, I believe, those who have attained only a low level of education, whose access to information is poor,[13] and who are so completely shut out from access to the centers of power that they feel themselves completely deprived of self-defense and subjected to unlimited manipulation by those who wield power. There are, moreover, certain types of popular movements of dissent that offer special opportunities to agitators with paranoid tendencies, who are able to make a vocational asset out of their psychic disturbances.[14] Such persons have an opportunity to impose their own style of thought upon the movements they lead. It would of course be misleading to imply that there are no such things as conspiracies in history. Anything that partakes of political strategy may need, for a time at least, an element of secrecy, and is thus vulnerable to being dubbed conspiratorial. Corruption itself has the character of conspiracy. In this sense the Crédit

---

[13] In this respect it is worth pointing out that in later years, when facilities for realistic exposure became more adequate, popular attacks on "the money power" showed fewer elements of fantasy and more of reality.

[14] See, for instance, the remarks about a mysterious series of international assassinations with which Mary E. Lease opens her book *The Problem of Civilization Solved* (Chicago, 1895).

Mobilier was a conspiracy, as was the Teapot Dome affair. If we tend to be too condenscending to the Populists at this point, it may be necessary to remind ourselves that they had seen so much bribery and corruption, particularly on the part of the railroads, that they had before them a convincing model of the management of affairs through conspiratorial behavior. Indeed, what makes conspiracy theories so widely acceptable is that they usually contain a germ of truth. But there is a great difference between locating conspiracies *in* history and saying that history *is,* in effect, a conspiracy, between singling out those conspiratorial acts that do on occasion occur and weaving a vast fabric of social explanation out of nothing but skeins of evil plots. . . .

Nevertheless, when these qualifications have been taken into account, it remains true that Populist thought showed an unusually strong tendency to account for relatively impersonal events in highly personal terms. An overwhelming sense of grievance does not find satisfactory expression in impersonal explanations, except among those with a well-developed tradition of intellectualism. It is the city, after all, that is the home of intellectual complexity. The farmer lived in isolation from the great world in which his fate was actually decided. He was accused of being unusually suspicious,[15] and certainly his situation, trying as it was, made thinking in impersonal terms difficult. Perhaps the rural middle-class leaders of Populism (this was a movement of farmers, but it was not led by farmers) had more to do than the farmer himself with the cast of Populist thinking. At any rate, Populist thought often carries one into a world in which the simple virtues and unmitigated villainies of a rural melodrama have been projected on a national and even an international scale. In Populist thought the farmer is not a speculating businessman, victimized by the risk economy of which he is a part, but rather a wounded yeoman, preyed upon by those who are alien to the life of folkish virtue. A villain was needed, marked with the unmistakable stigmata of the villains of melodrama, and the more remote he was from the familiar scene, the more plausibly his villainies could be exaggerated.

It was not enough to say that a conspiracy of the money power against the common people was going on. It had been going on ever since the Civil War. It was not enough to say that it stemmed from Wall Street. It was international: it stemmed from Lombard Street. In his preamble to the People's Party platform of 1892, a succinct, official expression of Populist views, Ignatius Donnelly asserted: "A vast conspiracy against mankind has been organized on two continents, and it is rapidly taking possession of the world. If not met and overthrown at once it forebodes terrible social convulsions, the destruction of civilization, or the establishment of an absolute

---

[15] Frederick L. Paxson: "The Agricultural Surplus: a Problem in History," *Agricultural History,* Vol. VI (April 1932), p. 58; cf. the observations of Lord Bryce in *The American Commonwealth* (New York, ed. 1897), Vol. II, pp. 294–5.

despotism." A manifesto of 1895, signed by fifteen outstanding leaders of the People's Party, declared: "As early as 1865–66 a conspiracy was entered into between the gold gamblers of Europe and America. . . . for nearly thirty years these conspirators have kept the people quarreling over less important matters while they have pursued with unrelenting zeal their one central purpose. . . . Every device of treachery, every resource of statecraft, and every artifice known to the secret cabals of the international gold ring are being made use of to deal a blow to the prosperity of the people and the financial and commercial independence of the country." [16]

The financial argument behind the conspiracy theory was simple enough. Those who owned bonds wanted to be paid not in a common currency but in gold, which was at a premium; those who lived by lending money wanted as high a premium as possible to be put on their commodity by increasing its scarcity. The panics, depressions, and bankruptcies caused by their policies only added to their wealth; such catastrophes offered opportunities to engross the wealth of others through business consolidations and foreclosures. Hence the interests actually relished and encouraged hard times. The Greenbackers had long since popularized this argument, insisting that an adequate legal-tender currency would break the monopoly of the "Shylocks." Their demand for $50 of circulating medium per capita, still in the air when the People's Party arose, was rapidly replaced by the less "radical" demand for free coinage of silver. But what both the Greenbackers and free-silverites held in common was the idea that the contraction of currency was a deliberate squeeze, the result of a long-range plot of the "Anglo-American Gold Trust." Wherever one turns in the Populist literature of the nineties one can find this conspiracy theory expressed. It is in the Populist newspapers, the proceedings of the silver conventions, the immense pamphlet literature broadcast by the American Bimetallic League, the Congressional debates over money; it is elaborated in such popular books as Mrs. S. E. V. Emery's *Seven Financial Conspiracies which have Enslaved the American People* or Gordon Clark's *Shylock: as Banker, Bondholder, Corruptionist, Conspirator.*

Mrs. Emery's book, first published in 1887, and dedicated to "the enslaved people of a dying republic," achieved great circulation, especially among the Kansas Populists. According to Mrs. Emery, the United States had been an economic Garden of Eden in the period before the Civil War. The fall of man had dated from the war itself, when "the money kings of Wall Street" determined that they could take advantage of the wartime necessities of their fellow men by manipulating the currency. "Controlling it, they could inflate or depress the business of the country at pleasure, they could send the warm life current through the channels of trade, dispensing peace, happiness, and prosperity, or they could check its flow, and completely para-

---

[16] Frank L. McVey: *The Populist Movement* (New York, 1896), pp. 201–2.

lyze the industries of the country." [17] With this great power for good in their hands, the Wall Street men preferred to do evil. Lincoln's war policy of issuing greenbacks presented them with the dire threat of an adequate supply of currency. So the Shylocks gathered in convention and "perfected" a conspiracy to create a demand for their gold.[18] The remainder of the book was a recital of a series of seven measures passed between 1862 and 1875 which were alleged to be a part of this continuing conspiracy, the total effect of which was to contract the currency of the country further and further until finally it squeezed the industry of the country like a hoop of steel.[19]

Mrs. Emery's rhetoric left no doubt of the sustained purposefulness of this scheme—described as "villainous robbery," and as having been "secured through the most soulless strategy." [20] She was most explicit about the so-called "crime of 1873," the demonetization of silver, giving a fairly full statement of the standard greenback-silverite myth concerning that event. As they had it, an agent of the Bank of England, Ernest Seyd by name, had come to the United States in 1872 with $500,000 with which he had bought enough support in Congress to secure the passage of the demonetization measure. This measure was supposed to have greatly increased the value of American four per cent bonds held by British capitalists by making it necessary to pay them in gold only. To it Mrs. Emery attributed the panic of 1873, its bankruptcies, and its train of human disasters: "Murder, insanity, suicide, divorce, drunkenness and all forms of immorality and crime have increased from that day to this in the most appalling ratio." [21]

"Coin" Harvey, the author of the most popular single document of the whole currency controversy, *Coin's Financial School,* also published a novel, *A Tale of Two Nations,* in which the conspiracy theory of history was incorporated into a melodramatic tale. In this story the powerful English banker Baron Rothe plans to bring about the demonetization of silver in the United States, in part for his own aggrandizement but also to prevent the power of the United States from outstripping that of England. He persuades an American Senator (probably John Sherman, the *bête noire* of the silverites) to co-operate in using British gold in a campaign against silver. To be sure that the work is successful, he also sends to the United States a relative and ally, one Rogasner, who stalks through the story like the villains in the plays of Dion Boucicault, muttering to himself such remarks as "I am here to destroy the United States—Cornwallis could not have done more. For the wrongs and insults, for the glory of my own country, I will

---

[17] Emery, op. cit., p. 13.   [18] Ibid., pp. 14–18.

[19] The measures were: the "exception clause" of 1862; the National Bank Act of 1863; the retirement of the greenbacks, beginning in 1866; the "credit-strengthening act" of March 18, 1869; the refunding of the national debt in 1870; the demonetization of silver in 1873; and the destruction of fractional paper currency in 1875.

[20] Ibid., pp. 25, 43.

[21] Ibid., pp. 54–5. For a more elaborate statement of this story see Gordon Clark: *Shylock: as Banker, Bondholder, Corruptionist, Conspirator* (Washington, 1894), pp. 88–99.

bury the knife deep into the heart of this nation." [22] Against the plausibly drawn background of the corruption of the Grant administration, Rogasner proceeds to buy up the American Congress and suborn American professors of economics to testify for gold. He also falls in love with a proud American beauty, but his designs on her are foiled because she loves a handsome young silver Congressman from Nebraska who bears a striking resemblance to William Jennings Bryan!

One feature of the Populist conspiracy theory that has been generally overlooked is its frequent link with a kind of rhetorical anti-Semitism. The slight current of anti-Semitism that existed in the United States before the 1890's had been associated with problems of money and credit.[23] During the closing years of the century it grew noticeably.[24] While the jocose and rather heavy-handed anti-Semitism that can be found in Henry Adams's letters of the 1890's shows that this prejudice existed outside Populist literature, it was chiefly Populist writers who expressed that identification of the Jew with the usurer and the "international gold ring" which was the central theme of the American anti-Semitism of the age. The omnipresent symbol of Shylock can hardly be taken in itself as evidence of anti-Semitism, but the frequent references to the House of Rothschild make it clear that for many silverites the Jew was an organic part of the conspiracy theory of history. Coin Harvey's Baron Rothe was clearly meant to be Rothschild; his Rogasner (Ernest Seyd?) was a dark figure out of the coarsest anti-Semitic tradition. "You are very wise in your way," Rogasner is told at the climax of the tale, "the commercial way, inbred through generations. The politic, scheming, devious way, inbred through generations also." [25] One of the cartoons in the effectively illustrated *Coin's Financial School* showed a map of the world dominated by the tentacles of an octopus at the side of the British Isles, labeled: "Rothschilds." [26] In Populist demonology, anti-Semitism and Anglophobia went hand in hand.

The note of anti-Semitism was often sounded openly in the campaign for

---

[22] W. H. Harvey: *A Tale of Two Nations* (Chicago, 1894), p. 69.

[23] Anti-Semitism as a kind of rhetorical flourish seems to have had a long underground history in the United States. During the panic of 1837, when many states defaulted on their obligations, many of which were held by foreigners, we find Governor McNutt of Mississippi defending the practice by baiting Baron Rothschild: "The blood of Judas and Shylock flows in his veins, and he unites the qualities of both his countrymen. . . ." Quoted by George W. Edwards: *The Evolution of Finance Capitalism* (New York, 1938), p. 149. Similarly we find Thaddeus Stevens assailing "the Rothschilds, Goldsmiths, and other large money dealers" during his early appeals for greenbacks. See James A. Woodburn: *The Life of Thaddeus Stevens* (Indianapolis, 1913), pp. 576, 579.

[24] See Oscar Handlin: "American Views of the Jew at the Opening of the Twentieth Century," *Publications of the American Jewish Historical Society*, no. 40 (June 1951), pp. 323–44.

[25] Harvey: *A Tale of Two Nations*, p. 289; cf. also p. 265: "Did not our ancestors . . . take whatever women of whatever race most pleased their fancy?"

[26] Harvey: *Coin's Financial School* (Chicago, 1894), p. 124; for a notable polemic against the Jews, see James B. Goode: *The Modern Banker* (Chicago, 1896), chapter xii.

silver. A representative of the New Jersey Grange, for instance, did not hesitate to warn the members of the Second National Silver Convention of 1892 to watch out for political candidates who represented "Wall Street, and the Jews of Europe." [27] Mary E. Lease described Grover Cleveland as "the agent of Jewish bankers and British gold." [28] Donnelly represented the leader of the governing Council of plutocrats in *Cæsar's Column,* one Prince Cabano, as a powerful Jew, born Jacob Isaacs; one of the triumvirate who lead the Brotherhood of Destruction is also an exiled Russian Jew, who flees from the apocalyptic carnage with a hundred million dollars which he intends to use to "revive the ancient splendors of the Jewish race, in the midst of the ruins of the world." [29] One of the more elaborate documents of the conspiracy school traced the power of the Rothschilds over America to a transaction between Hugh McCulloch, Secretary of the Treasury under Lincoln and Johnson, and Baron James Rothschild. "The most direful part of this business between Rothschild and the United States Treasury was not the loss of money, even by hundreds of millions. It was the resignation of the country itself INTO THE HANDS OF ENGLAND, as England had long been resigned into the hands of HER JEWS." [30]

Such rhetoric, which became common currency in the movement, later passed beyond Populism into the larger stream of political protest. By the time the campaign of 1896 arrived, an Associated Press reporter noticed as "one of the striking things" about the Populist convention at St. Louis "the extraordinary hatred of the Jewish race. It is not possible to go into any hotel in the city without hearing the most bitter denunciation of the Jews as a class and of the particular Jews who happen to have prospered in the world." [31] This report may have been somewhat overdone, but the identification of the silver cause with anti-Semitism did become close enough for Bryan to have to pause in the midst of his campaign to explain to the Jewish

[27] *Proceedings of the Second National Silver Convention* (Washington, 1892), p. 48.

[28] Mary E. Lease: *The Problem of Civilization Solved,* pp. 319–20; cf. p. 291.

[29] Donnelly, op. cit., pp. 147, 172, 331.

[30] Gordon Clark, op. cit., pp. 59–60; for the linkage between anti-Semitism and the conspiracy theme, see pp. 2, 4, 8, 39, 55–8, 102–3, 112–13, 117. There was a somewhat self-conscious and apologetic note in populistic anti-Semitism. Remarking that "the aristocracy of the world is now almost altogether of Hebrew origin," one of Donnelly's characters explains that the terrible persecutions to which the Jews had been subjected for centuries heightened the selective process among them, leaving "only the strong of body, the cunning of brain, the long-headed, the persistent . . . and now the Christian world is paying, in tears and blood, for the sufferings inflicted by their bigoted and ignorant ancestors upon a noble race. When the time came for liberty and fair play the Jew was master in the contest with the Gentile, who hated and feared him." *Cæsar's Column,* p. 37. In another fanciful tale Donnelly made amends to the Jews by restoring Palestine to them and making it very prosperous. *The Golden Bottle* (New York and St. Paul, 1892), pp. 280–1.

[31] Quoted by Edward Flower: *Anti-Semitism in the Free Silver and Populist Movements and the Election of 1896,* unpublished M.A. thesis, Columbia University, 1952, p. 27; this essay is illuminating on the development of anti-Semitism in this period and on the reaction of some of the Jewish press.

Democrats of Chicago that in denouncing the policies of the Rothchilds he and his silver friends were "not attacking a race; we are attacking greed and avarice which know no race or religion." [32]

It would be easy to misstate the character of Populist anti-Semitism or to exaggerate its intensity. For Populist anti-Semitism was entirely verbal. It was a mode of expression, a rhetorical style, not a tactic or a program. It did not lead to exclusion laws, much less to riots or pogroms. There were, after all, relatively few Jews in the United States in the late 1880's and early 1890's, most of them remote from the areas of Populist strength. It is one thing, however, to say that this prejudice did not go beyond a certain symbolic usage, quite another to say that a people's choice of symbols is of no significance. Populist anti-Semitism does have its importance—chiefly as a symptom of a certain ominous credulity in the Populist mind. It is not too much to say that the Greenback-Populist tradition activated most of what we have of modern popular anti-Semitism in the United States.[33] From Thaddeus Stevens and Coin Harvey to Father Coughlin, and from Brooks and Henry Adams to Ezra Pound, there has been a curiously persistent linkage between anti-Semitism and money and credit obsessions. A full history of modern anti-Semitism in the United States would reveal, I believe, its substantial Populist lineage, but it may be sufficient to point out here that neither the informal connection between Bryan and the Klan in the twenties nor Thomas E. Watson's conduct in the Leo Frank case* were altogether fortuitous.[34] And Henry Ford's notorious anti-Semitism of the 1920's, along with his hatred of "Wall Street," were the foibles of a Michigan farm boy who had been liberally exposed to Populist notions.[35]

---

[32] William Jennings Bryan: *The First Battle* (Chicago, 1897), p. 581.

[33] I distinguish here between popular anti-Semitism, which is linked with political issues, and upper-class anti-Semitism, which is a variety of snobbery. It is characteristic of the indulgence which Populism has received on this count that Carey McWilliams in his *A Mask for Privilege: Anti-Semitism in America* (Boston, 1948) deals with early American anti-Semitism simply as an upper-class phenomenon. In his historical account of the rise of anti-Semitism he does not mention the Greenback-Populist tradition. Daniel Bell: "The Grass Roots of American Jew Hatred," *Jewish Frontier*, Vol. XI (June 1944), pp. 15–20, is one of the few writers who has perceived that there is any relation between latter-day anti-Semites and the earlier Populist tradition. See also Handlin, op. cit. Arnold Rose has pointed out that much of American anti-Semitism is intimately linked to the agrarian myth and to resentment of the ascendancy of the city. The Jew is made a symbol of both capitalism and urbanism, which are themselves too abstract to be satisfactory objects of animosity. *Commentary*, Vol. VI (October 1948), pp. 374–78.

* Editor's note: The Jewish Leo Frank was convicted of the 1913 murder of a fourteen-year-old female employee of his Atlanta pencil factory. Mob spirit was very much in evidence throughout the course of the trial. After the governor of the state commuted Frank's death sentence, Watson initiated a campaign of abuse and vituperation that culminated in Frank's lynching.

[34] For the latter see Woodward: *Tom Watson*, chapter xxiii.

[35] Keith Sward: *The Legend of Henry Ford* (New York, 1948), pp. 83–4, 113–14, 119–20, 132, 143–60. Cf. especially pp. 145–6: "Ford could fuse the theory of Populism and the practice of capitalism easily enough for the reason that what he carried forward from the old platforms of agrarian revolt, in the main, were the planks that were most innocent

III. THE SPIRIT MILITANT

The conspiratorial theory and the associated Anglophobic and Judophobic feelings were part of a larger complex of fear and suspicion of the stranger that haunted, and still tragically haunts, the nativist American mind. This feeling, though hardly confined to Populists and Bryanites, was none the less exhibited by them in a particularly virulent form. Everyone remote and alien was distrusted and hated—even Americans, if they happened to be city people. The old agrarian conception of the city as the home of moral corruption reached a new pitch. Chicago was bad; New York, which housed the Wall Street bankers, was farther away and worse; London was still farther away and still worse. This traditional distrust grew stronger as the cities grew larger, and as they were filled with immigrant aliens. As early as 1885 the Kansas preacher Josiah Strong had published *Our Country,* a book widely read in the West, in which the cities were discussed as a great problem of the future, much as though they were some kind of monstrous malignant growths on the body politic.[36] Hamlin Garland recalled that when he first visited Chicago, in the late 1880's, having never seen a town larger than Rockford, Illinois, he naturally assumed that it swarmed with thieves. "If the city is miles across," he wondered, "how am I to get from the railway station to my hotel without being assaulted?" While such extreme fears could be quieted by some contact with the city, others were actually confirmed—especially when the farmers were confronted with city prices.[37] Nativist prejudices were equally aroused by immigration, for which urban manufacturers, with their insatiable demand for labor, were blamed. "We have become the world's melting pot," wrote Thomas E. Watson. "The scum of creation has been dumped on us. Some of our principal cities are more foreign than American. The most dangerous and corrupting hordes of the Old World have invaded us. The vice and crime which they have planted in our midst are sickening and terrifying. What brought these Goths and Vandals to our shores? The manufacturers are mainly to blame. They wanted cheap labor: and they didn't care a curse how much harm to our future might be the consequence of their heartless policy." [38]

Anglo-Saxons, whether Populist or patrician, found it difficult to accept

and least radical. Like many a greenbacker of an earlier day, the publisher of the Dearborn *Independent* was haunted by the will-o'-the-wisp of 'money' and the bogy of 'race.' It was these superstitions that lay at the very marrow of his political thinking." For further illustration of the effects of the Populist tradition on a Mountain State Senator, see Oscar Handlin's astute remarks on Senator Pat McCarran in "The Immigration Fight Has Only Begun," *Commentary,* Vol. XIV (July 1952), pp. 3–4.

[36] Josiah Strong: *Our Country* (New York, 1885), chapter x; for the impact of the city, see Arthur M. Schlesinger: *The Rise of the City* (New York, 1933).

[37] Hamlin Garland: *A Son of the Middle Border* (New York, ed. 1923), pp. 269, 295.

[38] Watson: *Andrew Jackson,* p. 326; cf. *Cæsar's Column,* p. 131: "The silly ancestors of the Americans called it 'national development' when they imported millions of foreigners to take up the public lands and left nothing for their own children."

other peoples on terms of equality or trust. Others were objects to be manipulated—benevolently, it was often said, but none the less firmly. Mary E. Lease, that authentic voice of inland Populism who became famous for advising farmers to "raise less corn and more hell," wrote a book in 1895 under the ingratiating title: *The Problem of Civilization Solved,* in which this ethnic condescension was rather ingenuously displayed. According to Mrs. Lease, Europe and America stood on the brink of one of two immense catastrophes—a universal reign of anarchistic terror or the establishment of a world-wide Russian despotism. The only hope of averting catastrophe was, as she put it, "the most stupendous migration of races the world has ever known, and thereby relieve the congested centers of the world's population of half their inhabitants and provide Free Homes for half of mankind." [39] She proposed a vast reshuffling of peoples in which the tropics in both hemispheres be taken over by white planters with Negroes and Orientals as "tillers of the soil." "Through all the vicissitudes of time, the Caucasian has arisen to the moral and intellectual supremacy of the world, until now this favored race is fitted for the *Stewardship of the Earth and Emancipation from Manual Labor.*" [40] This stewardship, far from being an imposition on the lesser breeds without the law, would be an act of mercy; it would take the starved and miserable ryots and coolies of the world and by giving them management and supervision provide them with the means of life, as well as rescue them from paganism. Such a change they would "hail with joy." [41]

The proposal for colonization under government supervision and with governmental subsidies was supplemented by a grand plan for what Mrs. Lease candidly called the partitioning of the world, in which the Germanic and Latin peoples would be united into two racial confederations, and the British and Russian empires checked and neutralized by other powerful states. The role of the United States in this world was to be the head of the federated American republics. Canada should be annexed—so also Cuba, Haiti, Santo Domingo, and Hawaii. The Latin republics would be fertile fields for colonization by the surplus population of the United States— which no longer had a public domain to give its citizens—and the North Americans would import "vast swarms of Asiatics as laborers for the plantations." Mrs. Lease felt that the Latins, like the Asiatics, would certainly benefit from this and that they ought to like it. Moreover, they owed the United States a debt of gratitude: "We stand, and have stood for years, ready to extend our blood and treasure in defense of Latin America against European aggression. Can they not *reciprocate* by giving us the leadership on this continent? If not, we should take it! We should follow the example of European nations and annex all we can and establish protectorates wherever possible in America." [42]

---

[39] Lease, op. cit., p. 17.   [40] Loc. cit.   [41] Ibid., pp. 31–2, 34, 35.   [42] Ibid., pp. 177–8.

Mrs. Lease's book, the work of a naïve but imaginative mind driven to the pitch of its powers by an extraordinary capacity for suspicion, was hardly as representative or popular as *Coin's Financial School* or *Cæsar's Column,* though its author was one of the indigenous products of Populist political culture. Mrs. Lease's peculiar ideas of *Weltpolitik,* her particular views on tropical colonization, were not common currency in Populist thinking. But other assumptions in her book could be found among the Populists with great frequency—the smug assumption of Anglo-Saxon superiority and benevolence, the sense of a need for some new area of expansion, the hatred of England, the fear of Russia,[43] the anxiety over the urban masses as a potential source of anarchy.

The nationalist fervor of Mrs. Lease's book also represents one side of a curiously ambiguous aspect of Populism. On the surface there was a strong note of anti-militarism and anti-imperialism in the Populist movement and Bryan democracy. Populists were opposed to large standing armies and large naval establishments; most of them supported Bryan's resistance to the acquisition of the Philippines. They looked upon the military as a threat to democracy, upon imperialist acquisitions as gains only to financiers and "monarchists," not to the people.[44] But what they chiefly objected to was institutional militarism rather than war itself, imperialism rather than jingoism. Under a patina of pacifist rhetoric they were profoundly nationalistic and bellicose. What the nativist mind most resolutely opposed was not so much war itself as co-operation with European governments for any ends at all.[45] Those who have been puzzled in our own time by the anti-European

---

[43] Since this was a commonplace in the nineteenth century, it would be too much to ascribe to Mrs. Lease any special prophetic stature.

[44] See W. H. Harvey: *Coin on Money, Trusts, and Imperialism* (Chicago, 1900), for an expression of popular feelings on these and other issues.

[45] The best illustration was the American bimetallist movement. It was only during the 1870's that the international gold standard can be said to have come into existence, and it did so on the eve of the long price decline of the "Great Depression." The desire of the silver interests in various parts of the world, together with those groups that sought in silver a means of raising the general level of prices, gave rise almost from the beginning to bimetallic movements nearly everywhere in western Europe. Even in England, the commercial center and the creditor nation which did not relish being paid its debts in depreciated currency, there were eminent statesmen who favored bimetallism; and the two greatest economists of the era, Jevons and Marshall, considered it seriously. But everywhere except in the United States the bimetallic movements looked to international action as the method of establishing a bimetallic standard; in the United States alone the silver interests adhered to the possibility of unilateral action. The constant expectation that the United States would act alone to maintain the price of silver was an impediment to action elsewhere. From the 1870's onward conservative American statesmen who sought to initiate action that would lead to an international bimetallic standard had been caught between the difficulty of lining up the other nations and the sharp impatience of domestic silver interests, which insisted with growing asperity as the years went by that reluctance to go it alone was treasonable. See J. B. Condliffe: *The Commerce of Nations* (New York, 1950), chapter xii, "The International Gold Standard"; Jeannette P. Nichols: "Silver Diplomacy," *Political Science Quarterly,* Vol. XXXVIII (December 1933), pp. 565–88. On the relation between silverism and isolationism, see Ray Allen Billington:

attitudes of men like Senator Taft* and General MacArthur, and by their alternating espousal of dangerously aggressive and near-pacifistic (or anti-militarist) policies, will find in the Populist mentality a suggestive precedent.

The Populists distinguished between wars for humanity and wars of conquest. The first of these they considered legitimate, but naturally they had difficulty in discriminating between the two, and they were quite ready to be ballyhooed into a righteous war, as the Cuban situation was to show. During the early nineteenth century popular sentiment in the United States, especially within the democratic camp, had been strong for the republican movements in Europe and Latin America. With the coming of the nineties and the great revulsion against the outside world, the emphasis was somewhat changed; where sympathy with oppressed and revolutionary peoples had been the dominant sentiment in the past, the dominant sentiment now seemed rather to be hatred of their governments. That there must always be such an opposition between peoples and governments the Populist mind did not like to question, and even the most democratic governments of Europe were persistently looked upon as though they were nothing but reactionary monarchies.[46]

After the success of *Cæsar's Column,* Donnelly wrote another fantasy called *The Golden Bottle,* in which this antagonism had a vivid expression. The first part of the story need not detain us: it deals with the life of one Ephraim Benezet of Kansas who is given a bottle that empowers him to turn iron into gold, a windfall which not surprisingly makes it possible for him to solve his own and the country's financial problems. Before long he is elected President, and after foiling a plot to kill him and checking a bankers' conspiracy to start a civil war, he delivers an extraordinary inaugural message. The one thing that prevents the American people, he tells them, from rising "to still higher levels of greatness and happiness" is the Old World. America is "united by a ligament to a corpse—Europe!" This begins an appeal to close the gates against further wretched immigrants from Europe who will be used by American capitalists to beat down the wages of American workingmen. "We could, by wise laws and just conditions, lift up the toilers of our own country to the level of the middle classes, but a vast multitude of the miserable of other lands clung to their skirts and dragged them down. Our country was the safety-valve which permitted the discontent of the Old World to escape. If that vent was closed, every throne in Europe would be blown up in twenty years. . . . For the people of the Old World, having to choose between death by starvation and resistance to tyrants, would turn upon their oppressors and tear them to pieces." There

---

"The Origins of Middle Western Isolationism," *Political Science Quarterly,* Vol. LX (March 1945), esp. pp. 50-2.

   * Editor's note: Robert A. Taft was a United States Senator from Ohio from 1938 to 1953.
   [46] See Harvey's *Coin on Money, Trusts, and Imperialism, passim.*

follows an appeal to the peoples of Europe to revolt against their rulers. The countries of Europe respond by declaring war, and in the great international conflict that follows, the United States comes to Europe as an invading liberator. President Benezet wins, of course, and frees even the Russians simply by making them literate. He also establishes a world government to keep the peace.[47]

It is no coincidence, then, that Populism and jingoism grew concurrently in the United States during the 1890's. The rising mood of intolerant nationalism was a nationwide thing, certainly not confined to the regions of Populist strength; but among no stratum of the population was it stronger than among the Populists. Moreover it was on jingoist issues that the Populist and Bryanite sections of the country, with the aid of the yellow press and many political leaders, achieved that rapport with the masses of the cities which they never succeeded in getting on economic issues. Even conservative politicians sensed that, whatever other grounds of harmony were lacking between themselves and the populace of the hinterland, grounds for unity could be found in war.

The first, and for the Populists the preferred, enemy would have been England, the center of the gold power. *Coin's Financial School* closed with a bitter philippic against England: "If it is claimed we must adopt for our money the metal England selects, and can have no independent choice in the matter, let us make the test and find out if it is true. It is not American to give up without trying. If it is true, let us attach England to the United States and blot her name out from among the nations of the earth. A war with England would be the most popular ever waged on the face of the earth . . . the most just war ever waged by man." [48] Some leaders of the Republican Party, which had attempted to appease the powerful silver sentiment in 1890 by passing the Sherman Silver Purchase Act, made a strategic move in the troubled year of 1894 to capture Western sentiment. On May 2 there opened in London an unofficial bimetallic conference in which American bimetallists were represented by Brooks Adams and Senator Wolcott of Colorado; fifteen prominent Senators, including outstanding Republicans, cabled their endorsement of international bimetallism. Senator Lodge proposed in the Senate to blackmail Britain by passing a discriminatory tariff against her if she did not consent to a bimetallic plan, a scheme nicely calculated to hold in line some of the Western silverite jingoes and Anglophobes.[49] ?

This proposal was defeated by the Cleveland Democrats, but the Demo-

---

[47] Ignatius Donnelly: *The Golden Bottle*, pp. 202 ff. "I would be sorry," said Donnelly in his preface, "if any one should be so foolish as to argue that the triumph of the People's Party means a declaration of war against the whole world." What concerns us here, however, is not the Populists' intentions in this sphere, which were doubtless innocent enough, but the emotions laid bare by Donnelly's fantasy.

[48] *Coin's Financial School*, pp. 131–2.   [49] Nevins, op. cit., pp. 608–9.

cratic Party's turn to make capital out of jingo sentiment came the next year with the excessively belligerent conduct of the Venezuela affair, one of the few really popular moves of the Cleveland administration.[50] A west-coast newspaper spoke for many Americans when it said: "We are at the mercy of England, as far as our finances go, and [war] is our only way out." [51] "War would be a good thing even if we got whipped," declared the silver Senator from Nevada, William M. Stewart, "for it would rid us of English bank rule." [52] And a Congressman from a strong Populist state wrote to congratulate Secretary of State Olney for having spiked the guns of Populism and anarchism with his vigorous diplomacy.[53] Olney was also urged by the American consul in Havana to identify the administration and the sound-money Democrats with a strong policy of mediation or intervention in the war in Cuba; it would either get credit for stopping the atrocities, for buying Cuba, if that was the outcome, or for "fighting a successful war, if war there be. In the latter case, the enthusiasm, the applications for service, the employment of many of the unemployed, might do much towards directing the minds of the people from imaginary ills, the relief of which is erroneously supposed to be reached by 'Free Silver.' " [54]

When the Venezuela matter was settled, the attention of jingoes turned toward Cuba. The situation of the oppressed Cubans was one with which the Populist elements in the country could readily identify themselves, and they added their voice to the general cry throughout the country for an active policy of intervention. After the defeat of Bryan, popular frustration in the silver areas, blocked on domestic issues, seemed to find expression in the Cuban question. Here at last was a point at which the goldbugs could be vanquished. Neither the big business and banking community nor the Cleveland and McKinley administrations had much sympathy with the crusading fever that pervaded the country at large, and there were bitter mutual recriminations between conservative and Populist papers. Wall Street was accused of a characteristic indifference to the interests of humanity; the Populists in return were charged with favoring war as a cover under which they could smuggle in an inflationary policy. One thing seems clear: "most of the leading Congressional backers of intervention in Cuba represented southern and western states where Populism and silver were strongest." [55] And it appears that one of the reasons why McKinley was advised

---

[50] On domestic pressures behind this incident, see Nelson M. Blake: "Background of Cleveland's Venezuela Policy," *American Historical Review*, Vol. XLVII (January 1942), pp. 259–77.

[51] James A. Barnes: *John G. Carlisle* (New York, 1931), p. 410.

[52] Nevins, op. cit., p. 641.

[53] Alfred Vagts: *Deutschland und die Vereinigten Staaten in der Welt politik* (New York, 1935), Vol. I, p. 511.

[54] Ibid., Vol. II, p. 1266 n.

[55] J. E. Wisan: *The Cuban Crisis as Reflected in the New York Press* (New York, 1934), p. 455; for the relation of this crisis to the public temper of the nineties, see Richard

by many influential Republicans to yield to the popular demand for war was the common fear, still meaningful in 1898, that the Democrats would go into the next presidential election with the irresistible slogan of Free Silver and Free Cuba as its battle cry.[56] Jingoism was confined to no class, section, or party; but the Populist areas stood in the vanguard, and their pressure went far to bring about a needless war. When the war was over, the economic and emotional climate in which their movement had grown no longer existed, and their forces were scattered and confused. A majority of them, after favoring war, attempted honorably to spurn the fruits of war by taking up the cause of anti-imperialism. Thomas E. Watson, one of the few Populists who had consistently opposed the war, later insisted that "The Spanish War finished us. The blare of the bugle drowned the voice of the reformer." [57] The cause of reform was, in fact, too resilient to be permanently crushed by a short war; but, for the moment, Free Cuba had displaced Free Silver in public interest, and when reform raised its head again, it had a new face.

As we review these aspects of Populist emotion, an odd parallel obtrudes itself. Where else in American thought during this period do we find this militancy and nationalism, these apocalyptic forebodings and drafts of world-political strategies, this hatred of big businessmen, bankers, and trusts, these fears of immigrants and urban workmen, even this occasional toying with anti-Semitic rhetoric? We find them, curiously enough, most conspicuous among a group of men who are in all obvious respects the antithesis of the Populists. During the late 1880's and the '90's there emerged in the eastern United States a small imperialist elite representing, in general, the same type that had once been Mugwumps, whose spokesmen were such solid and respectable gentlemen as Henry and Brooks Adams, Theodore Roosevelt, Henry Cabot Lodge, John Hay, and Albert J. Beveridge. While the silverites were raging openly and earnestly against the bankers and the Jews, Brooks and Henry Adams were expressing in their sardonic and morosely cynical private correspondence the same feelings, and acknowledging with bemused irony their kinship at this point with the mob. While Populist Congressmen and newspapers called for war with England or Spain, Roosevelt and Lodge did the same, and while Mrs. Lease projected her grandiose schemes of world partition and tropical colonization, men like Roosevelt, Lodge, Beveridge, and Mahan projected more realistic plans for the conquest of markets and the annexation of territory. While Populist readers were pondering over Donnelly's apocalyptic fantasies,* Brooks and Henry Adams were also bemoaning the approaching end of their type of civilization, and even the characteristically optimistic T. R. could share at

---

Hofstadter: "Manifest Destiny and the Philippines," in Daniel Aaron, ed.: *America in Crisis* (New York, 1952).

[56] Vagts, op. cit., Vol. II, p. 1308 n.   [57] Woodward: *Tom Watson*, p. 334.

* Editor's note: In his novel *Caesar's Column*.

moments in "Brooks Adams' gloomiest anticipations of our gold-ridden, capitalist-bestridden, usurer-mastered future." Not long after Mrs. Lease wrote that "we need a Napoleon in the industrial world who, by agitation and education, will lead the people to a realizing sense of their condition and the remedies," [58] Roosevelt and Brooks Adams talked about the threat of the eight-hour movement and the danger that the country would be "enslaved" by the organizers of the trusts, and played with the idea that Roosevelt might eventually lead "some great outburst of the emotional classes which should at least temporarily crush the Economic Man." [59]

Not only were the gentlemen of this imperialist elite better read and better fed than the Populists, but they despised them. This strange convergence of unlike social elements on similar ideas has its explanation, I believe, in this: both the imperialist elite and the Populists had been bypassed and humiliated by the advance of industrialism, and both were rebelling against the domination of the country by industrial and financial capitalists. The gentlemen wanted the power and status they felt due them, which had been taken away from their class and type by the *arriviste* manufacturers and railroaders and the all-too-potent banking houses. The Populists wanted a restoration of agrarian profits and popular government. Both elements found themselves impotent and deprived in an industrial culture and balked by a common enemy. On innumerable matters they disagreed, but both were strongly nationalistic, and amid the despairs and anxieties of the nineties both became ready for war if that would unseat or even embarrass the moneyed powers, or better still if it would topple the established political structure and open new opportunities for the leaders of disinherited farmers or for ambitious gentlemen. But if there seems to be in this situation any suggestion of a forerunner or analogue of modern authoritarian movements, it should by no means be exaggerated. The age was more innocent and more fortunate than ours, and by comparison with

---

[58] Lease, op. cit., p. 7. Thomas E. Watson wrote in 1902 a lengthy biography: *Napoleon, a Sketch of His Life, Character, Struggles, and Achievements,* in which Napoleon, "the moneyless lad from despised Corsica, who stormed the high places of the world, and by his own colossal strength of character, genius, and industry took them," is calmly described as "the great Democratic despot." Elsewhere Watson wrote: "There is not a railway king of the present day, not a single self-made man who has risen from the ranks to become chief in the vast movement of capital and labor, who will not recognize in Napoleon traits of his own character; the same unflagging purpose, tireless persistence, silent plotting, pitiless rush to victory . . ."—which caused Watson's biographer to ask what a Populist was doing celebrating the virtues of railroad kings and erecting an image of capitalist acquisitiveness for his people to worship. "Could it be that the Israelites worshipped the same gods as the Philistines? Could it be that the only quarrel between the two camps was over a singular disparity in the favors won?" Woodward, op. cit., pp. 340–2.

[59] Matthew Josephson: *The President Makers* (New York, 1940), p. 98. See the first three chapters of Josephson's volume for a penetrating account of the imperialist elite. Daniel Aaron has an illuminating analysis of Brooks Adams in his *Men of Good Hope* (New York, 1951).

the grimmer realities of the twentieth century many of the events of the nineties take on a comic-opera quality. What came in the end was only a small war and a quick victory; when the farmers and the gentlemen finally did coalesce in politics, they produced only the genial reforms of Progressivism; and the man on the white horse turned out to be just a graduate of the Harvard boxing squad, equipped with an immense bag of platitudes, and quite willing to play the democratic game.

Concluding Remarks

Walter T. K. Nugent

The foregoing chapters have narrated the story of the Populist movement in Kansas, with special reference to the relations between the Populists and non-American ideas, groups, and persons. Although a sizable body of literature appeared during the 1950's that asserted that the Populists were deeply hostile to things non-American, the Kansas story does not support those assertions. In fact, it supports something more like the opposite of each of the outstanding points of criticism.

The Populists have been accused of nativism, both of a personal kind and of an ideological kind; instead, they were friendlier and more receptive to foreign persons and foreign institutions than the average of their contemporary political opponents. They have been accused of "conspiracy-mindedness"; for them, however, tangible fact quite eclipsed neurotic fiction. They have been accused of anti-Semitism, both personal and ideological; instead they consistently got along well with their Jewish neighbors and consistently refrained from extending their dislike of certain financiers, who happened to be Jews, to Jews in general. They have been accused of chauvinism and jingoism, especially with reference to the Spanish-American War; instead, such lukewarm support as they gave collectively to Cuban intervention was based on quite different grounds, and as a group they strongly opposed the imperialism that the war engendered. Finally, they have been accused of selling out their vaunted reform principles by seeking political fusion with the Democratic party, especially in 1896, and thus of revealing a neurotic instability; but instead, fusion was for them a legiti-

Reprinted from *The Tolerant Populists: Kansas Populism and Nativism,* by Walter T. K. Nugent, by permission of The University of Chicago Press. © 1963 by The University of Chicago. All rights reserved. Pp. 231–243.

chauvinism

mate means to the accomplishment of real, if limited, reform. In the case of Kansas, the largest of the wheat-belt Populist states, the five principal criticisms of Populism voiced by recent writers not only do not square with the facts, but should be replaced with a viewpoint so much in contrast as to be practically the opposite. Briefly put, this viewpoint is as follows.

Populism in Kansas was a political response to economic distress. From the early days of the Farmers' Alliance, the progenitor of the People's party, to about 1892, relief of economic difficulty was virtually the sole reason for the party's existence; after 1892 this purpose was alloyed to some degree with the desire of the party to perpetuate itself as a political organism. In both periods, however, economic difficulties remained the party's chief reason for being, and relief of them its main objective. Populism called for the enactment of a set of legislative reforms by state and federal governments and accepted the extension of governmental power involved in such enactment. In its most complete and ideal form, the Populist program appeared in the national party platform of 1892, the "Omaha Platform," but this platform bore no more nor less relation to the practical operations of the party than platforms usually do. In Kansas the People's party placed its emphasis consistently on the three questions of land, money, and transportation, which were the issues causing greatest distress in that particular state. Since monetary reform seemed to have the broadest political appeal of all the forms called for in the Populist program, it received more stress than the rest of the program at the time (1894–97) when the party seemed to have its best chance of succeeding.

As Populism followed the ways of practical party politics in the program that it offered and in the issues it chose to stress, it took a practical approach to its sources of support as well. Economic distress cut across lines of religion, of nationality origins, of race, of previous political affiliation, even of occupation and of wealth and status. To so great an extent was this the case that it is not even accurate to say that the Populists accepted or sought the support of third-party men, Republicans, Democrats, immigrants of many kinds, organized labor, city dwellers, and others, to broaden their agriculturalist base. For these groups were in and of Populism from the beginning. The job of the party leaders was therefore not so much to attract new groups but to be sure that the party program appealed to each of those groups already there and to spread the Populist message to further individual members of the existing coalition, of which the lowest common denominator was a desire for one or more specific economic reforms.

As a result, large numbers of every politically consequential foreign-born group then in Kansas, with the exception of the Mennonites, became active Populists. Party leaders received this support warmly and eagerly, except for one or two occasions: the 1894 state convention and probably the one of 1890. At those times, certain influential leaders supported the non-economic issues of women's suffrage and prohibition so vocally that they led the party to take positions unacceptable to many foreign-born groups. Even here, however, the attitude of these leaders to the foreign-born was one of indifference not of hostility. The fact of the matter seems to be, to judge by statements made by the delegates on the floor of the 1894 convention, that many Populists were simply unconcerned with ethnic groups or foreign matters; they were neither favorable nor hostile, except when they thought they might justifiably appeal to ethnic bloc votes or when they cited examples of enlightened foreign institutions to document their own reform program. To the great majority of Populists, in 1894 and at other times, foreignness and certainly Jewishness were simply not affective categories. For practical political reasons, among others, the Populists expressed themselves favorably toward foreign groups, either abroad or close at hand. This was certainly true of the fusionists; it was true of the non-fusionists except when women's suffrage and prohibition got in the way; it was even true, at times, of the Middle-of-the-Road group,* which combined an anti-banker (including English, Anglo-Jewish, and Wall Street banker) rhetoric with some benevolence toward immigrants as individuals.

Many leading Populists were in fact first or second generation immigrants. In the 1890's the Populists surpassed the Republicans in the proportion of their state legislators who were foreign-born. Foreign-born Populists abounded among county-level officeholders, county committeemen, precinct workers, and delegates to county, district, and state political conventions. Wherever an ethnic group existed, there existed as well its Populist voters and Populist leaders, with the exception of the Mennonites, who were undeviatingly Republican. The Populists, however, had immigrant blocs of their own, especially on the frequent occasions of county and state-level fusion with the Democrats. The party organization appealed to foreign-language groups with pamphlets, newspapers, and campaign speakers. They presented much the same arguments to their polyglot audience as the party was making to the English-speaking voters. The only difference was in window dressing, such as testimonials from Prince Bismarck and from German political economists in support of silver coinage. At their 1894 state convention, and prior and subsequently in their newspapers, the Populists forthrightly condemned the American Protective Association, the most influential and widespread nativist organization since the Know-Nothings.

On three contemporaneous issues relating directly to immigrants, the Populists took positions that might seem at first glance to have been nativistic, but in each case their attitude to the immigrant was neutral or favorable. When they attacked "alien" landholding, they were attacking landlordism, not the immigrant small landholder. When they called for an end to contract or "pauper labor" immigration, they clearly excepted "worth-

---

* Editor's note: Populists opposed to fusion with the Democrats.

while" or "sturdy" immigrants and based their position on labor competition, not on racism. When their congressmen supported the Lodge-McCall literacy test to restrict immigration, they apparently did so as the only practical way to enact the bill's riders, which would have lessened labor competition, and almost never expressed approval of the philosophy of superior and inferior, desirable or undesirable, races put forward by Lodge and the Immigration Restriction League. In each of these three instances the Populists based their actions on reasonable economic grounds, if not especially perceptive or laudable ones. Their aim was to attract the political support of organized labor, of tenant farmers, and very likely of Irish-Americans.

The rhetoric of Populism was highly charged with nationalism, but it was a nineteenth-century kind of nationalism that did not include the nativistic or anti-Semitic characteristics of some twentieth-century right-wing nationalists. Only two foreign groups fell under the censure of any considerable number of Populists. This censure was a consequence of two issues firmly rooted in economic realities and in neither case did they grow out of or were they extended to racial or nativistic antagonism. The two groups were English or Anglo-Jewish financiers and English or Anglo-Irish landlords, respectively responsible in part for money stringency and for large landholding. Many Populists feared that the trend toward tighter money and tighter land would continue unchecked unless these two groups, *and their American or Gentile associates,* were stopped. In both cases the antipathy of the Populists clearly extended to all malevolent financiers, monopolists, and land barons, whether English or American, whether Jew or Gentile, whether native or alien. For the Populists, or many of them, to have laid their troubles at the door of a mixed group of English, Anglo-Jewish, and American capitalists may have been naïve and simplistic, but the point is that the common denominator of their hostility was not nativism or anti-Semitism but distrust and dislike of a truly unsympathetic economic class. In some cases their anti-English attitude transcended this economic base, since the economic problem meshed so well with the rather widespread anti-English attitude shared by many nineteenth-century Americans as part of the American Revolutionary tradition. But the English people escaped the censure placed upon certain financially powerful Englishmen, and Jewish fianciers escaped any blame whatever as Jews, although a few of them, as investment bankers, shared the criticisms heaped by the Populists, or rather, some of their more outspoken rhetoricians, upon the wickedness of powerful financial interests in general. This was certainly the case with the terms "Shylock" and "Rothschild," which appeared with some frequency in Populist literature but which were cachets not of Jewish conspiracy but of oppressive finance.

So far did Populist expressions of friendlinesss to Jews as individuals, in Kansas and elsewhere, to Jews as a group, to English immigrants, to English institutions such as co-operatives and public ownership of utilities, outweigh the expressions that might be construed with effort as Anglophobic or anti-Semitic, and so specious are the grounds upon which the Populists have been accused of Anglophobia, anti-Semitism, or nativism, that these accusations must simply fall without support. There is an exception that proves the rule. A handful of Populists sometimes let their antipathies include "racial characteristics" of these two groups, especially the English, and thereby they evidenced irrationality and prejudice. They were atypical. Many, in fact nearly all, of these Populists were attached to the Middle-of-the-Road Populist splinter group in 1894 and 1896. This group attempted to overthrow the recognized state leadership, whose reform credentials were at least as old and respectable as the dissidents'; it was in all probability subsidized by the Republican state organization; and it received the support of less than 1 per cent of the rank and file at the polls in 1896 and of the Populist press.

In what, then, did their nationalism consist? It is difficult to answer such a question, because to accuse such a pragmatic, anti-intellectual people as these agrarians of having possessed "concepts" or "ideas," much more a "system," is itself a distortion. They did, however, possess felt attitudes that were forced into words to form the rhetoric of their speeches and editorials. Needless to say, the scribes and leaders of Populism came closer than anyone else to expressing these views in logical form, subject, of course, to political exigencies. But it can be assumed that their rhetoric must have been congenial to the rank and file—otherwise they would have been unable to attract and to hold that rank and file. Nonetheless, the rhetoric is undoubtedly more radical, more logically organized, and much more explicit than the views of the mass of the party. In their rhetoric, Populist nationalism consisted of a feeling that the United States was a different kind of political society from any that had ever existed before and therefore more worth preserving than any previous one. America was not just another nation-state but an embodiment of certain ideals. It was the embodiment of democratic republicanism: a society where the people rule, where the governed consent to their governors, where the rights of life, liberty, and property are protected because this very protection is the object of their own self-government. It was the embodiment, too, of economic democracy: where resources wanted only honest labor to be translated into the reality of abundance, where opportunity was equal, where the distribution of the nation's wealth was equitable. It was the antithesis of Europe and Europe's corruption, decadence, parasitical upper classes, stagnation, and economic and political oppression. It was a place, in short, where the people rule for themselves and for the protection of their natural rights. Or, at least, so it should have been.

Yet who were the people? The answer is already implied. The people were those who believed in the ideals of democratic republicanism, of economic democracy, and of freedom from European conditions of life. The people were those who actively sought the preservation of those ideals. They were those who labored by their own hands, who had equal opportunities to labor and to accumulate, who used the resources of the United States to produce their own and the nation's wealth. They were those who created wealth rather than those who manipulated wealth already produced. Very often this legitimate wealth-producing activity was defined by the Populists as agricultural and laboring activity; those who farmed or labored were by definition the real people. This corresponded conveniently both to what might roughly be called the Jeffersonian-Jacksonian tradition and to the actual political bases of the People's party's support. Translated into the rhetoric of a political campaign, it often meant emphasizing "the producing classes" or the common bonds of "the farming and laboring people."

The conscious derivation for all of this was the American Revolution, and secondarily, the War of 1812. These struggles successfully created a nation embodying this set of ideals.[1] Such conscious roots made it easy, of course, for some Populists to look upon the machinations of English financiers as a third and final attempt by England to subjugate America. It was primarily through the American Revolution that a nation of, by, and for the people was created and through it that all that was wrong with Europe and Britain was left behind.

Consequently, it was up to the people—often implying the farmers and laborers—to see to it that this nation, this unique society, did not perish from the earth. Who threatened its extinction? Certainly not the refugee from European misery, at least so long as he, too, believed in American republicanism and opportunity. In this unique kind of nation the doors were open to those who wished legitimately to share its benefits. The goods of this nation were not to be shut up inside for the exclusive use of those already there but rather to beckon as to a flourishing haven those who wished to escape the oppression of a decadent Europe. The nation was, in Lincoln's words, a last, best hope of earth. The immigrant was to show his good faith in these ideals by becoming a citizen and remaining permanently (as the Populists' alien law provided) and by not attempting to destroy the opportunity of individuals already possessing it (as Populist demands for an end to "pauper labor" immigration showed). For an immigrant to take away the job of an American laborer was unnecessary anyway, since opportunity and America were virtually synonymous.

The "worthwhile" or "sturdy" immigrant was not, then, the enemy of American nationality. In fact, he seemed to justify the Populist approach to American nationality—certainly he did in the case of immigrant agricul-

---

[1] Except for frequent claims to have been at one time "Lincoln Republicans," few Populists looked back to the Civil War as a watershed for these ideals. Perhaps it was not yet sufficiently ancient and myth-ridden. Perhaps, too, this was another way of avoiding giving pause to the ex-Southerners attracted to the Populist ballot.

tural colonies in Kansas, which had been very successful—and he was therefore quite welcome. But who then *was* the enemy? To most Populists who thought about the matter beyond their immediate economic distress—and by no means all of them thought through their views of American nationalism with anything like the completeness that this sketch might imply—the enemy lay in certain recently emergent opportunities for malevolence. America was shifting from a predominantly rural and agricultural nation to one predominantly urban and industrial. This shift was in no way evil in itself. Populist spokesmen such as Senators Peffer and Harris had expressly denied any hope of turning back the clock, and if they were not absolutely delighted with a process that seemed to be toppling the farmers and their allies from political and economic predominance (if indeed they had ever possessed it), they were determined to live with such a trend. What is more, they were determined to see that these changes should benefit all the people and not just a few; that they should take place in such ways as to guarantee democratic republicanism and economic democracy. The majority of them therefore accepted industrialization but condemned monopoly, accepted banking and finance but condemned usury and financial sleight of hand, welcomed accumulation but condemned economic feudalism, welcomed enterprise but condemned speculation. It was not industry and urbanism that oppressed them, they thought, but their abuse.

For most Populists these considerations identified the enemy well enough. An appealing program, aimed conveniently at the relief of immediate distress as well as at the placing of new trends within the old ideals, could be constructed without further ado. A rhetoric quickly emerged that concerned itself with attacking landlordism, transportation monopoly, and money shortages, and this rhetoric remained the basic vehicle of Populist ideas from start to finish. In a minority of cases, however, it seemed convenient to personalize the enemy, and in doing so, some Populists passed the bounds of precise statement. At times, American financiers and monopolists such as the Belmonts, Morgans, and Vanderbilts, English financiers such as the Rothschilds, American and English land and mortgage loan companies, and prominent American statesmen such as Sherman, McKinley, and Cleveland, together seemed to form a common and inimical class dedicated to the people's overthrow. Ever since the Civil War this group seemed to have conspired to bring about the economic destruction of the farmers and their allies. This minority of Populists thereby dealt with the money question in terms of a "money power." Yet even they nearly all used the term "conspiracy" in a general sense to mean the common attitudes of an entrenched and powerful minority, and only a tiny proportion meant by the term an explicit conspiratorial agreement, as when they referred to Ernest Seyd and the "Hazzard Circular" * of the sixties and seventies. But most Populists

---

* Editor's note: It was alleged that European capitalists in 1862 had warned their

did not voice this line, a fact more remarkable if one grants that rhetoric tends to be more radical than the general feeling of its political following. This "conspiracy" was, in addition, a financial one and not a Jewish or English one. To look at a close-knit community of interest and to see in the mind's eye a conspiracy is not necessarily great irrationality but rather a lack of factual knowledge about the competitive methods of late nineteenth-century capitalism. If antibanker, antimonopoly, or anticapitalist statements formed fairly frequent themes in Populist rhetoric, Populists of every hue made it clear that it was usury, irresponsible economic power, and minority rule that they were opposing and not the industrial revolution, urbanism, or capitalism and banking as such. The abuse of new trends, not the trends themselves, had driven them, they felt, from their once uncontested eminence. Now they wanted to regain that eminence and accepted the fact that it could never again be theirs alone. If agrarian class predominance was over and done with, plutocratic class predominance should be scuttled before it progressed any further. Then economic democracy would be reborn.

The Populist view of American nationality, with its stress on democratic republicanism and economic democracy, was therefore intended to be at once majoritarian, individualistic, and humanitarian. That it was a nationalism naïvely humanitarian rather than aggressive appeared very clearly in the Populists' approach to the Cuban insurrection and the Spanish-American War. They sympathized deeply with the insurgent Cubans and viewed their uprising as a struggle for freedom and democracy much like the American uprising of the 1770's. In Kansas this sympathy expressed itself in a moral support for the insurrectionists that sprang from a confident view of their own moral righteousness. Nonetheless, the Populist press and Populist congressmen held back from armed intervention, took a cautious attitude to the blowing up of the *Maine,* restrained themselves from anything more vigorous than sympathetic gestures toward the Cubans in spite of the Spanish "despotism" and "Weylerism" they believed the Cubans to be suffering, and in unison with their Democratic neighbors hoped that war could be avoided. This was very close to the Republican position also. When war came, they supported it as everyone else did, but until then their humanitarian sympathy for the Cubans was checked by the fear that a war beginning with Cuban intervention could only benefit large financial interests. The Kansas Republicans' coolness toward Cuban intervention resulted mainly from the caution that McKinley maintained into April, 1898, and the desire of the Kansas Republicans to support their own administration. The Populists avoided the Republicans' scornful references to Cuban or Spanish racial inferiority and far more frequently than the Republicans

American counterparts by the "Hazzard Circular" that they had to co-operate after the war if control of money was to remain with "the international capitalist class."

took a humanitarian view of the matter. In Kansas the Populists were not violent jingoes. Furthermore, unlike the Republicans in their area, and other people elsewhere, the official Populist position on the question of American imperial expansion for commercial or military purposes, which arose after Dewey's victory in Manila Bay, was to join the Democrats in opposing expansion and in demanding that the United States leave the Philippines and other potential colonies alone. They were interested in the spread of American democratic ideals, in the overthrow of Spanish oppression of Cuba, if this could be done without the commitment of American armed forces, but not at all in American conquest or colonization. Populism in Kansas apparently lost many adherents because of this stand, but it remained the official party position nevertheless.

It is worth noting that Populist opposition to imperialism was much more firmly expressed than Populist sympathy to the Cuban insurrectionists, because the Democratic party was also much less firm on the latter question than on the former. As a matter of fact, official Populist rhetoric was tailored to fit the political exigencies involved in getting along with the Democrats not only on the war and imperialism issues but on most other questions as well. Political fusion with the Democrats on all levels marked Kansas Populism very strongly, and to some writers, fusion has meant that the Populists lacked any real dedication to the principles they so vigorously espoused. But the Populist movement chose political means to accomplish its program of economic reform; it was a political party, not a pressure group or an ideological front; for better or worse it therefore bound itself to use partisan methods. If one looks no further than the Omaha platform of 1892 to find out what Populism stood for and then observes that many planks in that platform were soft-pedaled in 1892 and later for the sake of fusion and political success, one might assume that Populist devotion to reform principles was a sham. But this is a superficial view. Fusion was the only apparent way to achieve any reforms, any accomplishment of any principles at all, and the degree to which the People's party was willing to fuse with the Democrats in Kansas was the degree to which it possessed political common sense. The identification of fusion with dedication to principle, rather than with a sellout, comes into even greater relief as soon as one recalls the shabby story of the Middle-of-the-Road Populists, those self-styled simon-pure reformers who almost certainly connived at the defeat of the reform party with the local Republican organization. The prevalence of fusion sentiment indicates as well the willingness of the Populists to seek out and accept the support of the foreign-born blocs that ordinarily made their political home in the Democratic party. It also indicates their pragmatic approach to political action, their willingness to use an obvious means at hand to achieve legitimate political ends, and their flexibility, which stood in such contrast to the rigidity of the Middle-of-the Road Populists.

The political horse sense that provided them with their receptivity to fusion was a natural outgrowth of the immediacy of the distress from which their movement sprang. It accounted, too, for the apparent anomaly of a radical program based on conservative ideals. For the Populists of Kansas were not a collection of rag-tag calamity howlers, ne'er-do-wells, and third-party malcontents, as William Allen White and others have suggested, but a large body of people of diverse occupational, wealth-holding, and status levels. As a group they were hardly distinguishable from their Republican neighbors, except for a probably higher mortgage indebtedness, and their greater degree of political and economic awareness. The great majority could be called "middle class," and they were interested in preserving what they considered to be their middle-class American ideals and substance. These were being threatened, they felt, not by the facts of industrialism and urbanism but by their existing *shape*. To change that shape, they settled upon the device of a political party.

Their view of the future was one in which many wrongs would have to be righted, many present trends would have to be redirected to conform to old ideals, for that future to become acceptable. Yet they were confident that this would happen. In several ways they were confused, ill-informed, and behind the times. They were unaware of urban problems, for example, and they never understood that money reform was basically a solution only to agricultural problems, if indeed to them, and not a solution for growing monopoly or for inequities of wealth distribution. Yet if this is true, it is true as well to acquit them of nativism, anti-Semitism, conspiracy-mindedness, jingoism, lack of principle, and of living in some neurotic agrarian dream world. They were bound together not by common neuroses but by common indebtedness, common price squeezes, common democratic and humanitarian ideals, and common wrath at the infringement of them. From this wrath rose the Farmers' Alliance, and from the Alliance their ultimate instrument of protest, the People's party. The Populists were far too concerned with land, money, and transportation, and also, later on, with the mechanics of winning and keeping public office, to have much time to worry about whether their ideals were mythical or their anxieties neurotic. Tight money and foreclosure sales were the products of nobody's imagination. Even in their rhetoric they were too busy preaching positive reforms in a depression to be concerned with racism or anti-Semitism or agrarian Arcadias; and in their practical political activities, they took all the help they could get.

The Populists were liberal nationalists bringing to radical social changes a radical response. By such means they meant to re-assert what they considered to be the fundamental ideals upon which their society had previously depended—in their view of history—and must continue to depend—in their view of political philosophy. They undertook this task in the Kansas of the 1890's, with its particular kind of social structure, its particular distribution of wealth and income, its specific economic conditions, and its peculiar laws and traditions. These particularities form the limits of historical analogy, and they give no grounds for making the Populists the gawky ancestors of Father Coughlin or of Senator Joseph R. McCarthy. They make it very difficult to call the Populists the descendants of the Jeffersonians and Jacksonians or the precursors of Progressivism or the New Deal, although with these movements the Populists shared a considerable body of ideals. They make it unrealistic even to equate the Kansas Populists with Populists of other regions or other states.

This particular set of facts, however, allows the Populists of Kansas to be judged on their own grounds. The verdict is very simple. They were people who were seeking the solution of concrete economic distress through the instrumentality of a political party. By this means they would not only help themselves but they would redirect, not reverse, the unsatisfactory trends of their time to correspond with the ideals of the past. This involved profoundly the political co-operation of the foreign-born, and it involved a deep respect and receptivity for non-American institutions and ideas.

VI

Politics in the Gilded Age:
Cynicism or
Modest Improvement?

INTRODUCTION

The significant developments of the years from the end of Reconstruction to the election of 1896 took place in the factories of America's growing industrial plant, in the burgeoning cities of the nation, in the vast spaces of the Great Plains, and in the world of ideas. Politics was slow to adjust to the fundamental changes that were occurring in American life, and neither party was prepared to deal realistically with the new problems created by industrialization and urbanization and by the revolutionary changes in the agricultural sector of the economy. Historians have generally written disparagingly of the politics and politicians of this era. They have pointed to the meagerness of the significant legislation emanating from Congress, the lack of principle in party behavior, and the low state of public morality.

Professor Richard Hofstadter agrees on the whole with the conventional interpretation of the politics of this era. In the selection that follows, which is extracted from his important study The American Political Tradition and the Men Who Made It, *Hofstadter deals with the politics of the late nineteenth century in essentially negative terms. His stress is on the corruption in American political life, the lack of distinction of the presidents of the era, the cynicism of party leaders and their everlasting pursuit of spoils, and the ineffectiveness of the reformers. He is highly critical of Grover Cleveland, generally regarded as the ablest of the presidents between Lincoln and Theodore Roosevelt.*

In the second selection of this set, Professor Ari Hoogenboom, the author of a book on the civil service reform movement in the post-Civil War era,[1] disputes the validity of some of the commonly held views regarding the politics of this period. Concentrating on the years before 1883, Hoogenboom complains that historians have relied on biased sources in reaching their conclusions regarding the degree of political immorality during this era and concludes that the age was not as corrupt as historians have generally indicated. He finds that there was slow but steady improvement during these years in the federal civil service and in the state of public morality.

---

[1] Ari Hoogenboom, *Outlawing the Spoils: A History of the Civil Service Reform Movement, 1865–1883* (Urbana: University of Illinois Press, 1961).

The Spoilsmen: An Age of Cynicism

Richard Hofstadter

Parties are not built by deportment, or by ladies' magazines, or gush.
Roscoe Conkling

Nothing is lost save honor! *Jim Fisk*

I

In the years from Appomattox to the end of the nineteenth century the
American people settled half their continental domain, laid down a vast
railroad system, and grew mighty in the world on their great resources in
coal, metals, oil, and land. There is no other period in the nation's history
when politics seems so completely dwarfed by economic changes, none in
which the life of the country rests so completely in the hands of the industrial entrepreneur. . . .

From the business of industry the business of politics took its style. Accumulating wealth and living richly, the industrialists set the model of
behavior for the less scrupulous politicians. The wealth they acquired and
enjoyed set standards of consumption and emulation; overflowing into politics, it multiplied among politicians opportunities for pecuniary enrichment. Standards of success in politics changed. It was not merely self-expres-
sion or public service or glory that the typical politician sought—it was
money. Lord Bryce found that the cohesive force in American politics was
"the desire for office and for office *as a means of gain.*" The spoilsmen
looked upon political power as a means of participating in the general
riches, of becoming wealthy in their smaller ways and by their lesser standards, as did the captains of industry. Never before had the motive been so
strong; never before had temptations been so abundant.

II

The parties of the period after the post-Civil War were based on patronage,
not principle; they divided over spoils, not issues. Although American po-

---

Reprinted from *The American Political Tradition and the Men Who Made It* by
Richard Hofstadter, by permission of Alfred A. Knopf, Inc. Copyright 1948 by Alfred
A. Knopf, Inc. Pp. 162–182.

litical parties are never celebrated for having sharp differences of principle, the great age of the spoilsmen was notable for elevating crass hunger for office to the level of a common credo. "The American parties now continue to exist, because they have existed," wrote Lord Bryce in *The American Commonwealth*. An eminent journalist observed to him as late as 1908 "that the two parties were like two bottles. Each bore a label denoting the kind of liquor it contained, but each was empty." In 1879 young Woodrow Wilson expressed in eight words his disgust with the degradation of American politics: "No leaders, no principles; no principles, no parties."

The Republicans were distinguished from the Democrats chiefly by being successful. From the war and Reconstruction onwards, when it sought actively to strengthen its social base by espousing the policies of American industrialists, the Republican Party existed in an unholy and often mutually hostile conjunction with the capitalistic interests. Capitalists, seeking land grants, tariffs, bounties, favorable currency policies, freedom from regulatory legislation and economic reform, supplied campaign funds, fees, and bribes and plied politicians with investment opportunities. Seward had said that "a party is in one sense a joint stock company in which those who contribute the most, direct the action and management of the concern." The interests owned important shares in both parties, but they occasionally grew restive under what they considered the excessive demands of the politicians. Until the 1880's, in fact, the machines depended very heavily upon the contributions of their officeholders to party treasuries, and it was not until businessmen, feeling their power, began to go into politics themselves on a more considerable scale that the parties came more fully under their sway. Before business learned to buy statesmen at wholesale, it had to buy privileges at retail. Fabulous sums were spent. A disgruntled Congressman from Ohio declared in 1873 that "the House of Representatives was like an auction room where more valuable considerations were disposed of under the speaker's hammer than in any other place on earth." Between 1866 and 1872, for example, the Union Pacific spent $400,000 on bribes; between 1875 and 1885 graft cost the Central Pacific as much as $500,000 annually. Little wonder that an honest Republican of the old school like Walter Q. Gresham could describe his party as "an infernally corrupt concern," or that Senator Grimes of Iowa, once an important leader, could say in 1870: "I believe it is to-day the most corrupt and debauched political party that ever existed." "One might search the whole list of Congress, Judiciary, and Executive during the twenty-five years 1870 to 1895," concluded Henry Adams, "and find little but damaged reputation."

The case of the Crédit Mobilier is a classic source in the ethical perspectives of the Gilded Age. The Crédit Mobilier was a construction company organized by the directors of the Union Pacific. As stockholders of the railroad they allowed to themselves, in their capacity as stockholders of Crédit Mobilier, exorbitant prices for the work of construction. Since the Union

Pacific was the beneficiary of almost ten million acres of public land, there was a danger that Congress might inquire too closely into the transaction. To forestall this, Oakes Ames, Congressman from Massachusetts and Union Pacific stockholder, distributed a block of shares in Crédit Mobilier among influential Congressmen. When the case was investigated by Congress in the campaign year 1872, Ames's conduct was "absolutely condemned" by a House resolution, passed 182 to 36. Significant, however, was the attitude of the Congressmen who immediately afterward surrounded Ames's desk to assure him that they had acted with reluctance, and that they had every confidence in the rectitude of his intentions. In the press there was widespread sympathy for Ames and the beneficiaries of his bribes, who, incidentally, were not similarly disciplined. Ames himself, without denying the facts, refused to acknowledge the slightest culpability. His distributing stock among Congressmen, he said, was "the same thing as going into a business community and interesting the leading business men by giving them shares." "I think," he wrote to a colleague, "a member of Congress has a right to own property in anything he chooses to invest in," and on another occasion he observed that "there is no difficulty in inducing men to look after their own property." The implication is unmistakable: it was to be expected that Congressmen would use their political power to look after their own investments, and there was nothing untoward about the whole proceeding.

A defense like this was made in confidence that a large segment of public opinion would sustain such conceptions of political morality. Such was the contemporary estimate of Benjamin F. Butler. During his service as Military Governor of New Orleans he had requisitioned from a bank of the city $80,000 which he never accounted for. Later, when a lawyer hired by the bank to sue Butler for the money—the suit was successful—reproached him with the remark that his neighbors in Lowell would think little of him for living on stolen funds, Butler replied: "The people would think I was a fool for not having taken twice as much." Mary Abigail Dodge reported that when John Bingham was taunted about possessing free shares in the Crédit Mobilier, he replied that he "only wished he had ten times more." Henry Adams concluded that the public did not care about reform: "The moral law had expired—like the Constitution."

There were, of course, untainted politicians, and they were esteemed. Grant was happy to have Hamilton Fish in his Cabinet, a man of conspicuous rectitude who adorned the group like a jewel in the head of a toad. The impeccable Carl Schurz became Secretary of the Interior under President Hayes.[1] Hayes and Harrison, two of the five Republican Presidents of the period, had tolerable reputations; but these two were as innocent of distinction as they were of corruption and they have become famous in Amer-

---

[1] Garfield writes of the appointment of this notorious reformer as though it were a bold experiment: "The appointment of Schurz is unfortunate and unwise, but still it ought to be confirmed to give the President a chance to test his policy."

ican annals chiefly for their obscurity. Their relation to underlying political realities is expressed in the retort of Boss Matt Quay to Harrison's remark upon his election in the close campaign of 1888. "Providence," breathed the aristocratic Harrison solemnly, "has given us the victory." "Think of the man," snorted Quay. "He ought to know that Providence hadn't a damn thing to do with it." Harrison would never know, he added, "how close a number of men were compelled to approach the gates of the penitentiary to make him President." Harrison found out soon enough what his role was expected to be. "When I came into power," he once lamented in Theodore Roosevelt's presence, "I found that the party managers had taken it all to themselves. I could not name my own Cabinet. They had sold out every place to pay the election expenses."

Of the remaining three presidents not much need be said. Grant's administrations are notorious for their corruption.[2] Hayes's successor, the sanctimonious Garfield, although essentially an honest and worthy soul, was tainted by a few minor scandals. Garfield's successor by virtue of assassination, Chester A. Arthur, had been before his vice-presidential nomination the major domo of Conkling's notorious New York Customhouse machine, a spoilsman's spoilsman. ("My God! Chet Arthur in the White House!" a friend was reported to have exclaimed.) Nevertheless Arthur, trying to rise to his office, sought conscientiously but ineffectually to promote a few reforms; ironically, his signature made the Pendleton Civil Service Act a law.

It was not the presidents who gave the machine its dynamic force, but the factional leaders and bosses of the Republican Party, men like Roscoe Conkling and James G. Blaine. In spite of their violent mutual animosity, these two seem now to have had much in common. Above all, both looked upon life as an amusing and rather profitable game of wits.

Conkling was incredible. Tall, elegant, showy—he wore white flannel trousers and florid waistcoats—he was voluptuously abandoned to his own egotism, which, as Henry Adams remarked, was so grotesquely comic that it rose above ridicule. An observer watching him perform in the Senate might have had difficulty deciding whether this was an actor burlesquing a senator or a senator burlesquing an actor. "A great fighter, inspired more by his hates than his loves," Garfield called him; he is best remembered for his malevolent interchanges with Blaine and his pitiless assault on George William Curtis and other reformers, whom he branded "the man-milliners, the dilettanti and carpet knights of politics." The New York *Times* once described him quite seriously as "a typical American statesman—a man by

---

[2] No one admired the great, capitalists more than Grant, who saw nothing incongruous about a president's accepting the most lavish gifts from the rich. As fully as Carnegie or Rockefeller he accepted the idea that Providence planned to turn over to these men the control of as much of the world as they could grasp. In what other era could a president say so complacently and so candidly, by way of advocating the acquisition of Santo Domingo, that if his policy had only been adopted, "the soil would soon have fallen into the hands of the United States capitalists"?

whose career and character the future will judge of the political standards of the present."

Conkling had come from a well-to-do New York family; it was characteristic that as a lawyer he tried and won his first case before his father, a judge who sat in the United States District Court. Well born and well married, he could indulge his fancies without resorting to personal corruption; he is not known to have accepted graft, but graft was the milieu in which he lived. One of Grant's most powerful supporters, master of the rich patronage of the New York Customhouse, he was a machine product par excellence, flagrantly contemptuous of reformers who tried to challenge orthodox politics. Of course a party was a machine run by machine methods, and how else did the proprietors of ladies' magazines propose to manage them?

> We are told the Republican party is a machine. Yes. A government is a machine; a church is a machine; an army is a machine . . . the common-school system of the State of New York is a machine; a political party is a machine.

Conkling was so steeped in the villainous practices of orthodox politics that he could conceive of reformers themselves as nothing but rival operators. "Their real object," he once proclaimed, "is office and plunder"—he could imagine no other intelligible end for political life. Therefore: "When Dr. Johnson defined patriotism as the last refuge of a scoundrel, he was unconscious of the then undeveloped capabilities of the word reform."

The magnetic Blaine was the most popular Republican of his time. Only once, in 1884, was he nominated by his party for the presidency, but in all other conventions from 1876 to 1892 he was a formidable possibility. His popularity persisted long after his spotty financial record became an open story to those who cared to read it; and while his little sins were a handicap that may have cost him the presidency, they never ruled him out of consideration.

Blaine's actual transgression was not especially gross by the standards of his fellows. As Speaker of the House he had been instrumental in killing a bill that would have blocked a land grant by the state of Arkansas to the Little Rock and Fort Smith Railroad. This he had done of his own volition and without any solicitations or inducements, so that he was technically clear of accepting an outright bribe. But he subsequently presumed upon this favor to secure a very liberal commission for selling the railroad's bonds to friends in Maine. The transaction turned out to be of no profit to him, because his friends lost on their investment, and Blaine, whose sense of private obligation was as healthy as his sense of public duty was frail, recompensed them for their losses. The incident, however, represented only one of a number of Blaine's railroad transactions; obviously the Republican leader, who had a sizable family and several homes and a taste for gracious living, spent more than the salaries of his offices.

It is not so much Blaine's relations with the railroads that are here significant, but the series of flagrant and well-dramatized lies to which they led. In 1876, not long before the party convention which was expected to nominate Blaine for the presidency, his various transactions with the railroads came under Congressional scrutiny. With heroic audacity Blaine made off with the private letters that held the most damaging evidence against him, selected innocent sequences from them to read on the floor of the House, and brilliantly turned upon his investigators with a false but plausible charge of scheming to suppress evidence that exonerated him. Although this bit of play-acting convinced Republican admirers of his innocence, anxiety took its toll from the protagonist, then at the height of his ambition. His friend and official biographer, Gail Hamilton, has left a memorable picture of him, lying ill on the sofa in his home, raising his clenched fist, and declaiming histrionically: "When I think, when I think, that there lives in this broad land one single human being who doubts my integrity, I would rather have stayed—" and finishing the sentence only with a flourishing gesture. Not long thereafter on a Sunday morning he fell in a faint all too conveniently at the door of the Congregational church that he attended.

All this, one is inclined to think, is too much. The New York *Evening Post* published during the campaign of 1884 a pamphlet documenting without difficulty ten separate lies Blaine had told about his private financial transactions. Blaine had even gone so far as to compose a letter to be sent to himself over the signature of Warren Fisher, an official of the Little Rock and Fort Smith Railroad. Fisher was to say in part—as Blaine wrote it:

> . . . your action was as open and fair as the day. When the original enterprise failed, I knew with what severity the pecuniary loss fell upon you and with what integrity and nerve you met it . . . your conduct was in the highest degree honorable and straightforward.

This testimony of James G. Blaine on behalf of James G. Blaine makes edifying reading. Here was the "Plumed Knight" of the Republican Party! A reputation built upon eulogies of the high protective tariff, which he believed to be the real source of American prosperity, on waving the bloody shirt over the conquered South, on twisting the British lion's tail for the benefit of his Irish and Anglophobic following, and on dubious and unsuccessful schemes for promoting imperialism in South America had to be protected, as though it were the most precious thing in the world, at the cost of the most desperate lies, desperately advertised.

Blaine has been accounted by both contemporaries and historians as a man of unusual intellectual faculties for a politician. His major intellectual effort, a massive two-volume history, *Twenty Years of Congress*, is still of some use; but its governing conception is simply that the Republic was safe only in the hands of the Republican Party, and it can be judged as well by what it omits as by what it includes. Blaine saw fit, for example, to say nothing at all of the corruptions and scandals of the Grant administrations. And this was characteristic: so much of his life was spent in obscuring the truth that falsehood and evasion blanket even his historical prose. By common testimony he was a man of intense personal charm, warm and tender in his private relationships, facile, clever, and winning in his public role. Yet he left behind him not a single constructive achievement, hardly even a constructive suggestion; his chief contribution to American politics was to lower its tone. Roscoe Conkling, when asked to campaign for him in 1884, snarled, out of his morbid hatred: "No thank you, I don't engage in criminal practice"; and for once Conkling was right: harmless as a private citizen, Blaine was an antisocial being in his public capacity. "When I want a thing," the Plumed Knight once said to his wife, "I want it dreadfully." It might have been the motto of a whole generation of Americans who wanted things dreadfully, and took them.

III

The isolation of the reformers was as characteristic as the cynicism and corruption of the regulars. Party warhorses, who tended to identify rapacity with manliness, looked upon "good" men in politics as dudes, freaks, immune to the spirit of their time not out of virtue but perversity—"man milliners," as Conkling said in his famous diatribe. Blaine referred to them in a letter to Garfield as "upstarts, conceited, foolish, vain . . . noisy but not numerous, pharisaical but not practical, ambitious but not wise, pretentious but not powerful." The tart Senator John J. Ingalls of Kansas, who believed that purity in politics is "an iridescent dream," described them as

> effeminate without being either masculine or feminine; unable to beget or to bear; possessing neither fecundity nor virility; endowed with the contempt of men and the derision of women, and doomed to sterility, isolation, and extinction.

This was savage, but it had some truth: in politics the reformers were both isolated and sterile. Intellectuals, obsessed with the abstract ideal of public service, businessmen tired of the cost of graft, patricians worried about the need of honesty in government, they did not know the people, and the people with good reason did not know them. While reformers were concerned with public uplift, farmers and workers were trying to stave off private downfall. The steady deflationary movement of prices was ruinous to farmers, whose history in this period was one of economic tragedies and largely futile struggles against money and monopoly. Industrialism brought down upon the working class that pall of oppression and misery which is found in every chronicle of the Industrial Revolution, and it was unrelieved by fitful and brutal labor struggles. Violent business fluctuations, the great depressions of the seventies and nineties, and the sharp crisis of the mideighties spread poverty and insecurity.

It is not surprising, therefore, that reformers who concentrated upon a Civil Service Act, the tariff, or exposing the peccadilloes of politicians did not excite mass enthusiasm. Single-minded concern for honesty in public service is a luxury of the middle and upper classes. The masses do not care deeply about the honesty of public servants unless it promises to lead to some human fruition, some measurable easing of the difficulties of life. If a choice is necessary, the populace of an American city will choose kindness over honesty, as the nation's enduring Tammanys attest. The rural masses look for statesmen of the cheap dollar.

Twice during the heyday of the spoilsmen organized reform movements arose within the Republican Party—in the liberal Republican movement that ran Horace Greeley for the presidency in 1872, and the Mugwump bolt of 1884, which helped to defeat Blaine. The chief purposes of the first were expressed by Godkin in 1870 when he called for a party "having for its object Tariff Reform, Civil Service Reform, and Minority Representation." Since the most flagrant corruption of the Grant administrations took place after 1872, and general discontent did not grow keen until after the panic of 1873, the movement was premature. In any case, it was not attractive to workers and farmers, and was hardly meant to be. Its candidate, the eccentric Greeley, was unable to throw even the vulnerable Grant on the defensive; when the campaign was over, finding himself the worst-beaten man in the history of the presidency, he grieved: "I was assailed so bitterly that I hardly knew whether I was running for the Presidency or the Penitentiary."

In 1884 some dissident Republicans, who were strong in the strategic state of New York, where the electoral vote was perilously close, refused to swallow Blaine's candidacy and helped elect Cleveland. But whatever these Mugwumps contributed to Cleveland's victory, economic radicalism was no part of it; indeed, a good part of Cleveland's appeal for them consisted in the fact that he yielded nothing to the Republican leadership in conservatism.

The fate of political reform was paralleled by the failure of economic reform. During the first Cleveland administration the Cullom committee, which had been investigating railroads, concluded that "upon no public question are the people nearly so unanimous" as that Congress should regulate interstate commerce. Congress accordingly gave "the people" the Interstate Commerce Act. But as Senator Nelson W. Aldrich, already the watchdog of the corporations, said, the act was "a delusion and a sham . . . an empty menace to the great interests, made to answer the clamor of the ignorant and the unreasoning"; Senator Cullom, the act's sponsor, described it as "conservative legislation" passed in the guise of a reform measure. Railroads were soon circumventing regulation by the Interstate Commerce Commission with ease. Six years after the law was passed, Richard Olney, Cleveland's Attorney General, advised the president of the Chicago, Burlington & Quincy that to ask for its repeal would be unwise:

The Commission, as its functions have now been limited by the courts, is, or can be made, of great use to the railroads. It satisfies the popular clamor for government supervision of the railroads at the same time that that supervision is almost entirely nominal. Further, the older such a commission gets to be, the more inclined it will be found to take the business and railroad view of things. It thus becomes a sort of barrier between the railroads and the people and a sort of protection against hasty and crude legislation hostile to railroad interests.

The second economic reform, the Sherman Anti-Trust Act, passed during the election year of 1890, likewise in response to public clamor against monopolists, was equally cynical in design. Republican Senator Orville Platt of Connecticut charged during the Sherman bill debate:

> The conduct of the Senate . . . has not been in the line of the honest preparation of a bill to prohibit and punish trusts. It has been in the line of getting some bill with that title that we might go to the country with. The questions of whether the bill would be operative, or how it would operate . . . have been whistled down the wind in this Senate as idle talk, and the whole effort has been to get some bill headed: "A Bill to Punish Trusts" with which to go to the country.

IV

The best defense of the two-party system is the argument that while it permits the majority party to govern, as it should, it also centralizes the opposition in a single minority group, thus preventing the dissipation of minority energy in sectarian disputes and checking any tyrannical tendencies on the part of the "ins." This argument has seldom fitted the facts of American life, where party differences have rarely been profound and party structure has been so rigid that minorities, instead of being focused in either major party when it was out, have rather had to sunder their traditional party ties and—in most cases—drown alone in the political seas.

The first post-Civil War victory of the Democrats, in 1884 (when they had the estimable assistance of the Mugwump Republicans), is one of the few exceptions to this American story of party loyalty; but the subsequent Democratic administration only confirmed the profound uniformity between Republican and Democratic principles. In Grover Cleveland, however, the Democrats at least had a man who stood out, if only for honesty and independence, as the sole reasonable facsimile of a major president between Lincoln and Theodore Roosevelt.

Grover Cleveland's father, Richard Falley Cleveland, was a poor, studious Presbyterian parson of modest abilities who raised a family of nine children on the niggardly salaries of his village pastorates, never taxed himself to rise in the ministry, and died at forty-nine, when Grover was sixteen. The son took on his father's moral imperatives and accepted his lack of ambition as normal. In him the balance between the call of duty, as he saw it, and the call of ambition was heavily weighted in favor of duty. Simple, sentimental, and unimaginative, he worked for security and comfort and expected little more. On the night of his election to the governorship of New York, at the age of forty-five, he wrote to his brother: "Do you know that if Mother were alive I should feel so much safer? I have always thought her prayers had much to do with my success."

The hardship of being thrown on his own resources at an early age made Cleveland neither bitter nor rebellious. A tinge of what psychologists call moral masochism may have made it easier for him to carry his early burdens and, in his later years, to bear the odium that fell upon him. Writing reminiscently about his first years in Buffalo as an underpaid law student and clerk, he declared that he "had adversity in abundance . . . actually enjoyed his adversities." His working habits were irregular: spurts of incredible energy and self-punishing conscientiousness were followed by spells of the easygoing laxity of bachelorhood. Corpulent, rugged, and amiable, falling quickly into the social tone of Buffalo, a thriving city with a large, *gemütlich* German population, Cleveland joined what Professor Allan Nevins aptly calls "the hotel lobby and bar-room set."

Cleveland's rise to power was rapid and freakish. In the spring of 1881 he was a well-established Buffalo lawyer with a comfortable livelihood and a brief history of conscientious and unaspiring tenure in two minor political offices. In the spring of 1885 he was in Washington, taking the oath of office as President of the United States. A series of chance events catapulted him upward. In 1881 a particularly flagrant Republican boodler was nominated for the mayoralty of Buffalo; the Democrats, searching for an aggressively honest opponent and remembering Cleveland's past services as sheriff, offered him a nomination, which he accepted without enthusiasm. The new Mayor dealt roughly with local grafters, winning himself a good reputation throughout New York Democracy just on the eve of a gubernatorial contest. Circumstances in the state happened to be favorable: New York County delegates who were revolting against Tammany and seeking a suitable candidate threw the nomination to Cleveland after a brief deadlock between two more prominent men. An equally fortuitous split in the New York State Republican Party between the followers of Governor Cornell and those of Conkling made Cleveland's election a certainty. The physical decline of Tilden and the impoverished state of Democratic leadership made Cleveland a logical choice for his party in 1884. His campaign opponent, Blaine, damaged by old sins, the defection of the Mugwumps, and the incredible "Rum, Romanism, and Rebellion" speech of the Rev. Samuel Burchard, lost to Cleveland by the slimmest margin: a change of some 600 votes in New York State could have swung the election the other way. It was through a series of improbabilities that a man of Cleveland's caliber became President in the Gilded Age.

The legacy of Samuel J. Tilden went to Cleveland. His chief advisers were Tilden protégés and lieutenants like Daniel Manning, the newspaper-owner who became his first Secretary of the Treasury, and the millionaire corporation lawyer William C. Whitney, recently mated with Standard Oil wealth. Such friends only confirmed Cleveland's views, which were conservative from the beginning; but they may also have insulated the politician from the broadening effect of contact with public opinion, which was so notable in changing the outlook of the two Roosevelts and Woodrow Wilson. It is disarming to find Whitney writing to President Cleveland in 1892:

> . . . the impression of you got by the people is that you do not appreciate their suffering and poverty . . . and have your ideas formed by Eastern money power, etc.—*the usual twaddle*. . . . As you said to me, it is unaccountable what ideas they get and where they get them.

Yet it was hardly a mistake for conservatives of the East to regard Cleveland as their own man or for many normally Republican businessmen to support him even as early as 1884. One of his most notable acts as Governor had been to veto a bill reducing elevated-railway fares in New York City from ten to five cents, in spite of the obvious popularity of the bill among the people of the city. Such acts had given Andrew D. White cause to exult that Cleveland had overcome his "sympathies for the working people" and to praise him for having "not the slightest germs of demagogism." After his first election Cleveland received from Jay Gould the telegraphic message: "I feel . . . that the vast business interests of the country will be entirely safe in your hands." When Cleveland turned back the tide of free silver, Respectability was rewarded for its confidence. The Republican Senator Allison told Horace White in 1894 that it was "God's mercy" that Cleveland had won over Harrison in 1892 because no Republican president could have secured repeal of the Sherman Silver Purchase Act. Many years later Woodrow Wilson, converted from Cleveland Democracy to progressivism, denied that Cleveland's administration had been Democratic at all—"Cleveland was a conservative Republican." "Too conservative," says Professor Nevins, "to be a great constructive statesman."

Cleveland regarded the duties of public office in the most serious light. "It seems to me," he wrote to an old friend in June 1885, "that I am as much consecrated to a service as the religionist who secludes himself from all that is joyous in life and devotes himself to a sacred mission." Vetoes had made him famous as Mayor and Governor, and from the very first he conceived of his presidential task as a negative one: he was the righteous executive; his assignment was to *police* other politicians, to prevent them from giving favors or taking graft. The key to his mind was his dislike of "paternalism" in government. The people, he believed, were entitled to economy, purity, and justice in their government, and should expect no more. "A fair field and no favor." Industry must not expect to be coddled by tariffs; veterans and their dependents must not expect overindulgence in pensions; railroad corporations must give strict account of their use of land grants. Cleveland's experience with the tariff was evidence of both the earnestness and the futility of his philosophy.

Carl Schurz recalled how Cleveland had asked him shortly after his election in 1884 what issues he should take up. When Schurz replied that he should strike at the tariff, the President-elect, visibly moved, replied candidly: "I am ashamed to say it, but the truth is I know nothing about the tariff. . . . Will you tell me how to go about it to learn?" He devoted the greater part of his annual message in 1887 to an attack upon high rates. Warned by the politicians that his aggressiveness on the tariff question would cost him re-election, he replied in characteristic tones: "What is the use of being elected or reelected unless you stand for something?" His fight for reform, however, was ineffectual; the Wilson-Gorman tariff was at one with the Interstate Commerce Act and the Sherman Anti-Trust Act.

Cleveland's philosophy of laissez-faire, like the classic theory, was dependent upon one grand assumption: things must work out smoothly without government action, or the whole system, coherent enough in theory, would fall from the weakness of its premises. That these were unrealistic Cleveland had to recognize by the time of his fourth annual message to Congress, written in December 1888, after his defeat by Harrison. This message rumbled with protests that might have been written by a Populist:

> . . . we find the wealth and luxury of our cities mingled with poverty and wretchedness and unremunerative toil. A crowded and constantly increasing urban population suggests the impoverishment of rural sections, and discontent with agricultural pursuits. . . .
>
> We discover that the fortunes realized by our manufacturers are no longer solely the reward of sturdy industry and enlightened foresight, but that they result from the discriminating favor of the government, and are largely built upon undue exactions from the masses of our people. The gulf between employers and the employed is constantly widening, and classes are rapidly forming, one comprising the very rich and powerful, while in another are found the toiling poor.
>
> . . . We discover the existence of trusts, combinations, and monopolies, while the citizen is struggling far in the rear, or is trampled to death beneath an iron heel. Corporations, which should be carefully restrained creatures of the law and the servants of the people, are fast becoming the people's masters.

Nevertheless, Cleveland held to the view that the government could do little to check the forces that brought such results. His only recourse was to appeal to businessmen to improve their morals and become trustees of the public. "Must we always," he asked pathetically of the Philadelphia Commercial Exchange in 1887, "must we always look for the political opinions of our business men precisely where they suppose their immediate pecuniary advantage to be found?" Business men should be "guided by better motives than purely selfish and exclusive benefit."

Lacking a more positive conception of social action, Cleveland fell quietly and naturally into an implicit partnership with the interests during the crisis of the nineties. The man who thought that tariffs and bounties were an unwarranted boon to business and a gross violation of justice and equity thought nothing of sending federal troops to break the Pullman strike in 1894, or of putting them substantially under the charge of a railroad attorney. Years later he asserted that he and others of responsibility in the strike were to be "congratulated" for the part they played. He was equally resolute in rebuffing the farmers over the silver question. One did not have to be a plutocrat, of course, to be a rigid adherent of the gold standard; but an equally rigid adherence to laissez-faire required Cleveland to deny the responsibility of the government to produce any alternative to free silver as a remedy for agrarian distress. Few men would have the blunt solidity to do what Cleveland did—or rather to fail to do what he failed to do. It demanded his far from nimble mind to display all the imbecile impartiality of a philosophy that lumped together both the tariff racketeers and the poor bedeviled farmers as illegitimate petitioners of the government. It has been said to Cleveland's credit that he was strong enough to resist popular pressures that no other man could have withstood; it can also be said that he turned his back on distress more acute than any other president would have had the *sang-froid* to ignore.

Cleveland, in short, had made a defect of his merits. He was not a cruel man, but he was dogmatic, obtuse, and insensitive. Making whatever allowance one will, there is something odd about a president's writing during a year of popular agony like 1895 to the man who acted as his broker: "You know rich investors like me have to keep an account of income in these days." The intended note of jocularity rings false. "I find," he writes soon again, "I am developing quite a strong desire to make money"—and curiously, "and I think this is a good time to indulge in that propensity." One is reminded of Carnegie's thoughtful words: "The man who has money during a panic is the wise and valuable citizen."

Certainly this is the spirit of the faithful bourgeois. And Cleveland, this product of good conscience and self-help, with his stern ideas of purity, efficiency, and service, was a taxpayer's dream, the ideal bourgeois statesman for his time: out of heartfelt conviction he gave to the interests what many a lesser politician might have sold them for a price. He was the flower of American political culture in the Gilded Age.

Spoilsmen and Reformers:
Civil Service Reform and
Public Morality

Ari Hoogenboom

The reaction of an American historian to the phrase "Gilded Age" is nearly as predictable as that of a Pavlov dog to a bell. Thoroughly conditioned, the historian thinks of corruption. He will condemn (often while enjoying) Senator Roscoe Conkling's affair with Kate Chase Sprague that Senator Sprague abruptly terminated by running Conkling off his property with a shotgun; Reverend Henry Ward Beecher's success at seducing his lady parishioners that resulted in the most spectacular trial of the nineteenth century; or capitalist Jim Fisk's insane infatuation for Josie Mansfield that led to his murder on the steps of the Fifth Avenue Hotel. A notorious libertine, ravisher of railroads, and corrupter of governments, Fisk achieved immortality thanks largely to two reformers, Charles Francis Adams, Jr., and his brother Henry, who described in intimate detail Fisk's sordid relations with both the Erie Railroad and public officials.[1]

Ever since the Adams brothers wrote their essays the immorality, especially the political immorality, of the Gilded Age has attracted historians. Using Fisk as an example, they insist that public and business morals matched private ones. On the municipal level there was New York's spectacularly corrupt Tweed ring, overshadowing the more modest activities of Philadelphia's gas ring and Washington's Boss Shepherd. State governments were also corrupt. The *Nation* reported in the spring of 1867 that votes of New York legislators were bought and sold like "meat in the mar-

---

[1] I am grateful to the University of Illinois Press for permission to reprint portions of my book, *Outlawing the Spoils* (Urbana, 1961). I am also grateful to the editor of *The Historian* for permission to reprint portions of my article: "An Analysis of Civil Service Reformers," *The Historian*, 23 (November 1960), pp. 54–78. See Charles Francis Adams, Jr., and Henry Adams, *Chapters of Erie and Other Essays* (Ithaca, 1960); Ishbel Ross, *Proud Kate* (New York, 1953), pp. 246–49; W. A. Swanberg, *Jim Fisk* (New York, 1959); Robert Shaplen, *Free Love and Heavenly Sinners* (New York, 1954).

ket." [2] And corruption was not limited to the Northeast. Southern governments, badly tainted during Reconstruction, found the Bourbon restoration only a slight improvement. In the West, United States Senator Samuel Clarke Pomeroy of Kansas failed of re-election in 1873 after allegedly attempting to buy a state senator's vote for $7,000.[3] And in the federal government itself, Oakes Ames bribed fellow congressmen with Credit Mobilier stock, the whisky ring of internal revenue agents and distillers defrauded the country of millions, and the Star Route frauds cost the Post Office Department millions. In textbooks and lectures the Gilded Age consistently outscandalizes any other age in our history.

These familiar misdoings, and others, account for the free association of corruption with the Gilded Age. But should the association be so free? Were these scandals typical? Are Jim Fisk and the Tweed ring full-blown symbols of an age or are they symptoms, traces of a disorder that was by no means general? [4] Was this age as corrupt as historians have implied, or was it a prim age whose scandals have been exaggerated by contrast? More basically, what is meant by corruption?

If political corruption is the violation of duty for a consideration, usually monetary, many frequently cited examples of Gilded Age corruption are of questionable validity. President Ulysses S. Grant's participation in Jay Gould's and Jim Fisk's scheme to corner the gold market, for instance, was naïve, not corrupt; ignorant, not immoral. The Salary Grab Act of 1873, while perhaps greedy, was not illegal. Indeed, salaries of high federal officials needed to be increased. John D. Sanborn's contract to collect delinquent taxes for a 50 per cent fee was not an invention of Secretary of the Treasury William A. Richardson but a new application of the ancient moiety system. Far more significant than the collection of moieties during this period was the public reaction resulting in their elimination in 1874. The resentment aroused by the Sanborn contract should be cited as an example of growing administrative efficiency.

And if, like George Washington Plunkitt, one differentiates between honest and dishonest graft, he further reduces the ranks of the corrupt. Honest graft, that estimable Tammany Hall politician said, was the profit that flowed from advance inside information on future government action. Why not make a little money on real estate, paving blocks, or what the occasion called for, if one could? Who was hurt by it? [5] And while one usually does not speak of George Washington Plunkitt, Andrew W. Mellon,

---

[2] *The Nation*, 4 (April 11, 1867), p. 286.

[3] C. Vann Woodward, *Origins of the New South 1877–1913* (Baton Rouge, 1951), pp. 66–74; Albert R. Kitzhaber, "Götterdämmerung in Topeka: The Downfall of Senator Pomeroy," *Kansas Historical Quarterly*, 18 (August 1950), pp. 243–78.

[4] *See* John W. Pratt, "Boss Tweed's Public Welfare Program," *New York Historical Society Quarterly*, 45 (October 1961), pp. 396–411, for a more charitable view of Tweed.

[5] William L. Riordan, *Plunkitt of Tammany Hall* (New York, 1948), pp. 3–8.

and George C. Humphrey* in one breath, they are perhaps spiritual brothers, with Plunkitt exceeding the other two in candor if not in profits. Before rejecting Plunkitt's distinction between honest and dishonest graft, one should observe that twentieth-century conflicts of interest more than match nineteenth-century honest graft. The Gilded Age has lost some of its dubious distinction.

The typical historian has been too loose in applying the term "corruption." Specifically, he labels a politically partisan civil service corrupt rather than inefficient; he equates the spoils system with corruption when honest spoilsmen far outnumber distonest ones; he pronounces Gilded Age politicians guilty of corruption for associating with corruptionists even while attacking guilt by association in his own day.

One apparent reason why the historian has exaggerated the corruption of the Gilded Age is his desire to enliven lectures and writings. All the world loves a scandal, and the historian is loathe to abandon the pleasure of dispensing "vicarious sin." More basically, the historian dislikes the dominant forces in the Gilded Age. The historian is usually liberal, more often than not a Democrat. He is, typically, hostile to big business, an advocate of government regulation, of strong executive leadership, and of a civil service staffed by experts. The post-Civil War era stands for all the historian opposes. It was an era of Republicanism, of big business domination, of few and ineffectual attempts at government regulation, of weak executives, and of an essentially nonprofessional civil service. The historian naturally dwells upon the shortcomings of the period, particularly on the failures of Ulysses S. Grant, whose political career both personifies all the historian abhors and symbolizes Gilded Age politics.

Another reason the historian has exaggerated corruption in this period is the bias of his sources. The most articulate individuals in this age were its severest critics. Their enforced inactivity (foolishly imposed by business and political opponents) gave them both a cause and the time for writing, while their enemies managed conventions and built railroads. Reformers' letters and writings, their journals and newspapers dominate footnotes with good reason. Take, for example, the *Nation* under the editorship of reformer Edwin Lawrence Godkin. Outstanding contributors and particularly Godkin, hard-working, hardheaded, a trifle hardhearted, and very hard-hitting, made the *Nation,* to quote James Bryce, "the best weekly not only in America but in the world." [6] When not quoting the *Nation,* the historian turns to George William Curtis' graceful editorials in *Harper's Weekly,* America's leading illustrated paper. For a quarter of a century Curtis was the most

---

* Editor's note: Mellon was Secretary of the Treasury from 1921 to 1932, and Humphrey was Secretary of the Treasury from 1953 to 1957.

[6] Rollo Ogden (ed.), *Life and Letters of Edwin Lawrence Godkin* (New York, 1907); William M. Armstrong, *E. L. Godkin and American Foreign Policy 1865–1900* (New York, 1957).

conspicuous civil service reformer in America. Among monthly magazines, both *Harper's* and the *Atlantic* reflect reformism, while the venerable old quarterly the *North American Review* could at times be considered a reform organ. Reformers dominated newspaper sources such as the *New York Evening Post* and the younger *New York Times*—in fact opposition to civil service reform by distinguished papers was almost limited to Whitelaw Reid's *New York Tribune*.

Finally, the reformers are the most quotable men in the period. Even though Jim Fisk could coin a beautiful phrase, the area of his interests and the level of his perception limits application of his words. Contrast his broad humor with the acid wit of Henry Adams' superb and readily available letters and his autobiography, *The Education*. Readers enraptured with Adams' prose also become enraptured with Adams' prejudices.

Reformers exaggerated the inefficiency and corruption of the Gilded Age. A typical instance was the estimate in January, 1866, by President Johnson's Revenue Commission that $12,000,000 to $25,000,000 were lost annually in the New York Customhouse. Six years later the Grant Civil Service Commission under the leadership of George William Curtis projected the earlier figures and estimated that one-fourth of the annual federal revenue was lost in collection. In the ensuing presidential campaign, liberal Republican Senator Lyman Trumbull, citing the commission's report, calculated that the corrupt Grant regime annually lost $95,830,986.22 of the nation's revenue. When an enraged Grant supporter protested and demanded to know the origin of these figures, the commission explained that its estimate was designed to provide the "most forceable illustration of the mischief of the system" and actually dated from "the administration of Andrew Johnson when the evils of the 'spoils' system culminated." The loss was not money collected and then stolen but money due the government and never collected. The commission also claimed that during Grant's administration deficiencies and defalcations under the internal revenue law had been reduced to one-seventh of those suffered during Johnson's term of office. "We regret," the commissioners concluded, "that in our desire to divest our report of any partisan character whatever and to make it as concise as possible, we failed to explain this statement, more in detail, & to show how ingenious and successful were the efforts of the administration to prevent the loss to which we alluded." [7] Quite obviously the commission had wished

---

[7] *See* U. S. Revenue Commission, "Revenue System of the United States," *House Executive Documents*, 39th Congress, 1st session, VII, No. 34, 44–51; Charles Eliot Norton (ed.), *Orations and Addresses of George William Curtis* (New York, 1894), II, 39; W. W. Belknap to John A. Logan, August 15, 1872, Logan papers, Library of Congress; "Senator Trumbull and the Revenue," *Harper's Weekly*, 16 (September 7, 1872), p. 690; Curtis to Belknap, August 25, 1872, and Curtis, Cattell, *et al.*, to Logan, September [?], 1872, Logan papers. For another exaggeration of statistics by reformers *see Congressional Globe*, 41st Congress, 3rd session, 400, 459–460, 666. In fairness to Johnson the improvement of the Internal Revenue Service, no doubt, resulted more from the drastic elimination and simplification of excise taxes than from Grant.

to paint the bleakest picture possible to demonstrate the need for reform. To accomplish this purpose the commission knowingly used an obsolete estimate since it testified that the internal revenue system was seven times more honest under Grant than under Johnson. The commission could hardly afford to have the spoils system reformed by spoilsmen.

Along with exaggerating corruption in the civil service, reformers embraced a devil theory respecting their enemies. Grossly overrating the organization of satanic spoilsmen, reformers' writings abound with reference to conspiracies and rings. In November, 1871, Charles Eliot Norton wrote Godkin from Dresden, Germany, "The whole country is, like New York, in the hands of the 'Ring,'—willing to let things go, till they get so bad that it is a question whether they can be bettered without complete upturning of the very foundations of law & civil order." So great was Norton's revulsion against rapacious capitalists that he questioned the further validity of the "systems of individualism & competition. We have erected selfishness into a rule of conduct, & we applaud the man who 'gets on' no matter at what cost to other men." Norton even approved the recent attempt of the Paris Commune to redress its grievances by force, and although he shared the typical reformer's aversion to violence, especially violence that would overturn social order, he advocated "occasional violent revolutionary action to remove deepseated evils." Norton's radicalism, though a temporary romantic aberration rather than a permanent view, reveals nevertheless a man deeply distressed, or more accurately frustrated, by repulsive politicians and capitalists. Norton was so frustrated that he advocated violent revolution to make men "more conscious of their duties to society." [8]

Norton revealed a good deal more of himself than of his homeland. The whole country was not in the hands of the "Ring," Tweed, whisky, or otherwise. All capitalists were not buccaneers like Jim Fisk, and there was no revolution. American reformers, with Norton among them, were content to espouse civil service reform, revenue reform, and hard money, a program they hoped would recreate the golden age of the past. But men with a program to reform society are hardly unbiased observers of that society. Obviously reform is achieved through "knocking" not "boosting" which explains the hypercritical bent of civil service reformers. The historian, however, faithfully reflects the reformers' dim view of the Gilded Age.

The cause of the reformers' dim view and their espousal of civil service reform can be found in their careers. Their morality, their heritage of Puritan virtue cannot be denied, but reformers recognized the evils of the spoils system only after it thwarted their ambitions. The career of the temporary revolutionary, Charles Eliot Norton, serves as an example. Son of Andrews Norton, Harvard Divinity School professor, and cousin of Charles W. Eliot, future president of Harvard University, Charles Eliot

---

[8] Norton to Godkin, November 3, 1871, Godkin papers, Harvard University.

Norton was born into the "best" Cambridge circles. After graduating from Harvard, he attempted a career in business but was not successful. Literature and the arts enthralled him; account books did not. Norton traveled widely abroad where he met George William Curtis, his life-long friend, and hobnobbed with the Brownings, Thackeray, Ruskin, Carlyle, and the Pre-Raphaelites. Before the Civil War Norton contributed to the *Atlantic*, sympathized with the antislavery cause although he personally did not care for abolitionists ("the most self righteous set of radicals"), and supported the Republican party. During the war he edited the Loyal Publication Society broadsides, which for three years helped shape northern public opinion by supplying editorials to local newspapers. With James Russell Lowell, Norton became co-editor of the *North American Review* in 1864, and in 1865 he joined with Godkin and others to found the *Nation*.[9]

The postwar world disenchanted Norton. He was suspicious of democracy, observing that it contributed to the unfortunate national "decline of manners." Norton had no use for Andrew Johnson but even less for radical Republican politicos. He opposed the impeachment of Johnson reasoning that "three months of Ben Wade are worse than two years of A. J." Johnson's acquittal encouraged Norton only because it enhanced reformers' opportunity to capture the Republican party. "I think," he wrote Godkin, "we have a better chance now than we had any right to expect so soon for reforming the party & freeing it from the burden of the sins of the extremists who have tried to usurp the leadership." As the election of 1868 drew near, Norton, like everyone else, fell under Grant's spell. " 'Honesty & Grant,' 'good-faith & Grant' must succeed," he wrote from Manchester, England. "Grant grows daily in my respect & confidence," Norton wrote Curtis after the election and rapturously described the president-elect as "so simple, so sensible, so strong & so magnanimous." Assuming Grant would be especially generous to the reform element, Norton added, "If you see a perfectly fit and easy opportunity, I should be glad to have you use it to suggest my name as that of a suitable person for the mission to Holland or Belgium." Although Curtis wrote to the newly appointed Secretary of State Hamilton Fish in Norton's behalf, nothing happened. The reformers' hope to reestablish themselves in their old stronghold, the diplomatic service, proved futile. A few months later, bitterly disillusioned after his season of hope, Norton wrote Curtis: "Grant's surrender, partial though it may be, to the politicians was an unexpected disappointment, but a very instructive one. His other mistakes were what might have been expected,—what indeed we ought to have been prepared for. But some of his appointments are disgraceful,—personally discreditable to him. . . . The question seems to be now

---

[9] *See* Kermit Vanderbilt, *Charles Eliot Norton* (Cambridge, 1959); and Sara Norton and M. A. DeWolfe Howe (eds.), *Letters of Charles Eliot Norton* (Boston, 1913); Norton to Godkin, July 20, 1866, Godkin papers.

whether the politicians,—'the men inside politics,'—will ruin the country, or the country take summary vengeance, by means of Jenckes's [civil service reform] bill, upon them." [10]

Norton's disappointments paralleled those of his friends, particularly those of George William Curtis. Exposed early to transcendentalism at Concord and Brook Farm, Curtis never escaped its influence. After the grand tour abroad, he embarked on a literary career, becoming one of the most popular writers of the 1850's and associate editor of *Putnam's Monthly*. When this magazine collapsed, Curtis assumed a debt he was not legally responsible for and paid it by lecturing on the lyceum circuit. An ardent Republican, Curtis supported the Lincoln administration from his editor's post on *Harper's Weekly*. He soon became a power in the New York Republican party, unsuccessfully ran for Congress in 1864, attempted to influence patronage distribution during Lincoln's administration, and was offered a diplomatic post in Egypt. Curtis was not opposed to the spoils system until it ceased to function satisfactorily for him and for his friends. [11]

Not only Johnson but politicians in general snubbed Curtis and his peers. In the fall of 1866 Charles Eliot Norton launched a campaign to elect Curtis United States senator. Although Curtis' sensitive nature was not a political asset, the *Nation* and several other journals strongly supported him. Success, however, did not follow. "Conkling is undoubtedly to be the man," Curtis wrote Norton in January, "but his friends and [Noah] Davis's and [Ira] Harris's—the three real contestants—have each declared for me as their second choice. Still even that would not bring it because I am not enough of a politician for the purposes of the men who make Senators." As if to prove his point, Curtis "declined absolutely" to unite with the weakest candidate against Roscoe Conkling, who was elected. A few weeks later Curtis, in answer either to public opinion or to personal frustration with politics, wrote in *Harper's Weekly* favoring the passage of the Jenckes civil service bill by the expiring 39th Congress. Although tardy, Curtis' espousal of civil service reform lasted until his death twenty-five years later. In this period he became its most conspicuous leader. [12]

Politicians continued to snub Curtis and each snub made him more of a reformer. In September, 1870, he played a prominent role in Conkling's behalf at the New York State Republican Convention. To give convention proceedings an air of respectability, Conkling men elected Curtis temporary

---

[10] Norton to Godkin, March 13, 1867, May 30, 1868, Godkin papers; Norton to Curtis, July 24, 1868, Norton papers, Harvard University; Norton to Curtis, January 29, 1869, *Ibid.*; Curtis to Norton, March 13, 1869, Curtis papers, Harvard University; Norton to Curtis, July 22, 1869, Norton papers.

[11] *See* Gordon Milne, *George William Curtis and the Genteel Tradition* (Bloomington, 1956), and Hoogenboom, *Outlawing the Spoils, passim.*

[12] *The Nation*, 3 (November 1, 1866), p. 341; *Ibid.* (November 29, 1866), p. 422; Curtis to Norton, January 2, 1867, Curtis papers; "Reform of the Civil Service," *Harper's Weekly*, 11 (March 2, 1867), p. 130.

chairman. Having won by a wide margin, Curtis delivered an impressive address, which he hoped would stampede the convention into nominating him for governor. When William Orton, head of Western Union and one of Conkling's chief allies, approached him about the nomination, Curtis, feigning disinterest, replied: "If it is evidently the wish of the Convention I will not decline. But I don't want the office and I entrust my name to your honorable care." Professional politicians made short work of the Curtis candidacy. He was nominated by an efficient Conkling lieutenant, Charles Spencer, who effectively confused Curtis supporters by later voting for another candidate. "In one word, my dear boy," Curtis wrote Norton, "I was the undoubted choice of the Convention and I had been disgracefully 'slaughtered' by my friends!" Curtis attempted to convince himself he was "glad" that he would not have to run. "The only real harm the affair can do me," he confided to Norton, "is that my influence will decline with those who think I want office!!" [13]

Politics held further disappointments for Curtis who remained loyal to the Republican party, headed Grant's Civil Service Commission, and supported Grant in the campaign of 1872. The president, however, snubbed Curtis after 1872. When the New York surveyor vacated his position, reformers considered the nomination of his successor a test case. Grant hesitated but, prodded by Curtis, nominated the deputy surveyor in accordance with the new civil service commission rules. Although reformers tasted victory, they again grew apprehensive when members of the Conkling machine bragged that Grant would withdraw the nomination. Two weeks later the nomination was indeed withdrawn with the assurance that reform methods would be used in selecting the new surveyor. A committee of three, including Curtis and Collector Chester A. Arthur, was named to select the customhouse employee best fitted for the post. Once more reformers' suspicions were allayed. But spoilsmen were to be the final victors. Curtis' serious illness kept the committee from holding an examination or making a report. In mid-March, George H. Sharpe, an active politician and the local United States marshal, was appointed without the committee's knowledge. Sharpe's appointment goaded an ill and testy Curtis into action. Three days after it was announced, he published a letter in the *New York Tribune* emphasizing that Sharpe's appointment was made without his knowledge or consent and ominously adding that "men do not willingly consent to be thus publicly snubbed." On March 18, 1873, Curtis resigned as chairman of Grant's Civil Service Commission.[14]

Curtis was more aggressive when he returned to his editorial work after his illness and resignation. Ignored by the administration and unable to realize his political ambitions, he attacked Grant's civil service policy with

---

[13] Curtis to Norton, September 17, 1870, Curtis papers.
[14] *The Nation,* 16 (February 20, 1873), pp. 126–27; *Ibid.,* 16 (March 20, 1873), p. 189.

special vigor. Curtis relished his new independence and was proud when the anti-administration *Springfield Republican* called one of his articles "another Bomb Shell." He acknowledged in an editorial that "public disbelief of the reality and thoroughness of the reform" was not surprising. "The President forbids political assessments upon subordinates, and issues an executive order virtually reproving the political officiousness of officers of the service. But, in total contempt of his orders, they levy assessments, desert their posts of duty, assume the management of all party assemblies, and continue to use patronage as a party lever." Grant could have inspired confidence in his administration, Curtis contended, if he had fired his corrupt brother-in-law who was collector of New Orleans, dismissed the postmaster at St. Louis for levying political assessments, filled New York Customhouse posts according to the rules, and required civil servants to attend to their duties instead of their party's needs. "Unless these things are done, constantly and consistently done," Curtis concluded, "the work of the Commission, faithful, able, and devoted as we know it to be, will be in vain, and the Republican party will have no right to claim that it has really reformed the civil service." [15]

Unlike Curtis, Henry Adams expected little from Grant and very quickly learned to expect nothing. "We here look," Adams wrote from Washington in February, 1869, "for a reign of western mediocrity, but one appreciates least the success of the steamer, when one lives in the engine-room." Two months later, Adams wrote with the satisfaction his family always seemed to feel when it had just suffered defeat: "My hopes of the new Administration have all been disappointed; it is far inferior to the last. My friends have almost all lost ground instead of gaining it as I hoped. My family is buried politically beyond recovery for years. I am becoming more and more isolated so far as allies go. I even doubt whether I can find an independent organ to publish my articles, so strong is the current against us." And a few days later Henry wrote his brother Charles Francis, Jr., the treasurer of the Social Science Association, which was agitating for civil service reform, "I can't get you an office. The only members of this Government that I have met are mere acquaintances, not friends, and I fancy no request of mine would be likely to call out a gush of sympathy." Nor could Henry obtain anything for himself. The administration was presumptuous enough to ignore the Adams family.[16]

With their ambitions thwarted, the Adams brothers forsook the conventional methods of political advancement and espoused civil service reform.

---

[15] Curtis to Norton, September 19, 1873, Curtis papers; "The Prospects of Civil Service Reform," *Harper's Weekly,* 17 (October 25, 1873), p. 938.

[16] Henry Adams to Charles Francis Adams, Jr., February 23, and April 29, 1869, and Henry Adams to Charles M. Gaskell, April 19 and June 20, 1869, in Worthington Chauncey Ford (ed.), *Letters of Henry Adams 1858–1891* (Boston, 1930), pp. 152, 156–57, 161–62. (By permission, Houghton Mifflin Company.)

In February Henry had recognized that the struggle against *"political corruption"* was more basic than free trade and its eradication would be more difficult than the antislavery crusade. By June he was writing an article called "Civil Service Reform," which he described as "very bitter and abusive of the Administration." Although Adams expected it to get him into "hot water," he believed he had "nothing to lose." Henry and his brothers, Charles Francis, Jr., and John Quincy, were "up to the ears in politics and public affairs, and in time," Henry hoped, "we shall perhaps make our little mark." [17]

The *North American Review* published and the *Nation* applauded Adams' article. In it Adams revealed reformers' disdain for the new men of politics and their concern over the passing of a more compatible political age. Two members of Grant's Cabinet, Ebenezer Rockwood Hoar and George S. Boutwell, epitomized the change. Boutwell, Adams stated, was "the product of caucuses and party promotion," but Hoar was "by birth and by training a representative of the best New England school, holding his moral rules on the sole authority of his own conscience, indifferent to opposition whether in or out of his party, obstinate to excess, and keenly alive to the weaknesses in which he did not share. Judge Hoar belonged in fact to a class of men who had been gradually driven from politics, but whom it is the hope of reformers to restore. Mr. Boutwell belonged to the class which has excluded its rival, but which has failed to fill with equal dignity the place it has usurped." [18]

The careers of Norton, Curtis, and Henry Adams demonstrate that the civil service reform movement fits into a pattern of those out of power versus those in power.[19] Reformers invariably wished to curtail the appointing power after they thought it had been abused, and to them abuse occurred when men of their own social station or political faction were not appointed to office. The post-Civil War political world was not what the "outs" expected it to be. In their disappointment they turned to reform.

The civil service reformer's political impotence accurately reflected his loss of social and economic power. He was out of step with the rest of society. The main tenet of his philosophy, laissez faire, was rendered obsolete by the post-Civil War industrial transformation of the United States. His ideas were largely ignored. He favored free trade in an age of growing protectionism. He demanded hard money when cries for currency expansion grew louder. He hated monopoly and rapacious capitalism when big business swept all before it. He disliked unions, strikes, and radicals, but these all became more common. He was engulfed in the city of his fathers

---

[17] Henry Adams to Edward Atkinson, February 1, 1869, and Henry Adams to Gaskell, August 27, 1869, *Ibid.*, pp. 151, 165–66.

[18] Henry Brooks Adams, "Civil Service Reform," *North American Review*, 109 (October 1869), pp. 443–75; *The Nation*, 9 (November 11, 1869), p. 415.

[19] *See* Hoogenboom, *Outlawing the Spoils, passim.*

by an increasing flood of immigrants from eastern and southern Europe. He opposed imperialism but in the twilight of his career witnessed America's most hypernationalistic war. The reformer stood for little government in a period when the civil service proportionately grew faster than the population. The reformer was an outsider, philosophically as well as politically.

Like its proponents, the civil service reform movement was essentially conservative. Its leaders were not interested in revolutionizing anything or even in recognizing the fundamental alteration industrialism had made in the pattern of American society. They were prosperous and to some extent were leaders of society, but their anticipations were much higher than their achievements. Without sacrificing the material gains of the present, civil service reformers wished to return to the attitudes of the good old days before Jacksonian democracy and the industrial revolution, when men with their background, status, and education were the unquestioned leaders of society. In their frustration, reformers attacked the hated spoilsmen's conspicuous source of strength, the civil service.

If zealous reformers exaggerated the corruption of government in the Gilded Age, what was the actual condition of the civil service? In 1865 it was at its nadir thanks to the Civil War which swelled its ranks abnormally and provided Republicans with an excuse, that of disloyalty, for firing more officeholders than ever before. There is more than rhetoric in Julius Bing's complaint, "At present there is no organization save that of partisanship; no test of qualification save that of intrigue." [20] Like most reformers, Bing, the clerk of the Joint Select Committee on Retrenchment who helped Thomas A. Jenckes lay the groundwork for the civil service reform movement, took a dim view of the civil service. Actually, the government would not have functioned at all if corruption and incompetence were as universal as reformers alleged. Nevertheless, professionalism was almost nonexistent in the civil service, and politics permeated it to the core.

At the end of the Civil War the bureaucracy was subdivided into seven departments employing 53,000 workers whose annual compensation amounted to about $30,000,000. Uncle Sam was then, as he is now, the largest employer in the United States. The Post Office Department, with an office in nearly every village, employed more than half of all civil servants. Next in size and in political importance was the Treasury Department with a large office in Washington, sizable customhouses in major port cities, and internal revenue agents dispersed throughout the country. The somewhat smaller Interior Department was also politically significant because of the Land, Patent, Indian, and Pension bureaus. The remaining War, Navy, State, and Justice departments controlled less patronage.[21]

---

[20] Julius Bing, "Our Civil Service," *Putnam's Magazine,* new series, 2 (August 1868), p. 233.

[21] Joint Select Committee on Retrenchment, "Civil Service of the United States," *House Reports,* 40th Congress, 2nd session, II, No. 47, 2, 7. Civil servants may actually have

Spoilsmen and Reformers: Civil Service Reform and Public Morality

The civil service lacked system. Uniformity in personnel policy outside of Washington was by accident rather than by design, and only a loose personnel system existed even in Washington where clerks were divided into four grades, compensated accordingly, and examined for competence upon appointment. Other evidences of a personnel system were the formal provision for supervision of clerks, the fixing of hours by Congress, the experimentation with efficiency ratings, and the tendency to reward the proficient with promotion. In practice, however, the personnel system was primitive. Examinations were farcical, nepotism was common, no real promotion policy existed, and there was neither a training program for new recruits nor provision for retirement.[22] In these respects the American bureaucracy was not unique. British personnel practices, despite progress toward reform, were also primitive, and those of private business were even more backward.

Tenure of civil servants was short and uncertain in the 1860's. Although every department could point to civil servants who had been in office for many years, these workers were the exception. They formed the working core of the civil service, provided continuity and consistency in administration, and trained new recruits. An example frequently cited is that of William Hunter, the second assistant secretary of state, who in 1868 had been employed in the State Department for thirty-nine years. Unlike Hunter, most civil servants held their positions only a short time and anticipated early dismissal. Tenure varied, with offices requiring a high degree of technical knowledge retaining their employees the longest. In 1868 twenty-seven of the fifty-five officers in the New York assay office had been employed more than ten years and forty-five of them had worked there more than six years. The office of the United States treasurer, however, is more representative. A tally taken in December, 1867, found that 219 of the 282 employees had been appointed within the preceding four years. Only five individuals had been employed over ten years.[23]

The training and backgrounds of civil servants differed widely. For positions requiring technical competence, such as jobs in assay offices and in the Patent Office, men of ability were secured and retained. In other offices, standards were less exacting. The 282 employees in the treasurer's office, for example, were a motley group. They numbered in previous occupations "7 accountants, 13 bankers, 18 bookkeepers, 27 clerks, 1 detective, 2 druggists, 1 editor, 5 farmers, 1 hackdriver, 1 housekeeper, 1 hotel steward, 16 laborers, 1 lawyer, 1 machinist, 1 manufacturer, 8 mechanics, 14 merchants, 2 messengers, 1 minister, 1 page, 1 porter, 1 postman, 2 salesmen, 1 sculptor,

---

numbered 70,000 in 1867. Civil service statistics are frequently contradictory and must be used with caution. See Paul P. Van Riper, *History of the United States Civil Service* (Evanston, 1958), pp. 56–59.

[22] Leonard D. White, *The Jacksonians* (New York, 1954), pp. 394–98. These generalizations on the personnel system of 1860 are applicable five years later.

[23] Joint Select Committee on Retrenchment, "Civil Service of the United States," pp. 23, 40, 203.

12 students, 1 surveyor, 24 teachers, 2 telegraphists, 1 county treasurer, 1 waiter, 1 washerwoman, 1 watchman, and of no particular occupation, 112." [24] These appointments were not the result of haphazard policy. They were the fruit of the spoils system.

The spoils system, though hoary in some aspects, had grown with democracy; it was no accident that the two developed side by side. With frequent elections decided by large numbers, democracy forced politicians to build elaborate organizations to influence voters. The best assets in building a "machine" were local, state, and federal employees whose jobs depended upon politicians. With the application of pressure these civil servants would contribute both time and money to their patron's political wars. Frequent elections, however, meant frequent changes, for winning politicians would force their enemies out of office. By 1865 the spoils system (like democracy) was well established and rested on three major principles: appointment primarily for political considerations, congressional dictation of most appointments, and rotation of officeholders.

Although the spoils system controlled more offices more completely than ever before, the stress of war exposed its deficiencies and stimulated interest in reform. In this way, the Civil War contributed both to the rise and to the fall of the spoils system. The needs of the public service itself and the prodding of obstreperous reformers like Norton, Curtis, and Adams, resulted in slow but steady improvement dating from the immediate postwar years. Public service under Grant was actually more efficient than under Lincoln and Johnson. During the Grant regime the internal revenue service improved and Congress abolished moieties. Although Grant earned the dubious distinction of abandoning civil service reform, no previous president had even experimented with it. Grant was not a civil service reformer, but he was decidedly more interested in reform than his predecessors just as his successors were far more committed to reform than he.

In Grant's cabinet the most maligned administrator was George S. Boutwell, the secretary of the treasury whom Henry Adams singled out as the personification of the spoils system. Yet from 1870 to 1872 Boutwell administered stringent tests in his department. He also appointed E. B. Elliott, a friend of reform who later became a civil service commissioner, to the treasury board of examiners. Elliott helped prepare a guide for treasury clerkship examinations designed to aid in hiring competent workers. These examinations especially stressed arithmetic, but also included a knowledge of weights, measures, bookkeeping, grammar, spelling, geography, history, and law. According to Elliott, admission to the Treasury Department under Boutwell was "invariably" at the lowest level and written examinations were "invariably" required for promotion. Elliott testified that enforcement of these rules was "steady & regular & firm, the standard moderate but persis-

---

[24] *Ibid.*, 40.

tently enforced examination in no case merely formal." He also stated that Boutwell's system, unlike competitive examinations, "took cognizance of special qualifications derived from experience in previous employment and of other special attainments." The first competitive examination in the United States civil service was held in Boutwell's department in 1870, when six third-class clerks were examined for vacancies in the next class. Although competitive, this examination was not open to all applicants.[25]

Inherent demands of the civil service necessitated reform in Boutwell's department. His connection with competitive and stringent examinations seems strange considering his opposition to civil service reformers and their intense dislike of him, but it was Boutwell's job to administer a large office. As a responsible official, he recognized the need for skilled employees, a need which increased as government functions multiplied and became more complex. Boutwell, like reformers, desired efficient workers and was prepared to use examinations to obtain them, but unlike reformers, he wished to continue making political appointments. Historians, relying mainly on such partisan sources as the *Nation,* have overlooked Boutwell's reform activities. What was actually an enlightened regime from the standpoint of personnel administration has been renowned as a blatant example of the spoils system.

The most important, the most publicized, and consequently the most maligned office in the country was the New York Customhouse. There, as in government service elsewhere, conditions gradually improved during the Gilded Age. In January, 1866, the New York Customhouse was the scene of frauds, waste, and incompetence; during the next five years removals numbered 1,678, the equivalent of twice the entire force or more than one removal per secular day. Daily collections of $480,000 (the chief source of federal revenue) and the intricacies of tariff legislation required a sensitive business organization, which the customhouse did not have. The cost of collecting revenue in the United States in 1874 was three, four, and five times that of France, Germany, and Great Britain respectively.[26]

The administration of the New York Customhouse improved steadily after Chester A. Arthur replaced Thomas Murphy as collector in 1871. Since Murphy and Arthur both belonged to the Roscoe Conkling faction of the New York Republican party, Arthur's political dirty work had already been accomplished. The change of collector brought no change in faction; tenure became more secure. Kept on his mettle by a series of investigations, Arthur was an able administrator who brought a measure of efficiency to the New York Customhouse.[27]

. . . Under President Hayes the administration of the New York Custom-

---

[25] "Civil Service Reform," I, 27, 31–35, 91–92, III, 558–559, Elliott papers, library of the U. S. Civil Service Commission, Washington, D. C.

[26] *See Congressional Record,* 47th Congress, 1st session, 79–85.

[27] George F. Howe, *Chester A. Arthur* (New York, 1934), pp. 48–49.

house further improved. Hayes attacked the Conkling machine by attempting to remove Arthur and naval officer Alonzo Cornell. After a long battle, Hayes prevailed. The original objective of displacing Conkling appears not to have been reform but the building of an administration party from the remains of the old Reuben Fenton machine. The administration stood to gain doubly by attacking Conkling—not only would reformers be pleased, but also a hostile faction that failed to deliver the New York vote in 1876 would be eliminated. Yet whatever Hayes originally intended, the struggle continued so long and its publicity was so great that he could do nothing but make the customhouse a showcase for reform. "My desire," he wrote Arthur's successor Edwin A. Merritt, "is that your office shall be conducted on strictly business principles, and according to the rules which were adopted on the recommendation of the civil service commission by the administration of General Grant. In making appointments and removals of subordinates you should be perfectly independent of mere influence. Neither my recommendation, nor Secretary Sherman's, nor that of any member of Congress, or other influential persons should be specially regarded. . . . Let no man be put out merely because he is Mr. Arthur's friend, and no man put in merely because he is our friend." [28]

Publication of Hayes's letter to Merritt brought praise from reformers, and this praise grew louder with publication of the new rules. These rules applied to all New York Customhouse and subtreasury appointees except a few officers of special trust. Appointments were to be made from the three candidates ranking highest on a competitive examination to be administered by one of three examining boards and observed by "well-known citizens." New appointees were to enter only at the lowest grade; other vacancies were to be filled by promotion within the customhouse.

Naval officer Silas W. Burt, an early and ardent civil service reformer, was the dynamic force behind the new customhouse rules. Although not opposed to competitive examinations, Collector Merritt believed the experiment would be short-lived and asked Burt to enforce the rules. "If you can revive this corpse you are entitled to all the glory," Merritt assured Burt. It was Burt's idea to invite prominent citizens, particularly editors, to observe examinations, an idea that George William Curtis enthusiastically approved. Twelve citizens were invited to each examination, and Curtis attended them all to explain the proceedings. "The editors who attended," Burt later recalled, "were specially interested and their impressions, always favorable, were reflected in their papers." Editors favoring the spoils system, however, invariably declined invitations.[29]

Despite his lukewarm attitude toward the competitive system, Merritt pleased reformers. Even the *New York Times* (highly critical of Hayes)

---

[28] Hayes to Merritt, February 4, 1879, Hayes papers, Hayes Library, Fremont, Ohio.

[29] Silas W. Burt, "A Brief History of the Civil Service Reform Movement in the United States," pp. K-L, in the Burt Writings, New York Public Library.

admitted in July that "after four months' experience, it is simple justice to say that the reform has been applied there [the New York Customhouse] in good faith, and with a degree of pertinacity, a patient attempt to make it successful, and an enlightened appreciation of its nature and its scope, which have been an agreeable disappointment to the doubters." An energetic civil service reform leader, Dorman B. Eaton, later reported to Hayes that Merritt's administration of open-competitive examinations was highly successful. Never before, according to Eaton, had so much time been given to proper work and so little to partisan politics. Economy, efficiency, promptness, and high morale characterized the service. Even though political activity had not been entirely eliminated, Eaton was encouraged by its decline. Reformers rightly thought that Burt was responsible for the success of the president's pilot program.[30]

The New York Customhouse was not the only federal office in the nation showing improvement. Under Thomas L. James, a Conkling Republican, reform in the New York Post Office was in certain respects even more advanced than in the customhouse. When James was appointed in March, 1873, "incompetency, neglect, confusion, and drunkenness" that staggered "credulity" prevailed in the post office. James found 400 to 600 neglected bags of mail scattered throughout the building, and on one occasion a book clearly addressed to Vice President Schuyler Colfax was delayed for months. James replaced this chaos with system. He dismissed drunkards and incompetents but conducted no partisan proscription. He set up examinations and despite political pressure refused to hire unworthy applicants. By May, 1879, he decided that non-competitive examinations were not adequate and instituted open-competitive examinations a few weeks after they were established in the New York Customhouse. Eaton and New York businessmen were proud of their post office. In 1880, the volume of mail had increased one-third over 1875, yet the mails were delivered for $20,000 less, and collections and deliveries had been increased.[31]

Despite improvement of government service and a growing awareness even among spoilsmen that further improvement was necessary, the civil service in the Gilded Age was not yet reformed. Until 1883 it was basically nonprofessional and was characterized by lack of training, insecure tenure, and low morale. Politicians whose interests were local dominated the civil service, and the government worker, frequently owing his position to the turn of events in a congressional district, was understandably provincial in outlook. A civil service reform law requiring that appointments be made on the basis of open-competitive examinations could not pass Congress. The

---

[30] Dorman B. Eaton, "Civil Service Reform in the New York City Post Office and Custom House," *House Executive Documents*, 46th Congress, 3rd session, XXVIII, No. 94, 35–37; Curtis to Burt, August 18, 1879, Burt Collection, New York Historical Society; *New York Times,* July 9, 1879.

[31] Eaton, "Civil Service Reform," pp. 39–43.

charges of corruption leveled by the reform press usually failed to convince most Americans. Rising industrialists, urban laborers, and rural farmers did not support civil service reform. Only after President Garfield's assassination by an insane office seeker did reformers have a simple, emotion-packed illustration which the previously uninterested masses could easily understand. The spoils system equaled murder. Goaded by an aroused public opinion, Congress approved the Pendleton Act in 1883.

Under the Pendleton Act the trend toward improvement accelerated. The power of the Civil Service Commission grew with the steady increase of classified positions. An unprofessional civil service became more professionalized. Better educated civil servants were recruited and society accorded them a higher place. Thanks to secure tenure local political considerations gave way in civil servants' minds to the national concerns of a federal office. Business influence and ideals replaced those of the politician.[32]

Although these changes outlined the future development of the American bureaucracy it is well to recall that the roots of change were in the Gilded Age. Curiously the reformers, the assiduous cultivators of those roots of change, frequently refused to recognize that improvements in the public service had resulted indirectly from their labor. In fact, prior to the Pendleton Act the more improved the public service became the more shrill were reformers' protests over public immorality. Their noise not only obscured improvements but also gave the profession of politics a disreputable name it does not deserve, a reputation that even now discourages the reform-type from entering politics. It is indeed ironic that the Gilded Age is indebted to the reformers for its tarnished reputation as well as for its improvement in public morals.

---

[32] *See* Ari Hoogenboom, "The Pendleton Act and the Civil Service," *American Historical Review*, 64 (January 1959), pp. 301–18.

VII

The Spanish-American War:
Did the American Businessman
Influence the Decision for War?

INTRODUCTION

Although the American people and their political representatives evidenced relatively little interest in overseas territorial expansion in the 1870's and 1880's, the United States became increasingly concerned with its imperialist destiny in the final decade of the century. The imperialist mood of the 1890's manifested itself in many ways, the most important of which was the decision of the United States to go to war with Spain in 1898.

Because so much of the writing on the subject has emphasized the economic motivation for imperialism and because some of the American expansionists of the late nineteenth century justified imperialism in economic terms, it is not surprising that American historians should have sought to ascertain the extent to which the American business community influenced the American decision for war. The definitive answer to this question appeared to have been given by Professor Julius W. Pratt in the middle 1930's, in an article that first appeared in the Hispanic American Historical Review[1] *and was then incorporated with minor changes in the same author's* Expansionists of 1898. *Pratt argued that aside from businessmen directly or indirectly interested in the Cuban sugar industry, "an overwhelming preponderance of the vocal business interests of the country strongly desired peace." He concedes that by the middle of March, 1898, business opinion was becoming less certain that war would have a damaging effect on the economy and that some business journals were beginning to regard war as inevitable; but this did not mean that the business community thought war desirable or was seeking to influence the President to pursue a policy that would lead to war. Prior to the beginning of the war, according to Pratt, American businessmen, although much interested in the expansion of American trade overseas, did not look to the acquisition of colonies as the means of achieving this end. It was not until after the outbreak of the war that the business community was converted to imperialism.*

The Pratt thesis concerning businessmen and the Spanish–American War has recently been challenged by Walter LaFeber in his book The New Empire, *from which the second selection on this topic is taken. LaFeber emphasizes in his work "the economic forces which resulted in commercial and landed expansion," because these forces appear to him to have been "the most important causes and results in the nation's diplomatic history" during the last half of the nineteenth century.[2] With regard to the Spanish–American conflict, LaFeber contends that the American business community*

---

[1] Julius W. Pratt, "American Businessmen and the Spanish–American War," *Hispanic American Historical Review,* XIV (May 1934), 163–201.

[2] Walter LaFeber, *The New Empire: An Interpretation of American Expansion, 1860-1898* (Ithaca: Cornell University Press, 1963), p. viii.

was not "monolithic" in its opposition to war. By the middle of March, 1898, as he sees it, "important businessmen and spokesmen for the business community were advocating war." Among the factors that influenced McKinley's policy regarding Cuba during the final month of peace, LaFeber stresses as "perhaps most important, the growing belief of many sections of the business community that somehow the disturbances on the island would have to be terminated before the United States could enjoy full prosperity."

The Business Point of View

Julius W. Pratt

. . . It is pertinent . . . to enquire whether the war with Spain and the accompanying acquisition of insular possessions were, in reality, the results of economic pressure; whether, that is, business interests in the United States shared the aspirations of such intellectuals as Mahan, Lodge, Roosevelt, and Beveridge.

So reliable a scholar as Professor H. U. Faulkner has asserted that "the great cause for the war" with Spain is to be found in the fact that by 1898 the United States was "sufficiently advanced for financial imperialism," implying that the war was fought for markets and fields for investment.[1] This interpretation was directly contradicted by the late James Ford Rhodes, who declared quite as categorically that "the financial and business interests of the country were opposed to the war."[2] We may well enquire, therefore, what was, in reality, the attitude of American business both to the war (or to the intervention in Cuba, which brought on the war) and to the question of territorial expansion.[3]

We may begin with a generalization, the evidence for which will be presented as the chapter proceeds. American business, in general, had strongly opposed action that would lead to war with Spain. American business had been either opposed or indifferent to the expansionist philosophy which had

From Julius W. Pratt, *Expansionists of 1898: The Acquisition of Hawaii and the Spanish Islands (Baltimore:* The Johns Hopkins Press), pp. 232–257, 266–267. Reprinted by permission.

[1] H. U. Faulkner, *American Economic History,* pp. 624–625.
[2] J. F. Rhodes, *The McKinley and Roosevelt Administrations,* p. 55.
[3] The discussion which follows is adapted, with slight changes, from the writer's article, "American Business and the Spanish–American War," *Hispanic American Historical Review,* XIV, 163–201.

arisen since 1890. But almost at the moment when the war began, a large section of American business had, for reasons that will become apparent, been converted to the belief that a program of territorial expansion would serve its purposes. Hence business, in the end, welcomed the "large policy" and exerted its share of pressure for the retention of the Spanish islands and such related policies as the annexation of Hawaii and the construction of an isthmian canal.

One public man to whom the welfare of American business was of so much concern that he may almost be considered its spokesman in the Senate, was McKinley's friend, Mark Hanna. No one was more unwilling than he to see the United States drift into war with Spain. To Hanna, in the words of his biographer, "the outbreak of war seemed to imperil the whole policy of domestic economic amelioration which he placed before every other object of political action." [4] Hanna's attitude appears to have been identical with that of leading business men. This conclusion is based not only upon the few published biographies of such men,[5] but also upon the study of a large number of financial and trade periodicals, of the proceedings of chambers of commerce and boards of trade, and of material in the *Miscellaneous Files* of the Department of State, containing numerous letters and petitions from business men and organizations.

That business sentiment, especially in the East, was strongly anti-war at the close of 1897 and in the opening months of 1898, is hardly open to doubt. Wall Street stocks turned downward whenever the day's news seemed to presage war and climbed again with information favorable to peace.[6] Bulls and bears on the market were those who anticipated, respectively, a peaceable and a warlike solution of the Cuban question.[7] The "jingo," in Congress or the press, was an object of intense dislike to the editors of business and financial journals,[8] who sought to counteract his influence by anti-

---

[4] Croly, *Marcus Alonzo Hanna*, p. 278.

[5] *Cf.* A. Carnegie, *Autobiography of Andrew Carnegie,* chap. xxviii; B. Alderson, *Andrew Carnegie: The Man and His Work,* pp. 101–102; C. Adler, *Jacob H. Schiff, His Life and Letters,* I, 308–309; J. G. Pyle, *Life of James J. Hill,* II, 77; G. Kennan, *E. H. Harriman,* I, 170; II, 1; H. A. Gibbons, *John Wanamaker,* I, 371–376. Carnegie, Schiff, and Hill were strongly anti-war and anti-imperialist. John Wanamaker supported the war and raised a regiment (which never saw service); there is no evidence in his biography that he was interested in annexations. Harriman's Union Pacific Railroad profited from American operations in the Philippines. It is not hinted that he foresaw this or worked for it. His business relations with the Far East did not begin till 1905. Biographies of Morgan, Rockefeller, Frick, Robert Bacon do not discuss the attitude of those men to the war or imperialism. For an apparently contradictory opinion of the attitude of business men, expressed by Thomas Beer, see *infra,* note 51.

[6] *Cf. Wall Street Journal,* December 3, 31, 1897; January 25, April 21, 1898; *Railway World,* XLII, 105, 217 (January 29, February 26, 1898).

[7] *Wall Street Journal,* December 31, 1897; February 17, 1898.

[8] *Ibid.,* November 18, December 3, 1897; *Railway World, loc. cit.; Banker and Tradesman,* XXVI, 78 (February 23, 1898); *American Banker,* LXIII, 528 (March 30, 1898); *Journal of Commerce and Commercial Bulletin,* November 27, 1897; *Commercial and Financial Chronicle,* LXV, 597 (October 2, 1897).

war editorials in their columns.[9] Boards of trade and chambers of commerce added their pleas for the maintenance of peace to those of the business newspapers and magazines.[10] So marked, indeed, was the anti-war solidarity of the financial interests and their spokesmen that the jingoes fell to charging Wall Street with want of patriotism. Wall Street, declared the Sacramento *Evening Bee* (March 11, 1898), was "the colossal and aggregate Benedict Arnold of the Union, and the syndicated Judas Iscariot of humanity." Senator Thurston, of Nebraska, charged that opposition to war was found only among the "money-changers," bringing from the editor of *The American Banker* the reply that "there is not an intelligent, self-respecting and civilized American citizen anywhere who would not prefer to have the existing crisis culminate in peaceful negotiations." [11]

This anti-war attitude on the part of several leading financial journals continued up to the very beginning of hostilities. The New York *Journal of Commerce and Commercial Bulletin* declared on February 28 that the only possible excuses for war would be (1) a finding by the naval board investigating the "Maine" disaster that the ship had been destroyed by an official act of the Spanish Government; or (2) a refusal by Spain to make reparation if the board should hold that she had failed to exercise due diligence in safeguarding the vessel. Either of these events it held to be almost inconceivable. The *Commercial and Financial Chronicle* expressed the belief on March 12 that the opposition of the financial interests would yet prevent war; and on April 2 the same journal branded as "monstrous" the proposition to settle the Cuban and "Maine" questions by war while the slightest chance remained for a peaceful solution. On April 16, after the House of Representatives had passed the Cuban resolutions, the Boston *Journal of Commerce* declared: "Sober second thought had but little to do with the deliberations. . . . The members were carried off their feet by the war fever that had been so persistently worked up since the Maine explosion. . . ." [12]

The reasons for this attitude on the part of business are not far to seek. Since the panic of 1893 American business had been in the doldrums. Ten-

---

[9] *Journal of Commerce and Commercial Bulletin,* February 28, 1898; *Commercial and Financial Chronicle,* April 2, 1898; Boston *Journal of Commerce,* LII, 40 (April 16, 1898); *Drugs, Oils and Paints,* XIII, 401 (April, 1898); *Railway World,* XLII, 241-242 (March 5, 1898); *Banker and Tradesman, loc. cit.; Daily Commercial News and Shipping List,* March 25, 1898.

[10] Chamber of Commerce of the State of New York, *Fortieth Annual Report, 1897–1898,* p. 127; Boston Chamber of Commerce, *Thirteenth Annual Report, 1898,* pp. 115–116; Baltimore Board of Trade, *Report of President and Directors for Year Ending September 30, 1898,* p. 67; Philadelphia Board of Trade, *Sixty-Sixth Annual Report,* pp. 50–51; Cleveland Chamber of Commerce, *Fiftieth Year,* p. 66; Indianapolis Board of Trade, *Annual Report for Year Ending June 1, 1898,* p. 20. Of the resolutions printed in these reports, some spoke out strongly against war; others merely commended President McKinley's conservative course in seeking a peaceful solution of the Cuban question.

[11] *American Banker, loc. cit.*

[12] *Com. and Fin. Chron.,* LXVI, 641; *Boston Jour. of Com.,* LII, 40.

dencies toward industrial revival had been checked, first by the Venezuela war scare in December, 1895, and again by the free silver menace in 1896.[13] But in 1897 began a real revival, and before the end of the year signs of prosperity appeared on all sides. The New York *Commercial* conducted a survey of business conditions in a wide variety of trades and industries, from which it concluded that, "after three years of waiting and of false starts, the groundswell of demand has at last begun to rise with a steadiness which leaves little doubt that an era of prosperity has appeared." January, 1898, said the same article, is "a supreme moment in the period of transition from depression to comparative prosperity." [14] This note of optimism one meets at every turn, even in such a careful and conservative sheet as the *Commercial and Financial Chronicle*. As early as July, 1897, this paper remarked: "We appear to be on the eve of a revival in business"; and in December after remarking upon the healthy condition of the railroads and the iron industry, it concluded: "In brief, no one can study the industrial conditions of today in America without a feeling of elation. . . ." [15] The *Wall Street Journal* found only two "blue spots" in the entire country: Boston, which suffered from the depressed demand for cotton goods, and New York, where senseless rate cutting by certain railroads caused uneasiness. "Throughout the west, southwest and on the Pacific coast business has never been better, nor the people more hopeful." [16]

A potent cause for optimism was found in the striking expansion of the American export trade. A volume of exports far in excess of those of any recent year, a favorable balance of trade of $286,000,000, and an especially notable increase in exports of manufactures of iron, steel, and copper, convinced practically every business expert that the United States was on the point of capturing the markets of the world. "There is no question," said one journal, "that the world, generally, is looking more and more to the United States as the source of its supply for very many of the staple commodities of life." [17] Especially elated were spokesmen of the iron and steel industry. Cheaper materials and improved methods were enabling the American producer to undersell his British competitor in Europe and in the British possessions,[18] and Andrew Carnegie was talking of a great shipbuilding yard near New York to take advantage of these low costs.[19] The

---

[13] G. H. Hull, *Industrial Depressions . . . or Iron the Barometer of Trade*, pp. 161–173.

[14] New York *Commercial*, January 3, 1898. The only flaw in the picture was continued depression in the cotton goods industry.

[15] *Com. & Fin. Chron.*, LXV, 134, 1046 (July 24, December 4, 1897).

[16] *Wall Street Journal*, December 23, 1897.

[17] *Banker and Tradesman*, XXVI, 297 (April 20, 1898). *Cf. American Banker*, LXIII, 178 (February 2, 1898); *Age of Steel*, LXXXIII, No. 1, p. 57 (January 1, 1898); *Rand-McNally Bankers' Monthly*, XV, 19 (January, 1898); *Statistical Abstract of the U. S.*, 1931, p. 488.

[18] *Iron Age*, December 9, 1897, p. 22; *Banker and Tradesman, loc. cit.; Railway World*, XLI, 837 (August 21, 1897).

[19] *Daily Commercial News and Shipping List*, March 7, 1898.

Iron Age, in an editorial on "The Future of Business," foretold the abolition of the business cycle by means of a better planned economy, consolidation of railroads and industries, reduction of margins of profit, higher wages, and lower prices to consumers.[20]

To this fair prospect of a great business revival the threat of war was like a spectre at the feast. A foreign complication, thought the *Commercial and Financial Chronicle* in October, 1897, would quickly mar "the trade prosperity which all are enjoying." Six months later (April 2, 1898), after a discussion of the effect of war rumors on the stock exchange, it declared: ". . . Every influence has been, and even now is, tending strongly towards a term of decided prosperity, and that the Cuban disturbance, and it alone, has arrested the movement and checked enterprise."[21] The *Banker and Tradesman* saw in the Cuban complication the threat of a "material setback to the prosperous conditions which had just set in after five years of panic and depression." The same journal summarized a calculation made by the Boston *Transcript* showing that in February, 1898, the wave of prosperity had carried the average price of twenty-five leading stocks within $5\frac{1}{2}$ points of the high for the preceding ten years and 30 points above the low of 1896, and that the Cuban trouble had, in a little over two months, caused a loss of over ten points, or more than one-third of the recent gain.[22] "War would impede the march of prosperity and put the country back many years," said the *New Jersey Trade Review.*[23] The *Railway Age* was of the opinion that the country was coming out of a depression and needed peace to complete its recovery. "From a commercial and mercenary standpoint," it remarked, "it seems peculiarly bitter that this war should have come when the country had already suffered so much and so needed rest and peace."[24]

The idea that war could bring any substantial benefits to business was generally scouted. It would endanger our currency stability, interrupt our trade, and threaten our coasts and our commerce, thought the *Commercial and Financial Chronicle*. It would "incalculably increase the loss to business interests," said the *Banker's Magazine;* while the *United States Investor* held that war was "never beneficial from a material standpoint, that is, in the long run."[25] The *Railroad Gazette* predicted that war would result in "interruption of business enterprise of every kind, stopping new projects and diminution of the output of existing businesses and contraction of trade everywhere." Railroads would lose more than they would gain. Even

---

[20] *Iron Age,* December 23, 1897, pp. 19–20.
[21] *Com. & Fin. Chron.,* LXV, 597–599; LXVI, 636.
[22] *Banker and Tradesman,* XXVI, 326 (April 27, 1898). *Cf. ibid.,* XXVI, 130 (March 9, 1898).
[23] *New Jersey Trade Review,* March 1, 1898.
[24] *Railway Age,* XXV, 215, 253 (April 1, 15, 1898).
[25] *Com. & Fin. Chron.,* LXVI, 308 (February 12, 1898); *Banker's Magazine,* LVI, 358 (March, 1898); *U. S. Investor,* IX, 529 (April 9, 1898).

arms manufacturers were not all agreed that war would be desirable.[26] Journals speaking for the iron and steel industry also argued that war would injure business. It "would injure the iron and steel makers ten times as much as they would be benefited by the prevailing spurt in the manufacture of small arms, projectiles and steel plates for war ships," in the opinion of one of these.[27] The *American Wool and Cotton Reporter* of New York and the *Northwestern Miller* of Minneapolis agreed that war was never materially beneficial in the long run, while trade journals in Atlanta, Chattanooga, and Portland, Oregon, saw as fruits of the approaching conflict only destruction, debt, and depressed industry.[28]

Many conservative interests feared war for the specific reason that it might derange the currency and even revive the free-silver agitation, which had seemed happily dead. The subsidence of that agitation and the prospect of currency reform were among the hopeful factors at the close of 1897.[29] It was not uncommonly charged that the jingoes were animated in part by the expectation that war would lead to inflation in paper or silver. The New York *Journal of Commerce,* in an editorial on "The Breeding Grounds of Jingoism," had called attention to the fact that the jingoes were generally silverites, including in their number "the financiers who desire to force bankruptcy on the country as a means of breaking down the gold standard," and had quoted with approval an editorial from another paper charging that Senator Morgan's championship of the Cuban insurgents was part of "his wild scheming in the interest of the silver standard." [30] The *Commercial and Financial Chronicle* endorsed this view, declaring that many of the Cuban agitators "are only interested in the establishment of a free-silver standard, a plan which they think war would advance." [31] Similar views were expressed by the *American Banker* of New York, the *United*

---

[26] *Railroad Gazette*, XXX, 236 (April 1, 1898). As to the position of arms and ammunition manufacturers, it is interesting to find a representative of a New York firm engaged in that trade writing to the Secretary of the Interior in March, 1898, in behalf of a peaceful settlement in Cuba. M. Hartley to C. N. Bliss, March 16, 17, 1898. *Miscellaneous Letters* (Dept. of State), March, 1898, II. Hartley represented Hartley and Graham, of New York, associated with the Union Metallic Cartridge Co. and Remington Arms Co.

[27] *Iron and Steel*, LXXII, No. 15, p. 10 (April 9, 1898). *Cf. Iron Age*, March 17, 1898, p. 21; *Age of Steel*, LXXXIII, No. 10 (March 5, 1898).

[28] *American Wool and Cotton Reporter*, XII, 439 (April 7, 1898); *Weekly Northwestern Miller*, XL., 667 (April 29, 1898); *"Dixie," A Monthly Journal Devoted to Southern Industrial Interests*, XIV, No. 5, pp. 21–23 (May, 1898); *Tradesman*, XXXIX, 60 (May 1, 1898); Portland (Ore.) *Board of Trade Journal*, XI, 6 (May, 1898).

[29] *Wall Street Journal*, November 18, December 31, 1897.

[30] New York *Journal of Commerce and Commercial Bulletin*, May 21, June 5, 1897. A. W. Dunn relates that Senator Pettigrew, of South Dakota, said to him: ". . . I want a war with Spain, because I believe it will put us on a silver basis." A. W. Dunn, *From Harrison to Harding*, I, 232.

[31] *Com. & Fin. Chron.*, LXIV, 974; LXVI, 308 (May 22, 1897; February 12, 1898). *Cf.* John D. Hicks, *The Populist Revolt*, p. 390. "The voting of bond issues to aid in financing the war drew fire from the Populists, who would have preferred issues of treasury notes, . . ."

States Investor of Boston, and the *Rand-McNally Bankers' Monthly* of Chicago. The last-named quoted from a speech of Secretary of the Treasury Gage, delivered in Chicago in February, 1898, in which he had declared that "it would be scarcely possible for this nation to engage in war in its present condition . . . without a suspension of specie payments and a resort to further issues of Government notes." A war of any duration, in the opinion of the *United States Investor,* would certainly derange the currency and reduce business to a gambling basis.[32]

Something of a freak among New York financial journals was the *Financial Record,* which, in November, 1897, denounced "the cowardice of our Administration in refusing the phenomenally brave Cubans the commonest rights of belligerency" as "a disgrace to the United States," and argued that war with Spain, far from depressing securities or injuring business, "would vastly increase the net earning power of every security sold on our market today." [33] The mystery of this jingo attitude is explained when we discover that this journal had been a warm advocate of the free coinage of silver.

Business opinion in the West, especially in the Mississippi Valley, appears to have been less opposed to war and less apprehensive of its results than that of the Atlantic coast. The Kansas City Board of Trade, at the beginning of 1897, had urged recognition of Cuban independence.[34] The Cincinnati Chamber of Commerce, at a meeting on March 29, 1898, adopted "amidst much enthusiasm" resolutions condemning Spain for cruelties to the Cubans and the destruction of the "Maine" and calling for a "firm and vigorous policy which will have for its purpose—peacefully if we can, but with force if we must—the redress of past wrongs, and the complete and unqualified independence of Cuba." [35] The Chicago *Economist* denied that war would seriously hurt business or endanger the gold standard and asserted that the liberation of Cuba, by peace or war, would mean another star of glory for the United States and would produce "results of the highest value to mankind." [36] The *Rand-McNally Bankers' Monthly,* of the same city, while opposing war, called attention to the fact that while the war scare had demoralized the stock market, "general business activity

---

[32] *American Banker,* LXII, 912–913; LXIII, 394 (May 26, 1897; March 9, 1898); *United States Investor,* IX, 368 (March 12, 1898); *Rand-McNally Bankers' Monthly,* XV, 294 (April, 1898). T. S. Woolsey, in his *America's Foreign Policy,* pp. 13–14, remarked that currency reform would be impeded by any unusual complication, such as a war, and added: "This, perhaps, will suggest a certain subtle connection between Jingoism and the fiat money advocates."

[33] *The Financial Record, An Investors' Manual,* November 4, 17, 1897.

[34] The proposal of the Kansas City Board of Trade was forwarded with a request for endorsement, to the Philadelphia Board of Trade, which rejected it. Philadelphia Board of Trade, *Sixty-Fourth Annual Report,* p. 15.

[35] *Fiftieth Annual Report* of the Cincinnati Chamber of Commerce and Merchant's Exchange, p. 49.

[36] *The Economist, A Weekly Financial, Commercial and Real-Estate Newspaper,* XIX, 233, 322 (February 26, March 19, 1898).

apparently received an impetus." [37] Similarly the *Age of Steel* (St. Louis), while much preferring peace, "when not secured at the price of national honor," comforted its readers with the thought that although foreign trade might suffer, home trade and industries would be stimulated by war.[38] A St. Louis bank president, Mr. Lackland, believed that war would "cause a boom in many lines of business in this country . . . and give employment to a large number of persons who are now out of work." [39] The Chattanooga *Tradesman* stated on March 1, 1898, that a "small prospect" of war had already stimulated the iron trade in certain lines and had benefited the railroads by hurrying forward shipments of grain and other commodities in anticipation of war prices.[40] The *Mining and Scientific Press,* of San Francisco, while holding that, in general, war "lets loose havoc and waste, and entails destructive expense," conceded that "to nearly everything related to the mining industry the war will be a stimulus." [41]

Even in New York, business men saw some rays of light piercing the war clouds. Stock market operators, according to the *Wall Street Journal,* just after the "Maine" explosion, "did not look for any great break in the market, because actual war with Spain would be a very small affair compared with the Venezuela complication with Great Britain." Their expectation was for a drop in stocks at the beginning of hostilities, followed by a resumption of the recent advance. In fact, the first shock might well be followed by a boom.[42] "The nation looks for peace," declared *Dun's Review,* March 5, "but knows that its sources of prosperity are quite beyond the reach of any attack that is possible." *Bradstreet's* contrasted the jumpiness of Wall Street over war news with "the calm way in which general business interests have regarded the current foreign complications," and *Dun's Review* of March 12 stated that no industry or branch of business showed any restriction, while some had been rapidly gaining, that railroads were increasing their profits while speculators sold their stocks, and that there was a growing demand for the products of all the great industries.[43]

Despite such expressions as these, there seems little reason to question the belief that an overwhelming preponderance of the vocal business interests of the country strongly desired peace. By the middle of March, however, many organs of business opinion were admitting that a war with Spain might bring no serious disaster, and there was a growing conviction

---

[37] *Rand-McNally Bankers' Monthly,* XV, 199–201 (March, 1898).

[38] *Age of Steel,* LXXXIII, Nos. 10, 11 (March 5, 12, 1898).

[39] St. Louis *Republic,* March 3, 1898.

[40] *The Tradesman,* XXXIX, 58 (March 1, 1898). The same paper, however, in its May issues, denied that any permanent good to business could result from war. *Supra,* p. 241.

[41] *Mining and Scientific Press,* LXXVI, 390 (April 9, 1898). In the issue of April 23, it remarked that war between the two chief copper-producing countries would occasion a boom in that metal. *Ibid.,* p. 438.

[42] *Wall Street Journal,* February 17, 24, 1898.

[43] *Dun's Review,* March 5, 12, 1898. *Bradstreet's,* XXVI, 161 (March 12, 1898). Similar views were expressed by the *Dry Goods Economist,* April 9, 1898.

that such a war was inevitable. In the Senate on March 17, Senator Redfield Proctor, of Vermont, described, from his own observation, the terrible sufferings of the Cuban "reconcentrados." Proctor was supposedly no sensationalist, and his speech carried great weight. The *Wall Street Journal* described its effect among the denizens of the Street. "Senator Proctor's speech," it said, "converted a great many people in Wall Street, who have heretofore taken the ground that the United States had no business to interfere in a revolution on Spanish soil. These men had been among the most prominent in deploring the whole Cuban matter, but there was no question about the accuracy of Senator Proctor's statements and as many of them expressed it, they made the blood boil." [44] The *American Banker*, hitherto a firm opponent of intervention, remarked on March 23 that Proctor's speech showed an intolerable state of things, in view of which it could not understand "how any one with a grain of human sympathy within him can dispute the propriety of a policy of intervention, so only that this outraged people might be set free!" It still hoped, however, for a peaceful solution, declaring that the United States ought to urge the Cubans to accept the Spanish offer of autonomy.[45] That this growing conviction that something must be done about Cuba was by no means equivalent to a desire for war, was clearly revealed a few days later. Rumors circulated to the effect that Spain was willing to sell Cuba and that J. P. Morgan's return from a trip abroad was connected with plans to finance the purchase. "There is much satisfaction expressed in Wall Street," said the *Wall Street Journal*, "at the prospects of having Cuba free, because it is believed that this will take one of the most disturbing factors out of the situation. . . . Even if $200,000,000 is the indemnity demanded it is a sum which the United States could well afford to pay to get rid of the trouble." Even $250,000,000, it was thought, would be insignificant in comparison with the probable cost of a war.[46]

It remains to examine the attitude of certain American business men and corporations having an immediate stake in Cuba, or otherwise liable to be directly affected by American intervention. Much American capital, as is well known, was invested in the Cuban sugar industry. Upon this industry the civil war fell with peculiarly devastating effect, not only cutting off profits on capital so invested, but also crippling a valuable carrying trade between Cuba and the United States. Naturally enough, some firms suffering under these conditions desired to see the United States intervene to

---

[44] *Wall Street Journal*, March 19, 1898. It was at this time that W. C. Beer, attempting to estimate the strength of war sentiment for the life insurance companies, noted (in the words of Thomas Beer) "that the solidarity of Wall Street was imperfect. John Jacob Astor wore a buttonhole of red, white, and blue flowers. John Gates, Thomas Fortune Ryan, Wm. Rockefeller and Stuyvesant Fish all were sounded before March 24, and were found to be feeling militant." Beer thought the only steady opponents of war were the life insurance people and the small bankers. Thomas Beer, *Hanna*, pp. 199–200.
[45] *American Banker*, LXIII, 489.   [46] *Wall Street Journal*, March 31, April 1, 1898.

end the war, though such intervention might lead to war between the United States and Spain. In May, 1897, a memorial on the subject bearing over three hundred signatures was presented to John Sherman, Secretary of State. The signers described themselves as "citizens of the United States, doing business as bankers, merchants, manufacturers, steamship owners and agents in the cities of Boston, New York, Philadelphia, Baltimore, Savannah, Charleston, Jacksonville, New Orleans, and other places, and also other citizens of the United States, who have been for many years engaged in the export and import trade with the Island of Cuba." They called attention to the serious losses to which their businesses had been subjected by the hostilities in Cuba and expressed the hope that, in order to prevent further loss, to reestablish American commerce, and also to secure "the blessings of peace for one and a half millions of residents of the Island of Cuba now enduring unspeakable distress and suffering," the United States Government might take steps to bring about an honorable reconciliation between the parties to the conflict.[47]

Another memorial, signed by many of the same subscribers, was presented to President McKinley on February 9, 1898, by a committee of New York business men. It asserted that the Cuban war, which had now continued for three entire years, had caused an average loss of $100,000,000 a year, or a total loss of $300,000,000 in the import and export trade between Cuba and the United States, to which were to be added "heavy sums irretrievably lost by the destruction of American properties, or properties supported by American capital in the Island itself, such as sugar factories, railways, tobacco plantations, mines and other industrial enterprises; the loss of the United States in trade and capital by means of this war being probably far greater and more serious than that of all the other parties concerned, not excepting Spain herself."

The sugar crop of 1897–1898, continued the memorial, appeared for the most part lost like its two predecessors, and unless peace could be established before May or June of the current year, the crop of 1898–1899, with all the business dependent upon it, would likewise be lost, since the rainy season of summer and fall would be required "to prepare for next winter's crop, by repairing damaged fields, machinery, lines of railways, &c." In view of the importance to the United States of the Cuban trade and of American participation "in the ownership or management of Cuban sugar factories, railways and other enterprises," the petitioners hoped that the President would deem the situation "of sufficient importance as to warrant prompt and efficient measures by our Government, with the sole object of restoring

---

[47] *Miscellaneous Letters* (Dept. of State), May, 1897, II. The memorial is covered by a letter from Geo. R. Mosle (of Mosle Bros., 16 Exchange Place, New York) to Hon. John Sherman, May 17, 1897. The list of signers is headed by Lawrence Turnure & Co.; August Belmont & Co. appear near the top.

peace . . . and with it restoring to us a most valuable commercial field." [48]

How much weight such pressure from special interests had with the administration there is no way of knowing. But it is to be noted that the pressure from parties directly interested was not all on one side. Mr. E. F. Atkins, an American citizen who divided his time between Boston and his sugar plantation of Soledad near Cienfuegos, Cuba, which he had developed at a cost of $1,400,000, had been able, through protection received from the Spanish Government and through a corps of guards organized and paid by himself, to continue operations throughout the period of the insurrection. He was frequently in Washington, where he had influential friends, during both the Cleveland and McKinley administrations and worked consistently against the adoption of any measures likely to provoke war.[49]

Unlike some of the sugar plantations, American-owned iron mines in Cuba continued to do active business despite the insurrection. Three American iron and manganese enterprises in the single province of Santiago claimed to have an investment of some $6,000,000 of purely American capital, a large proportion of which was in property which could easily be destroyed. "We are fully advised as to our status in case of war," wrote the representative of one company to the Assistant Secretary of State, "and that this property might be subject to confiscation or destruction by the Spanish Government." War between Spain and the United States, wrote the president of another company, "will very likely mean the destruction of our valuable plant and in any event untold loss to our company and its American stockholders." [50] An American cork company with large interests in Spain; a New York merchant with trade in the Mediterranean and Black Sea; a Mobile firm which had chartered a Spanish ship to carry a cargo of timber—these are samples of American business interests which saw in war the threat of direct damage to themselves.[51] They are hardly offset by the high hopes of an enterprising gentleman of Norfolk, "representing a party of capitalists who are enthusiastic supporters of the Gov-

---

[48] *Ibid.*, February, 1898, I. The memorial was signed by seventy persons or firms from New York and nearby cities; forty from Philadelphia; and sixty-four from Mobile. It was presented to the President on the morning of February 9, 1898, by George R. Mosle, Wm. Moore Carson, and George Turnure, and thereafter, at the President's suggestion, sent to Assistant Secretary Wm. R. Day. See accompanying letter from the committee to Mr. Day.

[49] E. F. Atkins, *Sixty Years in Cuba*, pp. 209, 212, 274, *et passim*. Atkins's attitude is illustrated by his query (p. 209) "whether the sentimental feeling of sympathy with the Cubans should outweigh the property interests amounting to some $30,000,000 of United States citizens in Cuba.

[50] Juragua Iron Co., Ltd. (per Josiah Monroe, Secy. and Treas.) to Day, Philadelphia, April 14, 1898. *Miscellaneous Letters* (Dept. of State), April, 1898, II. Spanish-American Iron Co. (per C. F. Rand, Pres.) to Day, New York, April 8, 1898. *Ibid.*, April, 1898, I.

[51] Armstrong Cork Co. to Secretary Sherman, March 8, 1898. *Ibid.*, March, 1898, I. John Duer to Department of State (telegram), March 28, 1898; R. H. Clarke (Mobile) to Hon. J. Wheeler, March 26, 1898. *Ibid.*, March, 1898, III.

ernment," who applied to the State Department for a letter of marque "to enable us to lawfully capture Spanish merchant vessels and torpedo boats," adding: "We have secured option on a fine steam vessel, and on receipt of proper documents will put to sea forth with." [52]

It seems safe to conclude, from the evidence available, that the only important business interests (other than the business of sensational journalism) which clamored for intervention in Cuba were those directly or indirectly concerned in the Cuban sugar industry; that opposed to intervention were the influence of other parties (including at least one prominent sugar planter) whose business would suffer direct injury from war and also the overwhelming preponderance of general business opinion. After the middle of March, 1898, some conservative editors came to think intervention inevitable on humanitarian grounds, but many of the most influential business journals opposed it to the end.[53]

We can now turn to the question whether American business was imperialistic; whether, in other words, business opinion favored schemes for acquiring foreign territory to supply it with markets, fields for capital investment, or commercial and naval stations in distant parts of the world. American business men were not unaware of the struggle for colonies then raging among European nations. Did they feel that the United States ought to participate in that struggle?

We have seen above that the rising tide of prosperity was intimately connected with the increase in American exports, particularly of manufactured articles. That the future welfare of American industry was dependent upon the command of foreign markets was an opinion so common as to appear almost universal. The New York *Journal of Commerce* pointed out, early in 1897, that the nation's industrial plant had been developed far beyond the needs of domestic consumption. In the wire nail industry there was said to be machinery to make four times as many nails as the American markets could consume. Rail mills, locomotive shops, and glass factories were in a similar situation. "Nature has thus destined this country for the industrial supremacy of the world," said the same paper later in the year.[54] When the National Association of Manufacturers met in New York for its annual convention in January, 1898, "the discussion of ways and means for extending this country's trade, and more particularly its export business, was, in fact, almost the single theme of the speakers," according to *Bradstreet's*, which added the comment: "Nothing is more significant of the changed attitude toward this country's foreign trade, manifested by the American manufacturer today as compared with a few years ago, than the

---

[52] C. R. Fowles to Secretary Alger, April 23, 1898. *Ibid.*, April, 1898, III.

[53] *Com. & Fin. Chron.*, LXVI, 732 (April 16, 1898); *Journal of Commerce and Commercial Bulletin*, April 23, 1898; Boston *Journal of Commerce*, April 16, 1898; *U. S. Investor*, IX, 529 (April 9, 1898).

[54] *Journal of Commerce and Commercial Bulletin*, February 24, May 27, 1897.

almost single devotion which he pays to the subject of possible export-trade extension." [55]

But if business men believed, prior to the opening of the war with Spain, that foreign markets were to be secured through the acquisition of colonies, they were strangely silent about it. To the program of colonial expansion which for almost a decade had been urged by such men as Mahan, Albert Shaw, Lodge, Roosevelt, and Morgan, business had remained, to all appearances, either indifferent or antagonistic. To the business man, such a program was merely one form of dangerous jingoism. A large section of business opinion had, indeed, favored plans for the building of a Nicaraguan canal with governmental assistance,[56] and some spokesmen for business had favored annexation of the Hawaiian Islands.[57] But beyond these relatively modest projects few business men, apparently, wished to go.[58] Two of the most important commercial journals, the New York *Journal of Commerce* and the *Commercial and Financial Chronicle,* had stoutly opposed both the canal scheme and Hawaiian annexation.[59] The former satirized the arguments of the proponents of both schemes. "We must certainly build the canal to defend the islands, and it is quite clear that we must acquire the islands . . . in order to defend the canal." The canal was not only unnecessary, but unless fortified at each end and patrolled by two fleets, it would be a positive misfortune. Such protection—"the price of jingoism"—

---

[55] *Bradstreet's*, XXVI, 66 (January 29, 1898). *Cf. American Banker*, LXII, 817 (May 12, 1897); *U. S. Investor*, IX, 400–401 (March 19, 1898); *Dry Goods Economist*, January 1, 1898; *American Wool and Cotton Reporter*, XII, 380 (March 24, 1898); *Tradesman*, XXXIX, 52 (June 15, 1898). The National Board of Trade, at its annual meeting in Washington in December, 1897, recommended various measures for the further extension of export trade. *Proceedings of the 28th Annual Meeting* of the National Board of Trade, pp. 337–338.

[56] The National Board of Trade, a federation of local boards of trade, chambers of commerce, etc., in all parts of the country, consistently urged construction of the canal. *Cf. Proceedings* of its 28th annual meeting, p. 335. *Cf.* also Indianapolis Board of Trade, *Annual Report for Year Ending June 1, 1898*, p. 18; Philadelphia Board of Trade, *65th Annual Report*, pp. 25–26; Merchant's Exchange of St. Louis, *Annual Statement of the Trade and Commerce of St. Louis for Year 1898*, p. 17; Chamber of Commerce of San Francisco, *48th Annual Report*, p. 18. The National Association of Manufacturers, at its January, 1897, meeting, took "strong ground in favor of the Nicaragua Canal." *Journal of Commerce and Commercial Bulletin*, January 25, 1897.

[57] *Cf. Bradstreet's* XXV, 386 (June 19, 1897); New York *Commercial*, April 30, 1898; San Francisco Chamber of Commerce, *48th Annual Report*, p. 18.

[58] Exceptions to this general rule were the *Financial Record*, which was pro-war (as shown above) and which also hailed the prospect of colonial responsibilities (June 23, 1897, March 23, 1898); and the New York *Commercial*, which thought the United States should not only annex Cuba and Puerto Rico but should also buy St. Thomas from Denmark for a naval station (March 31, April 8, 1898). The *American Banker*, in April, 1898, thought it would be good business to buy Cuba, pay for it in silver, and set it up as an American protectorate. It remarked: "A nation that borrows foreign capital, and in fact mortgages its resources to foreigners, must expect when it becomes unable to pay to be interfered with from without." *American Banker*, LVI, 517–520.

[59] *Com. & Fin. Chron.*, LXIV, 211–213, 1205–1207 (January 30, June 26, 1897); *Journal of Com. & Com. Bull.*, June 17, August 14, 1897.

might "easily cost us $25,000,000 a year, besides the lump sum that will be required for the original investment, and there is absolutely no excuse whatever in our commercial or our political interests for a single step in this long procession of expenses and of complications with foreign powers." [60] As for Hawaii and Cuba, neither was fit for self-government as a state,—and the American constitution provided no machinery for governing dependencies. The Hawaiian Islands would have no military value unless the United States were to build a great navy and take an aggressive attitude in the Pacific.[61] The *Commercial and Financial Chronicle* saw in colonies only useless outposts which must be protected at great expense, and the St. Louis *Age of Steel* warned lest the expansion of the export trade might "lead to territorial greed, as in the case of older nations, the price of which in armaments and militarism offsets the gain made by the spindle and the forge." [62]

Colonies were not only certain to bear a fruit of danger and expense; they were valueless from the commercial point of view. Did not the colonies of Great Britain afford us one of the most valuable of our export markets? [63] Did we not trade as advantageously with Guiana, a British colony, as with independent Venezuela? "Most of our ideas of the commercial value of conquests, the commercial use of navies and the commercial advantages of political control," said the New York *Journal of Commerce,* dated back to times when colonial policies were designed to monopolize colonial trade for the mother country.[64] The *Commercial and Financial Chronicle* believed that the current European enthusiasm for colonies was based on false premises; for although trade often followed the flag, "the trade is not always with the home markets of the colonizer. England and the United States are quite as apt to slip in with their wares under the very Custom-House pennant of the French or German dependency." [65] Outright opposition, such as this, to the idea of colonial expansion is not common in the business periodicals examined; much more common is complete silence on the subject. Positive and negative evidence together seem to warrant the conclusion that American business in general, at the opening of 1898, was either indifferent to imperialism, or definitely opposed. . . .

In the light of . . . [the] widespread and intense interest in the preserva-

---

[60] *Journal of Com. & Com. Bull.,* September 8, 1897.

[61] *Ibid.,* June 17, October 21, 1897. Similarly, the *U. S. Investor* regarded Hawaiian annexation as a "menace," and the *Banker and Tradesman* thought the people of Cuba were "incapable and unfit for self-government. . . . This country does not want Cuba." *U. S. Investor,* IX, 48 (January 8, 1898); *Banker and Tradesman,* XXVI, 161 (March 16, 1898).

[62] *Com. & Fin. Chron.,* LXVI, 446–448 (March 5, 1898); *Age of Steel,* LXXXIII, No. 1, p. 57 (January 1, 1898).

[63] Baltimore Chamber of Commerce, *43rd Annual Report,* p. 11. Address of the president, Robert Ramsay, January 31, 1898.

[64] *Jour. of Com. & Com. Bull.,* January 24, 1896.

[65] *Com. & Fin. Chron.,* LXV, 1147–1148 (December 18, 1897).

tion of the Chinese market, we can perhaps understand why American business, which had been, to all appearances, anti-war and anti-imperialist, was filled with sudden enthusiasm at the news of Dewey's victory at Manila Bay. Not only did the news dissipate all fears of a long and costly war and send stock prices rapidly upward;[66] still more important, it seemed to place in American hands, all unexpectedly, the key to the trade of the Orient. The attack on the Spanish fleet at Manila had been anticipated for months and well advertised by the American press.[67] Some papers had speculated upon the value of the islands as an American colony and had foreseen that a victory there might greatly alter our relation to the imbroglio in China.[68] But for most, this thought did not occur until arrival of the news that the Spanish fleet was destroyed and Dewey safely in possession of Manila Bay. Then, at last, business men joined the jingoes in their acclaim of imperial conquests. Senator Lodge's exclamation—"We hold the other side of the Pacific, and the value to this country is almost beyond recognition"—was matched by many a formerly conservative business journal. It was not the intrinsic value of the Philippines or their trade that most impressed American writers, though this angle of the subject was not overlooked.[69] Rather, their importance appeared to lie in their position as a gateway to the markets of Eastern Asia. . . .

---

[66] *Dun's Review*, May 7, 1898, said railway stocks had advanced on the average of $2.79 per share since the news, adding: "One day's work by the officers and men at Manila has given many days' work to thousands of people at home . . . and has placed all American industries and interests on a stronger footing for any conceivable future." Cf. *Jour. of Com. & Com. Bull.*, May 3, 1898; *Com. & Fin. Chron.*, LXVI, 874 (May 7, 1898).

[67] New York *Sun*, November 8, 1897, March 13, 1898.

[68] The *U. S. Investor*, IX, 624 (April 30, 1898) thought that such a victory, even if we did not retain the islands, "might pave the way for future interventions on the part of the United States in the affairs of the East." The *Financial Record*, May 5, 1898 (in an editorial written before receipt of the news of the battle), thought the Philippines" would be good trading material for getting our share of what is going in Asia." Cf. New York *Commercial*, April 27, 1898; New York *Sun*, April 29, 1898.

[69] The New York *Commercial*, May 7, 1898, declared the Philippines were "treasure islands"—"the richest islands in the world." Their development by American capital, it said (June 7), would stimulate the trade of the Pacific Coast and promote the establishment of new industries in the West. The *Daily Commercial News and Shipping List* of San Francisco also saw great possibilities of trade with the islands (May 13) and hailed the prospect of "Gold in the Philippines" (June 17). Cf. Chattanooga *Tradesman*, May 15, 1898.

Approach to War

Walter LaFeber

THE AMERICAN BUSINESS COMMUNITY
BEFORE THE WAR WITH SPAIN, 1897
TO FEBRUARY, 1898

During the eighteen months before the United States went to war with Spain, American businessmen began their most intensive search for foreign markets. A Mexico City newspaper marveled, in fact, that "enterprising manufacturers" in the United States "are able, by unremitting effort, to overcome the obstacles raised by the legislators at Washington." To outdistance the McKinley administration in the quest for foreign markets required some hard running. At approximately the same time the Mexico City journal printed its comment, McKinley was declaring that he wanted to climax his career by making the United States supreme in the markets of the world. These two factors—the intensive search by American producers for foreign markets, and the McKinley administration's urgent desire to aid the business community in this venture—are the two clues to understanding the economic aspects of the new empire in 1897 and 1898.[1]

. . . As the United States entered the new year of 1898, new syndicates and lobbying groups were organizing to advance American economic interests in the Orient. The Bureau of American Republics was having difficulty in meeting the mounting demand from businessmen who sought information and aid in finding new Latin-American markets. In March, 1898, the New York *Commercial Advertiser* could justifiably brag of the existence of "a new Monroe doctrine, not of political principles, but of commercial policy. . . . Instead of laying down dogmas, it figures up profits." [2] The Chattanooga *Tradesman* lost all restraint in proclaiming, "The Baltic trade properly belongs to the Americans, especially to those in the South." [3] In

---

From Walter LaFeber, *The New Empire: An Interpretation of American Expansion, 1860–1898* (Ithaca: Cornell University Press, 1963). © 1963 by the American Historical Association. Used by permission of Cornell University Press. Pp. 370, 378–379, 383–406.

[1] *Public Opinion*, July 8, 1897, 37; Leech, *Days of McKinley*, 142.

[2] Joseph P. Smith to McKinley, July 31, 1897, and Smith to Porter, Dec. 1, 1897, McKinley MSS; *Commercial Advertiser*, March 7, 1898, 6:2.

[3] Chattanooga *Tradesman*, Jan. 1, 1898, 102.

summary, the American business community would not suddenly discover the advantage of and need for foreign markets during and after the Spanish-American War. Indeed, the American businessman's quest for these markets was one of the most striking characteristics of the national scene in the months immediately preceding the war with Spain. The results of this war provided these businessmen with new opportunities for further economic expansion. But the war did not provide the impetus for this expansion. The impetus had been provided by the impact of the industrial revolution, especially the depression that followed the panic of 1893.

THE DECISION FOR WAR

. . . This interest in the Far East* was in the background—but the immediate background—when, in late March, McKinley decided to make ultimate demands of Spain. Sometime between March 18 and 27 the President decided that war was inevitable unless Spain was prepared to surrender Cuba, an action which the Sagasta ministry could not take without threatening its own political life and that of the Spanish monarchy. Several developments forced McKinley to make this decision at this time. The administration had concluded that the Sagasta reform program, hardly three months old, was a failure. Another reason was the President's fear that after the publication of the report of the "Maine" investigating commission Congress would be uncontrollable. This factor, however, probably played only a minor role when McKinley formulated his final policy. Two other factors were of greater importance: the fear of political repercussions on the Republican party, and, perhaps most important, the growing belief of many sections of the business community that somehow the disturbances on the island would have to be terminated before the United States could enjoy full prosperity.

Elections in 1897 had not gone well for McKinley's party, nor had more recent elections in New York and Kentucky. During the first three months of 1898 the President and other Republican leaders received many letters which drew bleak pictures of the party's future if the administration failed to deal with Cuba immediately. McKinley's letters on this point were capped with a long message from Henry Cabot Lodge on March 21. Lodge had recently returned from taking a private poll of Massachusetts opinion. The Senator first assured McKinley that the masses were firmly behind the administration. But, Lodge continued, "if the war in Cuba drags on through the summer with nothing done we should go down in the greatest defeat ever known before the cry 'Why have you not settled the Cuban question.' " Clarence Cary, who opposed a strong Cuban policy, wrote in the *Journal*

---

* Editor's note: The reference is to the threat to the Open Door posed by Russia and Germany in particular.

of Commerce in late March that mail was pouring in "even from conservative city districts" warning of the Republican losses which would inevitably result if the Democrats could "proclaim from every stump that it was they who forced the hand of the Republican President and with the aid of a few Republicans secured the liberty of Cuba." These letters, Cary concluded, were having a "potent effect." [4]

Most of the "conservative city districts" which Cary mentioned had long opposed war with Spain.[5] There were exceptions, however. The American business community was by no means monolithic in its opposition to war. To say as a generalization that businessmen opposed war is as erroneous as saying that businessmen wanted war. It is possible to suggest, however, that by the middle of March important businessmen and spokesmen for the business community were advocating war. It is also possible to suggest that at the same time, a shift seemed to be occurring in the general business community regarding its over-all views on the desirability of war.

Financial journals which advocated bimetallism had long urged a stronger attitude toward Spain in the hope that the resulting conflict would force the Treasury to pay expenses in silver. More important, business spokesmen in such midwestern and western cities as Cincinnati, Louisville, St. Louis, Chicago, San Francisco, and especially Pittsburgh were not reluctant to admit that they would welcome war. The Louisville *Commercial* believed, "Only a few of the eastern newspapers are pessimistic as to the business outlook at the beginning of war. . . . Everywhere in the west and south there is a disposition among businessmen . . . to keep their feet, and their heads, too." This journal was not reticent in providing its own viewpoint: if war occurred, transportation lines would prosper, "other enterprises would find more profit and securities would go up all along the line. Nor would the credit of the United States be in the least impaired." The Pittsburgh *Press,* mouthpiece for that area's booming steel interests, strongly supported the Cincinnati businessmen's resolutions that asked for war. The *Press* added, "It is not to be doubted that this expresses the feeling of the real business interests of the country. . . . The mistake made in some quarters is supposing that the stock jobbers are the business interests." [6]

The Pittsburgh *Press* represented one of the special interests that would benefit from war. The Pittsburgh Chamber of Commerce also advocated the use of force, and the Chattanooga *Tradesman* suggested one reason why: the "small prospect" of conflict, the *Tradesman* noted on March 1, "has

---

[4] Lodge to McKinley, March 21, 1898, McKinley MSS; *Journal of Commerce,* March 30, 1898, 1:5.

[5] Julius Pratt discusses this opposition in detail in ch. vii of his *Expansionists of 1898;* see also Boston *Herald,* March 6, 1898, 12:13; and *Journal of Commerce,* April 1, 1898, 6:2–3.

[6] Louisville *Commercial,* April 14, 1898, 4:1; March 5, 1898, 4:2; Cincinnati *Commercial Tribune,* March 30, 1898, 10:1; Pittsburgh *Press,* March 30, 1898, 4:1; Pratt, *Expansionists of 1898,* 243–244.

decidedly stimulated the iron trade." This journal, which did not want war, also commented, "Actual war would very decidedly enlarge the business of transportation," especially railroads. William E. Curtis wrote from Washington that the "belligerent spirit" which had infected everyone in the Navy Department, with the possible exception of Secretary Long, had been encouraged "by the contractors for projectiles, ordnance, ammunition and other supplies, who have thronged the department since the destruction of the *Maine*." These contractors, Curtis charged, had also assisted "correspondents of sensational newspapers in manufacturing canards and scare news." [7]

A strong possibility exists that the antiwar commercial journals in New York spoke for the less important members of that financial community. Russell Sage, claiming that he spoke "not only my own views on this point, but those of other moneyed men with whom I have talked," demanded that if the "Maine" was blown up by an outside force "the time for action has come. There should be no wavering." If war did occur, "There is no question as to where the rich men stand"; they would buy government bonds as they had during the Civil War and do all in their power to bolster the nation's war resources. W. C. Beer, who attempted to make a thorough survey of leading businessmen's opinion, concluded that "the steady opponents of the war among financiers were simply the life insurance men and small bankers." Beer found such giants as John Jacob Astor, John Gates, Thomas Fortune Ryan, William Rockefeller, and Stuyvesant Fish "feeling militant." On March 28 J. Pierpont Morgan declared that further talk of arbitration would accomplish nothing.[8]

Beer's findings can be supplemented with an analysis of the membership of the Cuban League of the United States. This organization began advertising in early 1897 that it would gladly receive donations to finance its efforts to free Cuba from Spanish control. As a part of these efforts, the league sold bonds for the Cuban Junta. This organization included such militants as Theodore Roosevelt, Colonel Ethan Allen, and Charles A. Dana. But the following conservative businessmen were among the Vice-Presidents: J. Edward Simmons, former President of the New York Stock Exchange, President of the Fourth National Bank of New York; Thomas F. Gilroy, builder and real estate operator in New York City; Chauncey M. Depew, railroad president and director of numerous railway and banking corporations; Thomas L. James, Chairman of the Board of Lincoln National Bank in New York City, President of the Lincoln Safe Deposit Company; John R. Dos Passos, New York lawyer who engaged in banking, corporate, and financial law and who had been active in the formation of large business amalgamations, including the sugar trust. Seated on the

---

[7] *Tradesman*, March 1, 1898, 58; *Journal of Commerce*, April 7, 1898, 6:3. Curtis' statement is in the Pittsburgh *Press*, March 16, 1898, 1:1.

[8] New York *Tribune*, Feb. 27, 1898, 5:1; Thomas Beer, *Hanna* (New York, 1929), 199–200.

Board of Directors were General Daniel Butterfield, Civil War hero, bank president, and Executive Officer of the Steam Boat and Ferry Company; and Colonel John Jacob Astor.[9]

A group of interests that depended upon Cuban trade formed another category of business support which demanded that the revolution be terminated. A group of importers, exporters, bankers, manufacturers, and steamship and vessel owners sent McKinley a petition in February, 1898, which noted that the fighting had created a loss of one hundred million dollars a year in business conducted directly with the island, not to mention the destruction of American properties on the island. The petition demanded peace before the rainy season in May; otherwise, the sugar crop of 1898 and 1899 would be ruined. Those who signed this petition included "a large number of well-known and influential firms" in New York City, the New York *Tribune* noted, and also the names of businessmen in Philadelphia and Mobile.[10]

The petition noted the immense losses suffered by property owners and merchants who had invested in the island itself. By early 1898 these persons were becoming alarmed about something other than the day-to-day destruction of property, although this was certainly troublesome. The State Department began receiving reports that, as Fitzhugh Lee phrased the problem, "there may be a revolution within a revolution." Conservative interests feared that continued Spanish rule or autonomy, no matter how developed, would result in Cuban radical forces gaining control of the government. A strong feeling was growing which demanded American intervention to end this threat. The American Consul in Santiago summarized this feeling on March 23, 1898: "Property holders without distinction of nationality, and with but few exceptions, strongly desire annexation, having but little hope of a stable government under either of the contending forces. . . . [B]ut such a move would not be popular among the masses." These interests, the Consul reported, regretted that Americans did not favor outright, immediate annexation. McKinley learned of this sentiment from a letter written by "a gentleman of high standing, who has close personal relations with influential Cubans who have favored the rebellion," as Levi P. Morton, former Vice-President under Harrison and a wheel-horse of the Republican party, described the author. This letter warned that the rebellion had to end quickly or the radical classes would come to power. The writer believed that educated and wealthy backers of the rebellion now wanted either annexation or autonomy under American control. "They are most pronounced in their fears," he continued, "that independence, if ob-

---

[9] *Review of Reviews*, XV (February, 1897), 137; *Who Was Who in America*, I (1897–1942) (Chicago, 1943).

[10] New York *Tribune*, Feb. 10, 1898, 2:3.

tained, would result in the troublesome, adventurous and non-responsible class" seizing power.[11]

Many of these businessmen in Cuba hoped that annexation could be accomplished through peaceful means, but they found themselves trapped when they realized that Spain would not surrender her sovereignty on American terms without war. Among those who were so trapped was Edwin F. Atkins, one of the largest American investors in Cuban plantations. He deprecated the possibility of war on behalf of the insurgents, especially since the protection provided by Spanish troops enabled his plantations to continue their harvests throughout the revolution. But as early as January, 1897, Atkins had written Lodge that the best thing that could happen would be the annexation of Cuba by the United States. Other investors, however, evaded this trap by hoping for, or openly advocating, forceful American intervention. Fitzhugh Lee wrote Day in January, 1898, "The Spanish merchants and property holders generally favor some form of intervention on the part of the United States, but are prevented from an open expression on the subject lest they be disturbed by the soldier element." The New York *Tribune* noted in a front-page story on March 14, 1898, that European, especially British, capital had been flowing into Cuba in the belief that the United States would shortly replace Spain as the sovereign power. "Large enterprises welcome peace or forcible intervention as the means of freeing them from burdens," the article continued. "The Government [of Cuba] owes everybody," the *Tribune* observed, especially the large utility and railroad companies.[12]

Perhaps the American business community exerted the most influence on the administration during the last two weeks in March when influential business spokesmen began to welcome the possibility of war in order to end the suspense which shrouded the commercial exchanges. Although other historians have touched briefly on this important change,[13] it should be noted that some important business spokesmen and President McKinley apparently arrived at this decision at approximately the same time.

During the first two months of 1898 the United States began to enjoy prosperous conditions for the first time in five years. The de Lôme and "Maine" incidents affected business conditions only in the stock exchanges, and even there the impact was slight. Business improved, especially in the West and Northwest. In early March very few business journals feared a return of depression conditions, and with the gold influx resulting from

---

[11] Lee to Day, Nov. 27, 1897, Consular, Havana; and Hyatt to Day, March 23, 1898, Consular, Santiago, NA, RG 59; enclosure in Levi P. Morton to McKinley, March 20, 1898, McKinley MSS.

[12] Atkins' views are in Lodge to Charles Francis Adams, Jan. 22, 1897, Letterbooks, Lodge MSS; Lee to Day, Jan. 18, 1898, Consular, Havana, NA, RG 59; New York *Tribune*, March 14, 1898, 1:6; Barrington to Salisbury, Nov. 11, 1897, Salisbury MSS.

[13] See especially Pratt, *Expansionists of 1898*, 246–247.

discoveries in Alaska and from the export surplus, even fewer business observers displayed anxiety over the silver threat.[14]

But in mid-March financial reporters noted that business in commodities as well as stocks had suddenly slowed. Henry Clay Frick had been optimistic in his business reports to Andrew Carnegie, who was vacationing in Scotland. But on March 24, Frick reported that "owing to uncertainty . . . of the Cuban trouble, business is rather stagnant." A Wall Street correspondent wrote on March 22 that "the last two days have been the dullest for many a month." On March 26 the *Commercial and Financial Chronicle* summarized the situation. No "sudden and violent drop in prices" had occurred. But the rapid progress in trade had stopped and now "frequent complaints are heard. The volume of trade undoubtedly remains large, but the reports speak of new enterprises being held in check." [15]

Businessmen had been particularly influenced by the speech of Senator Redfield Proctor of Vermont on March 17. Proctor was known for his conservative, antiwar disposition, an attitude he shared with his intimate friend, William McKinley. But the Senator had just returned from a visit to Cuba, a visit that had profoundly shocked him. Proctor discounted Spanish reforms as "too late," but he advised against going to war over the "Maine." The United States should use force, Proctor intimated, only to deliver the Cuban people from "the worst misgovernment of which I ever had knowledge." Conversations with businessmen in Cuba had provided him with most of his information; these men had declared "without exception" that it was too late for any more schemes of autonomy. They wanted an American protectorate, annexation, or a free Cuba. Although Proctor did not say so explicitly, none of these solutions was immediately possible without war with Spain. This speech deeply impressed almost all of the conservative and business journals which had opposed war. Many of these journals did not overlook Proctor's role as one of McKinley's "most trusted advisors and friends." Two weeks later the New York *Commercial Advertiser* looked back and marked this speech as the turning point in the road to war.[16]

This journal had steadily attacked the jingoes throughout January and February. But on March 10 it began to rationalize intervention not for "conquest," but for "humanity and love of freedom, and, above all, [the] desire that the commerce and industry of every part of the world shall have full freedom of development in the whole world's interest," especially "in that of nations in position to trade with it." In the week following Proctor's speech, important business opinion, tired of what the *Economist's* correspondent termed "the sudden revolutions of sentiment," began to fall

---

[14] *Bradstreet's*, March 12, 1898, 161, 170; March 19, 1898, 186; March 26, 1898, 202; *Economist*, March 5, 1898, 356; *Journal of Commerce*, March 26, 1898, 6:5.

[15] Frick to Carnegie, March 24, 1898, Carnegie MSS; *Economist*, April 5, 1898, 356; *Commercial and Financial Chronicle*, March 26, 1898, 590.

[16] The speech is in *Congressional Record*, 55th Cong., 2nd Sess., 2916–2919; *Public Opinion*, March 24, 1898, 358–360; *Commercial Advertiser*, April 2, 1898.

into line back of the *Commercial Advertiser*. The *Wall Street Journal* noted that Proctor's speech had "converted a great many people in Wall Street" who had formerly opposed war. The *Journal of Commerce* asked for "one result or the other" to end the "present uncertainty," and wanted to present Spain with an ultimatum. The Pittsburgh *Press* noted business indecision on March 19, then remarked, "The sooner the administration executes its Cuban program the better." The Philadelphia *Press*, which was quite close to the administration, reported on March 21 that McKinley would make his final decision during the next few days. On the same day as this *Press* report, Lodge wrote McKinley a long letter assuring the President: "I talked with bankers, brokers, businessmen, editors, clergymen and others in Boston," Lynn, and Nahant, and "everybody" including "the most conservative classes" wanted the Cuban question "solved." "They said," Lodge reported, "for business one shock and then an end was better than a succession of spasms such as we must have if this war in Cuba went on." [17]

Perhaps the most influential note the President received that week was a telegram from W. C. Reick, a trusted political adviser in New York City and city editor of the New York *Herald*. This message arrived at the White House on March 25: "Big corporations here now believe we will have war. Believe all would welcome it as relief to suspense." On March 27, the New York *Tribune* ran a front-page article which indicated that Reick's evaluation also applied to the London Stock Exchange, a financial institution which some American investors considered of more importance than the New York Exchange. "What is wanted first of all is relief from the suspense. . . . Even a declaration of war would be preferred by bankers and stockbrokers to the continuance of a stagnant market, with hourly flurries, caused by sensational journalism and the rumors of impending hostilities," the *Tribune* reported. If war occurred, a "speculators' movement" might result in a "temporary flurry in American stocks." But other investors would hold their securities "in confident expectation that these will rise with the increased movement of railway traffic caused by war." [18]

Two days after the receipt of Reick's telegram, McKinley and Day presented an ultimatum to Spain. This move climaxed a week of hurried consultations and policy changes. Before March 20 the President had considered purchasing the island or attempting to work out a plan which would

---

[17] *Ibid.*, March 10, 1898; *Economists*, April 9, 1898, 556; Pratt, *Expansionists of 1898*, 246; *Journal of Commerce*, March 14, 1898, 6:2–3; March 23, 1898, 6:1; Pittsburgh *Press*, March 19, 1898, 1:1; Philadelphia *Press*, March 21, 1898, 6:2; Lodge to McKinley, March 21, 1898, McKinley MSS.

[18] Reick to John Russell Young, March 25, 1898, McKinley MSS; New York *Tribune*, March 27, 1898, 1:6. The *Tribune* reported on March 25, 1898, 1:1, that a movement had begun on Lombard Street to stop the war by helping Spain pay an indemnity to the United States. American bankers were reported to be organizing the drive, supposedly with help from the Rothschilds. Diplomats doubted whether the bankers would achieve any success.

ensure American control while maintaining the trappings of Spanish sovereignty. Spain refused to sell the island, however, and the Junta and the rebels on the island would not listen to the second proposal. Now in the new climate created by Proctor's speech and the changing ideas of the business community, McKinley prepared to take more forceful steps. For the first time in the crisis the President called in a number of Democratic senators for consultations on March 22. Doubtlessly reflecting the changed attitudes of both McKinley and some business spokesmen, the war party in the Senate now claimed for the first time a majority of the forty-three Republicans, including representatives of the large corporations. These changes threatened to provoke Congress into its most belligerent outbursts on March 29 and 30.[19]

The President, however, was a week ahead of the war party on Capitol Hill. On March 20 Day instructed Woodford to ask Spain to restore peace in Cuba promptly and make a "full reparation" for the "Maine." Noting that "feeling in the United States very acute," Day declared that "April 15th is none too early date for accomplishment of these purposes" and threatened to lay the question before Congress if Spain did not respond properly. The Spanish government asked that these demands be delayed until the Cuban parliament met, that is, until the rainy season began. Woodford replied that such a delay was not possible. When the Spanish Foreign Minister, Pio Gullón, expressed surprise "at the apparent change in the attitude of the United States," Woodford said that there had been no change; the American government had always wanted peace. The American Minister then outlined four reasons why this peace had to come immediately: first, the terrible suffering in Cuba in which "during little more than three years" the deaths "had exceeded the births by nearly four hundred thousand"; the danger of sanitary conditions breaking down and plagues and diseases threatening the United States; the American dependence upon Cuban sugar and commerce; and, finally, "the large amounts of American capital invested in Cuba." "I emphasized," Woodford reported to McKinley, "the tremendous pecuniary loss which the people of the United States suffer and must suffer until peace is restored." [20]

Despite Spain's reluctance to meet Day's demands, Woodford cabled Washington on March 25 that he believed that Spain would grant a truce which would lead to negotiations with the rebels. If these negotiations did not result in peace by mid-September, Spain and the United States would "in such event jointly compel both parties in Cuba to accept such settlement

---

[19] Leech, *Days of McKinley*, 183, 184; *Journal of Commerce*, March 30, 1898, 1:5; Washington *Evening Star*, March 23, 1898, 1:1.

[20] Day to Woodford, March 20, 1898, Spain, Instructions, NA, RG 59; Barclay to Salisbury, March 28, 1898, F.O. 72/2068; Woodford to McKinley, March 22 and 24, 1898, Spain, Despatches, NA, RG 59.

as the two Governments should then jointly advise." Woodford's comments on this offer are especially crucial in view of what was to occur on April 9 and 10. The proposition, the American Minister told McKinley, "has the advantage of immediate truce and of practical recognition by Spain of an insurgent government with which the insular congress can deal. It also admits and even invites possible intervention by the United States. It may lead to the recognition of Cuban independence during the summer." On the same day, Woodford wrote the President: "A truce once established and negotiations begun, I see but two possible results. The one will be the independence of Cuba. The other may be annexation to the United States. Truce and negotiations in Cuba mean, in my respectful judgment, that the Spanish flag is to quit Cuba." [21] At this point the Spanish government refused to put forward such an offer formally. Two weeks later, however, Spain would take the initiative in offering such an armistice, and Woodford's comments on the meaning of a truce would again be relevant.

On March 26 Day attempted to prod the Sagasta regime by demanding that Cuban independence be worked out with American mediation during an armistice period. The following day the Assistant Secretary of State issued the first points of an ultimatum: first, an armistice until October 1 during which time the President would use his friendly offices to bring permanent peace to Cuba; second, "immediate revocation of reconcentrado order." The next day, Woodford reminded Day that under the Spanish Constitution the Ministry was powerless to recognize Cuban independence or nominal sovereignty. Only the Cortes could act on these issues, and this body would not meet until April 25. Day replied that the United States demanded the immediate promise of Cuban independence. On the 29th Day cabled that negotiations for an armistice must be concluded by March 31.[22]

The Spanish reply of March 31 renounced the *reconcentrado* orders (the Spanish further modified their position on this aspect of the negotiations on April 4 and 5), but would not promise an armistice at Spain's initiative. Woodford grieved over this last point as "a question of punctilio," forced upon the Spanish government by "Spanish pride" and the threat of revolution inside the nation. The Ministry realized, the American Minister reported, "that armistice now means certain peace next autumn." Woodford continued his efforts and on April 4 Day received a copy of the latest Spanish plan for Cuban autonomy. The Assistant Secretary tersely informed Woodford, "It is not armistice," but a Spanish appeal "urging the insurgents to lay down their arms and to join with the autonomy party. . . . The President's Message," Day concluded, "will go in Wednesday afternoon." McKinley did not send in his war message for another six days, how-

---

[21] Woodford to McKinley, March 24, March 25, Spain, Despatches, NA, RG 59.
[22] Day to Woodford, March 26, 27, 28, 1898, Spain, Instructions, and Woodford to Day, March 28, 1898, Spain, Despatches, NA, RG 59.

ever. He granted Fitzhugh Lee's request for time in order to remove American citizens from Havana.[23]

On April 9 Spain granted a suspension of hostilities "in order to arrange and facilitate peace on the island." Woodford cabled immediately that this move would mean "immediate and permanent peace in Cuba by negotiations" if Congress gave the President authority to conduct such discussions and full power to use the army and navy to enforce the results of the negotiations. The American Minister told McKinley that the talks would result in autonomy which the insurgents could accept, or complete independence, or cession of the islands to the United States. "I hope," Woodford asked, "that nothing will now be done to humiliate Spain as I am satisfied that the present Government is going and is loyally ready to go as fast and as far as it can." Day replied that the President "must decline to make further suggestions" to Spain, but "that in sending in his Message tomorrow the President will acquaint Congress with this latest communication." McKinley did append the Spanish offer to the end of his war message. Both the administration and Congress then proceeded to overlook the significance that Woodford attached to the offer. During the next nine days Congress debated the means, not the question, of intervention.[24]

McKinley had had the choice of three policies which would have terminated the Cuban revolution. First, he could have left the Spanish forces and the insurgents fight until one or the other fell exhausted from the bloodshed and financial strain. During the struggle the United States could have administered food and medicine to the civilian population, a privilege which the Spanish agreed to allow in March, 1898. Second, the President could have demanded an armistice and Spanish assurances that negotiations over the summer would result in some solution which would pacify American feelings. That is to say, he could have followed Woodford's ideas. Third, McKinley could have demanded both an armistice and Spanish assurances that Cuba would become independent immediately. If Spain would not grant both of these conditions, American military intervention would result. The last was the course the President followed.

Each of these policy alternatives deserves a short analysis. For American policy makers, the first choice was the least acceptable of the three, but the United States did have to deal, nevertheless, with certain aspects of this policy. If Spain hoped to win such a conflict, she had to use both the carrot

---

[23] Woodford to McKinley, March 31 and April 1, 1898, Spain, Despatches, Day to Woodford, April 4, 1898, Spain, Instructions, and Woodford to Day, April 4, 1898, Spain, Despatches, NA, RG 59. See also comment of Leech, *Days of McKinley*, 180; and Barclay to Salisbury, March 30, 31, April 1, 1898, F.O. 72/2068.

[24] Woodford to Day, April 9, 1898, Spain, Despatches, Day to Woodford, April 10, 1898, Spain, Instructions, "Memorandum" handed to Day from Spanish Minister on April 10, 1898, Notes from Spain, and Woodford to McKinley, April 10, 1898, Spain, Despatches, NA, RG 59.

of an improved and attractive autonomy scheme and the stick of an increased and effective military force. Spain could have granted no amount of autonomy, short of complete independence, which would have satisfied the rebels, and whether Americans cared to admit it or not, they were at least partially responsible for this obstinacy on the part of the insurgents. The United States did attempt to stop filibustering expeditions, but a large number nevertheless reached Cuban shores. More important, when the Spanish Minister asked Day to disband the New York Junta, the financial taproot of the insurgent organization, the Assistant Secretary replied that "this was not possible under American law and in the present state of public feeling." Woodford had given the Spanish Queen the same reply in mid-January. It was perhaps at this point that Spain saw the last hopes for a negotiated peace begin to flicker away.[25]

Seemingly unrelated actions by the United States gave boosts to the rebel cause. The sending of the "Maine," for instance, considerably heartened the rebels; they believed that the warship diverted Spanish attention and military power from insurgent forces. When the vessel exploded, the New York Junta released a statement which did not mourn the dead sailors as much as it mourned the sudden disappearance of American power in Havana harbor.[26] The Junta interpreted the passage of the $50,000,000 war appropriation measure during the first week of March as meaning either immediate war or the preparation for war. Under such conditions, it was not odd that the rebels were reluctant to compromise their objective of complete independence.

If the insurgents would not have accepted autonomy, no matter how liberal or attractive, then Spain might have hoped to suppress the rebels with outright force. To have done so, however, the Spanish government would have had to bring its army through the rainy season with few impairments, resume to a large extent the *reconcentrado* policies, and prevent all United States aid from reaching the rebels. The first objective would have been difficult, but the last two, if carried out, would have meant war with the United States. The State Department could not allow Spain to reimpose methods even faintly resembling Weyler's techniques, nor could the Department have allowed the searching of American vessels. McKinley and the American people hoped that Spain would stop the revolution, but they also insisted on taking from Spain the only tools with which that nation could deal with the Cubans.[27]

---

[25] *Spanish Correspondence and Documents,* 91–92; Ernest May comments, "When even this personal appeal to McKinley produced no results, the Queen and her ministers had to face the fact that the United States would not help to bring about a negotiated peace" (*Imperial Democracy,* 162–163).

[26] New York *Tribune,* Feb. 17, 1898, 10:1.

[27] Chadwick denies "that the desolation of Cuba was wholly or even mainly the work of the Spanish administration" and justifies "the right under international law" of Spain

Having found this first alternative impossible to accept, McKinley might have chosen a second approach: demand an armistice and ultimate pacification of the island, but attempt to achieve this peacefully over several months and with due respect for the sovereignty of Spain. This was the alternative Woodford hoped the administration would choose. He had reported during the two weeks before McKinley's message that the Spanish had given in time and time again on points which he had believed they could not afford to grant. In spite of the threat of revolution from the army, the Queen had granted a temporary truce. The American Minister continued to ask for more time to find a peaceful settlement. On April 11, the day the war message went to Congress, Woodford wrote the President, "To-day it is just possible that Moret* and I have been right [in our pursuit of peace], but it is too soon to be jubilant." [28] The American Minister sincerely believed that the negotiations during the period of truce could, with good faith on both the American and Spanish sides, result in Spain evacuating the island. This would have to be done slowly, however. No sovereign nation could be threatened with a time limit and uncompromising demands without fighting back. The fact that Spain would not grant McKinley's demand for immediate Cuban independence makes the Spanish-American War which began in April, 1898, by no means an inevitable conflict. Any conflict is inevitable once one proud and sovereign power, dealing with a similar power, decides to abandon the conference table and issue an ultimatum. The historical problem remains: which power took the initiative in setting the conditions that resulted in armed conflict, and were those conditions justified?

By April 10 McKinley had assumed an inflexible position. The President abjured this second alternative and demanded not only a truce, but a truce which would lead to a guarantee of immediate Cuban independence obtained with the aid of American mediation. He moreover demanded such a guarantee of independence before the Cortes or the Cuban parliament, the two groups which had the constitutional power to grant such independence, were to gather for their formal sessions.[29]

The central question is, of course, why McKinley found himself in such a position on April 10 that only the third alternative was open to him. The President did not want war; he had been sincere and tireless in his efforts to maintain the peace. By mid-March, however, he was beginning to discover that, although he did not want war, he did want what only a war could provide: the disappearance of the terrible uncertainty in Ameri-

---

to use the *reconcentrado* policies to stop the revolution. On the other hand, Chadwick believes American feeling correct in protesting the Spanish carelessness in feeding and caring for the *reconcentrados* (*United States and Spain*, 486–503).

* Editor's note: Segismundo Moret, Spanish Minister for Colonies.

[28] Woodford to McKinley, April 11, 1898, Spain, Despatches, NA, RG 59.

[29] Washington *Evening Star*, April 11, 1898, 2:3, has an interesting comment from an unidentified cabinet member on the meaninglessness of the Spanish truce offer.

can political and economic life, and a solid basis from which to resume the building of the new American commercial empire. When the President made his demands, therefore, he made the ultimate demands; as far as he was concerned, a six-month period of negotiations would not serve to temper the political and economic problems in the United States, but only exacerbate them.

To say this is to raise another question: why did McKinley arrive at this position during mid-March? What were the factors which limited the President's freedom of choice and policies at this particular time? The standard interpretations of the war's causes emphasize the yellow journals and a belligerent Congress. These were doubtlessly crucial factors in shaping the course of American entry into the conflict, but they must be used carefully. A first observation should be that Congress and the yellow press, which had been loudly urging intervention ever since 1895, did not make a maiden appearance in March, 1898; new elements had to enter the scene at that time to act as the catalysts for McKinley's policy. Other facts should be noted regarding the yellow press specifically. In areas where this press supposedly was most important, such as New York City, no more than one-third of the press could be considered sensational. The strongest and most widespread prowar journalism apparently occurred in the Midwest. But there were few yellow journals there. The papers that advocated war in this section did so for reasons other than sensationalism; among these reasons were the influence of the Cuban Junta and, perhaps most important, the belief that the United States possessed important interests in the Caribbean area which had to be protected. Finally, the yellow press obviously did not control the levers of American foreign policy. McKinley held these, and he bitterly attacked the owners of the sensational journals as "evil disposed . . . people." An interpretation stressing rabid journalism as a major cause of the war should draw some link to illustrate how these journals reached the White House or the State Department. To say that this influence was exerted through public opinion proves nothing; the next problem is to demonstrate how much public opinion was governed by the yellow press, how much of this opinion was influenced by more sober factors, and which of these two branches of opinion most influenced McKinley.[30]

Congress was a hotbed of interventionist sentiment, but then it had been so since 1895. The fact was that Congress had more trouble handling McKinley than the President had handling Congress. The President had no fear of that body. He told Charles Dawes during the critical days of February and March that if Congress tried to adjourn he would call it back into session. McKinley held Congress under control until the last two days of

---

[30] There is an excellent discussion of this point in Offner, "McKinley and the Origins of the Spanish-American War," 69–74; see also George W. Auxier, "Middle Western Newspapers and the Spanish-American War, 1895–1898," *Mississippi Valley Historical Review,* XXVI (March, 1940), 524, 532.

March, when the publication of the "Maine" investigation forced Thomas B. Reed, the passionately antiwar Speaker of the House, to surrender to the onslaughts of the rapidly increasing interventionist forces. As militants in Congress forced the moderates into full retreat, McKinley and Day were waiting in the White House for Spain's reply to the American ultimatum. And after the outbreak on March 31 McKinley reassumed control. On April 5 the Secretary of War, R. A. Alger, assured the President that several important senators had just informed him that "there will be no trouble about holding the Senate." When the President postponed his war message on April 5 in order to grant Fitzhugh Lee's request for more time, prowar congressmen went into a frenzy. During the weekend of April 8 and 9, they condemned the President, ridiculed Reed's impotence to hold back war, and threatened to declare war themselves. In fact, they did nearly everything except disobey McKinley's wishes that nothing be done until the following week. Nothing was done.[31]

When the Senate threatened to overrule the President's orders that the declaration of war not include a recognition of Cuban independence, the White House whipped its supporters into line and forced the Senate to recede from its position. This was an all-out battle between the White House and a strong Senate faction. McKinley triumphed despite extremely strong pressure exerted by sincere American sentiment on behalf of immediate Cuban independence and despite the more crass material interests of the Junta's financial supporters and spokesmen. The President wanted to have a free hand in dealing with Cuba after the war, and Congress granted his wishes. Events on Capitol Hill may have been more colorful than those at the White House, but the latter, not the former, was the center of power in March and April, 1898.

Influences other than the yellow press or congressional belligerence were more important in shaping McKinley's position of April 11. Perhaps most important was the transformation of the opinion of many spokesmen for the business community who had formerly opposed war. If, as one journal declared, the McKinley administration, "more than any that have preceded it, sustains . . . close relations to the business interests of the country," then this change of business sentiment should not be discounted.[32] This transformation brought important financial spokesmen, especially from the Northeast, into much the same position that had long been oc-

[31] Alger to McKinley, April 5, 1898, McKinley MSS; Offner, "McKinley and the Origins of the Spanish-American War,", 289–300.

[32] Chicago *Times-Herald* quoted in Cincinnati *Commercial Tribune*, Dec. 28, 1897, 6:2. The Chicago paper was particularly close to the administration through its publisher's friendship with McKinley. The publisher was H. H. Kohlsaat. Ernest May remarks, regarding McKinley's antiwar position in 1897 and early 1898, "It was simply out of the question for him [McKinley] to embark on a policy unless virtually certain that Republican businessmen would back him" (*Imperial Democracy*, 118). The same comment doubtlessly applies also to McKinley's actions in March and April.

cupied by prointerventionist business groups and journals in the trans-Appalachian area. McKinley's decision to intervene placated many of the same business spokesmen whom he had satisfied throughout 1897 and January and February of 1898 by his refusal to declare war.

Five factors may be delineated which shaped this interventionist sentiment of the business community. First, some business journals emphasized the material advantages to be gained should Cuba become a part of the world in which the United States would enjoy, in the words of the New York *Commercial Advertiser,* "full freedom of development in the whole world's interest." The *Banker's Magazine* noted that "so many of our citizens are so involved in the commerce and productions of the island, that to protect these interests . . . the United States will have eventually to force the establishment of fair and reasonable government." The material damage suffered by investors in Cuba and by many merchants, manufacturers, exporters, and importers, as, for example, the groups which presented the February 10 petition to McKinley, forced these interests to advocate a solution which could be obtained only through force.[33]

A second reason was the uncertainty that plagued the business community in mid-March. This uncertainty was increased by Proctor's powerful and influential speech and by the news that a Spanish torpedo-boat flotilla was sailing from Cadiz to Cuba. The uncertainty was exemplified by the sudden stagnation of trade on the New York Stock Exchange after March 17. Such an unpredictable economic basis could not provide the springboard for the type of overseas commercial empire that McKinley and numerous business spokesmen envisioned.

Third, by March many businessmen who had deprecated war on the ground that the United States Treasury did not possess adequate gold reserves began to realize that they had been arguing from false assumptions. The heavy exports of 1897 and the discoveries of gold in Alaska and Australia brought the yellow metal into the country in an ever widening stream. Private bankers had been preparing for war since 1897. *Banker's Magazine* summarized these developments: "Therefore, while not desiring war, it is apparent that the country now has an ample coin basis for sustaining the credit operations which a conflict would probably make necessary. In such a crisis the gold standard will prove a bulwark of confidence." [34]

Fourth, antiwar sentiment lost much strength when the nation realized that it had nothing to fear from European intervention on the side of Spain. France and Russia, who were most sympathetic to the Spanish monarchy, were forced to devote their attention to the Far East. Neither of these nations wished to alienate the United States on the Cuban issue. More im-

---

[33] *Commercial Advertiser,* March 10, 1898, 6:3; *Banker's Magazine,* LVI (April, 1898), 519–520.
[34] *Banker's Magazine,* LVI (March, 1898), 347–348; LVI (April, 1898), 520; Pittsburgh *Press,* April 8, 1898, 4:1; *Commercial and Financial Chronicle,* April 23, 1898, 786.

portant, Americans happily realized that they had the support of Great Britain. The *rapprochement* which had occurred since the Venezuelan incident now paid dividends. On an official level, the British Foreign Office assured the State Department that nothing would be accomplished in the way of European intervention unless the United States requested such intervention. The British attitude made it easy for McKinley to deal with a joint European note of April 6 which asked for American moderation toward Spain. The President brushed off the request firmly but politely. On an unofficial level, American periodicals expressed appreciation of the British policy on Cuba, and some of the journals noted that a common Anglo-American approach was also desirable in Asia.[35] The European reaction is interesting insofar as it evinces the continental powers' growing realization that the United States was rapidly becoming a major force in the world. But the European governments set no limits on American dealings with Spain. McKinley could take the initiative and make his demands with little concern for European reactions.

Finally, opposition to war melted away in some degree when the administration began to emphasize that the United States enjoyed military power much superior to that of Spain. One possible reason for McKinley's policies during the first two months of 1898 might have been his fear that the nation was not adequately prepared. As late as the weekend of March 25 the President worried over this inadequacy. But in late February and early March, especially after the $50,000,000 appropriation by Congress, the country's military strength developed rapidly. On March 13 the Philadelphia *Press* proclaimed that American naval power greatly exceeded that of the Spanish forces. By early April those who feared a Spanish bombardment of New York City were in the small minority. More representative were the views of Winthrop Chanler who wrote Lodge that if Spanish troops invaded New York "they would all be absorbed in the population . . . and engaged in selling oranges before they got as far as 14th Street." [36]

As the words of McKinley's war message flew across the wires to Madrid, many business spokesmen who had opposed war had recently changed their minds, American military forces were rapidly growing more powerful, banks and the United States Treasury had secured themselves against the initial shocks of war, and the European powers were divided among themselves and preoccupied in the Far East. Business boomed after McKinley signed the declaration of war. "With a hesitation so slight as to amount almost to indifference," *Bradstreet's* reported on April 30, "the business community, relieved from the tension caused by the incubus of doubt and uncertainty

---

[35] Dugdale, *German Documents*, II, 500–502; Porter to Sherman, April 8, 1898, France, Despatches, and Hay to Sherman, March 26, 28, 29, April 1, Great Britain, Despatches, NA, RG 59; *Public Opinion*, March 24, 1898, 360–361.
[36] Leech, *Days of McKinley*, 176; Philadelphia *Press*, March 13, 1898, 8:3; Garraty, *Lodge*, 191.

which so long controlled it, has stepped confidently forward to accept the situation confronting it oweing [*sic*] to the changed conditions." "Unfavorable circumstances . . . have hardly excited remark, while the stimulating effects have been so numerous and important as to surprise all but the most optimistic," this journal concluded.[37] A new type of American empire, temporarily clothed in armor, stepped out on the international stage after a half century of preparation to make its claim as one of the great world powers.

---

[37] *Bradstreet's,* April 9, 1898, 234, also April 30, 1898, 272, 282.

VIII

*Theodore Roosevelt
as Legislative Leader:
Success or Failure?*

INTRODUCTION

Whereas biographies of Theodore Roosevelt had previously been rather adulatory in tone, the publication in 1931 of Henry F. Pringle's charmingly written Theodore Roosevelt *ushered in a period during which historians either refused to take Roosevelt seriously or were highly critical of his actions. Pringle, Matthew Josephson, and others tended to minimize Roosevelt's accomplishments as President. His commitment to the cause of Progressivism was questioned, and he was pictured as a compromiser who was generally ready to settle for half a loaf when harder fighting might have gained the whole loaf.*

Thanks largely to the writings of George Mowry, John M. Blum, and Howard K. Beale and to the publication of The Letters of Theodore Roosevelt, *edited by Elting E. Morison, historians in the last two decades have begun to reappraise Roosevelt and to upgrade him in their evaluations. Today, Roosevelt the President is pictured as a leader who advanced the cause of Progressivism to a significant degree, who practiced the art of politics with consummate skill, who raised the office of the Presidency to a new stature, who asserted the supremacy of the national interest over any special interest, and who understood far better than most of his contemporaries both the nature of world politics and the role the United States would have to play in world affairs.*[1]

Both Matthew Josephson and John Blum, in the selections that follow, concentrate on Roosevelt's record as a legislative leader after his smashing triumph at the polls in 1904. The author and biographer Josephson argues that Roosevelt did not take advantage of the opportunity for positive leadership that his electoral triumph provided. Roosevelt, he contends, was not really devoted to the cause of reform and was bored by complex economic problems. In the crucial battle over the Hepburn Act, Roosevelt, according to Josephson, surrendered to the Old Guard and thus lost the fight for effective railroad regulation.

Blum, author of the brilliant The Republican Roosevelt *and associate editor of* The Roosevelt Letters, *takes direct issue with Josephson. The Yale history professor contends that Roosevelt was highly effective in his dealings with Congress and had a basic understanding of the problem of government control of business. In the fight for the Hepburn Act, Roosevelt, in Blum's opinion, maneuvered adroitly and ultimately secured from Congress precisely the sort of measure he wanted, a measure that "endowed the Interstate Commerce Commission with power commensurate with its task."*

---

[1] See, for example, Arthur S. Link, "Theodore Roosevelt in His Letters," *Yale Review,* XLIII (June 1954), 589–598.

The Politics of Reform

Matthew Josephson

The old Senators who still ruled Congress seemed surprisingly unhappy over the sweeping Republican party triumph of 1904.

"What is to be done now with our victory is a pretty serious question," wrote the canny Orville Platt of Connecticut to Aldrich.[1] It was a question that Theodore Roosevelt, too, asked himself continually.

Originally a political "accident," he had won more real power than any of the dreary Republican worthies who had preceded him in his office since Lincoln. He was not only the chief magistrate, but the unchallenged leader of his party organization, seated in the driving seat of the Steam Roller. The opportunity for positive leadership lay open for him, with the Presidential power less restricted by indirect controls than ever before, as a similar opportunity fell one day to a later Roosevelt after re-election in 1936.

Moreover he could say, in this great hour, that his re-election, which vindicated his principles, was owing

> not to the politicians primarily, although I have done my best to get on with them; not to the financiers, although I have staunchly upheld the rights of property; but above all to Abraham Lincoln's "plain people"; to the folk who worked hard on farm, in shop, or on the railroads, or who owned little stores, little businesses which they managed themselves. I would literally, not figuratively, rather cut off my right hand than forfeit by any improper act of mine the trust and regard of these people.[2]

No one could utter braver sentiments than T. R., nor with firmer conviction, at a given moment. His second inauguration, celebrated by a crowd of 500,000 persons who streamed into the capital, witnessed his liberation from pledges to the dead man he had succeeded. "I am glad to be President in my own right," he said to John Hay.[3]

From Matthew Josephson, *The President Makers* (New York: Harcourt, Brace and Company, 1940), pp. 175–182, 219–221, 226–236. Reprinted by permission. Although extracts from both Chapters VI and VII of the Josephson book are included in the selection, the title is that of Chapter VII.

[1] Stephenson, *op. cit.*, p. 250.
[2] Bishop, *op. cit.*, T. R. to Wister, Nov. 19, 1904, Vol. I, p. 345.
[3] Hay, *Diaries*, Vol. V, Nov. 8, 1904.

There is evidence that he weighed the trend of the recent elections, and the popular emotions that accompanied it, in serious spirit. One perhaps important symptom was the sharp rise of the tiny Socialist party, led by Eugene Debs, from 100,000 votes in 1900 to 400,000 votes in 1904. Roosevelt duly noted ,this when he remarked privately in February, 1905, that the growth of the Socialist party was "far more ominous than any Populist or similar movement in the past." [4] William Jennings Bryan, who also watched the popular pulse most carefully, told friends that he now feared the coming of socialism. The new party's rapid growth might lead soon to the capture of one of the older parties, as the Populists had managed to do in 1896. It was proof also "that the Democratic party has been too conservative to satisfy the reform element of the country." [5]

In serious vein, Roosevelt also pondered over the labor problem, though only a minority of American workers were Socialists, while the great majority pinned their hopes upon the economic action of the federated craft unions led by Samuel Gompers. In a long letter, written two days after the election to his Attorney General, Philander C. Knox (retiring now to enter the Senate), Roosevelt explored the possibilities of a Square Deal to labor. Hitherto, with Knox's aid, he had grappled chiefly with the great problems of the day that were connected with organized capital. To Knox, the conservative attorney for Carnegie, Roosevelt gave credit handsomely for having given shape to policies which were only "half-formulated" in his own mind. But once in the Senate, there would be occasion for Knox to give as deep thought to the problem of labor as he had given to that of capital.

> More and more the labor movement of this country will become a factor of vital importance. . . . If the attitude of the New York *Sun* toward labor, as toward the trusts, becomes the attitude of the Republican party, we shall some day go down before a radical and extreme democracy with a crash which would be disastrous to the nation. We must not only do justice *but we must show the wage-worker that we are doing justice.* We must make it evident that while there is not any weakness in our attitude, while we unflinchingly demand good conduct from them, yet we are equally resolute in the effort to secure them all just and proper consideration.

Here we see in this confidential, artless letter how Roosevelt still never falters in his desire to play the Great Mediator. His hope of upholding the democratic doctrine of "equality before the law" in the conflicts of capital and labor corresponded significantly with the English and European political reform movements of this time, which conceived of social legislation as concessions to be made in time, as a form of "ransom" paid in order to safeguard society and its prosperity. The concessions might be costly; yet, as a

---

[4] Pringle, *Roosevelt*, p. 368.
[5] E. E. Robinson, *American Political Parties*, p. 289.

Joseph Chamberlain intimated, their costs could be paid out of future profits, and would be outweighed by the gains in security from tragic upheavals.

Roosevelt argued:

> It would be a dreadful calamity if we saw this country divided into two parties, one containing the bulk of the property owners and conservative people, the other the bulk of the wage-workers and less prosperous people, generally; each party insisting upon, demanding much that was wrong, and each party sullen and angered by real and fancied grievances.

And what was the answer, what were the measures which, taken in time, would prevent such a fearful outcome? Roosevelt like the corporation lawyers Knox and Root wished to preserve the existing balance of property relations. Further than this he had no definite measures in mind, no timetable, no program. He seemed to offer only a standard, a kind of "moral" imperative, which his conservative colleagues often accepted, but as often wavered from, as it suited their material interests: ". . . Here in this republic, it is peculiarly incumbent upon the man with whom things have prospered to be in a certain sense the keeper of his brother with whom life has gone hard." For "the surest way to provoke an explosion of wrong and injustice is to be short-sighted, narrow-minded, greedy and ignorant. . . ." [6]

Yet vague as was the plan, and wavering the leader, it is true, as Herbert Croly later reflected, that Roosevelt groped in sound directions. His "new Nationalism" or "new Hamiltonianism," while strongly centralizing the government authority, made this augmented authority appear to be more responsive to the popular will; it served not as a bulwark against the rising tide of democracy, but as an effective instrument of the common national welfare. Even in compromise and failure, Rooseveltian leadership gave signs of what could be done; pointed to the "promise of American life."

"In internal affairs, I cannot say that I entered the Presidency with any deliberately planned and far-reaching scheme of social betterment," Roosevelt recollected in writing his autobiography. The more was the pity. What is remarkable at this stage is that, with a record-breaking victory to his credit, and holding an unchallenged position of leadership, Roosevelt confined himself so severely in his actual domestic policies.

While he wondered what to do with his victory, strong influence was brought to bear upon him to see to it that any reform or trust control activities should work, as he put it, "without paralyzing the energies of the business community." [7] From the West came two spokesmen of progressive measures, Governors Cummins and La Follette, with whom he held a long conference. La Follette advocated strong measures to control railroads and

---

[6] *T. R. Papers,* T. R. to P. C. Knox, Nov. 10, 1904.
[7] *T. R. Papers,* T. R. to Sir George Trevelyan, Mar. 9, 1905.

fix the rates they charged; Cummins urged a reduction of the tariff rates that would help, as he thought, to curb the trusts and lower the cost of living. Cummins, on leaving, expressed himself as satisfied with the interview, and counted upon Roosevelt's adherence to tariff reform. He recalled in later years that the President had shown him a passage in his forthcoming Message to Congress indicating as much.[8]

However, something very powerful moved Roosevelt at this juncture, and at almost the last hour before making public his message he veered and changed his mind. Senator Aldrich came to see him; Senator O. H. Platt likewise; and Speaker "Joe" Cannon also came to his desk. To Roosevelt's proposal to do something about tariff reform in the early future, Aldrich coolly answered: "Possibly." Senator Platt may well have reminded the President of the wisdom of holding to the "gentleman's agreement" of 1902 * to avoid forbidden subjects. Cannon was even more forthright, according to his own later account. A struggle over the tariff would probably end in failure, and would moreover prevent enactment of the railroad bill Roosevelt had set his heart upon. By telegram, the sentences in the Message of December, 1904, referring to tariff reform, already given out to the press, were "killed." [9]

The Message to Congress of December, 1904, which was to announce a Roosevelt who had "come into his own," and which had been awaited with burning curiosity, proved to be a most moderate document. In a spirit of humanity it recommended laws fostering workmen's compensation and restricting child labor. It was silent upon the tariff issue. Its proposals for the extension of government control over the railroads were the most important ones. Responding to bitter criticisms of existing freight rates, Roosevelt urged that Congress must accord a genuine power to the Interstate Commerce Commission—when complaints were brought—"to decide, subject to judicial review, what shall be a reasonable rate. . . ."

The terms of the Message were conciliatory. Great corporations, the President said, were "necessary," and for their "great and singular mental powers" the masters of corporations were entitled to large rewards. However, they must give due regard to the public interest.

Instant relief was felt now by the anxious railroad lobbyists and "railroad Senators" in Washington. Soon it became plain that, although an administration railroad bill was to be introduced in Congress, nothing would be done during the "Lame Duck" session, and that Roosevelt would not care to

---

[8] Stephenson, *op. cit.*, p. 235, citing memorandum of A. B. Cummins.

* Editor's note: The reference is to an agreement Roosevelt is alleged to have made with Senators Nelson Aldrich and Mark Hanna by which the President promised not to tamper with the tariff or the currency in return for a free hand in dealing with other problems.

[9] *Ibid.*, p. 462, memorandum of L. W. Busbey; cf. also L. W. Busbey, *Cannon*, pp. 208–209.

call a special session of the new, more liberal Congress, which would normally convene at the end of 1905. It was evident also that Roosevelt had as yet won no agreement of definite support for his bill from Aldrich and Cannon, who controlled Congress still with an unshaken grip. These men waited, and worked to gain time.

It was less well known that the great railroad master Edward H. Harriman, accompanied by his lawyer, quietly visited Washington several times in the winter of 1904–1905, and also in December, 1905, at the time of the new session of Congress. It is evident that in keeping with the friendly alliance between Harriman and Roosevelt, during the late campaign, Harriman was being "consulted" by those who advised the President in framing the proposed law. Yet Harriman disapproved of everything in the way of railroad legislation. He was not an easy man to please, and strain arose between the two aggressive men, more than a year before their public quarrel, almost immediately after the election to which Harriman had given such signal help.

The difficult course of Roosevelt's negotiations with both the railroad magnates and the Standpat leaders in Congress is reflected in certain letters to his Boswell, Joseph B. Bishop, and to Lodge. After a snarl of debate, the railroad reform bill, which had passed the House, died in the committee rooms of the Senate. It was evident that Roosevelt did not press the issue strongly and was easily resigned to waiting for another year, when perhaps the force of public opinion would come to his aid more strongly.

> My chief fear is lest the big financiers who, outside of their own narrowly limited profession, are as foolish as they are selfish, will force the moderates to join with the radicals in radical action, under penalty of not obtaining any at all. *I must prefer moderate action:* but the ultraconservatives may make it necessary to accept what is radical.[10]

In a similar vein he wrote to his old political mentor Lodge, saying that the railroads were opposing his reform bill vigorously and hoped to beat it. ". . . I think they are very short-sighted not to understand that *to beat it means to increase the danger of the movement for government ownership of railroads.*" [11]

These are scarcely the tones of one who, by a tremendous personal victory, had made himself the master of his party. Roosevelt's ventures in legislative leadership (actually very few) show instead that he accepted strict limitations of his power in this field; that he dreaded the wearisome, perplexing task of driving a definite program of legislation through Congress; that he feared the machinelike control of the Senate and the autocratic rule of Speaker Cannon, in the House, would be immune to direct attacks. This machine

---

[10] Bishop, *op. cit.*, Vol. I, p. 428, Mar. 23, 1905; italics mine.
[11] *T. R. Papers*, T. R. to Lodge, May 24, 1905; italics mine.

like control, especially in the lower House, remained unchallenged by both Roosevelt and Taft, until the insurrection led by Congressman Norris of Nebraska in 1910 suddenly overthrew it.

It was true that the President sought to rally public opinion to his side by making certain fighting speeches, such as that at Philadelphia, January 30, 1905. Here, waving his Big Stick a little, he declared that our free people would not tolerate longer the vast power of corporate wealth, unless "the still higher power" of controlling this wealth in the interests of the whole people were lodged "somewhere in the Government." He asked for "justice" in the way of submitting the railroads to more rigorous supervision by the Interstate Commerce Commission, and gave warning once more that, without such measures, our republic might founder like republics of olden times amid the destructive contests of the Haves and the Have-Nots, the Poor and Rich.

Yet it was all too plain that his mind was distracted by the pernickety controversies that arose over the terms and details of a new empowering act for the Interstate Commerce Commission. Complex economic or financial problems always ended by boring him, for his mind, as his friends knew, was wanting in the spirit of orderly logic necessary to a law-making program. His heart, his emotions, were turned elsewhere in 1905—during this time of painful domestic controversy, financial scandal, and popular unrest—to more distant fields, abroad, where a role of glory, infinitely simpler and more attractive to his nature, beckoned him. . . .

Theodore Roosevelt's sharp veerings, his lapses into reform, so to speak, can be understood only in relation to the growing pressure brought upon him by the radicals. Left to his own devices, he tended to wait, to hesitate, to temporize, like so many other professed reformers who were ready to believe that the mere occupation of office by themselves meant the winning of the battle. But the arrival of a La Follette, fresh from his provincial successes, to a leading place in national politics was a portent and a reminder.

Now Bryan, the "peerless leader" of the opposition party after 1904, began to urge radical policies for the Democrats. His influential weekly newspaper, *The Commoner,* kept up a constant fire of criticism upon Mr. Roosevelt, pointing out week after week the compromising features of his tactics. According to the indefatigable adversary, Roosevelt was dangerously "Hamiltonian" and believed that "the well-born were born to rule"—a very accurate judgment of the President's convictions. Great opportunities lay before the powerful President, said Bryan, but his own instincts led him to protect the "plutocracy," whatever he might say in his set speeches year after year. Bryan challenged him on a series of issues. What was President Roosevelt doing (1) to advance the Eight-Hour Day, even to the extent of enforcing it in the District of Columbia on government contracts? (2) What was he doing to bring about a constitutional amendment permitting "more democracy" through the Direct Election of Senators? (3) What of more vigorous prosecution of monopolies? Why were horse-thieves who broke the law given criminal punishment, while trust magnates who broke the law went unpunished? (4) Why was nothing done about the infamous court injunction used in labor disputes? (5) Why was there still no strict regulation of the railroads, after all these years? Why did President Roosevelt still oppose giving to the Interstate Commerce Commission the real power to initiate and fix railroad rates? What truth was there after all in the legend of the "iron man in the White House"? Bryan's organ asked.[12]

Thus after years of good fortune and comparatively smooth sailing Theodore Roosevelt faced an increasingly troubled and critical public opinion at home after 1904. Though he stood at the zenith of his power and glory, thanks chiefly to foreign exploits, his hesitations were noticed, his compromises were measured by would-be rivals for popular leadership.

The danger of party cleavage was always perfectly real to him. In the northwestern tier of states, hitherto staunchly Republican, he felt the constant clamor for downward revision of the tariff and increased trust prosecution. The clamor for more effective railroad regulation, led by La Follette and others, threatened to become a veritable "prairie fire." Yet for nearly two years, up to 1906, the clique of Aldrich and Cannon that still ruled Congress had warily forestalled legislative action.

The essence of Roosevelt's diplomacy, as Professor C. E. Merriam has pointed out, lay in pursuing tactics of combination, and in avoiding the "permanent consolidation of any one group against him. . . ." His "on the one hand" and "on the other hand" policy enabled him to hold the middle class, and alternately to attract and repel the labor group and the business group. "Broadly speaking . . . he was always detaching part of a group, commercial, labor or otherwise, and preventing solid opposition against him." [13] It was in very fear of a rupture within his party and of a combination of militant sectional and class movements, including Bryan, La Follette, and even Debs, that the Square Deal President now turned resolutely to the unpleasant business of writing large reforms into the statutes. For more than four years he had preached the Ten Commandments, yet no signal legislative achievements were credited to his name. . . .

By strenuous fighting for conservation, for pure-food and meat-inspection laws, and by frequent indictments of trusts, Roosevelt appeared to wage the struggle for reform with increasing vigor. His main objective, however, was still the passage of stronger laws regulating the railroads. To the press he stated frankly that the hour was late, that the people must have relief from the burdensome rates of the railroads. Yet in this contest he feared the outcome. The railroads, he felt, were "crazy" in their hostility. In the winter of 1906, while the railroad bill was being debated, Mr. Harriman and his

---

[12] *The Commoner*, Nov. 18, 1904; Dec. 9, 1904; Apr. 13, Apr. 20, 1906.
[13] Merriam, *Four American Party Leaders*, p. 34.

lawyer, Sidney Webster, came several times to Washington and expressed the strongest objection, not only to the railroad bill but to investigations of the Harriman lines being made by the Interstate Commerce Commission. It was plain that Harriman, who had raised $250,000 for the campaign of 1904, was becoming alienated, although in endeavoring to learn what he desired the President could get nothing but "general allegations or sweeping accusations" from him.[14]

In a public address on October 19, 1905, Roosevelt had already hinted that he would willingly accept *only a part* of the power he sought in order to regulate the railroads; it was a hint of compromise. His Message to Congress of December 9, 1905, whose main feature was the appeal for railroad control, also reiterated his prudent position of the year before: "My proposal is not to give the Interstate Commerce Commission power to initiate or originate rates generally, but to regulate a rate already fixed or originated by the roads, upon complaint and after investigation." The new rates to be established were to be, of course, "subject to review by the courts." Full publicity for the accounts of the railroad was another condition he favored.

The remarkable thing was that twenty years after the Interstate Commerce Act had become law, the Commission it established had almost no power to interfere with the activities of railroads. One of the members had even resigned lately, making public protests at the impotence of this regulatory body. Even its limited power had been stripped away—chiefly on the Constitutional ground of "due process"—by the remorseless reasoning of the Supreme Court, the court which Senator Aldrich was said to trust in as he trusted in Providence. The Commission could not of its own authority fix rates for the railroads, for such action might result in "confiscation." On the other hand, if a fair valuation of the railroad properties could once be established, as La Follette urged, then "reasonable" rates permitting fair profits might be fixed. But the very mention of government appraisal of the railroad properties and fixing of their rates aroused terror of a red Socialist revolution in Senatorial breasts.

In January the act enlarging the powers of the Interstate Commerce Commission, in line with the President's moderate views, was introduced in Congress by Representative Hepburn of Iowa. After brief debate, the bill was quickly passed by the Lower House—Speaker Cannon evidently offering no resistance—and committed to the charge of a committee of the Senate for consideration. Here, the leader of the "Railway Senators," the multi-millionaire Elkins of West Virginia, was chairman; beside him stood Nelson Aldrich, the "dictator," with divers faithful Republican followers. Tillman, on behalf of the Democratic minority in the Senate's Committee on Interstate Commerce, it was expected, would be able to accomplish nothing, and the bill would either be strangled by amendments or altogether killed.

---

[14] *T. R. Papers,* T. R. to Sidney Webster, Jan. 31, 1907.

The Old Guard was willing to grant power to the government commission, ostensibly to fix rates, upon complaints brought before it; provided, first, that complaint could be made difficult, costly, and infrequent. That is, a grain shipper with a grievance would be obliged to retain a lawyer and send him to Washington to defend his petition. In the second place, rate cases were to be reviewed after considerable delays, and judged before Federal courts, involving further costly legal process and (probably) very conservative judgment. This was what was meant by allowing for "broad court review" of railroad rate cases. Now the trouble with Hepburn's bill, as sent from the Lower House, was that it provided for no special intervention by the Federal courts, save those normally offered under the Constitution. Aldrich therefore prepared to amend the Hepburn Bill; it was rumored also that rather humorous, dilatory tactics were planned in the shape of a long series of "joke" amendments. Suddenly, to the astonishment of the Senate leader, one of the "regular" Republican members, Jonathan Dolliver of Iowa, rebelled, and with two other Republicans joined the Democratic minority to report the bill favorably.

Dolliver, the genial, studious giant with a pleasing gift for Lincolnesque oratory, long a popular and useful ornament in the conservative organization, had for several years, since 1903, shown signs of wishing to break from the leash. Like Governor Cummins of Iowa, who was soon to enter the Senate in place of the ancient Allison, Dolliver was sensitive to the strong current of discontent running again through the Granger states. Allison, who had reared him as his protégé since the '80's, and raised him to the party's Inner Circle, had often stayed Dolliver's hand when he thought to revolt, saying: "Don't do it now. Wait until I'm gone. I know it is wrong. . . . I have only a little while left, and I haven't got the strength to break away. But wait until I am gone. . . ." [15] Yet Dolliver now took a leading hand in the railroad bill, and prepared to issue a report in defiance of the Standpat dicta, saying nothing of "broad court review" and leaving the disposition of railway rate cases as the Lower House had voted it.

On the 15th of February, 1906, Aldrich had an interview with the President—possibly a stormy one—of which neither divulged anything to the public. Aldrich fought for delay, and even turned for aid to certain friends on the Democratic side of the Senate. Meanwhile Dolliver worked in close collaboration with Roosevelt to advance the new bill.

When the Senate's Committee on Interstate Commerce reported out the bill, it was seen that the Republican majority had split its vote. The Eastern faction, among them Aldrich, Foraker, Elkins, and Kean, opposed the Hepburn Bill; the Western Republicans, Dolliver and Clapp, joined with the Democratic minority under Tillman to bring about favorable recommendation. This development, undoubtedly forced by the crafty Aldrich, gave him

---

[15] La Follette, *Autobiography,* pp. 432–433.

the occasion for his astonishing maneuver by which "Pitchfork Ben" Tillman, the Southern radical Democrat, was designated to report the bill out
of committee without the official indorsement of the Republican party. Thus
if the bill came to grief or created evil consequences it would not be a Republican affair. Moreover Dolliver, who had hoped to sponsor the bill, was
out-flanked, while the President would be placed in an awkward position.
For not long ago Mr. Roosevelt had had a resounding personal quarrel
with the irascible Southerner Tillman and had barred him from the White
House.

Yet Tillman accepted his mission in good faith. As in the stirring campaign of '96, beside Bryan and Altgeld, he girded himself for a general on-
slaught upon entrenched corporate wealth and privilege, eager to garner
what credit he could for the Democratic party. The President, meanwhile,
after enjoying Aldrich's strange pleasantry, made conciliatory statements to
the press, declaring that he "did not care a rap" for personal difference, and,
in the interests of railroad reform, would co-operate unstintedly with the
Democratic leader, "Pitchfork Ben."

For sixty days, during the months of March and April, the Senate chamber
rang with a great "Constitutional debate" over railroad control. One by one
the conservative Republican orators arose and attacked a measure which
ostensibly had the support of their own administration. Foraker of Ohio, the
grey-haired hero of the Civil War, condemned the Hepburn Bill as "Democratic" in its inspiration. This old politician, not yet known as the "hireling"
of the Standard Oil Company that he was, was heard with respect when he
pleaded passionately for liberty to railroad owners. The policy of centralized
control that was embodied in the Hepburn Bill, he argued, would "feed on
itself . . . and spread like a conflagration until in some form or other it
comprehended and applied to every other kind of business, for such were the
teachings and plans of Socialism." [16]

Senator Philander Knox of Pennsylvania, formerly Attorney General in
Roosevelt's Cabinet, pointed out that the bill placed some ten billions of
railroad property under the arbitrary control of government agencies, "beyond the protecting clauses of the Constitution." He urged the inclusion of
an amendment providing for "broad judicial review" of all railroad rate
cases (which would be, in effect, an invitation to endless court suits). Otherwise, sacred rights, "painfully won from the tyrannies of the past, rights
adhering to the rich as well as to the poor, would be forfeited. . . . The
courts," cried Knox, in a ringing peroration, "are the guardians of our rights
and liberties." [17] Thus the theme of the opposition was the danger of a
tyranny of the poor over the rich!

While Aldrich and his Senatorial lawyers fought to defeat the Hepburn
Bill by ingenious constitutional arguments, or sniped at it with a series of

---

[16] *Congressional Record,* May 18, 1906.   [17] *Ibid.,* Mar. 28, 1906.

amendments, a crowd of Democratic and Republican "Granger" Senators, led by Tillman and Dolliver, defended the bill in torrents of words. They fought for "narrow court review," limiting the injunctive power of the Federal courts to suspend the government's action in railroad-shipper disputes; else, they contended, the floodgates of litigation would be opened. The issue was, simply put: should the Interstate Commerce Commission be given veritable power over the railways, or illusory powers that would be haltered in the courts?

The President for a time pursued the fight with uncommon force and resourcefulness, though Aldrich held the votes of forty Senators in his hand. As Mark Sullivan has recalled it, Roosevelt arranged with his admirers among the newspaper correspondents that a series of vigorous articles on the railroads and on Senators sympathetic to them should appear during the debate over the railroad control bill. In January, 1906, there appeared in the *World's Work* a powerful attack upon Senators Aldrich, Hale, Spooner, Elkins, Penrose, Foraker, Depew, and Kean, as "representatives of corporate business everywhere. . . ." In *McClure's Magazine* for March, 1906, Ray Stannard Baker published a careful, documented study of the evil tendencies of the railroads and their abuse of political privilege.[18] Rumors were circulated in the press, evidently inspired, that the President even hoped to send a few railroad presidents to jail, believing that it would have a wholesome effect on the situation.

News of sensational charges against the Standard Oil and the American Sugar Refining companies, developing from current investigations, was hinted at, as if held over the heads of the opposition. Also, in a series of public addresses during the early spring of 1906, Roosevelt made what then seemed radical proposals—proposals for an inheritance tax that would gradually level wealth, and for Federal laws regulating insurance companies within the District of Columbia. These were the days when Roosevelt thundered most heavily against the "malefactors of great wealth." Yet, whatever the popular effect of these broadsides, votes were still lacking in the Senate to encompass the passage of the Hepburn Bill, which he had made the spearhead of his program of economic reform.

In the early stages of the Senate deadlock, Roosevelt made great efforts to gather together a Senate majority. Through an intermediary he communicated privately with Senator Tillman, the Democratic floor leader, and made an "arrangement" for collaboration between the Democrats and himself. Tillman reported that he could count upon the aid of from twenty-six to twenty-eight of the Democratic contingent of thirty-three Senators. In addition, Dolliver promised the support of between twenty and twenty-two Western Republicans, making a majority of from forty-six to fifty votes out of ninety. The delicate negotiations for a coalition with the Democrats—

---

[18] Sullivan, *op. cit.*, Vol. III, p. 241.

a rather bold undertaking for a Republican President—were completed at a conference on April 14, 1906, in Attorney General Moody's office, both Tillman and Dolliver being present. Roosevelt, as Tillman declared, promised to "stand by" the coalition and contribute executive pressure in support of the bill, whose terms, providing for "narrow court review," were agreed upon.[19]

Roosevelt's public struggles with Aldrich often partook of the character of mock warfare. He respected and bowed before Aldrich's power. "My experience . . . has made me feel respect and regard for Aldrich," he told Taft in 1903, "as one of that group of Senators, including Allison, Hanna, Spooner, Platt of Connecticut, Lodge, and one or two others, who . . . are the most powerful factors in Congress." Though he disagreed with them radically on many questions they were "the leaders, and their great intelligence and power, and their desire . . . to do what is best for the government, makes them not only essential to work with but desirable to work with." [20]

To work instead with the Democrats, in order to pass a bill which Aldrich opposed, meant not only a break in the party harmony, but final departure from the President's tacit "gentleman's agreement" with the Standpatters. It was a decision before which Theodore Roosevelt hesitated deeply. Fortunately, conciliators were there to devise a compromise between the "narrow" and "broad" court review positions, difficult as that seemed. And then the magic of Aldrich accomplished the rest: subjection of the dynamic President, in his first large battle to lead Congress.

Aldrich's magic consisted at this time simply in his subterranean connection with friendly "Railway Senators" among the Democrats. The veteran Joseph Bailey of Texas, a florid, old-fashioned orator, with large black hat, sedate black suit, and string necktie, was at that time the real leader of the Democrats in the Senate. Though he publicly appeared to be sponsoring the "narrow" review clauses of the Hepburn Bill, as well as other popular measures urged by the Democracy, public scandal not long afterward stamped him as a partner in certain dubious oil enterprises that eventually came under the control of the Rockefeller clan. Legend also has pointed to him as the secret lieutenant of Aldrich on the Democratic side, who brought about, when needed, the sudden switch of two or three vitally necessary Democratic votes to the conservative side. For example, one of the amendments that Bailey proposed, an "anti-injunction" clause, had the air of being so radical that the Supreme Court would certainly nullify the whole railroad act.[21]

Tillman himself, according to his memorandum of the proceedings, "sus-

---

[19] Tillman's account, *Congressional Record*, May 12, 1906; Stephenson, *op. cit.*, pp. 307–308.
[20] *T. R. Papers*, Roosevelt to Taft, Mar. 13, 1903.
[21] S. H. Acheson, *Joe Bailey, The Last Democrat*, p. 201.

pected the Texan [Bailey] . . . of holding secret conferences with Aldrich," and, as he reported to Roosevelt, kept a close watch on his colleague, lest he "sell out." [22]

Just when victory over the Standpatters seemed assured—though with the dangerous help of a coalition of Democrats and Western Republicans of the La Follette type—the game passed from the President's hands. For at the Democratic caucus, on April 18, 1906, when noses were counted, to everyone's surprise it was found that several recruits were missing. This was all that Aldrich needed.

For Roosevelt the deadlock had been wearying, and the adventure of working with the Democrats, who would seek credit for railroad reform, politically hazardous. He pressed the distraught Tillman to produce the missing Democratic votes; but though Tillman pleaded for time, they were not found in the last two weeks of April. After having held the threat of a coalition with the Democrats over Aldrich's head, Roosevelt was now ready to abandon the comedy of intrigue, and to "trade" or compromise. He wished, as both Lincoln Steffens and La Follette complained, simply to "get something through"; he would content himself in the end with "half a loaf," when half a loaf was worse than none.

On May 4 Nelson Aldrich called at the White House. Reports of this secret interview held that the "dictator" of the Senate was suave and gracious in victory. Roosevelt, judging from his letter to Lodge, acknowledged his defeat in "sporting" fashion, and vowed that Aldrich, who represented only "ten per cent of the people," would be vanquished the next time. Meanwhile an election was approaching, and they must think of the fortunes of their party.[23]

A compromise amendment, made ready by the practiced Senator Allison, was now quickly produced. It had the language of strong railroad reform, but it offered the legal realities of *broadest court review* and restraint in favor of the railroads, in the shape of occult clauses permitting "interlocutory injunctions" and other court interventions which would limit government control. On the morning of May 4, 1906, it was understood in Washington that the harassed President had yielded suddenly and given his approval to the "Allison amendment," abandoning the Tillman-Dolliver reform coalition. When the Republican compromise terms were made known a week later, they were universally described as a "gold brick."

The vociferous Tillman and his fellow Democrats were outraged by the bad faith, and even "betrayal," they had suffered at the hands of the President. Roosevelt, they cried, had ended by yielding to Aldrich. He was "so constituted," as Senator Rayner of Maryland remarked, "that he cannot look at a trap without fooling with the spring." [24] The Hepburn Act emerged,

---

[22] Roosevelt to Allison, the New York *Tribune*, May 16, 1906.
[23] Lodge, *Correspondence*, Vol. II, p. 370.   [24] The New York *World*, May 12, 1906.

however, as a simon-pure Republican party measure, supported by the Old Guard. The embittered Tillman then disburdened himself of a remarkable "confession" on May 12, 1906, before the Senate, relating how the President had sought him out and agreed to use his services as leader of the opposition party, then cast him aside in order to effect a compromise with his own party leaders. Roosevelt issued angry denials from the White House; charges and countercharges filled the air with confusion as the memorable session of Congress drew to its close in June.

Roosevelt had been on the verge of forcing through Congress a measure that would have substantially increased the power of the Interstate Commerce Commission over railroad rates. It would have meant a bitter conflict within his own party, the possibility of overthrowing the old leaders and creating a new political alignment upon progressive and conservative beliefs. Instead he had recoiled, accepted a half-measure that brought no relief from the abuses that agitated a large part of the public. In defending himself, he argued that the bill he signed was the "same thing" that he had asked for; yet few believed him.[25]

As if to conceal his embarrassment, on May 4, 1906, the day when his compromise with Aldrich was announced, Roosevelt delivered his fiercest broadside against the industrial trusts in a message to Congress which laid bare the secret practices of the Standard Oil and sugar-refining trusts and the coal-carrying combination. He promised that his Attorney General would institute prosecutions against all these wrongdoers at an early date.[26] But one of the newspaper men present continued to question the President concerning the Hepburn Act amendments, and his explanations appeared labored. Finally, the reporter who had admired him exclaimed bluntly: "But Mr. President, what we want to know is why you surrendered." To this Roosevelt made no direct reply.[27]

---

[25] The Hepburn Act extended the authority of the Interstate Commerce Commission over pipe lines, express companies, sleeping-car companies, and railway terminals; it was given the power not to fix rates, but to nullify rates found unreasonable, on complaints of shippers. "Far from satisfying agrarian demands, the Hepburn Act only stimulated the progressive surge which was soon to induce a political earthquake. . . ." (C. A. and M. R. Beard, *The Rise of American Civilization*, Vol. II, p. 568.)

[26] The New York *World*, May 5, 1912.

[27] Stephenson, *op. cit.*, pp. 314–315, citing memorandum of Richard Hooker.

President, Congress, and Control

John Morton Blum

At no time was Theodore Roosevelt more intent on achievement, more attuned to opinion, or more conscious of the nice relationships within his party than in November 1904 when he had at last become President in his own right. "Stunned" though he may have been "by the overwhelming victory" he had won, he nevertheless turned at once to fashion a program for Congress. His pursuit of the objective in that program he most valued —a measure to regulate the railroads—demonstrated perhaps better than any other episode in his Presidency both his facility in dealing with Congress and his mature evaluation of the kind of public arrangement which would best permit necessary government control over industrial operations.

Roosevelt was never a speculative man. Thinking as he did primarily about specific issues, he understood and judged large problems in terms of their more limited parts. By his intent, furthermore, his actions spoke for him better than did his words. He made his points most convincingly when he dealt with situations instead of theories. His talents and his purpose are best understood, therefore, by examination of those activities he counted most significant. This was the importance of his railroad program. For it he exercised those qualities of executive leadership upon which successful Presidents must depend; with it he expected to provide the devices upon which the governing of an industrial society might depend.

On various occasions Roosevelt overcame the obstacles imposed by the American Constitution and party system. Again and again he arranged that his recommendations should embody or win the concern of party leaders who, reflecting conflicting regional and economic demands, often had little in common other than the desire to retain office. He maneuvered legislation past the gamut of committee hearings and congressional debates where powerful chairmen and adroit parliamentarians knew how to delay and divert, sometimes defeat, the consensus of the party. Prepared as he was to influence his party and Congress by mobilizing public opinion, careful as he was never to press his program beyond the limits he calculated as practicable, he nurtured bills for the inspection of meat-packing, for the definition and enforcement of pure food and drug standards, for the expansion of the navy. But of all the legislation Roosevelt proposed, he had to work hardest and most skillfully for his railroad program.

Conspicuous inequities in American industrial life drew Roosevelt's concentration to railroad regulation. Existing laws had failed to affect the practices by which railway managers, usually unwillingly, often solely to protect their properties, favored the largest, most ruthless industrial corporations. Faced, as they were, with enormous fixed costs—interest on huge bonded debts, depreciation on large and expensive equipment—railroads, to insure enough business to meet their overheads, acceded to the demands of such corporations as the Standard Oil Company, the Armour Company, and the American Sugar Refining Company for freight rates below those accorded to smaller shippers. Although the Elkins Act of 1903 forbade these discriminations, the law was continually violated outright. These violations the offenders could usually obscure by bookkeeping methods over which the Interstate Commerce Commission had no control. The Elkins Act, furthermore, was continually circumvented. Standard Oil and Armour, among many others, besides seeking rebates, obtained discriminatory favor by arranging to receive inordinately large fees from railroads for the use of private cars—such as oil or refrigerator cars—and private sidings and terminals which the corporations owned. Practices such as these helped large shippers to grow wealthier, to absorb their less-favored competitors, to increase thereby their control over markets, and consequently to set prices for their products higher than those that might otherwise have obtained. If the railroads suffered, they too often compensated for their losses by establishing seemingly excessive freight rates either on commodities—like grain and carbon black—whose producers were in no position to demand favors, or over routes where there was no competition for transportation services.

Determined to remedy these conditions, Roosevelt proposed that Congress give the Interstate Commerce Commission effective power over railroad accounts, over private railway equipment, and—most important—in modest degree, over railroad rates. To translate this recommendation into legislation, Roosevelt first created a controlled environment within his party and then adapted his views to parliamentary conditions. He established by his tactics a productive relationship between the executive and Congress. While his program was debated in the Senate, in the session of 1905–1906, Roosevelt defined explicitly the concepts of executive control essential to his more elaborate theses on political economy. During and immediately after the lame duck session of 1904–1905, by strategy as revealing of his purpose as was his later, more explicit definition, he committed the Republicans to railroad regulation and twice got through the House bills that embodied his policy.

Roosevelt's first negotiation necessitated the sacrifice of his announced intention to direct a revision of the tariff. It depended, however, on the continuing threat of tariff revision. The manner in which Roosevelt used tariff revision to advance railroad regulation and the reasons for which he subordinated the one issue to the other have meaning both as a revelatory instance of executive leadership and as an important indication of the central purpose of Roosevelt's political action.

Only two days after the election of 1904 Roosevelt informed Nicholas Murray Butler that he had "already begun the effort to secure a bill to revise and reduce the tariff." The President well understood the dimensions of this task. In his first term he had almost lost to the Republican standpatters his prolonged fight for reciprocity with Cuba. Yet even as his second term began he raised the whole tariff issue, because, he suggested in a heated moment, "we beat the Democrats on the issue that protection was robbery, and that when necessary we would amend or revise the tariff ourselves." This explanation, as Roosevelt knew, did violence to the facts. If the Republicans had any effective national issue in the campaign of 1904 other than Theodore Roosevelt and the Square Deal, it was certainly not tariff revision. The President had accepted a platform that complacently praised Dingleyism; he had strongly endorsed the principle of protection, chastised his Secretary of War for favoring tariff reduction in a campaign speech, and denounced the Democrats for their insistence that protection was robbery.

In his more candid and quiet moments, Roosevelt explained his position with less hyperbole and more effect. "I am convinced," he wrote, "that there is, among the good Republicans and among the masses of independent Democrats who supported us . . . , a very strong feeling in favor of what I prefer to call an amendment rather than a revision of the tariff laws." "My own judgment," Roosevelt confessed, "is that it is dangerous to undertake to do anything, but that it is fatal not to undertake it . . ."

This assessment of political sentiment had some validity. The Republican differences on the tariff were major and real. A considerable minority, primarily composed of Western agrarians, favored a general reduction of schedules. Others, for the most part representing Minnesota and Massachusetts shoe, woolens, and flour manufacturers, advocated reciprocity agreements, particularly with Canada, under which their constituents would benefit by cheaper raw materials and larger export markets. These revisionists contended that the party had promised the voters adjustment, though not abandonment, of the protective system. Failing this, they warned, the Democrats as they had in Massachusetts in 1904, would profitably exploit the tariff issue. They urged Roosevelt, therefore, to summon an extra session of Congress to deal with the tariff, preferably in the spring of 1905. Most Republican leaders, including the most powerful members of Congress, however, opposing any changes in the tariff and jealously guarding the principle of protection, asserted that the election returns evidenced popular satisfaction with the Dingley rates.

Sympathetic to the revisionists, Roosevelt also recognized their strength, but he lacked their conviction and, conscious of the greater strength of their opposition, he feared the divisive hostilities and probable futility that characteristically attended tariff debates. For him the tariff was a matter of expediency. Never willing to risk a division of his party that would endanger his favored measures on an issue about which he did not feel strongly, Roosevelt, in spite of his occasional hyperbole, approached revision with consummate caution. Yet because of the articulate minority support for revision, Roosevelt seized upon tariff discussions as a useful weapon. The prospect of revision, even of a tariff debate, alarmed the standpatters sufficiently to provide an effective disciplinary tool. For Presidential coöperation on the tariff, they were ultimately willing to reach an understanding with Roosevelt, perhaps even to strike a bargain, on railroad regulation.

To that end Roosevelt maneuvered skillfully. His problem was to talk of tariff revision firmly enough to frighten the Old Guard but gently enough not to alienate them. If in the process of negotiation and legislation he could arrange tariff modifications, the achievement would be welcome, but he considered it always incidental. From the very beginning the form of his tariff negotiations suggested that they were less an objective than a device. Roosevelt did not demand; he consulted. "When I see you," he informed the Republican whip in the House, "I want to take up the question of the tariff . . . It seems to me that our party ought to revise the tariff now, but of course I do not want to say anything about it unless the leaders of the House approve, because I realize thoroughly that the matter is primarily one for you all in the House." A week later he added that "an extra session, even if it was not held until the 1st of September [1905], would be most desirable," for, he feared, "if we wait until the regular session, . . . the Democrats will talk the matter over for a year and then we shall be swamped at the Congressional elections." Yet he acknowledged to one senator that "there should be only a few and moderate changes"; and even as he labeled protection "robbery," he assured the president of the American Iron and Steel Institute that he intended "of course, to abide by the general judgment of the party." Meanwhile Roosevelt's personal secretary had announced on November 19 that the President's forthcoming State of the Union message would not mention the tariff.

Clearly Roosevelt never considered the tariff worth a fight. Three weeks after telling Butler he had begun his "effort to secure" a revision, he confessed privately that the issue was practically dead. "The trouble," he explained, "is that there are large parts of the country which want no tariff revision, and of course their representatives are hostile to any agitation of the subject. They say, with entire truth, that neither in the platform nor in any communication of mine is there any promise whatever that there shall be tariff revision. They also say, with equal truth, that the tariff changes should not be great, and that those clamoring for tariff changes are certainly to be disappointed at whatever is done . . . I am going to make every effort to get something of what I desire . . . ; but I shall not split with my party on the matter . . ." Having shed all pretense that the party had a mandate for revision, Roosevelt several days later, again privately, admitted that he had no intention of tackling the tariff in the immediate future. "At present, . . ." he wrote Butler, "there is a strong majority against [amendment or reduction] . . . The minority . . . is entirely split up as to the articles on which the amendment should come . . . This means that unless circumstances change in the next sixty days it will be . . . worse than idle to call the extra session early."

It was not that Roosevelt had retreated. He had never really attacked. But before making his candid admissions to Butler, he had, with less candor, begun to bargain. Just before leaving Illinois for Washington, that arch-priest of protection, Speaker of the House Joe Cannon, had received from Roosevelt a disturbing draft, dated November 30, of a special message on the tariff that the President proposed sending to Congress. "While it is above all things desirable that the present tariff law should be kept in its essence unchanged," the draft read, "there may well be certain points as to which it can be amended. There may be some schedules that . . . should be changed . . . If it were possible to provide for reciprocity by a maximum and minimum scale to be applied in the discretion of the Executive, this should be done . . . In any event some of the schedules should now be examined . . ." If these modest proposals could not alarm the Speaker, they were certain at least to worry him. Carefully Roosevelt mitigated even worry, observing that he sent the draft "merely for the sake of having something which can be worked out, after you have consulted the men fresh from the people . . ."

Roosevelt timed the dispatch of the draft nicely. The Speaker was not to be allowed to forget that the tariff issue remained, even though the annual message, opening the last session of the Fifty-eighth Congress, said nothing of revision. He could not be allowed to forget, for that message voiced aggressively Roosevelt's demand for railroad regulation. "The government," Roosevelt instructed Congress, "must in increasing degree supervise and regulate the workings of the railways engaged in interstate commerce; and such increased supervision is the only alternative to an increase of the present evils on the one hand or a still more radical policy on the other. In my judgment, the most important legislative act now needed as regards the regulation of corporations is this act to confer on the Interstate Commerce Commission the power to revise rates and regulations."

With these words Roosevelt set off the battle over railroad regulation. On this issue the party was as divided as on the tariff. And the division, to Roosevelt's advantage, followed similar personal and sectional lines. The advocates of revision and reciprocity were also the proponents of regulation. Speaking for Western agrarians and grain dealers and for Massachusetts manufacturers, they wanted federal review of freight rates which had been, from their point of view, increasingly discriminatory. On the other hand, the standpatters, speaking either for or with the big business interests, had long resisted any departures from nineteenth-century *laissez faire.*

For the railroad program, to which there was strong Republican opposition, Roosevelt had genuine concern. He consulted Congress less and demanded more. It was "unwise and unsafe from every standpoint," he had concluded, "to fail to give the Interstate Commerce Commission additional power of an effective kind in regulating . . . rates." This, he believed, was an essential ingredient for his basic determination "that the Government should effectively shape the policy [of the] . . . Square Deal."

Thus fervently committed, but confronting a powerful opposition, Roosevelt capitalized on the divisions in Congress produced by regional and economic self-interest. The low-tariff, antirailroad group was to have one reform, the high-tariff, prorailroad group to hold one redoubt. Saving what he considered vital by sacrificing what he considered marginal, Roosevelt for the sake of railroad regulation jettisoned the draft of the special message on the tariff that had worried Cannon.

Toward this decision Cannon, by his own account, exercised his influence. The Speaker, and perhaps also Senator Nelson Aldrich, may have struck a bargain with Roosevelt on railroad regulation. The circumstantial evidence that there was some bargain or understanding is overwhelming. The alignments of economic self-interest provided fertile ground which Roosevelt had cultivated for such an understanding. The diminuendo in Roosevelt's private letters to Butler on tariff revision suggests that the President had settled his course in early December. Roosevelt's tariff conferences continued through the first week of January when, according to Cannon's account, he told the congressional leaders that revision would await the election of his successor. Cannon exaggerated, but shortly after that conference Roosevelt defined his position to a friend. "I am having anything but a harmonious time about the tariff and about the interstate commerce . . . ," he wrote. "On the interstate commerce business, which I regard as a matter of principle, I shall fight. On the tariff, which I regard as a matter of expediency, I shall endeavor to get the best results I can, but I shall not break with my party." And for the time being, with regard to the tariff, Cannon and the party were one. Two days later Roosevelt wrote Cannon: "Stop in here as soon as you can. I care very little for what the newspapers get in the way of passing sensationalism; but I do not want the people of the country to get the idea that there will be any split or clash between you and me on the tariff or anything else."

Roosevelt permitted no clash. He made no recommendation for specific or general revisions. Although he encouraged efforts for reciprocity arrangements with Canada and Newfoundland, he gave those efforts only desultory support in his dealings with Congress. At the other end of Pennsylvania Avenue, Cannon gave railroad legislation a clear track. The Speaker, it has been argued, saw to it that no bill passed until so late in the session that the Senate could not act. Actually Cannon had no need for such a scheme. The hearings of the House Committee on Interstate Commerce, as much as the debates on the floor, delayed approval of the bill. When it did finally come to a vote, it passed with a decisive majority of 309. Had it passed earlier, judging by the course of the railroad bill at the following session, it would have failed to get through the Senate before adjournment. And during the following sessions Cannon again presented no obstacles to railway regulation.

In the months following the expiration of the Fifty-eighth Congress, Roosevelt continued to rely on the threat of tariff revision. During that Congress the Senate Committee on Interstate Commerce began to hold hearings that continued through most of May 1905. Railroad executives, mobilized by Samuel Spencer, the chief of J. P. Morgan's railway division, and encouraged by sympathetic senators, used these hearings as a sounding board for opposition to Roosevelt. Outside of the committee room the railroads underwrote an expensive publicity campaign in which various business organizations, including the National Association of Manufacturers, came to their aid. With increasing fervor they rehearsed the dangerous folly of the President's proposals. As this propaganda received wide dissemination in the press, the enemies of regulation seemed to be gaining an upper hand.

Yet Roosevelt in this period displayed a measured optimism. Perhaps he suspected that the railroads would, as they did, overreach themselves. Doubtless he foresaw that investigations of the Standard Oil Company and the beef trust then under way would furnish much evidence to sustain him. Surely he had confidence that his speeches and those of his advisers would counteract the railroad propaganda. The President was continually at the hustings. In the winter at the Philadelphia Union League Club, later in Texas and Colorado, at Chautauqua and Chicago, along the southeastern seaboard, he spoke to adulating audiences of the righteousness, and yet the reasonableness, of his cause. If, in part, the prestige of his office drew them to hear him, the fervor in his falsetto persuaded them to listen. The overdrawn counterpropaganda of the railroads, whatever its merit in logic, could scarcely compete in a society primed by the muckrakers with the explosive personality of the President. Assertively he equated his view of rate-making with his then regnant dictum of a square deal for every man. He would restrain the perverters of privilege who by their manipulations of rates and rebates purloined the just profits of their honest competitors and threatened to provoke by their excesses the menace of socialism. This was a crisis (Theodore Roosevelt coped constantly with crises), but he would shackle greed and, routing the proponents of nationalization, save the railroads from themselves.

But Roosevelt did not confine his energies to the podium. In May he reminded the Old Guard that the tariff could still be an issue. To emphasize the tariff-railroad understanding that the battle of propaganda might otherwise have obscured, Roosevelt thrust at the standpatters' most sensitive spot. One guardian of protection had admitted the previous fall that the "strongest argument" for revision was that American manufacturers sold goods in foreign markets for less than they received at home. This condition, he then pointed out, while perhaps inequitable, was irremediable, for "no revision of the tariff which still left a protective margin could prevent" it. To challenge the differential in the export and domestic prices of protected commodities was to challenge the whole principle of protection. This was precisely what Roosevelt did.

On May 16, 1905, while the railroad propaganda was at its peak, an announcement that the Isthmian Canal Commission had decided to purchase supplies for the construction of the canal in foreign markets immediately staggered the standpatters. They were further shocked when Roosevelt flatly assumed all responsibility for the adoption of this "cheapest-market" policy. The New York *Times* called the announcement the "doom of Dingleyism." The steel industry's most active lobbyist and his reliable congressional echoes shared the view of the New York *Press* that the cheapest-market policy, repudiating the high-tariff mandate of 1904, was "a faithless service of outrage." The president of the National Association of Manufacturers and the secretary of the American Protective Tariff Association tersely labeled Roosevelt's action "un-American."

Less emotional observers noted that Roosevelt probably intended not to abandon protection but to call the attention of Congress to the whole subject of tariff adjustment. They were correct, for after succeeding admirably in just that, the President was satisfied. Three days after the announcement was made, Cannon conferred with Secretary of War Taft, who then rescinded the cheapest-market order, referring to the next Congress the question of canal purchases. Responsible, according to his own statement, for the order, Roosevelt must also have been responsible for the reversal.

The dramatic episode of the canal purchases served as Roosevelt's most forceful but not as his final reminder to the standpatters that the tariff remained a potential issue. In August, White House "leaks" inspired newspaper reports that the President contemplated calling an extra session of Congress to consider tariff revision. If he did not plant these rumors, Roosevelt at least used them. To his Secretary of the Treasury, an uncompromising protectionist, he wrote in the tone he had long used: "I entirely agree with all you say as to the dangers which accompany tariff revision—or any attempt at it, but as yet I am not sure whether there are not at least equal dangers in avoiding [it] . . . I want to go over the entire matter very carefully with all of the Congressional leaders before we decide which set of risks to take." Roosevelt quickly decided. It was scarcely necessary for him to consult his congressional leaders—they had understood each other for months. In mid-August, Taft, then in the Philippines, released a message from the President that there would be no extra session of Congress. The regular session, Roosevelt had already implied at Chautauqua and stated in private, would be, insofar as he could control it, devoted to rate regulation.

In December 1905, the Fifty-ninth Congress convened. During the fall, the campaigns in Massachusetts and Iowa had kept the tariff issue alive while Roosevelt, in the South, had focused on the railways. The President's annual message, silent, as it had been in 1904, on the tariff, made railroad regulation the central objective of the Administration. In the long struggle that ensued, the tariff once more provided a lever. In the House, a combination of Democrats and Administration Republicans passed a bill reducing the rates on Philippine products. Intended as an instrument of colonial policy, the measure was nevertheless considered by standpat Republicans to breach the principle of protection. Administration leaders in the Senate by their lassitude permitted it to die in committee while, like Roosevelt, they concentrated their energy and their power on the railroad bill. For this division of labor no explicit bargain need have been made, for all matters pertaining to the tariff continued in 1906 to be, as they had been since 1904, useful whips rather than real targets. By 1906 Roosevelt had abandoned all effort for tariff revision, yet essentially he abandoned only a bargaining instrument. At no time in his long public career did tariff revision much concern him. For eighteen months, however, he employed adroitly the specter of tariff agitation.

By defining tariff revision as a matter of expediency and railroad regulation as a matter of principle, Roosevelt established his own position. His life, he felt, was a quest for the moral. What he meant by morality was not always clear, but the concept had obvious components. In some cases, that which was moral was that which could be accomplished. Given two paper trusts to bust, Roosevelt had attacked the less offensive but legally vulnerable pool and ignored the more oppressive but legally secure holding company. By this criterion, railroad regulation was in 1904 more moral than tariff revision, for public and political opinion on the railways divided on nonpartisan lines and the Republican party was less committed to the Elkins Act as a line of defense than to the Dingley Act. That which was moral was also often that which was popular. In making a crucial test of the Sherman Antitrust Act, Roosevelt had prosecuted neither the largest nor the most monopolistic holding company. He had chosen, rather, a railroad merger that had been born of a discreditable stockmarket battle, that consisted of units long unpopular with shippers in the areas in which they ran, that had already been challenged by state authorities. Unlike Justice

Holmes, Roosevelt wanted to bring the voice of the people to bear on decisions. Showered as they were in 1904 by private and official disclosures of the iniquities of rebates, the evils of Armour, the machinations of Standard Oil, most of the people, particularly middle-class people, were less interested in the tariff than in direct controls of big business, especially the railways.

But Roosevelt's morality was not simply opportunistic. He felt that the central issue of his time pivoted on the control of business because this control determined conduct, and morality was for him a matter of conduct. He feared not the size but the policies of big business. He cared not about profits but about the manner of earning profits. This was the essence of the Square Deal. Roosevelt fought for railroad regulation because it was designed to control process. By his standard, tariff schedules—static matters —were as unimportant as an administrative agency overseeing day-by-day business arrangements was essential.

These dimensions of morality—practicability, popularity, and especially preoccupation with process—characterized Roosevelt's emergent progressivism. They permitted him to yield, when necessary, on details in order to advance his favored measures. They also persuaded him for reasons of policy as well as of tactics to arrange the understanding on tariff revision and railroad regulation that prepared the way for perhaps the most significant legislation of his Presidency.

Railroad rates could not be regulated, however, until Roosevelt, having committed the House to his policy, slowly brought the Senate also into line. In that second task, as in the persuading of the House, he exercised artfully the resources of office and person by which a President can lead Congress, in spite of the separation of powers imposed by the Constitution, to consummate his policies. Roosevelt's impressive ability to work within the structure of government, like his facility in managing the party, depended less on his arresting manner than on his appreciation of the institutions that shaped American political life. Like Edmund Burke, perhaps the greatest of British conservatives, Roosevelt valued the long wash of historical development, sometimes controlled, sometimes accidental, that had given form to the political society in which he lived. Both were wisely careful never to set up a system of their own. Like Burke, Roosevelt delighted in the processes by which political achievement and further institutional development were made possible. Both considered political peace the breathing-time which gave them leisure further to contrive. As he guided his railroad program through the Senate where formidable obstacles blocked his way, Roosevelt needed and took his daily gladness in situations "of power and energy," in government—as Burke described it—"founded on compromise and barter."

Behind all the political manipulation, beneath all the legalistic forensics, the issue was control. Theodore Roosevelt intended that an administrative agency should have the authority to rectify the inequities in the business of transportation. Nelson Aldrich, the resourceful leader of the President's opposition, intended that it should not. Roosevelt demanded that the Interstate Commerce Commission be invested with power to revise railroad rates. Here, he felt, lay the key to control. Aldrich, when he drew his lines, sought to transfer the final decision on rates from the commission to the courts, to leave the judiciary in its traditional, ineffectual, disorderly role of monitor of the price of transportation. President and senator, sensitive always to each other's strength, delighting in the test, came slowly to a crisis.

"I am well aware," Roosevelt stated in his annual message to Congress of 1905, "of the difficulties of the [railroad] legislation that I am suggesting, and of the need of temperate and cautious action in securing it. I should emphatically protest against improperly radical or hasty action . . . [But] the question of transportation lies at the root of all industrial success, and the revolution in transportation which has taken place during the last half-century has been the most important factor in the growth of the new industrial conditions . . . At present the railway is [the highway of commerce] . . . and we must do our best to see that it is kept open to all on equal terms . . . It is far better that it should be managed by private individuals than by the government. But it can only be so managed on condition that justice is done the public . . . What we need to do is to develop an orderly system, and such a system can only come through the gradually increased exercise of the right of efficient government control."

A year earlier Roosevelt had sent Congress only a paragraph on railroad legislation. Now he spelled out the elements of what he considered an orderly system of control. These he had derived from the accumulated findings of the Bureau of Corporations and the Interstate Commerce Commission and from the expert advice of the lawyers and railroad men in his Cabinet. Their recommendations, embodied in the Hepburn Bill with Administration guidance substantially as Roosevelt had announced them, covered every aspect of the railroad problem then recognized by the foremost authority on railroad economics in the United States. Grounded as it was on thorough study by essentially conservative men, much of Roosevelt's program provoked little congressional dissent.

The area of agreement was large. The Elkins Antirebate Act of 1903 had failed utterly to prevent the discriminations it explicitly forbade. Alive to this, and to the public's growing displeasure over the outrageous practices of Armour and Standard Oil, practices as harmful to the railroads as to the competitors of the favored, Congress shared the President's opinion that "all private-car lines, industrial roads, refrigerator charges, and the like should be expressly put under the supervision of the Interstate Commerce Commission . . ." Conscious of the experience of the government in investigating both railways and industrial concerns, Congress, like Roosevelt, had reached the commonsense conclusion that standardized records open to official inspection were a prerequisite for the determination of adequate policies of regulation as well as for the prevention of familiar abuses in corporation management. Congress was also willing, by providing for expeditious action in cases arising under the commerce act, to destroy "the weapon of delay, almost the most formidable weapon in the hands of those whose purpose is to violate the law." [1]

Had Roosevelt recommended and Congress agreed to nothing else, these provisions would in themselves have been worth-while but inadequate achievements. They did not fundamentally alter the existing relationship between the federal government and the railroads. They established no new device of regulation. The restriction of rebates, now strengthened, had earlier existed; the inspection of records, now facilitated, had long since begun; the expedition of trial for suits involving infractions of the Interstate Commerce Act had already been provided for suits arising under the Antitrust Act. Roosevelt's orderly system of efficient government control depended not on these precedents but on an innovation to which many in Congress were still openly hostile. The President proposed that the I.C.C. be given limited authority to make rates. As he carefully defined it, this was his central objective.

Roosevelt took his first and final position on rates in his annual message of 1904. He there considered it "undesirable . . . finally to clothe the commission with general authority to fix railroad rates." "As a fair security to shippers," however, he insisted that "the commission should be vested with the power, where a given rate has been challenged and after full hearing found to be unreasonable, to decide, subject to judicial review, what shall be a reasonable rate to take its place; the ruling of the commission to take effect immediately." The "reasonable rate," Roosevelt implied by his reference to the Supreme Court's interpretation of the Interstate Commerce Act, was to be only a maximum rate. This meaning he made explicit in 1905 when he requested that the commission receive power "to prescribe the limit of rate beyond which it shall not be lawful to go—the maximum reasonable rate, as it is commonly called."

Roosevelt's Attorney General had advised that legislation empowering the commission to set definite rate schedules—the objective of many Democratic and some Western Republican senators—might be declared unconstitutional. "The one thing I do not want," Roosevelt explained to one critic, "is to have a law passed and then declared unconstitutional." Furthermore, he argued, the authority to prescribe a maximum rate, while perhaps short of the ultimate ideal, promised immediate, substantial improvement in existing conditions. "If the Commission has the power to make the maximum rate that which the railroad gives to the most favored shipper, it

---

[1] Without Presidential prodding, the Senate added to the Hepburn Bill two important clauses, one imposing criminal penalties for certain violations, another, more significant, forbidding corporations producing such commodities as coal from owning the railroads that transported them.

will speedily become impossible thus to favor any shipper . . ." If, after a test, it should prove inadequate, he would then be willing to try to secure a definite rate proposition. "I believe," he explained to the impatient, "in men who take the next step; not those who theorize about the two-hundredth step."

Roosevelt intended primarily to protect individual shippers from excessive or discriminatory rates. He agreed that the maximum rate provision would afford little remedy for discrimination between commodities or between localities, but such discriminations seemed to him relatively impersonal. He cared less about freight classification and long and short haul differentials because he could not readily associate those matters with a doer of evil and a victim. Discriminations against a small shipper or exorbitant rates the President understood and despised. They were, he was sure, immoral. His interest had also political meaning, for the spokesmen of the shippers' organizations concentrated on the problems that a maximum rate provision could begin to resolve. They neglected to mention, and Roosevelt did not apparently recognize, that no recommendation in the annual messages or provision in the Hepburn Bill prevented shippers or their consignees from passing on rate burdens originating in any discriminatory devise to the still unorganized, essentially undiscerning consumers.

The maximum rate proposal, in many respects inadequate, properly labeled so by liberals of the time, nevertheless earned for Roosevelt the opprobrious criticism of a large part of the business community and the tenacious opposition of a near majority of the United States Senate. Modest as the proposal was, it challenged the most cherished prerogative of private management, the most hoary tenet of free private enterprise—the ability freely to make prices. This threat gave Roosevelt a reputation, persisting still among railway executives, of being a scandalous advocate of something closely akin to socialism. A more radical proposition, the President well knew, would have had no chance for success.

Roosevelt had constructed the Hepburn Bill with practiced care. Including as it did just enough to satisfy his purpose, it contained nothing that would alarm the marginal supporters without whom it could not survive. This was the last in a series of calculated tactics by which Roosevelt had prepared the parliamentary environment for his railroad program. "I have a very strong feeling," he acknowledged, "that it is a President's duty to get on with Congress if he possibly can, and that it is a reflection upon him if he and Congress come to a complete break." Avoiding a break, understanding his situation, he made the powers of his office and the talents of his person the instruments of viable leadership.

He had begun by trading tariff reform for railroad regulation. He had continued, after the adjournment of the lame duck session of the Fifty-eighth Congress, by taking his railroad issue, then the foremost national political problem, to the people. At the hustings his vigorous pleading won enthusiastic acclaim. His "plain people," for the most part, heard only the voice of their champion. Significantly, however, more careful, more cautious listeners, disregarding his dramatic allusions, at once could ascertain the moderation of his demands. Roosevelt's message was simple. His demands were not new. Indeed, Roosevelt added nothing to the principles or to the histrionics of the Granger and Populist railroad regulators of years gone by. But he did bring to their long-rejected national program a new respectability, an incomparable personal vitality, and assurances, impressive to thoughtful conservatives, that he, unlike his predecessors, would direct regulation to constructive ends.

The last was particularly important. By the fall of 1905 such reliable Republican senators from the West as Allison of Iowa and Spooner of Wisconsin, traditionally conservators of the status quo, now sensitive to the growing complaints of the farmers and shippers whose protests had preceded and exceeded Roosevelt's, realized that their political life rested upon an unprecedented capitulation to their constituents. In the President they recognized a safe sponsor for reform. If his language seemed at times extravagant, if his central purpose was a genuine departure from the past, he nevertheless, they knew from experience, guarded their party and, in the largest sense, their principles. This knowledge may also have comforted others who deeply distrusted the emotions Roosevelt evoked. Before the Fifty-ninth Congress convened, the roar of the President's crowds penetrated, perhaps, the cold quiet where Nelson Aldrich, by preference undisturbed, made policy. That master of the Senate, in any case, was thereafter willing to make a conciliatory gesture toward Roosevelt and his allies.

The President had set his stage. Reminded of the arrangements by which the tariff remained inviolate, the new House in February 1906, with only seven adverse votes, passed the Hepburn Bill. It provided for every objective of the Administration. The most thoughtful member of the I.C.C., Commissioner Prouty, told Roosevelt that it represented "an advance so extraordinary that he had never dared to suppose it would be possible to pass it." The President judged that it was "as far as we could with wisdom go at this time." Politically he was surely correct. Although an aroused constituency cheered the champions of the bill in the Senate, Nelson Aldrich, as debate began, had yet to surrender command of the chamber he had so long dominated. Roosevelt, until this time the aggressor, had now to adjust to the strength and the tactics of a talented oppositionist.

How unlike the President in many ways his adversary was: so urbane, so controlled, so indifferent to manifestations of approval, so patently disdainful of the string-tie statesmanship surrounding him; but, like Roosevelt, so bemused by the endless adventure of governing men! Did his friend Allison have, of a summer, to explain himself in ponderous periods from a rural podium? How dreary for Allison. Aldrich preferred the politics that the caucus controlled, the constituents one met graciously over liqueurs, the

measured exchanges between mutually respectful equals who understood
the manners and the meaning of their power. For all that, Aldrich was not
the less discerning, not the less tenacious. Many of the dreadful things that
Theodore did, the senator knew, he had to do. The people, after all, could
vote. The railroads were unpopular. Roosevelt could have his bill, but not
the way he wanted it. A gesture now, a delaying action—then, perhaps, the
worst would pass. Perhaps, again, it would not pass, the comfortable world
was changing. In that case, delay had of itself some value. And the means
to resist were familiar and strong.

Aldrich had a corps of allies: among the Republicans, the intractables, all
reliable, some expert parliamentarians, some outstanding men. There were
also among the Democrats those who regularly resisted any reform and
others, bound by quixotic tradition confounded with visions of miscegena-
tion, who could be made to shy at any extension of the federal executive
power. These were less reliable. Yet Aldrich in the past by prestige and by
persuasion had combined these parts into a solid phalanx to front, un-
budging, the bills that carried change.

Aldrich, disingenuous, moved quietly to bring the Hepburn Bill with its
objectionable clause on rates into the arena where he and his allies had
long had their way. While the measure lay before the Committee on Interstate and Foreign Commerce he labored at a disadvantage. There, with few
exceptions, his trusted assistants had no seat. There Roosevelt's friends,
making the President's moderation their own, seemed capable by coöperation with the Democratic committeemen of carrying crucial votes. There
Jonathan Dolliver, the junior senator from Iowa, then beginning the progressive period of his career, ably pleaded the case of the Administration.
Dolliver's continuing intimacy with Roosevelt and Attorney General Moody
made him as informed as he was ardent. If Dolliver could with the Democrats model the bill to Roosevelt's satisfaction and then bring it out of committee as a party measure, he would have thereafter a tactical advantage.
In these parts, Aldrich did not try to shape the bill in committee. He could
not have persuaded a majority to go his way, but he could and did persuade
a majority to ease his way. Seeming to yield, disarming Dolliver, Aldrich
permitted the Hepburn Bill to be reported unamended. Then, supported
by Democratic votes on which Dolliver had counted, he secured a motion
reserving to each committee member the right to propose amendments from
the floor. The issue, still unresolved, was now before the whole Senate.

The same Democratic votes sustained Aldrich's next move. Had Dolliver,
as he expected, been designated to guide the measure on the floor, he would
still have been an asset to the President and the bill might still have been
presented as the party's. Almost the senator from Iowa could see the
"Hepburn-Dolliver Act" engraved in history. The Democrats, however,
desiring some credit for regulating railroads, preferred that half that title
belong to them. This preference Aldrich exploited. He had won the Demo-

crats in the committee to reporting the bill for amendment from the floor by arranging to name as its floor leader one of their party, Benjamin Tillman of South Carolina. With that serpent-tongued agrarian as its guide, the bill could not be labeled "Republican." For Dolliver this was a staggering personal blow; for Aldrich, a beguiling triumph; for Roosevelt, an embarrassing problem in communication. The President and Tillman had long loathed each other. Only recently the senator had made one of his calculated, insulting attacks on Roosevelt's character. For years they had not spoken. Now Aldrich had forced them either to coöperate or to endanger the policy they both espoused. Whatever their course, furthermore, Aldrich had moved the bill into a position where he and his collaborators had an excellent chance of neutralizing it by amendment. "Aldrich," Roosevelt concluded irritably, had "completely lost both his head and his temper." The President had lost the first round.

Well before the Hepburn Bill reached the Senate, Aldrich and his associates had determined on the nature of their attack. Perhaps out of deference to the electorate, they refrained from a direct assault on the maximum rate clause. Instead, they concentrated on amendments by which they intended to endow the judiciary, the least mobile of the branches of government, with the authority to nullify and to delay the rate rulings of the I.C.C. In behalf of these amendments they debated not the economics of rate-making or the proprieties of privilege, but the constitutionality of the regulatory process, the orderly system that the President proposed to create.

Roosevelt had noted with care that the I.C.C. or a substitute commission "should be made unequivocally administrative." To an administrative body as opposed to an executive department, Congress could, he believed, within the meaning of the Constitution on the separation of powers, delegate the authority to fix maximum rates. This has become a commonplace assumption, the basis of a proliferation of alphabet agencies, but in 1906 men of disinterested conviction as well as those who were sheer obstructionists questioned the legality of combining in one body the quasi-legislative power of determining rates, even maximum rates, the quasi-judicial authority of deciding upon the validity of rates, and the quasi-executive function of investigation and enforcement. The unsuccessful railroad bill of 1905, attempting to resolve this constitutional difficulty, had included a clause, briefly resuscitated in 1910 by the Mann-Elkins Act, establishing a special court of commerce to review the rate decisions of the I.C.C. The Hepburn Bill as it emerged from the House, however, made no similar provision. Dodging the whole issue of judicial review, it said nothing at all about jurisdiction in cases arising under it.

On the question of judicial review, the proponents and the opponents of Roosevelt's program drew their lines. Contrasted to the large and varied significance of the whole railroad measure, this deployment seems at first

almost chicane. Yet since the debates on Hamilton's reports, American legislators had persisted in clothing their differences in constitutional terms.
Nor, in the case of the Hepburn Bill, was this lawyers' legacy meaningless.
Roosevelt envisioned a new kind of federal executive power to control the
complex processes of an industrialized state. He anticipated the methods of
the future. His opponents in the Senate, seeking to perpetuate the method
or lack of method of the past, relied upon the prevailing dicta of the American courts to prevent the executive from interfering in the day-by-day
operations of American business. In government based on law, this was in
1906 still a legal as well as an economic issue. Both sides assiduously spoke
the Constitution fair.

The President by no means denied the right of judicial review. He did
not believe that any legislation could "prevent . . . an appeal" from a ruling of the I.C.C. "The courts will retain, and should retain, no matter what
the Legislature does," he had asserted, "the power to interfere and upset
any action that is confiscatory in its nature." Yet Roosevelt also preferred
that judicial review should be limited essentially to procedural questions—
to a determination, in any mooted case, of whether the commission's
method of reaching the decision had been fair to the carrier. His opponents,
on the other hand, hoped to emasculate his program by providing explicitly
for broad judicial reinterpretation of the facts of each case. This would
have given the courts, considered friendly by the railroads, rather than the
commission, which the railroads feared, the real authority over rates.

By its reticence on the matter, the House's version of the Hepburn Bill
left to the courts themselves the determination of the scope of review.
Roosevelt expressed his satisfaction with this evasion. Attorney General
Moody, however, advised him that the measure, in order to pass the test of
constitutionality, needed an amendment affirming the right of the railroads
to have the courts review the commission's decisions. Roosevelt then considered it only desirable but not essential that the bill provide narrow review. As he began negotiations with the leaders of the Senate, he sought not
a limitation to procedural review but only an ambiguous declaration, consonant with the evasion in the unamended version, of the right of review.

Inherent in, but in Roosevelt's opinion subordinate to, the problem of
the scope of judicial review was the question of the time at which the rate
decisions of the I.C.C. should become effective. Roosevelt had asked that
they take effect "immediately," a stipulation the Hepburn Bill fulfilled to
his satisfaction by making them effective in thirty days. But if the railroads
took to court a decision of the commission, the long process of litigation
would postpone indefinitely the application of the revised maximum rate.
The House had avoided this problem. In the Senate, while the friends of the
railroads wanted just such a delay, the advocates of regulation endeavored to
construct some amendment that would prevent the use of injunctions to

suspend, pending the outcome of litigation, the rulings of the commission. Roosevelt when debate began preferred, but, as on the question of narrow review, did not insist that the use of injunctions be restricted.

Against the President's moderate, almost uncertain, position the prorailroad senators launched an offensive. Philander Chase Knox, who had while Attorney General seemed to endorse Roosevelt's program refused in a conference with Moody to reach an agreement on an amendment pertaining to judicial review. Moody's draft, supported by the President, protected the constitutionality of the Hepburn Bill without increasing the appellate jurisdiction of the courts. This was not enough for Knox. In conference he stated that he preferred the House's bill to Moody's amendment. To the Senate he proposed in February that the courts pass on the "lawfulness" of the commission's orders—a term Moody considered so vague as to invite continuing litigation on the economic details and constitutional implications of each rate order. Knox's broad definition of review, carrying as it did the prestige of its author, provided in compelling form precisely the objective of Aldrich and his allies. To graft upon the Hepburn Bill Knox's amendment or one just like it, Aldrich had maneuvered the measure out of committee and onto the floor.

Roosevelt, while Aldrich deployed, had not been idle. From the time the Hepburn Bill reached the Senate, even as it lay in committee, the President had begun to confer with his Republican associates about amendments. Like Aldrich, he had able collaborators. Most helpful of these were William B. Allison of Iowa and John C. Spooner of Wisconsin who, in other years, had with Aldrich and the now deceased O. H. Platt composed the Senate's inner council of control. Allison, of that Four the most sensitive to the tolerances of public opinion and the most skillful negotiator, "rendered," Roosevelt later recalled, "unwearied and invaluable service in the actual, and indispensable, working out of legislative business." Spooner, scarcely less gifted, had a large personal stake in the satisfactory resolution of the problem of regulation, for his home bastion rattled before the guerrillas of the insurgent La Follette. Allison and Spooner brought with them a loyal corps of lesser Western Republican veterans for whom freight rates had assumed pressing political importance. The President could also rely upon, though he would not confide in, the intense Republican left. Could these men clearly demonstrate their strength, others in the party would reluctantly go their way. Finally, there were the Bryan Democrats, Tillman, Bailey of Texas, and a few more cautious in thought and less erratic in deportment who would probably damn Roosevelt's bill but give it their votes.

So positioned, Roosevelt planned at first to carry the bill by sponsoring amendments which would attract the Republican center without alienating the bipartisan left. Throughout February and much of March, while the bill lay in committee, he sought only to perpetuate explicitly the ambiguities implicit in the House's version. The plan seemed feasible so long as the committee might fashion a party measure. But Aldrich's coup, preventing this, also permitted the senator to vitiate Roosevelt's influence with the uncertain. Naturally like Aldrich disposed to trust the judiciary to brake change, the Republican center, relieved of party discipline, now looked more favorably on broad review. Tillman as floor leader for the bill was scarcely fit by temperament or inclination to dissuade them. The President, consequently, had to adjust his strategy to Aldrich's *démarche*.

Roosevelt acted at once. As his personal, unofficial representative in the Senate he selected Allison, who could reach and convince a larger number of Republicans than could have any other possible agent. He arranged also to communicate with Tillman through ex-Senator William E. Chandler, a mutual friend and advocate of regulation. By this clumsy device, with Tillman's help and through Allison's negotiations, Roosevelt then set out to construct a new coalition. "Inasmuch as the Republican leaders have tried to betray me . . . ," he explained, "I am now trying to see if I cannot get . . . [the bill] through in the form I want by the aid of some fifteen or twenty Republicans added to most of the Democrats." For this purpose, involving as it did both the enthusiasm of Tillman and the loyalty of Allison, Roosevelt had to move cautiously but clearly to the left of his original position.

Largely to Allison fell the difficult task of seeking a formula which would solve the problems of judicial review and the use of injunctions to the satisfaction of the divers partners to the potential coalition. Aldrich, if not surprised, must have been a little hurt to find his friend working the other side of the aisle. The work was tedious. Senator after senator contributed to the dozens of amendments under consideration. Three of these sufficiently reveal the nature of Allison's predicament. That of Senator Long of Kansas, the well-advertised product of a White House conference held just at the time Roosevelt decided to rely upon a coalition, prevented, according to the consensus of the Senate, judicial reconsideration of the facts of a case. In endorsing it, the President, no longer equivocal, won the favor of the coalition's Republicans and populist Democrats. Yet this was not enough. Senator Bailey of Texas, Tillman's closest associate, and other persistent Jeffersonians opposed the amendment, as Aldrich expected they would, because it seemed to them an unwarranted extension of executive power. Both Tillman and Bailey, moreover, considered the injunction issue more important than judicial review. The Texan had introduced an amendment, endorsed by most Democrats, which deprived the courts of authority to issue temporary writs suspending rate orders. Although this proposal effectively prevented delay in the application of rate rulings, it seemed to Roosevelt and his harassed lieutenants to be clearly unconstitutional. As negotiations proceeded, the President feared that Aldrich might adopt Bailey's plan or any of several like it in order with Democratic support to write a law that the courts would promptly nullify. Roosevelt and Allison therefore sponsored as an alternative an amendment drafted by Spooner. It provided that whenever a court suspended a rate order the amount in dispute between the carrier and the commission should be placed in escrow pending the outcome of litigation. Spooner's plan at once prevented confiscation of railroad property without due process of law, protected the shippers, and eliminated any advantage for the railroad in seeking litigation simply to cause delay.

Had Roosevelt and Allison been dealing only with resilient men, such ingenuity as Spooner's might, in time, have permitted them to devise a winning compromise. Bailey, for one, began to trim toward Allison. But a few Republicans and Tillman Democrats remained so adamantly for narrow review, many other Democrats so firmly for broad review, that Spooner's promising solution for injunctions never commanded the serious attention of either extreme. Before Allison had a chance to homogenize these stubborn parts, Aldrich precipitated crisis. He, too, had been active across the aisle. On April 18, as he predicted, the Democratic caucus refused to follow Tillman and Bailey. Roosevelt's attempt at coalition had failed.

Aldrich, the second round his, doubtless hoped that Roosevelt would either capitulate or, as he had a few weeks earlier, move further left. The President could have consolidated a noisy defense by throwing in his lot with the La Follette Republicans and Tillman Democrats. He could with them have swelled the rising voices of protest. He might, by such a move, have earned a popularity beyond even that already his. But he would have lost his bill. Seeing this as clearly as did Aldrich, Roosevelt had already prepared once more to redeploy.

Six days earlier, sensing defeat, the President had begun to hedge. If he could not win with Tillman, he might still win on his own original terms without the Democrats. "I am not at all sure," he then wrote Allison, "but that the easy way will be to come right back to the bill as it passed the House, and with very few unimportant amendments to pass it as it stands." On April 22 Roosevelt told Knox, again his confidant, that this opinion was "evidently gaining ground." Indeed it was, for Nelson Aldrich turned toward Roosevelt after the Democrats turned away. The leaders of the President's Republican opposition by early May ceased to insist on an explicit statement for broad review. Perhaps Aldrich became impatient with the continuing delay in the work of the Senate brought about by the everlasting debate on regulation. Perhaps he decided that Republican solidarity was more important than Roosevelt's purpose was dangerous. Probably, however, he saw that he had miscalculated. When Roosevelt, refusing to list with the left, reverted doggedly to the ambiguous center where he had first stood, he impelled Tillman, La Follette, and their likes, his erstwhile allies, into embittered opposition. Their protestations, couched in their inevitable vocabulary of revolt, attested to the safe reasonableness Roosevelt had ever claimed as his own. The uncertain minds of the wavering Republican center might now hear Allison out—might now, as Allison and Spooner had, see in Roosevelt safety. By some new alignment, like that he had hoped Dolliver would muster, the President with Time in *Thermidor* might triumph. At least, so Aldrich may have reasoned. In any case he retreated.

He may also have drafted the amendment which, introduced by Allison, won a majority vote and thereby secured the enactment of the Hepburn Bill. Whether or not Aldrich drafted it, Allison's amendment, leaving the bill in effect as the House had written it, gave Roosevelt what he had started out to get. The authorship of the amendment, like the working of Aldrich's mind, remains obscure. Whoever wrote it, Allison guided it. His activities in the two weeks following the Democratic caucus may be accurately surmised. Leaving no records, the "unwearied and invaluable" senator from Iowa, camped in the cloakroom where he excelled, had fashioned for the President a compromise that satisfied enough Republicans to save the bill.

The Allison amendment covered both judicial review and the use of injunctions. With purposeful obscurity, it granted jurisdiction in cases arising under the Hepburn Act to the circuit courts but left the definition of the scope of review to the courts. In a flood of oratory over the meaning of the amendment, each senator interpreted it to suit himself and his constituents. Both sides claimed victory. Insofar as the amendment was described as a victory for either narrow or broad review, the claims were nonsense. The question of review remained in May as unsettled as it had been in February. Roosevelt had then asked for no more. Ultimately the Supreme Court, which he trusted so little, in the first decision involving rate rulings made his preference law by refusing to review the facts of the case.

The Allison amendment did affirmatively settle the matter of injunctions by empowering the courts to "enjoin, set aside, annul, or suspend any order" of the I.C.C. It also prescribed that appeals from the orders of the I.C.C. were to go directly to the Supreme Court with the calendar priorities of antitrust cases. The amendment did not, however, specify the grounds for suspension or establish an escrow scheme. There remained, consequently, the possibility of considerable delay before rate rulings took effect. Roosevelt had constantly expressed his preference for an arrangement less favorable to the railroads, but he had also continually indicated that he would accept a solution like that of the Allison amendment. On this matter Tillman and Bailey, but neither Aldrich nor Roosevelt, had been defeated.

Roosevelt was "entirely satisfied" with the Allison amendment, he pointed out, because he was "entirely satisfied with the Hepburn bill." The amendment, he informed a less satisfied representative of midwestern shippers, was "only declaratory of what the Hepburn bill must mean, supposing it to be constitutional . . . I should be glad to get certain [other] amendments . . . ; but they are not vital, and even without them the Hepburn bill with the Allison amendment contains practically exactly what I have both originally and always since asked for."

Characteristically, Roosevelt overstated his case. "Always since" did not apply, for in his maneuvers of late March and April, although only at that time, the President had asked for more. Tillman and Bailey, who had joined him then, with rankling disappointment attacked him for returning to what he had originally requested. Their attacks, often repeated by their friends, have persuaded two generations that Roosevelt, irresolute and insincere, deserting his friends, yielding to Aldrich, lost the battle for regulation. Surely his detractors felt this, but they erred. Roosevelt had made overtures to Tillman and Bailey only for tactical reasons. He had, temporarily and for parliamentary support, enlarged his earlier demands. When this did not produce sufficient support, he reverted for tactical reasons to his first position. In so doing he deserted his temporary allies, but he did not compromise his policy. Tillman and Bailey, proud veterans of the Senate, perhaps resented most the knowledge that they had been used. Doubtless their pain gave Aldrich, who had made Roosevelt woo them and leave them, some amused satisfaction.

His objective attained, Roosevelt exulted. "No given measure and no given set of measures," he believed, "will work a perfect cure for any serious evil; and the insistence upon having only the perfect cure often results in securing no betterment whatever." The Hepburn Act was not perfect. But, Roosevelt maintained, it represented "the longest step ever yet taken in the direction of solving the railway rate problem." This was a fair assessment. With his clear perception of political situations, Roosevelt had set the highest practicable goal. By his mastery of political devices, in contest with another master, he had reached it. The Senate, in the end, supplied the federal executive with authority beyond any antecedent definition to mitigate the maladjustments of a growing industrial society.

The Hepburn Act endowed the Interstate Commerce Commission with power commensurate with its task. By informed, expert decisions, it could at last alter the artificial configurations of a market that had long since ceased, in the classic sense, to be free. The courts inexpertly had judged transportation by criteria which, however precious in jurisprudence, bore little relation to the economics of the process. Released from the inhibition of judicial reinterpretations (the bond that Aldrich had sought to supply), endowed with weapons the carriers respected, the I.C.C. began to develop after 1906 the techniques of effective supervision. The need for further change of course remained. But the Hepburn Act provided the precedent, accepted by the courts and enlarged by later Congresses, by which federal regulatory agencies have promoted the national welfare. Now vastly ramified, the government by administrative commission remains, though somewhat shabby, a useful part of American political arrangements.

For a troubled people in a complex time perhaps only the executive could have become steward. Aldrich, in that case, fought history and Roosevelt only accelerated what no man could have prevented. But Roosevelt's reputation rests securely even in acceleration, for the inevitable sometimes takes too long, and he knew just what he did. His efforts in behalf of the Hepburn Act—a measure meaningful but moderate—demonstrated his skilled concern for creating the instruments he thought the nation needed. For an orderly administrative system, for the right of efficient federal controls, for the positive government of an industrial society, he mobilized in a crucial first skirmish the full powers of his office. And he won. . . .

Woodrow Wilson and
Progressivism:
Did the South Help Make
Wilson an Advanced
Progressive?

INTRODUCTION

In terms of ideas, the significant aspect of the election campaign of 1912 was the struggle between two types of progressivism, the New Freedom of Woodrow Wilson, with its plea for regulated competition and the restoration of the economic individualism of days gone by, and the New Nationalism of Theodore Roosevelt, with its advocacy of regulated monopoly and advanced welfare legislation. Upon assuming the Presidency, Wilson sought to persuade Congress to adopt a legislative program consistent with the principles of the New Freedom, and he specifically opposed certain legislative measures that comported better with the philosophy of the New Nationalism than with that of the New Freedom. Within a short time, however, Wilson was forced to modify his position somewhat, and eventually he espoused virtually the whole of the New Nationalist program. What accounts for this change in Wilson's policy?

In the first of the two selections that follow, Professor Arthur S. Link, the foremost Wilson scholar of our day, contends that a "Southern Agrarian" faction in Congress "helped to make Wilson an advanced progressive and helped to commit his administration to a broad program of welfare legislation." The contributions of this Southern group, Link declares, were "in many ways decisive" in pushing the Wilson administration away from the New Freedom and toward the New Nationalism.

Challenging Link on this point, Richard Abrams, who at the time the article here reprinted was written was a member of the research staff of the Dictionary of American Biography, *argues largely on the basis of an analysis of the votes of Southern members of Congress that there was no "co-ordinated" Southern radical faction in Congress, that the radicalism of the Southern group and the conservatism of Wilson have been exaggerated, and that in so far as Southerners deviated from administration policies, it was generally in the direction of conservatism rather than of radicalism.*

The South and the "New Freedom":

An Interpretation

Arthur S. Link

The election of Woodrow Wilson and Democratic majorities in the House and Senate in 1912 confronted the Democrats of the South with their most serious challenge since before the Civil War. They had come to power more because of the disruption of the Republican party than because their party now represented the majority opinion of the country, and the future of the Democratic party for many years to come would depend upon their performance during the next two years. But the question whether they were not too much rent by personal factionalism and too sectionally conscious to govern in the national interest remained yet to be answered.

Southern Democrats in 1913 controlled practically all important congressional committees; they had a large majority in the Democratic caucuses in both houses; they had a president apparently responsive to their wishes, and they had a goodly representation in the cabinet. Judged by all superficial appearances, at least, the South was "in the saddle." These, however, were only the outward signs of control. The fact that Southerners happened to be chairmen of certain committees may or may not be important. The important question is whether they used the power they possessed to achieve political and economic objectives that the South especially desired, and whether they helped to shape the character of Wilsonian reform.

Wilson came to the presidency in 1913 with a clear conception of what the Democratic party should do to right the wrongs that special privilege had allegedly perpetrated through the Republican party. He would have the Democrats revise the tariff to eliminate all features of special privilege to domestic industries, bring the national banks into effective cooperation and control, and work out a new code for business in order to restore competition and make impossible the misuse of power by the giant corporations. This was the sum and substance of the "New Freedom." The political and economic millennium was to be achieved by these simple expedients, all of

Reprinted from *The American Scholar*, Volume XX, Number 3, Summer 1951. Copyright © 1951 by the United Chapters of Phi Beta Kappa. By permission of the publishers. Pp. 314–324.

which were based upon the assumption implicit in Wilson's campaign addresses of 1912, namely, that the limits of federal authority under the Constitution would not permit, and wise statesmanship would not desire, the extension of federal authority directly into business operations or the use of that authority to change the social and economic relationships then existing among the various interest groups.

Wilson originally conceived of the New Freedom as the political means of implementing the doctrines of laissez-faire, by removing all kinds of special class legislation. It was, therefore, a program intended to meet the needs primarily of the business community. There was nothing in it for the farmers or laborers directly, although these groups presumably would benefit from lower tariff rates and the restoration of competition in business. But Wilson had no more idea of legislating to advance the interests of these particular groups than he did of granting subsidies to American manufacturers. It can be said, in brief, that the Wilsonian program had the one supreme objective of taking the government out of the business of subsidizing and directly regulating economic activity and of taking the country back to some mythical age when there was a perfect natural identification of economic interests.

The most significant fact about the first Wilson administration is that the New Freedom, as it was originally conceived by its author, survived for only a few months. It required only short contact with reality to convince Wilson that his elaborate doctrines of 1912 were inadequate to deal with such great concentrations of economic power as existed at the time. More important as a factor in moving him away from his laissez-faire position, however, were certain powerful political forces over which Wilson and his administration had no control and which, as it were, seized control of administration policy and pushed it far beyond the bounds that Wilson and his advisers had originally thought desirable. In effect, what occurred from 1913 to 1917 was that Wilson adopted many of the assumptions and almost the whole platform of Theodore Roosevelt's New Nationalism.

This metamorphosis in the Wilsonian program is the key to understanding the first Wilson administration. The Southern contribution toward bringing the administration to an advanced position with regard to the exercise of federal authority was considerable, but the character of this contribution was different from what has been generally assumed. The Southern Democrats in Congress were divided roughly into two factions. First, there was what might be called the administration faction, consisting mainly of committee chairmen like Oscar W. Underwood and Carter Glass, who, by and large, represented a political tradition and constituencies whose interests were more or less divergent from those of the more numerous Southern group. Members of the administration faction were for the most part conservatives, although most of them had no fundamental political principles, were loyal party men, and would follow Wilson's lead. Secondly, there was a larger faction that represented more accurately the political traditions and economic interests of the South—the spokesmen for the agrarian interests of the South, men like Claude Kitchin, Otis Wingo, James K. Vardaman and Robert L. Henry.

The Southern Agrarians of the Wilson period were the direct inheritors and now the prime articulators in the Democratic party of the philosophy underlying the Agrarian crusade—namely, that it was government's duty to intervene directly in economic affairs in order to benefit submerged or politically impotent economic interests. As it turned out, the existence and power of the Southern Agrarian group had important consequences for the Democratic party, the Wilson administration, and the nation. Whereas the administration faction usually followed the regular party line, the Southern Agrarians were often far to the left of it; and in the end they helped to make Wilson an advanced progressive and helped to commit his administration to a broad program of welfare legislation.

The program of the Southern Agrarians was aimed at benefiting the farmers almost exclusively. Although this had been true also of the Democratic program in 1896, Bryan and progressive Democrats in the North and West had moved beyond the almost pure agrarianism of 1896. There was a growing concern for the plight of submerged groups from about 1890 to 1913 and a consequent rise of a great movement for social justice. This phase of progressivism had not been totally absent in the South, but the Southern states were still overwhelmingly rural, and most Southerners had no conception of the grave social and economic problems raised by industrialization and urbanization.

Hence Southern progressives were more concerned with strengthening the political and economic position of the farmers, through regulation of railroads and corporations, a low tariff, the direct primary, and the like, than with tenement reforms, minimum wage legislation, or workmen's compensation legislation. But the important point about the Southern Agrarian program is not that it was limited in scope, but that its advocates were an important element in the Democratic party and that they were now in a position to give voice to their own demands.

The brief period when the philosophy of the New Freedom had any real authority was the few months in 1913 when the Underwood tariff bill was under discussion in Congress. There was little disagreement among Democratic congressmen, progressive or conservative, over the provisions of the bill, except for minor differences on the wool and sugar schedules. There was a much greater difference of opinion between the conservatives and the agrarian radicals, however, on the question of the reorganization of the banking system and the control of the money supply. It was here that the Southern Agrarians, acting with their colleagues from the West, first helped to move their party away from laissez-faire toward a dynamic concept of government.

In line with his New Freedom principles Wilson was inclined to favor the banking and monetary system proposed by the National Monetary Commission, one providing for a reserve association or associations owned and controlled by the bankers themselves. The original Glass bill, which had the tentative endorsement of the administration, provided for such an arrangement. But even before the federal reserve bill emerged from the House Banking Committee, there occurred a momentous struggle within the party councils that was not ended until the Agrarian leaders had won all their important demands. Secretary of State Bryan and Louis D. Brandeis persuaded the President that a banking bill which did not provide for exclusive governmental control, on the top level, was not only unwise but also would never be approved by the House caucus. This was true, incidentally, regardless of the position Bryan might have taken in the controversy.

Wilson was won over by the persuasive arguments of Bryan and Brandeis and the threats of the radicals. Thus the Glass bill, as it finally emerged from the House committee, provided for a decentralized reserve system, for government issue of federal-reserve currency, and for an over-all supervision and limited control of the new system by a central reserve board composed exclusively of presidential appointees. It marked, to all practical purposes, the demise of the New Freedom and the beginning of the rise to dominance of the progressives in the Wilson administration.

Bryan and the Western Democrats were now satisfied, but not the Southern Agrarian leaders. In spite of the radical changes that had been effected, the new banking system still would operate exclusively for the benefit of the business community. Here was the rub, as far as the Southern radicals were concerned. After tariff reform had been accomplished, their main objective was the establishment of a system by which farmers could obtain easier and cheaper credit. When the Glass bill was published, and the Southern Agrarians discovered that it included no provision for agricultural credit, they rose in rebellion and declared that they would help the Republicans defeat the measure if the administration did not concede their demands. The fight between the administration forces and the Southern Agrarians was bitter, and for a time threatened to defeat banking reform altogether. Suffice it to say that, in spite of the ridicule of the Eastern press and in spite of the opposition of the administration and of Wilson's spokesmen in the House, the Federal Reserve Bill as finally passed by Congress contained ample provisions for short-term agricultural credit. And this was true because Wilson realized that he must give in to the demands of the Southerners.

The philosophic foundations of the New Freedom were dealt another heavy blow during the formulation of an antitrust policy by administration leaders. It was Wilson's original idea that all that was required was to define precisely what constituted an unfair trade practice or illegal restraint of trade, so as to remove all element of doubt from the laws. The enforcement of the antitrust laws would be delegated, as before, to the Justice Department and the courts. Some of the Southern radicals proposed more drastic remedies, such as prescribing by law the percentage of the total production of a field of industry which one corporation would be allowed to control, or a high excess profits tax which would increase in direct proportion to the size of the industry; but they made no determined fight for these proposals. Wilson, therefore, gave the job of drawing up the measure to Representative Clayton of Georgia, chairman of the Judiciary Committee, and the bill that came out of his committee was simply a synthesis of current ideas, most of which were already embodied in the laws of many states. In addition, Representative Covington of Kentucky drew up at Wilson's request a bill providing for an interstate trade commission, which was to be an enlarged Bureau of Corporations and without any real authority over business practices.

Thus far Wilson had proceeded in line with his New Freedom concepts. At this point, however, an important turn in administration policy occurred. Brandeis, George L. Rublee, and Representative Stevens of New Hampshire visited the President and persuaded him to change the character of his antitrust program entirely. Under their direction, the Clayton bill was rewritten so as to provide for greater flexibility in defining an unfair trade practice and, more important, the interstate commerce commission was reconstituted as the Federal Trade Commission and given apparently vast authority over the day-to-day operations of the business world. The Covington bill had provided for nothing more than an investigatory body to serve as an adjunct of the Justice Department. In the revised bill, the Commission was established as an independent regulatory agency, empowered to supervise business practices and to issue cease and desist orders when it found that corporations were engaging in unfair practices. This last change marked the complete adoption by the Wilson administration of Roosevelt's program for the regulation of business.

The Southern leaders in Congress had nothing to do with bringing about this profound change in Wilson's antitrust policy. The Southern and Western Agrarian radicals, acting with a small Labor bloc in the House, worked hard, however, to have a provision inserted in the Clayton bill exempting farm and labor unions from the operation and application of the antitrust laws. This had been one of the major objectives of the American Federation of Labor since 1906 and had been given Democratic approval in the platforms of 1908 and 1912. Although Wilson was rapidly abandoning his New Freedom assumptions, he was not yet ready to go so far as to approve what was obviously legislation in the interest of particular classes. Since the first days of his administration he had resisted bitterly this move, and a bill specifically exempting farm and labor unions from antitrust prosecutions, which had been passed by the House in the previous session, was blocked by administration pressure. When the Clayton bill was under discussion in the House committee, however, the Agrarian and Labor bloc declared that they would guarantee its defeat unless Wilson gave in to their demands.

Thus faced with another major revolt within his party, Wilson resolved his dilemma by resorting, it must be admitted, to one of the most artful dodges in the history of American politics. The famous labor provisions of the Clayton bill were drawn by Representative E. Y. Webb of North Carolina, who had succeeded Clayton as chairman of the Judiciary Committee, and represented Wilson's attitude perfectly. On the face of it, the new provision did indeed seem to give the exemption and immunity from antitrust prosecutions that the farm and labor spokesmen were demanding. Actually, this was not the case at all. Farm and labor organizations were not to be construed by the courts as being, *per se,* combinations in restraint of trade, but they were in no way freed from the threat of prosecution if they violated the antitrust laws.

Wilson had completed his program of domestic reform by the fall of 1914. In his letters and public statements at the time, he made it clear that he thought everything had been done that was necessary to clear away special privilege and put all classes on an equal footing. Under the operation of the beneficient new laws, Wilson was sure that the nation would enjoy a long period of prosperity and economic freedom. As we have seen, he had been forced partially to abandon his earlier position and to make important concessions in order to get his program across. He was reconciled to the concessions he had been compelled to make, but he was absolutely determined to draw the line at the point it had reached by the fall of 1914.

In fact, a pronounced reaction against progressive policies had set in among Wilson and his advisers during the spring of 1914, and relations between the President and progressive leaders became exceedingly strained at this time. The following year, 1915, was practically barren of progressive accomplishments, except for . . . La Follette's Seamen's Act, which the administration had opposed and which Wilson almost vetoed. There were, however, several great political forces at work which were so strong that Wilson would be compelled to accommodate his program to satisfy their demands. One was the well-organized Agrarian movement for the establishment of a federal system of long-term rural credits. Another was the movement in behalf of federal social legislation, which was rapidly gaining momentum during this period. Another was the movement for women's suffrage, which was becoming so powerful that it would soon be dangerous for any politician to oppose it. Finally, there was the fact that the Progressive party was obviously disintegrating after 1914 and that the only hope the Democrats had of obtaining a national majority in 1916 was in winning a large minority of the former Bull Moosers to the Democratic side.

Wilson resisted this movement to extend the intervention of the federal government into the fields mentioned here as long as he could do so safely.

Then, when it became evident that the Democrats could win the election of 1916 only by adopting the New Nationalism, lock, stock and barrel, Wilson capitulated and supported the very demands he had so long opposed, as strongly as if he had been their originator. We do not have the space to discuss this last and most important phase of Wilsonian reform in any detail, except to consider the extent to which the Southern leaders contributed to the administration's final, complete surrender to the New Nationalism.

The main objective of the Southern Agrarian progressives after 1914 was the adoption of a federal rural credits bill. The first nationwide movement for long-term federal rural credit facilities had been inaugurated by the Southern Commercial Congress in 1913, and during the next year or two there was widespread discussion of the subject all over the country. In the spring of 1914 a joint subcommittee drew up the bill which was finally passed in 1916 and which would have passed in 1914 had not Wilson let it be known that he would veto the bill if Congress enacted it. Both Wilson and the Agrarian leaders proclaimed themselves advocates of a rural credits measure. What, therefore, was the root of the difference between them? Wilson would not agree to the establishment of a system involving direct subsidies or financial support by the government, and Wilson, Secretary of Agriculture Houston, and Carter Glass were insistent that the government should do no more than provide for the structure of a rural credits system, with capital and management to be provided by private sources. The Agrarian spokesmen, on the other hand, contended that any system which was not operated and financed by the government was bound to fail. But as this involved the direct intervention by the government in behalf of a special class, Wilson was absolutely adamant against it. The result was an impasse, with both sides holding out stubbornly for their own proposals until 1916, when Wilson accepted the Agrarian proposal for reasons of political expediency.

It was, in fact, in agricultural legislation that the Southern Agrarians had the greatest influence in the shaping of the later Wilsonian program. Their greatest contribution was undoubtedly the forcing of the Rural Credits Act of 1916, but they were also able to obtain the adoption of the Lever Warehouse Act in 1914, the Smith-Lever Act for rural extension work of the same year, the Smith-Hughes Act for vocational education, and the program of federal subsidies for highway improvement in 1916.

Southern influence was practically negligible, however, in the formulation of the remaining great social and economic legislation of 1916—the federal Workmen's Compensation Act, the Child Labor Law, the Adamson Act, and the act establishing the Federal Tariff Commission. But there still remain three other areas of legislation in which the influence of the Southern Agrarians was decisive and which merit notice here.

The first involved the question of what sort of military and naval bills Congress should enact in 1916. On this controversial subject the Southern progressives joined with radicals throughout the country in resisting the administration's designs greatly to increase the navy and to establish a large volunteer army. They were not successful in blocking the movement for a large navy, because the pressure here was too great. But they were signally successful in blocking Wilson's plans for military preparedness, indeed, in emasculating them.

The second field of legislation in which Southern progressive influence was decisive was the area of federal fiscal policy. Before the outbreak of the World War, Wilson and McAdoo were able to keep a firm grip on the formulation of tax policies, and their influence was conservative indeed. The tax structure that the Republicans had erected and which was weighted so heavily in favor of the upper classes was left practically undisturbed by the Wilson administration. An income tax provision was included in the Underwood Tariff Law, to make up the anticipated deficit resulting from the lower duties, but the rates were very low and the administration was quick to make it clear that it had no intention of using the income tax to effect a redistribution of wealth.

The outbreak of the war in Europe in the summer of 1914 caused a temporary disarrangement of the finances of the United States and resulted in a sharp decline in imports, which meant that the administration was faced with an alarming decline in revenues. To meet this emergency, McAdoo proposed a series of new excise taxes and a tax on freight shipments, such as had been applied during the Spanish-American War. The Southern and Western Agrarians rebelled at the administration's emergency tax program, claiming that it would throw the whole burden of carrying the country through the crisis on the masses and demanding instead an increase in the income tax. They were successful in eliminating the tax on freight shipments and in getting most of the new taxes put on alcoholic beverages and other luxuries. Even so, they did not like the emergency tax law and vowed that they would continue to fight all such consumption taxes.

With the opening of Congress in December, 1915, the Southern progressives found themselves virtually in control of the House Ways and Means Committee. Long before the new session convened, a majority of the committee declared in writing to the new chairman, Claude Kitchin of North Carolina, their determination to overhaul the tax structure and make it more democratic. The result was that during the winter and spring of 1916 the control of federal tax policy was literally taken out of the hands of the administration leaders and assumed by these Southern Agrarians and their Western allies. It was obvious by this time that some kind of preparedness measures would be adopted, and that either the government would have to find new sources of revenue or else resort to borrowing. The Republicans proposed a bond issue; the administration proposed new consumption and excise and increased income taxes. The Ways and Means Committee, however, replied with one of the most startling and significant tax bills in the history of the country. The Southern Agrarians, who had bitterly resisted the preparedness movement, saw now that new defense measures were inevitable; but they were determined that the people of the East, who had been most vociferous in support of preparedness, should pay for it. Kitchin said as much, in fact, before the House caucus when he explained the new tax bill, which greatly increased the income tax, levied the first federal inheritance tax in our history, and placed an excess profits tax on munitions manufacturers.

The last area in which Southern influence was decisive in determining the policies of the Wilson administration was the federal government's policy toward Negroes. Here the Southern contribution was definitely retrogressive and proved that it was impossible for white Southerners of all shades of opinion to get much beyond the rationale of slavery. Suffice it to say that Wilson practically sacrificed the Negroes on the altar of political expediency, by allowing segregation in the government departments, dismissal and downgrading of Negro civil servants in the South, and the like, in order to win Southern support for his program.

Yet in spite of this and other blind spots in the Southern progressive program, it must be concluded that the contributions of the Southern Agrarians were undoubtedly in many ways decisive in moving the Wilson administration away from a static laissez-faire program, to which it was originally dedicated, toward a dynamic, positive program of federal action. Although their program was limited in scope and motivated largely by class interests, the Southern progressives could claim as much credit as could several other major groups for the amazing metamorphosis in Democratic policy that occurred from 1913 to 1916. That is the real significance of their contribution.

275

Woodrow Wilson and the Southern

Congressmen, 1913–1916

Richard M. Abrams

During the Presidential campaign of 1912, Woodrow Wilson, in conjunction with Louis D. Brandeis, outlined the principles on which Wilson proposed to base a legislative program. As originally conceived, these principles—which have come to be known as the New Freedom—appeared to follow traditional assumptions of free enterprise and economic individualism. According to the New Freedom, the purpose of government was to remove all obstacles to the smooth operation of the mechanisms of the free market; logically this implied proscription of special privileges or favors which the government might extend to any interest or group. In a word, the New Freedom aimed to make *laissez faire* a practicable and just principle of government.

On the other hand, Theodore Roosevelt set forth a program of industrial progress and social welfare requiring active governmental intervention in the economic affairs of American society. According to the New Nationalism, as this program was called, business, farm, and labor consolidations were to be encouraged, underprivileged elements in society were to be given direct government benefits, and the government was to act in general as a mediator among the various contending interests. In brief, while the New Freedom emphasized decentralization of power in politics and economics, the New Nationalism emphasized concentration of power, in the name of efficiency, science, and progress.

The problem for the historian has been to understand how, if Wilson was committed to the New Freedom, so much legislation was passed during his first administration which does not appear to fit within the New Freedom's principles. Professor Arthur S. Link, the foremost student of the Wilson era, has been one of the first to attempt to resolve this problem.[1] He contends

From *The Journal of Southern History*, XXII (November 1956), 417–437. Copyright 1956 by the Southern Historical Association. Reprinted with permission of the Managing Editor.

[1] See especially Arthur S. Link, "The South and the 'New Freedom': An Interpretation," in *American Scholar* (New York, 1932–), XX (1951), 314–24; and *Woodrow Wilson and the Progressive Era, 1910–1917* (New York, 1954).

that although the "sum and substance" of Wilson's New Freedom was the elimination of special privilege by means of a thorough revision of the tariff system, the banking system, and the trust laws, before long certain radical forces compelled Wilson to use the powers of the government along lines prescribed by the New Nationalists. Prominent among these radicals was a large congressional faction of Southern agrarians, representing the true political traditions and economic interests of the South.

> The Southern Agrarians of the Wilson period were the direct in-heritors and now the prime articulators in the Democratic party of the philosophy underlying the Agrarian crusade—namely, that it was gov-ernment's duty to intervene directly in economic affairs in order to benefit submerged or politically impotent economic interests. . . . in the end they helped make Wilson an advanced progressive and helped to commit his administration to a broad program of welfare legislation.

By 1916, Professor Link concludes, Wilson had adopted the New National-ism "lock, stock and barrel." [2]

The purpose of this paper is to investigate the role of the Southern con-gressmen in the enactment of the domestic legislative program of Wilson's first administration; in part, perforce, it is to discover exactly who were the Southern agrarians to whom Professor Link refers. Were they a definite group or faction with a specific philosophy or program? What specifically did they accomplish? Were they indeed "radicals" or "progressives" in the sense understood by contemporary Americans?

To open the war on "privilege," President Wilson, in his inaugural ad-dress, summoned a special session of Congress to enact a tariff protecting no interests and earning only the revenue needed for normal governmental functions. Almost unanimously, the Southern congressmen (who comprised about 35 per cent of all congressional Democrats and commanded nearly all positions of power in Congress) co-operated fully with the administration in passing the Underwood Tariff Act.

Serious insurgency within the Democracy first arose during the contest over the bill to reform the national banking system, which the House took up while the Senate debated the tariff measure. Although the American business community had long recognized the need for a thoroughly reformed banking system, few agreed upon a definite plan. The principles of the New Freedom required a bill which, like the tariff measure, extended no govern-mental favors to any interest. It was natural, however, that whatever scheme the administration might choose, it would meet with heated opposition, not the least of which would be from the bankers and businessmen who had the most immediate material interest in the nation's financial structure.

---

[2] Link, "The South and the 'New Freedom,'" 316, 321. It is not clear just what states Professor Link includes in the "South." For the purposes of this paper, the "South" will be used to designate the eleven states of the Confederacy.

The bill initially drafted by Representative Carter Glass of Virginia, and used by the administration as the foundation for subsequent alterations, was essentially a conservative one, but the conservative banking community, unwilling to accept any reform it could not itself write, immediately protested to Washington. The chief opposition in Congress, however, came from those seeking a *less* conservative measure—a measure which would, through governmental intervention, provide easier credit for particular interests. Secretary of State William Jennings Bryan indicated that he and his congressional followers would oppose any plan not providing for federal control over the issue of currency, while Robert L. Owen of Oklahoma, chairman of the Senate Banking Committee, suggested that the Treasury Department directly control the entire banking system.[3] Hostility in Congress mounted among those who resented the "private" fashion in which the administration had drafted the bill, as well as among those who viewed the bill as "legalizing the money-trust" by leaving credit and the currency in bankers' control. In response to this hostility, the President called for advice from Louis D. Brandeis, on whom he had depended so often in the past campaign.

Brandeis persuaded Wilson to vest the power to issue currency in the government, and to limit the bankers to an advisory capacity. He pointed out that while it was desirable to pass a measure quickly, until then the only discussion of the issue had been "that organized by the bankers," so that the bill was too heavily influenced by this single source. Brandeis urged that time be allowed for the business and agrarian interests to make their suggestions. He added: "Nothing would go so far in establishing confidence among businessmen as the assurance that the Government will control the currency issue"—a sentiment which he shared with Owen.[4]

Although Wilson forced Glass to accept Brandeis' suggestions, an extremist element remained hostile. For the bill still omitted prohibition of interlocking directorates among national banks (one of the two major recommendations of the Pujo Committee of 1911–1912), it left the private bankers with considerable influence within the proposed Federal Reserve System, and it omitted provisions for long-term agricultural credit. When Glass made public the "compromise" bill on June 14, 1913, Robert L. Henry of Texas, chairman of the House Rules Committee and leader of the "radical agrarians" (as Professor Link refers to them), publicly blasted the measure.[5] The bill was formally introduced June 26, three days after the President addressed Congress declaring: "The control of the system of banking and of issue which our new laws are to set up must be public, not private, must be

---

[3] New York *Times*, April 30, 1913.

[4] Louis D. Brandeis to Woodrow Wilson, June 14, 1913, in Wilson Papers (Manuscripts Division, Library of Congress). Wilson had asked Brandeis to put in writing the major points of their discussion on June 12.

[5] New York *Times*, June 15, 1913; Ray Stannard Baker, *Woodrow Wilson, Life and Letters* (8 vols., Garden City, 1927–1939), IV, 164–65.

vested in the Government itself, so that the banks may be the instruments, not the masters, of business and of individual enterprise and initiative." [6]

While the bill was in committee, administration leaders conceded to insurgents only a few amendments, among which were prohibition of interlocking directorates and of loans by national banks in which their officers were interested.[7] The most serious challenge to the administration measure developed July 24, when J. Willard Ragsdale of South Carolina, following Robert Henry's lead, prepared a drastic substitute bill providing for an issue of currency based on warehouse receipts for cotton, corn, and wheat.[8] At this point, Wilson intervened, persuading Otis Wingo of Arkansas, leader of the committee rebels, to have proposals for agricultural credit introduced as a separate bill, and to take the banking bill into caucus where proceedings could be more confidential.[9]

On July 28 the Democrats on the committee voted 11–3 to send the bill to caucus beginning August 11—from where it emerged August 28 substantially unchanged. Before the Democrats caucused, however, the major accomplishment of the committee insurgents—banning interlocking directorates—was stricken from the bill (August 1), and August 22, in caucus, it was rejected again, 60–143. On the twenty-third Wingo's amendment, to limit the voting power of banks owning other banks in the election of regional reserve boards, was defeated 46–95. Henry's proposals for an "agricultural currency" based on warehouse receipts or liens on agricultural products, and to extend the maturity period of agricultural and commercial paper to six months, were repeatedly rejected; the only "concession" to the insurgents on this issue was an amendment adopted August 25 establishing the equality of agricultural and commercial paper.[10] Rebel strength slowly crumbled after Bryan (August 11) urged his supporters to end their opposition to the bill, and after the President issued a statement two days later promising that an agricultural credits bill would be introduced during the next session.[11] On the final day (August 28) the caucus voted 163 to 9 to reintroduce the bill into Congress.[12]

It is noteworthy that although during the caucus sessions the hostile press

---

[6] Quoted in Link, *Wilson and the Progressive Era*, 48.

[7] New York *Times*, July 13, 24, 1913; *American Year Book* (New York, 1911–   ), *1913*, p. 44.

[8] New York *Times*, July 25, 1913.

[9] *Ibid.*, July 26, 1913. Wilson feared that the intracommittee haggling would lead to an open breach among Democrats, and that the day-to-day decisions and reversals were jeopardizing business conditions, which showed signs of serious deterioration.

[10] *Ibid.*, August 29, 1913; *American Year Book, 1913*, p. 45; *La Follette's Weekly* (Madison, Wis., 1909–1929), March 21, 1914, p. 4. After the August 25 session the Henry-Ragsdale-Wingo forces contended they had won a victory, while the Glass supporters just as stoutly contended they had successfully resisted the insurgents. New York *Times*, August 26, 1913.

[11] Baker, *Wilson, Life and Letters*, IV, 174; *American Year Book, 1913*, p. 45.

[12] The nine were: Robert L. Henry, Joe H. Eagle, and Oscar Callaway of Texas, Thomas W. Hardwick of Georgia, George N. Neeley of Kansas, Thomas U. Sisson of Mississippi,

rang with reports of "open rebellion" and irreparable cleavages within the Democratic ranks, the opposition mustered on no occasion more than 35 per cent of the Democrats voting, and usually less than 25 per cent, of which a large number were from the Midwest. The one issue on which they showed the greatest strength, in and out of the caucus, was on a clause re-affirming the gold standard. Faced with last-minute pressure from Northern Democrats, Progressives, and Republicans, and with possible complications involving the Standard of Value Act of 1900, Glass had reluctantly accepted the clause on the final day of debate (September 18). Although some Demo-crats declared that the provision would be "a slap in the face" of the many silverites among them, it passed 299–68. Only 32 of the 68 were Southern Democrats.[13]

The roll call on the gold standard was one of the few in which the Demo-crats were not committed to a caucus pledge of party regularity, and, except for deference to the wishes of Carter Glass, were free to vote their convictions and interests. Significantly, several of those who persistently fought with the Henry-Ragsdale insurgents voted for the gold standard.[14] Thus, it appears that the composition of the insurgents was not only always small, it was con-tinually shifting; so that it is inaccurate to talk of a "radical" *faction* within the party threatening the stability of the administration.[15] This conclusion is supported by the only other important roll call available on the Glass Act in which the Democrats were not entirely bound by a caucus pledge: on a motion, December 20, to concur in a Senate amendment which in effect rewrote the Glass bill.

The Senate version contained two important additions to the bill received from the House on September 18: (1) a bank deposit guarantee clause; (2) an extension of the maturity period of loans on agricultural paper, from three to six months. The second was something for which agrarians had been striving since the early days of the Populists. Two wheat representatives from the Midwest and one cotton representative from the South[16] led the efforts for acceptance of the Senate measure, pointing out that a vote against

---

Charles O. Lobeck of Nebraska, and Frank Buchanan and H. Robert Fowler of Illinois. *La Follette's Weekly*, September 6, 1913, p. 9. Wingo's vote indicates that he was ap-parently reconciled with the administration leadership.

[13] *Cong. Record*, 63 Cong., 1 Sess., 5127–28. Significantly, the Progressives and progres-sive Republicans in the House voted 21–1 for the clause.

[14] For example, Hardwick of Georgia and Robert L. Doughton of North Carolina, to name but two.

[15] The jargon of contemporary observers made a "radical" out of every Democratic opponent of the administration during the banking and currency debates. Without defining terms any more carefully, these observers, and some historians, continued to use the epithet whenever referring to Democratic opposition to Wilson's policies. In most cases, however, the only sense in which most individual opponents might be considered radicals is in their occasional violation of party regularity.

[16] William H. ("Alfalfa Bill") Murray of Oklahoma, George A. Neeley of Kansas, and Hardwick of Georgia.

concurrence was a vote against long-term loan benefits for farmers. Glass meanwhile pleaded to be allowed to go into joint conference with a free hand.

The House defeated the motion for concurrence 59–295, with the Southern Democrats voting 22–68 against it, and with those previously among the insurgents badly split; for example, Wingo of Arkansas, Oscar Callaway and Joe H. Eagle of Texas, and J. Thomas Heflin of Alabama opposed the Senate measure, while Ragsdale of South Carolina, James L. Slayden of Texas, and Thomas U. Sisson and Samuel A. Witherspoon of Mississippi voted for it. Among the 22 Southerners voting for the Senate bill, moreover, were such stalwart conservatives as Martin Dies of Texas and Robert N. Page of North Carolina.[17]

Who, then, were the Southern "radicals" to whom contemporary observers (and many historians) frequently referred? If we consider them to have been those who voted differently from Carter Glass on either the Senate concurrence or the gold standard issues (thus taking in the maximum number of dissenters), they totalled 44, or about 40 per cent of all the Southerners. Included in this group, however, were many old-line conservatives, such as Dies, Page, Charles R. Crisp (Georgia), and William Adamson (Georgia). Had they been a real faction, with a program or a philosophy, had they acted together consistently under any pretext, these forty-four might have forced the administration to make major concessions. Instead, the "radicals" failed in their three prime goals: to ban interlocking directorates among national banks, to obtain long-term credits for farmers, and to have the government issue currency based on crop warehouse receipts; they even failed in their mightiest united effort—renunciation of the gold standard (and in this they encountered the almost unanimous opposition of the Northern and Western progressives).[18]

To say that before Glass introduced his revised bill in late June 1913, the "radicals" succeeded in forcing the administration to accept the responsibilities of directly controlling the national banking and currency system is to assume that the administration had, at that time, rather precise ideas on the details of its banking program.[19] The contrary is more likely true. Wilson sought a balanced measure which would be tolerable to both Congress and

---

[17] *Cong. Record*, 63 Cong., 2 Sess., 1307. In conference, as expected, Glass reduced the period of maturity for discountable paper to three months and eliminated the guarantee of bank deposits. H. Parker Willis, "The Federal Reserve Act," in *American Economic Review* (Ithaca, N. Y., 1911–   ), IV (1914), 12.

[18] By progressives I mean those non-Democrats who were elected to Congress in 1912 with Progressive party support, as well as some who were commonly recognized as progressives although, for various reasons, they kept the Republican party label (for example, Senators Robert M. La Follette and George Norris and Congressmen Charles A. Lindbergh and Irvine L. Lenroot). I count twelve such senators and twenty-seven such members of the House in the Sixty-Third Congress.

[19] See New York *Times*, June 14, 1913, on this point.

to the banking community (on whose co-operation success so largely depended). Once he decided on a specific measure and was content with its fairness, once he determined to fight for it through his congressional leaders, he won every major point.

On the subject of who was pushing whom into "advanced progressivism," the contest over the Federal Trade Commission is significant. If there was little agreement in 1913 on the kind of banking legislation needed, there was considerably less on exactly how to reform the trust laws. In fact, the progressives themselves were divided on fundamental policy. In the presidential campaign of 1912 the programs of the two major candidates differed significantly on how to cope with the problem of large aggregations of capital. Theodore Roosevelt proposed that government ought to regulate business consolidations in the public interest only by means of a strong commission; he decried antitrust acts as reactionary. Wilson denounced Roosevelt's program because he saw the likelihood of the corporations controlling the commission rather than the reverse, and because the entire scheme tended toward a paternalistic society dominated by the giant trust; he preferred to "regulate competition" (Louis Brandeis' phrase) rather than to "legalize the trusts"—to maintain competition by removing the conditions leading to trust formation.

As it developed, probably a majority of progressives, including those who joined Roosevelt's Progressive party, sought stronger *anti*trust laws. For example, "Bull Moose" Senator Joseph L. Bristow of Kansas wrote to Roosevelt on July 15, 1912, protesting against his New Nationalist program: "Many Progressives contend for a restoration of competition, believing that it would be better for the country and more conductive to industrial progress." Bristow had the hearty support of such progressive Republicans as Albert B. Cummins of Iowa, Moses E. Clapp of Minnesota, and William E. Borah of Idaho.[20]

Nevertheless, although Wilson had opposed the idea of a regulatory commission during the campaign, in June 1914 (in part because he was faced with a serious economic recession) he accepted a plan proposed by Brandeis and George L. Rublee for a commission which would define, investigate, and set governmental machinery in motion against unfair competition.[21] In doing so, Wilson actually surrendered no principles because the bill was designed to preserve competition and was not concerned with regulating monopoly or punishing fraudulent practices.[22]

The new bill consisted fundamentally of the old Covington bill, which

---

[20] George E. Mowry, *Theodore Roosevelt and the Progressive Movement* (Madison, Wis., 1946), 270.

[21] W. H. S. Stevens, "The Trade Commission Act," in *American Economic Review*, IV (1914), 840–55; Link, *Wilson and the Progressive Era*, 71–72.

[22] E. Pendleton Herring, "Politics, Personalities and the Federal Trade Commission," in *American Political Science Review* (Baltimore, 1906–), XXVIII (1934), 1016–29.

proposed an investigatory interstate trade commission to replace the Bureau of Corporations; it added, however, the notorious "Section 5," authorizing a Federal Trade Commission "to prevent the use of unfair methods of competition in interstate commerce." The provisions were made deliberately vague, in order to give the commissioners wide discretionary powers in determining unfair competition. In thus establishing a "quasi-judiciary" executive department, Wilson made his one real concession to [the] New Nationalism; and in doing so he drew the fire of many progressives as well as the Southerners in Congress.

On August 5, 1914, Democratic Senator James A. Reed of Missouri, an avowed enemy of the FTC, introduced a motion to define "unfair competition" in the bill. The motion was defeated 29–33, with five Southerners (including the radical James K. Vardaman of Mississippi) and two progressives for the motion.[23] Since the bill was a party measure, the Democratic vote for Reed's crippler indicated only those most strongly opposed to the idea of an FTC.

Better evidence for determining the Southerners who really favored the Trade Commission and were not merely deferring to administration policy, is provided by a roll call taken June 27, 1916. When Senator Henry F. Hollis of New Hampshire, who had led the pro-FTC forces in 1914, proposed an amendment reapportioning funds to increase the efficiency of the Commission, 14 out of 17 Southerners voted against Hollis, endorsing the claim of Senate Leader Thomas S. Martin of Virginia that the FTC was totally useless, inefficient, and extravagant. The amendment failed, 28–42.[24]

In May 1916 the Senate rejected the nomination of George Rublee to one of the five posts on the FTC. One of the principal issues of the nomination was Rublee's role in writing Section 5. Ten Southerners voted to approve the President's nominee, but nine opposed. Six of those who opposed strengthening the FTC would not oppose their leader's nomination, while only the inexplicable Vardaman voted for Hollis' amendment but against Rublee.[25]

The principal objections to the FTC Act centered on Section 5, one of the few parts of Wilson's entire trust program which offered something to the New Nationalists in the country. Not only did the Southerners have "noth-

---

[23] *Cong. Record,* 63 Cong., 2 Sess., 13314, 13319. James K. Vardaman is one of the very few Southerners who indeed deserves the label "radical" even apart from his role in the Glass Act debate; he may be called a radical because, like many progressives, he sought to commit the government to a program of welfare legislation.

[24] *Ibid.,* 64 Cong., 1 Sess., 10050, 10062. Vardaman (perverse as usual!), Luke Lea of Tennessee, and Morris Sheppard of Texas were the only three Southerners with Henry F. Hollis. Progressives William E. Borah of Idaho, Asle J. Gronna of North Dakota, Wesley L. Jones of Washington, and John D. Works of California opposed the amendment. Borah once declared: "I am opposed to it [the FTC] now, and I expect to be opposed to it so long as I retain my right mind." *Ibid.,* 63 Cong., 2 Sess., 14414.

[25] *Ibid.,* 64 Cong., 1 Sess., 7962, 8510. There was a direct correlation between the progressives' votes on Hollis' amendment and their votes on Rublee.

ing to do with bringing about this profound change in Wilson's antitrust policy," [26] but Wilson also had to face the opposition of many congressional progressives.[27]

If the southerners were reluctant to support the administration's "radical" FTC which put limits on "free competition," they were no more anxious to strengthen the antitrust laws. Charles A. Culberson of Texas, chairman of the Senate Judiciary Committee, successfully resisted all efforts to include in the Clayton Act (1) a provision making the settlement of a federal suit against a corporation for violation of the trust laws conclusive evidence in personal damage suits against that corporation, (2) penalties for conviction of price discrimination, rebates, and similar unfair trade practices, (3) effective prohibition of interlocking directorates, and (4) prohibition from interstate commerce of all corporations, except common carriers, capitalized at more than $100,000,000. Only four Southerners opposed Culberson with any consistency.[28]

Led by Culberson, Southerners also played a major role in crippling the efforts of labor to include in the Clayton Act explicit recognition of labor's claimed rights under the law. When Culberson's committee received the Clayton bill from the House it contained clauses (1) clearly limiting the issuance of restraining orders in labor disputes, (2) precluding a court interpretation of labor organizations *per se* as "conspiracies in restraint of trade," [29] and (3) prescribing trial by jury in contempt proceedings. When the committee released the bill, the first two clauses had been emasculated and the last had been omitted entirely. In the only roll call recorded in the

---

[26] Link, "The South and the 'New Freedom,'" 319.

[27] This is not the only evidence of the progressives' and the Southerners' reluctance to accept the New Nationalism. In an effort to exempt labor and farm organizations from the Sherman Antitrust Act, Congress attached a rider to the Sundry Civil Appropriations Bill of 1913 prohibiting the use of any money for prosecution of labor groups organized for the purpose of obtaining better wages or working conditions, or for anything "not in itself unlawful"; or of farm associations organized to maintain price levels. President Taft vetoed the bill, but it was reintroduced and passed almost immediately in the next Congress. Before passage in the Senate, a motion by Senator Jacob H. Gallinger, Republican of New Hampshire, to strike out the rider was defeated, 32–41; the progressive Republicans voted 8–3 for the motion. In the preceding debate Senator Norris of Nebraska pleaded that the measure was "an attempt . . . to differentiate between good trusts and bad trusts"; but his progressive colleague Borah replied with a sharp denunciation of price-fixing farm organizations and warned that it was "a very difficult matter" to determine when a trust became bad, and that creating supervisory federal bureaus to determine such matters invited a cumbersome, meddling government. In the end only La Follette, Norris, and Jones, among the progressives, voted against the Gallinger motion. *Cong. Record*, 63 Cong., 1 Sess., 1271, 1292.

[28] *Ibid.*, 63 Cong., 2 Sess., 13858, 13907, 14273, 14420–21, 14527.

[29] *American Year Book, 1914*, p. 16. Charles C. Carlin of Virginia, of the House Judiciary Committee, expressed his view to the President that the clause still did not exempt labor *acts* from such interpretations. Carlin to Wilson, about May 26, 1914, in Wilson Papers.

Senate only two Southerners joined with the progressives and some Northern Democrats in a vain attempt to replace the jury trial provision.[30]

Government control and operation of railroads had been one of the major demands of the agrarian rebels of the 1880's and 1890's, and had maintained its popularity among many progressives. On May 29, 1913, President Wilson wrote to Majority Leader Oscar W. Underwood of Alabama: "I am deeply interested in the passage of a bill authorizing the government to build a railroad in Alaska, and so soon as the pressure of Ways and Means work is off, I would very much value a conference with you." [31] Here was a measure close to the hearts of progressives and the "direct inheritors and . . . prime articulators in the Democratic party of the philosophy underlying the Agrarian crusade." [32]

In his first annual address Wilson requested an Alaskan railway system which "the Government should itself build and administer, and . . . ports and terminals [which] it should itself control in the interest of all who wish to use them for the service and development of the country and its people." [33] The bill was not a party measure, and so the Democrats were bound to no caucus pledge; although it still must be assumed that many simply followed the President's lead, those opposing the bill most probably expressed their genuine convictions on the role of the government in society. The issue of government participation in the railroad business was clearly drawn during the debate.

The bill passed the Senate 46–16, with 7 out of the 16 Southerners voting opposing it. The House passed the bill 232–86, with 49 of the 90 Southerners voting opposed. (The progressives in each house unanimously supported the act.) Of the 44 Southerners who harassed the administration in the Glass Act contest, 23 opposed the Alaska Act, only 11 favored it, and 10 abstained. Of the 11 for the act, only J. L. Eagle (Texas), Robert Henry (Texas), and P. E. Quin (Mississippi) had been consistently among the insurgents in the Glass Act fight, whereas a majority of the leading "radicals," including Slayden, Sisson, Wingo, Callaway, and Elder, opposed.[34]

By the end of 1914 the banking system, the tariff, and the trust laws had been drastically revised; the European war was contributing to the confusion and anxiety of depressed business; the President's patronage weapon was virtually exhausted so that his hold on Congress was considerably weakened; finally, the European conflict and a troublesome Mexican situation were absorbing more and more of Wilson's energy. Each or all of these facts may have led Wilson to indicate that he considered his major commitments to

---

[30] *Cong. Record,* 63 Cong., 2 Sess., 14417. Nathan P. Bryan of Florida and Vardaman were the two Southerners.

[31] Wilson to Oscar W. Underwood, May 29, 1913, in Wilson Papers.

[32] Link, "The South and the 'New Freedom,' " 316.

[33] *Cong. Record,* 63 Cong., 2 Sess., 45.   [34] *Ibid.,* 2250, 3646–47.

the electorate fulfilled and that he did not expect to push further domestic reforms.

With the President relinquishing the leadership of reform, only one major progressive bill passed Congress in 1915: La Follette's Seamen's Act. While the act was highly complex, causing serious international difficulties which would have killed any other bill and had already delayed this one several years, its popular human appeal served to dampen the opposition. Significantly, although the bill passed Congress with heavy majorities,[35] the only important opposition came from the South. From an examination of the debates on the bill and the roll calls on various motions and amendments, it is evident that eight Southern senators consistently opposed the popular measure, while eight supported it.[36] President Wilson signed the bill one day before the Sixty-Third Congress ended. Although it is true that he contemplated pocket-vetoing it, it is also true that until Secretary of State Bryan advised him that its safety provisions violated treaties with eighteen foreign powers, Wilson gave La Follette hearty encouragement.[37]

As the European war moved into its second year the Wilson administration came under increasingly heavy fire from Republicans and some non-office-holding Progressives (for example, Roosevelt and Albert J. Beveridge) for failing to take a firmer stand against German militarism; on the other hand, a large number of Democrats (especially from the South and the West) and the congressional progressives assailed the President for being "Anglophile" and for behaving too belligerently toward Germany. That year, nevertheless, Wilson regained both his will for leadership in domestic affairs and the power to enforce his will; for 1916 was an election year, and the mass of Democrats well knew that without President Wilson they had no hope of maintaining national power.

If the desire for victory kept the Democrats behind the President, Wilson's desire for re-election led him to make a series of moves designed to appeal to progressive-humanitarian interests. Wilson knew that unless he could capture the votes of the independent progressives, with whom labor and some farm interests had become associated in politics, his bid would fail. At the same time, the European war indirectly extended both the motive

---

[35] It passed both houses without a roll call—the Senate on October 23, 1913; the House on August 27, 1914, where at least a two-thirds vote was first necessary to suspend the rules in order to act on the motion for passage. *Ibid.*, 63 Cong., 1 Sess., 5791; *ibid.*, 63 Cong., 2 Sess., 14362.

[36] Various versions of the act had been pending for several years. *La Follette's Weekly*, March 29, 1913, pp. 14–15, contains three vote tabulations on the bill President Taft pocket-vetoed. See *Cong. Record*, 62 Cong., 3 Sess., 4587; *ibid.*, 63 Cong., 1 Sess., 5790, 5791; *ibid.*, 63 Cong., 3 Sess., 4817, for other roll calls especially the last, which records a vote on a last-minute crippler.

[37] For a fine brief statement on this matter see Link, *Wilson and the Progressive Era*, 61–63. Also *cf. Baker, Wilson, Life and Letters*, IV, 213, 364; Paul McKown, *Certain Important Domestic Policies of Woodrow Wilson* (Philadelphia, 1932), 82–83; Robert M. Lansing to Wilson, June 19, 1916, in Wilson Papers.

and the power of the administration to satisfy progressive demands, as the President found it necessary to center increasing power in the federal government.

President Wilson's nomination of Louis D. Brandeis to the Supreme Court on January 26, 1916, was the first of six major acts that year which appealed to progressive sentiment. For four months the Senate held up confirmation of the appointment while it conducted an unprecedented personal and professional inquiry. Leading the opposition among the Democrats were the Southerners, rebelling because Wilson had not consulted them in making the appointment, because they suspected it was a political appeal to the progressives (who currently were harassing the South on the child-labor issue), and because parts of the South, especially Georgia, had been whipped into an anti-Catholic and anti-Semitic frenzy, led by the old radical Tom Watson.[38] Party regularity ultimately prevailed, and on the final vote only one Democrat went on record against the President's nomination.

Wilson's nomination of the "radical" Brandeis marked no change in his attitude, for in 1913 he had to be dissuaded by his political advisers from naming Brandeis to his cabinet; if anything, the nomination indicated that Wilson's advisers had decided at last that, despite the South, in 1916 the Northern progressive vote must have prime consideration. On child-labor legislation, however, Wilson did reverse himself; as late as 1914 Wilson noted privately to his secretary, Joe Tumulty: ". . . in all frankness . . . no [federal] child labor law yet proposed has seemed to me constitutional." [39] Although, because of Southern opposition, a child-labor bill had languished in the Senate for almost four years, in 1916 it passed quickly once the President assumed leadership.

Southern representatives voted 41–43 against the bill that Wilson signed in 1916. Of the "radicals" of the Glass Act contest, 18 opposed child-labor legislation, while only 17 favored it. (Another four voted for the 1916 measure probably only because Wilson had demanded it; for previously they stubbornly opposed all federal legislation, including a 1913 bill designed simply to establish an investigatory Federal Children's Bureau.) Texas and Arkansas accounted for 76 per cent of those Southerners for federal legislation, although leading insurgent Oscar Callaway of Texas opposed all bills. In the Senate, four Southern textile states—North Carolina, South Carolina,

---

[38] Edward F. McClennen, Brandeis' law partner, wrote to Brandeis Attorney-General Thomas W. Gregory's advice "that no effort should be made by anyone which might arouse any suspicion that this appointment sprang from any 'Progressive' source or any other except purely Democratic. The strength is in Democratic party loyalty. . . . he believes activity by the Jews is not likely to help with Bourbon [Southern] Democrats. They know what this support means in the coming elections, without having it called to their attention." Alpheus T. Mason, *Brandeis: A Free Man's Life* (New York, 1946), 467–68. John K. Shields of Tennessee, Hoke Smith of Georgia, and Lee S. Overman of North Carolina led the Southern opposition.

[39] Link, *Wilson and the Progressive Era,* 59 n.

Georgia, and Alabama—plus Florida and Mississippi voted as a unit against all measures, although on the final vote in 1916 Underwood and Vardaman acquiesced. Only Thomas S. Martin and Claude A. Swanson of Virginia, Luke Lea and John K. Shields of Tennessee, Joseph T. Robinson of Arkansas, and Morris Sheppard of Texas consistently supported the reform.[40]

In his first annual address to Congress in December 1913 Wilson declared:

> The farmers, of course, ask and should be given no special privilege, such as extending to them the credit of the Government itself. . . . And yet the farmer does not stand upon the same footing with . . . [others] in the market of credit. He is the servant of the seasons. . . . He may give his note, but the season of its maturity depends upon the season when his crop matures. . . . And the security he gives is of a character not known in a broker's office or as familiarly as it might be on the counter of the banker. . . . Systems of rural credit have been studied and developed on the other side of the water while we left our farmers to shift for themselves in the ordinary money market.[41]

As we have seen, following the leadership of Carter Glass, Congress refused in 1913 to provide for long-term credits. Subsequent efforts to embody such provisions in a separate bill also failed—for which Wilson must bear heavy responsibility. For with the onset of the European war, the Mexican difficulties, and the business recession in 1914, the administration shied from further innovations and thus refused aid to the still vital reform currents. In the fall of 1914, however, Wilson did sign the Cotton Warehouse Act, which purported to facilitate better distribution of warehouses for (1) safer storage of crops throughout the nation and (2) better business methods in the handling of stored crops under license from the government, in order that warehouse receipts might be more readily acceptable as collateral for loans by banks.

If, in signing the bill, Wilson was yielding to the philosophy of the New Nationalism, the Southerners who pushed the bill were of a different mind. "It is emergency legislation," insisted Tom Heflin. "If the South were not in the distressed condition that she is [caused by the temporary shrinkage of the European market], and if the legislatures of the States were in session, we might go to the States and get this legislation." Although Heflin eventually won his point, he did not convince a large minority of the Southern "radicals" who voted against the bill because, as Robert Henry declared, it was "saturated, reeking, unduly intoxicated with rank federalism." [42]

In January 1916 Wilson was willing to go further than the warehouse

---

[40] There is no space here to present the roll calls and their significance on the various child-labor measures from 1912 on. See *Cong. Record*, 62 Cong., 2 Sess., 1578; *ibid.*, 63 Cong., 3 Sess., 3836; *ibid.*, 64 Cong., 1 Sess., 698, 2035, 12311, 12313.

[41] *Ibid.*, 63 Cong., 2 Sess., 44. One fourth of the entire message Wilson devoted to rural credits.

[42] *Ibid.*, 16204, 16210. Among the "radicals" who opposed the Warehouse Act were

measure provided—even to extend to the farmers "the credit of the government itself." Summoning Senator Hollis and Congressman Asbury F. Lever of South Carolina to the White House, he announced his support of their rural credits bill which had floundered in Congress for almost two years without administration support. The bill provided for the establishment of twelve farm loan banks, with the government purchasing up to $750,000 in bonds for the initial capital of each bank. What caused Wilson to endorse such a measure after insisting for years that it was "class legislation"?

One answer is provided by Wilson himself. In his third annual address the President declared that in order to prepare the country for mobilization, it was necessary to provide extensive borrowing facilities for farmers beyond those already provided by the Glass Act.[43] An equally important answer, however, is Wilson's desire for re-election and his need for the Western farm vote. Indeed, Wilson's summons to Hollis and Lever followed almost immediately a speech on January 9, 1916, by Frank G. Odell, secretary of the American Rural Credits Association, in which Odell stated: "The support of the farmers, which would be engaged by rural credits legislation, is necessary to the Democratic Party in the Middle West." [44]

Pressure from Southern interests could not have been crucial in Wilson's decision to press for rural credits act. He could hardly have feared the loss of Southern electoral votes. Moreover, if the Southerners had combined with the Western farm representatives any time before 1916, they might easily have forced Wilson to accept a rural credits system; instead, the project had to await administration leadership before it succeeded.

Another of Wilson's 1916 policy changes appealed to the Western farmers, while it antagonized the Southern agrarians. For years Western insurgents and Democrats in general, hoping to reduce the high and discriminatory tariff rates of Old Guard Republican design, had urged the creation of a nonpartisan tariff commission which could determine rates on a nonpolitical basis. Western farmers and progressives were nevertheless protectionists,[45]

Robert L. Henry, James L. Slayden, Thomas U. Sisson, and Samuel A. Witherspoon. By "radicals" I mean, as I have consistently meant in this paper in reference to the Southern congressmen, those who harassed the administration leaders on behalf of agrarian interests during the Glass Act debate.

[43] *Ibid.*, 64 Cong., 1 Sess., 99. Secretary of Agriculture David F. Houston, in his book *Eight Years with Wilson's Cabinet, 1913–1920* (2 vols., Garden City, 1926), I, gives the impression that the war emergency was principally responsible for the extension of the government's credit to the farmers.

[44] New York *Times*, January 10, 1916. William E. Gonzales, one of the leaders in Wilson's successful primary fight in South Carolina in 1912, wrote to Joseph P. Tumulty about the coming campaign: "Right now, it seems to me, is the time to catch the Progressives while their minds are open. . . . The National Committee should limit its efforts in the South to urging the newspapers to raise money; don't spend a stamp for anything else there." Gonzales to Tumulty, June 28, 1916, in Wilson Papers.

[45] See, for example, Robert M. La Follette's defense of the McKinley Tariff (which he had helped to write) in "The Farmer and the Tariff Bill," in *La Follette's Weekly*, December 14, 1912, pp. 1–2.

because they dealt largely in the domestic market. Southern cotton producers, on the other hand, depending chiefly on a foreign market, favored free trade. When the Old Guard fell in 1912, the triumphant Democrats bypassed demands for a commission; for President Wilson and the Democratic leaders favored a tariff for revenue only, and consequently had no use for a commission to adjust rates according to the marketing needs of American producers.

Although Wilson's sudden advocacy of a commission in January 1916 appealed to the progressives and Western farmers (as well as to Samuel Gompers and organized labor), and therefore may be considered a concession to them, we must not discard Wilson's own explanation that world conditions were changing so rapidly and unpredictably that a fact-finding and rate-adjusting commission was essential to carry out national policy.[46] Administration leaders feared that the commercial boom would collapse with the return of the European mercantile nations to peacetime trade and that Europe's surplus products would be "dumped" in the United States. In other words, Wilson's policy was not simply an election-year sop to the special interests of the West.

The European war (as well as the election campaign of 1916) created many circumstances with which the New Freedom, as originally conceived, proved inadequate to cope. With the disruption of international commerce in 1914, the revenue raised by the Underwood Tariff of 1913 could not meet government expenses; in the autumn Wilson called on Congress for an emergency revenue measure, suggesting traditional indirect taxes to raise the needed funds. The agrarians, especially the Southerners (who held the major committee posts), objected that additional excise taxes would hit hardest those who could least afford to pay, but since an income tax could not raise the money needed in the time required, Congress passed the administration's bill with no basic change.

It was natural for the South, where real estate still provided the major source of revenue, to lead in the drive for taxes on "intangible" wealth; not only had agrarians such as Claude Kitchin long fought for a national income tax, but many old-line Southern conservatives, from Joseph W. Bailey to John Sharp Williams, had been in the forefront of the fight. Although it is correct to say that the South led in the fight to increase income taxes during the first Wilson administration, it would be incorrect to mark Wilson as distinctly hostile to the idea. It is important to remember that Wilson had just forced through three great reform measures (plus the Alaska Railway Act, and repeal of the Panama Canal Tolls Act of 1911 in which he faced the opposition of almost every congressional leader); in addition, busi-

---

[46] See, for example, Wilson's explanation to the hostile Claude Kitchin of North Carolina, House majority leader. Wilson to Kitchin, January 26, 1916, in Wilson Papers. Pro-tariff business interests, of course, were quite as pleased as the Western farmers.

ness conditions were bad. The President preferred to consolidate his gains against the growing hostility and suspicion of conservative business.

In his third annual address, at the end of 1915, President Wilson again asked for additional revenues, this time advising: "We should be following an almost universal example of modern governments if we were to draw the greater part or even the whole of the revenues we need from the income taxes." [47] Congress responded by passing a bill in September 1916 which went far beyond the still conservative tax plan outlined by the administration. Instead of lowering the exempted income and surtaxable income levels, as Wilson requested, Congress doubled the tax rates and imposed a graduated estate tax. The revenue bill marked the first time the agrarians of the South and West (together with Northern labor representatives) successfully combined to press beyond the bounds set by the Wilson administration.[48]

Like the extended use of the income tax and other progressive innovations, the Adamson Act probably would not have passed except for the war in Europe. The act established the first federal eight-hour day law applying to nonfederal employment. In the summer of 1916 the four major railroad brotherhoods threatened to tie up the nation's railroad system unless demands for an eight-hour day and time and a half for overtime were met. Wilson stepped in to mediate a settlement. When the railroad managers refused Wilson's terms, the President went to Congress to enforce his settlement by legislative act. The act passed by almost a straight party vote.[49]

The Adamson Act was the last important domestic measure passed before the elections of 1916. It was symbolic of how far the Wilson administration had drifted from the original principles of the New Freedom. Apparently founded on principles requiring government abstinence in the unending struggle among contending interests in a free-market economy, the first Wilson administration culminated in a series of acts gauged to aid particular interests in their individual contentions. This paper has been devoted to the evolution of the change and to an analysis of the Southern contribution to it.

From the evidence, it is clear that both the radicalism of the Southern congressmen and the conservatism of Woodrow Wilson have been overestimated. It is also clear that the Southerners played a subordinate role in the Wilson administration's drift toward New Nationalism from 1913 to 1916.

As a group locally secure but long out of power nationally—and in low national repute—the Southern Democrats generally would not cross the one man who had a maximum of national respect and could give them the

---

[47] *Cong. Record,* 64 Cong., 1 Sess., 98.

[48] *Cf.* Link, *Wilson and the Progressive Era,* 192–96; Sidney Ratner, *American Taxation* (New York, 1942), 342–61.

[49] *Cong. Record,* 64 Cong., 1 Sess., 13655. The brotherhoods gave up their demands for time and a half for overtime.

rewards of national power.[50] Those Southerners who did oppose administration policies usually did so out of conservatism rather than radicalism. In one of the two most noteworthy exceptions to this fact—the opposition to the Glass bill—the "radical" Southerners won no important concessions from the administration; in the case of the income tax the Southern "radicals" successfully forced a progressive innovation upon a reluctant administration. In both cases, however, the term "radicals" must include many who were conservative and reactionary in all other instances. The term is justifiable only when it is understood that it does not necessarily represent a co-ordinated group within Congress, but simply those elements which, on various measures, favored further reforms. In fact, it is clear that whatever there was of a co-ordinated radical faction, its stable core was very small (perhaps fifteen or twenty congressmen), its periphery of drifters was highly mobile, and its political position was not consistently progressive.

Rather than being the masters of the administration's changing policy, the Southern congressmen were usually little more than the instruments of that policy. In almost every case, the immediate impulse for extending the government's power, authority, and credit on behalf of particular groups came from the administration in response to the exigencies of an impending national election and a world war. Wilson always subordinated his commitment to the New Freedom to his obligation—owed to himself, his country, and his party—to come out on top in both the international crisis and the election campaign of 1916. It was to fulfill this obligation that Wilson moved toward a more advanced progressivism during the years 1913–1916.

---

[50] The best example of this is the contest in 1913 over the repeal of the Panama Tolls Act, in which the mass of Southerners reversed themselves in deference to Wilson's wishes.

X

*The United States and
World War I, 1914–1917:
Did the Wilson Administration
Pursue a Policy of Neutrality?*

INTRODUCTION

Few aspects of American history since 1865 have been as productive of bitter argument among historians as the question of American entry into World War I and World War II. The debate has raged between those who have in the main defended the policies of the administrations in power when the United States became a belligerent in the two great wars and the so-called revisionists, who have been highly critical of the official version of how the nation became involved in war.

Following World War I the initiative in the evaluation of American neutrality between 1914 and 1917 was seized by the revisionists. Such writers as John K. Turner, Harry Elmer Barnes, and C. Hartley Grattan penned accounts of the American involvement in the war that were condemnatory of administration policy. (Professor Barnes' book, The Genesis of the World War, *was primarily concerned with the European origins of World War I, but Barnes also included a chapter on American intervention.) In the 1930's the revisionist case was most notably argued in books by Walter Millis, Edwin Borchard and William Potter Lage, and Charles C. Tansill.*

What has been called "the first historian's history of intervention" [1] *appeared in 1934, when Professor Charles Seymour's* American Diplomacy during World War I *was published. Seymour took issue with the revisionist position and pointed to the submarine as the chief cause for American entry into the war. Although new documentation has become available since Seymour wrote and although his view of American neutrality is regarded as too narrowly focused, Seymour's interpretation is considered to be basically sound by such recent defenders of Wilson's position as Professors Arthur S. Link and Ernest R. May.*

The revisionist position in the selections that follow is represented by Harry Elmer Barnes in a 1940 restatement of the thesis that he first presented in 1926. Barnes contends that the administration was far from neutral between 1914 and 1917, and he lays heavy stress on economic factors as the explanation for American entry into the war. Professor Link, by contrast, finds that Wilson was "substantially neutral in attitude" and that he strove desperately to the very end to keep the United States out of the war.

---

[1] Richard W. Leopold, "The Problem of American Intervention, 1917: An Historical Retrospect," *World Politics*, II (April 1950), 411.

The United States and the

First World War

Harry Elmer Barnes

We may now consider the forces, factors, and personalities which brought
the United States into the war.

The United States could not have been more perfectly set up for neutrality than it was in July and August, 1914. President Woodrow Wilson was a
lifelong and deeply conscientious pacifist. His convictions in this matter were
not emotional or impressionistic, but had been based upon deep study and
prolonged reflection. Moreover, he was married to a woman noted for pacific
sentiments and firm convictions on such matters. She strongly backed up her
husband in his pacific beliefs and policies. As Secretary of State, we had in
William Jennings Bryan the world's outstanding pacifist. His pacifism was
notably courageous; he was willing to stick by his guns even in the face of
malicious criticism.

Moreover, Wilson was almost uniquely well informed as to the essentials
of the European situation before war broke out in the summer of 1914.
He had sent his personal representative, Colonel Edward M. House, to
Europe to study the international situation and to report to him upon it.
Whatever his later mistakes, Colonel House sized up matters in Europe with
almost perfect sagacity and understanding in May, 1914. He concluded his
observations with the statement that "whenever England consents, France
and Russia will close in on Germany."

If one were to summarize, as briefly as this, the outcome of the years of
scholarly study since 1918, with respect to responsibility for the World War,
a more perfect estimate and verdict than Colonel House's phrase could not
be rendered in the same number of words. Further, the Colonel pointed out
that, whatever the Kaiser's emotional shortcomings, he wished for European
peace. On the other hand, he stated candidly that George V of England was
"the most pugnacious monarch loose in these parts."

When war broke out, President Wilson's statements were a model of neutral procedure. He issued a formally correct neutrality proclamation and

From *War in the Twentieth Century*, Willard Waller (Editor), Copyright © 1940. Reprinted by permission of Holt, Rinehart and Winston, Inc., publishers. Pp. 71–82.

went on to exhort his countrymen to be neutral in thought as well as in action. There is no doubt that he was completely neutral at heart in August, 1914. Less than three years later, however, in April, 1917, he went before Congress and told its members that "God helping her," this country could do no other than make war on Germany. Moreover, he returned from the Capitol to the White House and made statements to his secretary, Joseph P. Tumulty, indicating that, at the time of his war message, he had so far changed his attitude that he could not believe he ever had been neutral. He cited with approval an article by the correspondent of the *Manchester Guardian* stating that Mr. Wilson had always been sympathetic with the Allies and had wished to throw this country into war on their side just as soon as circumstances would permit.

We shall first briefly consider some of the reasons why Wilson altered his point of view, since no other set of circumstances could alone have forced us into the war, if Wilson had not been favorable to our entry by the spring of 1917.

First and foremost, we must take into account the fact that Wilson's intellectual perspective was predominantly Anglo-Saxon. He had little knowledge of, or sympathy with, continental European culture and institutions. His great intellectual heroes were such English writers as John Milton, John Locke, Adam Smith and Walter Bagehot. He did his graduate work in the Johns Hopkins University Seminar under Herbert Baxter Adams, where the "Anglo-Saxon Myth" [1] reigned supreme. Wilson was a persistent student and admirer of the English constitution and frankly regarded the British system of government as superior to our own.

Then Wilson had in his cabinet and among his ambassadors men who were intensely pro-English or pro-Ally in their sympathies. Such were Secretaries Lindley M. Garrison and David F. Houston. Walter Hines Page, our ambassador in London, was even more intensely pro-English than Wilson. Indeed, he frequently went to such excesses as to annoy the President. When Bryan was succeeded by Robert Lansing, the most crucial post in the cabinet went to another vehemently pro-English sympathizer. The biases of Page and Lansing made it difficult to pursue forthright diplomacy with Great Britain.

Another major difficulty lay in the fact that President Wilson and Secretary Lansing did not formulate and execute a fair and consistent line of diplomatic procedure. They had one type of international law for England and the Allies, and quite another for Germany. They all but allowed Great Britain to run wild in the violation of international law and of our neutral rights, while they insisted on holding Germany "to strict accountability."

England started out in 1914 by making a scrap of paper out of the Decla-

---

[1] *I.e.*, the idea that American political ideals and liberties are a heritage from a racially pure Anglo-Saxon England.

ration of London governing contraband in wartime. Next, we proceeded to allow her to make use of armed belligerent merchantmen as if they were peaceful commercial vessels. England violated our neutral rights far more extensively between 1914 and 1917 than she did before the War of 1812, even to the point of flying the American flag.

Wilson came to believe, however, that Great Britain was fighting for civilization and that so trivial a thing as international law must not be allowed to stand in her way. Wilson's Attorney-General, Thomas W. Gregory, tells of the rebuke which the President administered to certain cabinet members when they protested over the flagrant British violation of our neutral rights: "After patiently listening, Mr. Wilson said, in that quiet way of his, that the ordinary rules of conduct had no application to the situation; that the Allies were standing with their backs to the wall, fighting wild beasts; that he would permit nothing to be done by our country to hinder or embarrass them in the prosecution of the war unless admitted rights were grossly violated, and that this policy must be understood as settled." Bryan protested against our unfair and unneutral diplomacy and ultimately resigned because he could not square his conscience with it.

Secretary Lansing admits in his *Memoirs* that he made no real pretense of holding England to the tenets of international law. He tells us that after the sinking of the *Lusitania* he thought we should be fighting on the side of the Allies and that he was determined to do nothing which would prove embarrassing to us when we later took up our position as a military comrade of the Allied powers. He persisted in this attitude, even though he was honest enough to write after the war that in 1917 we had as good, if not better, legal grounds for fighting Britain as for fighting Germany.

Ambassador Page even went so far as to collaborate with Sir Edward Grey in answering the protests of his own government, an unparalleled procedure which, when revealed, outraged even so pro-Ally a journal as the *New York Times*.

We thus encouraged and perpetuated the illegally extensive British blockade, which provoked the German submarine warfare. In time, we made war on the latter, though it was our unneutral diplomacy which contributed, in large part, to the continuance of both the British blockade and the German submarine activities.[2]

Wilson was deeply affected by the criticisms to which he was subjected by prominent Americans sympathetic with the Allies and in favor of intervention on their side. He was stung by the famous speeches of Theodore Roosevelt on "The Shadows of Shadow Lawn," and by the latter's reference to Wilson's diplomatic statements as examples of "weasel words." He was par-

---

[2] From the studies of Professor Charles C. Tansill and others, it would seem that on the rare occasions when President Wilson and Secretary Lansing became outraged over the grossest British violations of our neutrality, Colonel House invariably appeared on the spot to prevent even a show of firmness on the part of our State Department.

ticularly annoyed by the statement of Elihu Root that "first he shakes his fist and then he shakes his finger."

On the other hand, Wilson was human enough to take note of the praise which was showered upon him by the press when he made a bellicose statement or led a preparedness parade. This contrasted sharply with the bitter criticism he evoked when he made a statesmanlike remark, such as that a country might be "too proud to fight," or that the only desirable peace would be "a peace without victory."

Wilson was also profoundly moved by the British propaganda relative to German atrocities and territorial ambitions. This was particularly true after Lord Bryce lent his name to the prestige and veracity of the propaganda stories as to German savagery. Of all living Englishmen, Bryce was probably the man whom Wilson most admired and trusted. When Bryce sponsored the propaganda lies, Wilson came to believe that they must have a substantial basis in fact. This helped on his rationalization that England was fighting the battle of human civilization against wild beasts.

Personal matters also played their rôle in the transformation of Wilson's attitude. His first wife died and a strong pacific influence was removed. He then courted and married a dashing widow who was sympathetic with the Allied side and friendly with Washington military and naval circles. She was also bitterly resentful of the criticism to which Wilson was subjected on account of his refusal to be stampeded into intervention. She appears to have wished him to take a stronger stand for intervention. The domestic influence on the President was, thus, completely transformed in character as a result of his second marriage. The publication of Mrs. Wilson's *Memoirs* does not make it necessary to modify this statement.

When, as an outcome of these various influences, Wilson had been converted to intervention, he rationalized his change of attitude on the basis of a noble moral purpose. As he told Jane Addams in the spring of 1917, he felt that the United States must be represented at the peace conference which would end the World War if there was to be any hope of a just and constructive peace. But Wilson could be at the peace conference only if the United States had previously entered the World War.

It is still asserted by many writers, such as Professor Charles Seymour, that the resumption of submarine warfare by Germany was the sole reason for Wilson's determination to enter the war on the Allied side. But we know that he had been converted to intervention long before January, 1917. A year earlier, he had sent Colonel House to Europe with a plan to put us in the war on the side of the Allies if Germany would not accept peace terms obviously unfavorable to her. But even such peace terms for Germany were rejected by the British leaders, who felt sure of American aid anyway and were determined to crush Germany. Yet this British rebuff did not lead Wilson to lose heart in his efforts to put this country into the war.

His next step was taken in this country. Early in April,[3] 1916, Wilson called into consultation Speaker Champ Clark of the House of Representatives and Congressional leaders Claude Kitchin and H. D. Flood, and sounded them out to see if they would support him in a plan to bring the United States into the war on the side of the Allies. This was the famous "Sunrise Conference" described later by Gilson Gardner in *McNaught's Monthly* of June, 1925. These men sharply refused to sanction any such policy, and Wilson allowed the campaign of 1916 to be fought out on the slogan, "He kept us out of war." Wilson did not dare to risk splitting the Democratic Party over entry into the war before the campaign of 1916 had successfully ended. The existence of the "Sunrise Conference" has been fully verified by Professor A. M. Arnett in his scholarly book on Claude Kitchin.[*]

Wilson was convinced after the failure of the "Sunrise Conference" that there was no hope of getting the country into war until after the election. The sentiment of the nation was for peace. If he was elected as an exponent of peace and then went into war the country as a whole would believe that he had done his best to "keep us out of war." He would have a united country behind him. Hence, he and Colonel House sent Governor Martin Glynn of New York and Senator Ollie James of Kentucky to the Democratic National Convention at St. Louis, in June, 1916, with instructions to make keynote speeches emphasizing Wilson's heroic efforts to keep us out of war.[†]

Thus was fashioned the famous slogan "He kept us out of war," which re-elected Woodrow Wilson to the presidency almost a year after Colonel House, following Wilson's directions, had declared that: "The United States would like Great Britain to do whatever would help the United States to aid the Allies." [4]

The campaign and election of 1916 were very really a referendum on war, and the people voted against war. This is illuminating as an illustration of the fallacy that a war referendum, such as the Ludlow Amendment,[‡] would,

---

[3] Professor Tansill believes that this conference was probably held in February rather than April. I still incline to credit the April date.

[*] Editor's note: Arthur S. Link has made it clear that the date of the conference was February 25. He insists that there is no "reliable" evidence that the President suggested that he desired American entry into the war. Wilson, in reply to questioning, simply declared that if an armed ship were torpedoed with a loss of American life, he would break relations with the Central Powers, and he had been told that this might lead to war. He indicated, however, that it was peace, not war, that he sought. Link, *Woodrow Wilson and the Progressive Era, 1910–1917* (New York: Harper & Brothers, 1954), pp. 212–13.

[†] Editor's note: The emphasis on the peace theme at the convention was not the result of Wilson's planning, according to Arthur Link. Link, *Wilson and the Progressive Era*, pp. 233–34.

[4] Grey of Fallodon, *Twenty-five Years*, Vol. II, p. 127; and B. J. Hendrick, *The Life and Letters of Walter Hines Page*, Vol. III, p. 279.

[‡] Editor's note: The Ludlow Amendment, a proposed amendment to the federal Constitution sponsored in the mid-1930's by Representative Louis Ludlow of Indiana, pro-

by itself alone, suffice to keep us out of war, but the election of 1916 does offer definite proof that Wilson was not pushed into war by popular demand.

The influence exerted by American finance upon our entry into the World War has been revealed in Ray Stannard Baker's *Life and Letters of Woodrow Wilson,* in the volumes of the Nye armament investigation, and in Professor C. C. Tansill's *America Goes to War.*

At the outset, the international bankers were not by any means all pro-Ally. Some, like the Morgan firm, were pro-British, and had been for years, while others, like Kuhn, Loeb and Company, manned chiefly by men of German derivation, were pro-German. But the financial interests of all the bankers soon came to be pro-Ally, for credit and loans to Germany were discouraged, while large loans were presently being made to the Allied powers.

On August 15, 1914, at the beginning of the war, Bryan declared against loans to any belligerent, on the ground that credit is the basis of all forms of contraband. President Wilson backed him up. For the time being, this position did not operate seriously against the Allies, for the balance of trade and investment was against the United States, and the Allied countries could pay for their purchases by cancelling the debts owed abroad by Americans. This situation took care of matters for a few months. But Allied war purchases became so great that, by the autumn of 1914, there was a credit crisis. The National City Bank addressed Robert Lansing, then Counsellor of the State Department, on this matter on October 23, 1914. Short-term credits to European governments were advocated. Lansing talked the matter over with President Wilson at once, and the latter agreed that the government would not interfere with such an arrangement. This information was transmitted orally to Willard Straight of J. P. Morgan & Company at the Metropolitan Club in Washington on the same night.

Shortly afterwards, H. P. Davison of the Morgan firm went to England and signed a contract to become the British purchasing agent in America. A similar contract was soon made with France.

The short-term loans sufficed for some months, but by the summer of 1915 Allied buying had become so extensive that the bankers saw that they must float loans here for the Allied countries if the latter were to continue to buy American munitions on a large scale. So they made strong representations to Colonel House and to the Secretary of the Treasury, W. G. McAdoo.

On August 21, 1915, McAdoo wrote a long letter to President Wilson, pointing out that great prosperity had come to the country as a result of the sale of munitions to the Allies, but that this prosperity could not continue unless we financed it through open loans to the Allies—i.e. selling Allied bonds in our own financial markets.

---

vided that Congress could not declare war, unless the United States or its possessions had been invaded, until a nation-wide referendum on the subject had been approved by majority vote.

On September 6, 1915, Secretary Lansing argued similarly in a letter to President Wilson, stressing the crisis that faced American business if the earlier ruling of Bryan and the President on American loans to belligerents was not rescinded. Colonel House supported this position. McAdoo and Lansing won their point. On September 8, 1915, Wilson assented to loans and the Morgan firm was once more given oral information. Very soon, the first public loan, the $500,000,000 Anglo-French loan, was floated.

The formal loans to the Allies—over $2,500,000,000 in all—financed their purchases for a little over a year, but their buying was so heavy that even the great investment banking houses could not take care of their needs. By January, 1917, the Allies had overdrawn their credit by nearly $500,000,000. Only Uncle Sam could save the great banking houses and the Allies. And Uncle Sam could help only if the United States were at war with Germany. We could not, as a government, lend money to a belligerent, unless we were at war with its enemy.

Just at this time the Germans renewed their unrestricted submarine warfare. The United States could now be led into the war, and the bankers would be repaid. They were repaid to the last cent. When the war was over, Mr. Thomas W. Lamont, of J. P. Morgan and Company, stated the facts relative to the attitude of his firm toward the World War and the belligerent powers:

> At the request of certain of the foreign governments the firm of Messrs. J. P. Morgan and Company undertook to co-ordinate the requirements of the Allies, and then to bring about regularity and promptness in fulfilling these requirements. Those were the days when American citizens were being urged to remain neutral in action, in word, and even in thought. But our firm had never for one moment been neutral: we didn't know how to be. From the very start we did everything we could to contribute to the cause of the Allies. And this particular work had two effects: one in assisting the Allies in the production of goods and munitions in America necessary to the Allies' vigorous prosecution of the war; the other in helping to develop the great and profitable export trade that our country has had.[5]

Most American industrialists naturally shared the attitude of the bankers. Since England controlled the seas, our sales were mainly to the Allied powers. We wished to see the Allies continue the war and win it. Upon their purchases depended most of our sales and prosperity, and upon their success and solvency depended the prospect of their being able to pay us in the end. The trade in munitions carried us from a depression in 1914 to boom years in 1915 and 1916.[6]

---

[5] *Manchester Guardian,* January 27, 1920.

[6] There has been much dispute as to whether we were forced into war by the loans and sales to the Allies or by the resumption of German submarine warfare early in 1917. In an important article in *Science and Society* (Spring, 1939) on "Neutrality and

By abandoning his neutral financial and industrial policy in favor of the Allies, President Wilson made it possible for the Entente Powers to enjoy an enormous advantage over the Central Powers in getting war supplies. The only way for the Central Powers to overcome it was to resume unlimited submarine warfare and try to sweep from the seas the ships that were carrying these supplies to the Allies.

It was our unneutral financing of the Allies that led to the resumption of German submarine warfare, and it was the resumption of this warfare which furnished the "incident" that enabled the war party in this country to put us into the conflict. It is, thus, perfectly clear that economic and financial pressure was the crucial factor which led us into war in 1917.

But no one need hold that President Wilson was moved primarily by any tender sentiments for the bankers. Both McAdoo and Lansing argued that it was essential to American prosperity to finance the Allies.

It was this general consideration of continued prosperity in 1915–16, and the relation of this to the prospects of the Democratic Party in the election of 1916, rather than any direct banker pressure on the White House, that bore in on Wilson's consciousness in the late summer of 1915, when he let down the gates to financing the Allies.

Yet, it is downright silly to contend that the bankers had no influence on Wilson's policy. If he did not listen to the bankers himself, he did listen very attentively to those who did heed banker pressure, namely, McAdoo, Lansing and House.

The active campaign for American preparedness and intervention was engineered by leaders of the war cult in the United States, such men as Theodore Roosevelt, Leonard Wood, Henry Cabot Lodge, "Gus" Gardiner, and the like. They led in the preparedness movement, the Plattsburg camp episode, and other steps designed to stimulate the martial spirit in America. The newspapers warmly supported this movement because of the circulation appeal which preparedness material supplied.

While there were notable exceptions, the majority of our newspapers were pro-Ally and pro-interventionist. Many of them were honestly sympathetic with the Allies. Others were deeply influenced by Allied propaganda. Some were heavily subsidized by the Allies. Still others were bought outright by Allied interests. Moreover, the Allies supplied all American newspapers with a vast amount of war-news material always favorable to the Allied cause. The newspapers also had a natural affinity for the bankers and industrialists who were their chief advertising clients. Finally, the newspapers were not unaware of the enormous circulation gains and increased advertising revenue which would follow our entry into the World War.

In the matter of propaganda the Allies had a notable advantage. They

---

Economic Pressures, 1914–1917" Professor Paul Birdsall shows that the two were inseparably tied together.

controlled the seas, the cables, and other means of communication. The Germans had only one crude and temporary wireless contact with the United States. Further, Allied propaganda was far better organized and more lavishly supported. It was also much more adroit than the German. As a result, a majority of Americans were led to believe in the veracity of the great batch of atrocity lies relative to the German invasion of Belgium, submarine warfare, and the like. This was particularly true after Lord Bryce put the force of his name and prestige behind the authenticity of such tales. Lord Northcliffe, who was in charge of British propaganda, in moments of unusual candor, stated that the Americans proved more gullible in such matters than any other people except the Chinese and called us "a bunch of sheep."

The ministers of the gospel also joined heartily in the great crusade to put us into the World War. Lining up behind such a stalwart as Newell Dwight Hillis, they preached a veritable holy war. They represented the Allies as divinely-anointed promoters of international decency and justice and the Central Powers as the servants of evil and the agents of savagery.

The net result of all this was that we entered the World War in April, 1917. We did so, even though there was no clear legal or moral basis for our so doing. If there ever was an instance in which the facts were clearly in accord with a neutrality policy it was in the spring of 1917. We should have fought both Germany and Britain or else neither. But the country went into war, with most of the citizens of the United States feeling that our self-respect and national honor demanded it. No other course seemed open to us.

Wilson and American Neutrality, 1914–1917

Arthur S. Link

WILSON AND THE PROBLEMS OF NEUTRALITY

For Woodrow Wilson and the American people, who had a positive disinclination to play the game of power politics, events on the international

From Arthur S. Link, *Wilson the Diplomatist* (Baltimore: The Johns Hopkins Press, 1957), pp. 31–90 *passim*. Reprinted by permission. The over-all title for the two chapters from this book was supplied by the editor.

stage intruded in an ironic if fateful way from 1914 to 1917. By the spring of 1915 the United States was the only great power not directly involved in the war then raging from western Europe to the Far East. Desiring only to deal fairly with both sides and to avoid military involvement, the President soon found that neutrality, as well as war, has its perplexities and perils.

The way in which Wilson met the challenges to America's peace and security raised by the death grapple between the opposing alliances has never been fully explained, notwithstanding scores of books and articles. Too often, historians, in company with public men, have looked for culprits instead of facts. Too often they have misunderstood the facts even when they found them. Too often they have written as if Wilson and his advisers made policy in a vacuum independent of the interplay of conflicting pressures. If we can see the President's policies of neutrality in the light of his convictions and objectives, the pressures and events (both domestic and foreign) that bore constantly upon him, and the alternatives between which he was often forced to choose—if we can do this, then perhaps we will see that his task in foreign policy at this juncture was not as simple as it has sometimes been described.

Among the most pervasive pressures controlling Wilson's decisions throughout the period 1914–1917 were the attitudes and opinions of the American people concerning the war and America's proper relation to it. Few presidents in American history have been more keenly aware of risks that the leader runs when he ceases to speak for the preponderant majority. "The ear of the leader must ring with the voices of the people. He cannot be of the school of the prophets; he must be of the number of those who studiously serve the slow-paced daily need." Thus Wilson had written in 1890;[1] thus he believed and practiced while formulating his policies toward the belligerents in the First World War.

The dominant American sentiment throughout the period of nonintervention can be summarily characterized by the single adjective "neutral." This is not to say that Americans had no opinions on the merits of the war and the claims of the opposing alliances, or that there were no differences among the popular reactions. It is simply to state the fairly obvious fact that the preponderant majority, whose opinions played a decisive role in shaping Wilson's policies, did not believe that their interests and security were vitally involved in the outcome of the war and desired to avoid participation if that were possible without sacrificing rights that should not be yielded. The prevalence and astounding vitality of neutralism, in spite of the severest provocations and all the efforts of propagandists on both sides, formed at once the unifying principle of American politics and the compelling reality with which Wilson had to deal from 1914 to 1917.

On the other hand, it would be a large error to imply that Wilson was a

---

[1] T. H. Vail Motter (ed.), *Leaders of Men* (Princeton, N. J., 1952), p. 43.

prisoner of the public opinion of the majority, and that his will to adopt sterner policies toward one group of belligerents or the other was paralyzed by the stronger counterforce of neutralism. Actually, the evidence points overwhelmingly to the conclusion that Wilson personally shared the opinions of the majority, in brief, that he was substantially neutral in attitude, and that his policies were controlled as much by his own convictions as by the obvious wishes of the people. . . .

It followed in Wilson's mind . . . that all the belligerents shared to some degree in the responsibility for the war and that one could not ascribe all blame to one side or the other. Nor could one use simple explanations in talking about conflicting war objectives. It was clear to Wilson that all the belligerents sincerely believed that they were fighting for their existence, but that all of them desired a smashing victory in order to enhance their power, win new territory, and impose crushing indemnities upon their enemies. Because this was true, Wilson reasoned, the best kind of settlement would be a stalemate in which neither alliance would have the power to impose terms upon the other.

In his fundamental thinking about war in general, moreover, Wilson shared in a remarkable way the assumptions of the majority of Americans. Like most of his fellow-citizens, he abhorred the very thought of using violence to achieve national objectives; indeed, he was reluctant to use even the threat of force in diplomacy. Like the Socialists, independent radicals, and a large majority of southern and western farmers, he suspected that the financiers and industrialists favored preparedness and a strong foreign policy in order to increase profits and provoke a war that would end the reform movement at home. Like the majority of Americans, he was willing to think of fighting only as a last resort and then only as a means of defending rights that no civilized nation could yield.

Fortified by these convictions, Wilson struggled hard and on the whole successfully to be impartial in thought as well as in deed, as he had asked the American people at the outbreak of the war to do. In fact, he succeeded in this impossible undertaking far better than most of his contemporaries and his historical critics. His method was to rely upon the general assumptions that he was sure were sound and then virtually to seal himself off from the passionate arguments and indictments of partisans of either alliance, by simply refusing to listen to them. "I recall," Secretary Lansing afterward wrote, for example, "that . . . his attitude toward evidence of German atrocities in Belgium and toward accounts of the horrors of submarine warfare . . . [was that] he would not read of them and showed anger if the details were called to his attention." [2]

This does not mean that Wilson was able completely to subordinate emotional reactions and personal feelings. Like the majority of Americans, he

---

[2] The Diary of Robert Lansing, November 20, 1921, MS in the Library of Congress.

was to a degree pro-British; on two, perhaps three, occasions during the two and a half years of American neutrality he avowed to close friends his personal sympathy for the Allied cause. But it would be a difficult task to prove that Wilson's pro-British sympathies were ever controlling or indeed even very strong. At no time did he act like a man willing to take measures merely to help his supposed friends. On the contrary, all his policies were aimed either at averting American participation on Britain's side or at ending the war on terms that would have denied the spoils of victory to Britain and her allies. If this is too big an assertion to be taken on faith, then perhaps the reasons for making it will become apparent as we see the way in which Wilson executed policies toward the two leading antagonists.

All authorities, whether friendly or hostile to Wilson, would agree that the acid tests of his neutrality were the policies that he worked out and applied vis-à-vis the British from 1914 to 1917. He has been most condemned by that group of historians highly censorious of his policies, generally known as revisionists, on this score—for becoming the captive of pro-Allied influences within his administration, for condoning such sweeping British control of neutral commerce that the Germans were forced to resort to drastic countermeasures, for permitting American prosperity to become dependent upon loans and exports to the Allies, in short, for permitting a situation to develop that made it inevitable that the United States would go to war if the success of Allied arms was ever seriously threatened.

Like most fallacious arguments, this one contains a certain element of plausibility. Wilson did condone a far-reaching British maritime system. American neutrality did work greatly to the benefit of the Allies. The error arises in saying that these things occurred because Wilson and his advisers necessarily wanted them to occur.

Perhaps the best way to gain a clear understanding of why Anglo-American relations developed as they did from 1914 to 1917 is to see how the policies that decisively shaped those relations emerged in several stages in response to certain pressures, events, and forces. The first stage, lasting from August, 1914, to about August, 1915, was in many ways the most critical, because the basic American response to the war and to the British maritime system was formulated then. That response was governed in the first instance by two domestic realities: the overwhelming, virtually unanimous, American desire to be neutral, and the pressures in the United States for a large measure of free trade with Britain's enemies.

In view of the prevailing American sentiment at the outbreak of the war, a policy of strict official neutrality was the only possible course for the United States government. This fact prompted the President's official proclamations of neutrality, supplemented by his appeal to the American people for impartiality in thought; the subsequent working out by the State Department of the elaborate technical rules to preserve American neutrality;

and the establishment of a Joint State and Navy Neutrality Board to advise the various departments upon the correct interpretation of international law.

One cannot read the records revealing how these policies were formulated without being convinced that their authors were high-minded in their determination to be fair to both sides. Indeed, Wilson and the man who chiefly influenced him in the formulation of the rules of neutrality, Secretary of State Bryan, were so intent upon being fair to the Germans that they adopted policies during the first months of the war that were highly disadvantageous to the British, if not unneutral. One was to prevent the sale of submarine parts, and hence parts for any naval craft, by a private American firm to the British government, on the ground that such a sale would be "contrary to . . . strict neutrality." Wilson persisted in supporting Bryan in this matter, in spite of advice from Counselor Lansing and the Joint Neutrality Board to the effect that their position was contrary to international law.

Infinitely more damaging to the Allies was the administration's second effort to lean over backward in being "strictly" neutral—the ban of loans by American bankers to the belligerent governments that the President permitted Bryan to impose in August, 1914. From a technical viewpoint, the ban was not unneutral, but it was highly prejudicial to the Allies because its effect was potentially to deny them their otherwise legal right to purchase supplies in the American market. These two incidents are not to be understood as revealing any anti-British bias on the part of Wilson and Bryan, although British officials at the time were convinced that they did. I mention them only to show what an important role the administration's desire to be impartial played in the formation of policies vis-à-vis the British during the early period of American neutrality.

The other pressure shaping American policies at this time was the force of combined demands at home for the virtually free transit of American ships and goods to the European neutrals and the belligerent Central Powers. So powerful were these demands, especially from cotton growers and exporters and their spokesmen in Congress, that Wilson personally sponsored two measures highly disadvantageous to the British and unneutral in fact as well as in spirit. One was a change in the ship registry law, put into effect by an act approved August 18, 1914, which made it easy for German or other foreign shipping firms to take out American registry for their vessels. The other was a plan to establish a federal corporation to purchase German ships in American ports and to use them to carry supplies to the belligerents, particularly to Germany. Wilson applied heavy pressure to obtain congressional approval of this, the so-called ship-purchase bill, during the short term from December, 1914, to March, 1915; he failed only because of a stout senatorial filibuster.

In negotiations with the British government during the early months of the war, Wilson fought hard in response to domestic pressures to keep the channels of international commerce open to American ships and goods. He did not go as far in defense of neutral rights as some of his predecessors, but he did suggest a code so sweeping that an enforcement of it would have meant almost total destruction of the British system of maritime controls. Specifically, the President first proposed on August 6, 1914, that the belligerents adopt the rules of naval warfare laid down in the Declaration of London of 1909, a convention never ratified by Great Britain or the United States, which permitted the free transit of all goods except those obviously contraband. When the British rejected this suggestion, the President came back on October 16, proposing a compromise that would have still seriously impaired the effectiveness of British sea power. When this effort also failed, Wilson then announced that his government would assert and defend all its rights under international law and treaties.

I have described these policies and proposals because they so clearly reveal Wilson's neutral intentions and what he would have done in matters of trade had he been able to make the rules himself. But he obviously could not follow his personal preferences alone or respond only to domestic pressures. In seeking to assert and defend American neutral rights he ran head-on into a reality as important as the reality of the pressures at home. It was the British determination to use sea power to prevent American ships and goods from going to the sustenance of the German economy and military forces.

British assumption of a nearly absolute control of the seas washing western Europe began with relatively mild measures in August, 1914, and culminated in the suppression of virtually all commerce to the Central Powers in March, 1915. For the British, this was not a question of adhering to the laws of blockade or of violating them, or of doing things merely to be nice to American friends. It was a question of achieving their supreme objective, to deprive their enemies of vital raw materials and goods, without risking the alienation of the United States. The controlling fact for the British was the necessity of preserving American friendship, in order to assure the uninterrupted rhythm of the North Atlantic trade. As the British Foreign Secretary at the time frankly put it:

> Blockade of Germany was essential to the victory of the Allies, but the ill-will of the United States meant their certain defeat. . . . It was better therefore to carry on the war without blockade, if need be, than to incur a break with the United States about contraband and thereby deprive the Allies of the resources necessary to carry on the war at all or with any chance of success. The object of diplomacy, therefore, was to secure the maximum of blockade that could be enforced without a rupture with the United States.[3]

---

[3] Viscount Grey of Fallodon, *Twenty-Five Years, 1892–1916* (2 vols.; New York, 1925), II, 107.

The crucial question all along, therefore, was whether the United States, the only neutral power strong enough successfully to challenge the British measures, would acquiesce or resist to the point of threatening or using force. The American response during the formative period of neutrality was, in brief, to accept the British system and to limit action against it to a vigorous assertion of American legal rights for future adjudication. All this is too well known to require any further exposition. What is not so well understood are the reasons why Wilson and his advisers acquiesced in a solution that denied the objectives that they and a large segment of the American public demanded. These reasons may be briefly summarized, as follows:

First, the British maritime system, in spite of American allegations to the contrary, enjoyed the advantage of being legitimate and usually legal, or nearly so, by traditional criteria. It was legitimate rather than fraudulent, and legal rather than capricious or terroristic, in its major aspects because the British did in fact hold undisputed sea supremacy and were therefore able to execute their controls in an orderly fashion. In asserting their own rights, the Americans could not well deny the advantages that accrued to the British by virtue of their sea power. The British, for example, had an undoubted right to establish a blockade of the Central Powers, and the American attempt to persuade the London government to use techniques effective only in the days of the sailing ship did not have much cogency in the twentieth century.

Second, much of the success of the British in establishing their control depended upon the way in which they went about it. Had they instituted their total blockade at the outset of the war, the American reaction would undoubtedly have been violent. Instead, the British applied their controls gradually, with a careful eye upon American opinion, using the opportunities provided by recurrent crises in German-American relations to institute their severest measures.

Third, the British were careful never to offend so many American interests at one time that retaliation would have been inevitable, or any single interest powerful enough by itself to compel retaliation. There was the case of cotton, which the officials in London were determined to prevent from going to Germany because it was an ingredient of gunpowder. Not until a year after the war began did they put cotton on the list of absolute contraband; even then they went to the extraordinary length of underwriting the entire American cotton market in order to avert an irresistible southern pressure in Congress for retaliation.[4] In addition, although they were ruthless in enforcing their blockade, the British took careful pains to avoid any serious injury to American property interests. They confiscated only the most obvious contraband; in all doubtful cases they paid full value for

---

[4] For a full discussion, see my "The Cotton Crisis, the South, and Anglo-American Diplomacy, 1914–1915," in J. C. Sitterson (ed.), *Studies in Southern History in Memory of Albert Ray Newsome, 1894–1951* (Chapel Hill, N. C., 1957), pp. 122–38.

cargoes or ships seized. Their objective was to control, not to destroy, American commerce.

Fourth, there was great significance in the language and symbolism that the British Foreign Office used in defending the measures of the Admiralty and Ministry of Blockade. By justifying their maritime system in terms of international law and the right of retaliation, and (at least before the summer of 1916) by making an honest effort to meet American objections half way when possible, the British made it almost inevitable that the Washington authorities would have to reply in the same language, thus giving a purely *legal* character to the issues involved and for the most part avoiding raising the issues of sovereignty and inherent national rights. The significance of this achievement can be seen in the conviction of Wilson and the majority of Americans that the Anglo-American disputes did involve only property rights, which should be vindicated only by an appeal to much-controverted international law. Moreover, by appealing to the American government and people in the name of friendship and by always professing their devotion to the cause of humanity, the British succeeded in evoking strong feelings of sympathy and understanding on the other side of the water.

Finally, the British were able partially to justify their own blockade measures as legitimate adaptations to a changing technology by pointing to precedents established by the Washington government itself during the American Civil War. To be sure, the British drew some incorrect analogies (as Lansing pointed out) between American and British practice; even so, their main contention—that the American government had also stretched the rules of blockade to allow for technological changes—was essentially correct.

Wilson's refusal to challenge the British maritime system, in short, to break the British blockade, was almost inevitable in view of the facts we have just reviewed, *if the President's objective was simply to maintain as best he could the neutral position of the United States.* An absolute neutrality was in any event impossible because of the total character of the war and America's importance in the world economy. It often happened that any action by the United States inevitably conferred a benefit on one side and thereby injured the other, at least indirectly. In these circumstances, neutrality often consisted of doing the things that would give the least unwarranted or undeserved advantages.

By this standard, it would have been more unneutral than neutral for Wilson to have broken the British maritime system by enforcing highly doubtful technical rights under international law. Judged by practical standards rather than by the often conflicting criteria of neutrality, Wilson's acceptance of the British system seems realistic and wise—indeed, the only choice that he could have made in the circumstances. This is true because the results of destroying the British blockade would have been the wrecking of American friendship with the two great European democracies and the probable victory of the Central Powers, without a single compensating gain for the interests and security of the United States. Only the sure achievement of some great political objective like a secure peace settlement, certainly not the winning of a commercial advantage or the defense of doubtful neutral rights, would have justified Wilson in undertaking a determined challenge to British sea power.

The second stage in Anglo-American relations, lasting from the summer of 1915 to the late spring of 1916, saw the development of the natural economic consequence of the American adjustment to tightening British control of the seas. That consequence was the burgeoning of an enormous war trade between the United States and the Allies. The United States became the storehouse and armory of the Allies neither because there was any conspiracy on the part of certain pro-Allied leaders in Washington to make American prosperity dependent upon an Allied victory, nor because American businessmen and bankers were willing to incur the risks of war in order to increase their profits. The United States became the storehouse of the Allies for the simple reason that Great Britain and not Germany controlled the seas.

The war trade itself was entirely neutral. Indeed, any action by the United States government to impede it, unless undertaken for overriding political motives, would have been grossly prejudicial and unneutral. If it had been permitted to develop in a normal way, this commerce would have raised no important problems in the relations of the United States with the Allies. A problem of the first magnitude did arise, however, because the President, in the summer of 1914, had permitted Secretary Bryan to enforce his own private moral views by imposing a ban on loans by American bankers to the belligerents.

There was no difficulty so long as the British and French governments could find gold and dollars to settle their adverse trade balances. By the summer of 1915, however, Allied gold and dollar resources were near the point of exhaustion; and American insistence upon a continuation of cash payments could result only in gravely damaging the Allied economies and ending the North Atlantic trade altogether. Credit could be found only in the United States, but credit meant floating loans, and loans to the belligerents were as much a political as an economic question because of the existence of Bryan's ban.

It is well known that the State Department under Bryan's direction substantially relaxed its credit embargo during the spring of 1915 and that Wilson and Bryan's successor, Lansing, lifted the ban altogether a few months later, at a time when the credit needs of the Allied governments were demonstrably acute. Even though the full facts bearing upon this matter have been available to scholars for more than twenty years, the reasons for the administration's reversal are still not properly understood.

Bryan's ban could not survive the development of the war trade on a large scale because, in the first place, it (like the Embargo of 1808) was potentially nearly as disastrous to the United States as to the Allies. American material well-being was in large measure dependent upon foreign trade, and particularly upon trade with the Allied world. Such trade was possible during wartime only if American businessmen were willing to do for the Allies what they always did for solvent customers in temporary straits, namely, sell them goods on credit.

The most important reason that Bryan's embargo could not survive, however, was that it was an essentially unneutral policy that impeded the growth of the chief economic consequence of American neutrality, the legitimate war trade. The credit embargo and the war trade could not both survive. The former gave way because Wilson finally realized that it would be as unneutral to interfere with the extension of credit as it would be to stop the flow of goods. Bryan's ban was in a sense, therefore, a casualty chiefly of American neutrality. . . .

The second stage in Anglo-American relations also witnessed the apparent convergence of the diplomatic policies of the two countries on the high level. During the summer and autumn of 1915 Colonel Edward M. House, Wilson's confidant and principal adviser on foreign policy, conceived a plan by which the American and British leaders would join hands to press for an end to the war through Wilson's mediation. The British Foreign Secretary, Sir Edward Grey, replied that his government would cooperate only if the Washington administration were willing to go beyond simple mediation and would agree to join a postwar international organization established for the purpose of effecting disarmament, maintaining freedom of the seas, and preserving peace. Wilson hopefully consented, and House went to Berlin, Paris, and London in January, 1916, to lay the diplomatic basis of mediation.

In London, House worked out in documentary form with Grey and the other members of the British Cabinet the specific terms of Anglo-American co-operation. Initialed by House and Grey on February 22, 1916, and known as the House-Grey Memorandum or Agreement, this document declared that President Wilson was ready, upon hearing from England and France that the time was ripe, to propose that a conference be called to end the war. Should the Allies accept and Germany refuse the invitation, the United States would "probably" enter the war against Germany. Should the conference meet and Germany refuse to accept a reasonable settlement, then the United States would also "probably" enter the war on the Allied side.

To the so-called revisionists the conclusion of the House-Grey Agreement is irrefutable proof that Wilson had abandoned neutrality and meant to take the country into war at the first opportunity. To remove all doubt that this was true, they point to what happened during the weeks immediately following the initialing of the agreement.

While House had been carrying his negotiations in London to a successful conclusion, Wilson and Lansing had undertaken to avert the possibility of conflict with Germany over the issue of submarine attacks against armed merchantmen by proposing that the Allies disarm their merchant ships and that U-boats follow the old rules of cruiser warfare in attacking them. Using the President's suggestion as a pretext, the German authorities announced on February 10, 1916, that submarines would attack *armed* enemy merchantmen without warning after February 29. Then without warning Wilson and Lansing reversed themselves and announced that the American government would insist upon the right of Americans to travel on ships defensively armed and would hold the German government to strict account for the loss of any American lives on armed merchantmen. Adhering doggedly to this position in the face of a threatened rebellion in Congress, the President proceeded to use the opportunity afforded by the torpedoing without warning of the French Channel packet *Sussex* by a German submarine, "in contravention of earlier pledges," to threaten a break in diplomatic relations with Germany and to force the Imperial government to make sweeping concessions in its conduct of submarine warfare.

To the revisionist critics, the case is so clear that it needs no further proof. The House-Grey Agreement, they say, was conceived and concluded for the purpose of promoting early American intervention. Wilson at once sought to accomplish this goal by taking a position on armed merchant ships that was bound to provoke a crisis with Germany, and by pressing the German government so hard during the *Sussex* controversy that a break in relations would probably ensue. The plan failed, the revisionists explain, only because the violent opposition in Congress convinced the President that the lawmakers would never approve a declaration of war to uphold the right of Americans to travel on belligerent armed merchant ships, and only because the German authorities proved to be more conciliatory than Wilson had expected.

The revisionists are correct in asserting that the conclusion of the House-Grey Agreement marked the beginning of a new and epochal phase in Wilson's policies toward the belligerents. Otherwise they have missed the entire meaning of the affair, for the House-Grey Agreement was in Wilson's purpose *not an instrument of intervention, but a means of averting American involvement.* The truth of this important generalization will perhaps become evident when we recall the realities of the American diplomatic situation during late 1915 and early 1916, and when we understand Wilson's motives and intentions in devising a solution.

The overshadowing reality confronting the makers of American foreign policy at this time was the grave possibility of war with Germany over the submarine issue. It caused Wilson and Lansing, for example, to abandon ambitious plans for further intervention in Mexico. It speeded the American acquiescence in the British maritime system. Most important, it prompted the President and his advisers to search for ways to avert the rupture that might draw the United States into the maelstrom.

One way out of the predicament was to come to a full understanding with the German government over the issues involved in the submarine controversy. This is what Lansing attempted to do and almost succeeded in accomplishing during his negotiations over the *Lusitania* affair. Another way out and a surer means of averting the peril of American involvement in the future was to bring the war itself to an end through Wilson's mediation. It seemed at the time that the best hope of peace lay in Anglo-American co-operation for a peace of compromise, specifically in the kind of co-operation detailed in the House-Grey Agreement.

Thus Wilson approved this plan of mediation, but with a full realization that certain obligations and risks were involved. There was the necessity of giving positive assurances to the Allies, for they would have been at a fatal disadvantage in a peace conference without American support, in view of the strategic advantages that the Germans then enjoyed on the Continent of Europe. There was, moreover, the risk of war if the Germans refused to approve an armistice or proved to be unreasonable at a peace conference after agreeing to end the fighting. However, Wilson gave the necessary assurances in the belief that the risk of war involved was insignificant as compared to the greater danger of hostilities with Germany if he could not somehow bring the war to an end. This, then, was his dominant motive in sending House to Europe in January, 1916, and in approving the House-Grey Agreement at the cost of Lansing's proposed compromise for submarine warfare.

In the final analysis, our judgment of Wilson's mediation plans must depend upon the kind of settlement that he had in mind and for which he was willing to run the risk of war in order to achieve peace. It is clear that Wilson envisaged a "reasonable" settlement based upon recognition that the war was a stalemate and upon a return for the most part of the *status quo ante bellum*. It meant, Wilson also hoped, the kind of settlement in which all the belligerents would forego annexations and indemnities, put aside past differences, and joins hands with the United States to create a new international order. In his final discussions with the British Cabinet, Colonel House made it clear that this, and this only, was the kind of settlement that Wilson was prepared to use the House-Grey Agreement to achieve. In other words, as House told the British leaders, the President would "throw the weight of the United States on the side of those wanting a just settlement—a settlement which would make another such war impossible." [5]

Granted that Wilson's purpose was a genuinely neutral mediation, we can almost hear the critics say, how can one explain his seemingly provoca-

---

[5] The Diary of Edward M. House, February 14, 1916, MS in the Yale University Library.

tive stand during the crises over armed merchantmen and the *Sussex?* Was he not making such a bold assertion of American rights in the hope that the German government would deny them and thereby give him an excuse for going to Congress for a declaration of war?

The answer, again, is that Wilson was trying desperately to prepare the way for peace and not for war. He and Lansing had proposed the disarming of merchant ships in the hope that this would facilitate a definitive understanding with Germany. But, as House and Page pointed out in urgent telegrams from London, such a proposal was unneutral in spirit and if implemented might mean the destruction of the British merchant marine; and Wilson's insistence upon it would assuredly disqualify him as a mediator acceptable to the Allies. Wilson suddenly reversed himself on the armed ship issue, therefore, primarily in order to restore his neutral standing. Then, following the conclusion of the House-Grey Agreement, the President pressed the Germans for guarantees of good behavior in the conduct of their submarine operations. But he did this with agonizing reluctance because of the risk of war involved and only in order to create a situation in which he might begin to move for peace.

All of Wilson's actions during the third and final stage in American neutrality, lasting from early May, 1916, to early February, 1917, confirm these conclusions. I will discuss his efforts to avert American involvement and his plans for peace in the next . . . [chapter]. Let us now see how he had meanwhile worked out his response to the continuing challenge of the submarine, and why.

So long as the British controlled the seas and the Germans commanded the strategic territories and resources of Europe, the American task of neutrality was the relatively easy one of accepting a *de facto* situation and of pursuing the most impartial policies possible within this framework of power. Thus Wilson permitted the German invasion of Belgium to pass without protest, even though some Americans contended that he was morally obliged to denounce such a gross violation of international law; thus he accepted the British maritime system. In this situation of actual stalemate, there was little likelihood of an Anglo-American rupture and no possibility of a German-American conflict, because there were no points of friction between the two governments. But the German decision to attempt to break the stalemate by using an untried weapon, the submarine, created a situation of great peril for the United States because it raised the issue of fundamental national rights and made it exceedingly difficult for the President to continue to steer a neutral course. Before we see how he struggled to find some adjustment to this new situation, let us consider for a moment some of the underlying factors that helped to govern German submarine policy and Wilson's response.

First, German decisions regarding the use of the submarine were determined almost exclusively by internal and objective considerations—the number of submarines on hand and their calculated effectiveness, the military situation in Europe and how it might be affected by American intervention, and the like—and in no essential way by American policies vis-à-vis the British, or by the rules of international law for cruiser warfare. . . . That is to say, calculations of sheer military advantage or disadvantage and not American or even British maritime policies dictated the way in which the Germans would prosecute their underseas campaign.

Second, the submarine was in 1915 a new weapon of naval warfare. This was an important fact, for it meant that there was no special international law to govern its use when the rights of neutrals were involved. The only laws that could be applied were the rules of cruiser warfare, which required attacking warships to warn merchant ships before sinking them and to make provision for the safety of passengers and crew. The trouble was that the submarine was not a cruiser, but a frail craft that had to rely upon deception and quick striking power for safety and effectiveness. If its use had been an issue only between the belligerents, then international law would not have been much involved. But international law was directly involved, because its provisions defined not only the rights of neutrals, but their obligations to the belligerent powers as well. Having chosen a course of neutrality under international law, Wilson had to work within accepted rules in formulating his response to the submarine challenge insofar as American rights were concerned. The Allies, understandably, would not consent to modifications to permit enemy submarines to operate at their peak deadly efficiency; their refusal made it difficult for Wilson to insist upon changing the rules without seeming to be unneutral in spirit and without in fact conferring enormous advantages upon the Germans.

Third, all questions of international law aside, a great power like the United States could not view the submarine blockade as a legitimate weapon, one that should be considered and perhaps accepted on grounds of expediency or necessity. This was true because at the time of its inauguration in February, 1915, the submarine blockade was actually a sham, since the Germans were then able to keep at most only seven U-boats at one time in all the waters surrounding the British Isles. The Germans, in fact, inaugurated the "blockade" with four submarines in service in the area. A year later, at the time of the *Sussex* crisis, the German Admiralty could send only eleven or twelve submarines into western waters at one time. Knowledge of these facts decisively influenced the way in which Wilson and his advisers viewed the so-called blockade and formulated policies regarding it, for it was one of the oldest and most generally recognized rules of international law that a blockade must be effective in order to be legal.

Fourth, unlike the Anglo-American disputes over trading rights, which involved only property interests, the German submarine campaign as it was often prosecuted raised an issue which no great power should ever evade or arbitrate—the safety and welfare of its people in pursuits and areas where they have a right to be. It is almost inconceivable that Wilson and the American people could have thought of going to war with the British over issues of search and seizure or of blockade. It is also inconceivable that they would not have been willing to think in terms of war with a government that permitted, indeed, instructed, its naval commanders to slaughter Americans indiscriminately upon the high seas.

It would, however, be a mistake of almost fatal magnitude to conclude, as so many writers have done, that Wilson's response to the submarine challenge was a simple and automatic reaction governed entirely by these factors. Although they played an important role, Wilson actually formed and executed, not a single consistent submarine policy, but a series of policies in response to changing issues and circumstances and in response to his own larger diplomatic objectives.

His first policy was formed in answer to the original German proclamation of submarine warfare. Avoiding the more difficult issue raised, the one involving the right of Americans to travel in safety on belligerent ships, Wilson replied by simply but strongly affirming the right of American vessels to use the seas subject to limitations permitted by international law, and by warning that the United States would hold Germany to a "strict accountability" (Counselor Lansing's words) for lives and property lost as a consequence of illegal submarine attacks against *American neutral* shipping. It was the only position that the President could have taken without abandoning the pretense of neutrality and national dignity, and the Germans soon retreated and gave such sweeping guarantees regarding American ships that this issue was never again a point of conflict between the two governments before 1917.

There still remained the necessity of devising a policy to deal with the more controversial issue of the right of American citizens to travel and work on *belligerent* merchant ships under conditions of safety specified by international law. When a German submarine sank the British liner *Falaba* without warning in March, 1915, killing an American citizen, Wilson's advisers in the State Department squared off in a momentous debate over the formulation of a proper response. One group, headed by Secretary Bryan, argued that American interests were not sufficiently involved to warrant a stern protest against submarine attacks on Allied ships, even when Americans were traveling on them, and that the spirit of neutrality demanded that the United States condone German violations of international law as it had done with British violations. The other group, headed by Counselor Lansing, replied that the attack on the *Falaba* had been such a flagrant infraction of international law that the United States must protest uncompromisingly in order to defend its neutrality and honor.

The records reveal that Wilson would have preferred to avoid any involvement while the two giant belligerents fought it out on the seas. In legal theory he agreed with Lansing, but he was so strongly moved by Bryan's pleading that he had apparently decided by the end of the debate over a *Falaba* note to make no protest at all. This is the course that he would probably have followed in the future if the Germans, by confining their underseas campaign to attacks against Allied cargo ships and by showing a desire to avoid the loss of American life, had made it possible for him to find a means of adjusting to the new situation.

A policy of noninvolvement, however, became impossible when a German U-boat sank the British passenger liner *Lusitania* without warning on May 7, 1915, with the loss of almost 1,200 civilians, including 128 Americans, men, women, and children. Wilson had to make some positive response now, so atrocious was the deed in the eyes of the American people, so flagrant was the violation of elemental national rights, so unneutral and degrading would be an acceptance of the terror campaign against the North Atlantic passenger liners.

The strategic facts of the situation—the German inability to maintain any effective blockade of the British Isles and the consequent serious dangers to Germany from a break with the United States—would have justified the President in peremptorily demanding prompt disavowal and guarantees. Wilson's response, however, reflected his own desire and that of the majority of Americans to preserve neutrality and to avoid taking any position short of yielding essential rights that might lead to hostilities with Germany. Thus all during the summer of 1915 Wilson pounded out notes on his typewriter, for the sole purpose of persuading the German government to disavow the sinking of the *Lusitania* and to abandon its campaign against unarmed passenger vessels. Threatening to break relations after a U-boat sank the liner *Arabic* on August 19, 1915, Wilson finally won the promise that he demanded.

By the end of the summer of 1915 the President had thus worked through two stages of policy and had won immunity from ruthless submarine attacks on American neutral ships and unarmed belligerent passenger liners. Up to this time, at any rate, Wilson had been patient, conciliatory, and firm only in his demand that the Germans give up measures that had already taken American lives and threatened untold others.

The third stage in the formulation of Wilson's policies toward the submarine, lasting from the early autumn of 1915 through the *Sussex* crisis in the spring of 1916, saw the President attempting to reach a definitive understanding with the Berlin authorities over all phases of submarine warfare against merchant shipping. The issue was daily becoming more difficult to solve by the application of traditional law, because the Allies since March, 1915, had been arming some passenger and cargo ships and ordering them to attack submarines that showed "hostile intent." But Wilson and Lansing persisted in trying to find a solution in spite of the obstacles because they (or Wilson, at any rate) and the majority of Americans still earnestly desired to avoid conflict over merely technical issues.

By patient negotiation Lansing finally won something resembling a German apology for the loss of American lives on the *Lusitania* and an implicit reaffirmation of the *Arabic* pledge. In order to hasten this German concession and to avert even the possibility of future contention, Lansing proposed his *modus vivendi* of January 18, 1916 (already mentioned), designed to provide a new code to govern the German underseas campaign against maritime commerce. This was the proposal that the Allies disarm their merchant ships and that the German submarines observe the rules of cruiser warfare in attacking them.

Adoption of the proposal by the opposing belligerents, or by the United States and Germany alone, would have achieved Wilson's objective of a comprehensive settlement of the submarine issue. And yet, for reasons that we have already seen, Wilson jettisoned the *modus vivendi* in order to save the House-Grey Agreement. Soon afterward, during the *Sussex* controversy (as we have also seen), he launched a new campaign to force the German government to conduct submarine operations against all merchant ships, armed and unarmed, within the rules of cruiser warfare.

Wilson's rejection of the opportunity to come to a seemingly definitive understanding with Germany seems altogether logical and wise when we remember his objectives and the circumstances in which he made these decisions during the third stage in German-American relations. Wilson's supreme objective now was peace through his own mediation. Mediation seemed possible at this time only through the co-operation of the British government. But the British would co-operate only if they believed that the President was genuinely neutral, and certainly not if he insisted upon a code of submarine warfare that minimized the risks to Americans at the expense of British sea power to the advantage of an essentially illegitimate weapon.

Mediation was a noble objective with such great benefits to the United States that it justified taking a few risks to achieve. But Wilson could have followed no other course than the one he followed during the crises over armed merchantmen and the *Sussex,* even if his objective had been merely to maintain American neutrality. In the circumstances prevailing in the late winter of 1916, Wilson had to choose between continuing to accept the British maritime system, mooted by American Civil War precedents, or acquiescing in the challenge to that system, the German submarine blockade. The first was legitimate because it was based upon *de facto* power as well as legal precedent; the second was not legitimate because it was still a paper blockade without any power of effective enforcement. By insisting upon adherence to traditional rules insofar as the rights of Americans were concerned, Wilson was not at this time depriving the Germans of a weapon essential for their survival or one the free use of which would bring them victory at this time. This, essentially, was the reason that they yielded (for the time being) to Wilson's demands in the *Sussex* crisis. By insisting upon the adoption of Lansing's *modus vivendi,* on the other hand, Wilson in effect would have changed the traditional rules and aimed a heavy blow at the British maritime system, and only for the illusory purpose of averting the possibility of a conflict with Germany.

The final test of any foreign policy is whether it serves the national interest. If it was to the interest of the United States to avoid participation in the war at any cost, regardless of its outcome, and if implementing the *modus vivendi* would have averted all possibility of American involvement, then Wilson's policies at this time were unwise. This generalization, however, is faulty in all its assumptions. To begin with, American interests would be best served by a stalemate and by a peace of reconciliation through Wilson's mediation, not by driving the Allies into sullen opposition, thereby making mediation impossible, and not by promoting a German victory. More important was the fact that implementing the *modus vivendi* would not have prevented the conflict with Germany that Wilson wished to avoid. As we now know, and as Wilson did not know, conflict would come inevitably when the Germans had enough submarines to institute an effective blockade. In that event neither right nor law nor concessions by the United States would dissuade the Germans from making an all-out bid for victory through a devastating attack upon all maritime commerce to the Allied nations.

With the conclusion of the *Sussex* crisis, Wilson's task of erecting a solid structure of neutral policies to govern relations with Britain and Germany was complete, and the next great effort of American foreign policy would be aimed at the higher goal of peace. Operating within the limitations imposed by American public opinion, external realities, and his own conception of the right role for the United States to play, Wilson had made the only kind of adjustments possible in view of American rights and duties as the leading neutral power. He was now in a position from which he could launch his peace campaign. Thus by virtue of Wilson's leadership, American neutrality was not merely a fact in the spring of 1916, but the most important and the most hopeful fact of international life at the time. . . .

WILSON AND THE DECISIONS FOR WAR

The interval between May 1, 1916, and February 1, 1917, was one of the fateful turning points of modern history, because the decisions that the leaders of the great powers made during this brief period determined the future of mankind for generations to come. It was a time of gloom, because by the spring of 1916 the war had become a bloody stalemate in the trenches and upon the seas, and its futile continuation could mean only the attrition and perhaps the ruin of Western civilization. It was also a time of hope, for, as events turned out, statesmen had the opportunity to end the war on terms that might have promised a secure and peaceful future. . . .

Wilson made the first decision during the period under review. It was to press for mediation under the terms of the House-Grey Agreement, a choice almost foreordained by developments that I described in the preceding chapter. Indeed, he began even before the end of the *Sussex* crisis, only to encounter a firm refusal by Sir Edward Grey, the British Foreign Secretary, who made it plain that he preferred American belligerency and that he did not have much hope for the President's mediation in any event.

Undaunted by these early rebuffs, Wilson, assisted by Colonel House, returned to the task with a new zeal born of the hope engendered by the happy resolution of the *Sussex* affair and his and House's still strong belief that the British leaders sincerely wanted peace. From May 10 through July 15, 1916, the two American leaders applied a mounting pressure upon the British Foreign Office, appealing, pleading, and warning that British refusal to co-operate with the President would drive the United States into complete isolation and compel the Washington government to re-examine its attitude toward British maritime measures. As Wilson put it:

> We are plainly face to face with this alternative, therefore. The United States must either make a decided move for peace (upon some basis that promises to be permanent) or, if she postpones that, must insist to the limit upon her rights of trade and upon such freedom of the seas as international law already justifies her in insisting on as against Great Britain, with the same plain speaking and firmness that she has used against Germany. And the choice must be made immediately. Which does Great Britain prefer? She cannot escape both. To do nothing is now, for us, impossible.[6]

In the beginning Grey tried to avoid a plain refusal by saying that the time for calling a peace conference was not yet ripe, and by urging the President to raise the question with the French government, which he knew would reject outright any suggestions of peace. But when pressed for a direct answer, the Foreign Secretary finally had to reply frankly that the Allies, and not the United States, would decide when the time for peace talks had come, and that there was no chance of implementing the House-Grey Agreement so long as the Allies had any hope of winning a military decision. In addition, other spokesmen of the British and French governments, who were not as much personally involved as Grey, made it plain by private conversation and public statement that the Allies would regard any mediation move by the President as a hostile act designed to deprive them of their chance of victory. . . .

Wilson's response was a decision with momentous possibilities for good or for ill—to strengthen American neutrality and then to press forward in his own independent campaign for peace. It was the grand culmination of American neutrality and the almost inevitable outgrowth of pressures and

---

[6] Wilson to E. M. House, May 16, 1916, the Ray Stannard Baker Collection of Wilson Materials, Library of Congress.

events at home and abroad that were converging during the summer and autumn of 1916 to cause a radical shift in American foreign policy.

One of these events was Wilson's mounting anger with the British and his growing disillusionment about the merits of the whole Allied cause as a consequence of the British rejection (as he saw it) of his right hand of fellowship. Going far beyond mere irritation, this anger and disillusionment culminated in convictions powerful enough to affect national policy—that the Allies were fighting for selfish motives and domination, and that they would prolong the carnage rather than consent to a fair and liberal settlement.

Developments in the official relations of the United States and Great Britain during the summer and autumn of 1916 also speeded the disillusionment in Washington and prepared the way for a change of American policy. To state the matter briefly, the Admiralty and Ministry of Blockade tightened the British maritime system to the point of denying the last vestiges of the freedom of the seas. This they did by such measures as the search and seizure of American mail, carrying the economic war to America by forbidding British subjects to have any dealings with neutral individuals and firms suspected of trading with the Central Powers, and attempting to bring all American shipping under British control by denying shipmasters the right to purchase coal in distant British ports if they refused to submit to the Admiralty's control.

A force of even greater power propelling Wilson toward policies of stern neutrality and independent mediation was the extraordinary growth of American neutralism following the settlement of the *Sussex* affair. In part it was the result of a sharp increase in anti-British sentiment as a consequence of the tightening of the maritime system and the American revulsion against the ruthless way in which the British army suppressed the Irish Rebellion in April, 1916. In larger measure it was a reflection of the overwhelming desire to avoid participation in a war the outcome of which did not concern most Americans. Whatever the causes for its spectacular increase, neutralism became the reigning passion during the summer and autumn of 1916. . . .

There was a final and irresistible force propelling Wilson toward a new diplomatic course at this time—his fear that the war was entering a new and more desperate stage in which the aggressions of the belligerents might drive the American people to war in sheer anger. If this happened, then Americans would be fighting in blind defense of national rights, not knowing really why they fought, and only to the end that one side might win a smashing victory and thus be able to impose a peace that could not endure. . . .

It was to avoid being caught in such a predicament as this that Wilson embarked upon the policies that I will now describe.

First, he began to move in a really menacing way to defend alleged American neutral rights in the face of the new British maritime measures. No longer couched in friendly terms, the State Department's protests now accused the London government of "lawless" conduct and warned that the United States would not tolerate the continuation of "repeated violations of international law." To give teeth to these warnings, Wilson obtained legislation from Congress in early September empowering him to deny clearance and port facilities to ships of any nation that discriminated against American commerce, and to use the armed forces to enforce the prohibition. In addition, he persuaded the Federal Reserve Board to warn American bankers to exercise caution in financing the war trade with the Allies.

The consequences of this new sternness—a sharp increase in Anglo-American tension and vigorous protests from London—were also a calculated component of Wilson's plan. His grand objective was independent mediation, and such mediation would be possible only from a posture of severe neutrality. In other words, mediation could succeed only if the President convinced the British that he meant to use his powers of retaliation to force them to co-operate, and the Germans that he was determined to compel as much respect for American rights from their enemies as he had from them.

Wilson proceeded with his preparations for a climactic peace campaign once the voters had decreed that he should have charge of foreign relations for another four years. Protracted discussions among Wilson, Lansing, and House during late November, 1916, pointed up the possibilities and dangers of the situation. The Allies were now even more violently opposed to peace talk of any kind than they had been during the preceding summer. The German leaders, on the other hand, were not only increasing their pressure on Wilson for a peace move, but were now even promising (at least so the German Ambassador in Washington said) to evacuate Belgium and France if the Allies consented to an armistice. There was the danger, therefore, as House and Lansing pointed out, that Germany would respond favorably to a call for peace and that the Allies would reject it. If this happened, the President's advisers further warned, then the United States might drift into a sympathetic alliance with Germany and into a naval war with England and Japan. Would it not be safer, House asked, to attempt to revive the House-Grey Agreement and to move for mediation under its terms?

These were weighty issues, and in dealing with them Wilson revealed for the first time his innermost thoughts about the war and America's duty toward the belligerents. Old plans like the House-Grey Agreement based upon the assumption of intimate Anglo-American co-operation were, he exclaimed, out of date. He must stand for peace alone, free and compelling, no matter what the risks might be. If the Germans responded favorably, he would work with them. If the Allies resisted, he would attempt to coerce them. There was the risk of a rupture and war, but he did not think that it was great.

"This morning in discussing these matters with the President," House wrote in his Diary on November 15, 1916,

> he went so far as to say that if the Allies wanted war with us we would not shrink from it. . . . He thought they would not dare resort to this and if they did, they could do this country no serious hurt. I disagreed with him again. I thought Great Britain might conceivably destroy our fleet and land troops from Japan in sufficient numbers to hold certain parts of the United States. He replied they might get a good distance but would have to stop somewhere.

Neither these somber warnings, which he did not take seriously, nor the call by the German government for a peace conference, issued on December 12, diverted Wilson from the course that he had decided to pursue, and he sent a message to the belligerent capitals on December 18, 1916. In order to avoid the appearance of supporting the German maneuver, the President eliminated a demand for the assembling of a peace conference and simply asked the belligerents to say frankly what they were fighting for and upon what terms they would consent to end the war. The whole world knew, however, that it was merely the first step in a bold campaign.

The time was now at hand when the belligerent leaders had to choose between peace and prolonging the war at the risk of incurring American intervention. To provide the opportunity for frank discussions, Wilson opened secret negotiations through Colonel House with the British Ambassador in Washington, with Sir William Wiseman, an agent accredited to the British Embassy, and with the German Ambassador to the United States. While waiting for their replies, moreover, the President went before the Senate on January 22, 1917, to describe the kind of settlement that he hoped to achieve.

The British gave their answer first, on January 26, 1917, when Wiseman told House that his government would agree to the meeting of an early peace conference, provided that the Germans returned a favorable reply to the President's appeal. It was a startling announcement in view of the hitherto bitter opposition of the British Cabinet to any suggestion of mediation and the Allied public answer of January 10, 1917, to Wilson's peace note, which had revealed ambitions so sweeping that they could be realized only by the defeat of Germany. . . .

At this point, however, it mattered comparatively little what the British said, or why they said it. Wilson had the power of life or death over the Allies and was prepared to use it to force them to the peace table, provided that the Germans approved his objectives and accepted his leadership. As he put it:

> If Germany really wants peace she can get it, and get it soon, *if she will but confide in me and let me have a chance.* . . . Feelings, exasperations are neither here nor there. Do they want me to help? I am

entitled to know because I genuinely want to help and have now put myself in a position to help without favour to either side.[7]

. . . The High Command had already made the decision by late December; it was confirmed by a conference of all leaders at Pless Castle on January 9, 1917. That decision was, in brief, to begin unrestricted submarine warfare against all shipping, belligerent and neutral, in the approaches to the British Isles and the eastern Mediterranean after January 31.

It was easily the most fateful decision made by any government during the course of the war, and the German records fully reveal the reasons for its adoption . . . on a basis of elaborate calculations the Admiralty spokesmen guaranteed absolutely to reduce the British to actual starvation within five months after the submarine blockade began. If this were possible, then Germany had it within her power to win a total victory and a settlement that would establish the Reich in an unassailable position. To the military leaders, who had despaired of winning the war in the trenches, it was an opportunity that could not be refused.

Fear of American belligerency no longer had any effect on German policy in such an atmosphere of confident expectation. The German leaders all assumed that a wholesale attack on American maritime commerce would drive the United States into the war. These same leaders also concluded that American belligerency would not make any difference. On the contrary, American participation would have certain positive advantages, for it would mean the diversion of huge quantities of food and matériel to an American army in training during the very period when the U-boats would be winning the war on the seas. But in any event, American participation was in the circumstances necessary to the success of the German plans, because the submarine blockade could succeed only if it were total, that is, only if American as well as British ships were prevented from carrying life-giving supplies to the beleaguered British Isles. Of course, no German leader wanted recklessly to provoke an American declaration of war; all Germans, however, were prepared to incur American belligerency if they could win the war by so doing. . . .

There remains only one further question, whether the Germans decided to go the whole length and to attack American shipping because they believed that the United States would enter the war in any case if they violated the *Sussex* pledge. In other words, did the Germans conclude that there was little point in confining unrestricted attacks to armed merchantmen or to *belligerent* shipping, armed and unarmed, because any deviations from the rules of cruiser warfare would provoke American intervention? This is an academic question, but an important one, because the answer to it sheds additional light upon Wilson's intentions and the German choice of alternatives.

---

[7] Wilson to E. M. House, January 24, 1917, R. S. Baker Collection, Library of Congress.

There is much evidence that by the end of 1916 Wilson was prepared to effect a sharp diplomatic withdrawal if both belligerent groups refused to heed his peace appeal. . . . It seems almost certain that he would have accepted unrestricted submarine attacks against *armed* merchantmen. On January 10, 1917, the German government informed the State Department that its submarines would hereafter attack armed merchant ships without warning, because these ships had all been offensively armed and instructed to attack submarines. The German proclamation was, technically, a violation of the *Sussex* pledge, but Wilson's only response was to indicate that he doubted that his earlier position on armed ships had been sound.

We can go further and say that it seems also possible that Wilson would not have broken diplomatic relations over unrestricted submarine attacks against all *belligerent* merchantmen, exclusive, perhaps, of passenger liners. . . .

The Germans never seriously considered adopting these limited alternatives, not because they believed that any infraction of the *Sussex* pledge would automatically provoke American intervention, but because they thought that they could win only by enforcing a total blockade. . . .

President Wilson's response to the German blockade proclamation lends additional evidence to my theory that the United States might not have broken diplomatic relations if the Germans had exempted American shipping from the wrath of their underseas campaign. The German Ambassador delivered copies of the German blockade announcement to Lansing and House on January 31, 1917. Wilson did not act like a man who had a predetermined course of action in mind. Even in the face of a German declaration of war against American commerce, he hesitated to take any step that might lead to war. He was willing, he told Lansing, to go to almost any lengths "rather than to have this nation actually involved in the conflict."

There was, however, only one decision that Wilson could now make. No great power could continue to maintain diplomatic intercourse with a government that promised to destroy its shipping and slaughter its citizens in violation of national and treaty rights and solemn pledges. . . . The remarkable thing is not that Wilson severed diplomatic relations as he did on February 3, but that he hesitated at all.

To engage in a debate at this point over the reasons for Wilson's severance of diplomatic relations with Germany would obscure a development that was vastly more important than the handing of passports to the German Ambassador. It was Wilson's announcement, made in an address to Congress on February 3, 1917, that the United States would accept the new submarine blockade and would not go to war, in spite of the break in relations, provided that the Germans did not carry out their threat to destroy American ships and lives. . . .

In short, Wilson was saying that he would follow a policy of watchful waiting and govern his future policies in response to what the Germans did.

If they spared American ships and lives, presumably upon American ships of all categories and upon belligerent unarmed passenger vessels, then he would do nothing. If they attacked American ships, then he would defend them by an armed neutrality. This, obviously, was not the language of war, such as Lansing had urged the President to use. It was the language of a man determined to avoid such full-fledged commitment as a war declaration would imply, willing in the worst event only to protect "our seamen and our people in the prosecution of their peaceful and legitimate errands on the high seas."

. . . As the days passed, however, the pressures for an end to watchful waiting and for the adoption of at least an armed neutrality mounted almost irresistibly. Members of the Cabinet, shipowners, a large majority of the newspapers, and a growing body of public opinion combined in the demand that the President either convoy merchantmen or arm them with naval guns and crews. Still protesting that the people wanted him to avert any risk of war, Wilson gave in to their wishes on about February 25. Going to Congress the following day to request authority to arm merchantmen and to "employ any other instrumentalities or methods that may be necessary and adequate to protect our ships and our people in their legitimate and peaceful pursuits on the seas," he carefully explained that he was not contemplating war or any steps that might lead to war. . . .

Although a small group of senators prevented approval of a bill authorizing Wilson to arm merchantmen, the President took such action anyway on March 9, 1917. . . .

By the middle of March, therefore, it seemed that Wilson had made his decision in favor of a limited defensive war on the seas. "We stand firm in armed neutrality," he declared, for example, in his second inaugural address on March 5, "since it seems that in no other way we can demonstrate what it is we insist upon and cannot forego." Yet on April 2 (he had meanwhile convened Congress for this earlier date), scarcely more than a month after he had uttered these words, he stood before Congress and asked for a declaration of full-fledged war. What events occurred, what forces were at work, what pressures were applied during this brief interval to cause Wilson to make the decision that he had been trying so desperately to avoid? We should perhaps put the question in a less positive way, as follows: What caused the President to abandon armed neutrality and to *accept* the decision for war?

There was first the fact that from the end of February to the end of March the Germans gave full evidence of their determination to press a relentless, total attack against all ships passing through the war zones that enveloped western Europe.

. . . the *immediate* reason why Wilson made his decision of war . . . was simply that the German assault upon American lives and property was so overwhelming and so flagrant that the only possible way to cope with it was to claim the status of a belligerent in order to strike at the sources of German power. "I would be inclined to adopt . . . [armed neutrality]," the President wrote only two days before he delivered his war message,

> indeed, as you know, I had already adopted it, but this is the difficulty: . . . To make even the measures of defense legitimate we must obtain the status of belligerents.[8]

Certainly Wilson had convinced himself that this was true, but I have a strong suspicion that he would have stood doggedly by his first decision to limit American action to a defense of rights on the seas if this decision had not been overridden by convictions, events, pressures, and ambitions that were themselves decisive in Wilson's final shift from armed neutrality to war, in forcing him to the conclusion that the *immediate* circumstances left the United States with no choice but full-scale participation.

One of the most important of these factors was the subtlest and the one for which the least direct evidence can be adduced. It was Wilson's apparent fear that the threat of a German victory imperiled the balance of power and all his hopes for the future reconstruction of the world community. We must be careful here not to misinterpret his thoughts and motives. There is little evidence that he accepted the decision for war because he thought that a German victory would seriously endanger American security, because he wanted to preserve Anglo-American control of the North Atlantic sea lanes, or because he desired to maintain the traditional balance of European power because it served American interests. Nor is there any convincing evidence that Wilson's attitude toward the objectives of the rival alliances had changed by the time that he made his final decision.

On the other hand, there was now a great and decisive difference in the relative position of the belligerents: The Allies seemed about to lose the war and the Central Powers about to win it. This, almost certainly, was a governing factor in Wilson's willingness to think in terms of war. Germany, he told Colonel House, was a madman who must be curbed. A German victory meant a peace of domination and conquest; it meant the end of all of Wilson's dreams of helping to build a secure future.

As the President pondered America's duty at this juncture in history, the answer must have seemed obvious to him—to accept belligerency, because now only through belligerency could the United States fulfill its mission to insure a just and lasting peace of reconciliation. This could be accomplished only by preventing a German victory and only by the assertion of such power and influence among the Allies as would come to the United States by virtue of its sacrifice of blood and treasure.

If the immediate events made a war resolution necessary, then the goal of a righteous peace was the objective that justified full-scale participation in Wilson's mind and raised that effort to a high and noble plane. It was, there-

---

[8] Wilson to Matthew Hale, March 31, 1917, Wilson Papers, Library of Congress.

fore, not war in anger that he advocated, not war sheerly in defense of national rights, but, as he put it in his war message,

> [war] for democracy, for the right of those who submit to authority to have a voice in their own governments, for the rights and liberties of small nations, for a universal dominion of right by such a concert of free peoples as shall bring peace and safety to all nations and make the world itself at last free.

The combined weight of official and public opinion was another pressure meanwhile driving Wilson toward acceptance of the decision for war. It was a fact of no little consequence that by the end of March every important member of the administration, including those members of the Cabinet who had heretofore opposed any bellicose measures, urged the President to admit that a state of war with Germany in fact existed. Public opinion had remained stubbornly pacific until near the end of February, 1917. Then the publication of the Zimmermann telegram, in which the German government proposed to Mexico a war alliance against the United States, the sinking of the *Laconia*, and, above all, the destruction of American ships in the war zones after mid-March generated a demand for war that grew with mounting crescendo in all sections and among all classes, until it seemed beyond doubt to be a national and a majority demand. It was further stimulated by news of the downfall of the czarist regime and the establishment of a provisional republican government in Russia—news that convinced many wavering Americans that the Allies were indeed fighting for democracy and also changed overnight the large and influential American Jewish community from a position of strong hostility toward the Allies to one of friendship.

This was all a development of profound importance for a leader as keenly sensitive to public opinion as was Woodrow Wilson. He could have joined forces with the large antiwar minority to resist the demand for war; indeed, he probably would have done so had he been convinced that it was the wise and right thing to do. The point is not, therefore, that public opinion *forced* Wilson to accept the decision for war, but that it facilitated doing what Wilson for other reasons now thought was necessary and right to do.

All this is said without any intention of implying that Wilson ever *wanted* war. The agony of his soul was great as he moved through the dark valley of his doubts. He had no illusions about the merits of the conflict into which he and his people were being drawn. He saw the risks of intervention, both to his own nation and to the world, with remarkable clarity. But he could devise no alternative; and he set aside his doubts in the hope that acting now as a belligerent, with all the power and idealism of the American people sustaining him, he could achieve objectives to justify the misery of mankind.

XI

The Defeat of the Versailles Treaty: Who Was Responsible, Wilson or Lodge?

INTRODUCTION

Following the conclusion of the armistice in November, 1918, Woodrow Wilson journeyed to France to play the role of peacemaker. He insisted that the covenant of the League of Nations be made an integral part of the Treaty of Versailles, and it was a treaty with the covenant included that the United States Senate was eventually asked to approve. The Senate, however, did not supply the two-thirds majority required for ratification of the treaty, with the result that the United States failed to become a member of the League.

Because the chief protagonists in the struggle for the ratification of the Versailles treaty were President Woodrow Wilson and Senator Henry Cabot Lodge, it is not surprising that there should be interest in the question as to which of the two was primarily responsible for the defeat of the treaty. Of course, it is perfectly clear that had Wilson not dissuaded his loyal followers in the Senate from voting for the Lodge reservations, particularly in the vote of March 19, 1920, the treaty would have been approved. In this tactical sense, Wilson, who thought that the electorate would ultimately compel the Senate to approve the treaty in a form acceptable to the President, was responsible for the defeat of the treaty (with the Lodge reservations appended). This still leaves unanswered, however, the question of Lodge's motivation during the treaty fight. Was Lodge really an irreconcilable on the League issue who added reservations to the treaty as the most likely way of securing its defeat and of thus blocking American entry into the League; or did Lodge wish to see the treaty approved and the United States enter the League, provided, of course, that his reservations were accepted?

Although not unmindful of Wilson's refusal to compromise, Professor Walter Johnson, writing in the midst of World War II, when thoughts were turning to the creation of a new world organization, concentrates his attention on Lodge. He pictures the Massachusetts senator as an irreconcilable at heart who used reservations as the means of preventing approval of the treaty. Professor Thomas A. Bailey, focusing in the selection that follows on the treaty vote of March 19, 1920, absolves Lodge of primary responsibility for the defeat of the treaty and directs his main shafts at Woodrow Wilson. "In the final analysis," he asserts, "the treaty was slain in the house of its friends rather than in the house of its enemies."

Senatorial Strategy, 1919–20 . . .

Walter Johnson

When, on September 1, 1939, the world was plunged into war for the second time in twenty-five years, many people turned their thoughts to the problem of creating some agency that in the future would have sufficient power to maintain world peace. Shortly after the United States entered the war, President Roosevelt told Congress that the American people were not going to be satisfied with just winning the war, but that they wanted to "maintain the security of the peace that will follow." Increasingly, more and more people have felt that if the United States had joined the League of Nations in 1919 or 1920 there would have been a strong possibility that now [1943] there would not be a war ravaging the earth. In a very blunt fashion Prime Minister Winston Churchill told the American Congress on December 26, 1941, that this war need not have happened had the peace-loving nations worked together during the past twenty years. In the light of this statement, why did the United States abstain from the league? Why did the United States shirk its responsibility as a major power and generally follow an irresponsible course in world affairs?

Unfortunately the Versailles Treaty, in which the League of Nations was incorporated, was not debated in the United States Senate purely on its merits. Instead of a reasonable atmosphere to discuss this proposed method of ending wars, the air of the Senate was one of bitterness, partisanship, and hostility. Some Senators, like Henry Cabot Lodge, had a deep personal hatred for Woodrow Wilson; some Senators were personally piqued that the President had not included any members of their body on the Peace Commission; some partisan Republicans did not want to pass a peace treaty drawn up by a Democratic President since this might insure a Democratic victory in 1920. Then, of course, certain Senators were influenced by their constituents: many German-Americans were opposed to the treaty because in their opinion it was too severe on Germany; many Italian-Americans were against the treaty because Italy had not been given Fiume; many Irish-Americans looked upon the treaty as an English plot to control the world and were particularly furious at England at that moment because of Eng-

From *The Antioch Review*, III, No. 4 (Winter 1943), 512–529. Reprinted by permission.

land's suppression of the Irish revolution; reactionaries were opposed to the treaty because it was not severe enough toward Germany; and, on the other hand, a number of liberals opposed the treaty because they felt that it was too harsh toward Germany.

When President Wilson presented the Versailles Treaty to the Senate on July 10, 1919, the Senate did not divide into two groups, one for the treaty and the other against. Instead, four groups were formed: (1) a protreaty group, composed of 43 Democrats and one Republican, who were for ratification without any qualifications; (2) the "mild reservationists," made up of about 15 Republicans, who were warmly for the treaty but desired reservations of a mild character; (3) the "strong reservationists," consisting of about 20 Republicans, who favored ratification but with "strong" reservations; and (4) the "irreconcilables," 12 Republicans and 3 Democrats, led by William E. Borah, who were opposed to ratification under any conditions.

The vast majority of the Senate, 80 out of 96, were for the treaty, although groups two and three wanted certain reservations. The problem of strategy was to present the question in such a way that the three groups favorable to the treaty could unite. The tragedy was that the treaty "failed of ratification not because a constitutional majority desired to reject the treaty but because the different groups in favor of the treaty were unable to agree on the conditions of ratification." When the two votes on ratification occurred (November 19, 1919,* and March 19, 1920) the treaty was defeated not by its enemies, the "irreconcilables," but by its most ardent friends. On both occasions when the treaty with reservations came to a vote, the reservationists voted for it and the "irreconcilables," in combination with the administration Democrats (group 1), voted against it. The administration Democrats did not want to defeat the treaty. They only wanted to defeat the treaty with reservations in order that a vote could be had under more acceptable conditions. In so doing they were acting on the advice of President Wilson, who wrote to Senator Hitchcock just before the first vote was taken: "I sincerely hope that the friends and the supporters of the treaty will vote against the Lodge resolution of ratification. I understand that the door will then probably be open for a more genuine resolution of ratification."

A majority of the Senators, then, desired to accept the treaty, but they could not devise the strategy necessary to bring this majority together on the vote. This favorable majority was backed up by a majority of the American public who, too, wanted to accept the treaty and entrance into the League of Nations. The *Literary Digest* conducted a poll of newspapers in April, 1919, and found that 718 were for ratification, 478 were for ratification with conditions, and only 181 were against ratification. For a long time,

---

* Editor's note: There were three separate votes on the treaty on November 19, 1919, two on the treaty with reservations and one on the treaty without any reservations. The treaty did not command a simple majority on any of these votes.

the idea of a league of nations had been growing in the United States. Theodore Roosevelt, speaking before the Nobel Prize Committee in 1910, advocated a League of Peace to prevent war from breaking out. After the outbreak of the World War, he wrote that "the great civilized nations of the world which do possess force, actual or immediately potential, should combine by solemn agreement in a great world league for the peace of righteousness." President Wilson was also thinking along the same lines in the fall of 1914. He told a friend that "all nations must be absorbed into some great association of nations whereby all shall guarantee the integrity of each so that any one nation violating the agreement between all of them shall bring punishment on itself automatically." Ex-President Taft expressed much the same opinion in October, 1914.

So many Americans were in agreement with these distinguished leaders that there was formed on June 17, 1915, a Committee for a League to Enforce Peace. Within a year the league had branches in almost every congressional district in the country. The organization felt that it was desirable for the United States to join a league of nations. Senator Lodge publicly gave his support to the proposal in 1916, as did Woodrow Wilson. On January 22, 1917, President Wilson told the Senate that one of the things necessary for permanent peace was a league of nations. On January 8, 1918, in his message to Congress setting forth the fourteen points on which he thought that the peace should be based, Wilson included a general association of nations to give "mutual guarantees of political independence and territorial integrity to great and small states alike" as the last point.

When Wilson sailed for Europe in December, 1918, to attend the peace conference, he did not have, however, a completely united country behind his desire to make a peace that would be permanent. In the mid-term Congressional elections, the Republicans had gained control of the Senate by a majority of two. Wilson, on October 25, 1918, had publicly asked the voters:

> . . . If you have approved of my leadership and wish me to continue to be your unembarrassed spokesman in affairs at home and abroad, I earnestly beg that you will express yourselves unmistakably to that effect by returning a Democratic majority to both the Senate and the House of Representatives. . . .

He pointed out that he wanted this because a Republican Congress would divide the leadership of the nation. The Republicans in Congress had been prowar but antiadministration, and this was no time for divided leadership. Furthermore, the election of a Republican majority in either house of Congress would be considered abroad to be a repudiation of his leadership. Theodore Roosevelt denounced this appeal and repudiated Wilson's Fourteen Points. Other Republicans like Charles E. Hughes, William H. Taft, and Will Hays, chairman of the Republican National Committee, stated they did not agree that Wilson's control of the government should be unhampered nor was it necessary for the country's welfare. In the months that followed, when Taft fought shoulder to shoulder with Wilson against the leadership of his own party in the Senate for the Versailles Treaty and the League of Nations, one leading writer has pointed out that Taft "must have wondered whether it might have been better to have given Wilson the continued control for which he asked. Wilson was destroyed in the conflict with a Republican Congress which followed the election of 1918. . . ." [1]

The election of a Republican Senate in 1918 should not necessarily be taken as evidence that the nation thereby repudiated Wilson's leadership. A majority of the people had long been Republican and Wilson had been elected in 1912 when the Republican party had split into two wings. In each of the elections from 1914 to 1918 the Republicans had slowly regained seats in Congress. When it is remembered that there is usually a reaction against the party in power at a midterm election when the Presidency is not at stake, the election of 1918 was not a great victory for the Republicans nor a great defeat for the President.[2]

As soon as the Armistice celebration had quieted, Senators Knox, Poindexter, and Reed attacked the proposal of a league of nations. Former Senator Albert Beveridge of Indiana had through his correspondence been urging the defeat of a league of nations for some time. He wrote Theodore Roosevelt and Will Hays that the Republican Party would be injured if Wilson's plans were not opposed. He wrote Henry Cabot Lodge, Republican majority leader and Chairman of the Senate Committee on Foreign Affairs, that the future of the party was in his hands and that its prospects would be "seriously, perhaps fatally, injured by the acceptance of Mr.

---

[1] Page 37 of D. F. Fleming, *The United States and the League of Nations 1918–1920* (G. P. Putnam Sons, 1932), upon which I have drawn for a number of details stated above.

Appeals similar to Wilson's had been made before. Lincoln in 1864 had warned the people against "swapping horses in midstream"; McKinley on October 11, 1898 had asked for the election of a Republican Congress as had Governor Theodore Roosevelt and H. C. Lodge (Fleming, pp. 48–49).

[2] Charles P. Howland, *American Foreign Relations* (New Haven: Yale University Press, 1928), pp. 239–246, in analyzing the result in each of the thirty-seven senatorial contests writes:

"The forces which determined the several elections were sometimes local, sometimes general. They included support for or hostility to prohibition; the tendency of the business interests, large and small, to back the Republican party; pressure for a high tariff in industrial districts; objection on the part of food producers and distributors to the fixing of food prices, especially as the South had profited enormously from unregulated cotton prices; resentment in the states where General Leonard Wood was popular that the administration had not permitted him to go to France; the attitude of the Non-Partisan League or of its anti-agrarian opponents, and the enthusiastic support by the women of those who had appealed for their new suffrages. There was virtually no issue contested and properly discussed which arose out of the policies that were the cause of our entering the war, of the degree of efficiency with which it was conducted, of the aims announced for the United States by its official spokesman, or of the effort which the United States was to put forth in the making of a durable peace."

Wilson's international plan, or any variation of it." With the Democrats winning prestige for the successful prosecution of the war, some Republican politicians felt that they could not permit that party also to write a successful peace, or victory for the Republicans in 1920 would be impossible.

When Congress reassembled in December, partisan attacks were made on the way the war had been conducted and on Wilson's decision to attend the peace conference in person. Wilson's failure to include any Senator in his peace commission rankled in the breasts of some Senators. In the next three months, the small group of irreconcilables, unalterably opposed to the League of Nations, seized the initiative in the Senate and assailed the idea of internationalism. The majority of Republicans who favored the league in some form or other remained quiet, and the country at large gained the impression that the peace was becoming a partisan issue.

Just what the role that Henry Cabot Lodge was playing in these months and those to come is not entirely clear. His apologists claim that he was honestly for a league of nations, with reservations. There is evidence, however, to demonstrate that he was out to kill the league under any circumstance, and that he considered the best way to accomplish this was through attaching reservations to the covenant. Lodge was a partisan Republican willing to sacrifice ideals or anything else to party loyalty. From 1893 to 1924, as a member of the Senate, he never departed from strict party regularity. In addition to party regularity, he hated Woodrow Wilson. Until Wilson's entrance into politics, Lodge had been known as "the scholar in politics," but this title, probably much to the bitterness of Lodge, then passed to Wilson. According to the estimate of Nicholas Murray Butler, "The figure that made the least appeal throughout all these years was that of Henry Cabot Lodge. He was able, vain, intensely egotistical, narrow-minded, dogmatic, and provincial."

Lodge was a master of parliamentary technique. By 1919 no one knew better than he the devices to be used to kill a treaty in the Senate. That Lodge would oppose a treaty drawn up by a Democratic President, and one whom he personally hated, seems obvious. In his public statements on the treaty, Lodge avoided any evidence of hostility toward the President. As Republican leader, it would have been unwise to have attacked the President. But in the book that Lodge wrote in 1925, justifying his conduct against the league, "his hatred for Wilson shines forth in its full intensity." [3]

Some of Lodge's personal associates, including a grandson, believe that Lodge sincerely was for the United States entering the league with reservations. Yet his daughter, who claimed to be close to him during the struggle, has stated:

---

[3] W. S. Holt, *Treaties Defeated By the Senate* (Baltimore, The Johns Hopkins Press, 1933), p. 263.

337

My father hated and feared the Wilson league, and his heart was really with the irreconcilables. But it was uncertain whether this league could be beaten straight out in this way, and the object of his reservations was so to emasculate the Wilson pact that if it did pass it would be valueless. . . . My father never wanted the Wilson league, and when it was finally defeated, he was like a man from whom a great burden had been lifted.[4]

Lodge, in his book, *The Senate and the League of Nations,* admitted that he had told Senator Borah, the leader of the irreconcilables, that "any attempt to defeat the treaty of Versailles with the league by a straight vote in the Senate, if taken immediately, would be hopeless, even if it were desirable" and that the thing to do was "to proceed in the discussion of the treaty by way of amendment and reservation."

There is other information to indicate that Lodge used reservations as a method of killing the league. According to Senator James E. Watson, Lodge planned to defeat the league through this technique. Watson said to Lodge, when the latter was planning the fight against the league:

"I don't see how we are ever going to defeat this proposition. It appears to me that eighty per cent of the people are for it. Fully that percentage of the preachers are right now advocating it, churches are very largely favoring it, all the people who have been burdened and oppressed by this awful tragedy of war and who imagine this opens a way to world peace are for it, and I don't see how it is possible to defeat it." He turned to me and said, "Ah, my dear James, I do not propose to try to beat it by direct frontal attack, but by the indirect method of reservations." "What do you mean by that?" I asked. "Illustrate it to me." He then went on to explain how, for instance, we would demand a reservation on the subject of submitting to our government the assumption of a mandate over Armenia, or any other foreign country. "We can debate that for days and hold up the dangers that it will involve and the responsibilities we will assume if we pursue that course, and we can thoroughly satisfy the country that it would be a most abhorrent policy for us to adopt." . . . Senator Lodge then went on for two hours to explain other reservations, and went into the details of the situation that would be thus evolved, until I became thoroughly satisfied that the treaty could be beaten in that way.[5]

There is also evidence that Lodge desired to kill the treaty by attaching reservations unacceptable to Wilson, in order that the responsibility for the defeat would then fall upon the President. Lodge wrote later:

There was another object which I had very much at heart, and that was that if we were successful in putting on reservations we should create a situation where, if the acceptance of the treaty was defeated,

---

[4] *The New York Herald Tribune,* March 7, 1930.
[5] James E. Watson, *As I Knew Them* (Bobbs-Merrill, 1936), pp. 190–191.

the Democratic party, and especially Mr. Wilson's friends, should be responsible for its defeat, and not the opponents of the treaty who were trying to pass it in a form safe for the United States.

As yet, evidence in the form of letters or memoirs, has not come to light which would definitely indicate that the irreconcilables knew that Lodge was fighting for them from the camp of the reservationists. However, Lodge was close to them during the fight and consulted with them on most major decisions. When former Senator Beveridge urged a more aggressive policy on Lodge to defeat the league, he replied agreeing with the ends sought but differing as to the method to obtain them.

The initial plans to attack the league were made by Lodge and Theodore Roosevelt in December, 1918. Although no draft of the league covenant had as yet been published, these two men planned to attack whatever league proposal the President brought home. On the floor of the Senate on December 21, Lodge made a speech, intended for the ears of the Allies, in which he warned that if certain "extraneous provisions"—i.e. The League of Nations—were to be found in the treaty of peace, then they would be struck out or amended by the United States Senate.

The text of the covenant of the league was first published in American papers on February 15, 1919. Immediately, the small minority of irreconcilables rallied to the attack. There can be no question that the majority of Republican Senators wanted the United States to join the league. They saw some shortcomings in it, but they felt that it was bigger than the shortcomings. The most active Senators in debate, however, were the opponents of the league. Lodge, as Republican leader, had a difficult time in preserving party unity, but he struck upon a device to accomplish this. On March 3, in the Senate, he introduced a resolution signed by thirty-seven* Republican Senators and Senators-elect of the next Congress to the effect that the peace treaty should be signed immediately and that the question of a "league of nations to insure the permanent peace of the world should then be taken up for careful and serious consideration." The real purpose of the round robin was to commit more than one-third of the Republican Senators to a policy of united, partisan action on the treaty. This policy was a victory for the irreconcilables, since one of them, Senator Brandegee, had first suggested it to Lodge. Although this was a victory for the irreconcilables, it was not a complete one. In order to gain the signatures of many Republican Senators, a statement had to be inserted in the resolution that the signers could not accept the constitution of the league "in the form now proposed." If changes were made, many of the signers were still free to accept the league.

When Lodge was discussing future plans, shortly after this round robin, with Borah, he had to admit that "the vocal classes of the community,

---

* Editor's note: The resolution was eventually signed by two additional Senators.

most of the clergymen, the preachers of sermons, a large element in the teaching force of the universities, a large proportion of the newspaper editors, and finally the men and women who were in the habit of writing and speaking for publication, although by no means thoroughly informed, were friendly to the league as it stood, and were advocating it." A month later Lodge admitted that a majority of the people favored the league. Outstanding Republicans outside the Senate, like former-President Taft and A. Lawrence Lowell, were actively campaigning for the league. When the covenant of the league was changed by the peace conference to meet the principal American objections, it was possible for the signers of the round robin to accept the league. Senator Hitchcock, the acting Democratic leader, had written Wilson: "A number of Republican Senators who signed Lodge's manifesto on the League of Nations will, in my opinion, vote for it nevertheless, if it is a part of the peace treaty. A still larger number will give it support if certain amendments are made." Taft and Lowell wired Wilson along the same vein, and the American delegation at Paris secured the consent of other nations to changes on certain points. These points were: (1) a recognition of the Monroe Doctrine by name; (2) exclusion of domestic questions like immigration and the tariff from the league's jurisdiction; (3) right of withdrawal from the league; (4) right to refuse to accept a mandate over territory.

When the new Congress met in special session on May 19, 1919 the irreconcilable Republicans gained a great advantage. The Republicans controlled the Senate by a majority of two, and thus they would have a majority on each committee. In control of the Committee on Foreign Relations, they could delay or hasten action on the treaty. When the composition of the committee was announced, of the ten Republican members six were openly irreconcilable. The other four were Lodge, the chairman, who was really irreconcilable; McCumber, the most outspoken Republican for the league; and two party regulars, Harding and New, who would follow the party leaders. Lodge seems to have deliberately packed the Republican membership of the committee with men hostile to the League. Thus he gained the power to keep the treaty in the committee's hands, while a campaign was launched to arouse public sentiment against the league. Millionaires H. C. Frick and Andrew W. Mellon contributed money, and a propaganda campaign consisting of mailings and speaking tours was started. The following advertisement is an example of their propaganda campaign:

Americans, Awake!
Shall We Bind Ourselves to the War Breeding Covenant?
It Impairs American Sovereignty!
Surrenders the Monroe Doctrine!
Flouts Washington's Warning!
Entangles Us In European and Asiatic Intrigues!
Sends Our Boys To Fight Throughout the World by Order of a League!
The Evil Thing With a Holy Name!

While this minority was working against the league, evidence continued to pile up of the great support that the league had among the people. Thirty-two state legislatures endorsed the league and two others made a conditional endorsement. Thirty-three governors of states, also, had endorsed a league of nations.

On July 10, the day after he returned from France, Wilson presented the treaty of peace to the Senate. The Committee on Foreign Affairs kept it in their hands for two months. They had to delay in this way in order to defeat the treaty, because, as one of the irreconcilables, Senator Moses, later said, if the rules of the Senate had permitted a quick vote, "the Versailles Treaty would have been ratified without reservation." In order to stall, the committee read the treaty aloud line by line. This required two weeks. Then, the next six weeks were devoted to permitting representatives of national groups that felt that the treaty was not fair to their homeland to vent their rage. It was natural for the irreconcilables to stir up this opposition to the treaty among foreign elements in the United States.

On September 10, the Committee on Foreign Relations presented its majority report to the Senate. The irreconcilables realized by now that they could not persuade the majority of the Republicans in the Senate to reject the treaty. Not one of the irreconcilables signed a report calling for rejection. Instead, they followed the advice of Lodge and proceeded "by way of amendment and reservation." With Lodge, Harding, and New, they recommended forty-five amendments and four reservations to the covenant of the league. The minority report, filed by six of the seven Democratic members, urged acceptance of the treaty without change. Senator McCumber, the tenth Republican on the committee, filed his own minority report in which he rebuked the partisanship of the majority:

> . . . Not one word is said, not a single allusion made, concerning either the great purpose of the League of Nations or the methods by which those purposes are to be accomplished.
>
> Irony and sarcasm have been substituted for argument and positions taken by the press or individuals outside the Senate seem to command more attention than the treaty itself. It is regrettable that the animosity which centers almost wholly against the League of Nations provisions should have been engendered against a subject so important to the world's welfare. It is regrettable that the consideration of a matter so foreign to any kind of partisanship should be influenced in the country, as well as on the floor of this Senate, by hostility toward or subserviency to the President of the United States. No matter how just may be any antagonism toward President Wilson, the aspirations and hopes of a wounded and bleeding world ought not to be denied because, under the Constitution, the treaty must first be formulated by him.

The majority report did not reflect the sentiment of the Senate. While the treaty was in committee, the debates on the floor of the Senate had demonstrated that the majority of the Republicans were going to vote for entrance into the league. Some wanted strong reservations, others mild, but both groups wanted acceptance of the treaty. The irreconcilables had failed to hold a majority to rejection, and admitted this in their majority report. Now their approach was to hold all Republicans together by a program of amendments or reservations. The Wilson Democrats had two courses of action. They might reach an agreement with the mild reservationists and detach them from the other Republicans, or they could refuse any concessions and possibly win some Republican Senators who would be willing to give up any reservations rather than have the treaty rejected.

It was this last course of action that they decided to follow. Wilson publicly made no suggestion that he might accept mild reservations. To his Senate leader, Hitchcock, he gave a list of reservations that he would accept if necessary, but Wilson took no public step to win the support of the mild reservationist Republicans. Wilson apparently felt that either it was not necessary to accept any reservations, or he was afraid that concessions so early might lead to further demands. In September, the President started on a tour of the nation to arouse the people to vigorous support of the league. On this tour he collapsed and returned to Washington, broken and paralyzed. With his collapse, the most powerful protagonist of the league could fight no more.

The debate in the Senate, following the reports of the Committee on Foreign Relations, was one replete with a great deal of demagoguery. The opponents of the league pandered to popular and national prejudices. They stated that the United States would become entangled in the broils of Europe; that the United States would lose its national sovereignty; that the league was a device for the British Empire to rule the world, since the Dominions as well as Great Britain had a vote; that the majority of countries in the league would be Catholic and thus the league would be under the Pope. They also tried to rally support by denouncing English activities in Ireland and the wrongs done to China in Shantung.

In October the voting began on the amendments. The mild reservationists joined with the almost solid Democratic membership, and all the amendments were defeated. On November 7, the voting began on the reservations, and then the mild reservationists joined with the rest of the Republicans to attach these to the treaty. When the treaty with fourteen reservations came to a vote on November 19, it was rejected by a vote of 39 to 55. Ratification was supported by the reservationist Senators and was opposed by the irreconcilables in combination with the Wilson Democrats, who voted for rejection in hopes of getting final ratification later on just the question of the league as it stood in the treaty of peace. McCumber, just before the vote was taken, pled with the administration Democrats to accept what could be obtained rather than lose everything, but Wilson sent a letter to them to vote against the treaty with reservations. Wilson did this in expectation that a favorable vote could be obtained without any reservations, and also that if the United States placed conditions on its entrance to the league, other nations might do the same and the league would be greatly weakened.

The Senate's action came as a shock to the nation. As one authority has written, "It seemed absurd that the national policy adopted should be the one advocated by only seventeen Senators. Common sense revolted at seeing the votes of seventy-eight Senators to enter the League nullified because they could not agree among themselves on the terms of entry." Immediately the Senate voted to reconsider the question in the next session. The bewilderment of the people at the action taken by the Senate can well be imagined from the observations of Ida Tarbell, who made a speaking tour of the west in the interests of the league in the summer of 1919:

> As the days went by, I sensed a growing bewilderment at the fight against the league. These people had listened for years to people they honored urging some form of international union against war. They had heard Dr. Jordan and Jane Addams preaching a national council for the prevention of war, President Taft advocating a league to enforce peace. In many of these towns there had been chapters of these societies. . . . With such a background, was it strange that many people in the Northwest should have been puzzled that the Congress of the United States was seemingly more and more determined that we should not join this first attempt of the civilized world to find substitutes for war in international quarrels?

When the demand swept the country for a compromise between the league Democrats and the reservationists even Lodge felt compelled to go into a conference on the question. He did so, however, from his own admission with no idea of compromising. He refused to admit that the treaty had been defeated because of verbal differences between the pro-league groups. According to Lodge, the difference between those who supported the treaty and those who opposed it was "not verbal, but vital and essential." By this he could only have meant that the difference between the irreconcilables (of which he really was one) and the administration Democrats was vital, because the difference between the reservationists (strong and mild) and the administration Democrats was one only of a verbal nature or at least of strategy.

A bipartisan conference met to discuss a method of common action between the reservationists and the Wilson Democrats. This conference failed, however, to work out a plan of action. The irreconcilables and the reservationists voted together to add reservations to the treaty, which were without essential changes from those of November 19. In spite of the fact that they voted for adding reservations to the league, on the question of ratification of the treaty with these reservations, there was no doubt but that the irreconcilables would vote against. The question was whether enough

Democrats would realize that there was no alternative but to vote for reservations or the treaty would be defeated. Again, however, Wilson wrote a letter from his sickbed urging his followers to oppose the treaty with the reservations. He still had faith that the public wanted the league, and he was willing to wait for the approaching presidential election to serve as a popular referendum on the subject.

The vote on March 19, 1920, on the question of ratification of the treaty with reservations, resulted in a majority of the votes cast being for the ratification, but not the requisite two-thirds majority, forty-nine being in favor and thirty-five being opposed. Some Democrats who had voted against in November voted *for* this second time, but there were still enough administration Democrats who carried out Wilson's desire that they vote against, and the treaty was defeated. For the second time, the responsibility for the defeat lies not alone with the irreconcilables but with the league's warmest friends. If Wilson had not been quite so uncompromising in his position, the treaty with reservations could easily have passed.

This possibility greatly disturbed some of the irreconcilables. One of them mentioned to Lodge that Wilson might accept the reservations and then the country would be in the league. Lodge's reply was:

> ". . . you do not take into consideration the hatred that Woodrow Wilson has for me personally. Never under any set of circumstances in this world could he be induced to accept a treaty with Lodge reservations appended to it!" "But," I replied, "that seems to me to be rather a slender thread on which to hang so great a cause." "A slender thread!" he answered. "Why, it is as strong as any cable with its strands wired and twisted together." [6]

That Lodge carefully estimated and studied Wilson at every step can be seen from Lodge's own book. After admitting that there was a possibility that the treaty might pass with the reservations, he observes that ". . . I also felt convinced that President Wilson would prevent the acceptance of the treaty with reservations if he possibly could. I based this opinion on the knowledge which I had acquired as to Mr. Wilson's temperament, intentions, and purposes." On the final page of his book Lodge repeats this same thought: "As the strenuous days which were filled by the contest over the League of Nations passed by, almost every one bringing its difficulty and its crucial question, I made no mistake in my estimate of what President Wilson would do under certain conditions."

Although President Wilson called for the presidential election of 1920 to serve as a great national referendum on the question of the league, it did not serve this purpose. The league was actively debated during the campaign, but the majority of seven million for Harding cannot be translated into a majority of seven million against the league. The Republican plat-

---

[6] James E. Watson, *op. cit.*, p. 200.

form was ambiguous, but it did advocate entrance of the United States into an international association of nations. In the platform committee there was a spectacular fight between the proleague Republicans and the irreconcilables. There was a move to adopt a plank favoring the league with the Lodge reservations, but Lodge prevented this plank from being included. This action of Lodge's tends to prove that he always had been an irreconcilable and had used reservations only as a technique to defeat the league.

During the campaign, Harding interpreted the plank on some occasions to be proleague and on other occasions to be antileague. This equivocal stand was, of course, designed to confuse the voters and muddle the issue. Near the end of the campaign Harding seemed more and more to favor an international league. All this time the Democrats were campaigning for the League of Nations without reservations. Outstanding Republicans like former-President Taft and Herbert Hoover campaigned for Harding and made it plain that they considered support for Harding equivalent to support of the League of Nations. On October 14, 1920, thirty-one leading Republicans, including Elihu Root, Charles E. Hughes, Henry L. Stimson, Herbert Hoover, and William Allen White, issued a public statement that a vote for Harding would be the surest way of indicating that the citizen favored joining the league.

Probably thousands of voters took these men at their word. In the light of their statement and the, at times, proleague stand of Harding, many proleague citizens undoubtedly voted for the Republican candidate. Calvin Coolidge, in a post-election statement, observed:

> I doubt if any particular mandate was given at the last election on the question of the League of Nations and if that was the preponderant issue. In the South, where there was decided opposition to the league, they voted the Democratic ticket. And as far as the League of Nations was concerned in the North, the vote was with equal and even greater preponderance in favor of the Republican ticket. Of course, many men voted thus who were in favor of the league. With them it became simply a question of supporting the Republican or Democratic party. So you can't say that there was a preponderance of votes against the League of Nations.

The entire story of the fight in the Senate and in the campaign of 1920 demonstrates that the American people never had the opportunity squarely to vote for the League of Nations. . . .

The Supreme Infanticide

Thomas A. Bailey

As a friend of the President, as one who has loyally followed him, I
solemnly declare to him this morning: If you want to kill your own
child because the Senate straightens out its crooked limbs, you must
take the responsibility and accept the verdict of history.

Senator Ashurst of Arizona (Democrat),
March 11, 1920

I

The treaty was now dead, as far as America was concerned. Who had killed
it?

The vital role of the loyal Democrats must be reemphasized. If all of
them who professed to want the treaty had voted "Yea," it would have
passed with more than a dozen votes to spare. If the strait-jacket of party
loyalty had not been involved, the necessary two-thirds could easily have
been mustered.*

In the previous November, the Democrats might have voted against the
treaty (as they did) even without White House pressure. But this time pressure had to be applied to force them into line, and even in the face of
Wilsonian wrath almost half of them bolted. On the day of the final balloting the newsmen observed that two Cabinet members (Burleson and Dan-
iels), possibly acting at the President's direction, were on the floor of the
Senate, buttonholing waverers. The day after the fateful voting Hitchcock
wrote Wilson that it had required the "most energetic efforts" on his part *to
prevent a majority of the Democrats from surrendering to Lodge.*

Desertion of the President . . . is no light offense in the political world,
especially when he has declared himself emphatically. Senators do not ordinarily court political suicide. Wilson still had the patronage bludgeon in
his hands, and having more than a trace of vindictiveness, he could oppose
renegade senators when they ran again, and in fact did so.

Reprinted with the permission of The Macmillan Company from Thomas A. Bailey,
Woodrow Wilson and the Great Betrayal (New York: The Macmillan Company, 1945),
pp. 271–287. Copyright 1945 by Thomas A. Bailey.

* Editor's note: The reference is to the vote on the treaty of March 19, 1920.

Many of the loyal Democrats were up for reelection in 1920. They certainly were aware of the effects of party treachery on their political fortunes. They knew—or many of them knew—that they were killing the treaty; they made no real effort to revive it; they must have wanted it killed—at least until after the November election.

One striking fact stands out like a lighthouse. With the exception of Hitchcock of Nebraska, Johnson of South Dakota, and Thomas of Colorado, *every single one of the twenty-three senators who stood loyally with Wilson in March came from south of the Mason and Dixon line.* Only four of the "disloyal" twenty-one represented states that had seceded in 1860–61. At the polls, as well as on the floor of the Senate, decent southern Democrats voted "the way their fathers shot." As between bothersome world responsibility on the one hand, and loyalty to President, party, section, and race on the other, there was but one choice. Perhaps world leadership would come eventually anyhow.

Democratic senators like Walsh of Montana and Ashurst of Arizona were not from the South. When the issue was clearly drawn between loyalty to party and loyalty to country, their consciences bade them choose the greater good. Ashurst had gone down the line in supporting Wilson; but several days before the final vote he declared, "I am just as much opposed to a White House irreconcilable as I am to a Lodge irreconcilable."

II

A word now about public opinion.

In March, as in November, more than 80 per cent of the senators professed to favor the treaty with some kind of reservations. All the polls and other studies indicate that this was roughly the sentiment of the country. Yet the senators were unable to scrape together a two-thirds vote for any one set of reservations.

The reaction of many newspaper editors, as before, was to cry out against the shame of it all—this indictment of the "capacity of our democracy to do business." We had astonished the world by our ability to make war; we now astonished the world with our "imbecility" in trying to make peace. How could we blame other countries for thinking us "a nation of boobs and bigots"? The Louisville *Courier-Journal* (Democrat), referring to our broken promises to the Allies, cried that we stood betrayed as "cravens and crooks," "hypocrites and liars."

Partisan Republican newspapers loudly blamed the stiff-backed Wilson and his "me-too" senators. Two wings of "irreconcilables"—the Wilsonites and the "bitter-enders"—had closed in to execute a successful pincers movement against the treaty. The New York *Tribune* (Independent Republican) condemned the "inefficiency, all-sufficiency and self-sufficiency of our self-named only negotiator," Woodrow Wilson. If the treaty died, said the

Tribune, the handle of the dagger that pierced its heart would bear the "initials 'W. W.'"

If Republicans scolded Democrats, Democrats scolded Republicans. Lodge and his cheap political tricks were roundly condemned, and the general conclusion was that "the blood of the Treaty stains the floor of the Republican wigwam." A few of the less partisan Democratic journals openly conceded that Wilson's obstinacy had something to do with the final result. William Jennings Bryan asserted from the platform that this "most colossal crime against our nation and the civilized world in all history" made his "blood boil." He began a vigorous campaign against the two-thirds rule in the Senate. "A majority of Congress can declare war," he cried; "it ought to be as easy to end a war as to begin it."

The leading liberal journals, as before, were sadly happy. They rejoiced that the result would clear the way for a renovation of the treaty, but they regretted that the pact had been defeated as a result of partisanship rather than as a result of the betrayal of Wilson's promises.

An impressive number of the more discerning editors deplored the fact that the issue was now in the dirty hands of politicians. An electoral referendum, it was felt, would merely confuse the issue; such a canvass could not possibly reveal anything more than was already known, namely, that *an overwhelming majority of the people wanted the treaty with some kind of reservations.*

III

Is it true that the invalid in the White House really strangled the treaty to death with his own enfeebled hands?

It is seldom that statesmen have a second chance—a second guess. They decide on a course of action, and the swift current of events bears them downstream from the starting point. Only rarely does the stream reverse itself and carry them back.

In November, Wilson had decided that he wanted deadlock, because he reasoned that deadlock would arouse public opinion and force the Senate to do his bidding. The tidal wave of public opinion did surge in, and Wilson got his second chance. But he threw it away, first by spurning compromise (except on his terms), and then by spurning the Lodge reservations.

There had been much more justification for Wilson's course in November than in March. In November he was sick, secluded, was fed censored news, and was convinced by Hitchcock that the strategy of deadlock was sound. In March, he was much improved in health, far less secluded, more in touch with the press and with the currents of opinion, though probably still not enough. He consulted even less with the Senate, presumably because he had made up his mind in advance to oppose the Lodge reservations. In November, there was a fair possibility of reconsideration; in March, it was clear that the only possibility lay in making the League an issue in the coming campaign. Wilson, with his broad knowledge of government and politics, should have seen that this hope was largely if not completely illusory. Perhaps he would have seen it had he not been blinded by his feeling for Lodge.

The evidence is convincing that Wilson wanted the issue cast into the hurly-burly of politics. He could not accept Lodge's terms; Lodge would not accept his terms. The only possible chance of beating the senator—and this was slim indeed—was to win a resounding mandate in 1920.

Yet this strategy . . . meant further delay. At Paris, the feeling at times had been, "Better a bad treaty today than a good treaty four months hence." Europe was still in chaos, and increasingly in need of America's helping hand. Well might the Europeans cry, "Better a treaty with the Lodge reservations today than a probable treaty without reservations after the election." Or as Dr. Frank Crane wrote in *Current Opinion,* "It is vastly more needful that some sort of League be formed, *any sort,* than that it be formed *perfectly.*" (Italics Crane's.)

Yet Wilson, for the reasons indicated, could not see all this clearly. Four days after the fatal vote he wrote Hitchcock, praising him for having done all in his power to protect the honor of the nation and the peace of the world against the Republican majority.

Mrs. Wilson, no doubt reflecting her husband's views, later wrote, "My conviction is that Mr. Lodge put the world back fifty years, and that at his door lies the wreckage of human hopes and the peril to human lives that afflict mankind today."

IV

To the very end Wilson was a fighter. When the Scotch-Irish in him became aroused, he would nail his colors to the mast. He said in 1916 that he was "playing for the verdict of mankind." His conception of duty as he saw it was overpowering. He once remarked that if he were a judge, and it became his duty to sentence his own brother to the gallows, he would do so—and afterwards die of a broken heart.

It is well to have principles; it is well to have a noble conception of duty. But Wilson, as he became warmed up in a fight, tended to get things out of focus and to lose a proper sense of values.

The basic issue in 1920 was the Hitchcock reservations* or the Lodge reservations. Wilson accepted those of Hitchcock while rejecting those of Lodge,

---

*Editor's note: Four of the five so-called Hitchcock reservations were drafted by President Wilson; the fifth was added by Senator Hitchcock. For the text of these reservations, see Bailey, *Woodrow Wilson and the Great Betrayal,* pp. 393–394.

which, he said, completely nullified the treaty and betrayed his promises to the Allies and to the American dead.

This . . . was a gross exaggeration. Minds no less acute than Wilson's, and less clouded with sickness and pride, denied that the Lodge reservations completely nullified the treaty. To the man in the street—in so far as he gave the dispute thought—there was little discernible difference between the two sets of reservations. How could one decry statements which merely re-affirmed the basic principles of the Constitution and of our foreign policy? To a vast number of Americans the Lodge reservations, far from nullifying the treaty, actually improved it. This was so apparent to even the most loyal Democrats in the Senate that Wilson could barely keep them in line.

In the final analysis the treaty was slain in the house of its friends rather than in the house of its enemies. In the final analysis it was not the two-thirds rule, or the "irreconcilables," or Lodge, or the "strong" and "mild reservationists," but Wilson and his docile following who delivered the fatal stab. If the President had been permitted to vote he would have sided with Borah, Brandegee, Johnson, and the other "bitter-enders"—though for entirely different reasons.

Wilson had said that the reservation to Article X was a knife thrust at the heart of the Covenant. Ironically, he parried this knife thrust, and stuck his own dagger, not into the heart of the Covenant, but into the entire treaty.

This was the supreme act of infanticide. With his own sickly hands Wilson slew his own brain child—or the one to which he had contributed so much.

This was the supreme paradox. He who had forced the Allies to write the League into the treaty, unwrote it; he who had done more than any other man to make the Covenant, unmade it—at least so far as America was concerned. And by his action, he contributed powerfully to the ultimate undoing of the League, and with it the high hopes of himself and mankind for an organization to prevent World War II.

V

The preceding dogmatic observations are of course qualified by the phrase, "in the last analysis."

Many elements enter into a log jam. Among them are the width of the stream, the depth of the stream, the swiftness of the current, the presence of boulders, the size of the logs, and the absence of enough lumberjacks. No one of these factors can be solely responsible for the pile-up.

Many elements entered into the legislative log jam of March, 1920. Among them were isolationism, partisanship, senatorial prerogative, confusion, apathy, personal pride, and private feuds. No one of them was solely responsible for the pile-up. *But as the pile-up finally developed, there was only one lumberjack who could break it, and that was Woodrow Wilson.*

If at any time before the final vote he had told the Senate Democrats to support the treaty with the Lodge reservations, or even if he had merely told them that they were on their own, the pact would almost certainly have been approved. So "in the last analysis" the primary responsibility for the failure in March rested with Wilson.

What about Lodge? If the treaty would have passed by Wilson's surrendering, is it not equally true that it would have passed by Lodge's surrendering?

The answer is probably "Yes," but the important point is that Lodge had far less responsibility for getting the treaty through than Wilson. If Lodge had yielded, he probably would have created a schism within his ranks. His ultimate responsibility was to keep the party from breaking to pieces, and in this he succeeded. Wilson's ultimate responsibility was to get the treaty ratified, and in this he failed. With Lodge, as with any truly partisan leader, the party comes before country; with the President the country should come before party, though unhappily it often does not.

It is possible that Wilson saw all this—but not clearly enough. He might have been willing to compromise if his adversary had been any other than Lodge. But so bitter was the feeling between the two men that Wilson, rather than give way, grasped at the straw of the election of 1920.

Lodge did not like Wilson either, but he made more of a show of compromising than the President. He actually supported and drove through amendments to his original reservations which were in line with Wilson's wishes, and he probably would have gone further had the "irreconcilables" not been on his back. He fought the crippling Irish reservation, as well as others supported by the "bitter-enders." Finally, he gave the Democrats a fair chance to reconsider their vote and get on the bandwagon, but they spurned it.

If Lodge's words mean anything, and if his actions were not those of a monstrous hypocrite, he actually tried to get the treaty through with his reservations. When he found that he could not, he washed his hands of the whole business in disgust.

The charge is frequently made that, if Wilson had yielded to his adversary, Lodge would have gleefully piled on more reservations until Wilson, further humiliated, would have had to throw out the whole thing.

The strongest evidence for this view is a circumstantial story which Secretary Houston relates. During a Cabinet meeting Wilson was called to the telephone, and agreed to make certain concessions agreeable to Lodge. Before adjournment the telephone rang again, and word came that Lodge would not adhere to his original proposal.

This story is highly improbable, because Wilson attended no Cabinet meetings between September 2, 1919, and April 13, 1920. By the latter date, all serious attempts at compromise had been dropped; by the earlier date the treaty was still before the Senate committee, and the Lodge reservations, though in an embryonic stage, were yet unborn. But, even if the story is true, it merely proves that Lodge veered about, as he frequently did under "irreconcilable" pressure.

In March, as in November, all Wilson had to do was to send over Postmaster General Burleson to the Senate a few minutes before the final vote with the quiet word that the Democrats were to vote "Yea." The treaty would then have passed with the Lodge reservations, and Lodge could hardly have dared incur for himself or his party the odium of moving to reconsider for the purpose of screwing on more reservations. Had he tried to do so, the "mild reservationists" almost certainly would have blocked him.

VI

A few days after the disastrous final vote, Wilson's only comment to Tumulty was, "They have shamed us in the eyes of the world." If his previous words said what he really meant, he was hardly more shamed by the defeat of the treaty than by the addition of the Lodge reservations. In his eyes it all amounted to the same thing.

If the treaty had passed, would the President have been willing to go through with the exchange of ratifications? Would he not have pocketed it, as he threatened to do prior to the November vote?

Again, if Wilson's words may be taken at their face value, this is what he would have done. He had not backed down from his pre-November position. His Jackson Day message and his letter to Hitchcock made it unmistakably clear that he preferred the uncertainties of a political campaign to the certainties of ratification with the Lodge reservations. The addition of the indefensible Irish reservation provided even stronger justification for pocketing the entire pact.

It is probable that some of the loyal Democrats voted as they did partly because they were convinced that Wilson was going to pigeonhole the treaty anyhow. From their point of view it was better that the odium for defeat should seemingly rest on Lodge rather than on their President. It also seems clear that Wilson preferred, as in November, to have the blood of the treaty on the Senate doorstep rather than on his. As he wrote to Secretary Colby, on April 2, 1920, the slain pact lay heavily on the consciences of those who had stabbed it, and he was quite willing to have it lie there until those consciences were either awakened or crushed.

Yet it is one thing to say, just before Senate action, "I will pocket the treaty." It is another, after the pact is approved and sent to the White House, to assume this tremendous responsibility. The eyes of the world are upon the President; he is the only man keeping the nation out of the peace which it so urgently needs; he is the one man standing in the way of the rehabilitation which the world so desperately demands. Public pressure to ratify in such a case would be enormous—probably irresistible.

Some years later Senator Hitchcock said that in the event of senatorial approval Wilson would possibly have waited for the November election. If he had won, he would have worked for the removal of the Lodge reservations; if he had lost, then the compulsion to go through with ratification would have become overpowering. By November more than six months would have passed, and by that time Wilson might have developed a saner perspective.

But this is all speculation. Wilson gave orders that the treaty was to be killed in the Senate chamber. And there it died.

VII

One other line of inquiry must be briefly pursued. Is it true, as some writers allege, that the thirty-odd Allied signatories of the original treaty would have rejected the Lodge reservations when officially presented? We recall that under the terms of the preamble these nations were privileged to acquiesce silently or file objections.

One will never know the answer to this question, because Wilson denied the other signatories a chance to act. But it seems proper to point to certain probabilities.

One or more of the Latin American nations might have objected to the reservation regarding the then hated Monroe Doctrine. Yet the Monroe Doctrine would have continued to exist anyhow; it was already in the Covenant; and these neighboring republics might well have swallowed their pride in the interest of world peace.

Italy probably would have acquiesced, and the evidence is strong that France would have done likewise. The Japanese could not completely overlook the Shantung reservation, but it was generally recognized in their press as meaningless, and for this reason it might have been tolerated, though not without some loss of face. It is noteworthy that the most important Japanese newspapers regretted the Senate stalemate as an encouragement to world instability, particularly in China.

Great Britain probably would have been the chief objector. The reservation on Ireland was highly offensive but completely innocuous, for the British lion had long endured Irish-American tail-twistings in pained but dignified silence. The reservation on six-to-one was a slap at the loyal and sacrificing Dominions, but it did not mean that their vote was to be taken away. Moreover, the contingency envisaged by this proviso was unlikely to arise very often, and in the long run would doubtless have proved inconsequential.

In sum, there were only two or three reservations to which the outside powers could seriously object. If they had objected, it is probable that a satisfactory adjustment could have been threshed out through diplomatic channels. For when it became clear that only a few phrases stood between the United States and peace, the dictates of common sense and the pressure of public opinion probably would have led to an acceptable compromise. If the Senate had refused to give ground in such a case, then the onus would have been clearly on it and not on Wilson.

The World Court is a case in point. In 1926 the Senate voted to join, but attached five reservations, four of which were accepted by the other powers. By 1935 a compromise was worked out on the fifth, but an isolationist uprising led by William Randolph Hearst and Father Coughlin turned what seemed to be a favorable vote in the Senate into a narrow defeat for the World Court. The one-third minority again triumphed, with the aging Borah and Johnson and Norris and Gore still voting their fears and prejudices.

But the World Court analogy must not be pressed too far. In 1920 Europe was in a desperate condition; the only real hope for a successful League lay in American cooperation. Unless the United States would shoulder its obligations the whole treaty system was in danger of collapse. In 1926 the powers could afford to haggle over the World Court; in 1920 there was far less temptation to haggle while Europe burned. The European nations were under strong compulsion to swallow their pride, or at the very worst not to drive too hard a bargain in seeking adjustment.

But this again is pure speculation. Wilson never gave the other powers a chance to act on the reservations, though Colonel House and others urged him to. He assumed this terrific responsibility all by himself. While thinking that he was throwing the onus on the consciences of the senators, he was in fact throwing a large share of the onus upon his own bent shoulders.

VIII

What were the reactions of our recent brothers in arms on the other side of the Atlantic?

The British viewed the Senate debacle with mixed emotions. The result had been a foregone conclusion, and there was some relief in having an end to senatorial uncertainty—at least this stage of it. Some journals were inclined to blame the two-thirds rule; others, the unbending doctrinaire in the White House. The London *Times* sorrowfully concluded that all the processes of peace would have to be suspended pending the outcome of the November election.

The French were shocked, though hardly surprised. The Paris *Liberté* aptly referred to the state of anarchy existing between the executive and the legislative in America. Other journals, smarting under Wilson's recent blast against French militarism, blamed the autocrat in the White House. "At the most troubled moment in history," gibed the Paris *Matin,* "America has a sick President, an amateur Secretary of State, and no Treaty of Peace. A President in the clouds, a Secretary of State in the bushes, and a treaty in the cabbage patch. What a situation!"

But the French did not completely abandon hope that America might yet honor her commitments. Meanwhile they would keep their powder dry and pursue the militaristic course which widened the growing rift between Britain and France, and which proved so fatal to the peace of Europe in the 1930's. The French finally became disgusted with German excuses (which were probably encouraged by America's defection), and in April, 1920, the month after the Senate rejected the treaty, their tanks rumbled into the Ruhr and occupied several German cities as hostages for reparations payments. Bullets were fired, and some blood was shed. This was but a dress rehearsal for the catastrophic invasion of the Ruhr in 1923.

The action—or rather inaction—of the United States had other tragic consequences. It encouraged German radicals in their determination to tear up the treaty: they were finding unwitting collaborators in Senator Borah and President Wilson. It delayed by many months, as British Foreign Secretary Curzon openly charged, the treaty with Turkey, thus giving the "Sick Man of Europe" (Turkey) a chance to prove that he was the "Slick Man of Europe." It held up the economic and moral rehabilitation of the Continent, and even hampered the work of relief then going forward. It further disillusioned the liberals of Europe and others who had clung to Wilson as the major prophet of a new order. It gave new comfort to the forces of disorder everywhere. It left the United States discredited, isolated, shorn of its prestige, and branded as a hypocrite and renegade. It marked the first unbridgeable rift in the ranks of the victorious Allies, a coalition that might have kept the peace. Instead they now went their separate ways, perhaps not as enemies, but certainly no longer as close friends. The United States was the first to break completely away.

America—and the world—paid a high price for the collapse of the treaty-making process in Washington. We are still paying it.

IX

One final question. Who won after all these months of parliamentary jockeying?

Lodge the master parliamentarian had not won—that is, if he really wanted the treaty with his reservations. As in November, he was unable to keep the "irreconcilables" in line on the crucial vote, and he was unable to muster a two-thirds majority. He finally had to confess failure of leadership, except in so far as he prevented a schism.

The Republican party had not won. Lodge had avoided a serious split with the "bitter-enders" by knuckling under when they laid down the law.

But the Republican leaders did not really want the issue in the campaign, and they had made strong efforts to keep it out. Now it was on their hands to cause them no end of embarrassment.

Wilson had not won. He has been praised for having kept the party ranks intact, and for having retained undisputed leadership of his following. But the Democrats in the Senate split 21 for the treaty to 23 against it, and that is hardly holding one's followers in line. Wilson lost irreparably because he did not get his treaty, even with reservations, and because he was doomed to lose again by insisting on a referendum where there could be no referendum.

The Democrats had not won. The treaty issue had caused a serious rift in the Senate, and Bryan, who was still a great leader, was on the rampage. Except for Wilson and some of his "yes men," there were few Democratic leaders who wanted this troublesome issue catapulated into the campaign. Yet there it was.

The United States had not won. It had won the war, to be sure; but it was now kicking the fruits of the victory back under the peace table. We had helped turn Europe into a scrap heap, and now we were scrapping the treaty. We were going to stand by the Allies—with our arms folded. We were throwing away the only hope of averting World War II.

The real victor was international anarchy.

XII

The Literature of the 1920's:
A Trivial Literature or a
Literature of "Useful Innocence"?

INTRODUCTION

In an article dealing with the "Shifting Perspectives on the 1920's" Professor Henry F. May has pointed out that "Like the Civil War itself, the cultural battles of the twenties have been fought again and again. Successive writers have found it necessary either to condemn or to praise the decade, though what they have seen in it to condemn or praise has differed." [1] *In the 1930's progressives and New Dealers among the historians and literary critics viewed the 1920's scornfully as a decade of reaction and spoke disparagingly of its literature as well. The outbreak of World War II in Europe and the subsequent involvement of the United States in the struggle led some to an even harsher view of the culture and literature of the 1920's. To the literary critics and literary historians Archibald MacLeish, Van Wyck Brooks, and Bernard DeVoto, most of the prominent literary figures of the 1920's were "irresponsibles" whose mordant and biased view of American society actually impaired the nation's morale. Today, by contrast, the literature of the 1920's is widely regarded as one of the decade's greatest achievements, and it is praised for its freshness, its insights, and its technical skill.*

Two contrasting views of the literature of the 1920's are presented in the selections that follow. The first piece is taken from a series of lectures delivered by Bernard DeVoto at Indiana University in 1943 and published in 1944. DeVoto, with the events of World War II very much on his mind, argues that it was not American civilization that was "bankrupt" in the 1920's "but the literary way of thinking about it." He dismisses "the official literature" of the 1920's as "a trivial literature" because littérateurs in their works rejected "democracy" and failed to recognize the dignity of man.

Frederick Hoffman, a professor of English, wrote his superb study of the literature of the 1920's, published in 1955, out of a conviction that "the 1920's had not so far been fairly portrayed." [2] *Hoffman contends that critics of the literature of the 1920's, like DeVoto, have not shown "respect for the values of literature." He defends the artist's right to have "a private view of public affairs," and he praises the writers of the decade for their "useful innocence."*

---

[1] Henry F. May, "Shifting Perspectives on the 1920's," *Mississippi Valley Historical Review*, XLIII (December 1956), 405.

[2] Frederick J. Hoffman, *The Twenties: American Writing in the Postwar Decade* (New York: The Viking Press, 1955), p. ix.

Waste Land

Bernard DeVoto

. . . I cannot take you through the literature of a decade in one lecture. I propose merely to examine the evidence of certain illustrations which seem to me to exhibit a relationship and a rough kind of harmony. They are all from the main current of the decade's literature, the official literature, the literature praised by writers themselves. They are also, whether consciously or unconsciously, within the final limitations imposed by the literary fallacy.*

Sinclair Lewis will be remembered as the author of four novels, *Main Street, Babbitt, Arrowsmith,* and *Elmer Gantry.* Our purpose would permit us to approach them in a number of ways. We might say that their rationale shows a progressive shift from the ideas of Mr. Van Wyck Brooks to those of Mr. H. L. Mencken. We might say that their description of America is considerably more sociological than anything we have previously considered. We might say that although they show an energetic repudiation of American experience it is not an irreconcilable repudiation or even a fundamental one. We certainly ought to say that they have a greater gusto than any other fiction of the period. They are first-rate novels, and Mr. Lewis may well be the best novelist of the decade. But I have time only to inquire whether something which they lack may not be a common, and significant, lack in the literature of the period as a whole. I propose merely to inquire what Mr. Lewis's novels praise.

The critics have never been sure whether Mr. Lewis was trying to truly represent the life of his time or to caricature it, and it seems likely that Mr. Lewis has shared their uncertainty. Satire, however, has an important prerogative. So long as we understand what a satirist is driving at, we cannot ask him to tell the whole truth about it. The faithful representation of reality which other kinds of novelists hold to be their highest duty lays no

---

From Bernard DeVoto, *The Literary Fallacy* (Boston: Little, Brown and Company, 1944), pp. 95–123. Reprinted by permission.

* Editor's note: As defined by DeVoto, "the literary fallacy assumes: that a culture may be understood and judged solely by means of its literature, that literature embodies truly and completely both the values and the content of a culture, that literature is the highest expression of a culture, that literature is the measure of life, and finally that life is subordinate to literature" (p. 43).

obligation on him. But also there is a touchstone to satire: it has points of reference which make its values clear. Thus the spirited portraiture in *Main Street* withholds you from asking whether some aspects of life in Gopher Prairie may not have been distorted or ignored until you wonder what the town is being held against for reference. You discover that the reference is to certain adolescent ideas of Carol Kennicott. And suddenly it appears that the Village Virus which has poisoned America consists of the failure of small towns to support productions of the one-act plays of Eugene O'Neill, to provide candlelight at dinner, and to sanction lounging pajamas as evening wear for housewives. The superb evocation of the city of Zenith in *Babbitt* distracts one from values until one comes to consider the side of George F. Babbitt with whom Mr. Lewis finally developed a warm friendship and to consider the few inhabitants of the city who are held to be living the good life. Whereupon there appears so trivial an imagination of deep experience, so shallow and unsophisticated a conception of emotional relationships and intellectual activity, that one sees at once what has been left out of Zenith. What has been left out is human profundity, whether admirable or base.

Finally, when a novelist creates heroes he comes out into the open. Mr. Lewis's understanding is illuminated for us by *Arrowsmith*. Here he not only undertakes to make a sociologist's survey of the entire field of medicine in America; he also undertakes to exalt the scientific ideal and to praise a way of life which he thinks of as heroic. We may dismiss the survey as within the prerogatives of satire, though Mr. Lewis's virtuosity blinds one to the ferocious injustice done to the Public Health Service, institutions like the Rockefeller Foundation, medical research in general, and the customary life of doctors. It is not that Mr. Lewis's Jacques Loeb, Professor Gottlieb, is contained altogether in a solution of romantic tears, or that his Metchnikoff, Dr. Sondelius, is a sophomore scientist seen sophomorically. It is rather that these characters show his conception of scientific inquiry to be debased. And in Martin Arrowsmith, the details of his career, his mind and thinking and emotions, his science and the larger science it is bound to, are romantic, sentimental, and above all trivial. Himself an adolescent whose experience is never mature or complex, he is portrayed in an adolescent conception of what he stands for. As a mind Martin suffers from arrested development, as a scientist he is a fool. Mr. Lewis does indeed picture certain genuine absurdities of scientific research in the book, but never the really dangerous absurdities. And the austerity, complexity, illuminations, frustrations, methods, goals, and conditions of scientific thinking never get into the book at all. The realities of science, worthy or unworthy, the great world of science in its entirety, are altogether passed by.

Is not the same true of Mr. Lewis's characters in general? Leora Arrowsmith is emotionally undeveloped. Ann Vickers is an immature mind and her emotions are childlike. Dodsworth is so simple a personality that one doubts if he could have managed a corporation. His wife Fran, who is

Lewis's most developed character, is not developed past a simple statement of frigidity, a statement which does not disclose either the content or the roots of frigidity. Maturity of mind, maturity of emotion, complexity of character or experience, profundity of aspiration, despair, achievement, or failure—they are not discoverable in these books. They are not present in America so far as these books try to be an index to America. Mr. Lewis is not at ease when he is on the side of his characters, he is at ease when he is deriding them, when they are his butts. But his attack on them consists of showing that they are without complexity, sophistication, true power, or genuine depth. Select whatever you will, love, lust, family affection, courage, meditation, fantasy, childhood, religion, socialism, education, friendship, villainy, pain—and you find it shallow. The lives explored are uncomplicated, the experience revealed is mediocre.

Again there is no point in asking whether some part of this may be a defect of the novelist, for even if any be, a greater part certainly originates in the literary fallacy. In Mr. Lewis's work a sizable portion of our literature went out to answer questions whose answers it had worked out as assumptions in advance. The rationale existed beforehand as a chart, and when literature inquired what American life was like, it knew in advance that American life would turn out to be trivial, shallow, and mediocre. It is a short step from mediocrity to contemptibility. In the mood to which Mr. Lewis brought more energy, talent, enjoyment, and even affection than anyone else, novelists for a long time conceived of fiction as an exercise in expressing the contemptibility of American life. True to the pattern of fads, fiction began to develop specific types. There was the farm novel: frustration, cretinism, bastardy, and the squalor of the soul. A current folkway of writers was to seek the good life on little farms in Connecticut, whence frustrate peasants had been driven out, but the novel of farm life as unspeakably degraded moved all across our geography till the Pacific Ocean put a boundary to it. There was the novel of Prohibition, the novel of the repressed high school teacher, the novel of the American male as an unskilled lover, the novel which daringly denounced the courthouse gang— but a more studious mind than I has made a list. An admirer of this fiction, which he called the novel of protest, once set out to name its principal themes, with no apparent knowledge that he was writing humor:—

> the American passion for "bigness" and success, high pressure salesmanship, shoddy commercial products, poor housing conditions in urban areas, the narrow, lethargic, platitudinous, and often hysterical mob mind, corruption in government, labor injunctions, racketeering, standardization in education, industry, and art, the deportation of radicals, the abridgment of our constitutional liberties, the contract system of prison labor, militarism, the subsidizing of large corporations, political patronage, blue laws, nationalism, the legalized extortion of big business, sweat shops in the needle trades, racial prejudice,

the stretch system in factories, inelastic marriage statutes, capital punishment, the entrance of religion into politics, imperialism, profiteering,
a nation half boom and half broke, jingoism, rate inflation by public
utilities, law evasions, our present jury system, election frauds, bigotry,
child labor, the Ku Klux Klan, and wage slavery of every kind.

Of this sort of thing criticism has lately been saying that fiction had
turned from experience to data, and that is true. But such a list merely
names some of the ways in which fiction was finding the Americans mediocre
or contemptible. One observes an omission: the list makes no finding that
literary persons are mediocre or may be considered contemptible. However,
in due time Mr. Hemingway was to close that gap.

By process of critical rationale, by dedication, by fashion, by a variety
of other avenues, writers have come to occupy the site chosen for them by
Mr. Brooks, for which Mr. Cabell found a suggestive name, the High Place.
Biography has become a study of mediocrity and contemptibility in our past,
apparently to excuse us by accusing our ancestors. Like fiction and criticism,
it is a withdrawal to the High Place. Some writers, following Harold
Stearns's manifesto,* are making a literal withdrawal. In American society
there is no joy nor light nor hope, no dignity, no worth; reality cannot be
found there and art cannot live. So the Artist will seek societies where art
can live, finding joy and hope and beauty, experience deep in the grain,
Paris, the French Riviera, Cornwall, the Mediterranean islands, Russia.
What life in America abundantly lacks exists abundantly in such places.
Thought is free there, art is the universal goal of human effort, writers are
universally respected, and human life has a claim on the interest of literary
men which in America it assuredly has not. But whether physical or only
spiritual, the withdrawal to the High Place has become an established mode
of literature and this mode dominates the literature to which the generality
of writers acknowledge allegiance. The dedication of the High Place may
be granted easily, but the illumination of its inhabitants seems to consist of
perceiving the inferiorities of their countrymen. Few writers ever spoke of
themselves in print as a superior class. The assumption is implicit in the
critical rationale, but it is customary to speak not of superiority but of
leadership. The superiority of the caste is the inferiority of the life withdrawn from. From the High Place, the Americans are the fall guys of the
world, sometimes dangerous as a mob, less often pitiful as well-meaning
boobs, but most often tawdry, yokelish, acquisitive, coarse, an undifferen-
tiated mass preyed on by mass passions and dominated by mass fears.

Turn now to Mr. Ernest Hemingway's fiction for evidence to carry us a
little farther. Here are memorable portraits of racketeers, thugs, hunters of

---

* Editor's note: After editing *Civilization in the United States* (1922), which deplored the state of American culture, Stearns concluded that the wise thing for a young
man to do was to leave the country.

big and small game, prizefighters, bullfighters, poolroom hangers-on, prostitutes, expatriate idlers, soldiers, a miscellany of touts, sportsmen, entertainers and the like, and some millionaires and writers of whom the principal assertion is that they are sexually impotent. Mr. Hemingway's themes are death, the fear of death, the defiance of death, and the dangers to which male potency is exposed—and it is easy to see what he praises. He praises aggressiveness, courage, male wariness, male belligerence, the instinctual life, war and fighting, sexual intercourse, and a few primary loyalties immediately associated with them. It is also easy to say what life is not, as his fiction represents life. Life, so far as it can be desired or respected, does not exist above the diaphragm. It is activated by digestion, the surge of adrenalin into the bloodstream at crises of danger or defiance, and the secretion of the testicles. His hero is a pre-Piltdown stage of man, a warily aggressive anthropoid who goes down fighting. Intellectual life does not exist even in rudimentary form, except that the contempt heaped on it grants it a kind of existence. There is no social life, there is not even a society. Pithecanthropus Erectus prowls a swamp so sown with danger that the honors, constraints, bonds, prohibitions, and decencies of men living together merely add another, extreme form of danger to it. They are weaknesses of less perfect animalities who have risen to the ethical and social development of, say, Cro-Magnon man; the superior, more primitive anthropoid merely uses them to destroy him. There is hardly even love, though Mr. Hemingway has written many love stories, one of which may well be the best of his period. Piltdown man couples with his female and the physical mating is clean, but the beauty of this function is corrupted when love tries to add spiritual associations to it. They are decadent—anything is decadent which may diminish male vigor or deflect its functioning. Life has grandeur in that it may aggressively defy violent death, and it has tragedy in that the defiance may be vain.

In short, the world most of us live in and the qualities by which we try to live are unrecognized in Mr. Hemingway's fiction. True, criticism has decided that the progress of world disorder finally led him to a great affirmation, and Mr. Geismar, whom I have quoted before, seems honestly to believe that the doom of civilization was averted and hope came back to the Western world when Mr. Hemingway found a cause he could believe in. Still, it does not appear that the dying murderer of *To Have and Have Not* has altered Mr. Hemingway's basic values when he has learned that adrenalin spurts in vain into the bloodstream of one man alone. Nor, after prayerful search, can I find that the values by which the life of men is to be judged have been altered in the novel to which Mr. Hemingway so presumptuously prefixed a quotation from John Donne. It is true that Mr. Hemingway's constant preoccupation with belligerence, cruelty, and inflicted death has contrived to associate itself with symbols in which the rest of us find values that ennoble life. But in the novel life is not ennobled by those symbols. The emphasis still suggests that though the sexual act may be very fine, the act of killing is an orgasm far surpassing it in intensity. The world for which Robert Jordan faithfully sacrifices his life appears to be, in prospect, still a swamp which men who are mere bowels and autonomic nervous systems will prowl to the same ends, though perhaps this time in bands of gangsters rather than as lonely killers. The novel is not aware, even in vision, of society as civilization or of life as something affected by the fore-brain.

From the beginning up to now, both implicitly and explicitly, with a vindictive belligerence, Mr. Hemingway has always attacked the life of the mind, the life of the spirit, and the shared social experience of mankind. Certainly he finds them contemptible; it is a legitimate guess that they scare him. The point is, however, that his disdain of intelligence, contempt of spirituality, praise of mindlessness, and adoration of instinct and blood-consciousness have many connections with other literary values held elsewhere in the general movement. They are related to the cult of pure esthetics, to the mystical cult of which D. H. Lawrence was the most gifted exponent in English, to the manias of doom that obsess Mr. Faulkner (who has much else in common with Mr. Hemingway), and to such clotted phobias as those that distinguish the work of Robinson Jeffers. If some areas of literature made a thesis of the inferiority of Americans, other areas exalted the thesis to make men inferior to the animals. It is a short step from thinking of the mob to thinking of the wolf pack, from the praise of instinct to war against reason, from art's vision of man as contemptible to dictatorship's vision of men as slaves. Such considerations, however, do not concern us. We have merely to repeat that Mr. Hemingway's fiction is separated from our common experience. By a different path he has come to the High Place. He is uncomfortable there for he finally comes to use the word "writer" as an epithet of contempt, as folklore has the wounded snake striking its fangs into its own body. But there he is and love, work, decency, achievement, aspiration, and defeat, as people know them who are neither writers nor bullfighters nor anthropoids, do not come within his awareness. Or, if they sometimes intrude on him, they only press the trigger of his scorn.

I think that we have enough clues now and may let the rest of the period's literature go undescribed, coming forthwith to the symbols which this literature agreed to accept as comprehending the whole. What this generation had to say about life, it was generally agreed, found final expression in Mr. Eliot's poem, "The Waste Land." I do not propose to add to the thousands of pages that have analyzed it, but only to mention the passage in which Tiresias, "Old man with wrinkled female breasts," is present at the tawdry seduction of the typist home at teatime by the young man carbuncular, the small house agent's clerk on whom assurance sits as a silk hat on a Bradford millionaire. Here thirty concentrated lines of verse render life in the modern world as a cheap inanity, love as a vulgar ritual without feeling or significance, and mankind as too unimportant to justify Mr. Eliot's hatred of Apeneck Sweeney.

It is a crucial passage, crucial not only in Mr. Eliot's poetry but in the literature of our time. All Mr. Eliot's other perceptions support it, down to the time when his forehead was crossed with ashes on the first day of a later Lent. In it an entire literary movement makes a final judgment. Literature looks at human beings and says that this is what their experience amounts to. It commits itself. Then, having made the commitment, Mr. Eliot went on to prophesy. He was right to do so. For if personality and experience in our time were justly rendered in this passage, then there could be little doubt that life must come out as he predicted.

> This is the way the world ends
> This is the way the world ends
> This is the way the world ends
> Not with a bang but a whimper.*

It happens that Mr. MacLeish had a moment of sharing this vision, and he envisaged the end of the world coming down upon a gaudy circus performance when "The armless ambidextrian was lighting A match between his great and second toe," and then above the white faces and dazed eyes of the audience

> There in the sudden blackness the black pall
> Of nothing, nothing, nothing—nothing at all.†

Literature, I say, had committed itself. It had made a final judgment. It had reached the end of a road. In homelier words, it had got out on the end of a limb. So then the end of the world arrived.

Who are the people to whom Mr. MacLeish has been appealing so passionately—on behalf of whom he has accused writers of being as irresponsible as common criminals? They are only that audience of white faces and dazed eyes whom even judgment day could not stir to an awareness of anything at all. And when the end of the world came no whimpering was to be heard, except perhaps a literary whimpering, but the typist home at teatime and young man carbuncular decided that the world should not end. Nothing whatever changed in the typist and the house agent's clerk when the bombers came over London or the shock of Pearl Harbor traveled across this country. But war provided an appeal of judgment. The typist and the clerk had fortitude, sacrifice, fellowship; they were willing to die as an act of

---

* From *Collected Poems 1909–1935* by T. S. Eliot, copyright, 1936, by Harcourt, Brace & World, Inc. and reprinted with their permission; from *Collected Poems 1909–1962* by T. S. Eliot with the permission of Faber and Faber, Ltd., London.

† From "The End of the World" by Archibald MacLeish. Reprinted by permission of Houghton Mifflin Company.

faith for the preservation of hope. They were hope, the soul and body of hope. They were staunchness, resolution, dedication. In fact they were incommensurable with what Mr. Eliot's poem had said they were. In "The Waste Land," I remarked, an entire literary movement made a final judgment on mankind. It committed itself. It got out on the end of a limb. But mankind turned out to be otherwise. It was not what literature had said it was. Furthermore, literature is now, temporarily at least, willing to accept the reversal of judgment. It has, temporarily at least, agreed to accept courage, fortitude, sacrifice, dedication, fellowship, willingness to die for the sake of the future—it has agreed to accept such attributes as a norm by which mankind shall be judged.

But perhaps it was the business of literature all along to take account of such attributes. It was not the typist and the young man carbuncular who were trivial. It was not their experience nor their emotions nor the realities they lived by that were trivial. It was the imagination of writers who passed judgment on them.

Return to the question I asked toward the beginning of these lectures. If one who was ignorant of American life during the 1920's, say Mr. Geismar, were to consult the books of, say, Mencken, Lewis, Hemingway, Dos Passos, and Wolfe in an effort to understand it, could he trust their description? I answered no. We have come far enough to turn that answer into an inquiry.

Consider the work of Mr. Dos Passos. No insincerity can be alleged against him, no malice, no kind of irresponsibility, especially the kind which Mr. MacLeish charges against the generation. Mr. Dos Passos has an austere conception of the responsibility of a novelist. All his fiction proceeds from a vision of life in America since the turn of the twentieth century, a vision of the time and the society as a whole. It is conceived with great power. It is worked out with a technical mastery which no contemporary has excelled. It is never suffered to depart from his vision.

One might, of course, hold that this vision is sometimes mistaken. Thus the damage done to our society by his Ward Moorehouses and Charley Andersons would indeed have been insignificant if such men had been what they seem to Mr. Dos Passos—if they had been just feeble timeservers or drunken lechers, antlike creatures carried crazily on chips by a great flood. But they were able to damage our society because that is precisely what they were not. Because Ward Moorehouse had a powerful intelligence which he employed in clearly calculated operations with effectively mastered tools. Because Charley Anderson, as a class, did not spend his time in debauchery but instead with an ascetic sobriety and an undeviating single-mindedness operated a mastered technology in his own service, toward ends which he did not in the least misconceive.

Specific inaccuracies, however, are less important for our study than the enveloping conditions in which Mr. Dos Passos's characters exist. They are always held to his vision with complete fidelity. But, ferocious as the injuries inflicted on them are, they do not move us much. These half-drugged men and women marching past milestones of indignity toward graceless deaths do not engage us to share their pain. The truth is that they hardly seem to suffer pain. Nothing theoretical or ideological is missing. Art has not failed to put any of its instruments at the service of life. Nevertheless these creatures, these integrations of behavior, are removed so far from us that they seem to be seen through a reducing glass. They lack a vital quality, they seem like automatons. It is as if, shall I say, the doom they meet is merely a literary doom.

If one sets against them the characters of the most considerable American novelist developed during the 1930's, James Farrell, one sees at once what the vital lack is. Mr. Dos Passos and Mr. Farrell conceive the function of fiction identically. But when a Farrell character is injured he bleeds, and when society wrongs one the reader is wronged with him, and this fails to happen in the Dos Passos novels. Certainly Mr. Dos Passos does not lack anger or compassion—nor the irony and pity which Mr. Hemingway found so funny when a bigger man than he praised them. But he remains on the High Place when looking at his people. His vision is afar off, from the mountain top. Whereas the monstrous cruelties inflicted on Studs Lonigan and the O'Neills, the monstrous brutalities they are forced to commit, are indeed monstrous precisely because they are not seen from the mountain top. They are monstrous because we feel that they are an intolerable impairment of human dignity. Precisely because human life is thought of as having inherent worth, things done to men may indeed be intolerable. Precisely because the experience of men has dignity there may be tragic experience. Precisely because men are not contemptible the cruelty and injustice inflicted on them can move us to say this must not be borne.

With Mr. Farrell for illustration, however, I have come outside the decade. It is proper to consider some who in that decade stood outside the official doctrines and made the affirmation I have found in him. But first let me a little generalize what we have said so far.

We have examined a system of ideas which held that American culture was barren and American life malformed, tawdry, and venal. From this the next step, soon taken, was to find the cultural traditions actively evil and the life they expressed vile. It is easy to say that from this literature was gone a sense of the heroic in our past. It is easy to say that American literature had lost all feeling of the greatness of America, whether past or present, and of its place in the Western world and its promise to civilization. It is easy to say that belief in the future, the very feeling of hope, was gone. But to say this is superficial, for much more was gone.

Not only heroes are scarce in this literature. In books which leading writers wrote and leading critics praised, the gospel of the established church, nothing is so rare as merely decent people. Where in the literature of the 1920's is the man or woman who lived a civilized life dedicated to the mature values of civilization? Where is the man who accepts the ordinary decencies and practises them with good will, meeting with self-respect and courage the human adventure of birth, growth, education, love, parenthood, work, and death? The man who is loyal to his friends, believes in his country, is a good citizen, loves his wife, works for his family, brings up his children, and deals resolutely with the vicissitudes, strains, anxieties, failures, and partial successes that compose our common lot? In the official Scriptures that man either does not exist at all or exists as an object of derision. Mr. Dos Passos overlooks him, he is beyond the concern of Mr. Faulkner, Mr. Hemingway says that he lacks maleness, and when Mr. Lewis abandons his amiable or occasionally dangerous fools he is unable to conceive that man above the level of a high school boy.

Here criticism usually demurs. The final phase of finance capitalism, the cynicism of an inflationary boom, Prohibition, racketeering, the decay of politics, the Scopes trial, the Sacco-Vanzetti case, innumerable other data of the same kind—such evidence as this, we are told, appalled writers, who were right to dissociate themselves from it altogether. With an odd pride Mr. Edmund Wilson has remarked that this generation of writers attacked their culture more unanimously and more continuously than any other known to history. Even so, a vagrant mind wonders why orthodox dogma was unable to perceive in America any will to oppose these things except among literary folk. One goes on to point out, moreover, that not only decency and righteousness are gone from the people whom this literature exploits but, as well, the simple basis of humanity. And that, one decides, makes merely silly the distress which criticism tells us was behind the exploitation. If man is a predatory animal, then surely it is silly of writers to blame him when he acts according to his nature. The wolf may not be hated for wolfishness nor the boob for stupidity: the anger of literature would be idiotic. But the idea that writers might be idiotic is abhorrent and so, summing up, one turns from it to say instead that literature's dissociation from common experience, achieved by systematic logic, results in a fundamental judgment, and a false judgment, on the nature of man. . . .

Let us, however, turn from what I have called the official literature of the 1920's—the body of writing which was accepted by most writers as composing the movement, and which was conscious of itself as representing the age. Nothing about the period is more remarkable than the fact that second-rate writers were commonly less susceptible to the literary fallacy than their betters. But I propose to speak of certain first-rate writers who stood outside the movement.

To name only a few, when one comes to Carl Sandburg, E. A. Robinson, Willa Cather, Stephen Vincent Benét, and Robert Frost one enters a world quite different from that of the poets and novelists I have discussed and the critics who made out work-sheets for them. It is certainly not a world sugary or aseptic, washed clean of evil, or emptied of hate, injustice, cruelty, suffering, failure, or decay. No one in the generation has written with fiercer anger of the exploitation of men than Mr. Sandburg. No one in the generation has more witheringly rebuked the ebbing from our consciousness of certain elements of greatness in our tradition than Miss Cather or Mr. Benét. In Mr. Frost's poetry there is a resentment of indignities inflicted on men so fierce that compared to it Mr. Lewis's protest seems no more than a rowdy bellow and Mr. Hemingway's a rather craven sob. The difference is not that these writers fail in any way to be aware of evil or that any of them fail to understand the indecencies of life. It is only a difference of opinion—a difference of opinion about the dignity of man. That is all but it is a final difference, one that can never be resolved.

The poetry of Robert Frost affirms what the orthodox literature of the 1920's denies: that human experience has dignity. Human feeling has finality. Grief may be hopeless and rebellion may be futile but they are real and so they are tragic. Tragedy may be immitigable but it *is* tragedy. The integrity of experience is common to us all and is sacred in us all. Life *has* sanctity; whether fulfilled or unfulfilled, it *is* worthy, it *can* be trusted, it *has* a dignity that cannot be corrupted. The experience of men has a fundamental worth which neither other men, nor God, nor a hostile fate can destroy. Hold the poems to any light, look at any edge or angle of them, and they always come to the same focus. A worthless hired man comes back to an adopted home to die with people who know his worthlessness. A woman once mad washes her dishes beside Lake Willoughby in the knowledge of what made her mad and the knowledge that she will be mad again. A lover of forest orchids whom the acquisitive society has crippled signs a legal release, knowing exactly what it was that cut off his feet. In them all is an infrangible dignity. On that infrangible dignity of man Frost's poetry stands foursquare and in Frost's poetry American literature of our time makes its basic affirmation. Man is the measure of things. Man's experience is the measure of reality. Man's spirit is the measure of fate.

The literature we have glanced at lacks this basic acknowledgment of the dignity of man. That is why it is a trivial literature—why the Waste Land of Mr. Eliot and the Solutrean swamp of Mr. Hemingway are less than tragedy, smaller than tragedy. Bulls and male sharks may die in agony, and perhaps there is beauty in the moment of total aggressive force going down before superior force, but though the pain they suffer may shock our nerves we cannot possibly feel their death as tragic. The diminished marionettes of Mr. Dos Passos do not move us to either pain or protest. Conceived as aggregations of reflexes, they lack the humanity which alone gives significance to suffering or cruelty. The frustration of an animal cannot be tragic. The accusation that any man is base or has done evil means nothing at all, unless baseness and evil are defections from the spirit of man. Injustice is an empty word unless man is the measure of justice. There can be no sin unless sin robs man of a state of grace.

That is why so many literary attitudes of our time led eventually to cynicism, heartbreak, or neurotic collapse. Out of them has come much penitence and much of that penitence is merely absurd. It was always possible to inquire "What art?" when someone told us long ago that a spirit bruised by the mediocrity of the life round it intended to seek healing in dedication to beauty. The same question disposes of several dozen literary confessions which have told us that the penitents found no life whatever in beauty, that the palace of art proved to be a house of the dead. Again, those who fled the culture of America, which stifled thought and forbade art and made war on freedom, were presently back from various European Utopias strangely shocked because something Utopian, something which clearly could not be charged against America, had interfered with thought and art and freedom. Another group were betrayed into a more painful bewilderment. They undertook to identify themselves with the workers of the world, only to perish of a dilemma. The blue jeans of the Noble Worker were ceremonial vestments by definition and yet, by earlier definition, the bodies they covered had been denied immortal souls. Three quarters of a literary movement died of internal friction.

Such fragile attitudes are unimportant. They merely move one to inquire whether the lack of intelligence observed was in the culture complained of or in the writers complaining. What counted was not the fragility of small attitudes but the falsity of the fundamental literary attitude. As the catastrophe of our time moved on to its last act, it became clear that literary thinking had got caught in a steel trap of its own making. Literature now found itself summoning men to die for institutions, traditions, possibilities, and hopes which it had lately described as either nonexistent or contemptible. And the men whom it summoned to die for them were the inferior creatures who had lately been incapable even of perceiving, still more of understanding, the values which could make them consent to die.

For it is clear to you that I have been talking about something which need not necessarily be phrased in literary jargon. I have been talking about democracy, I have been talking, in fact, about a very specific form of democracy which first became a faith, first established the tenets and developed the energy of a faith, and first brought that faith to the problems of men living together in society, here in America. It is true that not many writers of the 1920's formally or even consciously opposed democracy. It is proper to remember that a few did. There were some who formally analyzed democracy as a mob of inferior men, dominated by mob lusts and mob panics and conditioned by the swinishness of the average man. Such writers opposed democracy, and so did a number of the period's least stable minds, prettily coquetting with notions of American monarchy and various other lightly literary lunacies, though of course the stampede of literary men to formidable absolutisms, whether communist or fascist, was a phenomenon of the next decade. However, the sum was small and the effect unnoticeable even in the coterie press.

Apart from these, it is just to say that the writers of the period avowed an honest respect for the word "democracy." A word is only a word, however. American democracy is not a word but American men and women, the beliefs they hold about themselves and one another, institutions they maintain to safeguard their beliefs and to fulfill their hopes, and the goals, ideals, constraints, and prohibitions they share and mutually acknowledge. It was precisely these people and these ideas, feelings, institutions, traditions, and culture which the literature of the period rejected. For these people and their culture the orthodox writers of the period had, as their books prove, an antipathy ranging from mere disillusionment or mere distaste, through hatred, to contempt. No wonder, then, that when judgment day came so incomparably otherwise than Mr. Eliot had predicted, the ideas of many literary men became schizophrenic. Ordinary man must now save the democratic way of life. But one earlier premise held that that way of life was not worth saving. And another earlier premise held that those who must save it could not save it. Either premise seemed to make it impossible to take a stand.

But this merely repeats what I have just said in other words. The Christian view of life holds that men are entitled to primary respect because they are all the children of God—"inasmuch as ye have done it unto one of the least of these my brethren ye have done it unto me." The view of life, Christian or non-Christian, which in all ages is called humanistic holds that man is entitled to primary respect because only in man's consciousness can the universe be grappled with. And the democratic view of life holds quite simply that the dignity of man is unalienable.

But respect for this unalienable dignity is precisely what had been drained from the literature of the 1920's. Mr. MacLeish's indictment of modern American literature which I began by quoting says that writers failed to safeguard our democracy between the two great wars. There can be no appeal from that judgment. But they failed to safeguard it because they failed in primary respect for democratic man and primary understanding of his experience.

I have remarked that for several years now literature has been confessing its errors. The confession of such an error as this is a confession of betrayal. It amounts to a confession that what truly was bankrupt was not American civilization but the literary way of thinking about it. That way of thinking, it is now quite clear—it is temporarily clear even to writers—was not competent to bring in trustworthy findings. It was not an adequate, an accurate, or a dependable instrument. It would not give results that could be used. The principal effort of literature has, by its own confession, failed. It has failed because of the insufficiency of its means. It has failed because a people, a culture, and a civilization cannot be held to literary values.

371

Some Perspectives on the 1920's

Frederick J. Hoffman

1. THE SNOW OF 1929

Not long after October 1929 people began to regret the 1920's, to renounce the sins of a "wasted decade"; they admitted they had had a good time while "the gaudiest spree in history" had lasted, but they were ready now to assume the roles of adult, mature persons. No more pathetic reminder of the reformed playboy exists than Charlie Wales of Fitzgerald's story, "Babylon Revisited" (written in 1931). Wales returns to Paris, after an exile, to reclaim his life. He is properly humble, regretful, resolved; he has become "a new man," learned his lesson, and will his sister-in-law please restore his daughter Honoria to him? He will now be able to take care of her: sober, restrained, solvent, and anxious to identify himself with the human race, he feels that she will secure him in his new conviction. He now believes "in character"; he wants "to jump back a whole generation and trust in character again as the eternally valuable element."

Paris, the Babylon to which he has made his journey of contrition, is itself suffering a depression of the spirit. The streets are almost empty of tourists, where a few months before they had been gay and colorful. "The Poet's Cave had disappeared, but the two great mouths of the Café of Heaven and the Café of Hell still yawned—even devoured, as he watched, the meager contents of a tourist bus—a German, a Japanese, and an American couple who glanced at him with frightened eyes." Looking upon the waste, reflecting upon the pathos, Charlie Wales suddenly realizes "the meaning of the word 'dissipate'—to dissipate into thin air; to make nothing out of something."

The "waste" is both a moral and a dramatic problem. There are those who soberly endured the antics of their American contemporaries during the 1920's; now they have become their judges. But the morally correct do not enjoy their role; they have a sense not so much of wickedness resisted as of their having been cheated out of something. Marion Peters, the sister-in-law who has kept Charlie's daughter from him, "was a tall woman with worried eyes, who had once possessed a fresh American loveliness." Between

---

the two a quiet but intense struggle develops, a struggle of two equally strong determinations, for Honoria, the prize. If he should prove that one can morally survive the 1920's, the prize is his; if not, if there is the slightest doubt of his having fully reformed, Honoria remains with the "good woman," the woman who has sacrificed her "American loveliness" so that character might return to the American personality after an absence of at least ten years. Slowly, arduously, Wales works to regain her confidence. But the stain of the 1920's is hard to remove. Two of his friends reappear from out of the past; and, though Wales tries to keep them away, to prevent their violating the temple of his humble resolve, they do just that. The 1920's cannot be put away. The terrible crime of irresponsibility, which had led to the death of his wife, haunts the atonement at the very moment of forgiveness, and Wales is once more back at the beginning, without the reward he had wished for his patient efforts to redefine himself as a responsible human being:

> Again the memory of those days swept over him like a nightmare— the people they had met traveling; then people who couldn't add a row of figures or speak a coherent sentence. The little man Helen had consented to dance with at the ship's party, who had insulted her ten feet from the table; the women and girls carried screaming with drink or drugs out of public places—
> —The men who locked their wives out in the snow, because the snow of twenty-nine wasn't real snow. If you didn't want it to be snow, you just paid some money.

On January 2, 1950, *Life* magazine summarized the five decades of our century in one hundred pages of pictures and comment. As is usual on such occasions, the 1920's figured prominently, and there was nothing new or unexpected in the display. From Gilda Gray to Grover Whalen, the celebrities of the time were exhibited; and the brief preface reflected upon their meaning:

> When the 1920's ended in the crash it became fashionable (and merciful) to forget them, and they have been buried beneath recovery, war, and a new boom. It is startling to find the old headliners still looking as chipper as they do in these pictures taken in the past few months— startling, and pleasant. They were the life of the party and everyone loves them, even though it was not a party that the nation can afford to throw again.

What distinguishes this quotation from the Luce "capsule" is the quality of its metaphor; the 1920's were a "party" that resulted in a serious hangover. We still talk about the party but are properly repentant and resolved not to have another. The same metaphor is encountered in a collection called *The Pleasures of the Jazz Age* (1948), edited by William Hoddap: "Here is a ten-year-long weekend party in which they all participated and whose hangover never really started till the stock-market crash." These people had founded "an uncharted colony of freedom—even license—for refugees from reality." In other characterizations the 1920's were called "The Era of Wonderful Nonsense," the time of the "lost generation," the "Jazz Age," the age of Freud, Ziegfeld, and Coolidge.[1]

In a very real sense Fitzgerald, who had been in the vanguard of those establishing this image of the twenties, helped to make it a permanent view. When the decade died in the last months of 1929 Fitzgerald "tightened his belt"; and in subsequent years he wrote a series of pieces, for *Scribner's, Esquire,* and other magazines, in which he described both the pleasures and the agonies of atonement since undergone. Fitzgerald's Charlie Wales perhaps best symbolizes the crowd who "went to the party" and had to pay the check.[2]

The "golden boom," the "gaudiest spree in history," required in 1931 "the proper expression of horror as we look back at our wasted youth." In the 1930's Fitzgerald wrote about his "wasted youth," dwelling again and again upon its glamour and its misguided energy. The pages of *Tender Is the Night* (1934) are filled with judgments delivered upon the waste, the triviality, the pathetic effort to realize what in the decade had seemed hopelessly beyond realization.[3] The hero, Dr. Dick Diver, sacrifices his every talent, his last ounce of energy, to keep alive an illusion that has been doomed from the start. His struggle is not with the 1920's but with a complex of enemies who, in Fitzgerald's view, had made the decade what it was: easy wealth; the falsely sentimental view of life symbolized in the Rosemary Hoyt of the film *Daddy's Girl*; the inner weaknesses and tensions of its most gifted person; above all, its indifference to human responsibility—its inability to define the terms on which men *become* responsible. In the end

---

[1] See a recent "handbook" (*Backgrounds of American Literary Thought* by Rod W. Horton and Herbert W. Edwards, 1952): The 1920's "in reality . . . presented the rather sad spectacle of irresponsible youth having its last fling." Elsewhere it speaks of "the whoopie mentality of the happy-talking twenties" and employs the usual clichés concerning "national adolescence" and other reflections that recall Fitzgerald's remarks in the early 1930's. The authors do admit that there was talent in those years, that the young men "gave the nation the liveliest, freshest, most stimulating writing in its literary experience."

[2] Since the Depression had followed immediately upon the end of the decade, "perspectives" upon it were quickly achieved. But Fitzgerald had his personal reasons for looking back in such a way. It is of some interest to note that Nick Carraway, in the midst of the wild clamor of charge and countercharge at the Plaza Hotel, suddenly and sadly remembers that he has reached "the thirtieth year of his age."

[3] If one examines the history of the composition of this novel (begun almost immediately after *The Great Gatsby* was published in 1925), one can understand its pertinence as a commentary upon the decade. It began as an account of planned murder, in essentials exploiting the most sensational contemporary "copy." Gradually this quality of American life was toned down; and Fitzgerald moved toward the use of a hero who is endowed with the most affectingly "charming" good will and is (in his profession) a scientific minister to the decade's ills as well. See Arthur Mizener's *The Far Side of Paradise* for the story of the several plans that led to the novel of 1934.

Diver, on his "way out," his wife gone away with another man, pauses for a final "benediction" of that "prayer-rug" of Riviera beach that had been the scene of his greatest triumphs and his most painful defeats:

> "I must go," he said. As he stood up he swayed a little; he did not feel well any more—his blood raced slow. He raised his right hand and with a papal cross he blessed the beach from the high terrace.

In the quiet blasphemy of this gesture Diver dismisses the decade and himself; he had been identified with it and his talents and charm were exhausted to preserve in it a quality it had not wanted. He is through with it, and it with him.

In spite of the indifferent reception of *Tender Is the Night,* Fitzgerald's identification with the 1920's persisted. The two were indistinguishable in the public mind. A man of great talent, he had fought a losing battle with the temptations and the frivolities of the time. In loving them for their own sakes, he had forfeited his full right to judge them incisively. But Dr. Diver's final gesture is ironically a farewell to something pathetically lost when the decade ended. "Now once more the belt is tight," he said in November 1931 (*Scribner's Magazine*), "and we summon the proper expression of horror as we look back at our wasted youth."

> Sometimes, though, there is a ghostly rumble among the drums, an asthmatic whisper in the trombones that swings me back into the early twenties when we drank wood alcohol and every day in every way grew better and better, and there was a first abortive shortening of the skirts, and girls all looked alike in sweater dresses, and people you didn't want to know said 'Yes, we have no bananas,' and it seemed only a question of a few years before the older people would step aside and let the world be run by those who saw things as they were— and it all seems rosy and romantic to us who were young then, because we will never feel quite so intensely about our surroundings any more.[4]

Nevertheless the image of the twenties that remained most clearly in the public mind in 1950 was that established by Fitzgerald in 1920, exploited and all but exhausted by him in the following years, and then reassimilated in terms of a moral view of wistful regret in the 1930's.

---

[4] Fitzgerald's wife, Zelda, gave her own version of the 1920's in her only novel, *Save Me the Waltz* (1932). The heroine has to suffer the disadvantages of marriage to a celebrity; she turns to ballet dancing for salvation, as Mabel Dodge Luhan might have turned to Gurdjieff's rhythmic ceremonials. This tedious novel is valuable only for its annotations upon the Fitzgerald perspective: "They were having the bread line at the Ritz that year"; "People were tired of the proletariat—everybody was famous"; "Nobody knew the words to 'The Star-Spangled Banner'"; the expatriates sought "stimulation in the church and asceticism in sex." These are *New Yorker* captions; the conflict in "Alabama's" soul concerning allegiances and loyalties is patently contrived. The strongest impression one gets from reading this novel in 1953 is that the Fitzgeralds did have a "rough time" and that the violence of their hysterias must have disturbed his every paragraph and altered the punctuation of his every sentence.

It required more than Fitzgerald, however, to fix that impression upon the public mind. The crash of 1929 was, after all, not only a sign of moral collapse. It was a fact of economic history, and in the 1930's economic facts were also moral facts. The sturdy and persistent men of Marx watched the collapse of Wall Street with ill-concealed pleasure and began the 1930's with a determination to wipe the previous decade entirely off the record. "Social responsibility," all but absent from the American scene for ten years, according to the leftists, now became the major concern. The sad young men were welcomed back to America, on probation, and were asked to renounce their sinful past and promised reward for their assumption of doctrinal saintliness. The men who had made a pilgrimage to Moscow instead of indulging themselves in Babylon-on-the-Seine prepared themselves for the roles of moral spokesmen. A haunting sense of missed opportunities for "social good" overwhelmed the men and women of the 1930's, who looked back upon the "nation that for a decade had wanted only to be entertained." The apostles of social responsibility used the decade as a grim reminder: there but for the grace of Marx go I. The antics of the 1920's were "cute but horrible." Never had a more suitable demonstration appeared of the tragedy of social and moral dissipation. It was ideally suited to the Marxist text, which exploited it with great ease and convincing persuasion.

Mr. Roosevelt's liberals toned down the criticism a bit, but only because they wanted it to be less Marxist, more native to the grain of American social thought. The *New Republic* and the *Nation* regained their confidence and addressed themselves to the review of a tradition they thought had been lost when Sacco and Vanzetti were destroyed. The men who had begun their careers in the 1920's revised their points of view, addressing themselves eagerly and respectfully to great "social forces." John Dos Passos, whose John Andrews had risked and suffered all for art, now, in *U.S.A.,* relegated the aesthetic conscience to that corner of his trilogy called "The Camera Eye." Hemingway sought and found a social objective in the streets of Madrid, and later had his Robert Jordan defend the line that Lieutenant Henry had deserted. They were cured, or seemed to be. They came back to see what they had earlier ignored; and what they had previously seen they now ignored.

It was the leftists of the 1930's who were the first to count the cost, and they outlined the terms of payment in phrases of economic liability, which invariably had overtones of moral judgment. The early years of the *New Masses* (1926–1929) had anticipated the pattern of criticism: a pitiful waste of great talent and promise, because these people had not the slightest respect for society. They were pathetically unable to go beyond a childish "revolution" against the bad taste of their elders, ignoring in their rebellion the really disastrous sins committed by the older generation, the sins of capitalism. There was no doubt about it: the failure to understand the social economy was a consequence of the disrespect for any sensible tradition, American or Russian.

This view of the 1920's has not yet been entirely corrected or revised. In the 1940's the perspective was changed a bit, but it was just as much distorted by current moral and social urgencies. To the men who fought in World War II and survived it, the 1920's seemed either a period of amusing but stupid gaiety or a horrible and expensive example of what the "irresponsibles" could cost a nation with moral and military commitments to the world. In the 1950 reviews of the half-century provided in radio broadcasts and popular magazines, the 1920's appeared a grotesque world, remembered for sophomoric behavior and ingenious evasions of serious responsibility. The popular mind saw the decade only in the figure of the musical revue, in Hollywood's strange version of Jay Gatsby, or in the revival of Anita Loos's Lorelei.

The work of Van Wyck Brooks, Archibald MacLeish, Bernard DeVoto, and the editors of the *Saturday Review of Literature* sounded another kind of alarm. Their arguments combined a search for a creditable American past and an appeal for a sensible atomic future: according to them, the irresponsibles of the 1920's had either not known or not respected the American tradition. A simple formula was set up: personal responsibility is above all responsibility to one's neighbor, to one's group, and to the world at large. An explosion at Hiroshima, or anywhere, accelerates that sense of responsibility, should make man more vitally concerned than ever over the men who killed and the men who were killed. Isolationism of any kind was immoral. The historical event must hereafter be the constant locus of literary reference. Above all, one must respect one's America, as had Whittier and Twain and Whitman. There was no such respect in the 1920's; writers had given a distorted view of American life, mocking what was pardonable in it, ignoring what was admirable. When they dismissed H. G. Wells as a "Fabian schoolma'arm," spoke condescendingly of John Dewey, and welcomed the dismal historical metaphors of Spengler, they were committed to a grievous violation of literary proprieties—a violation that could lead only to the fascism of Ezra Pound and the solemnly obedient acceptance and defense of his unhappy views.

Such a judgment of the 1920's was a complex of both leftist and liberal views; the "Marxist" condemnation, relieved of its economic emphasis, became wholly moral and wholly traditional. Perhaps we could no longer claim that the writers of the twenties were responsible for the collapse of the American economy, but we could accuse them of having failed to provide a sufficient moral "readiness" for World War II; and we could also say that they gave us no clue to the awful responsibilities of the "atomic age."

Invariably these attacks upon the decade were the product of one form or another of moral disposition and prejudice. Fitzgerald's Charlie Wales recognized only the difficulties of atonement for serious human errors; Mike Gold described the "hollow men" (1941) as guilty entirely on the grounds of their indifference to the "right" issues or the right interpretation of them; Brooks, having earlier condemned the American past for its failure to meet his moral demands, in the late 1930's and the 1940's condemned those who had thus renounced the past; DeVoto accused writers of having committed the unpardonable sin of attending to their writing, to the neglect of certain subject matters that he thought indispensable to a proper understanding of our tradition; MacLeish called his own fellow writers of the 1920's irresponsibles for similar reasons. These critics, in their emphasis on what they thought was primarily important, in their insistence upon *their* reading of human nature and of its relationship to literature, almost invariably shared the special moral dispositions of their age.

In his lectures at Indiana University (*The Literary Fallacy*, 1944), De Voto passed many remarkable judgments upon the literature of the twenties. The principal accusation was contained in the phrase "the literary fallacy"; that is, the notion that evaluations of American life "as a whole" can be seen and realized exclusively in literary terms. Most of the writers whom DeVoto condemned "begin with the study of literature; most of them employ literary data exclusively. Practically all of them who extend their inquiry beyond literary data extend it by means of primarily literary ideas." This would not be a serious error, were it not that they also speak of such matters as "culture" and "civilization." But they do not know what these terms mean; they have confined their interests to form, to a narrow reading of human and cultural matters, and they have not studied the "things that matter." As a result they commit the error of assuming that what they have found within the range of their limited interests is generally or exclusively true. This is why we need not, or should not, take them seriously; their literature lacks a "basic acknowledgment of the dignity of man. That is why it is a trivial literature—why the Waste Land of Mr. Eliot and the solutrean swamp of Mr. Hemingway are less than tragedy, smaller than tragedy."

None of these critics showed respect for the values of literature, only a persistent attempt to command and direct the perceptions of literary artists in terms of an "extra-literary" set of moral imperatives. This was in part due to the "emergency" in which much of this criticism was written; during World War II almost nothing mattered but a "literature of crisis," a literature that reaffirmed what Brooks called "primary" values; and they found little or none of this "primary" literature in the 1920's. Having discovered that the writers of the 1920's were "indifferent" to the causes that led to World War II, they accused them of being irresponsible: that is, of having neglected their roles as spokesmen of a culture and thus having encouraged the public to remain indifferent and irresponsible.

All these critics were able to cite texts. The flapper of Fitzgerald's novels and stories, for example, repeated endlessly and apparently without variation her gestures of tired sophistication. " 'You see I think everything's terrible anyhow.' " Daisy Buchanan says in *The Great Gatsby*, "in a convinced way. 'Everybody thinks so—the most advanced people. And I *know*. I've been everywhere and seen everything and done everything.' " Through Fitzgerald and his imitators, every place seemed to take on the character of an undergraduate campus, and every person either to be living on one or in the memory of his having lived there.

Another text might be found in the pose of bright cynicism affected by Ben Hecht's newspaperman, Erik Dorn. The business of bootlegging, in which fortunes were quickly made by evading the law, was a background of *The Great Gatsby* and Dos Passos' *Manhattan Transfer*. Daisy's "advanced people" also wrote and published gloomy estimates of the melancholy results of World War I for a nation that had won it. Americans were better out of the "international gamble," which had been so patently exposed by the war (Dos Passos' *One Man's Initiation* and *Three Soldiers*; Hemingway's *A Farewell to Arms*). It was best to make "a separate peace"; desertion from public affairs was the only means of salvaging private dignity (*Three Soldiers, A Farewell to Arms, In Our Time*). Since the war had proved that the men in charge could not command respect, one was left with a problem of personal adjustment, deprived of past securities (*The Sun Also Rises*).

But no real tragic insight into the nature of man was possible in a time when the war had destroyed certain necessary illusions and the march of science had served to reduce all remaining ones. Beginning with Harold Stearns' *America and the Young Intellectual* (1921) and ending with Joseph Wood Krutch's *The Modern Temper* (1929), the decade offered one "proof" after another of moral and social incapacity. Both the village and the small city were riddled by prejudice, stupidity, callousness (Sinclair Lewis's *Main Street* and *Babbitt;* Carl Van Vechten's *The Tattooed Countess*). The clergy were transparently ridiculous and ungodly (Lewis's *Elmer Gantry*; Mencken's "Americana"). Political morality and intelligence had never reached so low a level, at least not since Mark Twain's Gilded Age (Lewis's *The Man Who Knew Coolidge*; weekly editorials in the *Nation,* the *New Republic;* Walter Lippmann in *Vanity Fair*). Numerous suggestions were offered for easy solutions of the human distress. Doctor Coué performed his "miracles" on one level of human response with as much effectiveness as Doctor Freud did on another. Edith Wharton's Mrs. Manford (*Twilight Sleep*) enjoyed an almost daily change of cult and "vision"; and the middle-aged ladies of Lewis's Zenith vied with Helen Hokinson's suburbanites in their search for the very latest word from the decade's multiple heaven.

The new social symbolism included many strangely acute designations of the period of adjustment: what Malcolm Cowley described as "significant gesture" became in the eyes of Hemingway's Count Mippipopolous the "values" of the good life, for his Nick Adams the right restraint in the use of the senses, for Jake Barnes the "pure line" of the matador artist. Fitzgerald's brooding ex-Yale man, Tom Buchanan, nibbled "at the edge of stale ideas" and invoked white supremacy as a means of explaining his own boredom and tension. His more sensitive and pathetic Abe North had "a code": he was against the burning of witches. The more articulate of the expatriates believed their social behavior to be closely associated with art, even when it was concerned entirely with the destruction of art. Dada was significantly concerned with destruction—the most vulgar gesture might be the most significant or the most effective. The aim was to invert the scale of decorum, to exalt vulgarity and explode convention. Mr. Babbitt was found daily in a thousand pieces in Montparnasse and Greenwich Village.

2. "SPIRITS GROWN ELIOTIC"

Of the general images the literature of the decade impressed upon us, two are especially vivid as "classical" reminders of the time: the "pathos of the adolescent" and the "unregenerate bohemian." For the first there is the evidence of many occasions. It is contained usually in a gesture, the very vagueness of which served to thrill its readers. Undoubtedly the great early success of Fitzgerald's *This Side of Paradise* was due to its appeals to the mind of the younger generation. Its most popular gesture comes in the last two pages: Amory Blaine speaks up for the new generation, endowing it with the privileges of its immaturity. This new generation, "grown up to find all Gods dead, all wars fought, all faiths in man shaken," was to be more brilliantly and more fully characterized in other texts; but no other work was able to endow it with quite the glamour of lonely defiance to be found in the novel's last lines:

> He stretched out his arms to the crystalline, radiant sky. "I know my-self," he cried, "but that is all."

Again, at the beginning of the decade, the moment of adolescent awareness was shown in Sherwood Anderson's *Winesburg, Ohio,* whose George Willard experiences for the first time "the sadness of sophistication":

> With a little gasp he sees himself as merely a leaf blown by the wind through the streets of his village. He knows that in spite of all the stout talk of his fellows he must live and die in uncertainty, a thing blown by the winds, a thing destined like corn to wilt in the sun.

This shock of realization is like a birth into a new world. Cynicism has not set in, nor has a philosophy grown. The protections accorded normal experience are removed, and the young man is forced into a world he can never really understand. This insistence upon the youth of the generation, upon its perilous freedom, proved a strong incentive to those who could claim to belong to the generation; it made those who didn't qualify wish to belong as well. In its many variations, it sounded a note of individual rebellion, of a determination to work outside conventional securities: Hemingway's Nick Adams makes a "separate peace"; Dos Passos' John Andrews calmly accepts the penalties of desertion; Floyd Dell's heroes and heroines run the gamut, from Iowa to Chicago to Greenwich Village; and Lieutenant Henry speaks for them all:

> That was what you did. You died. You did not know what it was
> about. You never had time to learn. They threw you in and told you
> the rules and the first time they caught you off base they killed you.

The range of experience varies, the definition achieves different shades and degrees of meaning. But the prevailing impression is that of the very young, frightened and puzzled and defeated at the start, but determined to formulate a code that both justifies and utilizes that defeat. This was part of the tone of the 1920's: a rhetorical quality quite different from the gestures made by Frank Norris's trapped superman or Theodore Dreiser's Hurstwood. It was a pathos realized too early, with neither the setting nor the incentive to give it the quality usually associated with "tragedy."

As for the attitude of the "unregenerate bohemian," it was even more roundly condemned by those who later criticized the decade, because it apparently ignored altogether what was usually recognized as "social experience." Far from being depressed by the period of his birth, the bohemian preferred to ignore it, except in satirical acknowledgment of its absurdity. The individual became an uncompromising anarchist, a radical of a kind that has almost vanished from the American scene since 1930. There were two variations of this attitude: one assumed that the aesthetic and the social conscience were the same; the other assumed there was no such thing as a social conscience, that there was no history but only persons. It was natural enough that this latter view should condemn the type of middle-class person Cummings had scornfully called the "official." Upton Sinclair proved to be the sole active survivor of progressive liberalism in the twenties, and Cummings was almost alone in his active sponsorship of aesthetic radicalism in the thirties. To affirm the value of the non-social personality was a difficult and unpopular task after 1929; even Maxwell Bodenheim marched in proletarian parades up Fifth Avenue in the thirties. But the basic point of view stated and dramatized in *The Enormous Room* was never altered thereafter by Cummings, except in details and kinds of reference.

Throughout the twenties writers shifted their ground uncomfortably with respect to the question of their debt to society. Of this maneuvering we have abundant evidence in Joseph Freeman's *An American Testament* and in the early history of the *New Masses*. But the position taken by Cummings is a partial sign of what in the decade was thought to be a most important privilege: that of aesthetic self-determination. From this point of view, most attacks were launched, trivial or profound or both, upon the restrictions and conventions of the world. The aesthetic radical retained a free and independent mind, refusing to permit any interference with his freedom. He was flattered to think that his views might be explained "scientifically," but he rejected without qualification the basic requirements of a scientific method. More often than not the "unregenerate bohemian" rejected philosophy as such altogether, thought himself possessed of finer instincts than the "prurient philosophers" of Cummings' poem.

The unregenerate bohemian was an extreme form of what has been an important contribution to modern culture: the emphasis, the *insistence,* upon the value of personal vision. The 1920's were one of a very few times when one could be respected for having a private view of public affairs. This private view applied not only to actual headline copy but to systems of philosophical thought, to scientific discoveries, to investigations of the nature of man and his world, and to theories of the writing and value of literature.

Much of the activity thus sponsored was of course reckless and irresponsible in its neglect of logic and in its sporadic enthusiasms. Nevertheless the literary activity of the decade stressed the very defensible assumption that the artist's sensibility is a legitimate means of gaining insight and knowledge that are indispensable to our total view of a culture. Since the artists of the decade realized the importance of their gift, they gave a special quality of insight into facts often unchallenged or misunderstood by others. For one thing, they pointed, not to the gifts of science, but to its dangers. They risked being called frivolous and ignorant, so that they might point out that science was not wholly good, that material progress may even be quite harmful, that an entirely satisfactory religious experience was all but impossible in a world that had "educated" itself beyond the need of it.

Perhaps their strongest (at any rate their loudest) activity consisted of their documentation of human absurdities. This criticism of the modern world, in spite of its frequent triviality, was both a profound and a necessary contribution to the knowledge we must have of our society. We realize now that for the most part it was correct and shrewd. Its value can be seen in several ways. One is its treatment of history, the act of taking the straight line of liberal prophecy and twisting it—rejecting the linear view of H. G. Wells for the cyclical view of Spengler. Another is the valuable distinction often drawn between scientific data and aesthetic—which suggested that mere science omitted much from what Ransom called "the world's body," and warned that a too narrow concern with abstract principle is almost as bad for life as it is for art. Again, this generation of critics described what they called a loss of taste in contemporary life. Vulgarity was clearly defined as a frantic and amoral desire to accumulate and to own goods; further, as the feeling that taste might be bought and did not need to be a responsible part of experience as a whole. The absurdities of the bourgeois mind and soul, the deformities of its architecture and its conscience, were never so fully documented. Perhaps the most valuable criticisms of the decade, and the most profound, were those which made it clear that defections of taste were not merely surface phenomena but betrayed an underlying inadequacy in our tradition and our culture.

These criticisms could not, after all, have remained effective had they pointed merely to superficial issues. The 1920's could make no more important contribution than is contained in their most jealously guarded thesis: that history and society are and remain abstractions until they are associated with personal experience. As Arthur Mizener has said (*Kenyon Review*, Winter 1950):

> . . . the situation, the moment in history, is not in itself tragic; it only provides the occasion on which the aware individual suffers the experience of unavoidable moral choices. No matter what the occasion, there is no tragedy where the forces of circumstance are not transmuted into personal experience.

If the twenties in America can be condemned seriously for a fault it is not for their vulgarity (there is vulgarity of some sort in any time) or for their immorality (immorality in any period is ordinarily a characteristic of the move toward moral redefinition). The greatest fault was their naïveté. Men and women were often quite literally and self-avowedly ignorant of tradition. They had chosen to be; they had rejected both sound and unsound generalities and thought. As a result they were open to every new influence that came along; in most cases there was no intellectual experience to use as a measure of validity. That is undoubtedly the reason so much of the discussion of ideas in the decade seemed the talk of an undergraduate newly and overly impressed by his introductory course in philosophy.

Perhaps the young men and women of the 1950's are immensely more sophisticated, learned, and disingenuous. The theories of Freud have been greatly extended, and the attitude toward them lacks the naïve enthusiasm of an earlier generation. The French masters of literature are now not only thoroughly known; they are being revaluated and their influence upon a handful of American poets now seems a part of ancient literary history. The mood in which bulletins from Moscow were received in the offices of the *Liberator* now seems incredibly naïve. Marxism has not only undergone numerous shifts in interpretation; there have been great changes of heart regarding the "crusade that failed." It is no longer possible to imagine (one no longer has the naïve expectancy to await) a doctrine's role in saving the world. The new generation is much wiser, much less likely to be taken in— one may say, less *capable* of being taken in. But in a very real sense the assertions so often made in the twenties now seem more sensible than they did in their own time. Certainly in our own postwar world we now are convinced (and not especially shocked to find) that evil actually does exist. We are aware of the peculiar failures of scientific research and suspicious of its direct application to human affairs.

It is perhaps unfortunate that we know so much and are so helpless at the same time. In looking back upon the 1920's perhaps we ought not to be worried about the "party we cannot afford to throw again," but rather about our loss of confidence in free, if erratic, inquiry, which we seem to have abandoned along with our naïveté. Our knowledge seems to lack the strength of will that accompanied the ignorance and the errantry of the 1920's. We become more sophisticated and more inflexible with each passing year. We are competent scholars, writers, thinkers, voters; we are properly shocked when one of our fellows commits an especially noticeable error against good taste and good manners. Why, then, are we restless, uncertain, and unhappy? Why is our literature not first-rate? Why are the majority of our critical essays written about the literature of the 1920's and not about that of our own time? Something must be true of that decade that has nothing to do with the big party they were supposed to have had. Perhaps they were more sane, less frivolous, than we have been led to believe.

The most intelligent and the most sensible attitude we can have toward the 1920's, as well as toward our own time, is to accept the saving grace of an irony directed at both. They are, both of them, times of war and of the effects of war. In neither time is it possible unqualifiedly to admire or simply to repudiate man's responsibility for what has happened. That irony is expressed with an especial relevance in Allen Tate's "Ode to Our Young Pro-Consuls of the Air" (1943)*. . . . The times, the poet says, have once more come round to war; and each citizen is again called upon "to take/His modest stake." We have responded to the call with full patriotism and with angry mechanical force. Once again humanity is simply divided into friend and foe; the enemy is "The puny Japanese" and "the German toad." Observing these demonstrations of moral and military might, the poet reflects upon what he had done (or might have done) to prevent these "enemies of mind" from resuming their quarrel.

There follows an ironic survey of the attacks upon the irresponsibles. The poet tries to recall past wars to present memory: the "Toy sword, three-cornered hat" of "York and Lexington"; the "Toy rifle, leather hat/Above the boyish beard" of the Civil War; then the "disorder" of Versailles, when

> Proud Wilson yielded ground
> To franc and pound,
> Made pilgrimage
> In the wake of Henry James

and its aftermath, when France "Opened the gate/To Hitler—at Compiègne." "In this bad time" the poet had no role, nor took any responsibility:

---

* Reprinted with the permission of Charles Scribner's Sons from *The Winter Sea* by Allen Tate, copyright 1945, by Allen Tate; and with the permission of Eyre & Spottiswoode (Publishers) Ltd. from *Poems 1920–1945*, by Allen Tate.

> He studied Swift and Donne,
> Ignored the Hun,
> While with faint heart
> Proust caused the fall of France.

Literature thus irresponsibly caused, or permitted, the disaster to happen. Yet, when our fortunes were most desperate, the critics rushed to the rescue of a faltering republic:

> Yet all that feeble time
> Brave Brooks and lithe MacLeish
> Had sworn to thresh
> Our flagging spirit
> With literature made Prime!

And, in response, our culture has revived, sprung to the defense of American ideals:

> Nursing the blague that dulls
> Spirits grown Eliotic,
> Now patriotic
> Are: we follow
> *The Irresponsibles!*

This is the spectacle of a nation aroused from its "Eliotic" sloth, cured of "the blague that dulls," transformed almost as if overnight by the magic of the "responsible word" from "Spirits grown Eliotic" to efficient and confirmed patriots. The poet ironically salutes the young men who have gone off to "win the world" on such short notice and after such a treacherous, defeatist past: with "zeal pro-consular," these "partisans/Of liberty unfurled!" will (once reminded of their duty) resume the task of civilizing the world.

The "Odè" concludes with a vision of the "saviors," the young men who have (because of "Brave Brooks and lithe MacLeish") thrown aside their indifference and resumed the traditional role, with the aid of "literature made Prime." The planes in which they travel on their liberating missions impress the poet with their "animal excellence," and he bids them success in finding their targets:

> Swear you to keep
> Faith with imperial eye:
>
> .   .   .
>
> Upon the Tibetan plain
> A limping caravan,
>   Dive, and exterminate
>   The Lama, late
> Survival of old pain.
> Go kill the dying swan.

The full, rich irony of this message to the "Young Pro-Consuls" comes simply from a shrewd penetration of certain falsely moral readings of American culture: first, that there is necessarily a direct relationship between literature and public life; second, that the moral responsibility for a present emergency can quickly and easily be ascribed to a literature that had not anticipated or prepared for the crisis; further, that the crisis can be met by searching for a "literature made Prime," by ignoring the totality of a culture and selecting only that part of it that is suitable to the occasion; finally, that the instruments of a war, which are the consequences of a total history and not just servants of an "ideal," can be used to return the world to sanity and rescue it from "the puny Japanese" and "the German toad."

The irony is addressed primarily to those who accused the writers of the 1920's of "the literary fallacy"—the critics who have been guilty of a larger "moral fallacy." For, as the poem suggests, literature is not maneuverable; a culture cannot be one thing at one time and its opposite immediately thereafter. An extreme neurosis of "social conscience" has led the judges of the 1920's into a trap of false criticism; it has assumed that the literature produced in the decade was cynically or irresponsibly (and thus dishonestly) engaged in corrupting an entire nation. These judgments suffer from a serious loss of perspective. The critics who made them have chosen to make what they need (what they will) out of the 1920's. They have insisted that literature should serve a moral objective of an extraordinarily narrow and limited kind. Since it has not seemed to do so, they have condemned it for not meeting their terms. This is not the way to a just or accurate estimate; it is a victim of its own narrowness of vision, and it cannot or should not endure beyond the limits of its occasion.

3. THE USES OF INNOCENCE

The positive values of the 1920's may perhaps best be suggested in the phrase "useful innocence." In the decade two generations collaborated in an exhaustive review of America's past greatness and present status. The one, the "old generation," contemporary with the Old Gang, surveyed the weaknesses of a tradition that had culminated in a war and an uneasy peace. The other generation, young in 1920 but old enough to have attended or participated in the ceremonies of 1914–1918, assumed the task of renewing that culture, of making it over according to new principles and what seemed newly acquired insights into human nature.

Of necessity, many of the writings of the decade were either important variants of old forms or new and original forms. No one can overemphasize the value of formal experiment in the 1920's. DeVoto and Brooks have complained about "moral failure" and the "literary fallacy." The truth is that the writers of the 1920's, finding a world that seemed cut free of the past, had to invent new combinations of spirit and matter and new forms of expressing the human drama. They were not aided by any secure ordering of social or religious systems. They were novelists of manners in a society distrustful of past definitions, poets of formalized insight into moral chaos. Their restless desire for the new was always motivated by their distrust of the old. *Form,* then, was a major concern, a major necessity. The careers of all important writers who began publishing in the decade are marked by a restless concern with literary form. Since the forms of the past had been generally associated with a tradition now abhorred, the new forms had perforce to be different, newly inspired, and newly seen.

When Gertrude Stein lectured on method, when Ezra Pound fulminated against softness and weakness of speech, they were speaking for a formal revolution that was also a moral revolution. The concern with form was basically a concern over the need to provide an aesthetic order for moral revisions. It is true that the best of our writers were preoccupied with literature; they were "whole men" in the genuine sense of being profoundly concerned with the moral value of literary form. Essential to the enlightenment the decade gave us was that sense of the significance of the aesthetic, of its essential nature. Such a preoccupation appears on the surface to be morally irresponsible; actually it is truly moral in the sense of its earnest desire to communicate the variants of the modern condition.

The great strength of the decade lay in its useful and deliberate innocence. Ideas habitually lose their vitality as the employment of them alters or is too closely aligned with social expediency. Naïve, innocent demonstrations of wrath over smugness, indolence, or hypocrisy are outward expressions of moral revision. The language communicates these ideas; when they descend from the level of genuine moral judgment to that of comfortable journalism, the language and the forms must be changed. The writers of the 1920's, concentrating on literary form, went about the business of morally redefining the function of the language and its association with present realities. To begin with the "new"—which is to say, the raw, unformed, unsupported, and unexplained present literary condition—is to begin innocently afresh, to explore "the thing seen" in terms of the "way it is seen."

Having rejected all precedents, the writers of the 1920's themselves became precedents for the literature of future decades. But it was in their literary, their aesthetic, successes that future writers saw merit. The narrator of Budd Schulberg's *The Disenchanted* (1950) wishes that he could accept the brilliant literary successes of Halliday and ignore the *man* who had achieved them. This narrator is a *naïf* of another decade, unable to see the tragic artist whole or judge him from any point of view other than the documentary morality of the 1930's. It is almost beyond the capacity of those who look at the 1920's, however carefully, to understand the close rapport between literary concentration and moral insight. The writers of the 1920's—or many of them——had both to *see* a world as it frankly was and to *re-establish* that world in their literary formulations. The very matter of Fitzgerald's moral extravagances (which are the substance of Halliday's past) is incorporated into his art; however imperfectly, that art formalized what would otherwise have been merely a series of sensational and superficial dissipations. The writers of the 1920's believed in everything, those of the 1930's in only one thing, those of the 1940's in nothing. The second and third groups borrowed from the first the means of formulating their one thing and their nothing. This fact startlingly, enduringly remains: the 1920's were an opportunity and a challenge offered to a group of persons who were freshly and naïvely talented, anxious to learn *how* to restate and redramatize the human condition, morally preoccupied with the basic problem of communicating their insights into their present world.

But the weight of tradition is always heavy upon the individual talent. The important truth of the decade is not that its artists rejected the past but that they looked at the past from an orientation psychologically different from that of previous decades. They did not borrow from tradition so much as they forced tradition to give to them precisely what they needed from it. They refused to accept without question the formal systems of judging and dramatizing the moral values of the human race, preferred to select what they would, and on their own terms, from what the past had to offer. As a result the literary history of the decade, like its moral history, is a mélange of contrivance, experiment, and revolt.

Invariably didactic precedent interferes with a genuine moral appraisal of such a time and such a phenomenon. The literary heroes of the time assist in perpetuating the confusion: they recant, they are "converted," they rebel against their rebellion, they grow old and do not dare to face impeachment. They cannot see, or do not wish to see, that what they did and were at one time was of the utmost importance for the state of their own health and of that of society at large.

This fact, that they do not now wish to see and that no one cares truly to see for them, remains of all the important positive legacies of the decade: the fact of useful innocence. They were truly, recklessly, innocently, rawly, tenaciously naïve. The emperor had worn no clothes after all. The world had not been saved. The health of society was not after all good. The Bridge did not lead us to Cathay. They therefore made—formally, aesthetically, and morally—what they could of the thing that they had seen. They often crossed the Atlantic in an attempt to see it from another perspective, to disengage themselves from its immediate nature only to see it more closely. They went to masters of French poetry, of seventeenth-century British drama, of nineteenth-century German philosophy and psychology, and took from them what "influences" they needed. But the best of them were from the beginning, and remained, endowed with talent, with reserves of irony, satire, and intelligent respect for the "right word." The best of them preserved in their work the exact *rapprochement* of experience with the act of experiencing, of action with the moral comedy of man acting.

When, as almost always, men complain of the 1920's that there was no steady adherence to the morally proper, they are narrowly right but fundamentally wrong. This was no time for Edith Wharton, as she admitted; in a genuine sense the opportunity for a formalized comedy of social manners had passed, and with it the opportunity to employ a fixed, traditional mode of moral examination. François Mauriac once said that if one were asked what is the most genuinely real human experience of personal agony, he would have to answer that it is the time immediately preceding his death, when the full weight of tradition and personal past bears upon an uncertain future, immediately foreseen. The moment of one's death is of such primary importance that the history of an entire culture can be relevant to it. This crisis in human experience requires all moral strength to meet it. But no one has sufficiently explored the role that form plays at such a time. The "comforts" that a culture offers then are either extremely reassuring or vaguely disturbing. When, as occurs so often in the literature of the 1920's, men say that "it does not mean anything to die," they would like to suggest that the agony of death is not attended by the solaces of a public moral security. It is indispensable to the health of any culture that this security be constantly examined, naïvely questioned, explosively rejected, and finally re-established and re-formed.

The "best of them" who did not die in 1914–1918, who came back to "frankness as never before," were possessed of a useful innocence in their approach to the world that was left them. They explored the corridors of history, inspected the meaning of a religion temporarily discredited; they formulated in several brilliant ways the most important of all symbolic figurations of our century—that of isolation, of the single, dispossessed soul whose life needs to be re-established in terms specifically new and unencumbered. They did not always succeed in defining this symbol, for themselves or for others. Many of their works suffered from intellectual colloquialism—which, like all other forms of colloquialism, loses its value as it loses its fresh relevance. But the great contributions to our ways of speaking about our ways of feeling have—in a manner still and always valuable—preoccupied themselves with the proper answers to the question Eliot's Gerontion put to himself at the beginning of the decade: "After such knowledge, what forgiveness?" After such experiences, what forms remain of meeting, defining, and sensibly tolerating the human condition?

XIII

*The New Deal and
the American Reform Tradition:
How New Was the New Deal?*

INTRODUCTION

There seems little question that a greater amount of significant reform legislation was enacted during the years of the New Deal (1933–1938) than during any other five-year period of American history. Indeed, it may very well be that more significant social and economic legislation was placed on the federal statute books during the New Deal era than during the entire history of the United States prior to 1933. What has intrigued historians, however, has not been the sheer bulk of this legislation but rather whether the reforms of the New Deal were consonant with the American tradition of reform or departed from that tradition.

Eric Goldman and Richard Hofstadter, authors of two of the most provocative books written on the subject of modern American reform, have taken opposite positions on this question. In his brilliantly written Rendez-vous with Destiny, *Professor Goldman relates the principal reforms of the New Deal to the New Freedom of Woodrow Wilson, the New Nationalism of Theodore Roosevelt, and the so-called "Associational Activities" of the 1920's. Although he notes that not all New Deal legislation can be neatly fitted into this framework, he nevertheless regards the statutes of the New Deal as basically within the confines of the reform tradition.*

Although Professor Hofstadter concedes in his Pulitzer-Prize winning Age of Reform *that "absolute discontinuities do not occur in history," what seems to him noteworthy about the New Deal is "the drastic new departure that it marks in the history of American reformism." He finds the New Deal different from Progressivism in the basic problems with which it attempted to deal and "in its ideas and its spirit and its techniques."*

The New Deal and Its Antecedents

Eric F. Goldman

SECOND HONEYMOON

The day after the Inaugural the new President proclaimed a four-day bank holiday, summoned Congress into special session, and started day-and-night White House conferences on emergency banking legislation. The bill was ready seventy-two hours later. The House of Representatives debated it thirty-eight minutes. The Senate debated it three hours. That night the President signed it. The Hundred Days were under way, the most controlled, directed, overpowered period in all the history of Congress.

Many of the bills whisked through Congress bespoke the central idea common to both principal reform traditions, the New Freedom and the New Nationalism—the belief that the best solution for economic and social ills was action by the federal government under strong executive leadership. The powerful leadership of Franklin Roosevelt set up federal protections for bank depositors and for all investors in stocks. Federal credit eased the burden of debt on farmers and householders, and federal guidance reorganized the railroads. A variety of federal devices made phony bankruptcy proceedings more difficult, imposed excess-profit and dividend taxes, created the Civilian Conservation Corps for the youthful unemployed, and raised prices by taking the country off the haloed gold standard. "Liberal" measures, the country called them, and quite clearly liberalism had come to mean not the Mencken-type emphasis of the Twenties but a full-blown revival of economic and social reformism. Talk of liberty in reform circles now was likely to produce a yawn, if not a scowl; opportunity, at least opportunity for the millions to have jobs, was the point.

The New Deal handling of the desperate unemployment problem produced the most sweeping reaffirmation of general progressive doctrine. For three years Herbert Hoover and the conservative press had been arguing that the use of large-scale federal funds for unemployment relief would bring about a dangerous political centralization, tear down the character of the recipients, and violate the economic law that the national debt cannot go beyond a fixed point without bankrupting the government. To these arguments, liberals of a dozen schools of thought made substantially one set of replies. Unemployment on its 1933 scale was too big a problem for the states and cities; environment shaped human character, and federal relief funds, by helping to remove squalor, would build character rather than injure it. The conservative appeal to economic laws was met by a barrage of Reform Darwinism,* even by a fresh Reform Darwinian formulation of economics. Well before the depression began, a number of economists had been developing theories which brushed aside the alleged economic law standing in the way of large-scale public spending. During the Thirties the long-time leader in world reform thinking, John Maynard Keynes, was rapidly developing these ideas into a persuasive system. The supposed economic law, Keynes argued in the authentic manner of Reform Darwinism, was simply the rationalization of upper-income groups who did not want to pay heavy taxes. There was nothing dangerous about running up a government debt. On the contrary, when private expenditures of money fell off, a sensible government would start "compensatory spending."

Franklin Roosevelt, together with a large segment of the liberal movement, distrusted the Keynes-type argument in the early New Deal days. At heart they hankered for a balanced budget. Yet the idea of large-scale federal spending on relief, with its implied contempt for rigid economics, its assignment of a key role to the national government, and its promise of quick alleviation of human distress, was a natural for the President and his following. Amid the roar of the Hundred Days, Congress passed a half-billion-dollar relief bill, and the President gave the administration of the money to a *de facto* Keynesian whose economics consisted largely of an urge "to feed the hungry, and Goddamn fast."

Harry Hopkins had always been in a hurry. He was already in a hurry when his father, a convivial jack-of-all-trades, finally settled the family in Grinnell, Iowa, and the homely youngster hustled his way to the title of "Big Man of the Class" at Grinnell College. On graduation, Hopkins almost took a job on a Montana newspaper; he almost did a dozen things; and somewhere in the middle of it all, a professor urged him to sign up as counselor in a boys' camp in New Jersey. A charitable boys' camp sat well with the son of a pious Methodist mother, who had bundled her five children off to church every Sunday and made them repeat the minister's points afterward. A boys' camp sponsored by influential people and near New York City had special attractions for the ne'er-do-well's son who was determined to find a place for himself in the exciting world of power. The professor did not have to urge long.

---

* Editor's note: Reform Darwinism, as Goldman defines it, was the faith of thoroughgoing evolutionists who believed that institutions "could and should change rapidly." They stressed the importance of environment and believed in man's ability to manipulate the environment in order to bring about a "better world."

Nor did Hopkins remain long in the camp organization. Quickly he was off to a series of successes in the social-work profession. By 1933 Hopkins had attained the number-one social worker's position in the nation, director of emergency relief in New York State, and a striking if somewhat mixed reputation. Associates knew him as a man who thought more swiftly than anyone working for, with, or against him, a first-class administrator with a habit of cutting through red tape like so much confetti, a wraith of quick cigarettes, frayed suits, curt sarcasms, and a highly developed ability to confuse advancing mankind with advancing Harry Hopkins.

Transferred to Washington to direct the New Deal relief program, Hopkins sat down at his desk before the workmen had moved it out of the hallway and in two hours spent more than five million dollars. During the ensuing months Hopkins's shabby little office in the old Walker-Johnson Building, with the faded paint and the water pipes up and down the walls, became the most swift-acting agency in all frenzied Washington. When somebody brought in a plan that "will work out in the long run," Hopkins snapped: "People don't eat in the long run—they eat every day." When inspectors from the Budget Bureau came around to see the "organizational chart," they heard that Hopkins had ordered: "I don't want anybody around here to waste any time drawing boxes. You'll always find that the person who drew the chart has his own name in the middle box." Out of the fury came striking new practices of unemployment relief, a devil for conservatives to flay, and an application of liberal doctrine so personal that its effects sank deep into the national mind.

The level-headed businessman, Frank Walker, discovered just how personal the application was when Roosevelt sent him on a tour to inspect the workings of the relief program. In his home state of Montana, Walker found former businessmen laying sewer pipes in their old business clothes because they had no money to buy overalls. And one of the ditch-diggers spoke for millions when he told Walker: "I hate to think what would have happened if this work hadn't come. . . . I'd sold or hocked everything I could. And my kids were hungry. I stood in front of the window of the bake-shop down the street and wondered just how long it would be before I got desperate enough to pick up a rock and heave it through that window and grab some bread to take home."

In the White House the lights burned late six or seven nights a week. Wearing out assistants by his energies, amazing intimates by his ability to toss off worries, Roosevelt kept prodding, brain-picking, quipping, politicking the Hundred Days ahead. Federal relief would alleviate distress; it could hardly cure a depression.

There was no lack of advice on the cure. The president of the Chamber of Commerce, a charwoman from Butte, the head of the AFL, Harvard classmates of Roosevelt, the third vice-president of Kiwanis, and some five thousand other people all brought or sent the President sure-fire remedies. Immediately around the President was the group of brilliant and contentious minds that the country had been calling the Brain Trust since the campaign of 1932. Yet amid all the babble, the proposals from informed and responsible people revealed a striking fact. Many business leaders and labor officials, Farm Bureau men and liberals, Brain-Trusters and Kiwanians, agreed on certain fundamentals of a recovery program.

Some concurrence from supposed ideological opposites was not surprising. Although the New Nationalism and the Associational Activities* outlook had important differences, they agreed on encouraging the formation of large economic units and on an important role for government in economic life. The depression of 1929, by presenting free enterprise in its most chaotic and inhumane form, brought an onrush of converts to the general idea of national planning of national economic units. New Freedomite reformers, who had so long battled any program that accepted the concentration of industry, now forgot their old battle in their concern with getting government controls over the existing situation. Businessmen who had railed at any system restricting their independence besought the government to tell them how to avoid bankruptcy. As the banks closed and the abyss seemed near in March 1933, free enterprise virtually abdicated. "There was hardly an industrial, economic, financial, commercial, reform, or agricultural leader who did not advance some idea of governmental intervention," the Washington insider Hugh Johnson has recalled. "A snowfall of paper plans drifted about the Capitol, and there was not one of them that would not, in some measure, have modified the Anti-Trust Acts."

The merger of Associational Activities ideas and New Nationalist thinking in a demand for national planning was plain in the Brain Trust. Raymond Moley, chief of the group, perfectly represented the coalescence in his own amiable, hardheaded self. As a boy in Berea, Ohio, Moley wept at the 1896 defeat of William Jennings Bryan, and as a young man he made a hero of Tom Johnson. Then, while the trust-busters kept on thundering and the trusts kept on growing, Moley began to wonder whether moralistic anti-big-business agitation was not trying to change the tides of economic development. As a professor of political science, first in the Midwest and then at Columbia, Moley sought solutions of the nation's ills that assumed the necessity of a battle against "ignorance" rather than against "sin." The nature of the proper enlightenment was not always clear. But the Moley who became important in the Roosevelt circle was a man who talked easily with people of an Associational Activities persuasion and who cited approvingly the Crolyite book that Theodore Roosevelt had quoted to the Bull Moose convention, Van Hise's *Concentration and Control*. The essential,

---

* Editor's note: The phrase is used by Goldman to connote the view of Herbert Hoover and others that government should assist the formation and activities of trade associations.

Moley was sure, was to end "the thoughtlessness and aimlessness" of free competition.

The merger of the New Nationalism and Associational Activities was no less striking in the relations of two important figures who gathered around Moley in the Brain Trust. No human beings could have seemed more different than Hugh Johnson and Rexford Tugwell. Johnson learned to spell to the whinnying of cavalry horses and the bawling of top sergeants at Fort Scott, Kansas, yelling to anyone who would listen to him: "Everybody in the world is a rink-stink but Hughie Johnson and he's all right!" Tugwell, the son of a prosperous farmer and cannery-owner in Sinclairville, New York, was raised to a genteel tradition of concern with community problems, almost to a Rooseveltian *noblesse oblige*. West Point remembered Johnson as the most talented hazer and the possessor of the biggest nose in the history of the school. The University of Pennsylvania recalled Tugwell as a handsome, smartly dressed ideologue, a gourmet with a special pride in his elaborate salads, who was given to practicing his sharp wit on bourgeois America and was more than likely to steer his date to a reform soirée. While Johnson was doing a hell-roaring border patrol along the Rio Grande, Tugwell was showing intimates a poem that included the lines:

> *I am sick of a Nation's stenches*
> *I am sick of propertied Czars. . . .*
> *I shall roll up my sleeves—make America over!*

The mature careers of the two men showed no more similarities. Johnson swashbuckled his way to a brigadier general's star, interrupting his military life only for tossing off children's books that were chock-full of carnage and last-minute touchdowns. Somewhere along the line, the Army discovered that its leathery-faced cavalryman, a perfect Captain Flagg in his tough talk and his sentimentality, also had a mind, a quick, perceptive instrument that expressed itself in curiously effective off-beat phrases. The Army sent Johnson to law school, then made him its principal representative on the War Industries Board of World War I. After the Armistice, Johnson resigned from the Army and entered business, first as an officer of the Moline Plow Company, later as one of the men who helped Bernard Baruch manage his web of interests. Still clattering across any room in a roar of Army attitudes, deeply involved with large-scale business, Johnson in 1933 seemed a caricature of the traditional reform type. Tugwell was close to being a typecase of the liberal professor. Settled at Columbia, he was entrancing classes by his iconoclasm and making a national reputation as a heretical agricultural economist. It was hardly surprising that at early Brain Trust sessions the relations between Tugwell and Johnson were a study in hostility, Tugwell holding Johnson off with witticisms, Johnson snapping and snarling at his debonair torturer.

Yet with the passage of a few months, Tugwell and Johnson were soon bending happily over the same charts and memoranda. Johnson had emerged from his service with the War Industries Board and his work with Baruch an ardent advocate of Associational Activities, though he added to Hoover's reliance on co-operation between government and economic units the belief that some degree of governmental compulsion should be used. Tugwell had emerged from his books and his indignation a highly involved economic thinker but fundamentally a New Nationalist. The line between Johnson's planning by partial co-operation and Tugwell's planning by overall compulsion was a wavering one, much too wavering not to be pushed aside by the impact of depression. The common denominator of their thinking in 1933, and of his own, was described by Moley when he wrote of the Brain Trust's "rejection of the traditional Wilson-Brandeis philosophy. . . . We believed that any attempt to atomize big business must destroy America's greatest contribution to a higher standard of living for the body of its citizenry—the development of mass production. . . . We recognized that competition, as such, was not inherently virtuous; that competition . . . created as many abuses as it prevented." So the Brain-Trusters, Moley summarized, turned "from the nostalgic philosophy of the 'trust busters,'" turned to national economic planning.

This was the kind of thinking swirling around the President during the Hundred Days, and it did not disturb him. In the period immediately preceding his election Roosevelt had begun to submerge the New Freedom element in his own thinking; he too could find little in trust-busting liberalism that seemed to apply to the emergency at hand. The real question for him, the real quarrel among his advisers, was not national planning versus free competition. The issue was: should the planning hew closer to the Associational Activities pattern, with its emphasis on noncompulsory relations between the government and economic life, or should it follow more the New Nationalist pattern of powerful federal controls?

Next to feeding the hungry, the most urgent problem was agriculture. Another good crop was on its way and, with farm prices already perilously low, another good crop could mean disaster.

Even during the campaign of 1932, while most of his program was still a cloud of generalities, Roosevelt edged toward a specific idea of national planning for agriculture. Shortly before the nominating convention, Tugwell began urging on Moley a plan that was the product of many minds but had been most actively propagandized by Professor Milburn L. Wilson, of the Montana State College. Wilson's proposal assumed that the American farmer could no longer depend on the foreign market. Instead of calling on the government to arrange dumping abroad, as the McNary-Haugen bill had done, Wilson argued that the government should plan crop-control at home by an elaborate procedure known as the "Domestic Allotment Plan." The Wilson program appealed to the planner in Moley; when Moley arranged a conference between Roosevelt and Tugwell, the plan appealed no less to the planner in Roosevelt. Roosevelt wanted to know more, and just as the convention was about to vote on the nomination, Tugwell wired Wilson to meet him in Chicago. The two men talked for a day in a hotel room; then Tugwell reported to Hyde Park on the long-distance phone. Roosevelt was sufficiently impressed to slip into his acceptance speech an endorsement of the basic Wilson principle that the federal government should make itself responsible for getting rid of farm surpluses without resorting to attempts at dumping abroad.

But just how was the responsibility to be fulfilled? Advocates of an Associational Activities tendency—most notably Hugh Johnson's friend George Peek—urged as little compulsion as possible. Peek argued long and ably that the chief mechanism for raising farm income should be a payment to the farmer for whatever money he lost by having to sell at a low price in foreign markets; only in years of superabundant yield should the actual size of his crop be curtailed, and then not until the crop was actually in growth. Professor Wilson, backed by a group including Tugwell, proposed crop curtailment, even in normal years and before planting, by offering attractive rentals to farmers on acreage taken out of production. The final legislation, the bill establishing the Agricultural Adjustment Administration, made the execution of either or both plans possible. But the Triple A plainly contained ample provisions to make it one of the boldest uses of national agricultural controls in the history of Western civilization.

The next week or so, the already famous Roosevelt smile was especially radiant. The President was busy with the final stages of a bill which, of all the New Deal legislation, was his labor of love. The idea of a Tennessee Valley Authority lit fires in a dozen cubicles of Roosevelt's mind. A TVA would provide a yardstick for power costs; it would mean a giant stride in conservation, an enthusiasm of Franklin no less than of Theodore Roosevelt; it would chain a capricious, destructive river to the development of one of the most depressed areas in the country.

Shortly before the bill went to Congress, its chief sponsor, Senator George Norris, came to dinner at the White House, and the two men, the Dutchess County patrician and the son of a Nebraska dirt farmer, sat talking enthusiastically over TVA's possibilities.

"What are you going to say when they ask you the political philosophy behind TVA?" Norris laughed.

"I'll tell them it's neither fish nor fowl," Roosevelt laughed back, "but, whatever it is, it will taste awfully good to the people of the Tennessee Valley."

Until midnight that evening the President squeezed dry his interlude, talking of forests and schoolhouses and the future, far away from the nagging present of hungry men and warring policies.

The next day the present returned with the jarring report that Congress was about to rush through a kind of industrial-recovery legislation which Roosevelt thoroughly disapproved. The President had not wanted to hurry industrial-recovery legislation. He felt that, though there was general agreement on the need for national planning, too much disagreement over key points still existed among important economic leaders. One school believed that industrial reorganization alone would bring recovery; another school insisted that industrial reorganization had to be accompanied by a pump-priming public-works program. There were also serious differences over the degree of governmental compulsion that should be involved. The President was reluctant to force the decisions. But now, with Congress getting out of hand, Roosevelt could wait no longer. He summoned the proponents of the more important plans among his aides, listened to them wrangle, then told them to go lock themselves in a room until they could agree on one bill.

After two days the conferees produced a bill, and the President accepted it with only minor modifications. With respect to the pump-priming issue, the National Industrial Recovery Act compromised, providing for public works but appropriating for them a sum much smaller than the ardent pump-primers wanted. The heart of the bill, the machinery for industrial planning, was less of a compromise. The codes were to be originally drafted by representatives of industry, which meant the trade associations in most cases; the antitrust laws were suspended; no prohibition was placed on price-fixing. All of these provisions had been major goals of business-minded planners since George Perkins's day. But the terms concerning hours, wages, and conditions of competition were to be written under the supervision of a federal administrator; they had to be approved by the President; and, once given White House approval, they carried the force of federal law. Herbert Hoover, speaking up from the deepest oblivion any living ex-President had ever known, was horrified. "Fascism, pure fascism," the advocate of Associational Activities called the enormous governmental powers granted to the National Recovery Administration.

Raymond Moley was jubilant. His Brain-Trusters, representing quite different approaches, had joined in giving the nation blueprints for both industry and agriculture which brushed aside the Wilsonian hostility to large-scale economic units and brought into actual fact a government-sponsored national planning. To the program of Associational Activities had been added the idea of federal compulsion, which men like Croly and Van Hise had long been advocating. The appointments of the top personnel of the Triple A and the NRA emphasized the way in which the New Deal was sweeping Associational Activities into a bolder pattern. None other than Baruch's assistant on the War Industries Board of World War I, George Peek, accepted the post as head of the Triple A. Another Baruch protégé, Hugh Johnson, not only moved into the top position of the NRA; he promptly began talking federal power in a way that made businessmen feel like so many captured peasants herded before the Czar.

Happily, Moley worked away on the draft of the Fireside Chat in which Roosevelt was to present the Triple A and the NRA to the public, working into the speech a huzza to the coming era of national planning. The President seemed to like the passage, and Moley pressed his advantage.

Did the President, Moley asked, realize to its fullest significance the "enormous step" he was taking? Did he realize that the Tripe A and the NRA were committing him to a sharp break not only with the conservative adulation of free enterprise but with the appeal for a return to free enterprise of New Freedom liberalism? Did he really approve, in its deepest meaning, this passage extolling national planning?

Roosevelt paused thoughtfully, then replied: "I never felt surer of anything in my life than I do of the soundness of this passage."

Uncle Ted, thrashing out his last years in impotent fury at Woodrow Wilson, had died too soon. For in the clear import of basic legislation and in the mind of the President of the United States, the nation was close to the repudiation of trust-busting and the dependence on compulsory federal planning which Theodore Roosevelt had appealed for under the name of the New Nationalism. . . .

LIBERALISM, AND THEN SOME

"Hugh," said Harry Hopkins, "your codes stink."

Hugh Johnson's face reddened, partly in anger, even more in surprise. When he took the job as NRA Administrator, Johnson knew that he was in for a rough time, but he did not expect sharp criticism from New Dealers, especially from so loyal a New Dealer as Harry Hopkins. Now, when the NRA was scarcely six months old, Hopkins proved only the first of many reformers who denounced the codes, and the criticism was increased by groups that liberals had long considered two of their prime concerns, the small businessmen and labor. Seven Cleveland grocers spoke for thousands of small businessmen when they wired the President: "NRA is the worst law ever passed by Congress." A Baltimore picket line expressed a common labor feeling with placards reading: "NRA means National Run Around."

By March 1934 the discontent was so great that President Roosevelt set up a National Recovery Review Board, under the chairmanship of Clarence Darrow. The seventy-six-year-old veteran of reform threw himself into the task as if it were his first case in Ashtabula. For four months, in the cramped heat of a Washington hotel suite, he drove his board through hearings on some three thousand complaints, only the infrequency of the old man's quips suggesting that this was to be his final important effort. And when Darrow sent his bulky three reports to the President, Hugh Johnson knew full well that he had lost much of liberal America.

"[In] virtually all the codes we have examined," the final Darrow report stated, "one condition has been persistent. . . . In Industry after Industry, the larger units, sometimes through the agency of what is called an Institute [a trade association], sometimes by other means, have for their own advantage written the codes, and then, in effect and for their own advantage, assumed the administration of the code they have framed. . . . To deliver industry into the hands of its greatest and most ruthless units when the protection of the anti-trust laws had been withdrawn was a grave error. It may safely be said that not in many years have monopolistic tendencies in industry been so forwarded and strengthened."

. . . The wrathful Darrow reports contained many overstatements or inaccuracies, and Hugh Johnson immediately boomed corrections across the nation. But the General's loudest roars could not drown out the fact that Darrow's basic contention was correct. Most of the codes had been written primarily by big business and were decidedly advantageous to big business. As a matter of fact, Darrow overlooked one choice subject for his sarcasm: in most important respects, the cotton, woolen, carpet, and sugar codes were copies, down to the last comma, of the trade-association agreements written during the Administration of Herbert Hoover.

The story of Triple A was less clear-cut. Industry was more completely dominated by large-scale producers than was agriculture, and the trade associations were more prepared, by their experience and by the nature of their field, to bend national planning to their own purposes. Yet the Triple A revealed the same tendency as the NRA. From the beginning of its operation, big-scale processors and distributors saw to it that their interests were generously protected. During the first three years of the New Deal, the total earnings of farmers leaped up, twenty-five per cent in 1933, fifteen per cent more in 1934, an additional sixteen per cent in 1935. But the new prosperity was not evenly spread. Large-scale farmers, organized in powerful associations, had their crops placed on the list for curtailment on highly favorable terms, while smaller and more weakly organized producers often were not on the lists at all or, if they were, benefited little from the program. Moreover, the Triple A assumed most of the risks of production for the landowner, but did not provide safeguards to prevent the landowner from passing on to tenants any unfavorable effect of the reduced acreage. "Proportionately at least," the historian Dixon Wecter has commented, "the principle—or application—of the AAA seemed to be: to him that hath it shall be given."

More and more, liberals who were concerned with agriculture began to sound like the Darrow Reports in their comments on the Triple A. Their indignation climaxed in the spring of 1935, when a group resignation removed from the Triple A some of its most devoted reform figures. To the liberal journals like the *Nation* this was a "purge" which spelled "the defeat of the social outlook in agricultural policy." The Triple A had succumbed to the "triumphant greed of the processors, distributors, and big producers." The *Christian Century,* an organ of liberal Protestantism, added: "What it all boils down to is that the old divergence between the NRA and the AAA—a matter of much conservative criticism a year or so ago—has been done away with. Both now . . . represent recovery programs . . . controlled by the big corporations involved, giving a subsidiary attention to the interests of the labor element, and hoping that the consumer will be satisfied with a few kind words and a seat out in the alley."

. . . Clarence Darrow, called before a Senate committee investigating the NRA, was melancholy and confused. "The concentration of wealth is going on," he told the Senators, "and it looks almost as if there were nothing to stop it. . . . I think this movement is going on faster than it ever did before, much faster. . . . If we do not destroy it there will be nothing but masters and slaves left before we get much further along." Darrow implied that the antitrust laws should be restored in full force; he also argued that "something like a socialistic system" was necessary. What the old warrior said was obviously contradictory, and it was obviously the struggle of a liberal caught in liberalism's worst domestic trouble.

The liberal in the White House was disturbed too. Though Roosevelt brushed aside the Darrow reports, he soon moved to bar price-fixing from future industrial codes; to set up an Industrial Appeals Board, which was to hear the complaints of small businessmen; and to get under way studies directed toward helping the low-income farmer. But the discontent with the NRA and the Triple A, particularly the irritation at the NRA, did not quiet. Worse still, the perversion of the purpose of New Deal planning meant that the whole structure was adding little to the nation's purchasing power, and recovery was stalling. Suddenly fate, in the form of a Brooklyn chicken-dealer, intervened. The Schechter poultry firm wanted to know what happened to its Constitutional rights if the Live Poultry Code told it how much it had to pay chicken-killers and which chickens were fit to sell. In May 1935 the Supreme Court answered by unanimously decreeing the NRA unconstitutional. Seven months later the Court knocked the other leg from under Roosevelt's New Nationalism by invalidating the crop-control sections of the Triple A. . . .

In the White House, testiness had long since disappeared. Only a short while after the invalidation of the NRA, Roosevelt was musing to Secretary of Labor Frances Perkins: "You know the whole thing is a mess . . . [and] we have got the best out of it anyhow. Industry got a shot in the arm. Everything has started up. . . . I think perhaps NRA has done all it can do. . . . I don't want to impose a system on this country that will set aside the anti-trust laws on any permanent basis." The President was back to his old self, impatient at the thought of permanence for the New Nationalism or any other ism, happily playing by ear.

Roosevelt could hardly improvise on the keyboard of American reform thought without hitting one chord constantly. Use the power of the federal government to smash concentrated wealth and to restore free enterprise;

use it simultaneously to lift the standard of living of the country's less favored groups; and, by both these moves, make opportunity more abundant —in short, the reform program conceived in the depression of 1873, erected into a powerful political force by decades of agitation, given effectiveness and respectability by the early Theodore Roosevelt and by Woodrow Wilson, kept alive even during the complacent Twenties. When Uncle Ted's New Nationalism failed, there was always the Jeffersonian New Freedom of the Chief.

Even in the middle of Roosevelt's New Nationalist period, two quite different facts had been reopening his mind to the New Freedom. The Roosevelt of the early Thirties had considerable sympathy for big business, and thought of government controls less as a crackdown than as a partnership between government and business. But during the NRA period the President discovered that corporation executives could prove highly unsatisfactory partners. Many openly flouted or skirted around all provisions of the NRA which were not entirely favorable to them, assailed most of the other New Deal measures, and spent millions of dollars trying to convince the country that Roosevelt was an egomaniacal Communist. By the time the President had to consider substitutes for the NRA, his irritation with big-business men had reached the point where he was remarking to intimates: "I get more and more convinced that most of them can't see farther than the next dividend."

Simultaneously, the President's mind was being moved in an anti-big-business direction by a push from the left. The shrewd, unscrupulous Senator Huey Long, clawing his way toward the Presidency, was not asking his audiences to wait for the workings of elaborate reforms, or to understand that there might be some point in co-operating with trust magnates. He was flailing his arms, pointing to his pockmarked face as evidence of the way the rich ground the poor, and announcing that after the election of 1936 "your Kingfish, Huey, asittin' in the White House, will know how to handle them moguls." By late 1935 the Kingfish had demagogued himself to a political strength which, if it could not move him into the White House, might possibly move Roosevelt out. A secret poll taken by the Democratic National Committee indicated that Long at the head of a third-party ticket would poll three to four million votes. This strength was not confined to the area around Louisiana but reached into pivotal Northern states—including a potential one hundred thousand votes in New York State, which could swing that big group of electors to the Republicans. Before the election an assassin's bullet ended the Long threat. But Roosevelt had learned to worry about what could happen to a reform President who did not reckon sufficiently with the anti-big-business feeling rooted in decades of American agitation. From the demagogic left and from the uncooperative right, the Jeffersonian reformer in Roosevelt was being pushed to the fore.

The New Deal never did pass over to a strict New Freedom pattern. The

Social Security Act, one of the most important bills passed after the invalidation of NRA, was no more Jeffersonian than it was New Nationalist; if it belonged to either pattern, it probably fitted better the Crolyan conception of the protective state. Nor did any one date or action mark the transition from the New Nationalism to the New Freedom. The shift came, in a blurred gradualism, after the invalidation of the NRA and the Triple A in 1935.

The change was marked by a slow turnover in the President's Brain-Trusters. By 1938 Washington was saying: "Moley is in opposition; Tugwell is in the city-planning business; and Hugh Johnson is in a rage," and the place of the early Brain-Trusters was being filled by a much larger group who shared an enthusiasm for New Freedom liberalism. Some of these men had been in the Administration almost from its start—most importantly, Harold Ickes and Harry Hopkins—and were now moving into the inner circle. Others were new figures, working together in shifting combinations, rising and falling in importance, men like Robert H. Jackson, Leon Henderson, Isador Lubin, and a half-dozen or more brilliant young graduates of Harvard Law School who had been placed in New Deal posts through the influence of the day's leading Jeffersonian legalist, Felix Frankfurter.

Early in the Hundred Days, one of these young lawyers showed up at a White House reception, maneuvered a friend into asking him to perform, and enchanted the President for two hours by singing Irish ballads, sea chanteys, and mountain laments. "You certainly stole the show, Tommy," the friend congratulated him. "I always steal the show," said Tommy Corcoran, and he always did. Springing somehow from a humdrum Rhode Island merchant family, Corcoran left Brown University loaded with prizes and then proceeded to equal Brandeis's record at Harvard Law School, a record that had seemed about as vulnerable as Babe Ruth's sixty home runs. The Hundred Days were not over before Corcoran was the unquestioned leader of Frankfurter's protégés, ranging airily through the government bureaus, making droves of friends and bringing the friends together for a session of songs and denunciations of big business, calling them all "my kids" from the senescence of his thirty-three years.

By 1934 Corcoran began admitting that one of his kids was his full equal, and at first friends were amazed at the choice. The anointed of the handsome, ebullient Tommy was a pale, shy ascetic, completely oblivious of pleasure or even comfort, who was shepherded around by Corcoran like a child at his first visit to an Automat. But Ben Cohen, Corcoran kept telling everyone, was something special, and everyone soon agreed. Cohen's legal powers aroused an admiration akin to worshipfulness, and his selfless absorption in public service won for the Corcoran-Cohen team a respect that Corcoran's pyrotechnics could never have achieved alone.

The team enjoyed a moment of importance in early New Deal days when, through Frankfurter's recommendation, Corcoran and Cohen were called on to draft the Securities and Exchange Act and the Securities Tax Bill. The President was impressed with their skill but these were not the days for militant Wilsonians. Corcoran and Cohen gained their real admission to the inner circle in 1935, when Roosevelt made one of the first important moves of his New Freedom period, the attack on holding companies in the power utilities field. The President asked the long-time trust-buster, Secretary of the Interior Harold Ickes, to supervise the working out of a bill, and, through Ickes's office, Corcoran and Cohen were assigned the detailed work.

The pair went at the task in a manner that was soon to be famous—all-night furies of work, with endless cups of sticky-sweet black coffee—and the bill that went to Congress would have delighted the heart of any trust-hating Populist. All holding companies in the power field, the "death sentence" clause provided, had to prove their social usefulness within five years or dissolve. When the provision provoked a savage battle in Congress, Corcoran bobbed up in the middle of the fight, artfully explaining and defending, dangling patronage before the eyes of reluctant Congressmen, rushing back and forth to the White House for reports and instructions. The holding companies were partially reprieved before Congress passed the bill, but the Corcoran-Cohen team was made. From then on, few important White House conferences did not include one or both of the men, at least four key laws were products of their legal wizardry, and "Tommy the Cork," as the President was soon affectionately calling the front man of the team, emerged as one of the two or three most inside New Deal insiders.

Shortly after the Holding Company Act went to Congress, Roosevelt sent to Congress a tax bill that was truculently anti-corporation. The President's "State of the Union" address of January 1936 bristled with phrases about the men of "entrenched greed" who sought "the restoration of their selfish power." All suggestions to revive the New Nationalist aspects of the NRA and the Triple A were brushed aside. Instead, the Administration pressed ahead with key legislation that bore the unmistakable New Freedom stamp. It went along with the Wagner-Connery Labor Act, probably the most bluntly anti-corporation legislation the United States has ever accepted, and pressed the Fair Labor Standards Act, with its ironclad provisions of minimum wages and maximum hours. A modified Triple A and other agricultural legislation, dropping much of the national-planning aspect of the original Triple A, aimed directly to improve the economic position of farmers and took especial care to promote the interests of the lowest-income group.

Amid this churn of legislation, the most symbolic of all New Freedom moves was made. In October 1937 a recession declared itself to the roar of crashing stocks, and the Corcoran group, attributing the recession to greedy price-fixing by monopolistic combines, urged on the President a series of bold steps, among them a general trust-busting campaign. Roosevelt was a willing listener, but the New Nationalist in him had not entirely disappeared. For the moment, the President decided, he would ask for a new housing act, hoping that this would stimulate employment. Beyond that, he would sit tight.

But Tommy Corcoran had no intention of sitting tight. The Administration was now being assailed on all sides, by conservatives for having caused the recession and by liberals for not ending it. To Corcoran it seemed as if the whole New Deal was on the run and something had to be done quickly. In a council of war instigated by Corcoran, a group of the new Brain-Trusters decided to gamble. They would go ahead on their own trust-busting campaign, hoping to stir the President into joining them but leaving him free to repudiate them at any time.

Assistant Attorney General Robert Jackson opened the campaign. In a radio speech written by Corcoran and Cohen, Jackson charged: "By profiteering, the monopolists and those so near monopoly as to control their prices have simply priced themselves out of the market, and priced themselves into the slump." In the excitement that followed, Corcoran asked Harold Ickes to speak and the Secretary responded with two blistering assaults on big capital. Washington was in a tumult. Conservative Senators demanded that Roosevelt immediately repudiate Jackson and Ickes. Ickes told his friends he slept with his hat hanging ready on the bedpost.

But the business indices were fighting on the side of the New Freedom trust-busters. As the recession worsened in the spring of 1938, Uncle Ted's New Nationalist nephew was overwhelmed by the Chief's disciple; Roosevelt, too, became convinced that the whole New Deal was threatened by selfish and shortsighted big capital. In March he reinvigorated the antitrust division of the Justice Department, naming as its chief the able, combative Thurman Arnold. The next month the President sent to Congress a strong message urging "a thorough study of the concentration of economic power in American industry and the effect of that concentration upon the decline of competition."

The New Nationalism and then the New Freedom—in a very real sense the New Dealers were right when they insisted that what they were doing hitched on to long-running American ideas. Yet there was something more to New Deal liberalism in both its New Nationalist and New Freedom phases, and the something more, as always, was connected with the climate of national opinion.

The New Deal, though it had given the country a way of coping with fear, had not entirely conquered it, and the common attitude was to go along with the New Deal enthusiastically but warily. If it could produce, fine; but there was always the reservation, accentuated by the recession of 1937, that the New Deal might not solve the problem. "Here we come, WPA!" the college boys wise-cracked, and millions beyond college age smiled understandingly.

The depression not only created a continuing uneasiness that another crash was round the corner; it brought into frightening focus a number of long-time trends that also spelled insecurity. Every year of increased urbanization and mechanization left thousands of individuals feeling more like an easily replaceable cog in the wheel, more alone in the impersonal crowd. By the late Thirties students of American society were also writing of "the specter of insecurity" raised by the steadily mounting percentage of the population who depended on someone else for a job, the growing proportion of women supporting themselves or contributing a vital portion to the family income, the ineluctable decline in independent farming. At the same time, the average age of the population was rapidly changing, with the age curve moving ever farther beyond the confidence of youth. It was the 1930's that, poignantly, kept Walter Pitkin's *Life Begins at Forty* at or near the top of the best-seller list for two solid years.

The general sense of insecurity was accompanied by a special restiveness among America's minority groups. They were not only, in fact, the least secure—the "last hired, the first fired," as the Negroes put it. By the 1930's the Negroes were more than half a century from slavery, and thousands of the newer immigrant families were raising a second or third generation on American soil. Often these later products of minority origins had the education and the manner to compete successfully for higher prestige positions and to move in higher-status circles, and the general liberal atmosphere of the Thirties encouraged their aspirations. Just because of this encouragement and the increased adaptation to the ways of the dominant groups, the enormous obstacles still standing in the way were the more frustrating.

Despite these developments, there is little evidence that any considerable part of the population gave up the faith in America as the land of opportunity. Too many generations had rooted their whole way of life in the belief; too many facts still proclaimed that the United States, more than any other country, did actually throw open the road for ambition. What happened was that millions of Americans were supplementing the credo of opportunity with a demand for laws that would guarantee them greater economic security and more equality in the pursuit of economic and social status. In case—just in case—economic opportunity did not knock, they wanted to be sure that the mailman would be around with a social-security check. In case—just in case—the social ladder proved too steep, they wanted laws which would guarantee that they would not be left on too humiliating a rung.

These trends showed themselves plainly in liberal thinking. Previous generations of reformers had been little concerned with security or equality brought about by law. The emphasis had been simply on creating a situation in which men could compete on reasonably even terms. Now, during both the New Nationalist and the New Freedom phases of the New Deal and increasing in intensity, a drive was being made to bring about greater security by legislation. The President himself laid down the line in 1934 when he placed "the security of the men, women and children of the Nation" first among the objectives of his Administration. The Social Security Act of 1935, of course, was the keystone of the Administration's security legislation, but a similar purpose marked a variety of New Deal legislation, ranging from the creation of the Home Owner's Loan Corporation in 1933 to the establishment of the Farm Security Administration in 1937. How far New Deal liberalism was ready to go in guaranteeing security was far from clear. Conservatives could only gloomily note the portents. The President spoke of a security program "which because of many lost years will take many future years to fulfill"; both the Farm Security and Resettlement Administrations were bringing group security ideas even into that sanctuary of individual relations, the medical field; and many powerful New Dealers were ready to agree with Eleanor Roosevelt when she declared: "In the nineteenth century . . . there was no recognition that the government owed an individual certain things as a right. . . . Now it is accepted that the government has an obligation to guard the rights of an individual so carefully that he never reaches a point at which he needs charity."

The New Deal made no concrete moves toward enforced equality, unless it was in its none too vigorous steps against segregation in public housing and against discrimination in employment on government contracts, but it smiled sympathetically on a liberal movement that was hurrying in that direction. The very tone of the New Deal was far more aggressively equalitarian than that of either Populism or progressivism. It was the New Dealer's President who told the Daughters of the American Revolution: "Remember, remember always that all of us, and you and I especially, are descended from immigrants." It was his wife who gladly permitted herself to be photographed while escorted by two Negro R.O.T.C. cadets.

Over much of previous progressivism had hung an air of patronizing the unfortunate, of helping the group that reformers often called "the little people." The attitude of the new liberalism was spoken with classic tartness when Joseph Mitchell presented his stories of "McSorley's Wonderful Saloon." The phrase "little people," Mitchell declared, was "repulsive. . . . There are no little people in this book. They are as big as you are, whoever you are." The point was carried to its further significance by a discerning, upper-income liberal, who added: "For quite a while I have lived in a commuter community that is rabidly anti-Roosevelt and I am convinced that the heart of their hatred is not economic. The real source of the venom is that Rooseveltism challenged their feeling that they were superior people, occupying by right a privileged position in the world. I am convinced that a lot of them would even have backed many of his economic measures if they had been permitted to believe the laws represented the fulfillment of their responsibility as 'superior people.' They were not permitted that belief. Instead, as the New Deal went on, it chipped away more and more at their sense of superiority. By the second term, it was pressing hard on a vital spot and the conservatives were screaming."

To many liberals, it was just these variations in reform that gave the New Deal its great strength. "This isn't a do-gooder tea club, patching things up here and there," one of the President's close associates exulted. "This is a real people's movement getting at the heart of the great modern problem, insecurity—insecurity in jobs and insecurity in feelings." Other liberals were not so confident. Even with the new concerns over economic security and social equality, American liberalism of the late Thirties was still fundamentally the New Freedom, and once it was tested over any considerable period of time, it could easily develop all the serious difficulties inherent in the New Freedom.

The New Deal was to have time only to begin the test of its variety of the New Freedom. For just as it was really swinging into its new phase, frenetic men across the oceans, whose interest in liberalism had always been minimal, decided to shove a different issue to the fore.

From Progressivism to the New Deal

Richard Hofstadter

THE NEW DEPARTURE

The Great Depression, which broke the mood of the twenties almost as suddenly as the postwar reaction had killed the Progressive fervor, rendered obsolete most of the antagonisms that had flavored the politics of the postwar era. Once again the demand for reform became irresistible, and out of the chaotic and often mutually contradictory schemes for salvation that arose from all corners of the country the New Deal took form. In the years 1933–8 the New Deal sponsored a series of legislative changes that made the enactments of the Progressive era seem timid by comparison, changes that, in their totality, carried the politics and administration of the United States farther from the conditions of 1914 than those had been from the conditions of 1880.

It is tempting, out of a desire for symmetry and historical continuity, to see in the New Deal a return to the preoccupations of Progressivism, a re-

Reprinted from *The Age of Reform: From Bryan to F.D.R.*, Vintage Edition, by Richard Hofstadter, by permission of Alfred A. Knopf, Inc. Copyright 1955 by Richard Hofstadter. Pp. 300–325.

sumption of the work of reform that had begun under Theodore Roosevelt and Woodrow Wilson, and a consummation of the changes that were proposed in the half-dozen years before the first World War. Much reason can be found for yielding to this temptation. Above all, the New Dealers shared with the Progressives a far greater willingness than had been seen in previous American history to make use of the machinery of government to meet the needs of the people and supplement the workings of the national economy. There are many occasions in its history when the New Deal, especially in its demand for organization, administration, and management from a central focus, seems to stand squarely in the tradition of the New Nationalism for which such Progressives as Herbert Croly had argued. Since it is hardly possible for any society to carve out a completely new vocabulary for every new problem it faces, there is also much in the New Deal rhetoric that is strongly reminiscent of Progressivism. Like the Progressives, the New Dealers invoked a larger democracy; and where the Progressives had their "plutocrats," the New Dealers had their "economic royalists." F. D. R., asserting in his first inaugural address that "The money changers have fled from their high seats in the temple of our civilization. We may now restore that temple to the ancient truths," sounds very much like almost any inspirational writer for *McClure's* in the old days.[1] On a number of particular issues, moreover, like the holding-company question, monopoly, and public power, one feels as though one is treating again, in the New Deal, with familiar problems—just as, in the crucial early days of 1933, the formation of a strong bloc of inflationist Senators from the West seemed to hark back to the Populist movement.

Still, granting that absolute discontinuities do not occur in history, and viewing the history of the New Deal as a whole, what seems outstanding about it is the drastic new departure that it marks in the history of American reformism.[2] The New Deal was different from anything that had yet happened in the United States: different because its central problem was unlike the problems of Progressivism; different in its ideas and its spirit and its techniques. Many men who had lived through Progressivism and had thought of its characteristic proposals as being in the main line of American traditions, even as being restoratives of those traditions, found in the New Deal an outrageous departure from everything they had known

---

[1] Naturally there was also some continuity in personnel, for F. D. R. himself was only one of a considerable number of American leaders who had been young Progressives before the war and were supporters of the major reforms of the thirties. However, one could draw up an equally formidable list—chiefly Republican insurgents of the Bull Moose era, but also many Democrats—who had supported Progressive measures and later became heated critics of the New Deal.

[2] Here I find myself in agreement with the view expressed by Samuel Lubell (op. cit., p. 3): "The distinctive feature of the political revolution which Franklin D. Roosevelt began and Truman inherited lies not in its resemblance to the political wars of Andrew Jackson or Thomas Jefferson, but in its abrupt break with the continuity of the past."

and valued, and so could interpret it only as an effort at subversion or as the result of overpowering alien influences. Their opposition was all too often hysterical, but in their sense that something new had come into American political and economic life they were quite right.

Consider, to begin, the fundamental problem that the New Dealers faced, as compared with the problems of the Progressives. When Theodore Roosevelt took office in 1901, the country was well over three years past a severe depression and in the midst of a period of healthy economic development. Its farmers were more prosperous than they had been for about forty years, its working class was employed and gaining in living standards, and even its middle class was far busier counting the moral costs of success than it was worrying about any urgent problems of family finance. When F. D. R. took his oath of office, the entire working apparatus of American economic life had gone to smash. The customary masters and leaders of the social order were themselves in a state of near panic. Millions were unemployed, and discontent had reached a dangerous pitch on the farms and in the cities.

Indeed, the New Deal episode marks the first in the history of reform movements when a leader of the reform party took the reins of a government confronted above all by the problems of a sick economy. To be sure, the whole nineteenth-century tradition of reform in American politics was influenced by experience with periodic economic breakdowns; but its political leaders had never had to bear responsibility for curing them. Jefferson in 1801, Jackson in 1829, and after them T. R. and Wilson—all took over at moments when the economy was in good shape. While each of them had experience with economic relapse—Jefferson in 1807 as the consequence of his embargo policies, the Jacksonians briefly in 1834 and again after 1837, T. R. briefly during the "bankers' panic" of 1907, and Wilson with a momentary recession just before the wartime boom—their thinking, and the thinking of the movements they reprsented, was centered upon sharing an existing prosperity among the various social classes rather than upon restoring a lost prosperity or preventing recurrent slumps.

The earlier American tradition of political protest had been a response to the needs of entrepreneurial classes or of those who were on the verge of entrepreneurship—the farmers, small businessmen, professionals, and occasionally the upper caste of the artisans or the working class. The goal of such classes had generally been to clear the way for new enterprises and new men, break up privileged business, big businesses, and monopolies, and give the small man better access to credit. The ideas of this Progressive tradition, as one might expect, were founded not merely upon acceptance but even upon glorification of the competitive order. The Jeffersonians, the Jacksonians, and after them most of the Progressives had believed in the market economy, and the only major qualification of this belief they cared to make stemmed from their realization that the market needed to be policed and moralized by a government responsive to the needs of the economic beginner and the small entrepreneur. Occasionally, very occasionally, they had argued for the exercise of a few positive functions on the part of the national government, but chiefly they preferred to keep the positive functions of government minimal, and, where these were necessary, to keep them on the state rather than put them on the national level. Their conceptions of the role of the national government were at first largely negative and then largely preventive. In the Jeffersonian and Jacksonian days it was to avoid excessive expenditure and excessive taxation, to refrain from giving privileged charters. Later, in the corporate era, it was to prevent abuses by the railroads and the monopolists, to check and to regulate unsound and immoral practices. It is of course true that some of the more "advanced" thinkers of the Populist and Progressive movements began to think tentatively of more positive functions for government, but it was just such proposals—the subtreasury scheme for agricultural credits and the various public-ownership proposals—that provoked the greatest opposition when attempts were made to apply them on a national scale.

The whole reformist tradition, then, displayed a mentality founded on the existence of an essentially healthy society; it was chiefly concerned not with managing an economy to meet the problems of collapse but simply with democratizing an economy in sound working order. Managing an economy in such a way as to restore prosperity is above all a problem of organization,[3] while democratizing a well-organized economy had been . . . in some important respects an attempt to find ways of attacking or limiting organization. Hence the Progressive mind was hardly more prepared than the conservative mind for what came in 1929. Herbert Hoover, an old Bull Mooser, while more disposed to lead the country than any president had been in any previous depression, was unprepared for it, and was prevented from adjusting to it by a doctrinaire adherence to inherited principles. F. D. R.—a fairly typical product of Progressivism who had first won office in 1910—was also unprepared for it in his economic thinking, as anyone will see who examines his career in the 1920's;[4] but he was sufficiently opportunistic and flexible to cope with it somewhat more successfully.

Hoover, an engineer born in Iowa, represented the moral traditions of native Protestant politics. An amateur in politics who had never run for office before he was elected President in 1928, he had no patience with the politician's willingness to accommodate, and he hung on, as inflexibly as the situation would permit, to the private and voluntary methods that had

---

[3] The closest thing to an earlier model for the first efforts of the New Deal was not the economic legislation of Progressivism but the efforts of the Wilson administration to organize the economy for the first World War. Hugh Johnson in the NRA and George Peek in the AAA were in many ways recapitulating the experience they had had in the War Industries Board under Bernard Baruch.

[4] See Frank Friedel's *Franklin D. Roosevelt: the Ordeal* (Boston, 1954), and his forthcoming volume on F. D. R.'s governorship.

always worked well in his administrative career.[5] F. D. R., a seasoned professional politician who had learned his trade straddling the terrible antagonisms of the 1920's, was thoroughly at home in the realities of machine politics and a master of the machine techniques of accommodation. Unlike Hoover, he had few hard and fast notions about economic principles, but he knew that it would be necessary to experiment and improvise. "It is common sense," he said in 1932, "to take a method and try it. If it fails, admit it frankly and try another. But above all, try something."

To describe the resulting flood of legislation as economic planning would be to confuse planning with interventionism. Planning was not quite the word for the New Deal: considered as an economic movement, it was a chaos of experimentation. Genuine planners like Rexford Guy Tugwell found themselves floundering amid the cross-currents of the New Deal, and ended in disillusionment. But if, from an economic standpoint, the New Deal was altogether lacking in that rationality or consistency which is implied in the concept of planning, from a political standpoint it represented a masterly shifting equipoise of interests. And little wonder that some of the old Republican insurgents shuddered at its methods. If the state was believed neutral in the days of T. R. because its leaders claimed to sanction favors for no one, the state under F. D. R. could be called neutral only in the sense that it offered favors to everyone.

Even before F. D. R. took office a silent revolution had taken place in public opinion, the essential character of which can be seen when we recall how little opposition there was in the country, at the beginning, to the assumption of the New Dealers that henceforth, for the purposes of recovery, the federal government was to be responsible for the condition of the labor market as a part of its concern with the industrial problem as a whole. Nothing revolutionary was intended—but simply as a matter of politics it was necessary for the federal government to assume primary responsibility for the relief of the unemployed. And, simply as a matter of politics, if the industrialists were to be given the power to write enforceable codes of fair practice, labor must at least be given some formal recognition of its right of collective bargaining. Certainly no one foresaw, in the first year or two of the New Deal, that the immense infusions of purchasing power into the economy through federal unemployment relief would be as lasting or as vital a part of the economy of the next several years as they proved in fact to be. Nor did anyone foresee how great and powerful a labor movement would be called into being by the spirit and the promise of the New Deal and by the partial recovery of its first few years. But by the end of 1937 it was clear that something had been added to the social base of reformism. The demands of a large and powerful labor movement, coupled with the interests

---

[5] Characteristically, also, Hoover accepted what might be called the nativist view of the Great Depression: it came from abroad; it was the product, not of any deficiencies in the American economy, but of repercussions of the unsound institutions of Europe.

of the unemployed, gave the later New Deal a social-democratic tinge that had never before been present in American reform movements. Hitherto concerned very largely with reforms of an essentially entrepreneurial sort and only marginally with social legislation, American political reformism was fated henceforth to take responsibility on a large scale for social security, unemployment insurance, wages and hours, and housing.[6]

Still more imposing was the new fiscal role of the federal government. Again, none of this was premeditated. Large-scale spending and unbalanced budgets were, in the beginning, a response to imperative needs. While other schemes for recovery seemed to fall short of expectations, spending kept the economy going; and it was only when F. D. R. tried in 1937 to cut back expenditures that he learned that he had become the prisoner of his spending policies, and turned about and made a necessity into a virtue. His spending policy never represented, at any time before the outbreak of the war, an unambiguous or wholehearted commitment to Keynesian economics. Here only the war itself could consummate the fiscal revolution that the New Deal began. In 1940 Lord Keynes published in the United States an article in which he somewhat disconsolately reviewed the American experience with deficit spending during the previous decade. "It seems politically impossible," he concluded, "for a capitalistic democracy to organize expenditure on the scale necessary to make the grand experiment which would prove my case—except in war conditions." He then added that preparations for war and the production of armaments might teach Americans so much about the potentialities of their economy that it would be "the stimulus, which neither the victory nor the defeat of the New Deal could give you, to greater individual consumption and a higher standard of life." [7] How remarkably prophetic this was we can now see. There had been under peacetime conditions an immense weeping and wailing over the budgets of F. D. R.—which at their peak ran to seven billion dollars. Now we contemplate budgets of over eighty billion dollars with somewhat less anguish, because we know that most of this expenditure will be used for defense and will not be put to uses that are politically more controversial. But, above all, we have learned things about the possibilities of our economy that were not dreamed of in 1933, much less in 1903. While men still grow angry over federal fiscal and tax policies, hardly anyone doubts that in the calculable

---

[6] As the counsel for the National Association of Manufacturers put it: "Regulation has passed from the negative stage of merely preventing unlawful and improper conduct, to the positive stage of directing and controlling the character and form of business activity. The concept that the function of government was to prevent exploitation by virtue of superior power has been replaced by the concept that it is the duty of government to provide security against all the major hazards of life—against unemployment, accident, illness, old age, and death." Thomas P. Jenkin: *Reactions of Major Groups to Positive Government in the United States* (Berkeley, 1945), pp. 300–1.

[7] J. M. Keynes: "The United States and the Keynes Plan," *New Republic,* Vol. CIII (July 29, 1940), p. 158.

future it will be the fiscal role of the government that more than anything else determines the course of the economy.

And what of the old Progressive issues? They were bypassed, sidestepped, outgrown—anything but solved. To realize how true this was, one need only look at the New Deal approach to those two *bêtes noires* of the Progressive mind, the machines and the trusts.

Where the Progressives spent much of their energy . . . trying to defeat the bosses and the machines and to make such changes in the political machinery of the country as would bring about direct popular democracy and "restore government to the people," the New Deal was almost completely free of such crusading. To the discomfort of the old-fashioned, principled liberals who were otherwise enthusiastic about his reforms, F. D. R. made no effort to put an end to bossism and corruption, but simply ignored the entire problem. In the interest of larger national goals and more urgent needs, he worked with the bosses wherever they would work with him—and did not scruple to include one of the worst machines of all, the authoritarian Hague machine in New Jersey. As for the restoration of democracy, he seemed well satisfied with his feeling that the broadest public needs were at least being served by the state and that there was such an excellent rapport between the people and their executive leadership.[8]

The chief apparent exception to this opportune and managerial spirit in the field of political reform—namely, the attempt to enlarge the Supreme Court—proves on examination to be no exception at all. F. D. R.'s fight over the Supreme Court was begun, after all, not in the interest of some large "democratic" principle or out of a desire to reform the Constitutional machinery as such, but because the Court's decisions had made it seem impossible to achieve the managerial reorganization of society that was so urgently needed. His first concern was not that judicial review was "undemocratic" but that the federal government had been stripped, as he thought, of its power to deal effectively with economic problems. Nor was this fight waged in the true Progressive spirit. The Progressives, too, had had their difficulties with the judiciary, and had responded with the characteristically principled but practically difficult proposal for the recall of judicial decisions. In short, they raised for reconsideration, as one might expect of principled men, the entire question of judicial review. F. D. R. chose no such method.[9] To reopen the entire question of the propriety of

---

[8] Of course to speak of democracy in purely domestic terms is to underestimate the world-wide significance of the New Deal. At a time when democracy was everywhere in retreat, the New Deal gave to the world an example of a free nation coping with the problems of its economy in a democratic and humane way.

[9] Indeed, in his message calling for reorganization Roosevelt declared that his proposal would make unnecessary any fundamental changes in the powers of the courts or in the Constitution, "changes which involve consequences so far-reaching as to cause uncertainty as to the wisdom of such a course." It remained for the leading senatorial opponent of the bill, Senator Burton K. Wheeler, to advocate an amendment to the

judicial review of the acts of Congress under a representative democracy would have been a high-minded approach to what he felt was a Constitutional impasse, but it would have ended perhaps even more disastrously than the tactic he employed. F. D. R. avoided such an approach, which would have involved a cumbersome effort to amend the Constitution, and devised a "gimmick" to achieve his ends—the pretense that the age of the judges prevented them from remaining abreast of their calendar, and the demand for the right to supplement the judiciary, to the number of six, with an additional judge for each incumbent who reached the age of seventy without retiring.

Students of the Court fight are fond of remarking that Roosevelt won his case, because the direction of the Court's decisions began to change while the fight was in progress and because Justice Van Devanter's retirement enabled the President to appoint a liberal justice and decisively change the composition of the Court.[10] It seems important, however, to point out that a very heavy price had to be paid for even this pragmatic attempt to alter a great and sacrosanct conservative institution. The Court fight alienated many principled liberals and enabled many of F. D. R.'s conservative opponents to portray him to the public more convincingly as a man who aspired to personal dictatorship and aimed at the subversion of the Republic.

If we look at the second of the two great foes of Progressivism, big business and monopoly, we find that by the time of the New Deal public sentiment had changed materially. To be sure, the coming of the depression and the revelation of some of the less palatable business practices of the 1920's brought about a climate of opinion in which the leadership of business, and particularly of big business, was profoundly distrusted and bitterly resented. Its position certainly was, in these respects, considerably weaker than it had been twenty-five years before. Still, by 1933 the American public had lived with the great corporation for so long that it was felt to be domesticated, and there was far more concern with getting business life on such a footing as would enable it to provide jobs than there was with breaking up the larger units. The New Deal never developed a clear or consistent line on

---

Constitution permitting Congress to override judicial vetoes of its acts. Charles A. and Mary R. Beard: *America in Midpassage* (New York, 1939), Vol. I, p. 355.

[10] Presumably it will always be debated whether the new harmony between Congress and the Supreme Court that developed even while the Court fight was going on can be attributed to Roosevelt's Court reform bill. Merlo Pusey in his *Charles Evans Hughes* (Vol. II, pp. 766 ff.) argues that the change in the Court's decisions was not a political response to the legislative struggle. He points out, among other things, that the New Deal legislation that came before the Court after the NRA and AAA decisions was better drafted. It is beyond doubt, however, that the resignation of Van Devanter was precipitated by the Court fight. Ibid., Vol. II, p. 761. The fact that advocates of both sides can go on arguing about who won the fight is the best evidence that the issue was satisfactorily settled. It aroused so much feeling that an unambiguous victory for either side would have been unfortunate.

business consolidation, and New Dealers fought over the subject in terms that were at times reminiscent of the old battles between the trust-busters and the trust-regulators. What can be said, however, is that the subject of bigness and monopoly was subordinated in the New Deal era to that restless groping for a means to bring recovery that was so characteristic of Roosevelt's efforts. The New Deal began not with a flourish of trust-busting but rather, in the NRA, with an attempt to solve the problems of the business order through a gigantic system of governmentally underwritten codes that would ratify the trustification of society. One of the first political setbacks suffered by the New Deal arose from just this—for it had put the formation of its codes of fair practice so completely in the hands of the big-business interests that both small businessmen and organized labor were seriously resentful. Only five years from the date of its passage, after the NRA had failed to produce a sustained recovery and had been declared unconstitutional by the Supreme Court, did the administration turn off and take the opposite tack with its call for an inquiry into corporate consolidation and business power that led to the Temporary National Economic Committee's memorable investigation.[11] Although at the time many observers thought that the old Progressive trust-busting charade was about to be resumed, the New Deal never became committed to a categorical "dissection" of the business order of the sort Wilson had talked of in 1912, nor to the "demonstration" prosecutions with which T. R. had both excited and reassured the country. The New Deal was not trying to re-establish the competitive order that Wilson had nostalgically invoked and that T. R. had sternly insisted was no longer possible. Its approach, as it turned out, was severely managerial, and distinctly subordinated to those economic considerations that would promote purchasing power and hence recovery. It was, in short, a concerted effort to discipline the pricing policies of businesses, not with the problem of size in mind, nor out of consideration for smaller competitors, but with the purpose of eliminating that private power to tax which is the prerogative of monopoly, and of leaving in the hands of consumers vital purchasing power.

History cannot quite repeat itself, if only because the participants in the second round of any experience are aware of the outcome of the first. The anti-trust philosophers of the closing years of the New Deal were quite aware that previous efforts to enforce the Sherman Act had been ceremonial demonstrations rather than serious assaults upon big business. Thurman Arnold, who was put in charge of the anti-trust program, was well known for his belief that earlier interpretations of the Sherman Act had actually concealed and encouraged business consolidation. In his account of the contemporary function of anti-trust prosecution Arnold put his emphasis

---

[11] There had been in the meantime, however, the assault upon the holding companies embodied in the so-called "death sentence" of 1935.

upon benefits for the consumer and repudiated the earlier use of the Sherman Act: "Since the consumers' interest was not emphasized, such enforcement efforts as existed were directed at the punishment of offenses rather than the achievement of economic objectives. Indeed, in very few anti-trust prosecutions was any practical economic objective defined or argued with respect to the distribution of any particular product. In this way the moral aspects of the offense, and that will-o'-the-wisp, corporate intent, became more important considerations than economic results. Anti-trust enforcement, not being geared to the idea of consumers' interests, became a hunt for offenders instead of an effort to test the validity of organized power by its performance in aiding or preventing the flow of goods in commerce. The result was that although the economic ideal of a free competitive market as the cornerstone of our economy was kept alive, no adequate enforcement staff was ever provided to make that ideal a reality. Such, broadly speaking, was the state of the Sherman Act from 1890 down to the great depression." [12]

But if such a position as Thurman Arnold's can be legitimately distinguished from the Progressive type of anti-trust, as I think it can, there are men today whose political thinking was forged in the service of the New Deal who go beyond him in repudiating anti-trust action as a mere attack upon size, and who take, on the whole, an acquiescent attitude toward big business. A few years ago John Kenneth Galbraith made quite a stir with his book *American Capitalism*, whose central thesis was that the process of business consolidation creates within itself a "countervailing power"—that is, that it brings about the organization not merely of strong sellers but of strong buyers as well, who distribute through large sectors of the economy their ability to save through organization.[13] In Galbraith's book, as in most recent literature in defense of bigness, it is not the effort at disorganization but the effects of counter-organization, in labor, agriculture, and government and within business itself, that are counted upon to minimize the evils of consolidation. More recently David Lilienthal, another graduate of the New Deal administrative agencies, has written a strong apologia for big business that followed Galbraith in stressing the technologically progressive character of large-scale industry in language that would have horrified Brandeis and Wilson.[14] It is not clear whether the attitudes of men like Galbraith and Lilienthal represent dominant liberal sentiment today—

---

[12] Thurman Arnold: *The Bottlenecks of Business* (New York, 1940), p. 263.

[13] This is a rather simplified statement of the thesis of Galbraith's *American Capitalism* (Boston, 1952). Students of the history of anti-trust ideologies will be particularly interested in Galbraith's strictures on the TNEC Report (pp. 59–60).

[14] Galbraith argues that "the competition of the competitive model . . . almost completely precludes technical development" and that indeed "there must be some element of monopoly in an industry if it is to be progressive." Ibid., pp. 91, 93, and chapter vii, *passim*. Cf. David Lilienthal: *Big Business: a New Era* (New York, 1953), chapter vi. For another such friendly treatment by a former New Dealer, see Adolph A. Berle: *The Twentieth Century Capitalist Revolution* (New York, 1954).

though it may be pertinent to say that their books brought no outpouring of protest from other liberal writers. The spectacle of liberals defending, with whatever qualifications, bigness and concentration in industry suggests that that anti-monopoly sentiment which was so long at the heart of Progressive thinking is no longer its central theme. The generation for which Wilson and Brandeis spoke looked to economic life as a field for the expression of character; modern liberals seem to think of it quite exclusively as a field in which certain results are to be expected. It is this change in the moral stance that seems most worthy of remark. A generation ago, and more, the average American was taught to expect that a career in business would and should be in some sense a testing and proving ground for character and manhood, and it was in these terms that the competitive order was often made most appealing.[15] Contrariwise, those who criticized the economic order very commonly formed their appeals within the same mold of moral suasion: the economic order failed to bring out or reward the desired qualities of character, to reward virtue and penalize vice; it was a source of inequities and injustices. During the last fifteen or twenty years, however, as Galbraith observes, "the American radical has ceased to talk about inequality or exploitation under capitalism or even its 'inherent contradictions.' He has stressed, instead, the unreliability of its performance." [16]

THE NEW OPPORTUNISM

The New Deal, and the thinking it engendered, represented the triumph of economic emergency and human needs over inherited notions and inhibitions. It was conceived and executed above all in the spirit of what Roosevelt called "bold, persistent experimentation," and what those more critical of the whole enterprise considered crass opportunism. In discussing Progressivism I emphasized its traffic in moral absolutes, its exalted moral tone. While something akin to this was by no means entirely absent from the New Deal, the later movement showed a strong and candid awareness that what was happening was not so much moral reformation as economic experimentation. Much of this experimentation seemed to the conservative opponents of the New Deal as not only dangerous but immoral.

The high moral indignation of the critics of the New Deal sheds light on another facet of the period—the relative reversal of the ideological roles of conservatives and reformers. Naturally in all ideologies, conservative or

---

[15] See, for instance, the touching letter quoted by Lilienthal (op. cit., p. 198), from a university graduate of the twenties: "We were dismayed at the vista of mediocre aspiration and of compartmentalized lives. The course of a big business career was predictable and foreclosed. It was also, as the personnel department pointed out, secure. The appeal of graduated salary raises and retirement on a pension was held out as the big lure. But in my high school days the appeal had been to ambition, a good deal was said about achievement and independence."

[16] Galbraith, op. cit., p. 70.

radical, there is a dual appeal to ultimate moral principles and to the practical necessities of institutional life. Classically, however, it has been the strength of conservatives that their appeal to institutional continuities, hard facts, and the limits of possibility is better founded; while it has usually been the strength of reformers that they arouse moral sentiments, denounce injustices, and rally the indignation of the community against intolerable abuses. Such had been the alignment of arguments during the Progressive era. During the New Deal, however, it was the reformers whose appeal to the urgent practical realities was most impressive—to the farmers without markets, to the unemployed without bread or hope, to those concerned over the condition of the banks, the investment market, and the like. It was the conservatives, on the other hand, who represented the greater moral indignation and rallied behind themselves the inspirational literature of American life; and this not merely because the conservatives were now the party of the opposition, but because things were being done of such drastic novelty that they seemed to breach all the inherited rules, not merely of practicality but of morality itself. Hence, if one wishes to look for utopianism in the 1930's, for an exalted faith in the intangibles of morals and character, and for moral indignation of the kind that had once been chiefly the prerogative of the reformers, one will find it far more readily in the editorials of the great conservative newspapers than in the literature of the New Deal. If one seeks for the latter-day equivalent of the first George Kennan, warning the people of San Francisco that it would do them no good to have a prosperous town if in gaining it they lost their souls, one will find it most readily in the 1930's among those who opposed federal relief for the unemployed because it would destroy their characters or who were shocked by the devaluation of the dollar, not because they always had a clear conception of its consequences, but above all because it smacked to them of dirtiness and dishonesty. In the past it had been the conservatives who controlled the settlement of the country, set up its great industrial and communications plant, and founded the fabulous system of production and distribution upon which the country prided itself, while the reformers pointed to the human costs, the sacrifice of principles, and drew blueprints to show how the job could be better done. Now, however, it was the reformers who fed the jobless or found them jobs, saved the banks, humanized industry, built houses and schools and public buildings, rescued farmers from bankruptcy, and restored hope—while the conservatives, expropriated at once from their customary control of affairs and from their practical role, invoked sound principles, worried about the Constitution, boggled over details, pleaded for better morals, and warned against tyranny.

Lamentably, most of the conservative thinking of the New Deal era was hollow and cliché-ridden. What seems most striking about the New Deal itself, however, was that all its ferment of practical change produced a very slight literature of political criticism. While the changes of the Progressive era had produced many significant books of pamphleteering or thoughtful analyses of society—the writings of such men as Croly, Lippmann, Weyl, Brooks Adams, Brandeis, the muckrakers, Socialist critics like W. J. Ghent and William English Walling—the New Deal produced no comparable body of political writing that would survive the day's headlines. In part this was simply a matter of time: the Progressive era lasted over a dozen years, and most of the significant writing it engendered came during its later phases, particularly after 1910; whereas the dynamic phase of the New Deal was concentrated in the six hectic years from 1933 to 1938. Perhaps still more important is the fact that the New Deal brought with it such a rapid bureaucratic expansion and such a complex multitude of problems that it created an immense market for the skills of reform-minded Americans from law, journalism, politics, and the professoriat. The men who might otherwise have been busy analyzing the meaning of events were caught up in the huge expanding bureaucracy and put to work drafting laws that would pass the courts, lobbying with refractory Congressmen, or relocating sharecroppers.

To this generalization there is one noteworthy exception: in his two books, *The Symbols of Government* and *The Folklore of Capitalism,* Thurman Arnold wrote works of great brilliance and wit and considerable permanent significance—better books, I believe, than any of the political criticism of the Progressive era.[17] But what do we find in these works, the most advanced of the New Deal camp? We find a sharp and sustained attack upon ideologies, rational principles, and moralism in politics. We find, in short, the theoretical equivalent of F. D. R.'s opportunistic virtuosity in practical politics—a theory that attacks theories. For Arnold's books, which were of course directed largely against the ritualistic thinking of the conservatives of the 1930's, might stand equally well as an attack upon that moralism which we found so insistent in the thinking of Progressivism.

Arnold's chief concern was with the disparities between the way society actually works and the mythology through which the sound lawyers, economists, and moralists attempt to understand it. His books are an explanation of the ritualistic and functionally irrational character of most of the superficially rational principles by which society lives. At the time his books were written, the necessity of coping with a breakdown in the actual workings of the economy had suddenly confronted men with the operational uselessness of a great many accepted words and ideas. The language of politics, economics, and law had itself become so uncertain that there was a new vogue of books on semantics and of works attempting to break "the tyranny of words," a literature of which Arnold's books were by far the most important. The greater part of Arnold's task was to examine, and to satirize,

---

[17] Thurman W. Arnold: *The Symbols of Government* (New Haven, 1935), *The Folklore of Capitalism* (New Haven, 1937). By 1941 the first of these works had gone through five printings; the second, fourteen.

the orthodox conservative thinking of the moment. This is not our main concern, but what is of primary interest here is the extent to which Arnold's thinking departs from, and indeed on occasion attacks, earlier Progressivism. The deviation of Arnold's system of values from the classic values of American Progressivism was clear from his very terminology. I noted, in discussing the Progressive climate of opinion, the existence of a prevailing vocabulary of civic morals that reflected the disinterested thinking and the selfless action that was expected of the good citizen. The key words of Progressivism were terms like *patriotism, citizen, democracy, law, character, conscience, soul, morals, service, duty, shame, disgrace, sin,* and *selfishness*—terms redolent of the sturdy Protestant Anglo-Saxon moral and intellectual roots of the Progressive uprising. A search for the key words of Arnold's books yields: *needs, organization, humanitarian, results, technique, institution, realistic, discipline, morale, skill, expert, habits, practical, leadership*—a vocabulary revealing a very different constellation of values arising from economic emergency and the imperatives of a bureaucracy.

Although primarily concerned with the conservatives of the present, Arnold paid his respects to the reformers of the past often enough to render a New Dealer's portrait of earlier Progressivism. He saw the reformers of the past as having occupied themselves with verbal and moral battles that left the great working organizations of society largely untouched. "Wherever the reformers are successful—whenever they see their direct primaries, their antitrust laws, or whatever else they base their hopes on, in actual operation—the great temporal institutions adapt themselves, leaving the older reformers disillusioned, like Lincoln Steffens, and a newer set carrying on the banner." [18] Respectable people with humanitarian values, Arnold thought, had characteristically made the mistake of ignoring the fact that "it is not logic but organizations which rule an organized society"; therefore they selected logical principles, rather than organizations, as the objects of their loyalties. Most liberal reform movements attempt to make institutions practice what they preach, in situations where, if this injunction were followed, the functions of the institutions could not be performed.[19] Where the Progressives had been troubled about the development of institutions and organizations, Arnold's argument often appeared to be an apotheosis of them.

At one point or another, Arnold had critical observations to make on most of the staple ideas of Progressive thinking. *The Folklore of Capitalism* opened with a satire on "the thinking man," to whom most of the discourse of rational politics was directed; and the thinking man was hardly more than a caricatured version of the good citizen who was taken as the central figure in most Progressive thinking. While Progressive publicists had devoted much of their time to preachments against what they called "lawlessness,"

---

[18] *The Symbols of Government,* p. 124.   [19] *The Folklore of Capitalism,* pp. 375, 384.

one of the central themes of Arnold's books was an analysis of law and legal thinking showing that law and respectability were so defined that a good many of the real and necessary functions of society had to go on outside the legal framework.[20] Similarly anti-Progressive was his attack on the anti-trust laws—a source of some amusement when he was later put in charge of the enforcement of these laws. But Arnold did not deny that the laws, as they had been interpreted by reformers, had had some use. Their chief use, as he saw it, had been that they permitted the organization of industry to go on while offering comfort to those who were made unhappy by the process. They had, then, a practical significance, but a far different one from that which the reformers had tried to give them. The reformers, how-ever, had had no real strategy with which to oppose the great trusts: "The reason why these attacks [against industrial organizations] always ended with a ceremony of atonement, but few practical results, lay in the fact that there were no new organizations growing up to take over the functions of those under attack. The opposition was never able to build up its own commis-sary and its service of supply. It was well supplied with orators and econ-omists, but it lacked practical organizers. A great cooperative movement in America might have changed the power of the industrial empire. Preaching against it, however, simply resulted in counterpreaching. And the reason for this was that the reformers themselves were caught in the same creeds which supported the institutions they were trying to reform. Obsessed with a moral attitude toward society, they thought in Utopias. They were inter-ested in systems of government. Philosophy was for them more important than opportunism and so they achieved in the end philosophy rather than opportunity." [21]

Arnold professed more admiration for the tycoons who had organized American industry and against whom the Progressives had grown indignant than he did for the reformers themselves. He spoke with much indulgence of Rockefeller, Carnegie, and Ford, and compared John L. Lewis with such men as examples of skillful organizers who had had to sidestep recog-nized scruples. "Actual observation of human society . . . indicates that great constructive achievements in human organization have been accom-plished by unscrupulous men who violated most of the principles which we cherish." [22] The leaders of industrial organization ignored legal, humani-tarian, and economic principles. "They built on their mistakes, their action was opportunistic, they experimented with human material and with little

---

[20] Cf. *The Symbols of Government*, p. 34: "It is part of the function of 'Law' to give recognition to ideals representing the exact opposite of established conduct . . . the function of law is not so much to guide society as to comfort it. Belief in fundamental principles of law does not necessarily lead to an orderly society. Such a belief is as often at the back of revolt or disorder."

[21] *The Folklore of Capitalism*, p. 220.   [22] *The Symbols of Government*, p. 5.

regard for social justice. Yet they raised the level of productive capacity beyond the dreams of their fathers." [23]

Not surprisingly Arnold also had a good word for the politicians, who, for all their lack of social values and for all the imperfections in their aims and vision, are "the only persons who understand the techniques of government." One would prefer a government in the hands of disinterested men, to be sure, but such men are so devoted to and satisfied with the development of good principles that they fail to develop skills, and hence fail to constitute "a competent governing class." Hence society is too often left with a choice between demagogues and psychopaths on one side, or, on the other, "kindly but uneducated Irishmen whose human sympathies give them an instinctive understanding of what people like." [24] Several pages of *The Folklore of Capitalism* were given to a defense of the political machines for the common sense with which they attack the task of government and for the humanitarian spirit in which their work is conducted.[25]

Taken by itself, Arnold's work, with its skepticism about the right-thinking citizen, its rejection of fixed moral principles and disinterested rationality in politics, its pragmatic temper, its worship of accomplishment, its apotheosis of organization and institutional discipline, and its defense of the political machines, may exaggerate the extent of the difference between the New Deal and pre-war Progressivism, but it does point sharply to the character of that difference.[26]

---

[23] Ibid., p. 125. [24] Ibid., pp. 21–2.
[25] *The Folklore of Capitalism*, pp. 367–72; cf. pp. 43, 114–15; cf. *The Symbols of Government*, pp. 239–40.
[26] There are many points at which Arnold yields to the need to seem hard-boiled and at which (rather like F. D. R. himself) he becomes flippant over serious questions. While such lapses have a good deal of symptomatic importance, I do not wish to appear to portray his writing as an attack upon political morality as such: it was not an effort to destroy political morality, but to satirize a particular code of morality that he considered obsolescent and obstructive, and to substitute for it a new one, the precise outlines of which were obviously vague. In my judgment, Arnold did not even successfully pose, much less answer, the very real and important questions that were suggested by his books concerning the relations between morals and politics, or between reason and politics. For a searching criticism see the essay by Sidney Hook in his *Reason, Social Myths, and Democracy* (New York, 1950), pp. 41–51 and the ensuing exchange between Hook and Arnold, pp. 51–61, which to my mind succeeds only in underscoring Arnold's philosophical difficulties. The great value of Arnold's books lies not in the little they have to say about political ethics, but in their descriptive, satirical, and analytical approach to the political thinking of his time, and in their statement of the working mood of a great many New Dealers.
I should perhaps add that my own comments in this area are not intended to be more than descriptive, for there are large questions of political ethics that I too have not attempted to answer. In contrasting the pragmatic and opportunistic tone of the New Deal with the insistent moralism of the Progressives, it has not been my purpose to suggest an invidious comparison that would, at every point, favor the New Deal. Neither is it my purpose to imply that the political morals of the New Dealers were inferior to those of their opponents. My essential interest is in the fact that the emergency that gave rise to

To emphasize, as I have done, the pragmatic and "hard" side of the New Deal is not to forget that it had its "soft" side. Not all its spokesmen shared Arnold's need to pose as hard-boiled.[27] No movement of such scope and power could exist without having its ideals and its ideologies, even its sentimentalities. The New Deal had its literature of inspiration and indignation, its idealistc fervor, its heroes and villains. The difference I hope to establish is that its indignation was directed far more against callousness and waste, far less against corruption or monopoly, than the indignation of the Progressives, and that its inspiration was much more informed by engineering, administration, and economics, considerably less by morals and uplift. For the New Deal not only brought with it a heartening rediscovery of the humane instincts of the country; it also revived the old American interest in practical achievement, in doing things with the physical world, in the ideal that had inspired the great tycoons and industry-builders of the Gilded Age but that afterwards had commonly been dismissed by sensitive men as the sphere only of philistines and money-grubbers.

At the core of the New Deal, then, was not a philosophy (F. D. R. could identify himself philosophically only as a Christian and a democrat), but an attitude, suitable for practical politicians, administrators, and technicians, but uncongenial to the moralism that the Progressives had for the most part shared with their opponents. At some distance from the center of the New Deal, but vital to its public support, were other types of feeling. In some quarters there was a revival of populistic sentiment and the old popular demonology, which F. D. R. and men like Harold Ickes occasionally played up to, chiefly in campaign years, and which Harry Truman later reflected in his baiting of Wall Street. Along with this came another New

---

the New Deal also gave rise to a transvaluation of values, and that the kind of moralism that I have identified with the dominant patterns of thought among the Progressives was inherited not so much by their successors among the New Dealers, who tended to repudiate them, as by the foes of the New Deal.

[27] I have been referred to David Lilienthal's *TVA: Democracy on the March* (New York, 1944) as an illustration of the idealism and inspirational force of the New Deal, and as a work more representative of its spirit than the writings of Thurman Arnold. Lilienthal's book is indeed more unabashedly humanitarian, more inspirational, more concerned with maintaining democracy in the face of technical and administrative change, more given to idealization of the people. It also shows, however, a dedication to certain values, readily discernible in Arnold, that would have been of marginal importance to all but a few of the Progressives. Like Arnold, Lilienthal is pleading the cause of organization, engineering, management, and the attitudes that go with them, as opposed to what he calls the "fog" of conventional ideologies. He appeals to administrative experience, technology, science, and *expertise,* finds that efficient devices of management "give a lift to the human spirit," and asserts that "there is almost nothing, however fantastic that (given competent organization) a team of engineers, scientists, and administrators cannot do today." (Pocket Book ed., New York, 1945, pp. ix, x, 3, 4, 8, 9, 79, 115.) In the light of this philosophy it is easier to see that Lilienthal's more recent defense of big business does not represent a conversion to a new philosophy but simply an ability to find in private organization many of the same virtues that as TVA administrator he found in public enterprise.

Deal phenomenon, a kind of pervasive tenderness for the underdog, for the Okies, the sharecroppers, the characters in John Steinbeck's novels, the subjects who posed for the FSA photographers, for what were called, until a revulsion set in, "the little people." With this there came, too, a kind of folkish nationalism, quickened no doubt by federal patronage of letters and the arts, but inspired at bottom by a real rediscovery of hope in America and its people and institutions. For after the concentration camps, the Nuremberg Laws, Guernica, and (though not everyone saw this so readily) the Moscow trials, everything in America seemed fresh and hopeful, Main Street seemed innocent beyond all expectation, and in time Babbitt became almost lovable. Where Progressivism had capitalized on a growing sense of the ugliness under the successful surface of American life, the New Deal flourished on a sense of the human warmth and the technological potentialities that could be found under the surface of its inequities and its post-depression poverty. On the far fringe there was also a small number of real ideologues, aroused not only by the battle over domestic reform but by the rise of world fascism. Although many of them were fellow travelers and Communists, we stand in serious danger of misunderstanding the character of the New Deal if we overemphasize the influence of this fringe either upon the New Deal core or upon the American people at large. It has now become both fashionable and, for some, convenient to exaggerate the impact of the extreme left upon the thinking of the country in the 1930's. No doubt it will always be possible to do so, for Marxism had a strong if ephemeral impact upon many intellectuals; but the amateur Marxism of the period had only a marginal effect upon the thought and action of either the administrative core of the New Deal or the great masses of Americans.[28] For the people at large—that is, for those who needed it most—the strength of the New Deal was based above all upon its ability to get results.

---

[28] Granville Hicks, in his *Where We Came Out* (New York, 1954), chapter iv, makes a sober effort to show how limited was the Communist influence even in those circles which were its special province. A complementary error to the now fashionable exaggeration of the Communist influence is to exaggerate its ties to the New Deal. Of course Communists played an active part in the spurt of labor organization until the experienced labor leaders expelled them, and in time Communists also succeeded in infiltrating the bureaucracy, with what shocking results we now know. But it was the depression that began to put American Communism on its feet and the New Deal that helped to kill it. The Communists, as consistent ideologues, were always contemptuous of the New Deal. At first they saw fascism in it, and when they gave up this line of criticism during the Popular Front period, they remained contemptuous of its frank experimentalism, its lack of direction, its unsystematic character, and of course its compromises.

XIV

The United States Enters World War II: Did the U. S. Maneuver Japan into the Attack on Pearl Harbor?

INTRODUCTION

As Wayne S. Cole has pointed out in an able analysis of the literature dealing with American entry into World War II, the controversy among historians regarding this question is to some extent a continuation of the debate that raged before Pearl Harbor between "interventionists" and "non-interventionists." The arguments employed between 1939 and 1941 by defenders and opponents of the administration's foreign policy have reappeared in the works of scholarship dealing with these years. As a matter of fact, some of the authors who have written on this subject were personally involved in the pre-Pearl Harbor controversy regarding the relations of the United States with the belligerent nations.[1]

The historians who have defended the foreign policy of the Roosevelt administration in the two years before Pearl Harbor (Cole uses the term "internationalist" to describe them) view the Axis powers as having constituted a threat to the security of the United States and have taken the position that the question of American entry into the war was by 1941 really beyond our power to control. In their opinion, the policies pursued by Roosevelt in 1940 and 1941 vis-à-vis Germany and Japan were, on the whole, the only policies consistent with our security and our principles. Regarding Germany as the greater threat to the United States, American policy-makers, they contend, hoped to avoid war with Japan, provided that this could be accomplished without jeopardizing our security and our interests and without abandoning our friends in the Far East. In the end, they assert, this proved impossible, and although the administration was aware that Japan would strike somewhere, it was genuinely surprised when the blow fell on Pearl Harbor.

The revisionists, by contrast, do not believe that the Axis powers were a threat to the security of the United States and contend that the decision for war or for peace was the administration's to make. Failing to provoke Germany into war despite a series of unneutral acts, Roosevelt, the revisionists argue, led the United States into the war through the back door by maneuvering Japan into the attack on Pearl Harbor. The United States, in their view, was unprepared for this attack because of the incompetence, or worse, of its civilian and military leaders in Washington.

The revisionist and the internationalist positions regarding American entry into World War II are represented here by Charles C. Tansill and Herbert Feis, respectively. Professor Tansill is the author of an impressive number of books in the field of American diplomatic history, including America Goes to War *(1938), generally regarded as the best of the revision-*

---

[1] Wayne S. Cole, "American Entry into World War II: A Historiographical Appraisal," *Mississippi Valley Historical Review*, XLIII (March 1957), 600–601.

ist books dealing with World War I. Tansill's revisionist interpretation of Japanese-American relations between 1937 and 1941, which follows, is taken from his Back Door to War: Roosevelt's Foreign Policy, 1933–1941 *and his essay in* Perpetual War for Perpetual Peace (*this essay is a somewhat condensed version of the treatment of the same subject in* Back Door to War).

Herbert Feis, who like Tansill has contributed importantly to the field of American diplomatic history, served as an economic advisor in the Department of State between 1931 and 1943 and as special consultant to the secretary of war from 1944 to 1946. His The Road to Pearl Harbor (*1950*) *is a study of the relations between the United States and Japan from 1937 to December 7, 1941. In the selection that follows Feis responds to some of the revisionist arguments concerning the events preceding the Japanese attack on Pearl Harbor.*

The United States Moves to War Against Japan

Charles C. Tansill

1. PRESIDENT ROOSEVELT DELIVERS A QUARANTINE SPEECH DIRECTED AGAINST JAPAN

Grew's dispatch* reached the Department of State on October 5. On this same day President Roosevelt made a famous address in Chicago in which he advocated a quarantine against aggressor nations.[1] His words of criticism and warning were directed chiefly against Japan and their baleful effect was all that Grew had feared. It was really big talk in a high key. He was actually far more worried about party reverses at home than about Japanese movements in Manchuria. An economic recession in the United States had made it clear that the big ballyhoo of New Deal politicians had suddenly

---

From *Perpetual War for Perpetual Peace*. Edited by Harry Elmer Barnes. Published by The Caxton Printers, Ltd., Caldwell, Idaho. Used by special permission of the copyright owners. Pp. 289–307, 310–313.

* Editor's note: A dispatch by Grew of September 15, 1937, advising against American action that might antagonize Japan.

[1] *Foreign Relations: Japan, 1931–1941*, I, 379–83.

turned very sour. The Morgenthau diaries give indisputable proof of the deep concern the administration felt with regard to the wide break in the economic structure of the nation.[2]

Joined with this bad news from the economic front was the hostile reaction in the press over the appointment of Senator Hugo Black to the Supreme Court. In September it was made known that Mr. Black had once hidden his face under the wide hood of a Klansman. In dismay he fled to Europe and President Roosevelt found it convenient to make a hurried trip to the Far West. It was highly expedient for him to make some address that would divert public attention from the widespread effects of economic recession and to cover the flight of the nimble Justice Black. A sharp denunciation of the Japanese advance in North China would draw a big herring across a noisome trail and, if it led to eventual war, there was the bright consolation that the war powers of the President are so indefinable and far-reaching that they would insure a long period of dictatorship.

The quarantine speech of October 5 had many macabre overtones designed to frighten the American people. Many parts of the world were experiencing a "reign of terror," and the "landmarks and traditions which have marked the progress of civilization toward a condition of law, order and justice" were being "wiped away." "Innocent peoples and nations" were being "cruelly sacrificed to a greed for power and supremacy" which was "devoid of all sense of justice and humane consideration." If this sad condition of affairs existed in other parts of the world it was vain for anyone to "imagine that America will escape, that it may expect mercy, that this Western Hemisphere will not be attacked, and that it will continue tranquilly and peacefully to carry on the ethics and the arts of civilization."

This attempt to frighten the American people and thus make them forget conditions at home was only partly successful. It is true that Justice Black was soon a "forgotten man" but business conditions grew so steadily worse that they could not escape notice. Moreover, a large part of the American press expressed the view that, if conditions abroad were so bad, it would be wise for America to adopt an isolationist attitude and stay away from trouble. There is no doubt that the President was "disappointed by the failure of the people to respond to his Chicago speech." [3] It was a bit of globaloney with such a strong smell that it took some years for American nostrils to get accustomed to it.

It is true, nonetheless, that the President's challenge to Japan marked a tragic turning point in our relations with that country. He had inaugurated a policy of pressure that eventually pushed America down the road to Pearl Harbor. Japan erected the first milestone along this road by the bombing of the *Panay* on December 12, 1937. A prompt apology and a large in-

---

[2] "The Morgenthau Diaries," *Collier's*, CXX (October 4, 1947), 20; *ibid.*, CXX (October 25, 1947), 85.

[3] James F. Byrnes, *Speaking Frankly* (New York: Harper & Brothers, 1947), p. 6.

demnity indicated that the Foreign Office was still anxious for peace, but the fact that such an incident had occurred gave support to the President's program of pressure upon Japan.

2. THE PRESIDENT PUSHES A PROGRAM
OF PRESSURE UPON JAPAN

The first item in this new program aimed at Japan was the sending of Admiral Royal E. Ingersoll to London in the latter part of December, 1937, with instructions to "explore with the British what we could do if we both found ourselves involved in war in the Far East with Japan." [4] When asked why he was sent to London in 1937 the Admiral replied that "everybody knew" that "sooner or later, we were all going to be involved in a war in the Pacific which would include the Dutch, the Chinese possibly, the Russians, the British, and ourselves." The only tangible result of these Anglo-American conversations in London was a "distribution of codes and ciphers." [5] It should be remembered, in this regard, that similar secret conversations between British and French officials in 1905 constituted the first link in the chain that bound the British to a policy of war with Germany in 1914.

While Admiral Ingersoll was engaged in conversations in London, the President had a press conference on January 8, 1938, in which he expressed the significant opinion that the time had arrived for "Congress to enact legislation aimed at the equalization of the burdens of possible war so that the whole nation will engage in war if we unfortunately have one." [6] Congress did not follow this suggestion. A majority of the members of both houses were still thinking of peace, not war. But the martial mood of the President and Secretary of State became apparent on July 1 when the Chief of the Office of Arms and Munitions Control sent a letter to "148 persons and Companies manufacturing airplane parts" stating that the "Government of the United States is strongly opposed to the sale of airplanes or aeronautical equipment which would materially aid or encourage" the practice of "bombing civilian populations from the air." The Japanese had been guilty of such a practice and therefore the Department of State would "with great regret issue any licenses authorizing exportation, direct or indirect, of any aircraft, aircraft armament, aircraft engines" or aircraft accessories to

---

[4] Testimony of Admiral R. E. Ingersoll during the *Hearings Before the Joint Committee on the Investigation of the Pearl Harbor Attack*, 79 Cong., 2 sess. (39 parts; Washington, D. C.: Government Printing Office, 1946), IX, 4272–73. (The *Hearings* will hereinafter be designated *Pearl Harbor Attack*.)

[5] *Ibid.*, pp. 4274–77.

[6] *The Public Papers and Addresses of Franklin Delano Roosevelt;* edited by Samuel I. Rosenman (13 vols.; New York: Random House, Inc., 1941), VII, 67.

Japan.[7] This "moral embargo" invoked against Japan led to further measures that forged an iron ring around that island empire and pushed it strongly in the direction of war with the United States.

In September, 1938, the President was so sure that the United States would soon "get into war" that he sent Harry Hopkins on a tour of airplane factories to see how production could be expedited. When Hopkins returned to Washington he was visited by Brigadier General George C. Marshall, who was later made Chief of Staff through the influence of Hopkins and Pershing. Marshall quickly caught the belligerent mood of the circle close to the President and it was not long before "several millions of dollars of WPA funds were transferred (secretly) to start making machine tools for the manufacture of small arms ammunition." [8]

While America was thus secretly preparing for what the President regarded as an inevitable war, the Japanese government was making pacific overtures to the United States. On May 16, 1939, a prominent Japanese made an important approach to Ambassador Grew concerning an improvement in Japanese-American relations. If the "democratic nations, especially the United States, could indicate to Japan that restoration of good relations with Japan is desired and that the way is open for Japan to align herself with the democratic nations, . . . those Japanese who are working for precisely those objectives would have their hand greatly strengthened." [9] On the following day the Japanese Minister of Foreign Affairs, Hachiro Arita, commented upon the dangerous activities of the Soviet government and the negotiations then going on in Moscow for an alliance between Britain, France, and the Soviet government. He then remarked that "there had been a suggestion that he give Mr. Grew an assurance that Japan would withhold any action to 'strengthen the Anti-Comintern Pact' until Mr. Grew returned to Washington and had an opportunity to discuss with his Government the possibility of making to Japan some 'gesture of welcome.' " Arita stressed the fact that Japan was "very anxious to avoid involvement in the affairs of Europe," but it was impossible to ignore the fact that "Russia straddled Europe and Asia, and that, whether Japan liked it or not, its [Russia's] policies and actions form a bridge by which events in the Far East and in Europe act and react on each other." It was possible that the danger of a tripartite pact between Britain, France, and Russia might compel Japan to enter into some arrangement with Germany and Italy. He could assure Mr. Grew, however, that the agreement under discussion with

---

[7] Joseph C. Green, Chief of the Office of Arms and Munitions Control, to 148 Persons and Companies Manufacturing Airplane Parts, July 1, 1938, *Foreign Relations, Japan: 1931–1941*, II, 201–2.

[8] Robert E. Sherwood, *Roosevelt and Hopkins* (New York: Harper & Brothers, 1948), pp. 100–101.

[9] Eugene H. Dooman to Secretary Hull, Tokyo, June 7, 1939, *Pearl Harbor Attack*, Part XX, pp. 4144–64.

Germany and Italy "would contain no military, political or economic clauses." [10]

On May 18, 1939, Grew had a long talk with Arita who once more insisted that an alliance between Britain, France, and Russia would probably push Japan into a closer understanding with Germany and Italy. He was equally insistent that Japan, in joining hands with Germany and Italy, had "no other purpose than to combat the destructive activities of the Comintern." If the United States, "not understanding the true position of Japan on this point, should base her future policies on such misunderstanding, it would bring about a deplorable situation not only respecting the relations between the United States and Japan but also in respect of the peace of the world." [11]

The next step by the Japanese government was an invitation to the United States to adopt a program whereby the two nations would jointly attempt to find a peaceful solution of the political differences that were leading to war in Europe. In discussing this matter with Prime Minister Hiranuma, Mr. Dooman, the American chargé d'affaires in Tokyo, asked the pertinent question whether the head of the Japanese cabinet "believed it likely that the American people would look with favor on American collaboration with Japan in approaching the difficulties in Europe when Japan herself was considered to be guilty of the same acts of which Germany and Italy stood condemned." Hiranuma replied that "if the Powers could come together to find by negotiation a solution of the world's troubles these issues involving American rights in China could be disposed of without difficulty." With reference to the conflict in the Far East he expressed the hope that "the American Government at least realized that Japan had not intended or expected to engage in war with China." [12]

Secretary Hull's answer, which did not arrive in Tokyo until the end of July, was negative and tart. Japan was advised to use its "influence toward discouraging among European governments, especially those governments with which your Government may have special relations, the taking of any action, or the pursuance of any policy, that might endanger the general peace." The establishment of world peace was made more difficult by "the continuance of armed conflict" in the Far East. The intimation was clearly given that if Japan was sincere in her desire to help the cause of peace in Europe she should give a better example in eastern Asia.[13]

In order further to emphasize the hostile attitude of the United States

---

[10] *Ibid.*, pp. 4148–50.

[11] Ambassador Grew to Secretary Hull, Tokyo, May 18, 1939, *Foreign Relations, Japan: 1931–1941*, II, 1–5.

[12] Mr. Dooman to Secretary Hull, Tokyo, May 23, 1939, *Pearl Harbor Attack*, Part XX, p. 4139.

[13] The Secretary of State to the Japanese Prime Minister, *Foreign Relations, Japan: 1931–1941*, II, 6–8.

toward Japan, the Department of State, on July 26, 1939, gave notice to the Japanese government that, after six months, the treaty of February 21, 1911, would expire.[14] This action was a severe blow to a Japanese cabinet that was desperately striving to arrive at some understanding with the United States. But Prime Minister Hiranuma disregarded this sharp rebuff and made another attempt to effect more friendly relations between Japan and the United States. On August 26, 1939, the Japanese ambassador (Horinouchi) had a long conversation with Secretary Hull. He gave assurances that his government "had decided to abandon any further negotiations with Germany and Italy relative to closer relations under the anti-Comintern Pact to which they have been parties for some time." After this conciliatory statement, he reiterated his "personal desire to clear up any misunderstanding or differences between our two countries and to restore the friendly relations heretofore existing." Mr. Hull's answer was one more example of his usual moral platitudes and the Japanese gestures of good will were in vain.[15]

While Secretary Hull was prating of peace, President Roosevelt was constantly thinking of war with Japan. Ambassador Grew saw this fact clearly in September, 1939. During the course of a conference with the President he took pains to point out that, if America placed an embargo upon oil exports to Japan, the result might be a Japanese effort to take the Dutch East Indies and thereby control the rich oil resources of Borneo. The President's reply showed that he was already thinking of war. If Japan decided upon such a step, American naval forces could "easily intercept her fleet." [16]

But Grew wished to prevent rather than provoke war with Japan. While the President was talking this belligerent bombast, Grew was confiding to his diary that the Department of State should "offer the Japanese a *modus vivendi*" and then commence negotiations for a new commercial treaty. In Japan the Shidehara policy of conciliation had once existed: "It can exist again." [17] To Grew the Japanese program, with its insistence upon "strategic protection against a future attack by Soviet Russia," did not appear too unreasonable. If America wished to change this program it should not try to do so through the employment of sanctions: "There must be no tone of threat in our attitude." [18]

It is evident that Grew did not appreciate the fact that the President's dislike of Japan had gone so deep and spread so far that it would lead inevitably to war. In defiance of Grew's advice against sanctions, a White House statement was issued once more invoking a moral embargo upon the

---

[14] Secretary Hull to the Japanese Ambassador, July 26, 1939, *Peace and War*, p. 475.

[15] Memorandum of a conversation between Secretary Hull and the Japanese ambassador (Horinouchi), August 26, 1939, *ibid.*, pp. 480–82.

[16] Herbert Feis, *The Road to Pearl Harbor* (Princeton, N. J.: Princeton University Press, 1950), p. 41, quoting from the manuscript diary of Ambassador Grew.

[17] *Ibid.*, p. 42.   [18] Grew, *Ten Years in Japan*, pp. 296–303.

shipment to Japan of "airplanes, aeronautical equipment and materials essential to airplane manufacture." [19] This statement of December 2 was followed by another one of December 20. This later pronouncement issued from the Department of State and contained the significant formula that "national interest suggests that for the time being there should be no further delivery to certain countries of plans, plants, manufacturing rights, or technical information required for the production of high quality aviation gasoline." [20] In 1940 there was a series of statements issued by the Administrator of Export Control which indicated a drastic curtailment of exports to Japan.[21] If embargoes could produce war the administration was determined to overlook no opportunity to exert pressure upon Japan along that line.

3. BRITAIN AND FRANCE ADOPT A POLICY OF APPEASEMENT TOWARD JAPAN

American pressure upon Japan was followed by Japanese pressure upon Britain and France. On March 30, 1940, Japan set up a "new Central Government of China" to be headed by Wang Ching-wei. Secretary Hull immediately announced that the Department of State would continue to recognize the government of Chiang Kai-shek "as the Government of China." [22] But the British Foreign Office was more conciliatory. On March 28, Sir Robert Craigie, the British ambassador in Tokyo, delivered an address in which he stated that Britain and Japan were "striving for the same objective, namely, a lasting peace and the preservation of our institutions from extraneous, subversive influences." [23] This address keynoted British policy. On July 17 the Burma Road was closed to shipments of war matériel to China.[24] France had already acceded to demands for a similar embargo upon supplies going to Chiang Kai-shek through Indochina. The Nationalist government in China was being effectively shut off from aid that was essential to her continuance in the war against Japan.

4. JAPAN CONCLUDES AN ALLIANCE WITH THE ROME–BERLIN AXIS

While Japan was exerting pressure upon Britain and France she was making overtures to the Rome-Berlin Axis. An alliance with these European dictatorships had been long in the making. Its most important Japanese sponsor was General Hiroshi Oshima, the Japanese ambassador to Germany. He and Ribbentrop were on intimate terms. In the summer of 1938 Ribbentrop in-

---

[19] *Foreign Relations, Japan: 1931–1941*, II, 202.   [20] *Ibid.*, pp. 203–4.   [21] *Ibid.*, 807–8.
[22] *Ibid.*, pp. 59–60.   [23] London *Times,* March 29, 1940.
[24] *Documents on American Foreign Relations, 1940–1941;* edited by S. Shepard Jones and Denys P. Myers (Boston: World Peace Foundation, 1941), III, 270–71.

quired if Japan would be willing to sign a treaty aimed at all the potential enemies of the proposed Rome-Berlin-Tokyo triangle.[25] Tokyo rejected this broad proposal [26] and in February, 1939, Prince Ito was sent to Berlin to acquaint Ribbentrop with the decision that Japan wished to limit the proposed treaty to action against Russia alone.[27]

In order to speed a decision by Japan to enter into an alliance with the Rome-Berlin Axis, Heinrich Stahmer hurried to Tokyo and insisted that the prime purpose in effecting the new political alignment was to keep America out of war.[28] Stahmer succeeded in silencing all Japanese opposition to the tripartite pact which was signed with great pomp in Berlin on September 27, 1940.[29] Article III pointed straight at the United States: "Japan, Germany and Italy . . . undertake to assist one another with all political, economic and military means when one of the Contracting Parties is attacked by a power at present not involved in the European War or in the Sino-Japanese Conflict." [30] There is evidence, however, that Japan extracted from Stahmer a secret oral understanding that she retain for herself the right to decide whether the *casus foederis* existed in any situation that might arise.[31]

5. JAPAN IS READY TO SACRIFICE HER POSITION IN CHINA FOR THE SAKE OF PEACE WITH THE UNITED STATES

But this tripartite pact of September 27, 1940, did not mean that Japan had abandoned all hope of a satisfactory arrangement with the United States. Quite the contrary! In November, 1940, Foreign Minister Matsuoka asked Bishop James E. Walsh, Superior General of the Catholic Foreign Mission Society of Maryknoll, New York, and Father J. M. Drought, of the same order, to undertake a special mission to Washington in order to impress upon the President and Secretary Hull the fact that the Japanese government "wished to negotiate a peace agreement: (1) an agreement to nullify their participation in the Axis Pact . . . (2) a guarantee to recall all military forces from China and to restore to China its geographical and political integrity." Other conditions bearing upon the relations of Japan and the United States were to be explored and agreed upon "in the conversations that it was hoped would ensue."

Bishop Walsh and Father Drought then had a conference with General

---

[25] Interrogation of General Oshima, February 4, 1946, *Record of Proceedings of the International Military Tribunal for the Far East* (Washington, D. C.: Department of State, 1946), Exhibit No. 497, pp. 6050–54.

[26] *Ibid.* [27] *Ibid.*, pp. 6063–71. [28] *Ibid.*, Exhibits Nos. 549, 550, 553, pp. 6323–93.

[29] William L. Shirer, *Berlin Diary* (New York: Alfred A. Knopf, 1941), pp. 532–37.

[30] *Foreign Relations, Japan: 1931–1941*, II, 165–66.

[31] H. L. Trefousse, *Germany and American Neutrality, 1939–1941* (New York: Bookman Associates, 1951), p. 71.

Muto, the director of the Central Bureau of Military Affairs, who assured them that "he and his associates in the Japanese Army were in accord with the efforts to reach a peace agreement."

Bishop Walsh and Father Drought hurried to Washington where (on January 23, 1941) they placed the whole matter before President Roosevelt and Secretary Hull during a long conference of more than two hours. They were told that the matter would be "taken under advisement," [32] and thus ended an anxious effort on the part of the Japanese government to find a path to peace, even though this path led to a renunciation of Japan's objectives in China and a tremendous loss of face.* It seems quite possible that the Far Eastern Military Tribunal brought to trial the wrong persons. It might have been better if the tribunal had held its sessions in Washington.

6. BLUEPRINT FOR ANGLO–AMERICAN CO-OPERATION
IN THE WAR ON JAPAN

Instead of acting upon the proposals of Bishop Walsh and Father Drought, the President and Secretary Hull initiated Joint Staff conferences in Washington from January to March, 1941. Delegations from Britain, Australia, Canada, and New Zealand surveyed with American representatives the many questions involved in the defense of the Pacific area against Japanese attack. During the session, which resulted in the ABC-1 Staff Agreement, the British delegation ardently argued that the defense of Singapore was so essential that the United States should be willing to divide the Pacific Fleet for that purpose. Although this proposal was rejected, the agreement did outline for American task forces some important operations that would be beneficial for Britain in the event both powers were involved in war with Japan.

The ABC-1 Staff Agreement was promptly approved by the Secretaries of the Navy and War; the President gave it no explicit approval.[33] It was soon apparent, however, that American military plans were profoundly affected by it.[34] The changes made in them were far more than mere technical details: they indicated a close community of thought and proposed

---

[32] *International Military Tribunal for the Far East*, Exhibit No. 3441, pp. 32979–85.

* Editor's note: It was decided at the January 23, 1941, conference that Bishop Walsh and Father Drought "should continue their informal contact with the Japanese Embassy" and, through the Postmaster General, with Secretary of State Hull. It was also decided to delay negotiations until the new Japanese ambassador, Admiral Nomura, arrived in Washington. Discussions with Nomura began in March "but the proposed Japanese concessions were gradually withdrawn or whittled away until they were unacceptable to the United States." William L. Langer and S. Everett Gleason, *The Challenge to Isolation, 1937–1940* (New York: Harper & Brothers, 1952), pp. 314–15, 320–21, 467–70; Julius W. Pratt, *A History of United States Foreign Policy* (New York: Prentice-Hall, Inc., 1955), p. 650.

[33] *Pearl Harbor Attack*, Part V, p. 2391.

[34] Admiral H. R. Stark to the Commanders in Chief of the U. S. Pacific Fleet; the Asiatic Fleet; and the Atlantic Fleet, April 3, 1941, *ibid.*, Part XVII, pp. 2462–63.

action between Britain and the United States. A blueprint had been drawn for an Anglo-American parallel policy. It would be carried out as soon as the President could find a pretext for doing so.

7. JAPAN PRESSES FOR PEACE WITH THE UNITED STATES

As Hitler moved toward war with Soviet Russia he began to think more and more of Japanese assistance in this projected struggle. In March, 1941, Ribbentrop strongly argued that Japan, in its own interest, should enter the war "as soon as possible." This intervention would not only destroy England's key position in the Far East but it would also "keep America out of the war." [35] On March 26 Matsuoka, the Japanese Foreign Minister, arrived in Berlin. On the following day Ribbentrop plied him with the usual Nazi line of argument. It would be "very advantageous if Japan should decide as soon as possible to take an active part in the war upon England." Japanese intervention would be "most likely to keep America out of the war." When Matsuoka bluntly inquired about the attitude of Germany toward America after Britain was defeated, Ribbentrop quickly answered that "Germany did not have the slightest interest in a war against the United States." [36]

Japan also did not have the "slightest interest in a war against the United States." The appointment of Nomura as ambassador to the United States was an indication of this fact. Admiral Nomura had been the Japanese naval attaché in Washington during the first World War and had formed a friendly relationship with Franklin D. Roosevelt, then serving as the Assistant Secretary of the Navy. His reception at the White House was cordial but the President frankly referred to the fact that relations between Japan and the United States were steadily "deteriorating." [37] At the State Department he soon discovered a studied policy of "coolness toward the Japanese."

On March 8 Hull and Nomura had their first conversation on Japanese-American relations. Subsequently they met more than forty times in vain endeavors to find some firm ground on which to build a new structure of friendship. Hitler viewed these negotiations with frank alarm. As Ribbentrop later remarked:

> The Fuehrer . . . saw the attitude of the United States "short of war" and he was worried . . . about groups in Japan who wanted to come to an arrangement with America. He was afraid that if an arrangement would be made between the United States and Japan, this would mean, so to speak, the back free for America and the ex-

---

[35] *Nazi Conspiracy and Aggression* (Washington, D. C.: Government Printing Office, 1946), P-S 1834, IV, 469–75.

[36] Memorandum of a conversation between Ribbentrop and Matsuoka, March 28, 1941, *Nazi-Soviet Relations, 1939–1941* (New York: Didier Publications, 1948), pp. 298–303.

[37] Memorandum by Secretary Hull, February 14, 1941, *Foreign Relations, Japan: 1931–1941*, II, 387.

pected attack or entry into the war by the United States would come quicker.[38]

Japan paid little attention to this pressure from Berlin and Nomura carried on his talks with Hull without much thought of the desires of the Rome-Berlin Axis. The Japanese government was willing to give two important pledges: (1) to use only peaceful measures in the southwest Pacific; (2) to go to the support of Germany only in the event that she was the object of aggression. In return for these pledges Japan wished America (1) to restore normal trade relations between the two countries; (2) to assist Japan to secure access to basic raw materials in the southwest Pacific area; (3) to exert pressure upon Chiang Kai-shek so that he would consent to certain peace terms; (4) if Chiang refused to yield to this pressure the American government would withdraw support from his regime; (5) and, finally, to lend friendly diplomatic assistance aimed at the removal of Hongkong and Singapore as doorways "to further political encroachment by the British in the Far East." Secretary Hull countered with a memorandum emphasizing the following points: (1) respect for the territorial integrity and the sovereignty of each and all nations; (2) support of the principle of noninterference in the internal affairs of other countries; (3) support of the principle of equality, including equality of commercial opportunity; (4) nondisturbance of the *status quo* in the Pacific except as the *status quo* may be altered by peaceful means.[39]

The discussion of these bases for a friendly accord was not helped by occasional verbal pyrotechnics on the part of Matsuoka. On May 14 he had a conversation with Ambassador Grew during the course of which he sharply criticized the attitude of the United States toward Germany. American attacks upon German submarines might bring into action Article III of the tripartite pact of September 27, 1940.[40]

This conversation was the subject of comment by Sumner Welles during a conference with the British ambassador. Lord Halifax inquired as to the progress of the Hull-Nomura talks. Was there any chance that they would have a successful outcome? Welles thought that the "chances might not be better than one in ten." He then handed to Halifax a copy of a letter Matsuoka wrote to Grew immediately after their conversation on May 14. It was written in such a rambling style that Halifax thought it "bore evidences of lunacy." Welles shared this impression but finally came to the conclusion that "it might be due to the fact that Mr. Matsuoka was understood to be drinking extremely heavily at this time and the mental state apparent

---

[38] Testimony of Ribbentrop at Nuremberg, September 10, 1945, *Nazi Conspiracy and Aggression*, Supplement B, pp. 1200–1201.

[39] *Foreign Relations, Japan: 1931–1941*, II, 407.

[40] Ambassador Grew to Secretary Hull, May 14, 1941, *ibid.*, pp. 145–48.

in the writing of this letter might be momentary rather than permanent." [41]

It is apparent that Matsuoka's belligerent state of mind was a result of the pressure from Berlin. Hitler would soon launch his attack upon Russia and he was particularly anxious that America remain neutral. But this Japanese threat failed to restrain Roosevelt. On June 20 an announcement was made in Washington that no more oil would be exported from American eastern ports (including the Gulf of Mexico) except to the British Empire and the Western Hemisphere. Two days later, Hitler's armies crossed the Russian frontier and the German offensive began to roll. When the news reached Tokyo, Matsuoka rushed to the Emperor and strongly argued that Japan should support Germany by immediately attacking Russia. He readily admitted that his program implied possible war with the United States. [42]

Although Konoye wished to apply a brake to the forward tactics of Matsuoka, the Japanese army leaders were restive, and liaison conferences on June 25 and July 2 mapped a new and dangerous program: (1) Japan should not rush into a conflict with the Soviets; (2) the triple alliance should not be abandoned; (3) Japan should move south into Indochina. [43] Knowledge of this decision reached Washington during the first week in July. The Japanese code had been broken and from July to December, 1941, the President and Secretary of State could read the instructions from the Japanese Foreign Office to Ambassador Nomura. [44] The projected Japanese drive to the south was soon familiar in all its details.

8. ROOSEVELT FREEZES JAPANESE FUNDS IN THE UNITED STATES

On July 16 the Japanese cabinet resigned. When Konoye was asked to form a new cabinet he dropped Matsuoka and named Admiral Toyoda as the new Foreign Minister. Toyoda was particularly fearful of further American embargoes upon the export of essential commodities to Japan. In the third week in July he sent an ominous instruction to Nomura in Washington: "Should the U. S. . . . take steps at this time which unduly excite Japan (such as . . . the freezing of assets), an exceedingly critical situation may be created. Please advise the United States of this fact and attempt to bring about an improvement in the situation." [45]

The efforts of Nomura to this end were in vain. On July 26 an order was

[41] Memorandum of a conversation between Sumner Welles and Viscount Halifax, May 17, 1941. 711.94/2207, MS, Department of State.

[42] "Memoirs of Prince Konoye," *Pearl Harbor Attack*, Part XX, p. 3993; see also the diary of the Marquis Koichi Kido in *International Military Tribunal for the Far East*, Exhibit No. 635.

[43] "Memoirs of Prince Konoye," *op. cit.*, pp. 4018-19.

[44] These intercepted decoded messages from Tokyo are given in detail in *Pearl Harbor Attack*, Part XII, pp. 1-316.

[45] Japanese Foreign Office to Ambassador Nomura, July 23, 1941, *ibid.*, pp. 4-5.

issued freezing Japanese funds in the United States. This meant an end to the export of oil to Japan. When Nomura called at the Department of State to inquire about the situation, Welles received him in his best frigid manner. Nomura expressed the hope that this restriction would not mean any "further deterioration in the relations of our two countries," but Welles parried this indirect query by remarking upon the extraordinary patience "which the United States had demonstrated in its relations with Japan during recent years." The Japanese ambassador quietly stated that he believed the best thing under the circumstances was to adopt some "compromise solution which would prove acceptable to both sides." Welles crisply replied that there was not the "slightest ground for any compromise solution." [46]

9. THE ATLANTIC CONFERENCE PUSHES AMERICA CLOSER TO A BREAK WITH JAPAN

Any thought of a compromise solution of Japanese-American difficulties was made more difficult by the decisions of the Atlantic Conference between Churchill and President Roosevelt. On August 9, 1941, in the Newfoundland harbor of Argentia, the first conference between these two statesmen was held. It was soon apparent that Britain was deeply disturbed about conditions in the southwest Pacific. According to a British suggestion, America was to state very frankly to Japan that any "further encroachment" in the direction of Malaya or the Netherlands East Indies would compel the United States to take measures that might lead to war. Welles wished to broaden the scope of American action. He would have the United States play the role of policeman in a very wide area in the Pacific. American forces should be ready to repel any Japanese thrust whether it was directed "against China, against the Soviet Union or against British Dominions or British colonies, or the colonies of the Netherlands in the Southern Pacific area." Churchill and Roosevelt were in hearty agreement with this wider formula, but the President was too cautious to broadcast it to the American public. [47]

Churchill did not secure at Argentia all the items in his program but he at least secured pledges that relieved many of his fears. In a speech in Parliament, January 27, 1942, he remarked: "The probability, since the Atlantic Conference . . . that the United States, even if not herself attacked, would come into a war in the Far East, and thus make final victory sure, seemed to allay some of these anxieties. . . . As time went on, one had greater as-

[46] Memorandum of a conversation between Sumner Welles and Ambassador Nomura, July 28, 1941, *Foreign Relations, Japan: 1931–1941*, II, 537–39.

[47] Memorandum of conversations at Argentia between President Roosevelt, Prime Minister Churchill, Sir Alexander Cadogan, Harry Hopkins, and Sumner Welles, *Pearl Harbor Attack*, Part IV, pp. 1784–92.

surance that if Japan ran amok in the Pacific, we should not fight alone." [48]

10. ROOSEVELT REFUSES TO MEET PRINCE KONOYE

In a statement he handed to the Japanese ambassador on August 17, Roosevelt carried out his pledge to Churchill. It was phrased in language that carried a definite warning against Japanese expansion:

> If the Japanese Government takes any further steps in pursuance of a policy . . . of military domination by force or threat of force of neighboring countries, the Government of the United States will be compelled to take immediately any and all steps which it may deem necessary toward safeguarding . . . the safety and security of the United States.[49]

A new issue now came up with reference to a meeting between Roosevelt and Prince Konoye. As early as August 7 the Japanese government had asked for such a meeting. It was now informed (August 17) that if it was ready to "suspend its expansionist activities" the Department of State would "endeavor to arrange a suitable time and place to exchange views."

In Tokyo Ambassador Grew was deeply impressed with the importance of a meeting between Konoye and Roosevelt. In a dispatch to Secretary Hull he thought such a conference would present an opportunity for "the highest statesmanship." [50] In the State Department, however, there was little enthusiasm for a Konoye-Roosevelt conference. In the Division of Far Eastern Affairs a memorandum was prepared which flatly stated: "The holding of the meeting between the President and the Japanese Prime Minister on the basis of the present status of the discussions between this country and Japan would result in more of disadvantage than of advantage as regards this country's interests and policies." [51]

Ambassador Grew strongly contested this viewpoint and cogently argued against a firm stand by the Department of State upon an inflexible program of principles in advance of a meeting between Roosevelt and Konoye. Political differences could be expressed in subtle shades that would not affront sensitive nations that objected to the conventional pattern of black and white. It would be best to go to such a meeting in a spirit that welcomed adjustment of existing difficulties; not in a spirit of challenge.[52] But Secre-

---

[48] Winston Churchill, *The End of the Beginning* (Boston: Little, Brown & Company, 1943), p. 33.

[49] *Foreign Relations, Japan: 1931–1941*, II, 556–59.

[50] Ambassador Grew to Secretary Hull, Tokyo, August 18, 1941, *ibid.*, pp. 565.

[51] Memorandum of the Division of Far Eastern Affairs, September 23, 1941. 711.94/2344, *Strictly Confidential*, MS, Department of State.

[52] Ambassador Grew to Secretary Hull, September 29, 1941, *Foreign Relations, Japan: 1931–1941*, II, 645–50.

tary Hull paid little attention to these admonitions from Grew. On October 2 he handed to Ambassador Nomura a statement that vetoed any idea of a Roosevelt-Konoye meeting. Before such a conference could be agreed upon there would first have to be a definite meeting of minds upon the agenda.[53] Sir Robert Craigie, the British ambassador in Tokyo, was sharply critical of the Hull attitude:

> By pursuing a policy of stalling, the United States is arguing about every word and every phrase on the grounds that it is an essential preliminary to any kind of an agreement. . . . It would be very regrettable indeed if the best opportunity for the settlement of the Far Eastern problem since I assumed my post here, were to be lost in such a manner. . . . Both the U. S. Ambassador in Japan and I are firmly of the opinion that it would be a foolish policy if this superb opportunity is permitted to slip by by assuming an unduly suspicious attitude.[54]

11. GENERAL MARSHALL AND ADMIRAL STARK OPPOSE AN ULTIMATUM TO JAPAN

When Hull insisted upon a continued "unduly suspicious attitude" toward Japan, the Konoye Ministry resigned (October 16). In the new cabinet General Hideki Tojo assumed the post of Prime Minister, with Shigenori Togo as the new Minister of Foreign Affairs. The story of the attempts of the Tojo cabinet to find some path to peace is a twice-told tale that does not have to be repeated here.[55] It has long been equally obvious that the highest officers in the American Army and Navy were deeply concerned about the rapid drift toward war and wanted to postpone the conflict for at least three months. But Chiang Kai-shek began a drive to hasten American intervention. On November 2 the Generalissimo wrote to Roosevelt that a new Japanese offensive against Yunnan might shake the morale of the Chinese Army and the Chinese people "to its foundation." For the first time in "this long war a real collapse of resistance would be possible" if the Japanese drive succeeded in taking Kunming.[56] But General Marshall and Admiral Stark resisted this Chinese pressure to push America immediately into the war. On November 5, after a review of the situation in the Far East, they strongly recommended that "no ultimatum be delivered to Japan." [57]

---

[53] Oral statement handed by Secretary Hull to Ambassador Nomura, October 2, 1941, *ibid.*, pp. 656–61.

[54] *Pearl Harbor Attack*, Part XII, p. 51.

[55] Feis, *The Road to Pearl Harbor*, pp. 282–325; Charles A. Beard, *President Roosevelt and the Coming of the War, 1941* (New Haven, Conn.: Yale University Press, 1948), pp. 496–516; Frederic R. Sanborn, *Design for War; a Study of Secret Power Politics, 1937–1941* (New York: Devin-Adair Company, 1951), pp. 377–425.

[56] *Pearl Harbor Attack*, Part XV, pp. 1476–78.   [57] *Ibid.*, Part XIV, pp. 1061–62.

12. JAPAN IS "MANEUVERED" INTO FIRING
THE FIRST SHOT AT PEARL HARBOR

The rejection of the Konoye-Roosevelt meeting was a real ultimatum to Japan, and after October 16 tension in Tokyo rapidly mounted. On November 5 instructions were sent to Nomura that November 25 would be the deadline in the negotiations in Washington.[58] This deadline was repeated in instructions on November 11.[59] From the intercepted Japanese radiograms, Secretary Hull knew all about this deadline. On November 15 Hull handed Nomura another one of his long oral statements. He knew that it could not be accepted by Japan. The bases for an agreement were a challenge. Complete control over "its economic, financial and monetary affairs" should be restored to China, and Japan should abandon any thought of preserving in China a "preferential position." [60]

Japan realized that this was really a challenge, but a last attempt was made to preserve peace. Saburo Kurusu was sent to Washington to assist Nomura. He had served as consul in Chicago and New York, and his happy marriage to an American girl had given him a personal interest in finding some road to accommodation. But Hull was hell-bent for war. The constant needling by Chiang Kai-shek had gotten under his skin and President Roosevelt felt pressure from his administrative assistant, Lauchlin Currie, also a warm admirer of Soviet Russia. At this point Owen Lattimore, American adviser to Chiang-Kai-shek, sent a strongly worded cablegram against any *modus vivendi* or truce with Japan: "Any *modus vivendi*" now arrived at with Japan would be "disastrous to Chinese belief in America." [61] For a week Currie had been "terribly anxious" because he feared that "Hull was in danger of selling China and America and Britain down the river." [62] In Chungking, Madame Chiang Kai-shek became "unrestrainedly critical" of the American government for its failure to "plunge into the war" and thus aid China.[63] From London word came from Churchill with reference to the situation in China: "There is only one point that disquiets us. What about Chiang Kai-shek? Is he not having a very thin diet?" [64]

Under the impact of these cablegrams Hull became hysterical. During a

---

[58] Japanese Foreign Office to Ambassador Nomura, November 5, 1941, *ibid.*, Part XII, p. 100.

[59] Japanese Foreign Office to Ambassador Nomura, November 11, 1941, *ibid.*, pp. 116–17.

[60] Oral statement handed by Secretary Hull to Ambassador Nomura, November 15, 1941, *Foreign Relations, Japan: 1931–1941*, II, 734–37.

[61] Owen Lattimore to Lauchlin Currie, November 25, 1941, *Pearl Harbor Attack*, Part XIV, p. 1160. See also *Hearings Before the Sub-Committee to Investigate the Administration of the Internal Security Act* (McCarran Committee), United States Senate, 82 Cong., 1 sess., Part I, pp. 156–57.

[62] *Hearings, ibid.*, pp. 157–58.

[63] Ambassador Gauss to Secretary Hull, Chungking, December 3, 1941. 711.94/2600, MS, Department of State.

[64] *Pearl Harbor Attack*, Part XIV, p. 1300.

telephone conversation with Secretary Stimson he remarked that he had just about made up his mind about any thought of a *modus vivendi* or truce with Japan—he "would kick the whole thing over." [65] This is just what he and President Roosevelt did on the following day, November 26. On that afternoon Hull handed to the Japanese diplomatic representatives a ten-point proposal which amounted to a sharp ultimatum: "The government of Japan will withdraw all military, naval, air and police forces from China and Indochina." [66] Both Hull and the President knew the Japanese government could not accept such a proposal: it was an invitation to war. It was not long before that invitation was accepted.

———

On* the morning of December 4, the Navy radio receiving station at Cheltenham, Maryland, intercepted a Japanese overseas news broadcast from Station JAP in Tokyo, in which there was inserted a false weather report, "east wind rain." On November 19 the Japanese Government had instructed its ambassador in Washington that such a weather forecast would indicate imminence of war with the United States.[67] After intercepting this Japanese instruction the radio receiving stations of the American armed forces were on the alert for the "east wind rain" message. As soon as it was translated, Lieutenant Commander Kramer handed it to Commander Safford with the exclamation: "This is *it*." Safford got in touch immediately with Rear Admiral Noyes who telephoned the substance of the intercepted message "to the naval aide to the President." [68]

According to the testimony of Captain Safford [in 1941 a Commander], the

> "winds" message and the change of the [Japanese] naval operations code came in the middle of the week: two days to Saturday and three days to Sunday. It was unthinkable that the Japanese would surrender their hopes of surprise by delaying until the week-end of December 13–14. This was not crystal-gazing or "intuition"—it was just the plain, common sense acceptance of a self-evident proposition. Col. Sadtler saw it, and so did Capt. Joseph R. Redman, U.S.N., according to Col. Sadtler's testimony in 1944. . . . The Japanese were going to start the war on Saturday, December 6, 1941, or Sunday, December 7, 1941.[69]

[65] Stimson diary, November 26, 1941; *Pearl Harbor Attack*, Part XI, p. 5434.

[66] Oral statement handed by Secretary Hull to Ambassador Nomura and Mr. Kurusu, November 26, 1941, *Foreign Relations, Japan: 1931–1941*, II, 766–70.

* Editor's note: The remainder of the text is reprinted, by permission, from *Back Door to War* by Charles C. Tansill, copyright 1952 by Henry Regnery Company. Pp. 650–652.

[67] Japanese Foreign Office to Ambassador Nomura, Tokyo, November 19, 1941. *Pearl Harbor Attack*, pt. 12, p. 154.

[68] George Morgenstern, *Pearl Harbor* (New York, 1947), p. 206.

[69] *Ibid.*, p. 211. The testimony of Captain Safford is given in detail in *Pearl Harbor Attack*, pt. 8, pp. 3555–3814.

For the next three days Commander Safford and Lieutenant Commander Kramer tried in vain to get some action out of their superior officers with regard to the implications of the "east wind rain" message. When they induced Captain McCollum to exert some pressure upon Admiral Stark he was given a sharp rebuke which so infuriated him that he later poured the whole story into the receptive ears of Admiral Kimmel. This disclosure led Kimmel to press for the Pearl Harbor investigations.

The unaccountable failure of high naval officers to convey a warning to Honolulu about the imminence of war was given additional highlights on the evening of December 6 when the Japanese reply to the American note of November 26 was sent secretly to Ambassador Nomura. It was intercepted by Navy receiving stations and decoded. When the President read this message to Nomura he at once exclaimed: "This means war!" He tried to get in touch with Admiral Stark but was informed that the chief of naval operations was at the National Theatre enjoying the delightful strains of *The Student Prince*.[70] The next day the Admiral's ears would be assailed by the crashing echoes of the attack upon Pearl Harbor.

It would ordinarily be assumed that the President, after reading this intercepted Japanese message, would hurriedly call a conference of the more important Army and Navy officers to concert plans to meet the anticipated attack. The testimony of General Marshall and Admiral Stark would indicate that the Chief Executive took the ominous news so calmly that he made no effort to consult with them.[71] Did he deliberately seek the Pearl Harbor attack in order to get America into the war? What is the real answer to this riddle of Presidential composure in the face of a threatened attack upon some American outpost in the faraway Pacific? This problem grows more complicated as we watch the approach of zero hour. At 9:00 A.M. on December 7, Lieutenant Commander Kramer delivered to Admiral Stark the final installment of the Japanese instruction to Nomura. Its meaning was now so obvious that Stark cried out in great alarm: "My God! This means war. I must get word to Kimmel at once." [72] But he made no effort to contact Honolulu. Instead he tried to get in touch with General Marshall, who, for some strange reason, suddenly decided to go on a long horseback ride. It was a history-making ride. In the early hours of the American Revolution, Paul Revere went on a famous ride to warn his countrymen of the enemy's approach and thus save American lives. In the early hours of World War II, General Marshall took a ride that helped prevent an alert from reaching Pearl Harbor in time to save an American fleet from serious disaster and an American garrison from a bombing that cost more than two thousand lives. Was there an important purpose behind this ride? This question looms constantly larger as we look further into the Pearl Harbor hearings.

---

[70] In this regard the testimony of Commander Lester B. Schulz is pertinent and colorful. *Ibid.*, pt. 10, pp. 4662–63.

[71] *Ibid.*, pt. 3, pp. 1049–1541; pt. 5, pp. 2096–2477.   [72] Morgenstern, *op. cit.*, p. 269.

When Colonel Bratton, on the morning of December 7, saw the last part of the Japanese instruction to Nomura he realized at once that "Japan planned to attack the United States at some point at or near 1 o'clock that day." [73] To Lieutenant Commander Kramer the message meant "a surprise attack at Pearl Harbor today." [74] This information was in the hands of Secretary Knox by 10:00 A.M., and he must have passed it on to the President immediately.

It was 11:25 A.M. when General Marshall returned to his office. If he carefully read the reports on the threatened Japanese attack (on Pearl Harbor) he still had plenty of time to contact Honolulu by means of the scrambler telephone on his desk, or by the Navy radio or the FBI radio. For some reason best known to himself he chose to send the alert to Honolulu by RCA and did not even take the precaution to have is stamped, "priority." As the Army Pearl Harbor Board significantly remarked: "We find no justification for a failure to send this message by multiple secret means either through the Navy radio or the FBI radio or the scrambler telephone or all three." [75] Was the General under Presidential orders to break military regulations with regard to the transmission of important military information? Did he think that the President's political objectives outweighed considerations of national safety? Was the preservation of the British Empire worth the blood, sweat, and tears not only of the men who would die in the agony of Pearl Harbor but also of the long roll of heroes who perished in the epic encounters in the Pacific, in the Mediterranean area, and in the famous offensive that rolled at high tide across the war-torn fields of France? New cemeteries all over the world would confirm to stricken American parents the melancholy fact that the paths of military glory lead but to the grave.

But the President and Harry Hopkins viewed these dread contingencies with amazing equanimity. In the quiet atmosphere of the oval study in the White House, with all incoming telephone calls shut off, the Chief Executive calmly studied his well-filled stamp albums while Hopkins fondled Fala, the White House scottie. At one o'clock, Death stood in the doorway. The Japanese had bombed Pearl Harbor. America had suddenly been thrust into a war she is still fighting.

---

[73] *Ibid.*, p. 275. See also the testimony of Colonel Rufus S. Bratton in *Pearl Harbor Attack*, pts. 9–10, pp. 4508–4623.

[74] *Ibid.*, p. 276.

[75] *Pearl Harbor Attack*, pt. 39, p. 95; Robert E. Ward, "The Inside Story of the Pearl Harbor Plan," United States Naval Institute *Proceedings*, LXXVII, No. 12 (December 1951), 1271–83.

War Came at Pearl Harbor:

Suspicions Considered

Herbert Feis

Ten years after victory, we look ruefully at the way the world has gone. It is right and natural to search out any errors of judgment or faults of character that have led us to our present pass. But such self-scrutiny can go awry if governed by a wish to revile rather than a wish to understand. Unless we are alert, that could happen as a result of the suspicions that have come to cluster around the way in which the United States became engaged in the Second World War—torch-lit by the Pearl Harbor disaster.

The more recently available sources have added but little to our knowledge of the events that led to our entry into the war. The books of memoirs written by Japanese witnesses have told us something more, especially about the struggle within the Japanese Government. But in my reading, while they may improve our knowledge of details, they do not change the fundamental view of this experience or its main features. In American and British records still kept secret there may be information or explanations that would do so. But even this I doubt. With no new great revealing facts to display, and no great new insights to impart, the most useful service would seem to be to act as caretaker of what is known, and in particular to deal with certain warped comments and inferences that seasonally must feel the straightening edge of evidence.

Of all the accusations made, the one most shocking to me is that Roosevelt and his chief advisers deliberately left the Pacific Fleet and base at Pearl Harbor exposed as a lure to bring about a direct Japanese attack upon us.

This has been diffused in the face of the fact that the Japanese High Military Command conference before the Imperial Throne on September 6, 1941, resolved that "If by the early part of October there is no reasonable hope of having our demands agreed to in the diplomatic negotiations mentioned above, we will immediately make up our minds to get ready for war against America (and England and Holland)." This is September 6. The plan for the attack on Pearl Harbor was not approved and adopted until

---

From *The Yale Review*, XLV (March 1956), 378–390. Copyright by Yale University Press. Reprinted by permission.

October; and Secret Operation Order #1, the execution of the plan, was not issued until November 5. The presence of the Pacific Fleet at Pearl Harbor was not a lure but an obstacle.

The literature of accusation ignores or rejects the real reasons why the Pacific Fleet was kept in Hawaii. It must do so, since one of the main reasons was the hope that its presence there would deter the Japanese from making so threatening a move south or north that American armed forces might have to join in the war. It scorns the fact that the American military plans —to be executed in the event that we became engaged in war—assigned vital tasks to this Pacific Fleet. A mind must indeed be distracted if it can believe that the American Government could, at one and the same time, use the Pacific Fleet as a target and count on having it as part of its main defending force.

A variant of this accusation, which at least does not require such a willingness to believe the worst, might also be noted—that despite ample knowledge that Pearl Harbor was about to be attacked, the American Government purposefully left it exposed and allowed the event to happen.

Those who do not find such an idea at odds with their view of the sense of duty and regard for human life of President Roosevelt and his chief advisers can find striking points about the occurrence that may be construed to correspond with this conception. How they glare out of the record in hindsight: Ambassador Grew's warnings; Secretary Hull's acute gleam put into words at least three times in Cabinet Councils in November that the Japanese attack might come "at any moment, anywhere"; the intercepted Japanese messages telling of the Japanese effort to secure minute information as to the location of the ships of our Pacific Fleet in the Harbor; carelessness in checking up on the protective measures taken by the local commanders; failure to use the chance to give an effective last-minute warning to Hawaii. How else, it is asked, can these be explained except in terms of secret and conscious purpose?

However, just as hindsight makes the failure of perception plain, so it also makes it understandable—but only by bringing back to mind the total circumstances. That can be done here only in the barest way. Up to then Japanese strategy had been wary, one small creeping step after another, from Manchuria to North China into China and down into Indo-China. American military circles came to take it for granted that it would go on that way. Then there was the fact that Japan's basic objectives lay to the south and southeast; there and there only it could get what it needed—raw materials, oil, and island bases to withstand the attack from the West. Expectation already set in that direction was kept there by impressive and accurate intelligence reports of movements under way. Against this flow of preconception, the signs pointing to Pearl Harbor were not heeded.

Such features of contemporary thinking within the American Government explain, though they do not excuse, the failure to discern that Pearl

Harbor was going to be attacked. To think the contrary is to believe that the President and the heads of the American Army, Navy, and Air Force were given to deep deception, and in order to have us enter the war were ready to sacrifice not only the Pacific Fleet but the whole war plan for the Pacific. This, I think, is the difference between history and police court history.

I have taken note of these accusations that have been built about the disaster at Pearl Harbor because they appeal to the sense of the sinister which is so lively in our times. But I am glad to turn to ideas and interpretations of broader historical import.

The first of these is that Roosevelt and the Joint Chiefs of Staff were obligated by secret agreements with Churchill and their British colleagues to enter the war at some time or other, in one way or other. Therefore, it is further supposed, the American authors of this agreement had to cause either Germany or Japan, or both, to attack us.

This view derives encouragement from the fact that the American Government *did* enter into a secret agreement about strategy with the British. The accord, known as ABC-1 Staff Agreement, adopted at Washington in March, 1941, set down the respective missions of the British and American elements in the event that the United States should be at war with Germany or Japan, or both; and subsequently the American basic joint war plan, Rainbow-5, was adjusted to fit this combined plan of operations. An attempt was made at a similar conference in Singapore soon after to work out a more detailed United States-British-Dutch operating plan for the Pacific. This attempt failed; but the discussion that took place there left a lasting mark on American official thinking, for the conferees defined the limits on land and sea beyond which Japanese forces could not be permitted to go without great risk to the defenders.

The ABC-1 agreement did not place the Roosevelt Administration under *political* obligation to enter the war against either Germany or Japan, not even if Japan attacked British or Dutch areas in the Far East. Nor did Roosevelt give a promise to this effect to Churchill when they met at Newfoundland in August, 1941. Up to the very eve of the Japanese assault the President refused to tell the British or Dutch what we would do. In short, the Government kept itself officially free from any obligation to enter the war, certainly free of any obligation to thrust itself into the war.

But I do think this accord conveyed responsibilities of a moral sort. After ABC-1 was adopted, production of weapons in the United States and the British Commonwealth took it into account; and the allocation of weapons, troops, ships, and planes as between threatened areas was based on the expectation that the United States would carry out the assignments set down in the plan.

Thus, it may be fairly thought, Roosevelt and his administration were obligated to try to gain the consent of Congress and the American people to play the part designated in the joint plans if Japanese assaults crossed the land and sea boundaries of resistance that were defined at these joint staff conferences. In the last November weeks when the end of the diplomatic talks with Japan came into sight, and General Marshall and Admiral Stark were asked what measures should be taken in face of the threatened Japanese advances, they advised the President to declare the limits defined at Singapore, and to warn the Japanese that we would fight if these were crossed. There is much reason to think this would have been done even had the Japanese not struck at Pearl Harbor and the Philippines, and this boundary would have been the line between peace and war. But this reaffirmation was made not as a measure required to carry out a secret accord, but because it was believed to be the best course.

A variant explanation of the way we dealt with Japan runs somewhat as follows: that Roosevelt was determined to get into the war against Germany; that he had to find a release from his public promises that the United States would not enter "foreign wars" unless attacked; that his efforts to do so by unneutral aid to Britain and the Soviet Union had failed because Hitler had refused to accept the challenge; and so he sought another door into war, a back door, by inviting or compelling the Japanese attack.

This interpretation, with its kick at the end, twists the record around its own preconception. The actions taken did not flow from a settled wish to get us into war. They trailed along the rim of necessity of the true purpose —which was to sustain resistance against the Axis. How many times the American Government refused to do what the British, French, Chinese, Russians, Dutch asked it to do, because it might involve us in actual combat!

This slant of reasoning about American action passes by the course of Japanese conduct which aroused our fears and stimulated our opposition: the way in which, despite all our pleas and warnings, Japan pressed on. By not recognizing that these Japanese actions called for American counteraction, it excuses them. Thus our resistance is made to appear as nothing else but a deceitful plot to plunge us into war. Furthermore, it dismisses as insincere the patient attempt to calm Japan by diplomatic talks, by offers to join in safeguarding its security.

There were influential individuals in the Roosevelt Administration who wanted to get into the war and indifferent as to how we got into it. Of these, Secretary of the Interior Ickes was, I believe, the most candid, at any rate in his diary entries. Secretary of the Treasury Morgenthau and his staff also had a positive wish that we should engage in war—but against Germany, not against Japan, for that might have brought a diversion of forces to the Pacific. Secretary of War Stimson thought that it would not be possible for Great Britain to sustain the fight unless we entered it; but toward the very end, particularly as it was becoming plain that the Soviet Union was going to survive the Nazi assault, he began to wish for delay. However, time and time again the memoirs and diaries record the impatience of these officials, and those who thought like them, with Hull's caution and Roosevelt's watchful indirection.

The most genuine point made by those who dissent, one that merits thorough analysis, is that the American Government, in conjunction with the British and Dutch, refused to continue to supply Japan with machines and materials vital to it—especially oil. It is contended that they thereby compelled Japan to resort to war, or at least fixed a time period in which Japan was faced with the need of deciding to yield to our terms or go to war.

In reflecting upon this action, the reasons for it must not be confused with the Japanese response to it. Japan showed no signs of curbing its aggressive course. It paid no heed to repeated and friendly warnings that unless it did, the threatened countries would have to take counter-measures. As when on February 14, 1941, while the Lend-Lease Act was being argued in Congress, Dooman, Counselor of the American Embassy in Japan and known to be a firm and straightforward friend of that country, carried back from Washington the message for the Vice-Minister for Foreign Affairs: that the American people were determined to support Britain even at the risk of war; that if Japan or any other country menaced that effort "it would have to expect to come in conflict with the United States"; and that the United States had abstained from an oil embargo in order not to impel Japan to create a situation that could only lead to the most serious outcome. Japan's answer over the following months had been to force its way further into Indo-China and threaten the Dutch East Indies.

This sustained proof that Japan was going on with its effort to dominate Asia, and the alliance pledging it to stand by Germany if that country got into war with the United States, made a continuation of trade with Japan an act of meekness on our part. Japan was concentrating its foreign purchases on products needed for war, while reducing civilian use by every means, and was thus accumulating great reserve stocks. These were enabling it to maintain its invasion of China without much strain, while continuing to expand its war-making power. Had *effective* restraints—note that I do not say *total* restraints—not been imposed, the American Government would have been in the strange position of having declared an unlimited national emergency, of calling upon the American people to strengthen their army, navy, and air force in great urgency, while at the same time nourishing the opponent that might have to be met in battle. This was a grave, if not intolerable, responsibility.

It is hard to tell how squarely the American and British Governments faced the possible consequence of their restrictive measures. My impression is that they knew the danger of war with Japan was being increased; that Japan might try to get by force the means denied it. The Japanese Government served plain warnings that this game of thrust and counterthrust might so end. These were soberly regarded, but did not weaken the will that Japan was not to have its way by threat.

Mingled with the anxiety lest these restrictive measures would make war more likely, there was a real hope that they might be a deterrent to war. Conceivably they would bring home to the Japanese people that if it came to war, they might soon run out of the means for combat, while the rapid growth of American military strength would make it clear that they could not in the end win. And, as evidence of these probabilities became plain, the conciliatory elements in the Japanese Government would prevail over the more militant ones.

This almost happened. But the reckless ones, those who would rather court fatality than accept frustration, managed to retain control of Japanese decision. The pressure applied by us did not prevent war, and may have brought the time of decision for war closer. The valid question, however, is not whether the American Government resorted to these restrictions *in order* to drive Japan to attack; it is whether the American Government failed to grasp a real chance, after the restraints had begun to leave their mark in Japanese official circles, to arrive at a satisfactory understanding that would have averted war. Twice, in the opinion of some qualified students of the subject, such a chance emerged, or at least appeared on the horizon of diplomacy. Were they real opportunities or merely mirages or decoys?

The first of these was the occasion when in the autumn of 1941, the Japanese Prime Minister, Prince Konoye, sought a personal meeting with the President. It is averred that the President's failure to respond lost a chance to avert the war without yielding any American principle or purpose. Some think the reason was that American diplomacy was inflexible, dull in its insight, and too soaked in mistrust. Others, more accusatory, explain the decision by a lack of desire for an agreement that would have thwarted the design for war.

Since there is no conclusive evidence of what Konoye intended to propose or could have achieved, comment on this subject must enter into "the boggy ground of what-might-have-been." Some observers, including Ambassador Grew, believe that Konoye could have made a real, and an irreversible, start toward meeting American terms. It will always be possible to think that this is so. But to the Americans in authority, the chance seemed small. Konoye was a man who in every past crisis had allowed himself to flounder between criss-cross promises; hence there was good reason to fear an attempt at deception. Such glimpses as we have of what he might have proposed do not support the view that he could have offered a suspension or end of the fight against China. His freedom to negotiate would have been subject to the conditions stated by those who had controlled Japan's course up to then —their price for allowing him to go to meet the President.

Even so, to repeat, it is possible that skilled and more daring American diplomacy might have handled the meeting so as to get a satisfactory accord;

or, failing that—and this is the more likely chance—to bring about so deep a division within the Japanese circle of decision as to have prevented war-like action. These alluring historical queries will continue to roam in the land of might-have-been.

But the risks were great. The echoes of Munich and its aftermath were still loud. The American Government might have found itself forced to make a miserable choice: either to accept an accord which would have left Japan free to complete its conquest of China and menace the rest of Asia, or to face a deep division among the American people. Any understanding with Japan that was not clear and decisive would have had unpredictable consequences. The Chinese Government might have felt justified in making a deal following our own. The Soviet Union, at this time just managing with the greatest effort and agony to prevent German victory, might also have chosen to compromise with Hitler rather than to fight it out. Specula-tions such as these must leave the subject unsettled. But in any case I think it clear that the American decision was one of judgment, not of secret intent. Konoye was not told that the President would not meet with him; he was told that he would not do so until more progress had been made toward defining what the Japanese Government was prepared to propose.

The same basic question had to be faced in the final crisis of negotiation in November, 1941: whether to relax restraints on Japan and leave it in a position to keep on trying to control much of Asia in return for a promise not to press on farther for the time being.

The opinion that the Japanese truce offer made at this last juncture ac-cepted the main purposes and principles for which the American Govern-ment had been standing may be summarily dismissed. It was ambiguously worded, it was silent about the alliance with Germany, and it would have required the American Government to end its support of China—for the last of its numbered five points read: "The Government of the United States undertakes to refrain from such measures and actions as will be prejudicial to the endeavors for the restoration of general peace between Japan and China." This scant and unclear proposal was at once deemed "entirely un-acceptable." Furthermore, there seemed little use and much possible dam-age in making a counter truce-offer of the same variety. The intercepted Japanese messages stated flatly that this was Japan's last and best offer. They told of the swift dismissal of a much more nearly acceptable one that Nomura and Kurusu asked their superiors in Tokyo to consider. A dead-line had been set. Thus it was all but sure that the reduced counter-offer which had been patched together in Washington would be unheeded. But it might shake the coalition to which by then the opponents of the Axis had pledged their lives and national destinies.

This seems to have been the thought uppermost in Hull's mind in recom-mending to the President that the counter truce-offer be withheld. As set

down in this historic memo of November 26, he had been led to this conclusion by the opposition of the Chinese, the half-hearted support or actual
opposition of the British, Dutch, and Australian governments, and the
further excited opposition to be expected because of lack of appreciation of
the importance and value of a truce. This I believe to have been the true
determining reason for a decision reluctantly taken. Even if by then Japan
was genuinely ready for reform, the repentance had come too late. The situation had grown too entangled by then for minor measures, its momentum
too great. Germany-Italy-Japan had forced the creation of a defensive coalition more vast than the empire of the Pacific for which Japan plotted. This
was not now to be quieted or endangered by a temporary halt along the
fringe of the Japanese advance.

Even though these reasons for dropping the idea of a truce may seem sufficient, they leave the question why the American Government could not
have given a softer and less declaratory answer. Why had it to give one so
"bleakly uncompromising"? It could have said simply that the Japanese offer
did not convey the assurances that would warrant us and the alliance for
which we spoke to resume the shipment of war materials to Japan and end
our aid to China. Why was it deemed advisable or essential at this juncture
to state fully and forcibly our maximum terms for a settlement in the
Pacific? Was it foreseen that, scanned with mistrust as it would almost surely
be, this would be construed as a demand for the swift abandonment of
Japan's whole program? Was it done, as the accusation runs, with the deliberate intent of banning any last chance for an accord? Of propelling the
Japanese attack?

That this was not the reason I am as sure as anyone can be on a matter of
this sort; but I can offer only conjecture as to what the inspiring purposes
were. Perhaps to vindicate past actions and decisions. Perhaps a wish to use
the dramatic chance to put in the record a statement of the aims for which
the risk of war was being accepted, and of the basis on which the Americans would found the peace when the time came. Such an idea was in accord with the usual mode of thought of the men in charge of the Executive
Branch of the Government and of most of the American people. It gave
vent to the propensity exemplified in Hull to find a base in general principles meant to be at once political standards and moral ideals. After long
caution, it appealed as a defiant contradiction of the Axis program. All this,
however, is surmise rather than evidenced history.

But I think it is well within the realm of evidenced history that the memo
of November 26 was not in any usual sense of the word an ultimatum. It
did not threaten the Japanese with war or any other form of forceful punishment if our terms were not accepted. It simply left them in the state of
distress in which they were, with the prospect that they might later have to
submit to our requirements. The Japanese Government could have, as

Konoye and Nomura pleaded with it to do, allowed the situation to drag along, with or without resuming talks with the American Government. Its power to make war would have been depleted, but neither quickly nor crucially. The armed forces and even the position in China could have been maintained.

Notably, the final Japanese answer which ended negotiations on December 7, 1941, does not accuse the American Government of confronting it with an ultimatum, but only of thwarting the larger Japanese aims. Part 14—the clinching part of this note—reads: "Obviously it is the intention of the American Government to conspire with Great Britain and other countries to obstruct Japan's efforts toward the establishment of peace through the creation of a New Order in East Asia, and especially to preserve Anglo-American rights and interests by keeping Japan and China at war. This intention has been revealed clearly during the course of the present negotiations. Thus, the earnest hope of the Japanese Government to adjust Japanese-American relations and to preserve and promote the peace of the Pacific through coöperation with the American Government has finally been lost."

This is a more nearly accurate description of the purposes of the American Government under Roosevelt than those attributed to it by hostile and suspicious American critics. Our Government did obstruct Japanese efforts, believing them to be unjust, cruel, and a threat to our national security, especially after Japan became a partner with Hitler's Germany and Mussolini's Italy and bent its efforts toward bringing the world under their combined control.

This determination stood on the proposition that it was better to take the risks of having to share in the suffering of the war than of finding ourselves moved or compelled to fight a more desperate battle against the Axis later on. The American Government, I believe, knew how serious a risk of war was being taken. But in its addresses to the American people it chose to put in the forefront the perils we would face if the Axis won, and to leave in the background, even to camouflage, the risks of finding ourselves plunged into wars which during the election campaign it had promised would not occur. Whether any large number of Americans were fooled by this, or whether most of them, in reality, were content to have the prospect presented that way rather than in a more blunt and candid way, I do not know.

This essay in interpretation has compelled me to recall and stress the aggressive Japanese assault—though I should have been glad to let that slip into the past. The passage of time does not alter facts, but it can bring a fuller and calmer understanding of them. It frees the mind for fairer appreciation of the causes and circumstances which impelled Japan along its tragic course and which impelled us to resist it. For both countries there are many common lessons. One of them is that continued friendliness requires mutual effort to relieve the other, to the extent it can, of deep cause for anxiety—the Japanese people of their anxiety over the means of living decently, the American people of anxiety about their security and power to defend the free world. Another is that they must both feel, speak, and act so honestly and steadily that their view of each other will be cleared of mistrust, and brightened by trust.

XV

The Yalta Agreements:
Surrender to Russia
or Wartime Realism?

INTRODUCTION

Of the various Allied diplomatic conferences during World War II, the most significant was the Yalta conference of February, 1945. It was the Yalta conference, as Paul Clyde has pointed out, that "cemented the military victory and shaped the broad outlines of the future." [1] *Far-reaching decisions were made with respect to Germany, Poland and eastern Europe, the Far East, and the United Nations. The initial reaction to the conference in the United States, before all the terms of the agreements were made public, was highly favorable; but as the Soviet Union extended its power and influence in Europe and Asia and as Soviet-American tension grew, the Yalta agreements were subjected to increasing criticism. To some of the more rabid critics of the Roosevelt and Truman administrations, Yalta became part of a gigantic conspiracy whose object was the promotion of international Communism.*

The journalist William Henry Chamberlin looks upon Yalta as a "moral and diplomatic debacle," "the climax of a gravely mistaken course in foreign affairs." He finds fault with all phases of the agreements and rejects the contentions of the defenders of Yalta. Professor John L. Snell and his associates take the other side of the argument. They assert that the Yalta agreements can only be understood in the context of the times and in the light of the emergence of a new balance of world power. They find the agreements on the whole reasonable and repudiate the charge that the Soviet view invariably triumphed at Yalta.

---

[1] Paul H. Clyde (Foreword), John L. Snell (Editor), *The Meaning of Yalta: Big Three Diplomacy and the New Balance of Power* (Baton Rouge: Louisiana State University Press, 1956), p. viii.

Appeasement at Yalta

William Henry Chamberlin

Morally, politically and militarily the Yalta Conference of February 4–11, 1945, was held under unfavorable conditions. The Soviet armies had recently launched a successful offensive. The memory of what proved to be the last German offensive, in the Ardennes region, was still fresh. The speed with which Germany would crumble before Eisenhower's offensive in the spring was not anticipated. Singularly faulty intelligence work had conveyed the impression that Japan still possessed large and effective forces in Manchuria.

The two leading figures in the American delegation, Roosevelt and Hopkins, were in very poor health and were committed by past attitudes to the policy of trusting Stalin and hoping for the best. The newly appointed Secretary of State, Edward R. Stettinius, possessed no visible qualifications for this office except an impressive shock of white hair, an adulatory attitude toward Roosevelt and a naive faith that all international problems could be solved by a determined application of good will and optimism.

A measure of the political judgment of Mr. Stettinius is furnished by his expression of opinion, four years after Yalta, that the Soviet Union at this conference made greater concessions than the United States, and that Yalta was an American diplomatic triumph.[1]

In his record of the Yalta proceedings Mr. Stettinius is effusive in his praise of one of his subordinates whose name inspires little confidence in most American minds today. Alger Hiss, according to Stettinius, "performed brilliantly" at Yalta, as in the Dumbarton Oaks conversations where preliminary details of the United Nations organization were worked out, at the San Francisco conference and the first meeting of the UN Assembly.[2] When Roosevelt asked Stettinius to get a lawyer to consult with him on the Polish boundary statement Stettinius promptly called for this "brilliant performer." [3]

Reprinted by permission from *Beyond Containment* by William Henry Chamberlin, copyright 1953 by Henry Regnery Company. Pp. 36–46. The title for this selection is the editor's.

[1] Edward R. Stettinius, *Roosevelt and the Russians* (Doubleday), p. 295. [2] *Ibid.*, p. 31.
[3] *Ibid.*, p. 270.

Of the other members of the American delegation only two, Averell Harriman, Ambassador to the Soviet Union, and Charles E. Bohlen, assistant to the Secretary of State and a Russian language expert who acted as translator, possessed a background of Soviet experience. There is nothing in the records of the conference to indicate that either Harriman or Bohlen did anything to avert moral and diplomatic debacle. Years later Harriman and Bohlen, nominated Ambassador to the Soviet Union by the Eisenhower Administration, were stubbornly maintaining that nothing was wrong with the Yalta Agreement except Soviet nonobservance of its provisions.

The principal decisions at Yalta, some revealed in a communiqué after the end of the meeting, some kept secret for a year or longer, dealt with the following subjects.

Poland. It was agreed that the eastern frontier of Poland should follow substantially the so-called Curzon Line, with minor digressions in favor of Poland. This was a ratification, for Stalin, of the spoils of his pact with Hitler. Poland was to receive accessions of German territory not precisely specified.

The existing Provisional Government of Poland was to be reorganized on a broader democratic basis, "with the inclusion of democratic leaders from Poland itself and from Poles abroad." The new government was to be called the Polish Provisional Government of National Unity and was to receive diplomatic recognition from the Big Three powers. This government was to be pledged to "the holding of free and unfettered elections as soon as possible on the basis of universal suffrage and secret ballot."

Germany. "We are determined to disarm and disband all German armed forces, break up for all time the German General Staff, remove or destroy all German military equipment, eliminate or control all German industry that could be used for military production, bring all war criminals to swift and just punishment and exact reparation in kind for the destruction wrought by the Germans; wipe out the Nazi Party, Nazi laws, organizations and institutions, etc." It was specified in the protocol of the conference that German labor might be used as a source of "reparations." A commission with American, Soviet and British representatives was set up to study the question of dismemberment of Germany.

The Far East. According to an agreement that was kept strictly secret at the time and that was published a year later, on February 11, 1946, the Soviet Union promised to enter the war against Japan "two or three months after Germany has surrendered and the war in Europe has terminated" on the following conditions:

That the status quo in Outer Mongolia be preserved. (Outer Mongolia, nominally a part of China, had been a Soviet protected state since 1921.)

That the southern part of Sakhalin with adjacent islands be returned to the Soviet Union.

That the commercial port of Dairen be internationalized, "the pre-eminent interests of the Soviet Union in this port being safeguarded, and the lease of Port Arthur as a naval base of the Soviet Union restored."

That the Chinese Eastern Railway and South Manchuria Railway (the principal railways of Manchuria) be operated by a joint Soviet-Chinese company, "it being understood that the pre-eminent interests of the Soviet Union shall be safeguarded and that China shall retain full sovereignty in Manchuria.

"That the Kurile Islands shall be handed over to the Soviet Union."

Declaration on Liberated Europe. There was to be mutual agreement between the three powers to concert their policies "in assisting the peoples of the former Axis satellite states of Europe to solve by democratic means their pressing political and economic problems." Interim government authorities were to be formed "broadly representative of all democratic elements in the population and pledged to the earliest possible establishment through free elections of governments responsive to the will of the people."

It was agreed that a conference to prepare the Charter of the United Nations should meet in San Francisco in April and that two of the affiliated Soviet Republics, the Ukraine and Byelorussia, should have individual seats in the UN Assembly. An agreement on Yugoslavia substantially confirmed the establishment of Tito's dictatorship, with one or two facesaving reservations, which, in practice, proved quite meaningless.

A separate important compact at Yalta, signed by Major General John R. Deane, chief of the United States military mission in Moscow, and Major General A. A. Gryzlov, on behalf of the Soviet Government, provided that all Soviet citizens liberated by the United States and all United States citizens liberated by the Soviet Union should be segregated from enemy war prisoners and maintained in separate camps until they had been handed over to their respective military authorities.

Here, in brief summary, is the factual content of the Yalta agreements. What is their moral and political significance?

First, the principle of self-determination for all peoples, emphasized in the first three clauses of the Atlantic Charter, was clearly scrapped, although professions of respect for the principles of the Atlantic Charter are sprinkled through the Yalta Declaration. The Soviet annexation of Eastern Poland, of Koenigsberg and past of East Prussia and the Polish authorized seizure of ethnic German territory were clearly against the will of the vast majority of the peoples concerned. There was no pretense in any of these changes of an honestly conducted plebiscite. These decisions created millions of homeless, embittered refugees and drew frontier lines that were unjust and unnatural and a very probable cause of future conflicts.

Second, the independence and territorial integrity of Poland were sacrificed. The legitimate Polish government in London, composed of representatives of all the leading political parties in pre-war Poland, was thrown over. A made-in-Moscow, communist dominated government which had come to

Poland in the wake of the Red Army, received the prestige of promised diplomatic recognition by the western powers. (In actual practice the "enlargement" of this government by the addition of Poles in Poland and abroad made no change in its domination by Moscow puppets.)

The Polish government in London was not a phantom. It had the undivided allegiance of hundreds of thousands of Poles who were fighting for the allied cause in the West, on land, on sea and in the air. It guided one of the most effective underground resistance movements in Europe.

It should not have been difficult to foresee how the pledges of "free unfettered elections" would work out, with Soviet-trained communists in charge of the police, the Red Army in occupation of the country and no safeguards for honest voting, such as the presence of foreign inspectors and American and British troop units, to counterbalance the effect of the Red Army. The effect of this abandonment of Poland was certain to be profound throughout Eastern Europe. For of all the countries in this area Poland had much the strongest legal and moral claim to American and British support. Polish resistance to Hitler's aggression had been the original occasion of the war. Poland had concluded an alliance with Great Britain on the eve of the outbreak of hostilities.

The treatment of Poland at Yalta offers a remarkably close parallel with the treatment of Czechoslovakia at Munich in 1938. If one substitutes Poland for Czechoslovakia, Stalin for Hitler, Roosevelt and Churchill for Daladier and Chamberlain the likeness is complete. Publicists of the Left showed (and sometimes still show) the same complacency about Yalta that some publicists of the Right displayed about Munich. There were the same distorted and irrelevant arguments to justify a shabby and dishonorable transaction, about Sudeten Germans in Czechoslovakia and Ukrainians in Eastern Poland. There was the same eagerness to find excuses for the rapacious dictator and there was the same impatient distaste with the protests of the victim against being murdered.

Harry Hopkins who, next to Roosevelt, bears the principal American responsibility for the Great Betrayal which reached its climax at Yalta, brushed the moral issue off with the remark: "The Poles are like the Irish. They are never satisfied with anything anyhow." And a junior diplomatic official in the United States told the Polish Ambassador that the Polish problem had to be settled because it had become "an intolerable headache"! [4]

Like Munich, Yalta must be set down as a dismal failure, practically as well as morally. For Hitler was not satiated by his acquisitions at Munich and Stalin was not appeased at Yalta. The human and industrial resources of Czechoslovakia became an asset for the Nazi war machine. Poland also, under its communist rulers, is being organized systematically against the West.

---

[4] Jan Ciechanowski, *Defeat in Victory* (Doubleday), pp. 383–84.

Third, the Yalta Agreement, besides foreshadowing the enslavement of tens of millions of people in Eastern Europe, represented, in two of its features, the endorsement by the United States of the principle of human slavery. One of these features was the recognition that German labor could be used as a source of reparations. This gave implied American sanction to the retention of large numbers of German war prisoners, years after the end of hostilities, as forced laborers in the Soviet Union, Great Britain and France. And the agreement that Soviet citizens who were found in the western zones of occupation should be handed over to the Soviet authorities amounted, for the many Soviet refugees who did not wish to return, to the enactment of a fugitive slave law.

Fourth, the secret clauses of the Yalta Agreement which offered Stalin extensive territorial and economic concessions in the Far East as the price of Soviet participation in the war against Japan were immoral, unnecessary and unwise. These secret clauses were immoral because they gave away effective control of Manchuria, the most industrialized part of China, without consulting with or even informing the Chinese Government, an ally since Pearl Harbor. They were unnecessary because Stalin would almost certainly have entered the war without any bribe.

Moreover, it was a case of paying Stalin a second time for something he had already agreed to do, presumably in consideration of lend-lease aid and the second front, without any bribe. When Cordell Hull visited Moscow in October, 1943, Stalin proposed to enter the war against Japan after the defeat of Germany. According to Hull, this offer was unsolicited and had no strings attached to it.[5]

Stalin repeated this promise at Teheran. But Roosevelt, without waiting for a request, suggested that the Soviet Union should have access to the key Manchurian port of Dairen.[6] Finding Roosevelt so eager to anticipate his wishes, Stalin began to raise his price.

During Churchill's visit to Moscow in October, 1944, the Soviet dictator consented to take the offensive against Japan three months after the defeat of Germany, but on two conditions. The United States was to build up reserve lend-lease supplies for the operation and the "political aspects of Russian participation" were to be clarified.[7]

It was typical of the Soviet attitude toward obligations that, although there were repeated promises of bases for the American air force in Eastern Siberia, no such bases were ever made available. The United States, however, continued unusual efforts to build up the Soviet military reserve stocks in Eastern Siberia.[8]

Finally, the invitation to the Soviet Union to take over the Kurile Islands, South Sakhalin and an economic stranglehold on Manchuria was unwise,

---

[5] *The Memoirs of Cordell Hull* (Macmillan), p. 1310.
[6] Robert Sherwood, *Roosevelt and Hopkins* (Harper's), p. 792.
[7] John R. Deane, *The Strange Alliance* (Viking), p. 247.   [8] *Ibid.*, p. 254.

from the standpoint of American national interests. To increase what was already a prospective formidable predominance of Soviet strength in the Far East after the war by giving the Soviet Union take-off points for threatening Japan (South Sakhalin and the Kuriles) and economic domination of Manchuria was not a demonstration of farsighted statesmanship.

Even now Yalta has its defenders. They are to be found mainly among the unreserved admirers of Franklin D. Roosevelt's foreign policy and among those who, because of wartime association with the Administration, feel that their personal prestige is bound up with the vindication of this conference. Their four principal arguments are:

(1) That Yalta gave Stalin nothing that he was not in a position to take, or had not taken, anyway.

(2) That there was moral value in obtaining such Soviet promises as "free unfettered elections in Poland" and "democratic processes" in the "liberated countries."

(3) That the Yalta concessions were necessary to keep the Soviet Union in the war against Germany and to bring about Soviet intervention in the war against Japan.

(4) That the only alternative to the Yalta Agreement was the politically impossible one of going to war with the Soviet Union.

The first of these arguments misses the political and moral heart of the Yalta issue. The question was not what Stalin might have taken by military force in Eastern Europe and the Far East, but what he could take with the approval of the western powers. The difference is extremely important. In the case of Poland, for instance, it would have been far more difficult to maintain a Soviet satellite regime if this regime had not received the endorsement of the western powers. Nor was there anything inevitable about the Soviet domination of Manchuria and North Korea. It is a reasonable assumption that a peace treaty could have been concluded with Japan months before the end of the war if there had been enough farsighted statesmanship to propose the same terms which were finally signed in San Francisco in 1951. Had this been done before the Soviet Government was able to intervene in the Far Eastern war the Korean-Manchurian door could have been bolted against Soviet intrusion.

Argument two seems to be on a par with praising a man as a financial genius because he accepted a number of bad checks from a fraudulent bankrupt. The Yalta promises were not the first international obligations on which Stalin defaulted.

The third argument is based on the assumption that Stalin's own interests did not prompt him to seek to deliver a knockout blow against the two powers which were the greatest potential checks against his ambitions, in Europe and in Asia, Germany and Japan. There was no reason to bribe him to continue a war in Europe or to start a war in Asia so clearly prompted by his own sense of interest.

Was there an alternative to the appeasement of Yalta, besides war? Of course there was. Suppose the United States and Great Britain before Yalta and at Yalta had committed themselves to a firm, uncompromising declaration that they would neither use the war as a means of territorial gain themselves nor recognize any annexations carried out by other powers in violation of the principles of the Atlantic Charter. The Soviet frontiers of 1939 (frontiers with which the Soviet Government before the war often expressed itself as entirely satisfied) and not one square foot of Polish, Latvian, Estonian, Lithuanian, Finnish, Rumanian, German, Chinese or Japanese territory beyond these frontiers would have been acknowledged as legal and valid.

Behind such a declaration would have stood the mightiest concentration of sea and air power the world had ever seen, a highly mechanized army and an American war economy capable of almost unlimited further achievement. On the other side would have been a Soviet Union devastated by invasion and bled white in manpower, dependent in the final drive to victory on American trucks, field telephones, canned food and other lend-lease supplies.

Moreover, at the time of Yalta the hope of a genuine liberation from Nazi tyranny was still high in Poland and other countries of Central and eastern Europe. Except in Czechoslovakia the communist parties in these lands were tiny minority groups, with no appreciable popular following. So hated was the very name communist in Poland that the revived Polish Communist Party, which had been written off as a bad fifth column investment by Moscow in the late thirties, tried to conceal its real nature by calling itself the Workers' Party.

In view of these circumstances, in view of Stalin's habitual caution in foreign affairs, the Soviet dictator might well have renounced his designs of conquest and been satisfied with the preservation of his original realm. And if Stalin had taken a tough and negative attitude the date of the cold war would have been advanced,—very much to the advantage of the West. For at the time of Yalta the power relation was less favorable to the Soviet Union than it became later, when the Soviet Union repaired its war damage, crushed all semblance of open dissent in the satellite countries and swung China against the West. It was not the least of the sins of Yalta that it helped to blind American and British public opinion to the threat of Soviet expansion and contributed to the mood of recklessly hasty demobilization as soon as the shooting war with the Axis was over. There was no corresponding demobilization on the Soviet side.

Yalta should not be regarded as an isolated accident or a piece of black magic. It was a consequence, as well as a cause, a consequence of the dry rot of appeasement which was already well advanced at the time of the Teheran Conference, if not earlier. But Yalta will be remembered as the climax of a gravely mistaken course in foreign affairs. It was the supreme example of giving Stalin an unlimited diplomatic blank check, of deserting friends and favoring enemies in the vain hope of appeasing a regime which, by its nature and philosophy, is unappeasable.

The Meaning of Yalta

John L. Snell et al.

GERMANY AND THE MEANING OF YALTA*

Some of the Yalta decisions affecting Germany were summarized in a press report on February 12. This public proclamation embraced certain decisions on which there was such general agreement that they required little or no discussion at Yalta; it included other statements which camouflaged the extent of the Soviet retreat on German matters at Yalta. In it the Big Three announced:

> It is our inflexible purpose to destroy German militarism and Nazism and to ensure that Germany will never again be able to disturb the peace of the world. We are determined to disarm and disband all German armed forces; break up for all time the German General Staff that has repeatedly contrived the resurgence of German militarism; remove or destroy all German military equipment; eliminate or control all German industry that could be used for military production; bring all war criminals to just and swift punishment and exact reparation in kind for the destruction wrought by the Germans; wipe out the Nazi Party, Nazi laws, organizations and institutions, remove all Nazi and militarist influences from public office and from the cultural and economic life of the German people; and take in harmony such other measures in Germany as may be necessary to the future peace and safety of the world. It is not our purpose to destroy the people of Germany, but only when Nazism and militarism have been extirpated will there be hope for a decent life for Germans, and a place for them in the comity of nations.

In a moderate bid for German action to shorten the war, the Big Three proclaimed: "The German people, as well as the German soldiers, must

---

From John L. Snell, editor, *The Meaning of Yalta: Big Three Diplomacy and the New Balance of Power* (Baton Rouge: Louisiana State University Press, 1956), pp. 70–74, 119–126, 152–166, 186–187, 205–208. Reprinted by permission.

* Editor's note: By John L. Snell.

realize that the sooner they give up and surrender, by groups or as individuals, the sooner their present agony will be over." [1]

This proclamation veiled the vast indecision of the great Allies in questions concerning Germany. They could not agree, and as long as Germany fought on they could not afford to disagree. But the prospects of Germany's early collapse had brought the western statesmen face to face at last with the greatest European dilemma of the twentieth century: how can the threat of German power be eliminated from Europe without leaving Soviet power dominant throughout the continent? Therein lies the essential meaning of Yalta so far as Germany—and much of Europe—is concerned.

Roosevelt was no conscious advocate of the balance-of-power concept but, like other American statesmen since Wilson, he supported a principle which was its corollary: that it was not in the interest of the United States for any one state in Europe to dominate the whole. Churchill, on the other hand, consciously followed a balance-of-power policy in his negotiations with the Russians concerning the future of Germany. Thus it came about that the discussions of Germany questions at Yalta revealed beneath the verbiage of conciliation toward Russia the hard rock of Anglo-American solidarity and moderation toward Germany. The Russians failed to win full satisfaction on a single one of the demands they raised at Yalta concerning Germany's future.

The credits and debits of Yalta concerning the German problem read as follows: Stalin demanded a decision to dismember Germany; Churchill and Roosevelt postponed any specific plans, though they agreed in principle to the possibility of dismemberment. Stalin demanded a decision to deindustrialize Germany and rebuild the U.S.S.R. with German equipment; the President and the Prime Minister refused to agree to deindustrialization and postponed consideration of reparations. The Russians hoped that the western boundary of Poland might be drawn by Big Three agreement at the Western Neisse River and that the Ruhr and Saar would be separated from Germany; both Roosevelt and Churchill were opposed. The single set of demands concerning Germany which were met fully at Yalta were those which Roosevelt and Churchill advanced there: France was to have a zone of occupation and to participate in the integrated administration of Germany through the Control Council.

The positive material reconstruction of Germany was not desired at Yalta by any of the participants, nor could it possibly have been planned there; Roosevelt and Churchill avoided committing themselves to the permanent destruction of Germany only at the risk of alienating their Moscow colleague. This situation, so unfavorable for Germany, was of Germany's own creation. Adolf Hitler had sought to conquer Europe while posing as

---

[1] *Yalta Papers*, 969–71; United States, Department of State, *The Axis in Defeat, a Collection of Documents on American Policy toward Germany and Japan* (Washington, n.d.), 8–9.

its savior against Bolshevism.[2] Hitler himself had offered Europe its choice of mistresses: Nazism or Bolshevism. But he had shown the opportunistic motivation of his egocentric ideology by outlawing his own nation against the western community. In February, 1945, it seemed certain that Europe would soon be rid of the ruthless and insatiable mistress whom Hitler had forced upon it; the era of German hegemony in European history was almost over, having been desperate in character but brief in duration. Was the second mistress which Hitler had offered, Russian communism, to be the only choice left after the debauchery into which Hitler had led Europe? This was the verdict of the Nazi newspaper *Völkischer Beobachter,* which headlined the Yalta communiqué as the "DEATH SENTENCE FOR EUROPE" and insisted that conference unity had been preserved only by the surrender of Roosevelt and Churchill to every demand Stalin raised.[3]

Ultimately a combination of American and British military and economic power broadened the choices facing Europe, but only after Germany and Japan were defeated and after it became crystal clear that Stalin thought in terms of the same two crude alternatives which Hitler had presented. In February, 1945, this was not fully apparent, and Hitler's Germany still held the Big Three together as it had made them "strange allies" in the first place. "We separated in the Crimea," Churchill has recalled, "not only as Allies but as friends facing a still mighty foe with whom all our armies were struggling in fierce and ceaseless battle." [4]

The Yalta negotiators had not solved "the German problem." But they had done an essential job of "papering over the cracks" in an alliance which could not be sacrificed until victory was won. This, in essence, was the best the Big Three at Yalta could do when they turned intermittently from the profound problem of Germany to consider the more immediately pressing difficulties which had been created by the Red Army's occupation of central-eastern Europe. . . .

EASTERN EUROPEAN EPILOGUE *

Early in the war Poland had emerged as the roughest testing ground of the possibility of maintaining amicable relations between East and West. Harry Hopkins once told Stalin that "the question of Poland *per se* was not so important as the fact that it had become a symbol of our ability to work out problems with the Soviet Union." [5] Uppermost in the American delegation's thoughts was winning Soviet acceptance of the United Nations blueprint and Russian participation in the Pacific war. Churchill declared at

---

[2] Paul Kluke, "Nationalsozialistische Europaideologie," *Vierteljahrshefte für Zeitgeschichte* (Tübingen and Munich), III (July, 1955), 240–75.

[3] Munich *Völkischer Beobachter,* February 13–16, 1945.

[4] Churchill, *Triumph and Tragedy,* 510.

* Editor's note: By Charles F. Delzell.   [5] Sherwood, *Roosevelt and Hopkins,* 898.

Yalta that his country "had no material interest in Poland." Britain's interests, he said, was "only one of honor" toward an allied state whose invasion had precipitated the war.[6] Stalin, on the other hand, took the uncompromising stand that for his country the Polish problem was not just a "symbol," nor a "question of honor," but one of "security." [7] Because of the relative weight which each of the Big Three assigned to the Polish issue, the nature of their prior agreements, and the realities of Russian military power in eastern Europe, there was little room at Yalta for successful bargaining against the U.S.S.R.

Nonetheless, Churchill and Roosevelt argued the Polish problem with Stalin for six days and nights. Obviously, it was not a question of what they would permit him to do but what they could persuade him to accept. In the protracted, exhausting discussions, Churchill, whose previous diplomatic engagements involved him in this region much more deeply than was the case with Roosevelt, doggedly carried the burden of western argumentation. He marshaled his points carefully and often eloquently, and in the drafting of the final agreements he endeavored, insofar as the limited time permitted, to weigh the import of every word. President Roosevelt preferred to play the role of moderator, but in the showdowns he usually aligned himself with Churchill. Roosevelt's exposition was not always so skillful, energetic, or persistent as that of the Briton, but it fully evidenced his concern for a really independent Poland as well as for lasting world peace. For his part, Stalin set forth with bluntness Soviet Russia's strategic interests, and he cleverly seized upon the weak points in the westerners' case. He reminded them that they should not expect him to be any less Russian than Clemenceau and Lord Curzon; he skillfully equated the legitimacy of his Lublin regime with that of de Gaulle in France; and employing the same arguments that Churchill had used recently in Greece to justify British measures, he argued persuasively that nothing must be allowed to jeopardize the security of the Soviet armies in Poland. The Russian leader was impervious to arguments based either on "high moral" principles or on the need for placating Polish-American voters. But sometimes he was willing to accept phraseology that enabled the West to "save face," especially if he felt certain that in the execution of the agreements he could have his own way.

Thus Roosevelt and Churchill were able to win a moral victory when they persuaded Stalin to agree with minor changes to the pledges contained in the somewhat loosely phrased Declaration on Liberated Europe. Certainly there was nothing reprehensible in the terms of this American-sponsored document, which called for "free" and "democratic" regimes in eastern Europe. But the present-day observer is inclined to marvel at the optimism of the Big Three when they declared: "We reaffirm our faith in

---

[6] *Yalta Papers*, 678–79.   [7] *Ibid.*, 679–81.

the principles of the Atlantic Charter, our pledge in the Declaration by the United Nations, and our determination to build in cooperation with other peaceloving nations a world order under law, dedicated to peace, security, freedom and general well-being of all mankind." [8] At the time of the Crimea conference there was still reason to hope that Stalin might honor his promises. Had he not scrupulously refrained from criticizing the British military operations in Greece, in accordance with his recent bargain with Churchill? When the evidence of Soviet lack of good faith in Rumania and other eastern countries was forthcoming a few weeks after Yalta, the United States and Britain were in an excellent position, thanks to the "Yalta Declaration," to make it clear to the world who was at fault.

On the subject of the Yugoslav agreements between Tito and Prime Minister Subašić, the British were able to win Soviet acceptance of pledges for a more parliamentary and constitutional type of government than then existed under Tito. What was regrettable in this was not the Yalta agreement but its violation.

The discussions of the perplexing Polish territorial problem ended by assigning to Soviet Russia the land east of the Curzon Line, except for minor rectifications in favor of Poland. No plebiscites were called for, and the action was taken without the consent of the Polish government in exile, although hardly to its surprise. The agreement thus violated the spirit of the Atlantic Charter. But it is impossible to see how the western statesmen could have prevented Soviet acquisition of this land, short of armed conflict with Russia, for the military balance of power in eastern Europe had shifted entirely in her favor by 1945. To ratify the shift or to repudiate the eastern ally? Therein lay the meaning of Yalta so far as the Polish problem was concerned.

Because of firm western opposition to "overstuffing the German goose" with millions of displaced people from Silesia, Stalin was forced to agree to leave the western frontier of Poland undefined. But in assenting to this, he undoubtedly foresaw that he could at a later time unilaterally assign a wide strip of the Soviet zone in Germany to Poland, thereby tightening his grip on a grateful Polish government. This he did a few months later, when he handed to Poland the territory east of the Oder and Western Neisse rivers.

On the issue of the Polish government, Churchill and Roosevelt could barely budge Stalin, in view of the Soviet recognition of the Lublin-Warsaw Committee of National Liberation a month before Yalta. There seems to be no reason to dispute the contention of Charles E. Bohlen, who was present at the conference, that on this subject only three courses of action were open to the western leaders: (1) they could have accepted the *fait accompli,*

[8] The Declaration on Liberated Europe is quoted in its final version in the Appendix of this volume.

doing nothing, which is what Stalin doubtless would have preferred; (2) they could have stood uncomprisingly behind the Polish government in exile, in which case probably no member of it would have returned to Poland; or (3) they could have attempted to get as many members as possible of the London group into a "reorganized" government.[9] Realistically, they chose the third course.

The crux of the negotiations was whether the Lublin-Warsaw regime should simply be "enlarged," as the Russians insisted, or completely "reorganized," as the West demanded. After six days of haggling, the agreement that emerged on paper was ambiguous at best. In deference to Stalin, no mention was made in the document of the government in exile, but reference repeatedly was made to the "Provisional Government which is now functioning in Poland." On the other hand, the western phrasemakers were able to insert a clause explaining that this provisional government would be "reorganized on a broader democratic basis . . . with the inclusion of democratic leaders from Poland itself and from Poles abroad." [10]

Admiral William D. Leahy commented to the President at the time that the Polish agreement was so elastic that the Russians could "stretch it all the way from Yalta to Washington without ever technically breaking it." Roosevelt readily conceded this. "I know, Bill—I know it. But it's the best I can do for Poland at this time." [11] Upon his return from the 14,000-mile trip, the President, in his last personal report to Congress, endeavored to put forth the best possible interpretation of the Polish compromise, but he scarcely concealed from his listeners that it was not entirely to his liking.[12] In the House of Commons Churchill was confronted with a full-dress debate on the Crimea conference between February 27 and March 1, and vigorous opposition was raised by some three dozen members who regarded the agreements as inconsonant with Britain's written and moral obligations to her Polish ally.[13] Most of the Poles abroad were in a rage, and on the Italian front General Anders threatened for a time to pull his Polish forces out of the line.[14] A great number of his soldiers decided to live permanently in western Europe.

From the vantage point of hindsight and an absolute standard of morality, one can readily concede the cogency of many of the criticisms levied against the agreements. But a fairer historical approach has been suggested

---

[9] United States Senate, 83rd Congress, 1st Session, *Hearings before the Committee on Foreign Relations: Nomination of Charles E. Bohlen, March 2, and 18, 1953* (Washington, 1953), 2–113.

[10] *Yalta Papers*, 973–74.   [11] Leahy, *I Was There*, 315–16.

[12] For the text of President Roosevelt's speech, see Leland M. Goodrich and Marie J. Carroll, *Documents on American Foreign Relations, 1944–45*, VII (Boston, 1947), 18–28.

[13] Churchill, *Triumph and Tragedy*, 401–402. Excerpts from the debate in the House of Commons are reprinted in R. Umiastowski, *Poland, Russia, and Great Britain, 1941–1945: A Study of the Evidence* (London, 1946), 509 *et seq.*

[14] Anders, *An Army in Exile*, 247–54.

by Churchill, notwithstanding the fact that he was an "interested party." He has reminded the world to judge the actions of statesmen on the basis of the limited knowledge available to them at the moment of their decisions and the over-all objectives that they considered to be pre-eminent.[15]

If the western leaders cannot escape responsibility for certain miscalculations, neither can many of the Polish politicians abroad. The war had left them "men without a country," yet they unrealistically and stubbornly insisted that virtually no political or territorial changes could be acknowledged in a region in which a great change in power relationships had, in fact, occurred. Clearly they could not hope to maintain an independent, viable state between the U.S.S.R. and the Soviet zone of Germany unless they were willing to collaborate with their all-powerful neighbor. Still, it is hard to blame the Poles for having been reluctant to give up a vast portion of their prewar state without a plebiscite and in the mere hope that the Communists would not attempt to subvert a fusion government. Churchill has stoutly insisted that if the Poles had been willing in 1941 or even as late as the autumn of 1944 to agree to the Curzon Line, Stalin might have been persuaded to permit the establishment of a truly independent but friendly government, much as he did in the case of Finland. This may be true, but the historian can not write in the subjunctive case.

Like the other decisions, the Yalta agreement on the Polish government rested on the assumption that the Kremlin would honor it. Instead, the dispute over "reorganization" as opposed to mere "enlargement" resumed almost at once, bedeviling the last weeks of Franklin D. Roosevelt's life and adding to the headaches of Harry S. Truman's first months in office. From Moscow, Ambassador Harriman in March informed Washington that Molotov refused to live up to the Yalta agreements regarding the future Polish government; and on April 7 Stalin protested to Roosevelt that the United States and British ambassadors in Moscow had departed from the principles of Yalta.[16] Just before his death in April, 1945, Roosevelt cabled Churchill with respect to the Polish controversy: "We must be firm . . . and our course thus far is correct." [17] However, the "reorganized" Polish government that eventually was formed and recognized by the Great Powers retained a majority of the cabinet seats for former members of the pro-Soviet Lublin committee. The elections which Stalin had promised within a few weeks after Yalta were postponed until January, 1947, and were of course neither "free" nor "unfettered." [18]

---

[15] Cf. Churchill, *Triumph and Tragedy*, 402.

[18] See *Yalta Papers*, 989–93, for the exchange of Russian and American protests of bad faith during March and April, 1945; cf. Harry S. Truman, *Year of Decisions* (Garden City, 1955), 15–16, 23–26, 37–39, 50, 71–79, 84–86, 107–109, 254–55, 263, 280–81, 320–22, 347–410, and *passim*.

[17] Churchill, *Triumph and Tragedy*, 454.

[18] Mikolajczyk, *Rape of Poland*, 180–202; Arthur Bliss Lane, *I Saw Poland Betrayed* (Indianapolis, 1948), 276–88.

The Soviet Union failed to live up to the Yalta agreements concerning central-eastern Europe, and western statesmen, especially Roosevelt, have been denounced as traitors or bemoaned as babes in the diplomatic woods for having accepted Stalin's promises. But the historical moment must be remembered and Yalta agreements on eastern Europe must be viewed as part of an entire complex of wartime problems. The fact that Roosevelt and Churchill had blocked Soviet pretensions in Germany made it difficult for them to resist all of Stalin's Polish demands and neither was ready to let the Polish problem rupture western relations with the Soviet Union; Japan remained to be defeated even after Nazism was crushed. Consideration of strategic problems in the Far East undoubtedly conditioned the Yalta bargaining of the West on all European questions. By the time the final agreements on central-eastern Europe were signed, Stalin had delighted both Roosevelt and Churchill by promising to enter the war against Japan. Diplomacy has ever been a "give-and-take proposition," and the global proportions of the Yalta give-and-take must be considered if the historical meaning of Yalta is to be understood. . . .

YALTA AND THE FAR EAST *

. . . in February, 1945, the secret Far Eastern agreement seemed "very reasonable." Indeed, to some it appeared to usher in "the dawn of the new day we had all been praying for and talking about for so many years." Shortly after the Yalta conference General MacArthur was quoted as having stated that Russian seizure of Manchuria, Korea, and possibly part of northern China was inevitable, and that to deny Port Arthur to Russia would be impractical. Less than a decade later the Yalta agreement was branded not only as a betrayal of American principles, but as downright "treason," and General MacArthur in 1955 characterized as "fantastic" concessions which in 1945 seemed "inevitable." [19] In 1948 and especially in 1952 the Far Eastern agreements at Yalta became major issues in American presidential elections.

The controversy over these agreements may well last as long as the Far East remains important in world affairs; it is likely to be reopened whenever the careers of Roosevelt, Churchill, and Stalin are evaluated. The whole controversy hinges on two basic questions, one of power and one of morality. The first: Was Russian entry into the war against Japan neces-

---

* Editor's note: By George A. Lensen.
[19] Leahy, *I Was There*, 318–19; Sherwood, *Roosevelt and Hopkins*, 870; Felix Wittmer, *The Yalta Betrayal: Data on the Decline and Fall of Franklin Delano Roosevelt* (Caldwell, 1953), 76; Letter from Col. Paul L. Freeman, Jr., to General Marshall (February 13, 1945), and memorandum from General George A. Lincoln to General Marshall (March 8, 1945), as cited in Department of Defense, "The Entry of the Soviet Union into the War against Japan," 50–52; statement of General MacArthur, New York *Times*, October 21, 1955.

sary? The second: Did Roosevelt and Churchill willfully and lightly sacrifice the interests of a third power and a friend, China?

Did defeat of Japan depend on Russian help? . . . Suffice it to state here that in February, 1945, no one could count upon the effective use of the atomic bomb in the war against Japan,[20] and that American planners estimated that eighteen months of fighting after the not yet attained German surrender and at least 500,000 American casualties—perhaps one million—might be required to subdue the Japanese, even with Russian help.[21] In the circumstances it is understandable that United States and British military strategists sought the destruction or at least the diversion of the Japanese forces on the Asian continent by Russian action. As late as July 24, 1945, the Combined Chiefs of Staff recommended Russian entry into the war against Japan "to assist in the execution of the over-all strategic concept." Roosevelt's successor, Harry S. Truman, has stated emphatically in his memoirs that even on this date, seven days after he had received news of the successful test explosion of the A-bomb, it was still of great importance to the United States to secure Soviet participation in the war against Japan.[22] In February, 1945, it was up to the President and the Prime Minister to make the political arrangements which the military needs seemed to require, and this they did. This may have been a mistake; quite clearly it was not "treason."

Had the Joint Chiefs of Staff and the President decided that Russian entry into the war against Japan was not desirable, would the Soviets have come to the same conclusion? Admiral William H. Standley, upon his return from ambassadorial duties in Moscow in October of 1943, had told Roosevelt: "I don't think you can keep Stalin out." During World War I Japan had invoked the Anglo-Japanese Alliance ostensibly to come to Britain's aid, but actually to conquer the former German possessions in China for herself. In 1945 Russia was America's ally in Europe; she might well have entered the Pacific war uninvited to help herself, with or without the pretext of aiding the United States. Then the sky would have been the limit. The conditional entry, negotiated at Yalta, put at least a paper restraint on Russian ambitions, and this was the only restraint anyone could have put on Stalin at Yalta in February, 1945.

The alternative to refusal of Russian help or failure to bargain for it would not simply have been to fight without Russian assistance; the exclusion of Russia would have aroused Russian apprehension if not hostility.

[20] Churchill, *Triumph and Tragedy*, 388–89; *Yalta Papers*, 383; Stettinius, *Roosevelt and the Russians*, 90.

[21] Churchill, *Triumph and Tragedy*, 388–89; Sherwood, *Roosevelt and Hopkins*, 867; Stettinius, *Roosevelt and the Russians*, 8–9; Harry S. Truman, *Year of Decisions* (Garden City, 1955), 265.

[22] Walter Millis (ed.), with the collaboration of E. S. Duffield, *The Forrestal Diaries* (New York, 1951), 51; Department of Defense, "The Entry of the Soviet Union into the War against Japan," 90–91; Truman, *Year of Decisions*, 236, 265, 381–82, 411.

Stalin was in a stronger bargaining position than the Joint Chiefs of Staff or Roosevelt realized, for Japan was ready to offer much to keep Russia neutral. As Japan's position grew more desperate during the war, so did the plans of her leaders. Expecting the co-operation of Communist Russia and the capitalist states to deteriorate if not end upon the defeat of Germany, Japanese admirals wanted their diplomats to negotiate a coalition or alliance with the Soviet Union and "apparently also hoped eventually to draw the Soviet Union into the Japanese war effort as a fighting member in good standing." Marquis Koichi Kido, the Lord Keeper or the Privy Seal, whose duty it was to advise the Emperor, looked to Russia for a possible alignment because she was "Oriental" in outlook. As Stalin had said to Matsuoka in April, 1941, "You are an Asiatic. So am I." Other Japanese felt that "the Soviet Union would want to see Japan retain a fairly important international position so that the two countries could ally themselves in the future against America and Britain." Stalin had asserted in 1941 that "the whole world can be settled" if Japan and Russia co-operate. In June, 1945, Koki Hirota, a former prime minister and onetime ambassador to Moscow, suggested to Jacob A. Malik, then Soviet ambassador to Japan, that "if the Soviet Army and the Japanese Navy were to join forces, Japan and the Soviet Union together would become the strongest powers in the world." [23]

The Japanese were prepared to make substantial concessions to Russia in order to bring her into the war on their side or, if this were not possible, to restrain her from taking up arms against Japan. Foreign Minister Shigenori Togo, for example, went so far as to suggest that Japan might have to return to her pre-1904 boundaries. Others would have given up even more. In the words of a former Japanese diplomat, the Japanese military leaders were "frightened out of their wits" at the thought of a new war with Russia and were willing to pay a heavy price to avoid one. After all, "If a ship is doomed what matters its cargo, however precious? Jettison the cargo as fast as possible, if only doing so may save the ship." [24]

Having been promised what they wanted at Yalta, the Russians rebuffed Japanese overtures. Had their conditions been rejected at Yalta, Stalin conceivably might have made his bargain with the Japanese instead of with Roosevelt. True, Russian entry into the war against Japan enabled Soviet historians to boast that "the Armed Forces of the Soviet Union played the decisive role in the crushing of the Japanese imperialism, in the final liberation of China from the Japanese usurpers," but had Russia chosen

---

[23] William H. Standley and Arthur A. Ageton, *Admiral Ambassador to Russia* (Chicago, 1955), 499; Robert J. C. Butow, *Japan's Decision to Surrender* (Stanford, 1954), 77, 86–87, 121–22; Toshikazu Kase (David Nelson Rowe, ed.), *Journey to the Missouri*, 131; Otto D. Tolischus, *Tokyo Record* (New York, 1943), 107.

[24] Kase, *Journey to the Missouri*, 169; Butow, *Japan's Decision to Surrender*, 84; Tolischus, *Tokyo Record*, 107.

to attain her ends by acting as a peace-loving mediator, her propaganda stock in these days of smiling imperialism would have been even higher in the Far East.[25]

There are other questions. Granted that Russian entry into the war against Japan was desirable, was the price paid for Soviet help too high? Were the concessions justified? Did Roosevelt "sell out" Nationalist China? Did Yalta pave the way for Russian domination of China? The best way to answer these questions is to take a closer look at the agreements.

The stipulation in the Yalta agreement that "the *status quo* in Outer-Mongolia (The Mongolian People's Republic) shall be preserved" implied Soviet domination of this area. This was contrary to the Sino-Soviet Treaty of 1924, which recognized Chinese sovereignty over Sovietized Outer Mongolia. But this sovereignty ceased to exist in the middle 1920's, and by the time of Yalta the Soviet Union had exercised *de facto* control there for about twenty years. The parenthetical inclusion of "the Mongol People's Republic" in the Yalta agreement merely strengthened later Russian arguments vis-à-vis the Chinese for Outer Mongolia's formal "independence." [26]

The provision that "the southern part of Sakhalin as well as all the islands adjacent to it shall be returned to the Soviet Union" provoked no American discussion. Professor Hugh Borton, then of the State Department, recommended that southern Sakhalin be treated as an international trusteeship, in view of its importance to both Russia and Japan. But somehow his memorandum had not been included in the Yalta Briefing Book.[27] Postwar disillusionment in America in the Yalta agreements led to the devaluation of experts, particularly professors. Actually, the Yalta records show that it was not the advice of the academicians which was taken that caused trouble, but that which was ignored.

The agreement that "the commercial port of Dairen shall be internationalized, the preeminent interests of the Soviet Union in this port being safeguarded and the lease of Port Arthur as a naval base of the USSR restored" has been criticized severely as a reversion to nineteenth-century imperialism. Harriman has tried to meet these objections by pointing out that "there is no reason from the discussions leading up to the Yalta agreements to presume that the safeguarding of the 'pre-eminent interests of the Soviet Union' should go beyond Soviet interests in the free *transit* of exports and

---

[25] G. Efimov, *Ocherki po novoi i noveishei istorii Kitaia* [Account of the Modern and Contemporary History of China] (Moscow, 1951), 401; V. Avarin, *Bor'ba za Tikhii Okean* [The Struggle for the Pacific Ocean] (Leningrad, 1947), 419; E. M. Zhukov (ed.), *Mezhdunarodnye otnosheniia na Dal'nem Vostoke (1870–1945)* [International Relations in the Far East (1870–1945)] (Moscow, 1951), 610–11.

[26] Gerald H. Friters, *Outer Mongolia and its International Position* (Baltimore, 1949), 149; State Department, *United States Relations with China*, 113, n. 2, and 117, n. 7; Charles Patrick Fitzgerald, *Revolution in China* (New York, 1952), 235.

[27] *Yalta Papers*, 385–88; Ernest J. King and Walter Muir Whitehill, *Fleet Admiral King, A Naval Record* (New York, 1952), 591–92.

imports to and from the Soviet Union," and that "President Roosevelt looked upon the lease of Port Arthur for a naval base as an arrangement similar to privileges which the United States has negotiated with other countries for the mutual security of two friendly nations." Be that as it may, the Russian desire to get back from the Japanese what they had lost in the Russo-Japanese War seemed on the whole reasonable[28]

The provision that the Chinese-Eastern Railroad and the South Manchurian Railroad, which provides an outlet to Dairen, should be jointly operated by a Soviet-Chinese company—with the understanding that "the pre-eminent interests of the Soviet Union shall be safeguarded and that China shall retain full sovereignty in Manchuria"—has encountered less criticism. China had never recognized Russia's sale of the Chinese-Eastern Railroad to Japan in 1935 and still clung to the Sino-Soviet agreement of 1924, which provided that the manager of the railway be a Soviet citizen. Furthermore, the curious geographical conformation of Russia's Maritime Province made joint operation highly logical. Last but not least, Roosevelt and other Allied leaders were still preoccupied with the thought of future security against Japanese aggression. Japan had put down roots in southern Manchuria that could not be destroyed by military defeat alone. China did not seem strong enough to neutralize this area. As one historian has put it: "To recognize Russia's legitimate economic and strategic stake in Manchuria under conditions that specified 'that China shall retain full sovereignty' was a solution far more conservative than to abandon the 'cradle of conflict' to the winds of fate." [29] It must also be remembered that Roosevelt was not "giving away" any Chinese territory which he or even the Chinese actually held, but what the Japanese had in fact conquered. The concessions at Yalta seemed the most effective way of winning Manchuria back for the Chinese, at least politically.

But whatever historical arguments there may have been for the cession of southern Sakhalin, Dairen, and Port Arthur, there were none to justify the transfer of the whole Kurile Archipelago to the Soviet Union. A State Department memorandum by Professor George H. Blakeslee, which unfortunately, like the memorandum by Professor Borton, was not included in the Briefing Book, recognized that Russia had "a substantial claim" to the northern Kurile Islands and a strategic interest in the central group. "There would seem, however, to be few factors which would justify a Soviet claim to the southern islands," the memorandum continued. "This transfer to the Soviet Union would create a situation which a future Japan would find difficult to accept as a permanent solution. It would deprive Japan of islands which are historically and ethnically Japanese and of waters which are

---

[28] State Department, *United States Relations with China*, 114, n. 3, 4; Leahy, *I Was There*, 318–19; Werner Levi, *Modern China's Foreign Policy* (Minneapolis, 1953), 240–41.
[29] William Appleman Williams, *American-Russian Relations, 1781–1947* (New York, 1952), 277.

valuable for fishery. If the southern islands should be fortified they would be a continuing menace to Japan." In view of the proximity of the Kurile Islands to the Aleutians and their consequent importance to the United States as a land bridge between Japan and Alaska, the memorandum recommended that the northern and central Kuriles should be placed under the projected international organization.[30] The advice of Professor Blakeslee was not considered at Yalta, where Stalin was assured that all the Kurile Islands "shall be handed over to the Soviet Union."

The Roosevelt-Stalin agreement qualified the provisions concerning Outer Mongolia, Dairen, Port Arthur, and the railroads by making them subject to concurrence by Chiang Kai-shek, but then proceeded to nullify this qualification by stating that "these claims of the Soviet Union shall be unquestionably fulfilled." Was this a "sell-out" of the Chinese government?

It is relevant to remember in this connection that Chiang Kai-shek's own policy from the middle of 1943 on was directed toward a *rapprochement* with the Soviet Union. For this he sought American mediation, suggesting to Vice-President Henry A. Wallace in June, 1944, that Roosevelt act as "middleman" between China and the U.S.S.R. Chiang was willing to go "more than halfway" to obtain a friendly understanding with the Soviet Union, partly because he hoped that this might induce the Russians to continue recognizing his government as *the* government of China and deprive them of incentive to support the Chinese Communists, and partly because he felt that obligating Russia to something by a treaty was better than leaving her a free hand.[31] It was only in later years, when the Nationalist government began to shift the blame for its own shortcomings upon the shoulders of the United States, that Nationalist officials "demanded American support as an atonement for the betrayal at Yalta." [32]

Postwar accusations of betrayal ignored the stipulation in the Yalta agreement that "the Soviet Union expresses its readiness to conclude with the National Government of China a pact of friendship and alliance between the USSR and China." The pact of friendship and alliance was not intended to betray China, but to strengthen it. As a Briefing Book paper stated, "The American Government's long-range policy with respect to China is based on the belief that the need for China to be a principal factor in the Far East is a fundamental requirement for peace and security in that area." And another paper, considering the "political and military situation in China in the event the U.S.S.R. enters the war in the Far East," recommended that the British and American governments "should make every effort to bring about cooperation between all Chinese forces

[30] *Yalta Papers*, 379–83.

[31] Levi, *Modern China's Foreign Policy*, 243–44; State Department, *United States Relations with China*, 550; Max Beloff, *Soviet Policy in the Far East, 1944–1951* (London, 1953), 29; "Statement of W. Averell Harriman," 3339.

[32] Levi, *Modern China's Foreign Policy*, 244.

and the Russian military command in order to prevent military developments from further widening the gap between the Communists and the Chinese Government and increasing the possibility of a disunited China after hostilities." In point of fact, the treaty which eventually was concluded between Nationalist China and the U.S.S.R., the Soong-Stalin agreements of August, 1945, was heralded by so pro-Nationalist a magazine as *Life* as a promise of "genuine peace" in the Far East.[33]

It was a weak China, unable to fill the power vacuum which the defeat of Japan would create, that the United States government dreaded. Stalin's recognition of the Nationalist government as the central authority in China was most reassuring, therefore, and subsequent Soviet statements were even more encouraging. Thus in June, 1945, the new President, Harry S. Truman, could inform his special representative in China, Patrick J. Hurley, that:

1. Stalin has made to us a categorical statement that he will do everything he can to promote unification under the leadership of Chiang Kai-shek.

2. That this leadership will continue after the war.

3. That he wants a unified stable China and wants China to control all of Manchuria as a part of a United China.

4. That he has no territorial claims against China, and that he will respect Chinese sovereignty in all areas his troops enter to fight Japanese.

5. That he will welcome representatives of the Generalissimo to be with his troops in Manchuria in order to facilitate the organization of Chinese administration in Manchuria.

6. That he agrees with America's "open door" policy in China.

7. That he agrees to a trusteeship for Korea under China, Great Britain, the Soviet Union, and the United States.[34]

Certainly this seemed to offer that promise of "a strong, stable, and united China" which was the objective set forth in the President's Briefing Book for the Yalta negotiations when it stated: "We regard Sino-Soviet cooperation as a *sine qua non* of peace and security in the Far East and seek to aid in removing the existing mistrust between China and the Soviet Union and in bringing about close and friendly relations between them." [35]

The same outlook underlay American-Soviet relations. "President Roosevelt and I saw alike with regard to Russia," wrote Cordell Hull. "We both realize that the path of our relations would not be a carpet of flowers, but we also felt that we could work with Russia. There was no difference of opinion between us that I can recall on the basic premise that we must and could get along with the Soviet Government." [36]

---

[33] *Yalta Papers*, 352, 356; *Life*, XIX (September 10, 1945), 42.

[34] Truman, *Year of Decisions*, 269.   [35] *Yalta Papers*, 356–57.

[36] Hull, *Memoirs*, II, 1467.

No one could have expected the Russians to enter the war against Japan for the sole purpose of saving American lives. It is understandable that some territorial agreement was reached. It is less understandable, however, that there was almost no discussion of Russian claims. It is by no means impossible that the Russians would have satisfied themselves with only the northern and central Kurile Islands. But nobody ever raised the question. Nor did anybody counter the other Russian demands. The Americans might have reminded Stalin that his demands violated not only Russia's treaty with Japan of 1925 but also her treaty with China of 1924. In the former she had declared that the treaty ending the Russo-Japanese War "remains in full force," and in the latter she had renounced "the special rights and privileges relating to all concessions in any part of China acquired by the Tsarist Government under various Conventions, Treaties, Agreements, etc." Probably Roosevelt felt that Stalin could not be swayed and that nothing would be gained by antagonizing him. But by agreeing that in 1904 Japan had been the aggressor, Churchill and Roosevelt put the finger on their own countries, for it was with English and American moral and financial support that Japan ventured to challenge Russia in apparent defense of the Open Door.

Roosevelt and Churchill missed a golden opportunity to remind Stalin of earlier Communist condemnations of the czarist government's role in the Russo-Japanese War and to accuse him, tongue in cheek, of "deviationism." But perhaps it was just as well, for when Churchill had reminded Stalin at Teheran in another connection of the old Communist slogan "no annexations and no indemnities," Stalin had only replied with a broad grin: "I have told you that I am becoming a Conservative." Stalin asserted at the end of the war that the Russian people had been looking forward to the defeat of Japan to liquidate the blemish cast upon their country in 1904, that "for forty years we the people of the older generation have waited for this day." This was contrary not only to the traditional party line but also to current Russian feelings. General Deane observed in Moscow that Russia's entry into the war against Japan evoked relatively little enthusiasm or interest.[37]

Yet, when all this has been said, it must be remembered that the United States did not "give away" at Yalta anything that it was within her power to withhold except by making war against her Russian ally. In the words of Secretary of War Henry L. Stimson, the concessions to Russia on Far Eastern matters which were made at Yalta were "generally matters which are within

---

[37] Harriet L. Moore, *Soviet Far Eastern Policy, 1931–1945* (New York, 1945), 159, 175; Iosif V. Stalin, "Obrashcheniia tovarishcha I. V. Stalina k narodu" [Speech of Comrade Joseph V. Stalin to the People], as cited by B. A. Romanov, *Ocherki diplomaticheskoi istorii russko-iaponskoi voiny 1895–1907* [Outlines of the Diplomatic History of the Russo-Japanese War, 1895–1907] (Moscow, 1947), 3; Winston S. Churchill, *Closing the Ring* (Boston, 1951), 398–99; Deane, *The Strange Alliance*, 311.

the military power of Russia to obtain regardless of U. S. military action short of war. The War Department believes that Russia is militarily capable of defeating the Japanese and occupying Karafuto [Sakhalin], Manchuria, Korea and Northern China before it would be possible for the U. S. military forces to occupy these areas. Only in the Kuriles is the United States in a position to circumvent Russian initiative. If the United States were to occupy these islands to forestall Russian designs, it would be at the direct expense of the campaign to defeat Japan and would involve an unacceptable cost in American lives." [38] Stimson's statement points to the essential meaning of Yalta, so far as American interests in the Far East were concerned. Yalta enabled the United States virtually to ignore the Japanese forces on the mainland of Asia and thus to concentrate upon the Japanese home islands. This was an asset which facilitated the exclusive postwar occupation by the United States of the real heart of Far Eastern industry—Japan.

It was not the Yalta agreement, but failure to live up to the agreement that furthered postwar conflict. Perhaps the breakdown in Russo-American co-operation was inherent in the amorality of Communism; perhaps it was due to the age-old inability of comrades-in-arms to remain comrades-in-peace. As Stalin said at Yalta: "It is not so difficult to keep unity in time of war since there is a joint aim to defeat the common enemy, which is clear to everyone. The difficult task will come after the war when diverse interests tend to divide the Allies." [39]

The Yalta agreements were not faultless, but their imperfections lay in the limitation of the human mind, in man's inability to gaze into the future. Churchill summed this up when, on the eve of Yalta, in one of his more humble moments, he wrote to Foreign Secretary Eden concerning the difficulty of long-range planning for a postwar world: "Guidance in these mundane matters is granted to us only step by step, or at the utmost a step or two ahead." [40] The Far Eastern sequel to Yalta has borne out Churchill's statement, and additional verification has been provided by the appearance of flaws in the plans for world order which the Big Three drafted there. . . .

THE BIG THREE AND THE UNITED NATIONS *

. . . [By agreeing to permit the Soviet Union to have three seats in the U. N. Assembly], Roosevelt saddened many liberal supporters, who felt that he had weakened his moral position vis-à-vis the Soviet Union. A few weeks after the conference, in explaining his position to the American dele-

---

[38] Department of Defense, "The Entry of the Soviet Union into the War against Japan," 70. See also *ibid.*, 20.

[39] James F. Byrnes, *Speaking Frankly* (New York, 1947), 44.

[40] Churchill, *Triumph and Tragedy*, 351.   * Editor's note: By Forrest C. Pogue.

gation to the San Francisco conference, the President stressed the fact that he had talked the Russians into taking fewer votes than they had demanded and into agreeing to an equal number of votes for the United States. He said that American delegates to the United Nations conference were free to vote as they pleased on the issue, but that he had told Stalin that if he were a delegate he would vote for the extra seats for the U.S.S.R. Senator Vandenberg, the leading Republican on the delegation, commented: "This will *raise hell*." [41] (Italics in the original.)

But, in the final analysis, Roosevelt's U. N. policy at Yalta must be praised or damned in terms of the desirability of obtaining British and Russian co-operation in the world organization. Without their support no U. N. could be founded or could work effectively; to get their support, compromise was essential. Therein lay the essential meaning of Yalta in the history of man's search for world order. Furthermore, it should be remembered that the Russians and British had accepted the American voting procedure, and that Roosevelt's strong stand against sixteen votes for the Soviet Republics held the Russians to the minimum number they would settle for. While the concession was something Roosevelt did not care to defend, it was not a serious blow to the U. N. Charter and it gave the Russians no great increase in power in the Assembly, as events have fully shown. Moreover, Roosevelt at Yalta won approval of pre-April negotiations regarding the troublesome question of territorial trusteeships for the U. N. . . .

Most important of all, Roosevelt won from Churchill and Stalin an agreement to call the United Nations Conference on World Organization before the war's end. At Yalta the President demanded that agreement be reached on details of the organization before the territorial concessions were made. He may have hoped, like Wilson, that such peace machinery might help remove injustices of the peace settlement. Had he lived to hear Vandenberg's defense of the U. N. Charter in June, 1945, just before the United States Senate overwhelmingly accepted membership in the United Nations, Roosevelt might have felt that the Republican senator from Michigan was speaking for him. Vandenberg declared that the United Nations organization served the intelligent self-interest of the United States; that it offered "our only chance to keep faith with those who have borne the heat of battle." And he added:

> I have signed the Charter with no illusions regarding its imperfections and with no pretensions that it guarantees its own benign aims; but with no doubts that it proposes an experiment which must be bravely undertaken in behalf of peace with justice in a better, happier, and safer world.

.   .   .   .

[41] Arthur H. Vandenberg, Jr. (ed.), with the collaboration of Joe Alex Morris, *Private Papers of Senator Vandenberg* (Boston, 1952), 159–60.

> Within the framework of the Charter, through its refinement in the
> light of experience, the future can overtake our errors. But there will
> be no future for it unless we can make this start. . . .[42]

Critics of the U. N. compromises at Yalta must ask whether the postwar
world has been better or worse for having had the United Nations to help
keep a semblance of East-West order in the midst of the "Cold War." After
ten years of U. N. contributions to world peace, the answer can hardly
remain in doubt. . . .

YALTA IN RETROSPECT *

. . . The meaning of Yalta cannot be grasped unless the conditions under
which the conference leaders worked are remembered. In February, 1945,
the Allied peoples generally agreed that Germany and Japan must be
severely punished and cured of aggressive tendencies. Agreement was widespread that Germany and Japan must be effectively disarmed and their
heavy industries restricted in order to prevent them from making war in
the future. The western powers generally acknowledged that the U.S.S.R.
had suffered terribly in the war and should receive compensation from the
common enemies. Thoughts of the postwar era were pervaded by a desire
to counterbalance the power of Germany and Japan by the force of the
"world policemen" who had co-operated to win the war. Roosevelt certainly
hoped, and probably believed until the last weeks before his death, that
he could sit down at a table with Stalin and Churchill and work out solutions to the problems of the world. The Big Three tended, as a result, to
give smaller states little opportunity to shape their own futures. The President strongly believed that Soviet expansive tendencies would be allayed
when the U.S.S.R. won security on its European and Asian frontiers.

Other assumptions likewise encouraged Roosevelt to overestimate the
possibilities of postwar co-operation with the Soviet Union. Knowledge
that Russia had been severely damaged in the early years of the war with
Germany led him to surmise that the U.S.S.R. might require a generation
to recover. Some Washington officials believed that the Soviet Union would
be dependent upon postwar economic aid for her recovery, and that for this
reason Stalin could be counted upon to maintain good relations with the
United States. In short, one must remember both the war-born opportunism and the hopes and fears of 1945: concessions which would shorten
the war and save lives would be acceptable to the people of the West; the
formation of a workable United Nations organization held hope for the
correction of any basic errors which might have been made in the various
peace arrangements; and, more realistically, it was feared that the Soviet

---

[42] United States House of Representatives, 79th Congress, 1st Session, *Congressional Record,* XCI, 6981–82.

* Editor's note: By Forrest C. Pogue.

Union might become the center of opposition to the West unless bound as closely as possible to its wartime allies.

All these factors powerfully asserted themselves when the Big Three met in the Crimean palace of the czar in February, 1945. But yet another factor loomed large in the conference at Yalta. The disintegration of Germany meant that the force which had dominated central Europe since 1938 was gone and that its place in central-eastern Europe would be taken by the Soviet Union. A disarmed Italy and a weakened France could not be expected to balance the enormous power of the Red Army. Britain, seriously drained of her capital wealth by the heavy exactions of the war and lacking the manpower reserves to challenge a potential enemy of Russia's strength, could not hope to redress the balance of Europe as she had for two centuries. The people of the United States viewed their exertions in Europe as temporary and hoped for their early termination; they were in no state of psychological readiness to take up Britain's traditional role. The approaching defeat of Japan threatened to create a power vacuum in the Far East like that which Hitler's defeat would leave in Europe. Thus concessions at Yalta inevitably reflected the powerful position of the Soviet Union in Europe and its potential power in the Far East. Personal diplomacy at Yalta came to grips with the basic realities of a new balance of power in the world at large, and the freedom of action of the individual statesman was greatly restricted by these impersonal forces. Therein lies the overriding fact about the conference; without its comprehension, the meaning of Yalta is sure to be missed.

Several courses were open to the western leaders at Yalta in dealing with the new set of power relationships. It was possible to make minimum concessions to Stalin and hope for Russian co-operation and goodwill; it was possible to break off discussions at the first sign of demands which would ratify the new power relationships or create a greater imbalance in world politics than already existed; and it was possible to state certain moral positions in indignant and ringing Wilsonian phrases. Roosevelt and Churchill selected the first course, believing and hoping that it would bring victory and at the same time save the peace. They gained something by forcing the Russians to put their promises on record; but they could not make Stalin keep his word. The United States and Great Britain have at least the moral right and, technically, the legal right to use Soviet violations as the basis for repudiation of Allied concessions at Yalta, for it was the Soviet breach of contract that started the "Cold War."

The Korean War: Who Was Right, Truman or MacArthur?

INTRODUCTION

When the Chinese Communists entered the Korean War in force, United Nations Commander General Douglas MacArthur, who but a few days previously had launched a general offensive to end the war, announced that "we face an entirely new war." In order to achieve victory in this "new war," the general proposed a naval blockade of the Chinese coast, the air bombardment of selected targets in China, the reinforcement of the U.N. troops in Korea by the soldiers of Chiang Kai-shek, "diversionary action" by the Chinese Nationalists against the Chinese mainland that might lead to "counter-invasion," and, apparently, the use of atomic weapons to seal off Korea from China. The Truman administration, which from the beginning of the Korean War had sought to keep the fighting limited lest Russian intervention be provoked and World War III initiated, refused to institute any of General MacArthur's suggestions. Unwilling to accept the limitations imposed upon his forces by the administration, MacArthur, in defiance of orders, publicly sought to promote his own views regarding the proper conduct of the war. The result was that on April 10, 1951, President Truman relieved the general of his various commands.

The constitutional right of the president as commander-in-chief to remove a general from his post is, of course, not subject to dispute, but this still "leaves unanswered the question of whether the government waged the [Korean] war in the most effective manner consistent with the limitation of war." [1] *In short, was the Truman administration correct in limiting the war to the extent that it did, or would it have been wiser for it to have adopted General MacArthur's recommendations in the hopes that this would have led to total victory in Korea? Beyond this question, the Truman-MacArthur controversy points up a whole congeries of questions concerning the ability of the American democracy to fight a limited war.*

The two selections that follow present conflicting points of view regarding the wisdom of MacArthur's proposals to enlarge the Korean War beyond the limits set by the Truman administration. Alvin J. Cottrell and James E. Dougherty criticize the Truman administration's conduct of the war, defend MacArthur's proposals for expanding the war, and stress what the United States lost by failing to win a decisive victory in Korea. The Korean War, in their opinion, "revealed the inadequacy of Western democratic governments to deal with a conflict situation which is protracted and kept indecisive."

The position of the Truman administration as it was presented at the

---

[1] Robert Endicott Osgood, *Limited War: The Challenge to American Strategy* (Chicago: University of Chicago Press, 1957), p. 173.

*joint hearings of the Senate Foreign Relations and Armed Services Com-
mittees following General MacArthur's return to the United States is summarized in a chapter taken from Professor John W. Spanier's book,* The
Truman-MacArthur Controversy and the Korean War. *The military and
political reasons for the administration's rejection of MacArthur's proposals
are set forth in this selection, and the gains that the administration believed
accrued to the United States because of the manner in which the war was
fought are indicated. Spanier, it is clear from other chapters of his book,
is by no means uncritical of the Truman administration's conduct of the
war, but he has considerably more sympathy for the administration's position than for that of MacArthur.*

The Lessons of Korea: War and
the Power of Man*

Alvin J. Cottrell and James E. Dougherty

The Korean War represented a crucial turning point in the struggle between the communists and the Free World. The manner of the American
response to the North Korean attack demonstrated to the communists the
West's ability to react swiftly and decisively to an act of outright aggression.
But more important still, the Korean War revealed the inadequacy of
Western democratic governments to deal with a conflict situation which is
protracted and kept indecisive. It was the experience of this war, more than
any other single factor, which has given rise, during the last two years, to
the debate over the readiness of the United States to wage so-called "limited
wars." This debate, insofar as it has centered upon the size and the mobility
of American tactical forces on the periphery of the Sino-Soviet bloc, completely misses the crucial point: namely that the problem of waging "limited
war" is essentially not one of military power but of political will.

Through the years 1950–1953, the United States was, in terms of sheer
military power, the superior contestant. Narrow limits were indeed imposed

From *Orbis*, II (Spring 1958), 39–65. Reprinted by permission.

* This article has been adapted from research materials utilized in the preparation of
the *Study on Protracted Conflict,* to be published in fall 1958 by Frederick A. Praeger
under the auspices of the Foreign Policy Research Institute of the University of Pennsylvania.

upon the Korean conflict, but "it was obviously the stronger Power which imposed them and made them stick." [1] It is fair to ask whether the United States, if it had in being all of the elaborate force levels called for by contemporary proponents of the "limited war" doctrine, would even now be able to avoid a repetition of Korea. Since the memory of the Korean War, with all its bitter frustrations, continues to permeate American thinking in the present discussion on weapons policy,[2] a review of United States strategy in that war may serve to remind us that mere possession of the requisite military power does not provide, by itself, an answer to our problem: namely how to meet the intermediate—"limited"—challenges of the communists.

IMPOSED LIMITATIONS ON THE WAR

The Korean War has been the only military conflict directly involving the United States and members of the communist bloc. The conflict was limited in several ways: The hostilities were confined to a precise geographical area. The nearby territory of Formosa was "neutralized" and the territory north of the Yalu River was declared off limits. The war was limited with regard to the nationality of the forces eligible to participate, for the armed forces of the Nationalist Chinese Government, a member of the Security Council, which urged U. N. members to resist the aggression, were not allowed to take part in the action. Furthermore, the war was limited as to weapons employed, types of targets selected and kinds of supplementary operations undertaken. Thus, weapons of mass destruction were not used; the rail and supply lines of the Chinese communists were not hit; and long range American aerial reconnaissance was ruled out.

It is significant that none of these limitations were or could have been forced upon the United States by the enemy. They all were voluntarily assumed by the United States. The reasons given for accepting these limitations were various, but practically all of them were reducible to fears of one sort or another: fear that the United States would alienate its European allies by prosecuting too vigorously a war in Asia; fear of antagonizing the Asian neutrals if Chiang's forces were utilized; and, above all, fear that the war, if it was not rigidly localized, would become general and global.

The difficulties encountered by the United States during the Korean War sprang in the first instance from a failure to view the struggle against the total strategic background. Probably the communists themselves did not foresee the full strategic implication of the border crossing on June 24,

---

[1] Bernard Brodie, "Nuclear Weapons: Strategic or Tactical," *Foreign Affairs,* XXXII (January 1954), 228.

[2] Cf., e.g., Henry A. Kissinger, *Nuclear Weapons and Foreign Policy* (New York, 1957), and Robert E. Osgood, *Limited War: The Challenge to American Strategy* (Chicago, 1957).

1950, and they may not have anticipated the prompt response of the United States and the U. N. Security Council. The United States entered the war for definite enough a purpose: the defense of a free nation against flagrant communist aggression. At the outset, the United States and its friends in the United Nations were under no misapprehension as to the fundamental issues, political and moral, raised by the attack on South Korea.

Some of the countries who later assumed a neutralist posture voted in the U. N. to resist the North Koreans. By October of 1950, when U. N. forces began their offensive to the Yalu, the General Assembly went beyond the original objective of merely defending South Korea and defined the U. N.'s goal as the establishment of a "unified, independent and democratic government in the sovereign state of Korea." This policy statement was intended and interpreted as an authorization for General MacArthur to move northward to the Yalu River.[3] In the same month, the situation changed ominously when the Chinese communists began to pour into Korea. Then the Korean War began to assume a different meaning: MacArthur called it an "entirely new war." The West was slow to evaluate the strategic consequences of the conflict with Communist China. Since the war had started over the Korean question, Western diplomats and commentators persisted in regarding it as a war over Korea, in which the additional features of Chinese communist intervention now had to be taken into account. A mental block obscured the full significance of the fact that the war was now between Communist China and the United States. It took the communists four months—from June to October 1950—to develop a novel strategy for turning Korea to their own strategic advantage.

Once the Chinese were in the fight, the unity of purpose of the United States and its allies in the U. N. began to flag. While India began to view Korea as an arena of the Cold War in which she vowed to be neutral, Great Britain "became anxious to minimize her responsibility for sponsoring the decisive resolution" concerning MacArthur's authority to cross the 38th Parallel.[4]

Once it was known that China was the antagonist, what were the decisions to be made by the United States? Some of these decisions, by their very nature, could not even be faced unless the United States formulated for itself a reasonably clear picture of the over-all Sino-Soviet strategy in Asia. Policy-making flows from analysis, and analysis hinges on framing the right questions. Several questions had to be asked, and at least hypothetical answers had to be given to them. There is some cause for wondering whether American policy-makers did pose the right questions in October 1950. Why did Communist China enter the Korean War? Did she come in

---

[3] Cf. *U. S. Policy in the Korean Conflict,* Department of State Publication 4263, Far Eastern Series 44, 1951, p. 17. The vote in the General Assembly was 47–5. India, fearing that action in North Korea would bring in Communist China, abstained.

[4] "The Record on Korea," *The Economist,* March 10, 1951, p. 526.

enthusiastically to defend herself against an American-U.N.-dominated Korea on her border, or did she come in somewhat reluctantly and fearfully as a result of Soviet cajolery, pressure and promises? Was Mao Tse-tung confident of his estimate of the Korean situation before committing himself? Or did he use the gradual build-up of "volunteer" forces during October to probe his enemy and thus to gauge the Western reaction to his move? Was Stalin prepared to divert sizable and much-needed resources from the Soviet Union to support the Chinese in the event of large-scale fighting? Were the communists prepared to face atomic conflict? What were the strategic implications of China's move for American interests in Japan, Formosa, Indochina, and elsewhere? What did the communist bloc really stand to gain in Korea? How great and how genuine was the danger that the Korean tinderbox would spark a world conflagration? What was the relation of American objectives in the Far East to American objectives in the NATO community? These and similar questions impinged upon the decisions which had to be made in the fall of 1950, particularly those concerning the role of Chiang's army, the application of an economic and naval blockade to China, going beyond the Yalu and using atomic weapons.

The gravest American error in Korea was the failure to respond decisively during the first few days of the Chinese communist intervention. Since the United States temporized in the face of Mao Tse-tung's probingly cautious, "unofficial" entry into the war, Mao was able gradually to build up his ground forces in North Korea. The initiative passed out of American hands, and the war became prolonged. The longer the war dragged on, the more often the debate within the United States over the Korean War raised the specter of general war. Whenever it was suggested that the United States take steps to regain the military initiative, the proposals were invariably rejected on the grounds that they involved the danger either of provoking general war or of offending the friends of the United States. The major proposals put forth for regaining the initiative concerned the use of Chiang Kai-shek's Nationalist forces on Formosa, the application of a blockade against China, operations beyond the Yalu River and the introduction of atomic weapons.

THE USE OF CHIANG'S FORCES

There may have been justification for the neutralization of Chiang's forces on Formosa by executive order of June 27, 1950, under which the Seventh Fleet was to protect Formosa and thus restrain Chiang from carrying out air or sea attacks against the mainland. Secretary of State Dean Acheson had argued that if Chinese troops from Taiwan were to join the U. N. forces in Korea, the Red Chinese might decide to enter the conflict precisely to weaken Chiang's army and thus diminish his capability of defending the island against a potential communist assault.[5] Another and perhaps the most important reason for the U. S. refusal to permit Chiang's participation was, in a sense, a political one, imposed upon the United States by foreign sentiment and by its own reluctance to offend that sentiment. It was summed up succinctly by W. Averell Harriman in the report which he gave to President Truman on his meeting with General MacArthur in early August 1950:

> He [General MacArthur] did not seem to consider the liability that our support of Chiang on such a move would be to us in the Far East. I explained in great detail why Chiang was a liability and the great danger of a split in the unity of the United Nations on the Chinese-Communist-Formosa policies; the attitude of the British, Nehru and such countries as Norway, who, although stalwart in their determination to resist Russian aggression, did not want to stir up trouble elsewhere.[6]

This decision to hold Chiang "under wraps" should have come in for review and modification as soon as Chinese intervention loomed seriously on the horizon. The argument about non-interference in the Chinese Civil War, if it ever had any validity, lost all its effectiveness in October 1950. When intelligence reports were received through Indian and British diplomatic channels concerning an impending Chinese military move into Korea, "intelligence reports" should have immediately been filtered through the same channels to the communists concerning an impending "deneutralization" of Formosa. Had this been done, Mao may well have reconsidered his policy of introducing "volunteers," who could conceivably have been recalled and publicly "chastised" for unauthorized activities. The pretext of "volunteers" reflected Mao's extreme caution. October and November 1950 were doubtless the critical months in the Korean War, when Mao scanned carefully American responses to his moves and took the measure of the U. N.'s firmness of purpose. The U. S. might at this point have blocked China from entering the war, and Mao could have recalled the "volunteers" with a minimum loss of face. General MacArthur, at the time of his dismissal, proposed that restrictions be removed from the deployment of Chiang's forces and that these forces be given substantial American logistical support against China. Regardless of how helpful Chiang's army may have been on the Korean peninsula, it is not mere hindsight to conclude that, had the Chinese Nationalists been poised for action across the Formosa Straits, the communists would not have felt free to remove sizable forces from the Fukien area for use in Korea. In his testimony to the Senate on the military situation in the Far East, General MacArthur stated:

---

[5] Harry S. Truman, *Years of Trial and Hope*, II (Garden City, 1956), 343.
[6] *Ibid.*, p. 352.

I believe that the minute you took off the inhibitions from the Generalissimo's forces it would result in relieving the pressure on our front in Korea. I believe that they would have tended to shift the center of gravity of their military mobilization down further south than they are at the present time.[7]

Among the arguments often advanced against accepting Chiang's offer of troops was that the United States might unwittingly commit itself to deploying American ground forces to achieve Chiang's major objective: re-establishing the Nationalist Government on the mainland.[8] This reasoning would have us believe that America could not have controlled the scope of its operations on the Chinese mainland, even though it had demonstrated its ability to impose precise limits on its Korean actions. The U. S. certainly could have supplied Chiang with enough material to allow him to carry out diversionary attacks against the Chinese communists without running the risk of being drawn into the morass of China. The United States could have reduced or cut off the aid to Chiang if and when his operations conflicted with American strategic objectives.[9] There is no need to conclude that Chiang's ambitions were bound to prevail over American interests. American policy-makers pondered all the possible alternatives before them and assumed fatalistically that, once a decision had been made, all its possible consequences, pleasant and unpleasant, would come to pass by some mysterious process over which they had no control.

ECONOMIC SANCTIONS

The question of invoking economic warfare measures against China raised problems of coalition diplomacy for the United States. There can be little doubt that an intensified application of economic sanctions against Communist China, reinforced by a naval blockade against communist shipping along the coast of China, would have greatly reduced the strength of the Chinese armies in Korea. Admiral Forrest Sherman, Chief of Naval Operations, made this statement during the Senate hearings:

A naval blockade by the United Nations would substantially reduce the war potential of Communist China. . . . China is not capable of taking countermeasures that could appreciably reduce the effectiveness of such a blockade.

A naval blockade by the United Nations would be advantageous

---

[7] Hearings, Senate Armed Services Committee, 82d Congress, 1st Session, 1951, *The Military Situation in the Far East,* Part I, pp. 266–267.

[8] Cf., for example, Harold M. Vinacke, *Far Eastern Politics in the Postwar Period* (New York, 1956), p. 240.

[9] General MacArthur told the Senate: "I have said that I can conceive of no condition in which I would attempt to land United States ground forces in continental China." Hearings, *cit. supra.,* Part I, p. 267.

from a psychological standpoint. It would demonstrate to the Chinese Communists, and to the neighboring Asian peoples, the power of the forces against communism—it would demonstrate the effectiveness of sea power, a power that the Chinese communists can do little to thwart.[10]

The general arguments against economic weapons were reducible to one, namely that they could have little effect because of the agricultural character of the Chinese economy and because China would still be able to receive goods from the Soviet bloc. *The Economist* stated its position in this way:

> It is and should remain the British argument that economic sanctions will do more harm than good. Because the main strategic materials from all sources—oil, for example—are already under embargo, very little of vital importance is going into China from the Western world. A greatly increased effort at control would produce only small additional results, which could have little effect on the slender war potential of Peking. . . . What is more, the strict application of sanctions means sooner or later that an American warship stops on the high seas ships bearing Indian jute to China. . . .[11]

American allies were firmly opposed to boycott and blockade, because such policies would have hurt their Far East trade, which totals several hundred shiploads per year. Britain, moreover, was concerned over the precarious position of Hongkong. Consequently, the United States was unable to expect its allies to favor General MacArthur's proposal for applying economic sanctions. Nevertheless, the failure to apply sanctions enabled China to protract the conflict without suffering any unusual economic strains. The fact that China was an underdeveloped agrarian nation made her almost totally dependent upon imports for the success of her first five-year plan. Every shipload of goods received in the eastern ports helped to lessen China's need for making demands upon her Soviet ally or the East European satellites. The supply lines from the Soviet Union to Korea, some 4,000 miles in length, were already operating under a heavy strain.[12]

---

[10] Hearings, *cit. supra.*, Part II, p. 1514. Admiral Sherman said that a blockade could seriously interefere with several war commodities, including rubber, petroleum, industrial chemicals, pharmaceuticals, machine tools, spare parts and electrical equipment. He pointed out that 78 million tons of shipping enter Chinese ports every year in about 2,500 foreign ships. *Ibid.*, p. 1512. See also the testimony of Admiral Turner Joy: "I believe the United Nations could have defeated the communists, or at least caused them to withdraw from the Korean Peninsula, had not the commander-in-chief of the Far East been restricted in the use of his forces, and had an effective United Nations (naval) blockade of Red China been established as soon as the Chinese entered the war." "The Korean War and Related Matters," *op. cit.*, pp. 22–23. For an account of the effective naval blockade against North Korea, see M. W. Cagle and F. A. Manson, *The Sea War in Korea* (Annapolis, 1957), pp. 299–300.

[11] "Korean Stalemate," *The Economist*, February 10, 1951, p. 298.

[12] According to Admiral Sherman, "practically all material from Russia to China must be transported via the Trans-Siberian Railway, which is known to be already overtaxed

Had the United States been able to persuade all the U. N. members who had branded China as an aggressor to cut off trade with her, the impact of an embargo upon Communist China's economy and war effort would have proved considerable. Mao was, no doubt, agreeably surprised to see that he was free to make strategic moves in Korea without being forced entirely to rely upon his own meager resources and those of his Soviet ally, who was ill-prepared to increase aid shipments. Central to the Chinese communist leader's concept of protracted war is the notion of altering the relative power distribution between oneself and the enemy, strengthening the former and weakening the latter by every available means.[13]

OPERATIONS BEYOND THE YALU

There were two principal suggestions for extending operations beyond the Yalu River. The first was to reconnoiter Manchuria and the Chinese coastal areas. As early as July 1950, the Air Force had contemplated flying high-level photo missions over Dairen, Port Arthur, Vladivostok and the Kuriles. When President Truman heard about these proposed flights over Soviet-controlled territory, he instructed Secretary of the Air Force Finletter not to allow his Far East commanders "to engage in activities that might give the Soviet Union a pretext to come into open conflict with us."[14] This decision to refrain from sweeping reconnaissance over Soviet areas on the Pacific coast may have been justified at the time, although such restraint precluded our gaining the very intelligence needed to corroborate the Central Intelligence Agency estimate that the U.S.S.R. did not intend to intervene on a large scale in the Far East. Certainly, official policy on reconnaissance should have undergone review when it became apparent that General MacArthur's post-Inchon offensive would take U. N. forces into North Korea or, at the very latest, when the State Department learned through Indian and British diplomatic channels that the Chinese communists had made a definite threat to intervene. Had reconnaissance been conducted, the request for authority to bomb the Yalu bridges could have been made in time to hinder the Communist Chinese build-up of massive ground armies in the Korean peninsula. The continued failure to reconnoiter the area above the Yalu even after MacArthur reiterated the need for such operations in the spring of 1951 was indefensible.

The second suggestion for going beyond the Yalu related to actual offensive operations in Manchuria, including "hot pursuit" of communist fighter

---

. . . inadequate and vulnerable. . . . Traffic along that railroad is particularly subject to easy disruption." Hearings, cit. supra., p. 1513.

[13] On the Protracted War in Selected Works of Mao Tse-tung, II (London, 1954), 189.

[14] Harry S. Truman, op. cit., p. 346. For the validity of this assumption—that the Soviets needed or wanted a "pretext" to become directly embroiled in the war—see below, pp. 501–2.

planes and the bombing of enemy supply routes and industrial centers. It should be made clear that at no time were ground force operations by American forces north of the Yalu contemplated. Air components alone could have executed whatever additional measures the Chinese intervention made imperative.

The limitations which the United States placed upon itself with respect to the use of air power along the Yalu not only prevented the carrying of the war into Manchuria but, furthermore, prevented the U. N. forces from holding their line of farthest advance because it deprived them of maximum effective air support. Air Marshal Sir John Slessor wrote as long ago as 1936: "The airplane is not a battlefield weapon—the air striking force is not as a rule best employed in the actual zone in which the armies are in contact." [15] Later, Slessor applied this maxim to the military situation which obtained in Korea:

> One of the strongest reasons for my dislike at the time of our advance to the Yalu in 1950 was that to do so would deprive the United Nations armies of the massive support of air power, unless we were prepared to spread the war into Manchuria, which for political reasons we were not prepared to do (whether or not those political reasons were good is irrelevant to this military point). And I am on record as being sure, when our armies were subsequently in retreat toward the thirty-eighth parallel, that as soon as they had come back far enough to restore to us the depth in the enemy's rear to enable the air to act freely again, the effect would be to retard and finally to arrest the communist advance.[16]

The communists held a unique advantage in being able to use Manchuria as a privileged sanctuary into which their MIG's could retreat after attacking American forces in Korea. On November 13, 1950, the State Department wired instructions to its embassies in six nations to inform the allied governments

> that it may become necessary at an early date to permit U. N. aircraft to defend themselves in the air space over the Yalu River to the extent of permitting hot pursuit of attacking enemy aircraft up to 2 or 3 minutes' flying time into Manchuria air space.
>
> It is contemplated that U. N. aircraft would limit themselves to repelling enemy aircraft engaged in offensive missions to Korea.
>
> We believe this would be a minimum reaction to extreme provocation, would not in itself affect adversely the attitude of the enemy toward Korean operations, would serve as a warning, and would add greatly to the morale of U. N. pilots. . . .[17]

---

[15] J. C. Slessor, *Air Power and Armies* (New York, 1936), p. 213, quoted by the same author in *Strategy for the West* (New York, 1954), pp. 127–128.
[16] J. C. Slessor, *Strategy for the West*, p. 128.   [17] Hearings, Part III, p. 1928.

The instructions made it clear that the United States was not seeking the concurrence of the governments concerned. Nonetheless, in the face of the "strongly negative responses" received from those governments, the State and Defense Departments decided that the plans for "hot pursuit" ought to be abandoned.[18] On this issue, too, coalition diplomacy came into conflict with tactical operations which were considered necessary or desirable from a military point of view.

After the United States' allies reacted unfavorably to the "hot pursuit" proposals, it was practically a foregone conclusion that General MacArthur's recommendations for more ambitious operations beyond the Yalu, i.e., bombing Manchuria, would be received with even less enthusiasm in the NATO capitals. General MacArthur frequently stressed the fact that his objective was not to extend the scope of ground operations into China itself, but rather to force China to remove herself from the Korean War by the continued application of added pressure on the Chinese supply lines in Manchuria.[19] Nevertheless, Canada's Lester Pearson publicly expressed doubts that his government could participate in any program in Asia involving commitments on the mainland of China, and the British House of Commons carried on a long discussion about war on the Chinese mainland if MacArthur's policies were adopted. Secretary of State Acheson testified to the Senate that he deemed it "highly probable" that the Sino-Soviet agreement of 1950 included a Soviet promise to assist China if the Manchurian Railway were subjected to a bombing attack by a foreign power.[20] Secretary Acheson did admit, however, that his views on the risk of direct Russian intervention were based on an analysis of Russian self-interest and treaty obligations, not on specific information from intelligence and diplomatic sources concerning Soviet intentions.[21]

THE USE OF ATOMIC WEAPONS

There is no question that of all the proposals advanced for regaining the initiative the suggestion to introduce atomic weapons in Korea was the one fraught with the most serious implications. Despite the fact that by the end of November 1950 approximately 400,000 Chinese had poured into Korea,[22] there were some credible reasons why atomic weapons should not have been used at that time. The American atomic stockpile was then earmarked primarily for use by the Strategic Air Command. The diversion of atomic weapons to Korea might have retarded the build-up of the West's far-flung system of atomic air bases, on which Western deterrent power hinged. Moreover, the technology of tactical atomic weapons and delivery systems had not been developed beyond its earliest stages when the fighting

---

[18] *Ibid.*, p. 1723.   [19] *Ibid.*, Part I, p. 259.   [20] *Ibid.*, Part III, pp. 1877–1878.
[21] *Ibid.*, Part I, p. 1859.
[22] *United States Policy in the Korean Conflict, cit. supra.*, pp. 22–23.

in Korea was at its peak; experiments with low-yield atomic weapons for use against troop concentrations in the immediate battle-zone had scarcely begun. Consequently, Americans and their allies, with the disturbing image of atomic bombs dropped by strategic aircraft on Hiroshima and Nagasaki still vivid in their minds, were unable or unwilling to distinguish between the tactical use of nuclear weapons against enemy armies in the field and their strategic use against urban populations deep in enemy territory.[23]

The West, therefore, cavilled at any suggestion that atomic weapons should or could be used in Korea. In particular the European allies of the United States, more vulnerable to atomic attack than the American Continent, took a less sanguine view of the atomic risks than some American policy-makers. On November 30, 1950, President Truman, perhaps in an effort to bring United States nuclear capability into close support of American diplomacy, hinted at a press conference that the introduction of atomic weapons into the Korean conflict was being discussed. "Naturally, there has been consideration of this subject since the outbreak of the hostilities in Korea, just as there is consideration of the use of all weapons whenever our forces are in combat. Consideration of the use of any weapon is always implicit in the very possession of that weapon." [24] If this guarded reference was intended to frighten the Chinese communists, the effort backfired. Before the news could have any impact on the strategic thinking of the Chinese communist leadership, the British Labour Government reacted to this veiled threat with open concern, and Prime Minister Clement Attlee hurried to Washington in order to obtain Mr. Truman's assurance that the Korean War would remain "conventional." Domestic critics voiced misgivings to the effect that, since the atom bomb had become a popular symbol of cataclysmic destruction, its use under any circumstances would set off an uncontrollable chain of events which would propel the world into an unwanted total war. Others argued that, even if global war would not be touched off by atomic warfare in Korea, the peoples of Asia would be even more deeply offended by a new exhibition of "American contempt for Asian lives" than they had been five years earlier at the time of Hiroshima and Nagasaki.

In retrospect, the American decision to forego the actual use of atomic weapons in Korea was the most defensible of all the negative decisions made in Washington. The "atomic question," in a sense, was a false one, for probably it would never have been raised had other conventional alternatives, which were available for dealing with Communist China's aggression, been adopted with vigor and determination.[25] It was one thing, however, to

---

[23] Cf. Raymond Aron, "Europe and Air Power," *The Annals of the American Academy of Political and Social Science,* CCIC (May 1955), 95.

[24] Harry S. Truman, *op. cit.,* pp. 395–396.

[25] The feasibility of the most important of these alternatives was lucidly expressed by Senator Ralph Flanders during the Senate hearings in June 1951: ". . . General Mac-

decide that the United States would not bring to bear its most powerful military weapon upon a given conflict situation; it was quite another thing to forfeit the psychological and political value inherent in the possession of the atomic bomb by communicating such a decision baldly to the enemy. The disclosure of our intentions may well have served to reassure our allies or to placate an ill-informed public incited by irresponsible party politicians and segments of the press. But however much the Western public may have wished to ignore the fact, the Korean War was fought in the atomic age, and one of the contestants in this war was an atomic power. Hence atomic weapons had a role to play in the strategy of the war, even if they were never actually employed.

Today, when nuclear weapons constitute such an important component of the Western defense establishment, it is essential that we read correctly the lessons of the Korean War with regard to the American decision not to use the atomic bomb. For some Americans, who for the first time had occasion to pass prior judgment upon the potential use of atomic weapons, the problem was a moral one. For others the problem was political, since they conceived of it in terms of Asian sentiments or NATO solidarity. These objections were, at least in the context of the Korean War, more logical than those which sprang from a fear that the use of atomic weapons was certain to touch off World War III. There are weighty reasons for concluding that the Soviet Union was willing to be drawn, in 1950–51, into a general war with the West neither in Korea nor, as some people feared, in Europe. In either case, the question confronting the Russians was identical: Were they ready for general war? It is clear now that the time was not at all appropriate for the Kremlin to risk large-scale conflict with the West had the latter applied additional pressure upon Communist China. Stalin was in no position to enter the Korean War openly. His Far East air force was not strong enough to stand a contest of attrition and replacement production with the United States. The Soviet Union, moreover, would have encountered serious logistic difficulties in attempting to establish and supply operational bases in North Korea, some 4,000 miles from the locus of Russian industrial power. Had the United States increased military pressure in Korea, one wonders how long the communist bloc would have attempted to match the West in a war in which technical equipment and material

---

Arthur's proposals on bombing Manchuria can be interpreted and executed in a way which involves a minimum risk of starting World War III. . . . All that would seem to be required would be that we have in Manchuria the same freedom of maneuver in the air, and perhaps in the air alone, not on land, to make our protection of the whole of Korea possible. . . .

"It seems to me to be foolish to talk about invading the mainland of China when the military objectives can be stated in so much more limited terms . . . (or) to assume that such a limited undertaking would start World War III. . . .

"It strikes me we are in a rather silly position, and that more resource and enterprise would diminish the serious risk of a war of attrition to which we are presently subjected without materially increasing the risk. . . ." Hearings, Part III, pp. 1945–46.

resources (rather than manpower, which was far more expendable for the communists) were being devoured at a steadily increasing rate. The Soviets, had they attempted to intervene massively against the United States in the Far East or launched an attack against Western Europe, could not have avoided the type of war which has long been the nightmare both of the Tsarist and bolshevik strategists: a two-front all-out war against a powerful enemy. During World War II, the Kremlin had been at pains to avoid a showdown with the Japanese while holding off the Germans in the West. By contrast, the United States, between 1942 and 1945, was strong enough to take on two powerful enemies on opposite sides of the globe.

Most important of all, Russian atomic stockpiles and strategic delivery capabilities were distinctly inferior to those at the disposal of the U. S. Communist conflict doctrine prescribes the postponement of the all-out, decisive engagement until overwhelming victory is assured. It is, therefore, unlikely that the Soviet Union would have allowed itself to be drawn into a war beyond its borders under circumstances as unfavorable as those surrounding the Korean War. When asked whether the bombing of Manchurian air bases would bring the Soviets into the conflict and thereby touch off World War III, General Mark Clark replied to the Senate Subcommittee investigating the War: "I do not think you can drag the Soviets into a world war except at a time and place of their own choosing. They have been doing too well in the Cold War." [26]

WAR BY TRUCE: PANMUNJOM

Despite the limitations which the United States imposed upon itself, it was the consensus of Western observers at the scene that the U. N. forces were on the verge of breaking through the communists' lines in June 1951. At this point, the communists feared that the United States was about to mount a tactical offensive in Korea, supported by the extension of air operations into Manchuria. They switched to a strategy of protracted truce negotiations to prevent being driven out of Korea and to demoralize the West by weakening its will to take up the fight again later. This was the second crucial junc-

---

[26] "The Korean War and Related Matters," *op. cit.*, p. 6. Yuri A. Rastvorov, former Lieutenant Colonel of the MVD, wrote that as time went on "it became apparent that the whole Korean adventure had been one of Stalin's worst blunders. Soviet army leaders realized that China was not prepared for a long war with a major power and could not be so prepared on short notice. Indeed, some of us wondered why the U. S. did not push the Korean war to a victorious conclusion. Had it done so, I believe that Stalin would have relinquished the entire peninsula without further Soviet intervention. . . . *At the end of 1950 Soviet atomic strength was as much bluff as reality. Moscow's ambiguous announcements about atomic explosions we discounted as mainly propaganda. For us in Japan, news of the U. S. atomic activities had highest priority. Moscow got some tips that A bombs from the U. S. were being shipped to Korea and many Soviet leaders feared that they might suddenly be used.*" "Red Fraud and Intrigue in Far East," *Life*, Dec. 6, 1954, p. 176 (editors' italics).

ture of the war. Just as the circumspect use of "volunteers" had enabled Mao's forces to enter the war with a minimum risk of provoking a commensurate action by the United States against China, the changeover to truce talks in June 1951 eliminated, for all practical purposes, any further danger that Mao's forces might suffer a serious military reversal. Thus the negotiations provided a perfect alibi for a Chinese withdrawal from the shooting war—with their major units intact and well-trained and with the prestige of having fought the United States to a stalemate. The first American strategic mistake had been the failure to act swiftly in November 1950 to counter the stealthy Chinese entrance into the war; the second major blunder by the United States was the virtual decision to accept the communist demand for a cessation of hostilities prior to the opening of truce negotiations.

Had the U. S. followed the World War I example of continuing the offensive until the armistice was actually signed, the Korean War might well have ended by mid-summer of 1951 on much more favorable terms for the Free World and for Korea. Instead, the United States gave the communists an invaluable breathing spell. . . .

KOREAN BALANCE SHEET

In the light of the contemporary debate over U. S. military strategy, it is important to review the after-effects of the Korean War. The Chinese communists used the war as a training school in which the most up-to-date technical weapons were available. Thus Korea helped them transform their ill-equipped revolutionary forces into a modern army.[27] Meanwhile, the "Resist America, Aid Korea" campaign conducted by Peking helped considerably to consolidate the new regime at home and to stiffen the political loyalty of the Chinese people.[28] China won and the United States lost considerable prestige in Asia, for this was the first time in history that an Oriental nation held the technically superior West at bay. The Korean War, moreover, gave tremendous impetus to the international communist campaigns for propagating pacifism, especially through such devices as the Stockholm Peace Appeal,[29] and strengthening neutralism throughout the

---

[27] Several thousand fighter pilots, both Chinese and Russian, had an opportunity to be tested under combat conditions. At the end of the war, China had an air force rated the world's third largest, primarily on the strength of 1,500 MIG's which were made available by the Soviet Union. Cf. Charles J. V. Murphy, "Defense and Strategy," special reprint from *Fortune,* Headquarters, Air Force ROTC, Air University, Maxwell Air Base, December 1954, pp. 21–23.

[28] Richard L. Walker, *China Under Communism: The First Five Years* (New Haven, 1955), p. 92.

[29] "No operative contradiction exists between pacifist propaganda and the launching of aggressive war. In Soviet thinking, pacifist propaganda cannot hit home unless the targets of that propaganda are actively engaged in fighting and unless, by their physical sufferings and psychological experiences, they are convinced of the absolute necessity of peace." Stefan T. Possony, *A Century of Conflict* (Chicago, 1953), p. 356.

Arab-Asian world. Neutralist India, originally a supporter of the U.N. decision to counter North Korean aggression, began to sound a strident note of hostility against the United States as soon as Communist China became a contestant; the defense of a small republic then became, in Indian eyes, a case of American intervention in Asian affairs. When, in mid-1951, the Soviet Union espoused the role of peacemaker, the Asians seemed to forget entirely that the war had been instigated by a puppet government armed by the Soviets. By manifesting a willingness to settle for a draw in Korea, the West virtually admitted that Communist China's right to intervene in the peninsula was equal to that of the United Nations.

The United States, by waging the kind of war it did in Korea from November 1950 on, allowed the strategic initiative to pass into the hands of an enemy leader who had frequently stressed in his military writings that an army, once it can be forced into a passive position or deprived of its freedom of action, is on the road to defeat. Mao Tse-tung fully realized that the side which enjoys superiority at the outset of the conflict need not retain the initiative throughout the campaign:

> In the course of a struggle, a correct or incorrect command may transform inferiority into superiority or passivity into initiative, and vice versa. . . . The inferior and passive side can wrestle the initiative and victory from the side possessing superiority and the initiative by securing the necessary conditions through active endeavour in accordance with actual circumstances.[30]

One of the most suitable means of achieving superiority and seizing the initiative from the enemy, Mao wrote, is to create illusions in the mind of the enemy, including the illusion that he is up against overwhelming strength. Mao applied his superior understanding of strategic principles in Korea to compensate for the overwhelming superiority of American technological power. Throughout 575 truce meetings, the communist leaders stalled for time. The Chinese communists built up their military power and international support, while the United States suffered all the "internal and external contradictions" which Mao had forecast for all his enemies: mounting casualty lists, consumption of war material, decline of troop morale, discontented public opinion at home and the gradual alienation of world opinion.[31]

The United States imposed upon itself a number of severe limitations in conducting the Korean War. The motivation for these restraints was largely a political one. American policy-makers hoped that, with a war policy of forbearance unprecedented in modern history, the United States would earn the respect both of its new Atlantic allies and the uncommitted peoples. This hope, unfortunately, proved to be an illusory one. The United States built up very little credit either in Europe or in Asia: Americans, in fact,

---

[30] Mao Tse-tung, *On the Protracted War, op. cit.*, II, 215.   [31] *Ibid.*, p. 189.

found themselves in the incredible position of having to defend themselves against charges of waging "germ warfare," forestalling the "natural integration" of Formosa with the Chinese Mainland, and preventing the restoration of peace in the Far East by keeping Red China out of the United Nations. While Europeans placed little credence in communist propaganda, most were inclined to blame the United States for placing too much emphasis on the conflict in Korea. Finally, few people in Europe and Asia believed that the United States deserved any praise for limiting the war—for American political leaders, in their efforts to justify the Korean policy, argued frequently that any extension of the war would lead to general war and risk of communist retaliation against the United States. American motives, consequently, were taken to be more selfish than altruistic.

The decision to meet communist aggression in Korea in June 1950 was both courageous and wise. But the United States failed to foresee the future implications of the outcome of the Korean War—that popular political support for all subsequent responses to communist peripheral attacks would to a large extent hinge upon the success of the first direct encounter between American and communist forces.

There can be little question but that Secretary of State Acheson was confronted by serious political problems during the course of the Korean War. The United States had scarcely begun to construct a defense of Europe through the North Atlantic Treaty Organization when the Korean War broke out. The Europeans, especially the British, were inclined to dissociate the crisis in the Far East from their security interests and feared that an American emphasis of Asia might slow down the development of the Atlantic Alliance. The United States, on the other hand, had historically been oriented more towards Asia than Europe, and emerged from World War II as the dominant power in the Pacific. Whereas Great Britain was in the process of reducing her political commitments in Asia, the United States, which had borne the greatest burden among the Western powers in fighting the Axis on both fronts, realized its growing strategic responsibilities in both theaters. This divergence of basic interests in the Western Alliance was aggravated by Mao's entry into the war.

There is no doubt, however, that the success of Communist China was in large measure due to Mao's strategy of delay and attrition. Had the United Nations been able to conclude the war with MacArthur's Inchon offensive, America would have been spared many a diplomatic dilemma. Mao, by entering the Korean War, shored up the faltering regime of North Korea and denied the U. N. a decision with finality. Then, by switching in June 1951 to "attritional" truce talks which lasted for two years, the communists were able to camouflage their flagging capabilities and resources and, at the same time, to wear down the American will to resume the kind of energetic initiative needed to bring the war to a successful conclusion.

The American people were increasingly dissatified with the conduct of the Korean War, which they found both frustrating and pointless. After the experience, in the twentieth century, of two world wars, both of which had ended in climactic, overwhelming victories, it was difficult for Americans to readjust their thinking to the notion of a war which, for two years, had to be fought out along the "line of scrimmage." What Americans objected to was not the fact that the war was kept limited, or waged at a level lower than that of a general war, but rather the fact that its limitations whittled down the real superiority of the United States. Since American policy-makers had posed a false dilemma—either a protracted stalemate or all-out war—popular opinion within the United States tended to conclude that American conventional forces had been misused in Korea. Perhaps the most serious effect of this was to inhibit the freedom of action of U. S. policy-makers when confronted by subsequent crises in so-called peripheral areas.

The communists, doubtless realizing to what an extent the Korean War had served as a conditioner of the American mind, were able to parlay their psychological gains in Korea into a swift victory in Indochina. A successful prosecution of the war in Korea by the United States might have either convinced the Chinese communists that a new adventure in Indochina should not be risked or, failing this, prepared the American people for intervention in Indochina.

In recent years, far too much criticism has been hurled at the Dulles policy of "massive retaliation" on the grounds that it did not prevent the loss of North Vietnam.[32] Such criticism, unfortunately, does not go to the root of the problem. Most of the critics of the declaratory policy of "massive retaliation" imply that statements of this sort are relatively worthless in meeting the intermediate range of communist military threats and that, first and foremost, the United States needs to increase its tactical force levels to fight limited wars in any part of the globe. Yet the experience of Korea shows clearly that the possession of forces "in being" does not of itself assure an effective defense against communist aggression. . . .

In the current quest for a sound military policy, the need for many different types of weapons is recognized as a matter of course. But, as Korea amply attested, hardware without courage and firmness of purpose is of little value. Mao Tse-tung, who now must be ranked with the great classical strategists, long ago warned against the fallacy of the mechanistic assumption that "weapons mean everything." He wrote that the view of the communists differs from that of the capitalist: "We see not only weapons, but also the power of man. Weapons are an important factor in war but not the decisive one; it is man and not material that counts." [33]

---

[32] Secretary Dulles made his statement concerning the possibility of retaliating "at times and places of our own choosing" on January 11, 1954. The communist assault on Dienbienphu was launched on March 13, 1954.

[33] Mao Tse-tung, *On the Protracted War* (Foreign Languages Press, 1954), p. 54.

The Administration's Defense:

The Meek Shall Inherit

John W. Spanier

MacArthur had condemned the Administration's Korean and Chinese policy in forthright and unequivocal terms. "I was operating in what I call a vacuum. I could hardly have been said to be in opposition to policies which I was not aware of even. I don't know what the policy is now." No doubt MacArthur overstated his case somewhat for dramatic effect, but his words illustrate the intensity of his frustration after Communist China's intervention. Washington was fighting an accordion war—up and down—at a "staggering" cost. "It isn't just dust that is settling in Korea . . . it is American blood." [1] His own plan, he maintained, would be decisive, and it would quickly achieve the desired results—victory in the field, a united Korea, and an end to hostilities. His only requirement was that the restrictions imposed upon him by the politicians in Washington should be lifted. It is to these two themes—the Administration's indetermination and his own resolution—to which MacArthur constantly returned. His course was positive; Truman's negative. He stood for victory; the President for stalemate. The choice was clear, the alternatives simple.

The Truman Administration, not unnaturally, saw MacArthur's strategy in a different light. It would, as Secretary of State Acheson emphasized, accept the "large risk of war with China, risk of war with the Soviet Union, and a demonstrable weakening of our collective-security system—all this in return for what? In return for measures whose effectiveness in bringing the conflict to an early conclusion are judged doubtful by our responsible military authorities." [2] The United States could not, therefore, allow its field commander's desire to achieve military victory in a local area to govern its

Reprinted by permission of the publishers from John W. Spanier, *The Truman-MacArthur Controversy and the Korean War.* Cambridge, Mass.: Harvard University Press, Copyright, 1959, by The President and Fellows of Harvard College. Pp. 239–256.

[1] *Military Situation in the Far East,* Hearings before the Committee on Armed Services and the Committee on Foreign Relations, United States Senate, 82d Cong., 1st Sess. (Washington, 1951), p. 30. This document will hereafter be referred to as *Senate Hearings.*
[2] *Ibid.,* pp. 325, 351, 354.

entire global foreign policy, particularly since his strategic recommendations were militarily unfeasible and politically undesirable.

To clarify these points, to emphasize them, and then once more to re-emphasize them, the Administration brought an impressive array of witnesses before the committee: Secretary of Defense Marshall, the Joint Chiefs of Staff, the Secretary of State, and ex-Secretary of Defense Louis Johnson. Altogether, they testified for almost a month, from May 7 to June 7 [1951]. MacArthur had testified for three days.

During his days on the witness stand, MacArthur had argued that his military program to defeat Communist China had received the endorsement of the Joint Chiefs of Staff, and that the limitations imposed upon him were political. The Joint Chiefs quickly denied both of these notions. They made it quite clear that they had opposed an extension of the war on strictly military grounds; in other words, their professional opinion was that MacArthur's program was militarily impracticable. Perhaps the most important military testimony in this respect came from the Air Force Chief of Staff. His testimony has suffered from gross neglect, partly no doubt, because it came near the end of the hearings when public interest was rapidly waning. Nevertheless, what General Hoyt Vandenberg had to say remains significant because he dismissed once and for all the notion that the Joint Chiefs had allowed their views to be colored by considerations not strictly professional.

In declaring his opposition to the bombing of Manchuria, General Vandenberg prefaced his remarks with the comment that the role of air power was not well understood in the United States. Strategic air power, he said, should be employed only for the destruction of the enemy's industrial centers. He did not doubt that the air force could lay waste the cities of Communist China and Manchuria, but the result might not be conclusive. In war, there could first of all be no guarantee, no certainty. More important, Communist China's arsenals lay in the Soviet Union; despite large-scale bombing of Manchuria and continental China, therefore, the Russians would still be in a position to supply the weapons of war from across the Manchuria border.[3]

Destruction of Red Chinese and Manchurian cities would, in addition, require "full" application of the Strategic Air Command's power. Anything less would be unable to achieve the task, since the rate of attrition would be too high. The air force would lose planes and crews more quickly than they could be replaced. The resulting loss would deprive the air arm of its capacity for "massive retaliation" against the Soviet Union. ". . . The United States Air Force, if used as a whole, can lay waste Manchuria and

---

[3] *Ibid.*, pp. 1378, 1402, 744, 887, 943.

[the] principal cities of China, but . . . the attrition that would inevitably be brought about upon us would leave us, in my opinion, as a Nation, naked for several years to come . . ." The bombing of Manchuria would require twice the number of bombers then available to the Strategic Air Command. Under present circumstances, therefore, the air force could not afford to "peck at the periphery." SAC must be kept ready for its principal role—to deter the Soviet Union from attack and to preserve the global balance of power; or, if it did not succeed in this task, to destroy the heart of international Communism's power, the Soviet Union's industrial complex. "While we can lay the industrial potential of Russia today [to] waste, in my opinion, or we can lay the Manchurian countryside [to] waste, as well as the principal cities of China, we cannot do both, again because we have a shoestring Air Force [87 wings]. We are trying to operate a $20 million business with about $20,000." [4]

It was, therefore, better to concentrate on the 200 miles of supply line in North Korea—"we can exercise very concentrated attacks on that supply line. If you extend the length another hundred miles back into Manchuria, you can get certain other bases, but with the same air power you would thin out your present attacks against the 200 miles of supply line that is Korea." [5]

Not only could the country not afford to attack Manchuria because the rate of attrition which the air force would suffer would undermine its deterrent capacity, but "going it alone" would seriously affect its over-all strength in another way. If we "went it alone" in Asia, we probably would have to "go it alone" in Europe. This would deprive the United States of its bases in both Europe and North Africa. The advantages of keeping these bases were obvious: bombers stationed near to the Soviet Union would have to load less gasoline and would be able to carry more bombs than planes flying in from farther away. Bombers striking from the continental United States would have to be refueled two or three times per mission. At that rate, a plane could render only two to three missions per month; from Europe and North Africa, the same plane could carry out fifteen to twenty missions every thirty days. Vandenberg estimated that minus its overseas bases, the United States would require an air force five to six times the size it at present possessed. European bases, while not therefore "absolutely essential," were "highly desirable." [6]

An economic blockade too would be limited in its effectiveness in bringing enough pressure to bear upon Communist China to quickly end the war. The limitation was, according to Admiral Sherman, dictated by two factors. The first consideration was the nature and stage of Communist China's economic development. This was still sufficiently lacking in indus-

[4] *Ibid.*, pp. 1398, 1399, 1379, 1385, 1393.   [5] *Ibid.*, pp. 887, 744, 507.
[6] *Ibid.*, pp. 1386, 884.

trialization and specialization that a blockade would not have the same immediate impact as it would on a more highly industrialized country. A blockade could only be an effective long-run weapon. . . .[7]

The second consideration limiting the effectiveness of a blockade of Communist China was the thoroughness with which China could be cut off from the essential supplies she had to import. The long Sino-Russian border would make any blockade incomplete. Admiral Sherman stressed that the loss of imports enforced by a naval blockade would force Communist China to rely more upon the Soviet Union, and thereby place an increasing drain on both the Soviet economy and the Trans-Siberian railroad. This long railway, which was subject to easy disruption by bombing, sabotage, or naval raiding parties, was already overtaxed and could not therefore adequately replace the supplies stopped on the sea; moreover, it could attempt to do so only at the expense of supplying the Soviet Union's own forces in the Far East.[8] The other members of the Joint Chiefs were less optimistic than Admiral Sherman. General Bradley, the chairman of the Joint Chiefs, qualified Sherman's analysis: the Trans-Siberian railroad could handle 17,000 tons a day in addition to its own tonnage-maintenance requirements. Russia had also built up supply depots and certain war industries to relieve the railway of some of its load during wartime. The implication was clear: Russian forces in the Far East had a "considerable military capacity": they could for a time get along with fewer supplies. This available tonnage could be switched to supply Communist China.

A blockade by itself could not, therefore, speedily terminate hostilities. A blockade could necessarily yield only slow results since it relied for effects principally on starvation and attrition. Only if combined with other military measures, such as air bombardment, could a naval blockade yield immediate results; short of such supplementary means, a blockade could not seriously hamper China's capacity to continue its conduct of the war. The Admiral also emphasized that the key to an effective United Nations naval blockade would be the wholehearted cooperation of our allies. Any effective blockade must include Port Arthur and Dairen, over which the Soviet Union exercised certain military rights and privileges under the Sino-Soviet treaty. The Russians would "very probably" demand unimpeded access to both ports; stopping her ships might provoke her entry into the war.[9] "If the United Nations should declare a naval blockade, the Russians would probably respect it, as they did the United Nations blockade of Korea. If the United States should declare a blockade unilaterally, the Russians might not respect it, and it is conceivable that they might oppose it by force." [10]

The implication of Admiral Sherman's words is clear: a unilateral blockade by the United States would signify the isolation of this country from

---

[7] *Ibid.*, pp. 1512–13.   [8] *Ibid.*   [9] *Ibid.*, pp. 1525, 1518, 1521, 1189.
[10] *Ibid.*, pp. 1514, 1517, 742.

its allies. Since this would for all practical purposes neutralize the United States Air Force, Moscow might be tempted to break the blockade of Dairen and Port Arthur. With NATO's massive retaliation nonexistent, the Strategic Air Command could, in the event of war, operate at only 15 to 20 per cent of its effectiveness. If, on the other hand, the United States imposed the blockade in cooperation with its Atlantic allies, any Soviet counteraction would risk the possibility of an immediate reaction by NATO, or more specifically, American strategic air power based on Western European and North African soil. "The fact is that our allies have been unwilling to join in a naval blockade of China, and have been slow to establish a tight economic blockade." [11]

Another reason for the need of a United Nations blockade was equally obvious; most of the strategic imports and ships carrying goods to Communist China bore the flags of non-Communist United Nations members. Sherman recommended that greater effort be concentrated on increasing the effectiveness of the economic blockade. In recent weeks, he said, United States efforts along these lines had been successful. The British government had prohibited any further sales of rubber for the rest of the year,[12] and the General Assembly had on May 18 by a vote of forty-five to four approved a resolution calling for an embargo on arms, ammunition, petroleum, and other materials of war, although as Secretary Acheson stressed, "Many countries were already doing this . . . ; others were not."

In expanding this point, Acheson emphasized that as early as 1948 the United States had agreed with its allies to draw up a number of lists of such items as arms, ammunition, implements of war and atomic energy whose export to the Soviet bloc would be restricted. These lists were expanded in 1949, so that by the end of that year the participating European nations had embargoed shipments to the Soviet bloc of about two-thirds of the industrial items which American experts then regarded as being of primary strategic significance. In both of the following years, the number of categories of goods not to be exported to the Communist sphere was augmented by approximately 50 per cent, and the total number of items restricted, or closely supervised to prevent excessive shipment, was increased threefold. The result was that by early 1951 about 90 per cent of the items the United States considered to be of strategic importance were already on the embargo lists. Since late 1949, moreover, certain specialized petroleum products, such as aviation gasoline and special lubricants, had also been embargoed to the Sino-Soviet bloc by the United States, England, and other governments. Acheson stressed that ever since the Chinese Communists consolidated their grip on the Chinese mainland, for many months before the outbreak of the Korean War, the British government had cooperated with the United States and the principal American and British oil com-

---

[11] *Ibid.*, pp. 1523, 1570, 1514, 882.   [12] *Ibid.*, pp. 1515–16.

panies in restricting shipment of petroleum products to those types and quantities clearly intended for civilian use. Immediately after the Communist attack in Korea, the British Admiralty had taken over all British oil stocks in the Far East and secured agreements by British companies to follow a sales policy parallel to that of American companies. The Hong Kong government had reinforced this policy by closely supervising the bunkering of vessels in Hong Kong and rationing shipments to Macao to prevent leakage to Communist China, by numerous seizures of illicit cargoes, confiscation of the ships involved, and the levying of severe fines on smugglers. It was possible that despite these measures small amounts of petroleum products may have been smuggled into the mainland, but, Acheson said, it "can be stated flatly, however, that . . . no significant shipments of petroleum products of military usefulness have been exported to Communist China from or through any place in the free world." Thus the "facts show there already exists on the part of the major industrial countries of the free world an economic embargo with respect to materials of primary strategic significance." The economic blockade made the naval blockade much less important. "I think it is clear that we cannot get nations to go further in regard to a naval blockade than they are willing to go on an economic blockade, since it is a more drastic sanction." [13]

Thus the Administration, particularly its military advisers, doubted the efficacy of winning the Korean War through the application of air power and the imposition of a naval blockade. MacArthur had always denied that his prescription would need few [many?] extra ground troops. General Collins, Army Chief of Staff, did not agree. The successful implementation of MacArthur's strategy would require the United States to send "considerably" more troops to Korea.[14] General Bradley, indeed, thought that a decision could be effected only if American troops were actually sent into China proper.

> Chairman Connally . . . if we have an all-out war, and the war should expand to include China, would it not almost inevitably follow that at some time in the future development of that, we would have to put ground troops on Chinese soil?
>
> General Bradley. To get decisive results, in my opinion you would . . . if you go to an all-out war with China, I think you would have to do something like the Japanese did. Go in and try to get a decision. I do not believe you could get any decision by naval and air action alone.
>
> Chairman Connally. Well, naval and air action as against China without ground troops would mean just sort of a holding proposition, would it not?
>
> General Bradley. Well, I think it would be a rather long-drawn-out affair in which you would try to knock out their centers of communi-

---

[13] *Ibid.*, pp. 1726–27.   [14] *Ibid.*, p. 1219.

cation and knock out as much of their industry as possible, possibly try to limit on supplies and food without taking any positive action inside China itself.[15]

The Communist army in Korea could be decimated; but it could not be defeated without hitting its center of power. The air force and navy could hamper China's capacity to fight; but they could not destroy it. If there were no alternative to military victory, there could also be no substitute to military invasion and occupation. MacArthur had himself recognized at the time of the North Korean aggression that air and naval forces alone would not suffice to halt the Communist attack; ground troops would be needed. If this was true for a Soviet satellite, it was certainly true for Communist China.

In any case, even if it were not necessary to employ American troops inside continental China, large reinforcements would be needed. An all-out war with Communist China would require "substantially" more naval, air, and ground power, as well as an increase in supply and service troops to support the forces at the front. These could not, however, be furnished without a more intensive program of mobilization and greater effort to produce the ammunition and other implements of war.[16]

Could these troops not be supplied by Nationalist China? The Joint Chiefs thought not. Chiang would need his troops to safeguard Formosa; and his soldiers were anything but first-class. General MacArthur's mission to Formosa had "indicated a state of readiness which didn't seem to be conducive of successful action by those troops . . ." The Nationalist troops "had very limited capabilities, particularly for offensive action. As General MacArthur himself had pointed out, they would have to have almost complete logistical support from ourselves, transportation furnished . . . their leadership, equipment, and training were all of such a state that they would be of limited use in offensive operations." [17] Any diversionary action against continental China would, in addition, require excessive United States naval and air support—excessive, that is, to the returns that could be expected from such an investment.[18] Nor was the reason purely the military's unfavorable estimate of Chiang's troops. Of greater importance, although not explicitly stated during the hearings, was the Administration's evaluation of Chiang Kai-shek's political prospects on the continent. The only circumstances under which Nationalist troops might reconquer vast portions of China, if not the whole mainland, would be if upon their landing, the Chinese Communist army rallied to Chiang Kai-shek as the French people and the Bourbon army had rallied to Napoleon upon his return to French soil from Corsica. In the Administration's opinion, it was precisely this confidence of the masses which Chiang lacked; its loss had accounted

---

[15] *Ibid.*, p. 745.   [16] *Ibid.*, pp. 882–883.   [17] *Ibid.*, pp. 619, 337, 673–674, 742, 886, 903.
[18] *Ibid.*, pp. 1584, 1620.

for his defeat in the first place, for his fall in four short years from "the undisputed leader" of the Chinese people to a "refugee" on a small island off the coast of China. It was extremely doubtful that a year's absence had restored the Chinese people's affection for their old leader.

There was, in short, no substitute for American troops. But concentrating American armed power in Korea meant stripping other areas of their forces, lowering the deterrent to Soviet intervention in these parts of the world, and increasing their vulnerability to attack. In fact, the attrition of American military strength, particularly air and ground strength, might well deprive the United States of its ability to counter emergencies elsewhere, and perhaps even weaken the United States sufficiently to attract a Soviet attack. This country could not therefore afford to engage "too much of our power in an area that is not the critical strategic prize." Yet, this is precisely what MacArthur's strategy would entail; nothing would probably delight the Kremlin more. It would, in General Bradley's famous phrase, "involve us in the wrong war, at the wrong place, at the wrong time, and with the wrong enemy." [19]

Indeed, it might also involve us with the right enemy, since bombing Communist China and inflicting a severe defeat upon the Soviet Union's closest and strongest ally would probably leave the Kremlin no alternative but to intervene. As Secretary Acheson said:

> We know of Soviet influence in North Korea, of Soviet assistance to the North Koreans and to Communist China, and we know that understandings must have accompanied this assistance. We also know that there is a treaty between the Soviets and the Chinese Communists. But even if this treaty did not exist, China is the Soviet Union's largest and most important satellite. Russian self-interest in the Far East and the necessity of maintaining prestige in the Communist sphere make it difficult to see how the Soviet Union could ignore a direct attack upon the Chinese mainland.

To be sure, General MacArthur had argued that the Soviet Union would not intervene if the United States and its allies acted with determination and without hesitation; the Administration, however, remembered that he had said the same thing just before Communist China had entered the battle. (It might have added that MacArthur's foresight had proven itself equally fallible on other occasions. In 1939, he had declared Japan would not attack the Philippines; proponents of such a view, he had said, failed to understand "the logic of the Japanese mind." If Japan did covet the islands, however, his Filipino forces would prove themselves more than a match for the invading army. In early 1941, he had doubted that the Japanese would commit suicide by attacking as mighty a naval power as the United States, but if Japan should launch such an attack, American,

---

[19] *Ibid.,* pp. 731–732, 1219.

British, and Dutch forces could handle her with half the forces they then had in the Far East!) Admittedly, the Administration had shared MacArthur's mistaken estimate of Peking's intentions before November 24; but it was unwilling to take a second chance. "I cannot accept the assumption," said Secretary Acheson, "that the Soviet Union will go its way regardless of what we do. I do not think that Russian policy is formed that way any more than our own policy is formed that way. This view is certainly not well enough grounded to justify a gamble with the essential security of our Nation."

There were a number of courses the Russians could follow. Acheson believed that "They could turn over to the Chinese large numbers of planes with 'volunteer' crews for retaliatory action in Korea and outside. They might participate with the Soviet Air Force and the submarine fleet." Or, the "Kremlin could elect to parallel the action, taken by Peiping and intervene with a half million or more ground-force 'volunteers'; or it could go the whole way and launch an all-out war. Singly, or in combination, these reactions contain explosive possibilities, not only for the Far East, but for the rest of the world as well." [20]

Hostilities with the Soviet Union at the present time had, however, to be avoided. Not only was a war unnecessary because Soviet imperialism had been contained and denied the fruits of its aggression; it was also undesirable because the United States might have to fight such a war alone. Our allies, as Secretary Acheson said,

> are understandably reluctant to be drawn into a general war in the Far East—one which holds the possibilities of becoming a world war —particularly if it developed out of an American impatience with the progress of the effort to repel aggression, an effort which in their belief offers an honorable and fair less catastrophic solution.
>
> If we followed the course proposed, we would be increasing our risks and commitments at the same time that we diminished our strength by reducing the strength and determination of our coalition.
>
> We cannot expect that our collective-security system will long survive if we take steps which unnecessarily and dangerously expose the people who are in the system with us. They would understandably hesitate to be tied to a partner who leads them to a highly dangerous short cut across a difficult crevasse.
>
> In relation to the total world threat, our safety requires that we strengthen, not weaken, the bonds of our collective-security system.
>
> The power of our coalition to deter an attack depends in part upon the will and the mutual confidence of our partners. If we, by the measures proposed, were to weaken that effort, particularly in the North Atlantic area, we would be jeopardizing the security of an area which is vital to our own national security.[21]

---

[20] *Ibid.*, pp. 1719, 741, 751. [21] *Ibid.*, p. 1719.

Allied fears of a large-scale war in the Far East and a corresponding shift of American power from Europe to the opposite side of the world—or World War III, which would probably see the Russians occupying their countries—were not the only reason for Washington's reluctance to test MacArthur's opinions about Soviet intentions. Even if the United States were willing to "go it alone" and alienate its allies, it had to resist this temptation for one simple reason—the United States was unready to fight a global war.

> Senator Johnson. General, from an over-all standpoint of the dispo-
> sition of our forces throughout the world, are we sufficiently strong to
> fight a successful holding action in the event the Soviet Union attacks
> at an early date?
> General Collins. Not as of the moment; no, sir. That applies particu-
> larly to Europe. I think that we have sufficient forces out in the Far
> East to hold there. I think that we have sufficient forces in Alaska to
> hold there. I do not think we have sufficient forces in Europe.

General Bradley was even more emphatic: "I would not be a proponent of a policy which would ignore the military facts and rush us headlong into a showdown before we are ready." [22]

Even in Asia, the Russians possessed the capacity to intervene and put up a good fight; contrary to General MacArthur's opinion, Administration witnesses considered Soviet power in the Far East "a very serious matter." They had "many thousands of planes in the other areas of Vladivostok, Dairen-Port Arthur, in Harbin, Manchuria, and troop concentrations at Sakhalin near to Japan." The Russians had over the past few years also been building up their Far Eastern industries, and they had "undoubtedly" been accumulating sufficient supplies to sustain their divisions "for a considerable length of time." [23]

Refusal to accept MacArthur's military program did not, therefore, in the opinion of the chairman of the Joint Chiefs, constitute "appeasement."

> There are those who deplore the present military situation in Korea
> and urge us to engage Red China in a larger war to solve this problem.
> Taking on Red China is not a decisive move, does not guarantee the
> end of the war in Korea, and may not bring China to her knees. We
> have only to look back to the five long years when the Japanese, one
> of the greatest military powers of that time, moved into China and
> had almost full control of a large part of China, and yet were never
> able to conclude that war successfully. I would say from past history
> one would only jump from a smaller conflict to a larger deadlock at
> greater expense. My own feeling is to avoid such an engagement if
> possible because victory in Korea would not be assured and victory over
> Red China would be many years away . . .

---

[22] *Ibid.*, pp. 1212, 1188, 1218, 732, 742, 745, 883–884, 896.
[23] *Ibid.*, pp. 360, 743, 1002–03, 1588.

Some critics of our strategy say if we do not immediately bomb troop concentration points and airfields in Manchuria, it is "appeasement." If we do not immediately set up a blockade of Chinese ports—which to be successful would have to include British and Russian ports—it is appeasement. These same critics would say that if we do not provide the logistical support and air and naval assistance to launch Chinese Nationalist troops into China it is "appeasement."

These critics ignore the vital questions:

Will these actions, if taken, actually assure victory in Korea?

Do these actions mean prolongation of the war by bringing Russia into the fight?

Will these actions strip us of our allies in Korea and in other parts of the world?

From a military viewpoint, appeasement occurs when you give up something, which is rightfully free, to an aggressor without putting up a struggle, or making him pay a price. Forsaking Korea—withdrawing from the fight unless we are forced out—would be an appeasement to aggression. Refusing to enlarge the quarrel to the point where our global capabilities are diminished, is certainly not appeasement but is a militarily sound course of action under the present circumstances.[24]

Did the rejection of MacArthur's program mean that the Administration would continue to "go on as before"? Would it continue to sacrifice American lives, as MacArthur had charged, "without justified purpose"? The answer to the first question was "yes," to the second "no." American lives in Korea had not been sacrificed in vain.

The operation in Korea has been a success. Both the North Koreans and the Chinese Communists declared it to be their purpose to drive the United Nations forces out of Korea and impose Communist rule throughout the entire peninsula. They have been prevented from accomplishing their objective.

It has been charged that the American and allied forces in Korea are engaged in a pointless and inconclusive struggle.

Nothing could be further from the fact. They have been magnificent. Their gallant, determined, and successful fight has checked the Communist advance and turned it into a retreat. They have administered terrible defeats to the Communist forces. In so doing, they have scored a powerful victory.

Their victory has dealt Communist imperialist aims in Asia a severe setback.

The alluring prospect for the Communist conspiracy in June 1950—the prospect of a quick and easy success which would not only win Korea for the Kremlin but shake the free notions of Asia and paralyze the defense of Europe—all this has evaporated.

---

[24] *Ibid.*, p. 733.

But the achievements gained by the United States and her friends were not simply negative:

> Instead of weakening the rest of the world, they have solidified it. They have given a more powerful impetus to the military preparations of this country and its associates in and out of the North Atlantic Treaty Organization.
>
> We have doubled the number of our men under arms, and the production of material has been boosted to a point where it can begin to have a profound effect on the maintenance of the peace.
>
> The idea of collective security has been put to the test, and has been sustained. The nations who believe in collective security have shown that they can stick together and fight together.
>
> New urgency has been given the negotiation of a peace with Japan, and of initial security arrangements to build strength in the Pacific area.
>
> These are some of the results of the attack on Korea, unexpected by —and I am sure most unwelcome to—the Kremlin.[25]

Korea had thus been a success. But how could fighting now be ended? Could this really be achieved without carrying the war into China as General MacArthur had recommended? Could the hostilities actually be concluded without risking the dire consequences pointed out by the government's witnesses? Their testimony seemed to suggest that the United States would continue to fight indefinitely, that is until Communist China finally tired of the war; this impression, needless to say, was not welcome to the American public, and must be attributed largely to the Administration's inability to clarify the nature of previous cold-war clashes and their relationship to the present war in Korea.

A comprehensive presentation of Administration policy would have clarified that in each of the East-West conflicts which had preceded Korea, both sides had aimed only at limited objectives and pursued these aims by limited means. The Soviet rulers had in no case aimed at a knock-out blow of the Western powers, since this purpose could have been achieved only by means of total war. Each Communist challenge had been met by the Western powers, particularly the United States, with an equally limited response; the West, too, had been reluctant to resort to global hostilities.

Each side had been unwilling to precipitate atomic warfare. The almost equal distribution of power between them and the very destructiveness of modern weapons had limited the objectives which they could safely seek. Both blocs had therefore surrendered the notion that they could impose their respective wills upon one another; neither pursued total military victory nor unconditional surrender.

---

[25] *Ibid.*, pp. 1716–17.

The means, in short, had limited the end, and necessity had become the mother of moderation. Consequently, the Administration believed: first, that the United States must restrain its efforts to counter expansionist Soviet moves to the restoration of the *status quo;* and second, that the Soviet government acted upon the assumption that if the Western nations resisted its thrusts successfully, it was safest to break off the engagement and accept the pre-crisis situation. In this context, the American government viewed the intermittent American-Soviet trials of strength as a series of conflicts whose aim it was to determine the precise location of the boundary which divided the Communist states from the free world; American containment would allow no further Russian encroachment beyond this line, and Soviet imperialism could satisfy its ambitions only at the risk of all-out war.

Berlin was an obvious case in point. The Russians had hoped to drive the Western allies out of the former German capital, and they had expected to achieve their objective by a land blockade of the city. The Western allies had refused to be intimidated, since they could have not withstood the political and psychological consequences of Berlin's fall. At the same time, the Atlantic allies had shared the Soviet Union's reluctance to pay the price of a full-scale war for a limited aim. Consequently, they had not tried to reopen the corridor into Berlin by sending tanks and troops to challenge the Red army; instead, they had limited themselves to the air lift. The Soviets had not challenged this effort, for they had realized that to have done so would have precipitated the total war which both sides hoped to avoid. The United States and the Soviet Union had been unwilling to take a risk of this magnitude in order to achieve a decisive result in Berlin. Consequently, the issue had been settled on the basis of the *status quo.* Neither side had won a victory in the traditional sense of the word; instead, both sides had accepted the stalemate.

Nor had the blockade been settled quickly; it had taken fifteen months for the crisis to pass. Patience, firmness, and determination had been needed to execute this policy, since it had required the application of just enough pressure to achieve its objective, but not so much pressure that it would have precipitated a world war. As Secretary Marshall explained, "We have brought to bear whatever has been necessary, in money and also manpower, to curb the aggressor; and we have sought in every possible way to avoid a third World War." Berlin had been an expensive operation; nevertheless, it had been a better alternative than a total war and the vast destruction which such a holocaust would have inflicted upon all sides.[26]

Korea fell into the same category as Berlin. It was "only the latest challenge in this long, hard, continuing world-wide struggle. We are applying there the same policy that has been successfully applied in the attempted aggressions that preceded it elsewhere in the world." [27] This war, too, was

---

[26] *Ibid.*, pp. 365–366, 731.   [27] *Ibid.*, p. 366.

being fought under certain ground rules. The Chinese Communists possessed a "privileged sanctuary" in Manchuria, but the United States possessed a similar sanctuary in Japan, Okinawa, and South Korea, particularly around the main port of Pusan. "They are not bombing our ports and supply installations," said General Bradley, "and they are not bombing our troops." [28]

The objective too was limited. The purpose of the fighting was to restore the situation that had existed before the North Korean attack on June 25, 1950. When Senator Alexander Smith said that he was "a little bit confused" by the idea of "stopping where we began," Acheson replied:

> Senator, if you accomplish what you started out to do, I don't think that is synonymous with saying you stopped where you began.
>
> We started out to do two things. One is repel the armed attack and the other is to restore peace and security in the area.
>
> Now, if we do these two things, we have done what we started out to do, and I should think that is success.

Thus, without admitting outrightly that the Administration had abandoned the goal of a militarily unified Korea, the Secretary of State informed the Communists that it was willing to call a cease-fire on the 38th Parallel. The price for a united Korea was too high; the *status quo* was therefore acceptable.[29]

To be sure, Acheson had always insisted that the United States had never harbored any other aim, but this explanation will not withstand critical examination. That the attempt to unify Korea by force had been made, but that circumstances had necessitated acceptance of the present solution, is evident from General Bradley's testimony:

> General Bradley . . . as we went farther north and the United Nations again came out with a resolution to establish a unified Korea, united and free Korea; that was the mission they gave to General MacArthur in late September. [Actually the United Nations resolution was approved on October 7, though Bradley is correct when he says that the mission was originally assigned to MacArthur by Washington in late September.]
>
> Senator Cain. And yet to carry out that mission from a military point of view or that objective from a political point of view, it will, before we are through, if we do not change that mission, be required to defeat the enemy and to repel him, not from South Korea but we must repel the enemy from Korea, or otherwise, sir, how can we make Korea a free, independent, and democratic nation?
>
> General Bradley. Well, I think we could have an intermediate military objective . . .[30]

---

[28] *Ibid.*, pp. 751, 892.   [29] *Ibid.*, p. 1786.   [30] *Ibid.*, p. 955.

In late September and early October, the Administration had argued that the parallel had to be crossed to safeguard South Korea's security; for if North Korea were not defeated, South Korea might be subjected to a further attack at some future date when the enemy had recovered his strength and reorganized his army. Administration witnesses did not repeat this argument after Communist China's intervention, even though the threat to South Korea's future existence remained—only, of course, on a more potent scale. This time they explained that although a cease-fire on the 38th Parallel would only reaffirm the position that had existed at the time of the initial challenge, it could be made to contain safeguards to deter another invasion. Why such an arrangement had not been considered in October of 1950 was not said; but the implication was that it had not then been a question of accepting such a cease-fire or nothing. The opportunity for a militarily united Korea had been rendered possible by the destruction of the North Korean army. Circumstances had now changed. The *status quo* had been restored at the 38th Parallel and the Administration was willing to call an end to the fighting on this line.[31]

There remained only one question: would the Chinese Communists, as the Russians before them, settle on the basis of the 38th Parallel, the line from which the North Korean advance had originally started? Secretary Acheson believed they would, although he could not predict the time when this would happen. But Berlin had taken fifteen months to settle; Greece eighteen months; Korea was then in its tenth month. Hope for an early finish of the fighting, however, was good for several reasons. First, "the offensives of the enemy have been broken and thrown back with enormous enemy casualties. These defeats . . . present grave problems for the Communist authorities in China. While the manpower resources of China are vast, its supply of trained men is limited. They cannot cover up their casualties. They cannot gloss over the draft of more and more men for military service." Second, the "Chinese Red leaders have betrayed their long-standing pledge of demobilization and the military demand for man power has, instead, been increased." And third, "Peiping has also broken its promises of social and economic improvement. In the great cities, dependent on imported materials, unemployment increases. The regime has not lightened the burdens of the people. It has made them heavier." The dissatisfaction caused by this increasing toll of dead and injured, as well as by the broken pledges, were already "reflected in a sharp increase in repressive measures, and in propaganda to whip up the flagging zeal of their own people. In the light of all these factors," Acheson concluded, "I believe that the aggression can best be brought to an end with a minimum risk and a minimum loss, by continuing the punishing defeat of the Chinese in Korea." The infliction of heavy casualties on the Chinese army, the destruc-

---

[31] *Ibid.*, pp. 1053–54.

tion of its morale and "trained fabric" would, in other words, bring the Chinese Communists to negotiate an end to hostilities without the risk of World War III.[32]

Shortly after Acheson made this statement, the Communists made their first move to end the war. On June 23, 1951, the Russian delegate to the United Nations, Jacob Malik, intimated that the Soviet Union was ready for a cease-fire in Korea. The Communists, therefore, having also tried unsuccessfully to conquer the entire Korean peninsula, had finally decided to incorporate the stalemate on the 38th Parallel into the almost global stalemate along the line determined in previous engagements.

The meek had inherited; they had restored the Republic of Korea to its prewar boundaries; they had managed to avoid an enlarged war and its attendant dangers in the Far East; they had preserved the unity of the Atlantic community and through the rearmament program increased their power several times; and they had husbanded their strength to balance Russian power and to create "unassailable barriers" in the path of Soviet expansion. They had refused to dissipate their military power on the periphery of the Communist empire, but had conserved it for its primary function, the continued denial of Communist ambitions and the encouragement of trends within the Soviet political and social system which would so increase its strains and stresses that they would moderate the ambitions of its leaders.

It was this article of faith upon which the Administration's case, in the final analysis, rested: Soviet imperialism could be contained without the horror of another global conflict, that the indefinite frustration of the Kremlin's appetite could cause the regime to become more accommodating and negotiate outstanding issues, and to accept a live-and-let-live attitude based upon the realities of military strength and the necessity of compromising with power. "For no mystical, Messianic movement—and particularly not that of the Kremlin," George Kennan had predicted, "can face frustration indefinitely without eventually adjusting itself in one way or another to the logic of that state of affairs." United States containment policy, therefore, "has it in its power to increase enormously the strains under which Soviet policy must operate, to force upon the Kremlin a far greater degree of circumspection than it has had to observe in recent years, and in this way to promote tendencies which must eventually find their outlet in either the break-up or the gradual mellowing of Soviet power." [33] Or, as Secretary Acheson expressed it during the hearings: ". . . what we must do is to create situations of strength, then I think that the whole situation in the world begins to change so far as the potentialities of the Soviet Union being able to achieve its present purposes is concerned; and with that change there comes a difference in the negotiating positions of

---

[32] *Ibid.*, pp. 1717–18.   [33] Kennan, pp. 127–128.

the various parties, and out of that I should hope that there would be a willingness on the side of the Kremlin to recognize the facts which have been created by this effort of ours and to begin to solve at least some of the difficulties between east and west." [34] Time, in short, *was* on the side of the United States and her allies—if the Western powers could remain united, contain further Communist expansion, and preserve the balance of power on the basis of the *status quo*.

---

[34] *Senate Hearings*, p. 2083.

XVII

*A Catholic Is Elected President:
What Factors Determined the
Outcome of the 1960 Election?*

INTRODUCTION

Twenty years of Democratic occupancy of the White House came to an end when Dwight D. Eisenhower decisively defeated Adlai E. Stevenson in the presidential election of 1952. Although Eisenhower repeated his victory in 1956, the Democrats apparently remained the majority party throughout the years of his presidency. In the election of 1960, Richard M. Nixon, Eisenhower's vice-president, was the Republican candidate, and John F. Kennedy, the second Catholic nominated for the presidency by his party, was the Democratic choice. The contest proved to be the closest in terms of the popular vote of any presidential election since 1884: Kennedy's popular vote exceeded that of Nixon by only 112,881.

The authors of the two selections on the election of 1960 approach the problem of Kennedy's victory from quite different and contrasting points of view. Theodore White, in his Pulitzer Prize-winning The Making of the President, 1960, *is more impressed with the fact that Kennedy won the election than that he won by such a small margin. In the first selection that follows, White analyzes the factors that enabled Kennedy to overcome the advantages that Nixon, in White's opinion, enjoyed at the outset of the campaign. White recognizes religion as an issue in the election, but he does not appear to regard it as the most important issue nor does he offer a judgment as to whether in itself it aided or injured Kennedy with the voters. White sees American tolerance, in the final analysis, as a major cause for Kennedy's triumph.*

The authors of the second selection, all of them associated with the University of Michigan's Survey Research Center, which has conducted many significant studies of American voting behavior, single out the religious issue as the most important factor in determining the outcome of the 1960 presidential election. The question they seek to answer is why Kennedy, as the representative of the majority party, did not win by a margin more indicative of the strength of his party. They conclude that Kennedy's religion substantially reduced his popular vote and accounts for the narrowness of his triumph.

To Wake as President

Theodore H. White

Men will examine the figures of the 1960 vote for decades, and as yet we cannot tell whether they will examine them as they did those of 1860, which closed an era of American history, or as they examine the figures of 1932, which opened one. . . . But however the chroniclers will read the vote, they, too, as we, must start with the bare bones of tabulation.

John F. Kennedy was elected President on November 8, 1960, by 303 electoral votes, drawn from 23 states, to 219 votes for Richard M. Nixon, drawn from 26 states. One state, Mississippi, was carried by a slate of eight independent electors who, with seven other Southerners (from Oklahoma and Alabama) voted for Senator Harry F. Byrd of Virginia. The margin of this electoral vote, so apparently substantial, is however a tribute not to the victor but to the wisdom of the Constitutional Fathers who, in their foresight, invented the device of the Electoral College, which, while preserving free citizen choice, prevents it from degenerating into the violence that can accompany the narrow act of head-counting. On the same day the American people returned to Congress a Senate of sixty-four Democrats and thirty-six Republicans and a House of Representatives of 262 Democrats and 175 Republicans, a gain for the Republicans of two Senate seats and twenty-one House seats.

In the head-counting of the popular vote, 68,832,818 Americans voted for President, or 64.5 per cent of the 107,000,000 Americans old enough and eligible to vote by census estimate. This participation (which ranged from a high of 80.7 per cent in Idaho to a low of 25.6 per cent in Mississippi) was the highest recorded participation in numbers and percentage of any American national election.

John F. Kennedy received 34,221,463 of these votes (49.7 per cent), or 112,881 votes (one tenth of one per cent of the whole) more than Richard M. Nixon, who drew 34,108,582 (49.6 per cent of the total). Thirteen minority-party candidates divided the remaining 502,773 (0.7 per cent) votes of this total. This margin of popular vote is so thin as to be, in all reality, nonexistent. If only 4,500 voters in Illinois and 28,000 voters in Texas had

From *The Making of the President 1960* by Theodore H. White. Copyright © 1961 by Atheneum House, Inc. Reprinted by permission of Atheneum. Pp. 350–359.

changed their minds, the sum of their 32,500 votes would have moved both those states, with their combined fifty-one electoral votes, into the Nixon column. Thus giving him an electoral majority of two, these 32,500 votes would have made Richard M. Nixon President of the United States.

Analysis of the meaning of the national vote must begin, then, by separation, proceeding from the gross figures, which can be established with hard accuracy, to the finer and more delicate speculations on the subdivisions of the vote, which attempt to illuminate the privacy of American minds.

Only when one begins to cluster the individual states into natural groups does the blur and confusion first dissolve into a rough pattern. Dividing America into its eight major regions, one finds that of the eight fairly distinct geographical communities in the nation, Richard M. Nixon carried five and John F. Kennedy but three.

One learns much by scanning the separate totals of these areas—for here there are true margins, thin but real.

The most decisive single expression of will for Richard M. Nixon came from the block of five predominantly farm states (Iowa, North Dakota, Kansas, South Dakota, Nebraska). Here, in the culture of the small town and the old America, in the Protestant homesteads of traditional Republican allegiance, Nixon led by a margin of 598,362 votes out of a total of 3,395,088 (with 58.8 per cent of the whole). He scored well in the block of eight states that sprawl across the Rocky Mountains (Montana, Idaho, Colorado, Utah, Wyoming, Nevada, Arizona, New Mexico), where he led Kennedy by 192,313 votes out of 2,641,593 cast, or 53.6 per cent of the whole. The margin thinned somewhat in the five border states (Kentucky, Missouri, Oklahoma, Tennessee, West Virginia), which provided Nixon with a margin of 263,033 votes out of 5,837,945 cast, or 52.2 per cent. Here, in these traditionally Democratic yet Bible-loving and Protestant regions, religion played a heavy role—in only six states of the Union did Nixon outrun the Eisenhower percentages of 1956, and two of these were in border country (Tennessee and Oklahoma; the other four were in the Deep South: Georgia, Alabama, Mississippi, South Carolina). His lead was pared yet further in the six industrial Midwestern states that ring the lakes (Illinois, Michigan, Indiana, Minnesota, Wisconsin, Ohio), where Nixon led by 462,-778 out of 17,607,696 cast (with 51.3 per cent of the whole). This, the industrial heartland of the country, still remains the greatest single base of Republican strength. Finally, the five Pacific states (California, Oregon, Washington, Hawaii, Alaska) provided his thinnest margin—107,461 votes out of 8,733,361, or 50.6 per cent.

These five geographic regions of the land, sweeping in a huge lopsided crescent from the shores of the Pacific to the Appalachians, together gave Mr. Nixon a margin of 1,623,967 votes. That these were not enough to affect the delicate amplification of the Electoral College was simple because

Mr. Kennedy had *his* margin where it counted—in the populous Northeast and the Old South.

Of the three regions that Kennedy claimed, New England, as expected, performed best. In the six states (Maine, New Hampshire, Vermont, Massachusetts, Rhode Island, Connecticut) of this, the most heavily Catholic section of the country, and his native ground, Kennedy ran up a margin of 603,587 votes out of 4,977,169 cast, or 56.0 per cent of the total—almost, but not quite, as good as Nixon's margin in the five farm states. Ten states of the Old South (Alabama, Arkansas, Florida, Georgia, Louisiana, Mississippi, North Carolina, South Carolina, Texas and Virginia), came next in expression of loyalty—yielding a plurality of 530,693 votes out of 8,865,501 cast, or 52.9 per cent. Here . . . came the greatest and most significant Republican gains in the national election, a gain which, by proper strategic planning, might have been amplified enough to give Nixon victory and revolutionize American politics. Finally (the fruit of Kennedy's own determined strategy) came the great block of five Middle-Atlantic states (New York, New Jersey, Pennsylvania, Maryland and Delaware), which gave him a lead of 601,570 votes out of 16,372,790 cast, or 51.5 per cent—a thin lead in percentiles, but large enough in size and distribution to give him all 105 electoral votes of the region. Altogether, these three Kennedy regions provided a margin of 1,735,851 votes, or just enough votes in just the right places to give him victory—as he had planned it.

For never was planning and decision of greater importance in any campaign than in that of 1960—for supreme planning calculates both underlying force and vagrant accident, and provides enough underlying force to take advantage of or protect against accident; which is what the Kennedy planning, in essence, achieved; and which is why afterwards no Republican candidate in recent years, not even Thomas Dewey, has been more bitterly, if privately, denounced by his closest associates of campaign and headquarters than Richard M. Nixon. For unforeseen accidents happened on both sides; yet the Nixon strategy—or lack of it—made the Republican most vulnerable. . . .

The first of the Kennedy strategies had been a regional one, decided by the candidate alone, on the night of his nomination, by his choice of Vice-President. He felt he had New England locked up; that he must campaign personally for the big Northeastern industrial states; that Lyndon B. Johnson must be his Lord Constable for the Old South. These grand calculations worked. Of the nine big states, Kennedy carried seven: New York, Pennsylvania, Michigan, Illinois, Texas, New Jersey, Massachusetts. Nixon carried only two: Ohio and California. It was in these big states that Kennedy invested the greatest part of his time and personal effort, while Nixon sought to spread himself over all fifty states of the union. New England proved indeed to be in the bag; and Lyndon Johnson proved indeed able to captain the Southern electoral drive. Had Kennedy carried only one other state except those envisioned in this strategy (and he did carry Minnesota, Missouri, Nevada, New Mexico, West Virginia and Hawaii), this strategy would still have given him a majority of the Electoral College.

Within this larger regional strategy of voting, a subordinate but nonetheless major calculation must be signaled. This was Kennedy's October decision to hammer away at the great suburban belts in the large states—suburbs that in the past decade have been traditionally Republican. He left it to his big-city bosses to firm up the traditionally Democratic ethnic blocs inside the big cities, into which Eisenhower had previously cut so heavily. He himself hammered at the suburbs around Chicago, Philadelphia, New York and Baltimore, appealing to the younger voters in the developments, as he had learned to do in his native Massachusetts. A Lou Harris survey early in the campaign had come up with the oddly interesting fact that while fewer than 30 per cent of American families *now* send their children to college or junior college, no less than 80 per cent hope in the future to send children to college. In the suburbs, early and late, Kennedy hammered at educational themes within the broader theme of We Must Move, and the "young marrieds," worried about their children, must have hearkened. In the suburbs of the top fourteen Northeastern metropolitan areas he was able to increase the Democratic percentage in these naturally Republican girdles from the 38 per cent netted by Adlai Stevenson in 1956 to 49 per cent in 1960. On the East Coast, his gains in the Protestant suburbs of Baltimore and Buffalo were of the same order as his gains in the heavily Catholic suburbs of New York and Boston. (His record as the vote moved West was definitely not as good: moderate in the suburbs of Chicago and disastrous in the suburban outer fringe of Los Angeles; in Los Angeles a clear amount of the fall-off was due to mismanagement of the California campaign, where Kennedy ran farther behind his Democratic ticket mates than in any major state of the Union.)

The most precise response of result to strategy lay, however, in the Negro vote. And this was overwhelmingly for Kennedy. It must be remembered that as Kennedy entered the Democratic Convention in Los Angeles, he was the *least* popular among Negroes of all Democratic candidates; many Northern Negro politicians preferred even Lyndon Johnson to Kennedy. Hard work (chiefly by the Civil Rights Section, led by the able Sargent Shriver and Harris Wofford) and the master stroke of intervention in the Martin Luther King arrest,* not only reversed this Negro indifference to him, but gave him a larger share of the Negro vote than Stevenson had received in

---

* Editor's note: The Rev. Martin Luther King was arrested in Atlanta on October 19, 1960, for participating in a "sit-in" in a department store and was sentenced to four months' imprisonment. John Kennedy called Mrs. King to express his concern, and Robert Kennedy later appealed to the Georgia judge who had sentenced King to release the prisoner. King was then released on bail pending an appeal. Nixon took no action in the affair.

1956 (although not quite as large a share as Stevenson had had in 1952). In analyzing the Negro vote, almost all dissections agree that seven out of ten Negroes voted for Kennedy for President—the Gallup Poll estimating 70 per cent, the IBM calculations estimating 68 per cent. In Detroit, Negro percentages ran at 8 to 1 or better; in the five Negro wards of Chicago's swollen South Side, the percentage ran approximately 4 to 1. And not only did the Northern Negro vote Democratic—so did the Southern Negro, in a complete reversal of form. In Memphis, Tennessee, Ward Thirty-five, a typical Negro ward, switched from 36 per cent Democratic in 1956 to 67 per cent Democratic in 1960; similar staggering switches occurred in South Carolina, in Georgia and in Texas. Some Negro political leaders claim that in no less than eleven states (Illinois, New Jersey, Michigan, South Carolina, Texas, Delaware, Maryland, Missouri, North Carolina, Pennsylvania, Nevada), with 169 electoral votes, it was the Negro community that provided the Kennedy margin of victory. This statement is interesting only as an example of wind in the sails of men who propose to move fast; it bears no relation to reality. Yet it is difficult to see how Illinois, New Jersey, Michigan, South Carolina or Delaware (with 74 electoral votes) could have been won had the Republican-Democratic split of the Negro wards and precincts remained as it was, unchanged from the Eisenhower charm of 1956. Nor can one avoid the observation that as October stretched on to November, and the economic downturn of the winter began to be felt, unemployment began to bite, as it always does, most sharply on Negro unskilled workers. ("Mister," said a Chicago Negro discussing his vote with me in 1960, "they could put a dog at the head of that ticket and if they called him Democratic I'd vote for him. This hoolarium about civil rights doesn't mean anything to me—it's the man that puts money into my pocket that counts.")

There remains, then, in examining the vote, the most controversial of all areas of reflection: the Catholic-Protestant cleavage in American life. For there is little room to argue about how American Catholics and Protestants voted in 1960—only about what the generally accepted (and valid) figures mean.

American Catholics voted preponderantly for John F. Kennedy. They had, indeed, voted preponderantly Democratic ever since the Irish first arrived in New York and Boston a century ago. But during the 1950s they had voted so heavily for the Republicans (or Dwight D. Eisenhower) that their return to the old pattern of voting at about 3 or 4 to 1 Democratic provokes the perplexing question of whether they were voting by faith, by political conviction or by resumption of interrupted habit. The extremes of research of Catholic voting in 1960 are those of Dr. George Gallup (who held that 78 per cent of all Catholics voted for Kennedy, in social breaks that ranged from 65 per cent for college-educated, prosperous Catholics to 83 per cent for poorer, grade-school-educated Catholics) to that of the IBM data computers that held that only 61 per cent of all Catholics voted for Kennedy. Not all Catholics, it should be noted, voted alike—for them, too, the past has many threads and sometimes the threads tangle. Italian Catholics (most analysts agree) voted about 70 per cent for Kennedy, Polish Catholics about 68 per cent. There is controversy about the margin by which Kennedy held or won back his Irish-Catholic fellows—the IBM data computers insist that about 68 per cent of definable Irish-Catholic voting units went for Kennedy, whereas the Kennedy staff grieves that in many areas (as in Hudson County, New Jersey) the expected Irish-Catholic vote fell so far below anticipation as to jeopardize election in close states.

The most interesting performance of the minor communities in the Catholic subcommunity of America was that of the German-Catholic-Americans. Where their vote can be isolated, it is estimated that it was 50 per cent Kennedy, 50 per cent Nixon. Here, in the German-Catholic-American vote, one sees two different kinds of past straining and tugging at the voter: an American of German ancestry must see a Democrat as one who belongs to the party that has twice led this country into war against the old fatherland; as an American Catholic, he must see a Catholic candidate as one, like himself, of a minority hitherto excluded. The two pressures of the past clash.

Perhaps the best demonstration of how this clash worked out in voting practice in 1960 happened in Wisconsin. In Wisconsin, political reporters talk of the "ten Catholic counties"—meaning those ten Wisconsin counties that, alone, voted both for Alfred E. Smith for President in 1928 and for state aid for parochial-school buses in 1938. These counties are populated largely by German and Irish Catholics. In the spring primary between Humphrey and Kennedy, these ten counties voted overwhelmingly *for* Kennedy *against* Humphrey, as if to prove that, between two Democrats, they preferred their coreligionist. But in the November election, when a Republican (Protestant) and a Democrat (Catholic) stood before them, and religion was confused with politics, they split—five for Nixon, five for Kennedy.

There is no doubt that millions of Americans, Protestant and Catholic, voted in 1960 primordially out of instinct, kinship and past.

One cannot examine the structure of the voting returns in Oklahoma, Tennessee, Utah, Florida, Kentucky, Oregon, Indiana, Ohio or Wisconsin without finding transparent evidence in precise counties and precincts that millions of Protestants could not tolerate the thought of a Catholic sitting in the White House. Equally, one cannot examine returns from New York, Illinois, Pennsylvania, and New England without recognizing that millions of Americans, equally blind, voted *for* Kennedy only because he *was* a Catholic. One has, for example, that marvelously clear pattern of interlocking bigotries of such a county as Nelson County, Kentucky. There, four predominantly Baptist precincts gave Kennedy only 599 votes (35 per cent) and Nixon 1,095 votes (65 per cent); yet in the same county, five predominantly Catholic precincts gave Kennedy 1,285 (88 per cent) and Nixon 174 votes (12 per cent). One has the pattern (if one wishes to analyze patterns further) of the three predominantly Irish precincts of Philadelphia with a permanent registration of 53 per cent Republican—which in 1960 went for Kennedy by 70 per cent. And the contrasting pattern, if one wishes, of the town of New Amersterdam in Montana, which had voted *for* Democrat Lee Metcalf, a Protestant, for Congressman in 1958, by 287 to 34; yet which in 1960, when he ran for United States Senator and was denounced by the local opinion makers as the candidate of the "Catholic Party," voted *against* him by 260 to 40.

Over all, there can be no doubt that the great majority of Catholics voted for Kennedy; and, situated as they were by history in the Northeast, they cast their votes in the big states, which counted most. All other matters but this were planned and mobilized by Kennedy—the concentration of campaigning in the Northeast, the emphasis on civil rights and protection of the Negroes, the cultivation of suburbia and the advocacy of a new important program of federally aided education. The Catholic vote, it is true, was counted in all Kennedy calculations as being committed to him in advance; yet this vote alone was *not* planned, nor was it mobilized. For even when the Catholic vote is added to the Negro vote, the Jewish vote and the suburban vote, one still has no true picture of what happened in the election of 1960 nor how its totals came about. For John F. Kennedy, as other Democrats before him, was not elected only by a federation of American minorities—nor does his Presidency rest on that fact, nor did his campaign at its highest and most important level plan that kind of victory.

In the long sight of history, John F. Kennedy cast his appeal, *above all*, to the overwhelmingly Protestant majority of the American people, and ran uphill to convince them that whatever differing pasts and heritages they brought to 1960, they shared a common future and common conviction for the years ahead.

It was this, indeed, that was the greatest success of Kennedy planning.

For the addition of minorities in no way explains the Kennedy total of triumph. No estimate or analysis of the final vote denies that in the final Kennedy constituency of 34,000,000 votes, the number of Protestants who voted for him materially outweighed the number of Catholics and Jews combined. The high estimate (IBM) is that 46 per cent of all American Protestants voted for John F. Kennedy, or 22,500,000—making almost two thirds of his total. The low estimate (Dr. George Gallup) is that only 38 per cent of all American Protestants voted for John F. Kennedy—which still comes to some 18,600,000 of his 34,000,000 constituency, or critically more than half of his majority. If the exact percentage of Protestants who voted for Kennedy is forever indefinable, the truth must nevertheless lie somewhere between the low and high estimates; thus the Kennedy victory is a triumph of many facets—a triumph first of American tolerance and of the enlightened leadership of contemporary Protestant churchmen, a triumph next of the planning of the man who became President, a triumph finally of the American spirit, which is unafraid. Which invites us once more, in the afterlight of the election totals, to examine the strategies of the two candidates.

If Nixon were to win, he had need only to move forward from the Eisenhower base of Peace and Prosperity; the country was indeed at peace and, until the late fall downturn, more prosperous than ever before in history. To urge it forward, he need only have been bold, been strong, and offered visions. The past, both immediate and remote, weighed in his favor, and to this pressure of the past he need only add a minimum sense of future in which all could hope for more. Instead he tangled in words, locked himself on issues thrust at him by his rival, defending and retaliating when he should have been leading. He offered no vision of a greater future to any minority—Catholic or otherwise—within a moving, broadening American future that might win them from their past; and to the great majority Protestant stock of the country he offered, with utmost honor, no fear of religion—yet nothing to offset the emotions Kennedy sought to arouse in order to tug them, by hope, from their instinct and fear.

For Kennedy, the problem was equally clear, if different as in a mirror image. It was to stir the nation with a sense of anticipation strong enough to overcome the hidden and unspoken reluctance of millions of Americans to abandon their past—and not only the past of religion, but the pride of the Anglo-American peoples who had fought the Civil War, who had built America's industry, had cleared its plains, who found themselves still unable to recognize in the third or fourth generation of the immigrant hordes those leadership qualities that run in the tradition of Lincoln, Roosevelt, Adams, Hay, Wilson, Roosevelt, Stimson.

It was seventy years ago that Senator Robert F. Hoare (Rep.) of Massachusetts, replying to a European inquirer, declared, "The men who do the work of piety and charity in our churches, the men who administer our school system, the men who own and till their own farms, the men who perform skilled labor in the shops, the soldiers, the men who went to war and stayed all through, the men who paid the debt and kept the currency sound and saved the nation's honor, the men who saved the country in war and have made it worth living in peace, commonly and as a rule, by the natural law of their being find their places in the Republican party. While the old slave-owner and slave-driver, the saloon keeper, the ballot box stuffer, the Ku Klux Klan, the criminal class of the great cities, the men who cannot read or write, commonly and as a rule, by the natural law of their being, find their congenial place in the Democratic party."

One has only to travel through the Midwest or upper New York and New England today to find the echo of this generations-old statement. If

Joseph P. Kennedy had become an apostate Catholic and baptized his son an Episcopalian at birth in Trinity Church, Copley Square, Boston, John F. Kennedy would, nonetheless, have had to run against the same sense of the past and the same unease that the American people felt when they considered putting their destiny into new hands. Consciously or unconsciously, therefore, in all his elegant quotations from Franklin and Jefferson, from Lincoln and Roosevelt, from Thoreau and from Emerson, Kennedy sought to identify himself with this past. (At times, indeed, following him about the country was like attending a peripatetic and anecdotal course in American history.) And out of this past he attempted to urge all Americans to move forward with him to a common future.

The fact that he succeeded at all is, in retrospect, more startling than the narrowness of his margin. He had, of course, the entire future to himself—no other Republican candidate has ever so willfully conceded so vast an area to a Democratic opponent without struggle. But his problem was fantastic nonetheless. For politics is the slow public application of reason to the governing of mass emotion. And it is rare that reason can reach an entire people without clarification by disaster—such as the disaster of the depression in America in 1932, or defeat in battle of the Germans in 1945. Kennedy spoke to a peaceful and prosperous people in the year 1960, a people for whom the crises of swelling problems lay still unclear years ahead. He insisted that they must move to meet those obscure crises—which he did not define—and urged them to give into his untested hands the greatest of all crises, war and peace, without ever telling them how he meant to meet it. It was on this above all that he won—a sense of purpose, in a year of malaise; a sense of confidence, in a future that darkened. . . .

Stability and Change in 1960:

A Reinstating Election

Philip E. Converse, Angus Campbell, Warren E. Miller,

Donald E. Stokes

John F. Kennedy's narrow popular vote margin in 1960 has already insured this presidential election a classic position in the roll call of close
American elections. Whatever more substantial judgments historical perspective may bring, we can be sure that the 1960 election will do heavy
duty in demonstrations to a reluctant public that after all is said and done,
every vote does count. And the margin translated into "votes per precinct"
will became standard fare in exhortations to party workers that no stone
be left unturned.

The 1960 election is a classic as well in the license it allows for "explanations" of the final outcome. Any event or campaign strategem that might
plausibly have changed the thinnest sprinkling of votes across the nation
may, more persuasively than is usual, be called "critical." Viewed in this
manner, the 1960 presidential election hung on such a manifold of factors
that reasonable men might despair of cataloguing them.

Nevertheless, it is possible to put together an account of the election in
terms of the broadest currents influencing the American electorate in 1960.
We speak of the gross lines of motivation which gave the election its unique
shape, motivations involving millions rather than thousands of votes. Analysis of these broad currents is not intended to explain the hairline differences in popular vote, state by state, which edged the balance in favor of
Kennedy rather than Nixon. But it can indicate quite clearly the broad
forces which reduced the popular vote to a virtual stalemate, rather than
any of the other reasonable outcomes between a 60–40 or a 40–60 vote
division. And it can thereby help us to understand in parsimonious terms
why a last feather thrown on the scales in November, 1960, could have
spelled victory or defeat for either candidate.

From *The American Political Science Review*, LV (June 1961), 269–280. Reprinted
by permission.

Stability and Change in 1960: A Reinstating Election

I. SURFACE CHARACTERISTICS OF THE ELECTION

Any account of the election should not only be consistent with its obvious characteristics as they filtered clear from raw vote tallies in the days after the election, but should organize them into a coherent pattern of meaning as well. These characteristics are, of course, the ones that have nourished post-election speculation. In addition to the close partisan division of the popular vote, the following items deserve mention:

(1) *The remarkably high level of turnout.* About 62.7 percent of estimated adults over 21 voted in the 1952 election, a figure which had stood as the high-water mark of vote turnout in recent presidential elections. The comparable turnout proportion for the 1960 presidential election appears to have been 64.3 per cent.[1]

(2) *Upswing in turnout in the South.*[2] The South appears to have contributed disproportionately to the high level in turnout. Outside the South, the increase in total presidential votes cast in 1960 relative to the 1956 election was about 7 percent, a figure scarcely exceeding estimated population growth in this period. In the South, however, presidential ballots in 1960 increased by more than 25 per cent relative to 1956, an increase far outstripping population growth in this region.[3]

(3) *Stronger Republican voting at the presidential level.* On balance across the nation Nixon led Republican tickets, while Kennedy trailed behind many other Democratic candidates, especially outside of the Northeast. These discrepancies in the partisanship of presidential voting and ballots at other levels were not, of course, as striking as those in 1956. Nevertheless, their political significance has an obvious bearing on the future expectations of the two youthful candidates, and therefore occasions special interest.

(4) *The stamp of the religious factor in 1960 voting patterns.* While the Kennedy victory was initially taken as proof that religion had not been

---

[1] Estimates of turnout lack much meaning except as raw vote totals are stated as a proportion of the potential electorate. Whereas the number of adults over 21 in the nation is known with reasonable precision, the number of adult citizens over 21 who are "eligible" according to any of several possible definitions depends on cruder estimates, which can be quite diverse. For the 1952 figure we employ here Table No. 446 for the "Civilian Population 21 Years and Older," *Statistical Abstract of the United States* (1958 edition). The 1960 figure rests on an estimated 107 million adults over 21.

[2] The South is defined throughout this article to include 15 border and deep Southern States. Texas, Oklahoma, Arkansas, Kentucky, West Virginia and Maryland (but not Delaware) are included and form the western and nothern boundaries of the region.

[3] Population growth in areas such as Texas and Florida includes the immigration of American citizens from outside the South who are more accustomed to voting in every election than are Southerners. It seems almost certain, however, that there was a real increase in motivation among long-term Southern residents as well. The factor of population change was quite insufficient to account for the 1960 increase in Southern turnout.

important in the election, all serious students of election statistics have since been impressed by the religious axis visible in the returns. Fenton, Scammon, Bean, Harris and others have commented upon the substantial correlation between aggregate voting patterns and the relative concentration of Catholics and Protestants from district to district.

Of these surface characteristics, probably the last has drawn most attention. Once it became clear that religion had not only played some part but, as these things go, a rather impressive part in presidential voting across the nation, discussions came to hinge on the nature of its role. It could safely be assumed that Kennedy as a Catholic had attracted some unusual Catholic votes, and had lost some normally Democratic Protestant votes. A clear question remained, however, as to the *net* effect. The *New York Times,* summarizing the discussion late in November, spoke of a "narrow consensus" among the experts that Kennedy had won more than he lost as a result of his Catholicism.[4] These are questions, however, which aggregate vote statistics can but dimly illuminate, as the disputed history of Al Smith's 1928 defeat makes clear. Fortunately in 1960 the election was studied extensively by sample surveys, permitting more exact inferences to be drawn.

The national sample survey conducted by the Survey Research Center of The University of Michigan in the fall of 1960 had features which give an unparalleled opportunity to comment on the recent evolution of the American electorate. The fall surveys were part of a long-term "panel" study, in which respondents first interviewed at the time of the 1956 presidential election were reinterviewed.[5] In the fall of 1956 a sample of 1763 adults, chosen by strict probability methods from all the adults living in private households in the United States, had been questioned just before and just after the presidential election. This initial sample was constituted as a panel of respondents and was interviewed again in 1958 and twice in connection with the 1960 presidential election.[6] These materials permit the linking of 1960 and 1956 voting behavior with unusual reliability.[7]

---

[4] *New York Times,* November 20, 1960, Section 4, p. E5.

[5] Results of the 1956 survey, considered as a simple cross-section sample of the nation, are reported in Campbell, Converse, Miller and Stokes, *The American Voter* (New York, 1960). There are natural difficulties in any attempt to retain contact with a farflung national sample over periods of two and four years, especially in a population as geographically mobile as that of the current United States. Of the original 1763 respondents interviewed twice in 1956, nearly 100 had died before the 1960 interview. Others had been effectively removed from the electorate by advanced senility or institutionalization. Of the remaining possible interviews, numbering somewhat over 1600 people, more than 1100 were successfully reinterviewed in the fall of 1960. The 1956 social, economic and political characteristics of the 1960 survivors show almost no sign of deviation from the characteristics of the larger pool of original 1956 respondents. Therefore, although attrition may seem substantial, there is no evidence of alarming bias.

[6] The sequence of interviews in 1956, 1958 and 1960 was carried out under grants from the Rockefeller Foundation. The 1960 sample design provided not only contact with the 1956 panel which, due to aging, no longer gave an adequate representation of the 1960

II. THE EVOLUTION OF THE ELECTORATE, 1956–1960

The difference in presidential election outcome between 1956 and 1960 might depend upon either or both of two broad types of change in the electorate. The first includes shifts in the physical composition of the electorate over time due to non-political factors, *i.e.*, vital processes. Some adult citizens who voted in 1956 were no longer part of the eligible electorate in 1960, primarily because of death or institutionalization. On the other hand, a new cohort of voters who had been too young to vote in 1956 were eligible to participate in the 1960 election. Even in a four-year period, vital processes alone could account for shifts in the vote. In addition, changes in the electoral vote, though not in the nationwide popular vote margin, might result from voters changing their residences without changing their minds.

Secondly, there are obviously genuine changes in the political choice of individuals eligible to vote in both elections. Such citizens may enter or leave the active electorate by choice, or may decide to change the partisanship of their presidential vote.

The contribution of these two types of change to the shift in votes from a 1956 Eisenhower landslide to a narrow 1960 Kennedy margin—a net shift toward the Democrats of almost 8 percent—may be analyzed. Somewhat less than 10 percent of the eligible 1956 electorate had become effectively ineligible by 1960, with death as the principal cause.[8] Older people naturally bulk large in this category. The felt party affiliation or "party identification" expressed in 1956 by these "departing" respondents was somewhat Republican relative to the remainder of the sample.[9] Nonetheless, these people cast a vote for president which was about 48 percent Democratic, or 6 percent *more Democratic* than the vote of the 1956 electorate as a whole.

---

electorate, but also a set of additional interviews filling out an up-to-date cross-section sample of all adult citizens living in private households in 1960. Analysis of the additional interview material is being carried out under a grant from the Social Science Research Council. Both the panel and cross-section bodies of data contribute, where appropriate, to materials in this article.

[7] The longitudinal analysis of political change permitted by a panel design can only be poorly approximated in simple cross-section surveys, where deductions must rest on the respondent's recollection of his behavior in time past. Most analysts have justly felt uncomfortable with recall materials of this sort, since it has been clear that the accuracy of a vote report declines rapidly as time passes. In both 1958 and 1960, we asked our respondents to recall their 1956 vote. The results, as compared with actual reports collected just after the 1956 election, demonstrate forcefully the inaccuracies which accumulate with time.

[8] Throughout this article, the "eligible electorate" is taken to consist of those non-institutionalized citizens over 21. Negroes disqualified in many parts of the South, for example, are included in this bounding of the electorate, as well as those who had moved too recently to have established new voting residences in 1960.

[9] The concept of party identification is treated in detail, Campbell *et al.*, *op. cit.*, p. 120 ff.

Although this appears to be a contradiction, it is actually nothing more than a logical consequence of existing theory. The high Republican vote in 1956 depended on a massive defection to Eisenhower by many people identified with the Democratic party. Since the strength of party attachments increases as a function of age, and since defections are inversely related to strength of party identification, it follows that 1956 defection rates were much higher among younger citizens than among older.[10] The data make it clear that the group of older people voting for the last time in 1956 had cast a much straighter "party vote" than their juniors. Only about 5 percent of these older Democrats had defected to Eisenhower, as opposed to about a quarter of all Democrats in the electorate as a whole. So both things are true: this departing cohort was more Republican than average in party identification but had voted more Democratic than average in 1956. If we remove them from the 1956 electorate, then, we arrive at a presidential vote of about 60 percent for Eisenhower among those voters who were to have the option of voting again in 1960. Hence the elimination of this older group from consideration increases the amount of partisan change to be accounted for between 1956 and 1960, rather than decreasing it.

Comparable isolation of the new cohort of young voters in 1960 does very little to change the picture. Little more than one half of this new group of voters normally votes in the first election of eligibility;[11] furthermore, in 1960 its two-party vote division differed only negligibly from that of the nation as a whole. As a result, its analytic removal leaves the vote among the remainder of the electorate nearly unchanged. By way of summary, then, differences in the 1956 and 1960 electorates arising from vital processes do not explain the 1956–1960 vote change; if anything, they extend the amount of change to be otherwise explained.

We may further narrow our focus by considering those people eligible in both 1956 and 1960, who failed to join the active electorate in 1960. A very large majority of these 1960 non-voters had not voted in 1956, and represent Negroes in the South as well as persistent non-voters of other types. Among those who *had* voted in 1956, however, the vote had been rather evenly divided between Eisenhower and Stevenson. As with the older voters, removal of this group leaves an active 1956–1960 electorate whose vote for Eisenhower now surpasses 60 percent, broadening again the discrepancy between the two-party divisions in the 1956 and 1960 votes. The final fringe group which we may set aside analytically is constituted of those citizens eligible to have voted in 1956 who did not then participate, yet who joined the electorate in 1960. The fact that young voters often

---

[10] Our theoretical understanding of this net of relationships is suggested *ibid.*, pp. 161–167.

[11] Participation rates by age in 1960 follow rather nicely the rates indicated *ibid.*, Fig. 17-1, p. 494.

"sit out" their first presidential election or two indicates part of the composition of such a group. Once again, however, these newly active citizens divided their ballots in 1960 almost equally between the two major candidates, and the residual portion of the 1960 electorate changes little with their removal.

By this point we have eliminated all the fringe groupings whose entry or departure from the active electorate might have contributed to change in the national vote division between 1956 and 1960. We come to focus directly, then, on the individuals who cast a vote for Kennedy or Nixon in 1960 *and had voted for president in 1956* (Table I). As we see, paring away the fringe groupings has had the total effect of increasing the net shift in the vote division between the two years from 8 percent to 11 percent. If we can explain this shift it will be clear that we have dealt with those broad currents in the electorate which brought the 1960 election to a virtual stalemate.

Naturally, the most interesting features of Table I are the cells involving vote changers. In a sequence of elections such as the 1956–1960 series it is

TABLE I. 1956–1960 VOTE CHANGE WITHIN THE ACTIVE CORE OF THE ELECTORATE

1960 Vote for ↓	1956 Vote for		Total %
	Stevenson %	Eisenhower %	
Kennedy	33	17	50
Nixon	6	44	50
	39	61	100

Note: Since we usually think of vote shifts in terms of proportions of the total electorate, percentages in this table use the total vote as a base, rather than row or column totals.

a temptation to assume that about 8 percent of the Eisenhower voters of 1956 shifted to Kennedy in 1960, since this was the net observable change between the two years. Much analysis of aggregate election statistics is forced to proceed on this assumption within any given voting unit. However, we see that the net shift of 11 percent in the vote of the active 1956–1960 electorate in fact derived from a gross shift of 23 percent, over half of which was rendered invisible in the national totals because counter-movements cancelled themselves out.

A traditional analysis of these vote changers would specify their membership in various population groupings such as age and occupation category, union membership, race and the like. However, results of this sort in 1960 are so uniform across most of these population groupings that they seem to reflect little more than national trends, and change seems at best loosely connected with location in various of these specific categories. If we took the fact in isolation, for example, we might be struck to note that union members voted almost 8 percent more Democratic in 1960 than in 1956. However, such a figure loses much of its interest when we remind ourselves that people who are not labor union members also shifted their votes in the same direction and in about the same degree between 1956 and 1960. Such uniform changes characterize most of the standard sociological categories.

There is, of course, one dramatic exception. Vote change between 1956 and 1960 follows religious lines very closely. Within the 6 percent of the active 1956–1960 electorate who followed a Stevenson-Nixon path (Table I), 90 percent are Protestant and only 8 percent are Catholic. Among the larger group of Eisenhower-Kennedy changers, however, only 40 percent are Protestant and close to 60 percent are Catholic. In the total vote in 1956 and 1960, Protestants show almost no net partisan change. Eisenhower had won 64 percent of the "Protestant vote" in 1956; Nixon won 63 percent. Meanwhile, the Democratic proportion of the two-party vote among Catholics across the nation skyrocketed from a rough 50 percent in the two Eisenhower elections to a vote of 80 percent for Kennedy. These gross totals appear to substantiate the early claims of Kennedy backers that a Catholic candidate would draw back to the Democratic party sufficient Catholics to carry the 1960 election. Furthermore, it appears that Kennedy must have gained more votes than he lost by virtue of his religious affiliation, for relative to Stevenson in 1956, he lost no Protestant votes and attracted a very substantial bloc of Catholic votes.

The question of net gains or losses as a result of the Catholic issue is not, however, so simply laid to rest. The data cited above make a very strong case, as have the aggregate national statistics, that religion played a powerful role in the 1960 outcome. The vote polarized along religious lines in a degree which we have not seen in the course of previous sample survey studies. Moreover, the few interesting deviations in the 1960 vote of other population groupings, to the degree that they are visible at all, seem with minor exceptions to reflect the central religious polarization. That is, where a group exceeded or fell below the magnitude of the national shift to the Democrats, it is usually true that the group is incidentally a more or less Catholic group. The central phenomenon therefore was religious; the question as to its net effect favoring or disfavoring Kennedy remains open.

In a strict sense, of course, the answers to this question can only be estimated. We know how the election came out, with Kennedy a Catholic. We cannot, without major additional assumptions, know what the election returns might have been if Kennedy were a Protestant and all other conditions remained unchanged. We can make an estimate, however, if we can assume some baseline, some vote that would have occurred under "normal" circumstances. A number of such baselines suggest themselves. We might work from the 1956 presidential vote, as we have done above (42 percent Democratic); or from the more recent Congressional vote in 1958 (56 percent Democratic); or from some general average of recent nation-wide votes. But it is obvious that the simple choice of baseline will go a long way toward determining the answer we propose to the question of net religious effect. If we choose the 1958 vote as a baseline, it is hard to argue that Kennedy could have made any net gains from his religion; if we choose the 1956 presidential vote, it is equally hard to argue that he lost ground on balance.

Indeed, the most cogent arguments documenting a net gain for Kennedy —those accounts which appear to express the majority opinion of election observers—use the 1956 presidential vote quite explicitly as a baseline. Yet the second Eisenhower vote seems the most bizarre choice for a baseline of any which might be suggested. The vote Eisenhower achieved in 1956 stands out as the most disproportionately Republican vote in the total series of nation-wide presidential and Congressional elections stretching back to 1928. In what sense, then, is this extreme Republican swing plausible as a "normal vote?" Its sole claim seems to lie in the fact that it is the most recent presidential election. Yet other recent elections attest dramatically to the extreme abnormality of the 1956 Eisenhower vote. In the 1954 Congressional elections the nation's Democrats, although they turned out less well than Republicans in minor elections, still fashioned a solid majority of votes cast. The fall of 1958 witnessed a Democratic landslide. Even in 1956, "underneath" Eisenhower's towering personal margin, a Democratic popular vote majority exceeding that which Kennedy won in 1960 appeared at other levels of the ticket. Finally, if 1956 is taken as a normal baseline and if it is true that Kennedy did score some relative personal success in 1960, how can we possibly explain the fact that other diverse Democrats on state tickets around the nation tended to win a greater proportion of popular votes than he attracted?

It seems more reasonable to suggest that Kennedy did not in any sense *exceed* the "normal" vote expectations of the generalized and anonymous Democratic candidate; rather, he fell visibly below these expectations, although nowhere nearly as far below them as Adlai Stevenson had fallen. This proposition is congruent not only with the general contours of election returns in the recent period, but with the great mass of sample survey data collected in the past decade as well. With this proposition we can draw into a coherent pattern the several surface characteristics which seemed intriguing from the simple 1960 vote totals. With it, we can locate the 1960 election more generally in the stream of American political history.

III. THE BASIC VOTING STRENGTH
OF THE TWO PARTIES

We have found it of great explanatory value to think of election results as reflecting the interplay of two sets of forces: stable, long-term partisan dispositions and short-term forces specific to the immediate election situation. The long-term partisan dispositions are very adequately represented by our measures of party identification. The stability of these dispositions over time is a matter of empirical record.[12] Their partisan division over any period, as it may favor one party or the other, provides the point from which one must start to understand any specific election. This underlying division of loyalties lends itself admirably to the goal of indicating what a "normal" vote would be, aside from specific forces associated with the immediate election.

In these terms, the basic Democratic majority in the nation is scarcely subject to dispute. Year in and year out since 1952, national samples of the American electorate have indicated a preference for the Democratic party by a margin approaching 60–40. However, since no election in recent years has shown a Democratic margin of this magnitude, it would be as absurd to take a 60–40 Democratic majority for a baseline as it would be to work from the 1956 presidential vote. Actually there is little temptation to do so. Over the years large amounts of information have been accumulated on the behavior of people identifying with the two major parties, and it is clear that the realistic voting strength of the Democrats—and this is the sort of baseline which interests us—falls well short of a 60–40 majority. The fact that heavy Democratic majorities in the South are concealed by low voting turnout is but one factor which reduces realistic Democratic strength. Outside the South, as well, Democrats under the same conditions of short-term stimulation are less likely to vote than Republicans.

It is possible to manipulate the data in such a fashion as to take into account all of the significant discrepancies between nominal party identification and realistic voting strength. We thereby arrive at a picture of the vote division which could be expected in the normal presidential election, if short-term forces associated with the election favored neither party in particular, but stood at an equilibrium. In such circumstances, we would expect a Democratic proportion of the two-party popular vote to fall in the vicinity of 53–54 percent.[13] Outside of the South, such a vote would fall short of a

---

[12] The absence of any significant change in the distribution of party loyalties throughout the Eisenhower period is best illustrated by Table 6–1, *ibid.*, p. 124. Distributions drawn in 1959 and 1960 continue the same pattern. Furthermore, there is no evidence that this surface stability of party identification is concealing a great flux of compensating changes beneath the surface. There have indeed been one or two slow, modest evolutions since 1952 which do involve compensating changes and hence are not visible in simple distributions. Nevertheless, our panel data show strikingly that among all the political orientations which we measure, partisan identification is by far the most stable for individuals over the periods which our data cover.

[13] This figure should be taken to indicate a rough range. It would vary upward or downward slightly according to the assumptions made concerning the overall proportion of the electorate turning out. While the computations underlying this estimate are tedious, their rationale is entirely straightforward. Turnout rates and the two-party vote division within each of seven categories of party identifiers have shown remarkable regularities over the range of elections which we have studied. These rates are not constant

50–50 split with the Republicans; within the South there would be a strong Democratic majority exceeding a 2-to-1 division.

Short-term forces associated with a specific election may, according to their net partisan strength, send the actual vote in that election deviating to one side or the other of the equilibrium point. In 1952 and 1956 the popularity of Eisenhower constituted one such force, and this force was strongly pro-Republican. The distortions produced in the behaviors of party identifiers of different types have now become familiar. If the net partisan force is strong, as in 1956, identifiers of the favored party vote almost *en bloc,* without defection. The small group of "independents" who do not commit themselves to either party divide very disproportionately in favor of the advantaged party, instead of dividing their vote equally as in the equilibrium case. And members of the disfavored party defect in relatively large numbers, as Democrats did in 1956. A useful description of any specific election, then, is an account of the short-term forces which have introduced these strains across the distribution of party identification.

In such a description, the existing division of deeper party loyalties is taken for granted. Its current character is not to be explained by the immediate political situation. The point is made most clearly by the 1960 election. The fact that the Democrats enjoyed a standing majority was in no way a consequence of the personal duel between Kennedy and Nixon, for it was a majority created long before either candidate became salient as a national political figure, and long before most of the campaign "issues" of 1960 had taken shape. In this perspective, then, we can consider some of the forces which drew the 1960 vote away from its equilibrium state.

IV. SHORT-TERM FORCES IN THE 1960 ELECTION

Popular vote tallies show that Kennedy received 49.8 percent of the two-party vote outside of the South, and 51.2 percent of the popular vote cast in the South. The vote outside the South is almost 1 percent more Democratic than our equilibrium estimates for this part of the nation. In the South, however, the Democratic deficit relative to the same baseline approaches 17 percent. Naturally, some short-term forces may balance out so that no net advantage accrues to either party. But the comparisons between our baselines and the 1960 vote suggest that we should find some short-

---

from election to election, but do vary for each type of identifier quite dependably as a function of the net balance of short-term partisan forces characterizing the specific election. While we have observed no election which registered a perfect equilibrium of these forces, we have observed situations in which net forces were Democratic (e.g., 1958) as well as Republican (e.g., 1952 or 1956). It is therefore possible to compute the turnout rate and two-party vote division which could be expected for each type of party identifier in the intermediate case in which short-term forces are balanced. The estimate employed above derives from a summation of these computations across categories of identifiers, weighted in a fashion appropriate to represent the entire electorate.

term forces which gave a very slight net advantage to Kennedy outside of the South, and yet which penalized him heavily within the South.

As in all elections that attract a wide degree of public attention, a number of short-term forces were certainly at work in 1960. A comprehensive assessment of these forces must await further analysis. However, there can be little doubt that the religious issue was the strongest single factor overlaid on basic partisan loyalties in the 1960 election, and we have focused most of our initial analyses in this area. Fortunately we know a great deal about the "normal" voting behavior within different religious categories, and can use this knowledge to provide baselines which aid in estimating the net effect of Kennedy's Catholicism upon his candidacy.

The Catholic Vote. As we have observed, the vote division among Catholics soared from a 50–50 split in the two Eisenhower contests to an 80–20 majority in the 1960 presidential vote. However, it is hard to attribute all of this increment simply to the Kennedy candidacy. In the 1958 election, when there were mild short-term economic forces favoring the Democratic party, the vote among Catholics went well over 70 percent in that direction. Ever since our measurements of party identification began in 1952, only a small minority—less than 20 percent—of Catholics in the nation have considered themselves as Republicans, although a fair portion have typically styled themselves as "Independents." Most of what attracted attention as a Republican trend among Catholics during the 1950's finds little support in our data, at least as a trend peculiar to Catholics. To be sure, many Democratic Catholics defected to vote for Eisenhower in 1952 and 1956. So did many Democratic Protestants. As a matter of fact, the defection rate among Democratic Catholics in 1952 was very slightly less than among Democratic Protestants, and in 1956 was very slightly more. In neither case do the differences exceed sampling error. There is some long-term evidence of a faint and slow erosion in the Catholic Democratic vote; but this has been proceeding at such a glacial pace that the 1956–1960 vote trends which we are treating here dwarf it completely. There is no reason to believe that the short-term personal "pull" exerted on Democrats generally by Eisenhower had a different strength for Catholics than for Protestants. The myths that have arisen to this effect seem to be primarily illusions stemming from the large proportion of Democrats who are Catholics. Their loss was painful in the two Eisenhower votes. But they were at the outset, and remained up to the first glimmer of the Kennedy candidacy, a strongly Democratic group.

We may specify this "normal" Democratic strength among Catholics by applying the same operations for Catholics alone that we have employed for the electorate as a whole. In the equilibrium case, it turns out that one would expect at least a 63 percent Democratic margin among Catholics. The difference between 63 percent and the 80 percent which Kennedy achieved can provisionally be taken as an estimate of the increment in

Democratic votes among Catholics above that which the normal, Protestant Democratic presidential candidate could have expected.

We can readily translate this 17 percent vote gain into proportions of the total 1960 vote, taking into account levels of Catholic turnout and the like. On such grounds, it appears that Kennedy won a vote bonus from Catholics amounting to about 4 percent of the national two-party popular vote. This increment is, of course, very unequally divided between the South and the rest of the nation, owing simply to the sparse Catholic population in the South. Within the 1960 non-Southern electorate, Kennedy's net gain from the Catholic increment amounts to better than 5 percent of the two-party vote. The same rate of gain represents less than 1 percent of the Southern popular vote.

The Anti-Catholic Vote. Respondents talked to our interviewers with re-markable freedom about the Catholic factor during the fall of 1960. This is not to say that all respondents referred to it as a problem. There were even signs that some Protestant respondents were struggling to avoid men-tion of it although it was a matter of concern. Nonetheless, nearly 40 per-cent of the sample voluntarily introduced the subject before any direct probing on our part in the early stages of the pre-election questionnaire. Since this figure certainly understates the proportion of the population for whom religion was a salient concern in 1960, it testifies rather eloquently to the importance of the factor in conscious political motivations during the fall campaign.

These discussions of the Catholic question, volunteered by our respond-ents, will, in time, provide more incisive descriptions of the short-term anti-Catholic forces important in the election. Our interest here, however, is to estimate the magnitude of anti-Catholic voting in terms of otherwise Demo-cratic votes which Kennedy lost. In such an enterprise, our material on the political backgrounds of our respondents is most useful.

We focus, therefore, upon the simple rates of defection to Nixon among Protestants who were identified in 1960 with the Democratic party. As Figure 1 shows, this defection rate is strongly correlated with regularity of attendance at a Protestant church. Protestant Democrats who, by self-description, never attend church, and hence are not likely to have much identification with it, defected to Nixon only at a rate of 6 percent. This rate, incidentally, is just about the "normal" defection rate which we would predict for both parties in the equilibrium case: it represents the scattered defections which occur for entirely idiosyncratic reasons in any election. Therefore, for Democrats who were nominal Protestants but outside the psychological orbit of their church, the short-term religious force set up by a Catholic candidacy had no visible impact. However, as soon as there is some evidence of identification with a Protestant church, the defection rate rises rapidly.

Although Protestant Independents are not included in Figure 1, they show the same gradient at a different level of the two-party vote division. The few Protestant Independents not attending church split close to the theoretically-expected 50–50 point. Then the Nixon vote rises to 61 percent in the "seldom" category; to 72 percent for the "often" category; and to 83 percent for the Protestant Independents attending church regularly. This increment of Republican votes above the "normal" 50–50 division for Independents matches remarkably the increment of Republican votes above the "normal" figure of 6 percent in the case of the Democrats.

We customarily find in our data certain substantial correlations between church attendance and political behavior. The correlation between church attendance and vote among Protestant Democrats and Independents is not, however, one of these.[14] The strong associations seem linked in an obvious way to the 1960 election. We need not assume, of course, that each defection pictured here represents a sermon from the pulpit and an obedient member of the congregation. Social science theory assures us that whether through sermons, informal communication or a private sense of reserve toward Catholicism, the faithful Protestant would react more negatively to the presidential candidacy of a Catholic than would more indifferent Protestants.[15] It remains notable, however, that Democrats who were at the same time regular Protestants defected to Nixon at rates far exceeding those which Eisenhower had attracted in 1952 or 1956.

We may use Figure 1, then, as a tool to estimate the magnitude of the anti-Catholic vote. It is easily argued that the area below the dotted line in Figure 1 represents "normal" defections within each category of church attendance, and that the votes represented by the triangle above the dotted line are votes which Kennedy lost on religious grounds. It is then a simple mechanical matter to convert this triangle into proportions of the popular vote for South and non-South.

On the surface, Figure 1 seems to say that the impact of the religious factor was very nearly the same, North and South, for the Southern gradient of defections is only slightly higher than the non-Southern gradient. If we think of the impact of short-term forces *on individuals* as a function of their party and religious loyalties, this conclusion is proper. Indeed, as we consider in later analyses the impact by different types of Protestantism, it may well be that the character of the impact will show no remaining regional difference whatever. However, to construe Figure 1 as suggesting that the *magnitude* of the anti-Catholic effect was about the same in votes cast

---

[14] Re-examination of earlier data shows a faint residual relationship between Republican voting and church attendance among Democratic Protestants which is not statistically significant. In 1956, the rank-order correlations involved were about 05 both within and outside the South. On the other hand, the comparable coefficient for Independents in 1956 was negative, —.04. The text ignores these variations as probably inconsequential.

[15] This is simply a special case of propositions concerning group identifications more generally, discussed in Campbell *et al., op. cit.,* ch. 12.

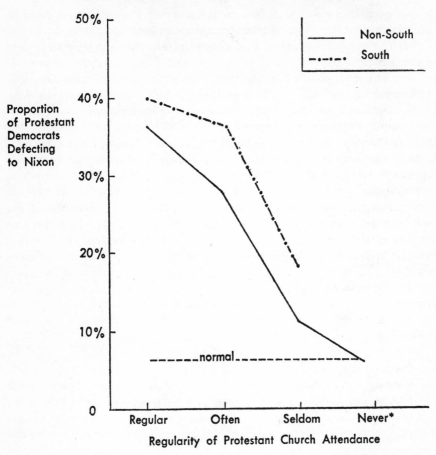

FIGURE 1. *Defections to Nixon among Protestant Democrats as a Function of Church Attendance.*

in North and South, is quite improper. The differences between the regions turn out to be substantial.

We must consider first that less than two-thirds of the active non-Southern electorate is Protestant, whereas within the South the electorate is almost completely (95 percent) Protestant. Secondly, Protestants are more faithful church-goers in the South than outside it. Quite specifically, we find that over half of the Southern presidential vote is cast by Protestants who go to church regularly, whereas less than 20 percent of the vote outside the South comes from regular, church-going Protestants. Finally, of the minority outside the South who are Protestant and attend church regularly, only a small proportion are Democratic identifiers: Republicans clearly predominate in

---

* The number of Protestant Democrats who "never" attend church in the South is too small for inclusion.

this category. In the South, the situation is reversed, with regular Protestants being far more often than not Democratic identifiers.

This conjunction of regional differences means that the defecting votes represented in Figure 1 are of vastly different sizes, South and non-South. It turns out that outside the South regular, church-going Protestants who are Democrats cast only about 5 percent of the total non-Southern vote. Within the South, however, regular church-going Protestants who are Democrats contributed over 35 percent of the total Southern vote. Thus it is that the anti-Catholic impact in the South turns out to involve a much larger share of the votes than elsewhere. The anti-Catholic vote in the South fulfills our search for a short-term force of strong net Republican strength in that region.

Summing up these apparent anti-Catholic votes as proportions of the total vote in the South, the non-South, and the nation as a whole, we can compare them with our estimations of the bonuses received by Kennedy from Catholics. Table II shows the balance sheet.

TABLE II. OFFSETTING EFFECTS OF THE CATHOLIC ISSUE,
1960 DEMOCRATIC PRESIDENTIAL VOTE

Area	% of 2-party vote in area
Outside the South, Kennedy's "unexpected" . . .	
Gains from Catholics	5.2%
Losses from Protestant Democrats and Independents	−3.6
NET	+1.6%
Inside the South, Kennedy's "unexpected" . . .	
Gains from Catholics	0.7%
Losses from Protestant Democrats and Independents	−17.2
NET	−16.5%
For the *nation as a whole,* Kennedy's "unexpected" . . .	
Gains from Catholics	4.3%
Losses from Protestant Democrats and Independents	−6.5
NET	−2.2%

There is every reason to believe that these preliminary estimates underestimate the importance of religion in the 1960 vote and, in particular, under-estimate the magnitude of the anti-Catholic vote. We have at no point taken account, for example, of the possibility that certain Republican identifiers, exposed to short-term forces which would normally have produced defections to the Democrats, may have been inhibited from such defection by Kennedy's Catholicism. In the midwest there were signs of a "farm revolt" favoring the Democrats which failed to materialize in the presidential balloting. At lower levels on farm belt tickets one finds that major Democratic candidates consistently surpassed "normal" Democratic expectations. Yet Kennedy seems to have been peculiarly insulated from any of this profit-taking: in these areas he lagged behind other major Democrats by a rather consistent 5 percent. It is difficult not to believe that at lower levels of office net short-term forces were favoring the Democrats, and Republican identifiers were defecting at unusual rates. Analyses may show that religion was a primary force inhibiting such defections at the presidential level.

Other early glimpses of our data also suggest the estimates of anti-Catholicism in Table II are conservative. It is likely that a number of non-religious short-term forces generated by the campaign itself were favorable to Kennedy on balance. As a number of other surveys reported, Nixon held a substantial lead over Kennedy in the early stages. At the outset, Kennedy was little known to the public: he stood primarily as the Democratic candidate and a Catholic. As the campaign went on, other and non-religious aspects of the Kennedy image filled in, and the public impression was usually positive. In this crucial shift in sentiment during the campaign, the television debates probably played an important role. Although there were Democrats who reacted warmly to Nixon's performance, our materials show quite strikingly that the net response to the debates favored Kennedy, as has been commonly supposed. In case studies, a reading of interviews has already turned up numerous Protestants of varying partisanship who were much more impressed by Kennedy as a candidate than by Nixon, yet who could not bring themselves to vote for a Catholic. In the measure that Kennedy's attractiveness as a candidate exceeded Nixon's and other short-term forces apart from religion were favoring the Democrats, the total popular vote should have been drawn to the Democratic side of the equilibrium point. The fact that it stayed instead on the Republican side may represent further damaging effects of religion for Kennedy.[16]

Refined analyses at a later date will permit us to estimate more adequately the role which all the major motivational factors, including religion, played in the 1960 outcome. For the moment, however, it is impressive the degree to which the surface characteristics of the 1960 election become intelligible even when viewed simply as the result of an "ancient" and enduring division of partisan loyalties overlaid by a short-term cross-current of religious motivation.

Normally we would expect a national vote falling as close to its equilibrium point as the 1960 case to be a relatively low-turnout election. That

---

[16] Two other motivational patterns associated with religion in 1960 deserve note. There were undoubtedly broad-minded Protestants who were drawn to a Kennedy vote out of a desire to see the religious precedent broken and hence buried; and there were undoubtedly Catholics who were drawn away from a Kennedy vote out of fear that the fact of a Catholic president would keep the religious issue uncomfortably prominent. It is hard to find instances of these viewpoints in our sample, however, and it is to be assumed that their incidence was slight.

is, a vote near the equilibrium point suggests either weak short-term forces or else a balance of stronger forces creating conflict in individuals and thereby lowering their motivation to vote. It is rare that forces strong enough to compel indifferent citizens to come out and vote do not also favor one party over the other quite categorically.

In 1960, however, the motivational picture underlying the vote was somewhat different, and can best be understood by separating the Protestant South from the rest of the nation. In the South, of course, a strong and unidirectional short-term force was reflected in a sharp departure from equilibrium and a surge in turnout, as fits normal expectations. What is abnormal is that this strong Republican short-term force raised motivation in a Democratic preserve, rather than diluting it through conflict. It is likely that conflict *was* created, especially where Democratic partisanship was strong. "Strong" Democrats in our sample made virtually no contribution to the 1960 rise in Southern turnout. The increase came from weaker Democrats, whose participation increased so radically over 1952 and 1956 that their turnout even surpassed that of strong Democrats in very exceptional fashion. For these voters, it seems likely that such forces as anti-Catholic feelings rapidly overcame relatively weak party loyalties and left strong motivation to turn out.

While turnout elsewhere did not show the same remarkable surge which appeared in the South, it remained at the fairly high level characteristic of the 1952 and 1956 elections, despite a partisan division of the vote near the regional equilibrium point. Strong balancing forces appear to have been in operation which did not create much conflict within individuals. The reason is clear: to the degree that religious motivations were engaged, forces were conflicting between groups rather than within individuals. Non-Southern Catholics, predominantly Democratic, were exposed to strong unidirectional short-term forces motivating them to get out and vote for Kennedy. Non-Southern Protestants, predominantly Republican, were exposed to contrary forces, at least where Protestant religious fidelity was strong. Thus the vote fell near the equilibrium point, but there was rather high turnout as well.

The other surface characteristics of the election are equally intelligible in these terms. Despite his position as majority candidate, Kennedy very nearly lost and tended to run behind his ticket. In the northeast, where concentrations of Catholics are greatest, his relation to the rest of the ticket was not generally unfavorable. The penalty he suffered becomes visible and consistent in the Midwest, where Catholics are fewer and Protestant church attendance is more regular. In the South, and for the same reasons, the differences between the Kennedy vote and that of other Democrats become large indeed. Everywhere, if one compares 1956 vote statistics with 1960 statistics, the course of political change is closely associated with the religious composition of voting units.

There was some relief even outside the more committed Democratic circles when the Kennedy victory, slight though it was, demonstrated that a Catholic was not in practice barred from the White House. Yet it would be naive to suppose that a Catholic candidate no longer suffers any initial disadvantage before the American electorate as a result of his creed. Not only did Kennedy possess a type of personal appeal which the television debates permitted him to exploit in unusual measure, but he was also the candidate of a party enjoying a fundamental majority in the land. Even the combination of these circumstances was barely sufficient to give him a popular vote victory. Lacking such a strong underlying majority, which Al Smith most certainly lacked in 1928, it is doubtful that the most attractive of Catholic presidential candidates in 1960 would have had much chance of success. It remains to be seen how far the experience of a Catholic president may diminish the disadvantage another time.

V. THE 1960 ELECTION IN HISTORICAL PERSPECTIVE

In a publication which appeared a few months prior to the 1960 elections[17] we posed the question of "how long a party can hope to hold the White House if it does not have a majority of the party-identified electorate." We had identified the two Eisenhower victories as "deviating elections," in which short-term forces had brought about the defeat of the majority party. We had not found any evidence in our 1952 or 1956 studies that these short-term forces were producing any significant realignment in the basic partisan commitments of the electorate. We felt that unless such a realignment did occur, "the minority party [could] not hope to continue its tenure in office over a very extended period."

We now know that the eight-year Eisenhower period ended with no basic change in the proportions of the public who identify themselves as Republican, Democrat, or Independent. If there had been an opportunity in 1952 for the Republican party to rewin the majority status it had held prior to 1932, it failed to capitalize on it. The Democratic party remained the majority party and the 1960 election returned it to the presidency. It was, to extend the nomenclature of our earlier publication, a "reinstating" election, one in which the party enjoying a majority of party identifiers returns to power. The 1960 election was remarkable not in the fact that the majority party was reinstated but that its return to power was accomplished by such a narrow margin. We had recognized the possibility that "the unfolding of national and international events and the appearance of new political figures" might swing the vote away from its natural equilibrium. We now see that such a deflection did occur and that it very nearly cost the majority party the election.

---

[17] Campbell *et al., op. cit.*, ch. 19.

Philip Converse, Angus Campbell, Warren Miller, Donald Stokes

It may be argued that the deficit the Democratic presidential candidate suffered from his normal expectation did not derive from damaging circumstances which were specific to the 1960 election but from a progressive weakening in the willingness of some Democratic partisans to support their ticket at the presidential level. It has been suggested that some voters who consider themselves to be Democrats and customarily favor Democratic candidates at the lower levels of office may have come during the Eisenhower period to have a perverse interest in favoring Republican candidates for president, either because of notions of party balance in government, because of local considerations in their states, or simply out of admiration for Eisenhower.

Important differences no doubt exist between voting at the presidential level and voting for a congressman. Our studies have shown, for example, that the popular vote for lesser offices is a more party-determined vote than the vote for president and varies around the normal equilibrium vote figure within a much narrower range than does the presidential vote.[18] However, the supposition that Kennedy failed to win a normal Democratic majority because of a cadre of Democrats who are covertly Republican in their presidential voting is not supported by our data.

Table I has already demonstrated that the overall shift in partisanship of the vote between 1956 and 1960 cannot be explained as a simple unilateral movement of erstwhile Eisenhower Democrats. The election did not depend, as was often supposed, upon the number of Eisenhower Democrats whom Nixon could retain as "covert Republicans." Our panel materials show that if Nixon had been forced to depend only upon the Eisenhower Democrats whom he retained, he would have suffered a convincing 54–46 defeat, assuming that other Democrats had continued to vote for Kennedy. He did not suffer such a defeat because he drew a new stream of Democratic defections nearly sufficient to put him in the White House.

The patterns of short-term forces in the 1960 election were independent of those shaping the 1956 election, then, in the sense that they affected a new set of people, on new grounds. There were Democrats susceptible to Eisenhower in 1956; there were Democrats sensitive to religion in 1960: the two sets of people do not intersect much more than one would expect by chance. In short, there is little evidence that the two Eisenhower elections had created a set of Democrats peculiarly disposed to vote for a Republican presidential candidate.

Analysis of our 1960 data is not sufficiently complete to enable us to describe the entire pattern of forces to which the electorate was reacting on Election Day. We do not know, for example, what the partisan impact of international affairs, which had favored the Republican candidate so

---

[18] Angus Campbell, "Surge and Decline: A Study of Electoral Change," *Public Opinion Quarterly*, Vol. 24 (Fall 1960), pp. 397–418.

strongly in the preceding two elections, was in the 1960 election. We do not know the effect of the Negro discrimination issues. We do not know in detail as yet how the personal attributes of the major candidates, other than their religious affiliations, were evaluated by the public. We feel confident, however, that we will not find any short-term force which moved as large a fraction of the 1960 electorate as did the issue of a Catholic president. This was the major cause of the net departure of the vote totals from the division which the comparative underlying strength of the two parties in 1960 would have led us to expect. After two consecutive "deviating" elections won at a presidential level by the minority party, the 1960 election reinstated the Democratic party. But short-term forces generated by the immediate 1960 situation once again favored the Republicans on balance, and the difference in votes which separated this "reinstating election" from a third "deviating election" was slight indeed.